"A magisterial textbook, but much more than a textbook. Every aspect of biblical hermeneutics is thoroughly explored in a readable, engaging, and stimulating manner. The real joy of the book, however, lies in the subtitle: 'for hearing God in Scripture.' This transforms the hermeneutical task from an exercise between a reader and an object (the Bible) to an encounter between a listener and a person (God). The former requires good and proper methods, tools, and wisdom, all of which matter greatly. The latter calls for response, faith, repentance, and obedience, all of which matter even more. Bartholomew not only explains both dimensions but also models them again and again. From the subtitle on the opening page, we move in a fitting way to the closing chapter on preaching the Bible. For if the ecclesial context of authentic biblical hermeneutics is crucial, then the church needs to know again the story we are in, which requires renewed commitment to preaching the whole counsel of God from the whole canon of Scripture. This book provides ample resources for just such a challenge."

—**Christopher J. H. Wright**, Langham Partnership

"This book is a versatile tool for research. It could serve as a textbook in biblical hermeneutics but equally well as a source for complementary readings on inspiration, canon, exegesis, revelation, the definition of theology, the historical and contemporary practice of biblical interpretation, the relationship between theology and biblical exegesis, and the role of the Bible in preaching, Christian spirituality, and missionary work. As a Catholic, I see and welcome in it a great openness to both the riches of patristic studies and the recent waves of what is often called *ressourcement*. Equally gratifying is Bartholomew's personal example of listening to not only a large corpus of Protestant biblical research but also a large variety of voices promoting biblical theology in the Catholic Church, past and present."

—**Denis Farkasfalvy**, University of Dallas; abbot emeritus of the Cistercian Abbey of Our Lady of Dallas

"A book that stands out in a crowded catalog of hermeneutics texts, *Introducing Biblical Hermeneutics* deserves careful attention. With characteristic erudition and lucidity, Bartholomew provides a Trinitarian hermeneutic that carries the reader all the way from devotional reading of Scripture to the ecclesial reception of the preached Word. The reader learns to read Scripture humbly and prayerfully, seeking not only information but also transformation by the living Christ. Along the way, Bartholomew masterfully relates biblical interpretation to biblical theology, systematic theology, philosophical hermeneutics, preaching, and the disciplines of the modern university. A unique and thought-provoking addition to the field of hermeneutics."

—**Bruce Ashford**, Southeastern Baptist Theological Seminary

Introducing Biblical Hermeneutics

A Comprehensive Framework *for* Hearing God in Scripture

Craig G. Bartholomew

Baker Academic
a division of Baker Publishing Group
Grand Rapids, Michigan

© 2015 by Craig G. Bartholomew

Published by Baker Academic
a division of Baker Publishing Group
P.O. Box 6287, Grand Rapids, MI 49516-6287
www.bakeracademic.com

Paperback edition published 2023
ISBN 978-1-5409-6820-3

All rights reserved. No part of this publication may be reproduced, stored in a retrieval system, or transmitted in any form or by any means—for example, electronic, photocopy, recording—without the prior written permission of the publisher. The only exception is brief quotations in printed reviews.

The Library of Congress has cataloged the hardcover edition as follows:
Bartholomew, Craig G., 1961–
    Introducing biblical hermeneutics : a comprehensive framework for hearing God in Scripture / Craig G. Bartholomew.
        pages cm
    Includes bibliographical references and indexes.
    ISBN 978-0-8010-3977-5 (cloth)
    1. Bible—Hermeneutics. I. Title.
BS476.B37 2015
220.601—dc23   2015014074

Unless otherwise indicated, Scripture quotations are from the New Revised Standard Version of the Bible, copyright © 1989, by the Division of Christian Education of the National Council of the Churches of Christ in the United States of America. Used by permission. All rights reserved. Any italics in these quotations are added for emphasis.

Scripture quotations labeled NIV are from the Holy Bible, New International Version®. NIV®. Copyright © 1973, 1978, 1984, 2011 by Biblica, Inc.™ Used by permission of Zondervan. All rights reserved worldwide. www.zondervan.com

Baker Publishing Group publications use paper produced from sustainable forestry practices and post-consumer waste whenever possible.

Dedicated to Cal and Inés Seerveld
with gratitude and hope

Contents

Preface ix
Abbreviations xi

Part 1 Approaching Biblical Interpretation
1. Biblical Interpretation *Coram Deo* 3
2. Listening and Biblical Interpretation 17

Part 2 Biblical Interpretation and Biblical Theology
3. The Story of Our World 51
4. The Development of Biblical Theology 85

Part 3 The Story of Biblical Interpretation
5. The Traditions within Which We Read 113
6. Early and Medieval Jewish Biblical Interpretation 158
7. Renaissance, Reformation, and Modernity 193
8. Canon 251

Part 4 Biblical Interpretation and the Academic Disciplines
9. Philosophy and Hermeneutics 281
10. History 335
11. Literature 376
12. Theology 431
13. Scripture and the University: *The Ecology of Christian Scholarship* 463

Part 5 The Goal of Biblical Interpretation

14. The "Epistle" to the Hebrews: *But We Do See Jesus*   487
15. Preaching the Bible for All It's Worth: *The Resurrection of the Sermon and the Incarnation of the Christ*   523

Bibliography   547
Subject Index   592
Scripture Index   603
Author Index   608

Preface

As I write the preface to this work, it is Lent in the church's calendar, a time in which we prepare for the great feast of Easter. It is an appropriate time in which to finish a book on biblical hermeneutics and evocative of George Steiner's description of Holy Saturday: "But ours is the long day's journey of the Saturday. Between suffering, aloneness, unutterable waste on the one hand and the dream of liberation, of rebirth on the other."[1] Holy Saturday is, if you like, the Lent of Holy Week.

We live in that interim between the coming of the King and the final consummation of the kingdom. Final liberation is assured, yet still, so often, "ours is the long day's journey of the Saturday." Scripture is given to us for *this* journey, and thus it feels appropriate to complete this work in the middle of Lent.

In one sense this book has been years in the making. My work in hermeneutics goes back to my doctoral dissertation, "Reading Ecclesiastes," supervised by Gordon Wenham and Christopher Norris, to whom I remain deeply grateful. Some fourteen years ago I started, with generous funding and help from the British and Foreign Bible Society, the Scripture and Hermeneutics Seminar (SAHS). In its initial nine-year phase it published eight volumes[2] and provided me with an opportunity to meet and learn from many of the major biblical and theological—and other—scholars of our day. The Seminar has since published *Hearing the Old Testament* (Eerdmans, 2012; coedited with David Beldman), and about the same time as this book is published, so too will be another SAHS volume: *A Manifesto for Theological Interpretation*, coedited with Heath Thomas. I have drawn on my years of work on biblical hermeneutics, but writing this volume has enabled me to consolidate my work, draw it all together, and develop it in many fresh and new ways.

I owe a huge debt to the Bible Society; to all those who have participated in the SAHS throughout the years; to Rosemary Hales, who faithfully

---

1. G. Steiner, *Real Presences: Is There Anything in What We Say?* (London: Faber & Faber, 1989), 232.
2. See www.stgeorgesonline.com/centre.

administered the project; and to the University of Gloucestershire, which provided a first home for it. SAHS is now housed in the St Georges Centre for Biblical and Public Theology.[3] I am glad to acknowledge the help of my research assistant: Josh Walker. Redeemer University College also graciously provided me with a grant to help in the final stages of editing.

Many friends have read chapters and helped me to develop my thinking in this area. Special thanks go to Heath Thomas, Bruce Ashford, David Beldman, Justin Orr, Alan Mittleman, Bryan Dyer, Jim Kinney, and so many others. The deficiencies that remain are entirely mine. Chapter 3 of this book emerged in part from a chapter that Michael Goheen and I wrote together, and I acknowledge his missional expertise and input.[4]

Readers should note that throughout the book more detailed discussions of issues that arise are in a smaller font. Biblical hermeneutics is a vast domain and these sections allow me to go into more detail on particular issues. The text can be read without these but my hope is that you will find these forays of interest and that they will enhance your reading of the book.

In this past year I have gotten to know some of the staff of Logos Bible Software, and I appreciate their making available to me their product, an indispensable resource in the latter stages of this project. Faithlife is an amazing company, and their product is first rate. The Theological College of the Canadian Reformed Church, based in Hamilton, made their excellent library available to me, for which I am truly grateful.

It is a pleasure once again to work with Jim Kinney and his team at Baker Academic. Their editorial process and marketing are rigorous, and one is grateful for such practice.

I am delighted to dedicate this book to my good friends Calvin and Inés Seerveld. Cal is a philosopher and aesthetician but has a long-standing interest in biblical interpretation and enjoys few things more than working away at the Hebrew and Greek text.[5] It was while working under Oscar Cullmann on a Fulbright scholarship that Cal experienced something of an epiphany when he was locked in his living quarters translating Romans from the Greek into German! That rigor and spirit pervades his work. He is also a great guy, and Inés is a lovely, quiet, and altogether genuine person. She bakes the best muffins! Their friendship is a blessing.

3. www.stgeorgesonline.com/centre.
4. C. G. Bartholomew and M. W. Goheen, "Story and Biblical Theology," in *Out of Egypt: Biblical Theology and Biblical Interpretation*, ed. C. G. Bartholomew et al., SAHS (Grand Rapids: Zondervan, 2004), 144–71.
5. See most recently C. Seerveld, *Biblical Studies and Wisdom for Living* (Sioux Center, IA: Dordt College Press, 2014). See also http://www.seerveld.com/tuppence.html.

Abbreviations

Old Testament

Gen.	Genesis	2 Chron.	2 Chronicles	Dan.	Daniel
Exod.	Exodus	Ezra	Ezra	Hosea	Hosea
Lev.	Leviticus	Neh.	Nehemiah	Joel	Joel
Num.	Numbers	Esther	Esther	Amos	Amos
Deut.	Deuteronomy	Job	Job	Obad.	Obadiah
Josh.	Joshua	Ps(s).	Psalms	Jon.	Jonah
Judg.	Judges	Prov.	Proverbs	Mic.	Micah
Ruth	Ruth	Eccles.	Ecclesiastes	Nahum	Nahum
1 Sam.	1 Samuel	Songs	Song of Songs	Hab.	Habakkuk
2 Sam.	2 Samuel	Isa.	Isaiah	Zeph.	Zephaniah
1 Kings	1 Kings	Jer.	Jeremiah	Hag.	Haggai
2 Kings	2 Kings	Lam.	Lamentations	Zech.	Zechariah
1 Chron.	1 Chronicles	Ezek.	Ezekiel	Mal.	Malachi

New Testament

Matt.	Matthew	Eph.	Ephesians	Heb.	Hebrews
Mark	Mark	Phil.	Philippians	James	James
Luke	Luke	Col.	Colossians	1 Pet.	1 Peter
John	John	1 Thess.	1 Thessalonians	2 Pet.	2 Peter
Acts	Acts of the Apostles	2 Thess.	2 Thessalonians	1 John	1 John
Rom.	Romans	1 Tim.	1 Timothy	2 John	2 John
1 Cor.	1 Corinthians	2 Tim.	2 Timothy	3 John	3 John
2 Cor.	2 Corinthians	Titus	Titus	Jude	Jude
Gal.	Galatians	Philem.	Philemon	Rev.	Revelation

General

AD	anno Domini, in the year of the Lord	IVP	InterVarsity Press
BC	before Christ	JEDP	hypothetical sources of the Pentateuch: Jahwist/Yahwist, Elohist, Deuteronomist, Priestly
BT	biblical theology		
BTM	Biblical Theology Movement	KJV	King James Version
ca.	*circa*, approximately	loc.	location/s (in an ebook)
cf.	*confer*, compare	LXX	Septuagint, Greek translation of the Old Testament
chap(s).	chapter(s)		
CTH	contemporary traditional homiletics	MT	Masoretic Text (versification for the Hebrew)
d.	died	NC	New Criticism
DSS	Dead Sea Scrolls	NIV	New International Version
ed(s).	editor(s), edited by, edition(s)	NKJV	New King James Version
e.g.	*exempli gratia*, for example	NRSV	New Revised Standard Version
esp.	especially, page/s referenced	NT	New Testament
ET	English translation/versification	OG	Old Greek
et al.	*et alii*, and others	OT	Old Testament
etc.	*et cetera*, other things of this sort	pbk.	paperback
exp.	expanded	PN	Patriarchal Narratives
fl.	flourished	rev.	revised (by)
FS	Festschrift	SAHS	Scripture and Hermeneutics Seminar
ibid.	*ibidem*, in the same place (as immediately preceding)		
		SBL	Society of Biblical Literature
idem	the same (author as just mentioned)	trans.	translated by, translator(s)
		v(v).	verse, verses
i.e.	*id est*, that is		

Series, Collections, and Reference Works

AB	Anchor Bible
ABD	*Anchor Bible Dictionary*. Edited by D. N. Freedman. 6 vols. New York: Doubleday, 1992
AGJU	Arbeiten zur Geschichte des antikum Judentums und des Urchristentums
ANF	*Ante-Nicene Fathers*. Edited by A. Robertson and J. Donaldson. Buffalo: Christian Literature Co., 1885–96. http://www.ccel.org/index/title/A
AOAT	Alter Orient und Altes Testament
AUSS	*Andrews University Seminary Studies*
BA	*Biblical Archaeologist*
BASOR	*Bulletin of the American Schools of Oriental Research*
BBR	*Bulletin for Biblical Research*
BCOTWP	Baker Commentary on the Old Testament Wisdom and Psalms
BDAG	W. Bauer, F. W. Danker, W. F. Arndt, and F. W. Gingrich. *Greek-English Lexicon of the New Testament and Other Early Christian Literature*. 3rd ed. Chicago: University of Chicago Press, 2000
BDB	F. Brown, S. R. Driver, and C. A. Briggs, eds. *Hebrew and English Lexicon of the Old Testament*. Oxford: Clarendon, 1907

BETL	Bibliotheca ephemeridum theologicarum lovaniensium
BIOSCS	*Bulletin of the International Organization for Septuagint and Cognate Studies*
BIS	Biblical Interpretation Series
BSac	*Bibliotheca sacra*
BTIC	B. S. Childs. *Biblical Theology in Crisis*. Philadelphia: Westminster, 1970
BTONT	B. S. Childs. *Biblical Theology of the Old and New Testaments: Theological Reflection on the Christian Bible*. Minneapolis: Fortress, 1993
BZAW	Beihefte zur Zeitschrift für die alttestamentliche Wissenschaft
CBQ	*Catholic Biblical Quarterly*
CCSG	Corpus Christianorum: Series graeca. Turnhout: Brepols, 1977–
CD	Karl Barth. *Church Dogmatics*. Edited by G. W. Bromiley and T. F. Torrance. Translated by G. W. Bromiley et al. First pbk. ed. 4 vols. in 14. Edinburgh: T&T Clark, 2004
ConBOT	Coniectanea biblica: Old Testament Series
DDC	Augustine of Hippo. *De doctrina christiana*. In *On Christian Teaching*. Translated by R. P. H. Green. Oxford: Oxford University Press, 1997
EJT	*European Journal of Theology*
ExpTim	*Expository Times*
FC	Fathers of the Church. Washington, DC: Catholic University of America Press, 1947–
FRLANT	Forschungen zur Religion und Literatur des Alten und Neuen Testaments
HAR	*Hebrew Annual Review*
HAT	Handbuch zum Alten Testament
HB/OT	M. Sæbø, ed. *Hebrew Bible / Old Testament: The History of Its Interpretation*. Göttingen: Vandenhoeck & Ruprecht, 1996–
HPE	C. Kannengiesser, ed. *Handbook of Patristic Exegesis*. 2 vols. The Bible in Ancient Christianity. Leiden: Brill, 2004. 2 vols. in 1, 2006
HTR	*Harvard Theological Review*
HUCA	*Hebrew Union College Annual*
Int	*Interpretation*
IOTS	B. S. Childs. *Introduction to the Old Testament as Scripture*. Philadelphia: Fortress, 1979
ISBE	*International Standard Bible Encyclopedia*. Edited by G. W. Bromiley. 4 vols. Grand Rapids: Eerdmans, 1979–88
ITS	*Indian Theological Studies* (Bangalore)
JAAR	*Journal of the American Academy of Religion*
JETS	*Journal of the Evangelical Theological Society*
JQR	*Jewish Quarterly Review*
JR	*Journal of Religion*
JSJSup	Journal for the Study of Judaism: Supplement Series
JSNT	*Journal for the Study of the New Testament*
JSNTSup	Journal for the Study of the New Testament: Supplement Series
JSOT	*Journal for the Study of the Old Testament*
JSOTSup	Journal for the Study of the Old Testament: Supplement Series
JSS	*Journal of Semitic Studies*
JTS	*Journal of Theological Studies*
KAT	Kommentar zum Alten Testament

KEK	Kritisch-exegetischer Kommentar über das Neue Testament
LCC	Library of Christian Classics
LNTS	Library of New Testament Studies
NAC	New American Commentary
NCBC	New Century Bible Commentary
NICNT	New International Commentary on the New Testament
NICOT	New International Commentary on the Old Testament
NIGTC	New International Greek Testament Commentary
NovT	*Novum Testamentum*
NovTSup	Supplements to Novum Testamentum
NPNF²	*Nicene and Post-Nicene Fathers*. Second Series. Edited by P. Schaff and H. Wace. Translated by W. H. Fremantle, G. Lewis, and W. G. Martley. Buffalo: Christian Literature Co., 1893. http://www.ccel.org/search/fulltext/post-nicene
NTPG	N. T. Wright. *The New Testament and the People of God*. Christian Origins and the Question of God 1. Minneapolis: Fortress, 1992
PG	Patrologia graeca. Edited by J.-P. Migne. 162 vols. Paris, 1857–66; index, 1912
PSB	*Princeton Seminary Bulletin*
RB	*Revue biblique*
SAHS	Scripture and Hermeneutics Seminar
SBLDS	Society of Biblical Literature Dissertation Series
SBT	Studies in Biblical Theology
SCS	Septuagint and Cognate Studies
SJT	*Scottish Journal of Theology*
SNTSMS	Society for New Testament Studies Monograph Series
TCW	*Tydskrif vir Christelike Wetenskap*. Bloemfontein, South Africa
TDOT	*Theological Dictionary of the Old Testament*. Edited by G. J. Botterweck, H. Ringgren, and H.-J. Fabry. Translated by J. T. Willis, G. W. Bromiley, and D. E. Green. Grand Rapids: Eerdmans, 1974–2006
TTZ	*Trierer theologische Zeitschrift*
TWOG	C. H. H. Scobie. *The Ways of Our God: An Approach to Biblical Theology*. Grand Rapids: Eerdmans, 2003
VT	*Vetus Testamentum*
VTSup	Supplements to Vetus Testamentum
WA	D. Martin Luthers Werke: Kritische Gesamtausgabe [Weimarer Ausgabe]. Edited by J. K. F. Knaake, G. Kawerau, et al. 127 vols. Weimar: Böhlau, 1883–
WA BR	*Briefwechsel*. Correspondence
WA DB	*Die deutsche Bibel*. The German Bible and its prefaces
WA TR	*Tischreden*. Table talk
WBC	Word Biblical Commentary
WTJ	*Westminster Theological Journal*
WUNT	Wissenschaftliche Untersuchungen zum Neuen Testament
ZAW	*Zeitschrift für die alttestamentliche Wissenschaft*

PART 1

Approaching Biblical Interpretation

1

Biblical Interpretation *Coram Deo*

> In this way I hope to be able to show most clearly to my readers that hermeneutics is no esoteric teaching but the theory of a practice.
>
> Hans Robert Jauss[1]

Introduction

It is hard to overestimate what is at stake in biblical interpretation. According to Hebrews, "in these last days he [God] has spoken to us by a Son, whom he appointed heir of all things, through whom he also created the worlds" (Heb. 1:2). Similarly in 1 John we read:

> We declare to you what was from the beginning, what we have heard, what we have seen with our eyes, what we have looked at and touched with our hands, concerning the word of life—this life was revealed, and we have seen it and testify to it, and declare to you the eternal life that was with the Father and was revealed to us—we declare to you what we have seen and heard so that you also may have fellowship with us; and truly our fellowship is with the Father and with his Son Jesus Christ. (1 John 1:1–3)

---

1. H. R. Jauss, *Wege des Verstehens* (Munich: Wilhelm Fink, 1994): "Auf diese Weise hoffe ich, meinen Lesern am klarsten darlegen zu können, dass Hermeneutik keine esoterische Lehre, sondern die Theorie einer Praxis ist" (8).

If for a moment we defamiliarize ourselves with these texts, step back, and quietly reflect on them, we begin to sense the enormity of their claims:

> In these last days . . . God has spoken . . . by a Son . . . through whom he created the worlds . . . what was from the beginning . . . what we have seen . . . what we have touched . . . the word of life . . . we declare to you.

If these claims are true, then their implications are huge, and they connect with our deepest needs. In Ecclesiastes, Qohelet observes in chapter 3 that God has put eternity in our hearts, but we cannot find out what God has done from the beginning to the end.[2] We are creatures who need to know the true, grand story of which we are part, and Qohelet fingers the frustration and despair that follow when this need is not met. Hebrews and 1 John tell us, however, that it has been met.

This is truly good news, and not least for the present. We live amid turbulent times, and some in the West would have us embrace and celebrate the nihilism that postmodernism has brought in its wake. Roy Brassier in his *Nihil Unbound*, for example, asserts that

> the disenchantment of the world deserves to be celebrated as an achievement of intellectual maturity, not bewailed as a debilitating impoverishment. . . . Nature is not our or anyone's "home," nor a particularly beneficent progenitor. Philosophers would do well to desist from issuing any further injunctions about the need to re-establish the meaningfulness of existence, the purposefulness of life, or mend the shattered concord between man and nature. . . . Nihilism is not an existential quandary but a speculative opportunity.[3]

One needs to reflect on this statement in relation to the above passages. In my opinion such a shocking view is possible only amid the bloated comfort of the West, which has enjoyed some seventy years of relative peace and affluence. By comparison, the Brazilian theologian Leonardo Boff evokes the experience of far too many in our world: "There is a suffering humanity whose way of the cross has as many stations as that of the Lord when he suffered among us in Palestine."[4] Boff is equally clear that it is not just humanity but the entire creation that groans amid these stations of the cross. For the poor of our world, an increasing number

---

2. See C. G. Bartholomew, *Ecclesiastes*, BCOTWP (Grand Rapids: Baker Academic, 2009), 166–67.

3. R. Brassier, *Nihil Unbound: Enlightenment and Extinction* (Basingstoke, UK: Palgrave Macmillan, 2007), xi.

4. L. Boff, *Passion of Christ, Passion of the World: The Facts, Their Interpretation, and Their Meaning Yesterday and Today*, trans. R. R. Barr, 2nd ed. (Maryknoll, NY: Orbis Books, 2001), ix.

of whom are found in the West, whose lives are already characterized by disenchantment, meaninglessness, and displacement, it would be absurd and evil to encourage them cheerfully to embrace nihilism as a "speculative opportunity."

There is much darkness in our world, and Jesus, John tells us, is the light of the world. He dispels the darkness, brings healing, and helps our world find its way toward the goal of rest that God has in mind for it. It is in the Bible that we find the authoritative witness to Jesus. Indeed, the great joy of the Spirit is to use Scripture to open us up to the reality of the Lord Christ. If, as I like to think of it, Scripture is that field in which is hid the pearl of great price, then healthy biblical interpretation that keeps on excavating this pearl is vital not just for the life of the church but also for the life of the world. Thus, there is indeed much at stake in biblical interpretation.

What does healthy biblical interpretation look like?

A Trinitarian Hermeneutic

I assume—although this can no longer be taken for granted—that (Christian) biblical scholars aim to excavate "the truth" when they interpret the Bible. However, "truth" is not as simple as it may seem. It has become common to hear the view expressed that one must pursue the truth wherever it takes one. While a real openness to the evidence is indispensable, the problem with this approach is that the view of truth involved is rarely explicit and tends to presuppose a view of truth as autonomous, value-free research. Postmodernism has rightly helped us to see that such a view is a myth: all of us approach the world in particular ways and with particular foundational commitments. In my view, true progress would be made if scholars brought their foundational commitments out into the open and if the academy, including such organizations as the American Academy of Religion and the Society of Biblical Literature, fostered a *genuine pluralism* in which different foundational commitments were allowed to come to expression so that the real, in-depth dialogue could begin.

So, what are my foundational commitments? I take it for granted that, for Christians, our understanding of the world must take as its starting point the God revealed in Scripture and articulated in the tradition. This means that any biblical hermeneutic worth its salt must be *christocentric*. One cannot take seriously the quotes from Hebrews and 1 John above and avoid this. As Karl Barth says of Jesus: "This man is the secret of heaven and earth, of the cosmos created by God."[5] Similarly Lesslie Newbigin asserts that Christ is the

---

5. K. Barth, *CD* III/1:21.

clue to the whole of creation.⁶ And as Thomas Aquinas put it, "He was also full of truth, because the human nature in Christ attained to the divine truth itself, that is, *that this man should be the divine Truth itself*. In other men we find many participated truths, insofar as the First Truth gleams back into their minds through many likenesses; but Christ is Truth itself."⁷ However, precisely because such a hermeneutic is christocentric, it will be *trinitarian*. In Jesus's Jewish context of monotheism, the New Testament awareness of him as "truly God" made the postcanonical development of the doctrine of the Trinity inevitable.

There are many biblical entrances into the concept of truth, but here I will follow several theologians in entering through John's Gospel.⁸ The question of truth comes famously to the fore in Pilate's interrogation of Jesus in John 18:28–19:16a. At stake is whether Jesus is "king of the Jews." Jesus replies that he "came into the world to testify to the truth" and that "everyone who belongs to the truth listens to *his* voice" (18:37 altered). As Herman Ridderbos notes:

> Jesus' kingship consists in the utterly unique authority with which he represents the truth in the world. His birth and coming has no other purpose than to "bear witness" to the truth, in the absolute sense in which the Fourth Gospel continually speaks of the truth: Jesus testifies to what "he has seen and heard of the Father" (cf. 3:31–36), indeed to the truth that he himself is (14:6) and for which he answers with his life, person, and work. By speaking of himself as "witness," Jesus—standing before the judgment seat of Pilate—is using the language of the courtroom (cf. 1 Tim. 6:13), but not as the accused testifying on his own behalf but as the one who, in the suit that God brings against the world, has come to testify against the rule of the lie and for the "truth," that is, for God and for God's claim on the world. In that testimony Jesus' kingship consists.⁹

In postmodern idiom, Pilate replies, "What is truth?" Doubtless, many today, in the tradition of Nietzsche, would see Pilate as the winner of this debate. However, Jesus, by reversing his role in the interrogation and thus reframing Pilate's

---

6. L. Newbigin, *The Gospel in a Pluralist Society* (Grand Rapids: Eerdmans, 1989), 103–15.

7. Thomas Aquinas, *Commentary on the Gospel of Saint John*, 8, 188 (Kindle edition), Kindle loc. 1576–78, with added emphasis.

8. So, e.g., B. D. Marshall, *Trinity and Truth* (Cambridge: Cambridge University Press, 2000), 1–3; H. U. von Balthasar, *Theologik*, vol. 2, *Wahrheit Gottes* (Einsiedeln: Johannes-Verlag, 1985), 13–23; idem, *Theologik*, vol. 3, *Der Geist der Wahrheit* (Einsiedeln: Johannes Verlag, 1987), 61–75; L. Newbigin, *The Light Has Come: An Exposition of the Fourth Gospel* (Grand Rapids: Eerdmans, 1982).

9. H. N. Ridderbos, *The Gospel of John: A Theological Commentary* (Grand Rapids: Eerdmans, 1997), 596.

court case in the context of a larger narrative,[10] alerts us unequivocally to the resistance that a trinitarian view of truth affords to the relativism of so much postmodernism.[11] The reader of John's Gospel knows the answer to Pilate's question: Jesus himself is the answer. "Truth is not simply personal; for John truth is a person. Even this is too weak: truth is not just any person, but this human being in particular: Jesus of Nazareth, and among human beings only he. Knowing what truth is and deciding about truth, so this Gospel suggests, finally depend on becoming adequately acquainted with this person."[12] However, Jesus is not the truth all by himself but by virtue of his unique relationship with the Father (John 5:30) who sent him into the world and by his unique relationship with the Spirit whom he sends into the world (16:13–14). "So as John's Gospel and Letters depict it, 'truth' is an attribute of the triune God. Indeed, truth is in some deep sense identical with the persons of the Trinity. Apparently both saying what truth is and deciding what is true depend on identifying the triune God, and on being the subject of his community-forming action."[13]

It is this trinitarian view of God that distinguishes the Christian church from other communities. The post-Enlightenment legacy in theology was to marginalize the doctrine of the Trinity.[14] The latter half of the twentieth century, however, partially in the context of the reaction to modernity signified by postmodernism, witnessed a remarkable flowering of trinitarian theology. Undoubtedly the father of this renaissance was Karl Barth,[15] but major contributions were also made by Jürgen Moltmann, John Zizioulas, Colin Gunton, and many others. This renaissance is of great importance to biblical hermeneutics because "prime reality" for the Christian is the God who has come to us in Jesus, and epistemologically it is essential that a biblical hermeneutic take

---

10. A. Lincoln (*Truth on Trial: The Lawsuit Motif in the Fourth Gospel* [Peabody, MA: Hendrickson, 2000]) examines the centrality of the lawsuit to John's Gospel; see esp. 123–38. He also comments that "Jesus' assertion to Pilate, then, puts his judge on trial regarding the truth" (129). Regarding Pilate's famous question, P. Duke (*Irony in the Fourth Gospel* [Atlanta: John Knox, 1985]) writes, "The dramatic irony of the question lies in our knowledge that the one to whom the question about truth is asked is himself the Truth" (130).

11. See B. D. Marshall, *Trinity and Truth*, 168–69, for a cogent defense of the view that Scripture does indeed provide us with a God's-eye view of our world.

12. Ibid., 2.

13. Ibid., 2–3.

14. This is esp. true of twentieth-century English theology. According to B. Hebblethwaite ("Recent British Theology," in *One God in Trinity: An Analysis of the Primary Dogma of Christianity*, ed. P. Toon and J. D. Spiceland [London: Samuel Bagster, 1980]): "The most striking feature of recent British trinitarian theology—at least where England is concerned—is the frankness with which orthodox trinitarianism is being questioned or even rejected.... Indeed the collapse of trinitarian theology is an inevitable consequence of the abandonment of incarnational Christology" (158).

15. See K. Barth, *CD* I/1, *The Doctrine of the Word of God*, chap. 2.

this prime reality as its starting point. An exciting development of our time is that a multitude of scholars have come to this view via a variety of theological traditions. Some, like Hans Frei, George Lindbeck, and B. D. Marshall, have journeyed to this point via the Barthian tradition; others, like Alvin Plantinga and Nicholas Wolterstorff, via the neo-Calvinist tradition; others via the Catholic and Orthodox traditions. All of this group that I am referring to have in common Marshall's point that "Christians can and should have their own ways of thinking about truth and about deciding what to believe."[16]

For Christians, "God" is the prime reality from which everything else is to be understood. And in Christian thought the doctrine of the Trinity specifies the meaning and reference of "God"; as such, it is the primary Christian doctrine with major epistemic significance, and not least in relation to the Bible.[17] The link between the Trinity and the Bible is unavoidable:

> The action whereby the Spirit induces us to love God by sharing in the mutual love of the Father and the Son is epistemically decisive: from it ultimately stems our willingness *to hold true the narratives which identify Jesus and the triune God, and to order the rest of our beliefs accordingly*. We cannot love the triune God, let alone love him with his own love, unless we hold a complex collection of beliefs which together pick out and describe the actions in time by which this God identifies himself in the world, and thereby makes his life available to our desires.[18]

James Barr articulates this quite clearly: "All Christian use of the Old Testament seems to depend on the belief that the one God who is the God of Israel is also the God and Father of Jesus Christ."[19] Again: "All our use of the Old Testament goes back to this belief. What is said there that relates to 'God' relates to our God. Consequently that which can be known of our God is known only when we consider the Old Testament as a place in which he is known."[20]

How then does the doctrine of the Trinity shape a biblical hermeneutic?

1. *A trinitarian hermeneutic approaches the Bible as authoritative Scripture.* The doctrine of the Trinity commits us to the view that Scripture as a whole is authoritative in that it adequately renders Jesus Christ and thus God to us.[21]

---

16. B. D. Marshall, *Trinity and Truth*, xi.
17. I take it that the "immanent" and the "economic" Trinity are one and the same.
18. B. D. Marshall, *Trinity and Truth*, 209, with added emphasis.
19. J. Barr, *Old and New in Interpretation: A Study of the Two Testaments*, 2nd ed. (London: SCM, 1982), 149.
20. Ibid., 153–55; cf. C. Seitz, *Figured Out: Typology and Providence in Christian Scripture* (Louisville: Westminster John Knox Press, 2001), 4–6.
21. See K. J. Vanhoozer, *The Drama of Doctrine: A Canonical Linguistic Approach to Christian Theology* (Louisville: Westminster John Knox, 2005), 286–88.

2. *A trinitarian hermeneutic approaches the Bible* as a whole *as Scripture*. The Old Testament by itself is not Christian Scripture, nor is the New Testament by itself; they function as such only within *tota Scriptura*. We do not read the Old Testament truthfully unless we read it as the Old Testament, which is "fulfilled" in the New. Thus a trinitarian hermeneutic commits us to biblical theology and typology, with their quest for the inner unity of the Bible. In chapter 3 (below) I will argue for the primacy of a narrative approach to biblical theology, on the basis of which (in chap. 4) a variety of other approaches find their place.

3. *A trinitarian hermeneutic views ecclesial reception of Scripture as primary*. B. D. Marshall, quoted above, states, "Knowing what truth is and deciding about truth, so this Gospel suggests, finally depend on becoming adequately acquainted with this person." It is above all through Scripture in the context of the ecclesia that we become acquainted with "this person." Scripture is primarily God's Word to God's people, and thus communal, ecclesial reception is primary, as I will argue in chapter 2. This alerts us to the importance of tradition and the reception history of the Bible (chaps. 5–7) and also raises, as we will see, the question of the relationship between ecclesial interpretation and academic interpretation. In my view *both*, and this follows logically from the above quote, should operate out of a trinitarian hermeneutic, with the aim of academic interpretation being to deepen ecclesial reception. This envisages a healthy relationship between the two, with each potentially correcting the other, but *not* with one being committed and the other "neutral."

4. *A trinitarian hermeneutic exalts and humbles academic interpretation*. As is true throughout the history of the church, academic work in the service of biblical interpretation is vital and indispensable, a holy endeavor. But it is not the royal route to the truth of the Bible apart from the ecclesia. I like to think of biblical scholars hunched over their desks as akin to those who worked so hard to break the Enigma code in World War II; indispensable work, but only part of a larger endeavor, and probably not the front line of the battle. Academic interpretation is a partner to ecclesial reception of the Bible, which operates at the front line of its reception. Historically such an understanding has not detracted from the best and most rigorous scholarship; rather, it has been its raison d'être. It has spurred scholars on to extraordinary achievements, and we need to recover such rigor and courage in our day. At its best, Christianity has produced scholars and exegetes of the caliber of Augustine, Aquinas, Calvin, Barth, and Bonhoeffer; it is scholarship of this caliber that a trinitarian hermeneutic will embody.

5. *A trinitarian hermeneutic will attend to the discrete witness of the Testaments*. Too often a christological hermeneutic has been imposed on the Old

Testament, thus restricting its voice from being heard on its own terms.[22] A trinitarian hermeneutic alerts us to the historical unfolding of God's revelation in the economy of his world and does full justice to his revelation of himself in and through the life of his elect, the ancient Near Eastern people Israel, culminating in Jesus. The emphasis on perichoresis in trinitarian doctrine similarly points in this direction as it stresses that while all three persons of the Trinity are involved in all their acts, the Father is particularly associated with creation and Israel, the Son with the fulfillment of redemption, and the Spirit with mission. In this area Barr rightly declares: "It is an illusory position to think of ourselves as in a position where the New Testament is clear, is known and accepted, and where therefore from this secure position we start out to explore the much more doubtful and dangerous territory of the Old Testament. . . . Insofar as a position is Christian it is related to the Old Testament from the beginning."[23]

As Brevard Childs therefore observes, a trinitarian hermeneutic will attend to what he calls the discrete witness of the Testaments.[24] God's revelation of himself in the life of Israel, an ancient Near Eastern nation, will be taken with full seriousness, and all critical tools will be brought to bear in articulating this witness. Critical tools are, however, never neutral, and their underpinnings may require reconfiguration in relation to the epistemic priority of the Trinity; yet the historical dimension of Israel's life and Jesus's life will be open to rigorous scrutiny.

Does this mean that Christians should read the Old Testament with no sense of the further acts in the story? This is simply not possible, but it does mean that we should be sensitive to the "otherness" of the Old Testament where it does not fit easily with our New Testament sensibilities. Vanhoozer states: "Of all the canonical dialogues, perhaps the most important is that between the Old and New Testaments. Bakhtin rightly cautions us against thinking of dialogue as the merging of two or more voices into one. . . . In a genuine dialogue, each voice retains its integrity, yet each is also mutually enriched."[25] "Dialogue" is, however, a limited metaphor for the relationship

22. On this issue, see C. R. Seitz, "Christological Interpretation of Texts and Trinitarian Claims to Truth," *SJT* 52 (1999): 209–26; and F. Watson, "The Old Testament as Christian Scripture: A Response to Professor Seitz," *SJT* 52 (1999): 227–32.
23. Barr, *Old and New in Interpretation*, 153–55.
24. B. S. Childs, *BTONT* 95–118; see also idem, "The Nature of the Christian Bible: One Book, Two Testaments," in *The Rule of Faith: Scripture, Canon and Creed in a Critical Age*, ed. E. Radner and G. Sumner (Harrisburg, PA: Morehouse, 1998), 115–26.
25. Vanhoozer, *Drama of Doctrine*, 290–91. B. S. Childs ("On Reclaiming the Bible for Christian Theology," in *Reclaiming the Bible for the Church*, ed. C. E. Braaten and R. W. Jenson [Edinburgh: T&T Clark, 1995], 1–19) also makes use of the metaphor of dialogue: "The

between the Testaments because the doctrine of the Trinity implies that in the canon of Scripture (the subject of chap. 8) God speaks with one voice, not two. But Vanhoozer's point is well taken: a trinitarian hermeneutic will listen to the Old Testament on its own terms, trusting that the voice of the Father will be found to be in concord with that of the Son and of the Spirit. McCann's work on the Psalter is an excellent example of this sort of hermeneutic in practice.[26]

The notion of reconfiguring critical approaches (referred to above) is important. Methods are never philosophically and theologically neutral, and we should avoid uncritically importing methods of interpretation that at root are in epistemological conflict with the epistemic primacy of the Trinity.[27] Thus Tom Wright, for example, in his *The New Testament and the People of God*, notes that we need a more Jewish and less Greek form criticism for the Gospels.[28] The bifurcation between biblical studies and theology has often meant that methods are regularly applied to the Bible with the built-in assumption that God can neither act nor speak; clearly this sort of emphasis is ruled out by a trinitarian hermeneutic.

This is not to suggest that a trinitarian hermeneutic provides an easy option out of the many issues that historical criticism, literary analysis, and postmodern interpretation have raised in relation to the Bible. At their best all these approaches involve *very* close readings of the Bible, and the data they point to cannot and should not be ignored. But data is never neutral: it always comes within a particular framework or paradigm so that, as philosophers of science have declared, all theory is underdetermined. A trinitarian hermeneutic should not avoid any of these issues, but as Stephen Neill noted of a theology of history in relation to New Testament interpretation, it provides the appropriate ring within which solutions may and should be found.[29]

Chapter 10 deals with biblical interpretation and history, and chapters 11–12 with literature and theology. Chapter 9 deals with philosophy and biblical interpretation. A distinctive of this volume is its insistence that theology and

---

dialogical move of theological reflection that is being suggested traverses the partial and fragmentary grasp of reality found in both Testaments to the full reality that the church confesses to have found in Jesus Christ" (15).

26. J. C. McCann Jr., *A Theological Introduction to the Book of Psalms: The Psalms as Torah* (Nashville: Abingdon, 1993).

27. See C. G. Bartholomew, "Uncharted Waters: Philosophy, Theology, and the Crisis in Biblical Interpretation," in *Renewing Biblical Interpretation*, ed. C. G. Bartholomew, C. Greene, and K. Möller, SAHS 1 (Grand Rapids: Zondervan, 2000), 1–39.

28. N. T. Wright, *NTPG* 427.

29. S. Neill and N. T. Wright, *The Interpretation of the New Testament, 1861–1986*, 2nd ed. (Oxford: Oxford University Press, 1988), 366.

philosophy cannot be bracketed out of biblical interpretation. As I hope to show, such bracketing simply leaves unnamed theologies and philosophies to shape one's scholarship unconsciously. As the quote from Jauss at the outset of this chapter indicates, properly understood hermeneutics is no esoteric teaching but the theory of a practice. Done well, hermeneutics deepens and enriches our practice of engagement with the Bible as Scripture.

6. *A trinitarian hermeneutic rightly discerns the goal of reading the Bible.* So much academic exegesis falls short of what *must* be the goal of a trinitarian hermeneutic: obedient attention to God's address through his Word. From a trinitarian perspective any hermeneutic that fails to make this its goal is woefully inadequate. Athanasius makes the point that God is not incommunicative; he is always speaking![30] The Trinity reveals God to us as the living and true God: "God is fullness of being: 'ocean of essence.'"[31] And as Charles Wood rightly states, "To read the Bible, at least if one is properly prepared and disposed toward the task, is, on this view, to be addressed by God."[32] This is not for a moment to shortchange the rigor of biblical scholarship, but it does position all the hard work within the trajectory between an initial receptive listening and a final receptive listening. In chapter 2 I discuss ecclesial reception and lectio divina. The final chapter (15) is about preaching the Bible. Such an academic trinitarian hermeneutic begins with, proceeds with, and is consummated in communion: "To fall in love with this God, to be drawn into the love of this Father and this Son for one another, seems an outcome which only their Spirit can bring about."[33] Thus prayer and being present to God should accompany the hermeneutical process, both academic and ecclesial, from beginning to end and back again. It is the Spirit who leads ordinary Christian readers *as well as* the academic into the truth of Scripture.[34] Trinitarian biblical interpretation will proceed from him, through him, and to him.

30. H. Bavinck, *The Doctrine of God*, trans. W. Hendriksen (Edinburgh: Banner of Truth, 1978), 282.
31. Ibid., 330.
32. C. M. Wood, *The Formation of Christian Understanding: Theological Hermeneutics* (Eugene, OR: Wipf & Stock, 2000), 39.
33. B. D. Marshall, *Trinity and Truth*, 208.
34. B. D. Marshall (ibid., 180–216) and J. B. Webster (*Word and Church: Essays in Church Dogmatics* [Edinburgh: T&T Clark, 2001], 80) both notice the sinful resistance to approaching Scripture as God's address. Webster writes, "Crucially, this means that to read Scripture well is to undergo a chastening of the will, even, perhaps, 'the death of the subject and of the will.' Anything less would fail to take seriously the eschatological character of Christian life and therefore of Christian reading" (*Word and Church*, 80). For analyses of the role of the Spirit in interpretation, see B. D. Marshall, *Trinity and Truth*, 180–216; and K. J. Vanhoozer, "The Spirit of Understanding: Special Revelation and General Hermeneutics," in *Disciplining Hermeneutics: Interpretation in Christian Perspective*, ed. R. Lundin (Grand Rapids: Eerdmans,

As Jean Vanier poignantly expresses it,

> At one moment in time
> the "Logos"
> became flesh
> and entered history.
> He came to lead us all
> into this communion,
> which is the very life of God.[35]

A trinitarian hermeneutic will therefore always have as its goal to hear God's address, to facilitate communion. This is not to deny the cognitive, propositional element in God's communication but instead to insist that "an important aspect of truth gets lost when testimony is 'objectified.' Simply to preserve the content is to catch only half the sacred fish."[36] As Magrassi explains, "The passage that leads to the understanding of Scripture leads to life in Christ. When the Scriptures are opened, he admits us to his private domain. Every deeper reading of the text is a movement toward him. The essential task of exegesis . . . is to apply everything to the mystery of Christ. . . . He is the one center where all the lines of the biblical universe meet."[37]

7. *A trinitarian hermeneutic does not close down but opens up interpretation of the Bible.* A trinitarian hermeneutic is one among many approaches to the Bible in our increasingly pluralistic academy. However, we should not take this to imply that from a Christian perspective one approach is as valid as another, so that a trinitarian hermeneutic is simply a matter of personal preference. From a Christian perspective a trinitarian hermeneutic is the right and truthful way to read Scripture, the way that will yield a truthful understanding of the Bible.

But this way is spacious and fecund and creates room for a variety of genuinely theological readings of the Bible. As Seitz says,

> Concern with the figural linguistic world of Scripture did not mean single-meaning exegesis! No one reading Justin, Irenaeus, Clement, Origen, the Antiochenes, or Athanasius should expect anything like uniformity, yet all of them,

---

1997). H. de Lubac (*Scripture in the Tradition* [New York: Crossroad, 2000]) asserts, "Just as he is the exegesis of Scripture, Jesus Christ is also its exegete. . . . It is he and he alone who explains it to us, and in explaining it to us he is himself explained" (106–7).

35. J. Vanier, *Drawn into the Mystery of Jesus through the Gospel of John* (Ottawa: Novalis, 2004), 17.

36. Vanhoozer, *Drama of Doctrine*, 288.

37. M. Magrassi, *Praying the Bible: An Introduction to Lectio Divina*, trans. E. Hagman (Collegeville, MN: Liturgical Press, 1998), 44.

including Origen, bear a decided family resemblance. The dynamic character of scripture in its two-testament form does not allow for propositional or technical flattening, given that this witness is received in faith, under the guidance of the Holy Spirit, disciplined by prayer, eucharistic fellowship, and the teaching of the church in its baptismal interrogatories and creedal affirmations.[38]

Similarly Thiselton declares, "The inexhaustible, multilayered, multifunctional polyphony of biblical texts transcends repeatedly any single way of saying it; but this does not, need not, and should not invite the disastrous hospitality to radical pluralism that brings anarchy."[39] A trinitarian hermeneutic is radical in that it does exclude certain readings of the Old Testament: Seitz notes how a trinitarian hermeneutic opposes the "historicism" rampant in contemporary Old Testament studies;[40] Achtemeier shows how a theological hermeneutic is incompatible with the "developmentalism" of so much Old Testament study;[41] and we have noticed above how a trinitarian hermeneutics resists any theological move that disengages with Scripture as Scripture. Having said this, a trinitarian hermeneutic invites us to the feast of Scripture with its endless possibility of theological interpretation. In chapter 14 we will focus on the Epistle to the Hebrews as an example of such interpretation. As Neuhaus comments in his foreword to Oden's *Requiem*,

> Origen, Irenaeus, Cyril of Alexandria, Thomas Aquinas, Teresa of Avila, Martin Luther, John Calvin, John Wesley—the names fall trippingly from Oden's tongue like a gourmet surveying a most spectacular table. Here are arguments [and we would say interpretations of the Bible] you can sink your teeth into, conceptual flights of intoxicating complexity, and truths to die for. Far from the table, over there, *way* over there, is American theological education, where prodigal academics feed starving students on the dry husks of their clever unbelief.[42]

8. *A trinitarian hermeneutic takes God's address for* all of life *seriously*. It is astonishing how much content of the Old Testament is filtered out by commentators or simply overlooked. Take politics, for example: the Old Testament is jam-packed with political content, but commentators rarely engage

---

38. Seitz, *Figured Out*, 8–9.
39. A. C. Thiselton, "Communicative Action and Promise in Interdisciplinary, Biblical, and Theological Hermeneutics," in *The Promise of Hermeneutics*, by R. Lundin, C. Walhout, and A. C. Thiselton (Grand Rapids: Eerdmans, 1999), 138.
40. Seitz, *Figured Out*, 82–86.
41. E. Achtemeier, "The Canon as the Voice of the Living God," in Braaten and Jenson, *Reclaiming the Bible*, 123–24.
42. R. Neuhaus, "Foreword," in *Requiem: A Lament in Three Movements*, by T. C. Oden (Nashville: Abingdon, 1995), 10.

this in depth.[43] Acts (3:15) describes Jesus as the "Author of life"! With Jesus as the creator-redeemer, we would expect a trinitarian hermeneutic to open our eyes to find God addressing the whole of life as he has made it. Bavinck explains that

> the thoughtful person places the doctrine of the Trinity in the very center of the full-orbed life of nature and mankind. The confession of the Christian is not an island in mid-ocean but a mountain-top overlooking the entire creation. And it is the task of the Christian theologian to set forth clearly the great significance of God's revelation for (and the relation of that revelation to) the whole realm of existence. The mind of the Christian is not satisfied until every form of existence has been referred to the Triune God and until the confession of the Trinity has received the place of prominence in our thought and life.[44]

Trinitarian interpretation will take with the utmost seriousness what John Stott has called double listening: one ear to the Scripture, and the other to our cultures, with a view to discerning God's address to all of life today.[45] This is not nearly as common as it should be among Christian commentators. In this volume we attend to this issue in chapter 13, on the ecology of Christian scholarship and the role of the Bible in such work.

Conclusion

Isaiah 55 is an extraordinary chapter, ranging from an invitation to a feast, to the Davidic king and the nations, the transcendence of Yahweh, the word that goes out from Yahweh's mouth, and going forth with joy. How does one answer the invitation to this feast? Isaiah 55:2–3 provides the answer: "Listen carefully to me. . . . Incline your ear, and come to me; listen, so that you may live." It is as biblical hermeneutics inhabits the trajectory *from* listening *to* listening that it finds its place and is enabled to flourish. Thus Jean-Louis Chrétien poignantly testifies in his engagement with Augustine's *Sermon 288*, on John the Baptist:

---

43. O. O'Donovan in *The Desire of the Nations: Rediscovering the Roots of Political Theology* (Cambridge: Cambridge University Press, 1996) is exemplary in this respect.

44. Bavinck, *Doctrine of God*, 329. On a trinitarian worldview, see B. D. Marshall, *Trinity and Truth*, chap. 5. B. D. Marshall states, "Believing the gospel (that is, the narratives which identify Jesus and the triune God), therefore, necessarily commits believers to a comprehensive view of the world centered epistemically on the gospel narrative itself. On such a view there will be no region of belief and practice which can isolate itself from the epistemic reach of the gospel" (118).

45. J. Stott, *The Contemporary Christian* (Downers Grove, IL: InterVarsity, 1992), 29.

The voice cries out in truth when it lifts itself incandescently towards its own silence, so that "the voice of the Bridegroom" may be heard. Its ultimate joy, its perfect and plenary fulfillment, which is therefore to fail and be broken, is to fall silent in order to listen, after having invited others to be silent and listen, after having resounded and thrown the flames of its cry only for the sake of silence's excess over the cry. "Voices fade away in proportion as the Word increases," adds Saint Augustine.[46]

---

46. J.-L. Chrétien, *The Call and the Response*, trans. A. A. Davenport (Bronx, NY: Fordham University Press, 2004), 64.

2

Listening and Biblical Interpretation

> Does not the ear test words as the palate tastes food?
>
> Job 12:11

> The church is properly a hearing church before it is a speaking church.
>
> John Webster[1]

> But Christians have forgotten that the ministry of listening has been entrusted to them by the one who is indeed the great listener and in whose work they are to participate. We should listen with the ears of God, so that we can speak the Word of God.
>
> Dietrich Bonhoeffer[2]

Even in its acts of construing and interpreting, in bringing a communicative interest to bear upon the text, the Christian reading act is a kind of surrender. Above all, faithful reading is an aspect of *mortificatio sui*, a repudiation of the

---

1. J. B. Webster, *Word and Church: Essays in Church Dogmatics* (New York: T&T Clark, 2001), 36.
2. D. Bonhoeffer, *Life Together; Prayerbook of the Bible*, Dietrich Bonhoeffer Works 5 (Minneapolis: Fortress, 1996), 99.

desire to assemble all realities, including texts, including even the revelation of God, around the steady centre of my will.

Dietrich Bonhoeffer[3]

The patient consciousness knows that its attentiveness and expectation [*son attention et son attente*] give it no hold over God. . . . Liturgy never ceases to tell us that being-in-the-world is not the definitive, and it represents the initial and not the originary.

Jean-Yves Lacoste[4]

In recent years theological interpretation has drawn attention to the divide between biblical studies and theology. This cleavage has been damaging to both disciplines. However, a renewal of the relationship between these two *academic* disciplines does not go nearly far enough in addressing the root of the issue. The underlying issue is that of the nature of Scripture and the appropriate mode of receiving it. Academic work, including biblical studies and theology, concentrates on analysis; Scripture asks first to be *listened to* as God's address.[5]

There are a multitude of ways in which one could approach the issue of listening to Scripture as God's Word. Liturgical churches retain a sense of this overwhelming reality with their response to every reading of Scripture: "This is the Word of the Lord. . . . Thanks be to God!" Jesus used parables to provoke his audience to listen attentively, hence his repeated, "Let those who have ears to hear, hear." At the center of Ecclesiastes we find a characteristic wisdom *and* liturgical insight: "Approach to listen" (4:17 MT [5:1 NRSV]).[6] If we are looking for a patron saint for biblical interpretation, I would propose Mary, Martha's sister. While Martha is bustling around, Mary is attending to *the one thing necessary*; quiet attentive listening to Jesus.

The narrative of Jesus at the house of Martha in Luke 10:38–42 has attracted considerable attention in the history of interpretation, not least in relation to the priority of the *vita contemplativa*. The setting of the contemplative life against the working life is a false dualism, although, undoubtedly, some are called primarily to one or the other. In the Greek "the better part" is actually "the good [ἀγαθήν] part." Van Prinsterer is thus right in saying, "One thing is needful, but when we

---

3. Ibid., 43–44.
4. J.-Y. Lacoste, *Experience and the Absolute: Disputed Questions on the Humanity of Man*, Perspectives in Continental Philosophy (Bronx, NY: Fordham University Press, 2004), 91–92.
5. K. Barth (*CD* I/1:51) rightly states that theology cannot claim to be proclamation. Proclamation is the *presupposition* of theology, so that theology originates in listening.
6. See C. G. Bartholomew, *Ecclesiastes*, BCOTWP (Grand Rapids: Baker Academic, 2009), 201–5.

possess that one thing the fruits of it should be manifest in everything.... The fear of the Lord is the beginning of knowledge, but the beginning is not the whole of it; the whole of knowledge embraces the other elements as well, in which the beginning is worked out."[7] The point of this narrative is that, for everyone, "the one thing needful" is indispensable. And what is this one thing needful? The answer is given in Mary's action: she sat at Jesus's feet and *listened* to what he was saying. It is such listening that is the primary way in which to receive Scripture.

Augustine provocatively says that he knows what Mary was doing: she was eating Jesus!

> For Mary was intent on the sweetness of the Lord's word. Martha was intent, how she might feed the Lord; Mary intent how she might be fed by the Lord. By Martha a feast was being prepared for the Lord, in whose feast Mary was even now delighting herself. As Mary then was listening with sweet pleasure to His most sweet word, and was feeding with the most earnest affection, when the Lord was appealed to by her sister, how, think we, did she fear, lest the Lord should say to her, Rise and help your sister? For by a wondrous sweetness was she held; a sweetness of the mind which is doubtless greater than that of the senses. She was excused, she sat in greater confidence.[8]

One of Kierkegaard's edifying discourses is titled *Purity of Heart Is to Will One Thing*. As we will see elsewhere, in his corpus Kierkegaard embodies a rich style of listening to Scripture. In this book he has a chapter with the subtitle "The Listener's Role in a Devotional Address."[9] He stresses the personal engagement of the reader, the role of silence, and warns against listeners becoming "critical theatergoers."[10] The good listener "pays attention to himself, to how he listens, and whether during the address he, in his inner self, secretly talks with God."[11] The listener "stands openly before God."[12]

A Philosophy of Listening

Lest we think that a recovery of such listening will be easy, a word of caution is in order. Chrétien recognizes that "listening requires patience, effort, hard work, and obedience."[13] Fiumara points out in detail the extent to which listening has been lost in our culture today, and not least in academia.[14] Working in the continental philosophical tradition, she excavates lost elements of Greek words such as *logos* and *legein*. Our Western tradition, she rightly

---

7. H. Van Dyke, *Groen van Prinsterer's Lectures on Unbelief and Revolution* (Jordan Station, ON: Wedge, 1989), Lecture I, 11–12.
8. Augustine, *Sermon 54 on the New Testament* 1, www.newadvent.org/fathers/160354.htm.
9. S. Kierkegaard, *Purity of Heart Is to Will One Thing* (New York: Harper & Row, 1938, 1948), 177.
10. Ibid., 181.
11. Ibid.
12. Ibid.
13. J.-L. Chrétien, *The Call and the Response*, trans. A. A. Davenport (Bronx, NY: Fordham University Press, 2004), 68.
14. G. C. Fiumara, *The Other Side of Language: A Philosophy of Listening* (London: Routledge, 1995). The overprivileging of sight has a long history. Fiumara reports Heraclitus's belief that "the eyes are more exact witnesses than the ears" (ibid., 41). Derrida wished to privilege writing, as he understood it, over speech; I wish to privilege listening over speech and writing.

maintains, is logocratic: "In the tradition of Western thought we are thus faced with a system of knowledge that tends to ignore listening processes"[15] so that we are left with only half the meaning of *logos*, "a partial sense of *logos* understood precisely as a capacity for ordering and explaining, detached from any propensity to receive and listen."[16] Heidegger refers to language as the "house of being,"[17] but how, asks Fiumara, can we "host being" in such a diminished house?

Fiumara is sympathetic to Gadamer's dialogical approach to understanding but cautions against privileging *our* questions. There is no method to learn listening; it requires careful attentiveness. Lack of attention to listening has left us with a kind of epistemological benumbment. "The inability to listen . . . can only result in a surrender to the pull of benumbing trends."[18] Listening should be epistemologically central; indeed, it functions like a midwife, opening the way to thought. Listening involves focused concentration and consequently "the reawakening of our epistemic potential."[19] "The exercise of listening to oneself and to others, even if only occasionally, may be of help in the attempt to restore the core of inner functions as a premise for the integration of a 'life of thought' which is often too dissipated and devoid of strength. The attitude toward listening implies a basic trust—almost a hope."[20] Attentive, reciprocal listening is alone capable of stimulating intellectual wonder.

Intriguingly, Fiumara attends to the role of silence in listening.[21] "In my opinion the creation of an empty space, or distance, within a dialogic relation might be the only way of letting the deeper meanings and implications of that relationship emerge."[22] Inner silence is crucial to listening: indeed, the advancement of listening depends on "one's ability to reenter one's own self."[23] Fiumara refers to this silence as "inner listening": "The search for personal identity seems to coincide with heeding one's own inner expression; a message whose origin is so deep . . . that, evidently, one opts from a contact anchored to listening rather than to the logical interrogation advocated by the Sophists."[24]

15. Ibid., 1.
16. Ibid., 10.
17. M. Heidegger, *Letter on Humanism* (1949), §145, wagner.edu/psychology/files/2013/01/Heidegger-Letter-On-Humanism-Translation-GROTH.pdf.
18. Fiumara, *Other Side of Language*, 84.
19. Ibid., 83.
20. Ibid., 162.
21. Ibid., chap. 7.
22. Ibid., 102.
23. Ibid., 115.
24. Ibid., 131.

Within the Christian tradition contemplation of the Christ child has been a fertile site for reflection on silence, particularly in the seventeenth century,[25] although this emphasis is already found in Augustine, who, in one of his Christmas sermons speaks of Christ as "unspeakably wise, wisely speechless as an infant."[26] "The *Verbum infans* is Speech that does not speak, that cannot speak, Speech deprived of speech. In coming to reveal himself to us, the Word began by becoming silent."[27] Bourgoing notices: "On the cross, Jesus was deprived of the effects of his power and his glory, but not of his wisdom nor of his speech, for he spoke there; but in the manger he said not a word, he spoke not. The Shepherds hailed him, the Magi came from the East to adore him, and yet this divine wisdom manifested itself not at all, the Word of God became silent."[28]

The Word's silence calls forth our silence. Grou says, "Reason loses itself here, it must adore, and hold itself in silence."[29] Chrétien, in a masterful reflection on George de La Tour's *Adoration of the Shepherds*, observes that all the adults in the painting are "intensely silent." "They adore the silent Word in silence, in silence and by silence. . . . This silence, in every respect is central; . . . their silence too belongs to him. . . . He is the Master of silence, and they are only his servants."[30]

Not surprisingly, Chrétien goes on to attend to the silence of listening.[31] He refers to Rembrandt's remarkable engraving titled *La Petite Tombe* (see fig. 2.1).[32] Only Jesus's body is open; he has his arms raised with his somewhat heavy head inclined: "He too listens, and he speaks only because he listens, for the words that he says he does not say on his own."[33] Apart from the child in the foreground, all in the audience exhibit "extreme attention, and thus . . . a profound silence as well."[34] In my reading of the work, one enters the engraving through the figure of the child and circles to the right until one encounters the image of a bearded man leaning forward in rapt attention. He almost looks as though he is on the move into Jesus's words! Major says of this work that "Rembrandt here accomplished the impossible: he made the portrait of a voice."[35] However, as Chrétien notes, "But the portrait of a voice can be made only by showing us the dimension of silence from which it proceeds and the dimension of silence to which it addresses itself: this is

25. Notably Cardinal Pierre de Bérulle (1575–1629) and François Bourgoing (1585–1662).

26. Augustine of Hippo, *Essential Sermons*, trans. E. Hill (Hyde Park, NY: New City, 2007), 245.

27. J.-L. Chrétien, *Hand to Hand: Listening to the Work of Art*, trans. S. E. Lewis (Bronx, NY: Fordham University Press, 2003), 44.

28. Ibid., 45, quoting R. P. F. Bourgoing, *Méditations sur les vérités et excellences de Jésus-Christ Notre-Seigneur* (Paris, 1636; or later ed.), 1:446–47.

29. Chrétien, *Hand to Hand*, 46, quoting J. N. Grou, *L'intérieur des Jésus et de Marie* (Paris, 1829), 2:228–89.

30. Chrétien, *Hand to Hand*, 47–48.

31. See also J.-L. Chrétien's remarkable chapter "The Hospitality of Silence," in his *The Ark of Speech*, trans. A. Brown (New York: Routledge, 2004), 39–75. Chrétien notes that silence is the precondition of listening and of vision. He quotes Herman Melville (*Pierre, or The Ambiguities* [New York: Harper & Brothers, 1852]), the author of *Moby-Dick*, who asserts, "All profound things, and emotions of things are preceded and attended by silence. . . . Silence is the invisible laying on of the Divine Pontiff's hands upon the world" (16.1.240). Chrétien rightly distinguishes different types of silence, all related in one way or another to speech.

32. J. S. Held ("Rembrandt and the Spoken Word," in *Rembrandt Studies* [Princeton: Princeton University Press, 1991], 164–83) argues that human speech and listening are the acts constitutive of Rembrandt's work.

33. Chrétien, *Hand to Hand*, 50.

34. Ibid., 49.

35. Quoted in ibid., 50.

what Rembrandt understood so profoundly."[36] In a Christmas sermon, Tauler says, "This is why you must fall silent: then the Word of this birth will be utterable within you and you will be able to hear it.... It is in the midst of silence, at the very moment when all things are plunged into the greatest silence, where the true silence reigns, it is then that one truly hears the Word, for if you wish God to speak, you must be silent; for him to enter, all things must come out."[37]

The silence required for listening to the Word requires a self-emptying for, as Chrétien notes, "The Word is always speaking within us, but we do not pay attention to it, we cover up its voice with our own inner tumult."[38] Chrétien takes his metaphor of *the ark of speech* from Noah's ark; he perceptively comments, "Our voice cannot build the ark of speech, in which everything will be given shelter and received, unless it be in proportion to the hospitality of its silence."[39]

There is much here to unpack in relation to biblical hermeneutics. Fiumara perceptively opens up the integral relationship between listening and analysis. Our analysis of texts will be hindered and distorted if it does not begin with listening.[40] Nevertheless, when it comes to Scripture in particular, it is important, as we will see below, to distinguish an approach that is predominantly one of receptive listening, yet includes analysis—and the predominantly analytical approach of biblical studies, which nevertheless should be rooted and sustained in listening. According to Chrétien, "The first hospitality is nothing other than listening.... And is not the ultimate hospitality, that of the Lord, the hospitality that falls, dizzyingly, into the luminous listening of the Word, listening to it so as to speak, speaking so as to listen to it? Listening is big with eternity."[41]

Theologically listening is an extension of our being creaturely; it is a manifestation of creaturely humility. As Gabriel Marcel rightly states, "At the root of humility lies the more or less unexpressed assertion, 'By myself, I am nothing and I can do nothing except in so far as I am not only helped but promoted in my being by Him who is everything and is all-powerful.'"[42] As Marcel says, humility is a mode of being and should not be confused with humiliation. Prophetically, Marcel argues that for many today a hubris akin to that of Prometheus has become an "habitual disposition,"[43] with a consequent confusing of humility and humiliation. For Marcel, humility involves

36. Ibid., 50.
37. J. Tauler, *Sermons*, trans. É. Hugueny et al. (Paris: Cerf, 1991), 17, 20.
38. Chrétien, *Ark of Speech*, 54.
39. Ibid., 74.
40. A. G. Sertillanges (*The Intellectual Life: Its Spirit, Conditions, Methods* [Washington, DC: Catholic University of America Press, 1998]) advises the intellectual, "Learn to listen; and listen first, to anyone" (74).
41. Chrétien, *Ark of Speech*, 9.
42. G. Marcel, *The Mystery of Being*, vol. 2, *Faith and Reality* (South Bend, IN: St. Augustine's Press, 2001), 85–86; cf. Chrétien, *Call and the Response*, 66–67.
43. Marcel, *Mystery of Being*, 87.

Figure 2.1 Rembrandt's engraving *La Petite Tombe*

a creative receptivity and an authentic transcendence. In line with Jacques Ellul and others,[44] Marcel rightly observes that humility is incompatible with *technique*, insofar as the latter sees scientific method as the royal route to truth across the gamut of created life.[45] Ellul says of technique that "we are dealing with what is basically a power covering the full range of human life. This expansion of technology to human groups, to human life, is one of the essential characteristics of our world."[46] To a significant extent modern biblical study is an expression of modernity with concomitant strengths and weaknesses. A serious weakness is the overwhelming embrace of method and thus *technique*, in Ellul's sense of the word,[47] as the key to interpretation, an approach that marginalizes, if not eliminates, listening.

---

44. See works by W. H. Vanderburg, who did his postdoctoral work under J. Ellul and has developed Ellul's work in important ways; and G. Grant, *Technology and Justice* (Toronto: Anansi, 1986).

45. On technique, see J. Ellul, *The Technological Society* (New York: Knopf, 1964).

46. W. H. Vanderburg, ed., *Perspectives on Our Age: Jacques Ellul Speaks on His Life and Work* (New York: Seabury, 1981), 38.

47. See ibid., 31–57; Ellul, *Technological Society*, 3–60: "The technical operation includes every operation carried out in accordance with a certain method in order to attain a particular end" (19).

Biblical hermeneutics needs to recover the primacy of creative receptivity, of listening. This is not for a moment to undermine the role of analysis but to insist that listening and analysis are linked by, as Fiumara notes, "a message whose origin is so deep." Clearly the way we approach biblical hermeneutics is at the outset irrevocably related to our view of the world. The scant attention to listening in much work on biblical interpretation is an indication of the extent to which biblical studies has been shaped by some of the least attractive aspects of modernity. Starting with listening provides us with an opportunity to redirect biblical hermeneutics along healthier lines.

The Shema

With regard to this, a central text for both Jews and Christians is the *šĕmaʿ* (Shema) of Deuteronomy 6:4–9.[48] In 6:3–4 the imperative *šĕmaʿ*, which could well be translated as "Listen!"[49] alerts the Israelites to the fundamental importance of *listening* to God's address mediated through Moses. This connects with the church's root metaphor for Scripture: it is God's Word/address, and the attitude of reception it calls for is *respectful listening*. In the light of the Shema, this is obvious: what alternative attitude would be more appropriate than a trembling, open receptivity? And yet, as we know, Moses's speeches are a constant reminder that for the Israelites an alternative response of unbelief and autonomous disagreement was in practice all too prevalent.

In its modern guise biblical studies is largely an heir to the Enlightenment legacy, in which rational analysis with its focus on what *we* can *see* is primary. The visual metaphor—albeit a particular version—replaces the auditory.[50] What Karl Barth says of modernist dogmatics is as true of too much modern biblical interpretation:

> Modernist dogmatics is finally unaware of the fact that in relation to God man has constantly to let something be said to him, has constantly to listen to something, which he constantly does not know and which in no circumstances

---

48. There is a great deal of literature on the Shema; see, e.g., D. I. Block, *How I Love Your Torah, O Lord! Studies in Deuteronomy* (Eugene, OR: Cascade Books, 2011), 73–97; R. W. L. Moberly, *Old Testament Theology: Reading the Bible as Christian Scripture* (Grand Rapids: Baker Academic, 2013), 7–40.

49. Block translates *šĕmaʿ* as "Listen" (*How I Love*, 73).

50. This is not to assert that the auditory metaphor is somehow better than the visual. Both are subject, in Al Wolters's terms (*Creation Regained: Biblical Basics for a Reformational Worldview* [Grand Rapids: Eerdmans, 1985]), to structure and direction. In Gen. 1 the visual metaphor is very positive, whereas in Gen. 3 it is negative. In Ps. 119, a great example of creative receptivity, the visual is a dominant metaphor in a positive sense; cf. 119:6, 15, 18, 37, 82, 105, 123, 148.

and in no sense can he say to himself. Modernist dogmatics hears man answer when no one has called him. It hears him speak with himself.[51]

Analysis of the Bible has a vital place, as we will see, but when it comes to biblical interpretation, the replacement of listening with *our* seeing turns Deuteronomy 6 and the Christian tradition on its head. Such a visual hermeneutic embraces the Enlightenment elevation of *right method*, a seduction to which both conservatives and liberals have fallen prey. On the right and the left, method is exalted, whether it be the grammatico-historical method or the historical-critical or the postmodern smorgasbord of methods; all such academic approaches presuppose that if we just get the method of analysis right, true (or playful) readings will result. And method is all about analysis, about what *we* can *see* in the text.

The Shema and the understanding of Scripture as God's Word insist that prior to analysis comes listening. Such a hermeneutic privileges trust and hospitality toward the Word because of the Real Presence of God that underlies it. In secular literature the closest approximation to such a hermeneutic is that articulated by George Steiner in his *Real Presences*.

George Steiner's *Courteous* Hermeneutic

Steiner's overt use of eucharistic lexicography (*Real Presences*) to articulate his view of language indicates Catholic influence, which is mediated to an extent by Heidegger, but Steiner's stronger theological commitments also distinguish him from Heidegger.[52] From the outset in *Real Presences*, Steiner is clear that any coherent account of language and communication needs to be supported by a theology of God's presence.[53] Steiner is acutely aware of the interpretative crisis of our time—secondary critical reflection on literature and art has become an end in itself, and in this Secondary City we are hindered from directly encountering art and literature, and thus the Bible. Steiner relates this crisis in artistic encounter and interpretation to a loss of the transcendent. Such a time radically misconceives hermeneutics, which rightly understood is "the enactment of answerable understanding, of active

51. K. Barth, *CD* I/1:61–62.
52. See George Ward, "Heidegger in Steiner," in *Reading George Steiner*, ed. N. A. Scott and R. A. Sharp (London: Johns Hopkins University Press, 1994), 180–204, esp. 199–200.
53. Cf. K. Barth, who says, "Even the realities and truths distinct from Him [God] and us which usually form the concrete occasion and subject of human speech exist from Him and to Him. Hence there is no genuinely profane speech. In the last resort, there is only talk about God" (*CD* I/1:47).

apprehension."[54] Steiner correctly discerns theological reasons behind our consumer society's preference for the secondary. We prefer not to confront the real presence or the absence thereof. Amid all the secondary theory we welcome the one who can secularize the mystery and call of creation![55]

According to Steiner, humans have great and unbounded freedom when it comes to language. There is no limit to the chain of signs, and it is the way we think about this infinity that shapes our practice of interpretation. "Inhabiting language, . . . both the act of interpretation and that of assessment, hermeneutics and criticism, are inextricably enmeshed in the metaphysical and theological or anti-theological question of unbounded saying."[56] An effect of this, according to Steiner, is that language cannot ultimately be verified or falsified.[57] Generally we proceed by appealing to consensus and tradition (the canonic), but this is never decisive.[58]

The consequent turn to theory to make reading of language scientific is like trying to catch the wind.[59] The principles of indeterminacy and of complementarity, as understood in particle physics, are central to all interpretation. Each text is singular. For Steiner there is a gap, therefore, between all theories and the process of understanding. Theory has value, but only if it is aware of its reductiveness. Theories are best understood as narratives of moments of illumination while dealing with texts.[60] Steiner describes the claim to theory in the humanities as impatience systematized; he claims that today this impatience has assumed nihilistic urgency.

How have we reached our present state? For Steiner, there has been a monumental break in our understanding of the word-world relationship. Our understanding of language and discourse had previously been underwritten by trust, by the assumption that being is "sayable." According to Steiner, this contract was broken in a major way for the first time during the decades from the 1870s to the 1930s. "*It is this break of the covenant between word and world which constitutes one of the very few genuine revolutions in spirit in Western history and which defines modernity itself.*"[61] So decisive is this shift for Steiner that he distinguishes two major phases in our "inward history,"

---

54. G. Steiner, *Real Presences: Is There Anything in What We Say?* (London: Faber & Faber, 1989), 7; see p. 9 for his emphasis on performance and on ingestion of the text so that it becomes part of the pacemaker of one's consciousness.
55. Ibid., 39.
56. Ibid., 59.
57. Ibid., 61, 68.
58. Ibid., 68.
59. "Chasing after wind" is an idiom central to Ecclesiastes (e.g., 1:14, 17).
60. Steiner, *Real Presences*, 86.
61. Ibid., 93, with original emphasis.

the first being that from the beginnings of recorded history to the late nineteenth century. This is the phase of the "saying of being." The second is that which follows this phase, the time of the after-Word, of the epilogue, "an immanence within the logic of the 'afterword.'"[62]

Steiner discerns this monumental shift in Western consciousness in Mallarmé's understanding of language as embodying "real absence" and in Rimbaud's deconstruction of the first-person singular as encapsulated in his "*Je est un autre*." Mallarmé rejects the "covenant of reference" and argues that nonreference constitutes the true genius of language.[63] "Where Mallarmé alters the epistemology of 'real presence' (theologically grounded) into one of 'real absence,' Rimbaud posits at the now vacant heart of consciousness the splintered images of other and momentary 'selves.'"[64]

Steiner identifies four great currents of the "after-Word" that followed this revolution in consciousness: that of Wittgenstein, post-Saussurean linguistics, psychoanalysis (Freud, Lacan), and the indictment of language in *Sprachkritik* (Fritz Mauthner, Karl Kraus). For Steiner, Nietzsche's "death of God" and Freud's implicit secularization of the psyche are footnotes to the breach represented by Mallarmé and Rimbaud. In Derrida and deconstruction, Steiner discerns the nihilistic consequences of the after-Word: "In a time of epilogue and after-Word, a critique such as deconstruction *must* be formulated."[65]

Steiner recognizes the grounds for refuting deconstruction, but the problem is that deconstruction can live quite comfortably with the critique it engenders. In Steiner's opinion, deconstruction is, on its own terms, irrefutable. The real alternative is to ask what would happen if we take theology and metaphysics seriously![66]

> [Steiner] chooses not to waste time on polemic: because what Paul Ricoeur calls "the dismantled fortress of consciousness" is not to be "restored or made foolproof by replacing this or that fallen brick." . . . He sees with absolute clarity that the most essential repudiation lying at the heart of the whole deconstructive enterprise is a theological repudiation, and thus, as he feels, the one kind of faith (in unfaith) may only be countered by another kind of faith.[67]

62. Ibid., 228.
63. Ibid., 96.
64. Ibid., 99.
65. Ibid., 120. The Italian philosopher Giorgio Agamben (*The Time That Remains: A Commentary on the Letter to the Romans*, trans. P. Dailey [Stanford, CA: Stanford University Press, 2005]) says of Derrida's philosophy that "Deconstruction is a thwarted messianism, a suspension of the messianic" (103).
66. Ibid., 134.
67. N. A. Scott, "Steiner on Interpretation," in Scott and Sharp, *Reading George Steiner*, 1–13, esp. 4.

In Steiner's words, "The issue is, quite simply, that of the meaning of meaning as it is re-insured by the existence of God. 'In the beginning was the Word.' There was no such beginning, says deconstruction; only the play of sounds and markers amid the mutations of time."[68] This alternative architecture of language and literature/art is the subject of the third section of *Real Presences*, to which we will come below.

In the Christian tradition a remarkable recovery of *being as sayable* is found in Chrétien's *The Ark of Speech*.[69] Chrétien takes the image of the "ark" from Noah's ark! His reflection on Adam's naming of the animals is acute and representative of his view of language as hospitality.

> Much more essential, and worthy of consideration, is the fact that this story makes human speech into the *first ark*. The animals have been gathered for human speech and brought together in this speech, which names them long before they are brought together . . . in Noah's ark to be saved from the flood and the destruction it brings. . . . Their first guardian, their first safeguard, is that of speech, which shelters their being and their diversity. This is true for more than just the animals. No protective gesture could take responsibility for the least being if the latter had not been taken up into speech.[70]

Like Steiner, Chrétien relates his view of language to *creation*: "In the account of creation given in the first chapter of Genesis, we see brought into play, so that the game of the world can be played, a word and a gaze—and they are inseparable."[71] Paul Celan was not the first to notice the common root of *denken* (think) and *danken* (thank), but as Chrétien notes, "To think is to thank, but for this to be true, to thank must be to think really and truly, in other words to see."[72] For Chrétien,

> The world itself is heavy with speech, it calls on speech and on our speech in response, and it calls only by responding itself, already, to the Speech that created it. How could it be foreign to the word, when it subsists, through faith, only by the Word? . . . The speech we utter about the world does not come from beyond the world, it is no more a stranger to the world than we are.[73]

As with Steiner, a grammar of creation makes all the difference in the world to reading. In the Christian tradition the world has often been likened to a

---

68. Steiner, *Real Presences*, 120.
69. See esp. Chrétien's chapter "The Offering of the World" in *Ark of Speech*, 111–48.
70. Chrétien, *Ark of Speech*, 2.
71. Ibid., 115.
72. Ibid., 119.
73. Ibid., 129.

book, and Chrétien observes that "within the book, God has created readers: us. Reading must of course be learnt, and requires, in our present condition, effort and patience; the fact remains that this book is not written in an unintelligible language."[74] By virtue of the way God has made the world, including human beings, being is sayable!

In order to articulate a vision of interpretation that does justice to our experience of the other, Steiner invokes the metaphor of *courtesy*, just as Chrétien invokes the metaphor of *hospitality*. Steiner is worth quoting at length on this point.

> The phenomenology of courtesy would organize, that is to say, quicken into articulate life, our meetings with each other, with the beloved, with the adversary, with the familiar and the stranger. . . . Classically, where branch and leaf are highest, *cortesia* qualifies the last ambush or the final tryst which is the possible venue—the coming, the coming to a place—of God. . . . We lay a clean cloth on the table when we hear the guest at our threshold. In the paintings of Chardin, in the poems of Trakl, that movement at evening is made both domestic and sacramental. . . . What we must focus, with uncompromising clarity, on the text, on the work of art, on the music before us, is an ethic of common sense, a courtesy of the most robust and refined sort.[75]

Such courtesy allows the object of interpretation precedence over the reader, thereby reversing the direction of our Secondary City. The movement toward reception and understanding embodies an initial act of trust. The guest may turn antagonistic, but in order to open the door, we have to gamble on trust.[76] Steiner discerns three levels of philological reception of a text. Lexical-grammatical study is, for Steiner, the opening of the door to a text. The second level is that of sensitivity to syntax. The third level is that of the semantic.[77]

Steiner notes that this passage into meaning always entails interaction with *context*, and the latter is unbounded. However, contra deconstruction, "the fact that there cannot be, in Coleridge's macaronic phrase, any *omnium gatherum* of the context that is the world, does not mean that intelligibility is either wholly arbitrary or self-erasing. Such deduction is nihilistic sophistry."[78]

---

74. Ibid., 141.
75. Steiner, *Real Presences*, 148–49.
76. Ibid., 156.
77. Here cf. Steiner's fourfold understanding of the hermeneutic motion, in *After Babel: Aspects of Language and Translation*, 3rd ed. (Oxford: Oxford University Press, 1998), 312–16: Understanding starts with trust, then comes aggression, then incorporation, and finally the enactment of reciprocity.
78. Steiner, *Real Presences*, 163.

The dialectic of context alerts us to the impossibility of a systematic theory of meaning in anything but a metaphoric sense. Art and literature are expressions of human freedom, and such freedom always has as a corollary the sort of radical doubt of deconstruction. But between the illusion of absolute presence and the play of deconstruction "lies the rich, legitimate ground of the philological."[79]

It is a mistake to ignore the historicity of texts. We welcome them now, but this immediacy is always historically informed.[80] As the metaphor of courtesy implies, a good reading is never complete and final; its falling short guarantees the otherness of the text. But such limitation does not reduce the presence before us to absence or falsehood.

In the transcendent is where Steiner grounds the experience of otherness in art. There is human creation because there is creation.

> So far as it wagers on meaning, an account of the act of reading, in the fullest sense, of the act of the reception and internalization of significant forms within us, is a metaphysical and, in the last analysis, a theological one. The ascription of beauty to truth and to meaning is either a rhetorical flourish, or it is a piece of theology. . . . The meaning of meaning is a transcendent postulate. To read the poem responsibly ("respondingly"), to be answerable to form, is to wager on a reinsurance of sense. It is to wager on a relationship . . . between word and world, but on a relationship precisely bounded by that which reinsures it.[81]

Steiner has brought an incisive, theological critique to bear on literary and hermeneutical developments. In the 1970s the literary turn in biblical interpretation brought with it many positive developments. Although Steiner has not written extensively on biblical interpretation, in his review of *The Literary Guide to the Bible* he articulated the theological weaknesses of some literary approaches to the Bible with rare precision:

> The question is: Does this "Literary Guide" help us to come to sensible grips with the singularity and the overwhelming provocations of the Bible—a singularity and a summons altogether independent of the reach of current literary-critical fashions? Does it help us to understand in what ways the Bible and the demands of answerability it puts upon us are like no others? Of this tome . . . a terrible blandness is born. . . . We hear of "omelettes," of "pressure cookers," not of the terror, of the *mysterium tremendum*, that inhabits man's endeavours to speak to and speak of God. . . . The separation, made in the name of current

---

79. Ibid., 165.
80. See ibid., 168–78, for Steiner's nuanced discussion of biography and intentionality.
81. Ibid., 216.

rationalism and agnosticism, between a theological-religious experiencing of Biblical texts and a literary one is radically factitious. It cannot work.[82]

From the above, it is clear just what a fertile view of interpretation Steiner's courteous hermeneutic yields, and just how helpful this is for biblical interpretation. Suffice it here to indicate some of the insights in Steiner's hermeneutic for biblical interpretation.

Steiner's warm and human hermeneutic[83] is miles away from Derrida's cold hermeneutic, which hands us over to the flux of history.[84] The text is given priority, and there is an ethics of interpretation acknowledging that one can do all sorts of things with texts but which insists that "answerable understanding" is the reader's first responsibility, and *how can one answer without listening?* Criticism is allowed a full role in exegesis, but it is made subsidiary to the text, the reading of the text, and encounter with it. Texts do have rights,[85] and while right method cannot guarantee the right reading, there is every hope that if approached courteously, with all the philological rigor that Steiner insists on, they will yield their treasures—albeit never completely—to their readers. Like Gadamer, Steiner by no means rejects method but repositions it within a larger context.[86] Steiner resists the polarities of determinacy and indeterminacy of textual interpretation and leaves us with a rigorous and hopeful, yet humble, hermeneutic.

Steiner goes a long way toward exposing the reason why listening to texts and especially Scripture is so politically incorrect nowadays. The underlying reason is religious but comes to us clothed in contemporary philosophies of language, literary theories, and hermeneutics, most of which either ignore theology or are opposed to it, at least in its orthodox form. A depth recovery

---

82. G. Steiner, "Books: The Good Books," *The New Yorker*, January 11, 1988, 94–98, esp. 96–97, reviewing *The Literary Guide to the Bible*, by R. Alter and F. Kermode (Cambridge, MA: Harvard University Press, 1999).

83. G. Steiner ("A Responsion," in Scott and Sharp, *Reading George Steiner*) defines true criticism and reading as a "debt of love." In contrast, he reports that he has "felt our age and climate to be one of *invidia*, of the sneer" (276).

84. J. D. Caputo (*Radical Hermeneutics: Repetition, Deconstruction, and the Hermeneutic Project* [Bloomington: Indiana University Press, 1987], 187–206) describes Derrida's interpretation of interpretation in this way. Contra my perspective, E. Wyschogrod ("The Mind of a Critical Moralist: Steiner as Jew," in Scott and Sharp, *Reading George Steiner*, 151–79) argues that Steiner is closer to Derrida than Steiner's critique suggests.

85. Contra R. Morgan with J. Barton, *Biblical Interpretation* (Oxford: Oxford University Press, 1988), 7.

86. On Gadamer and method, see the important essay by G. B. Madison, *The Hermeneutics of Postmodernity: Figures and Themes*, Studies in Phenomenology and Existential Philosophy (Bloomington: Indiana University Press, 1988), 25–39. H.-G. Gadamer is not an advocate of truth *or* method, but of *Truth and Method* (New York: Seabury, 1975).

of biblical interpretation *must* therefore attend to hermeneutics and its theological underpinnings with all that this discipline now entails. The following chapters are not an unnecessary detour, as some proponents of theological interpretation argue, but an indispensable route if we are to understand our present context and find genuinely healthy ways forward.

Steiner's approach gives some indication of how interpretation of Scripture may differ from interpretation of other books. There is a tendency for Steiner to treat all "great works" as canonical in a similar way, but Steiner's encouragement to Old Testament scholars to revisit the issue of the authorship of the Bible[87]—reporting that on a good day he can imagine Shakespeare writing his plays but cannot similarly conceive of the speeches of God in Job—indicates an understanding of the peculiar provocations of the Bible. And it is surely true that to read Scripture without making these provocations a focus is woefully inadequate.

That Steiner's hermeneutic is overtly theological and rooted in the "grammars of creation"[88] is a strength and not a weakness. There is certainly room for clearer articulation of the theology that underlies Steiner's type of hermeneutic, but, contra Robert Carroll,[89] in general Steiner's grammars of creation are precisely the sort of foundation a biblical hermeneutic requires. As Chrétien says, "A song that offers the world to the light of its origin, which illuminates it by virtue of offering it, and illuminates itself as the place where it comes to offer itself—such is the horizon of all human speech, and already the horizon of the air that we breathe in and out."[90]

If all interpretation (of texts) is underwritten by a theology of real presences, then how much more so is Scripture as God's Word. Steiner and Chrétien perceptively recognize the fundamental importance of the relationship between language and creation; indeed, Scripture comes to us in Hebrew, Aramaic, and Greek as the deposit—like the silt of a river—resulting from God's engagement with Israel, culminating in the incarnation of the Word. Christians confess that these historically produced writings are the authoritative witness to the God who has come to us in Christ, so that as we listen to them, we hear God's address. The Real Presence of the trinitarian God underlies Scripture in a unique

---

87. G. Steiner, lecture given to the Society of the Old Testament in the UK; cf. Steiner's comments on Job in his *Grammars of Creation* (London: Faber & Faber, 2001), 36–42.

88. This is also the title of Steiner's 1990 Gifford lectures.

89. Robert Carroll ("Toward a Grammar of Creation: On Steiner the Theologian," in Scott and Sharp, *Reading George Steiner*, 262–74, esp. 265) finds theological difficulties with Steiner's grammars of creation, but these are not telling. See O. O'Donovan, *Resurrection and Moral Order: An Outline for Evangelical Ethics* (Grand Rapids: Eerdmans, 1986), for how compelling and creative a view of creation order can be.

90. Chrétien, *Ark of Speech*, 145.

way, and it is in and through his Word that he addresses us and gives himself to us. God's Real Presence in Scripture is related to his Real Presence in the world and thus in texts other than the Bible. In this sense Vanhoozer is right that all texts require a trinitarian hermeneutic,[91] but Scripture remains unique among texts and thus makes its own unique demands, as we will see below.

Liturgical Proclamation and *Lectio Sacra*

> It may be expedient here to recall that liturgy engages one as a "soul" more than as a "consciousness."[92]

> In Christ there was re-created the form of man before God. . . . "Formation" consequently means in the first place Jesus's taking form in His Church. . . . The Church, then, bears the form which is in truth the proper form of all humanity. . . . She has essentially . . . to do . . . *with the whole man in his existence in the world with all its implications.*[93]

The vocative "Israel" in Deuteronomy 6:4 alerts us to the fact that God's Word is addressed primarily to his gathered people.[94] Theologically this means that the gathered church is the primary context for the reception of the Word. Magrassi rightly observes how it is in the liturgy that the Word is living and active *maximally* although not *exclusively*.[95] The gathering of the ecclesia is God's appointed place where he promises to meet with his people. We gather for a multitude of reasons but primarily in order to eat and drink of Christ, and so to become like him and thus ever more fully human. And Scripture is that field in which is hid the pearl of great price. As Newbigin stated, "We go to the Bible to meet Christ, our present and Living Lord."[96]

---

91. K. J. Vanhoozer, *Is There a Meaning in This Text? The Bible, the Reader, and the Morality of Literary Knowledge* (Grand Rapids: Zondervan, 1998), 455–56.

92. Lacoste, *Experience and the Absolute*, 91.

93. D. Bonhoeffer, *Ethics*, trans. N. H. Smith (London: SCM, 1995), 20–21, with added emphasis.

94. This is not to undermine the implications of God's address for all creation: Ps. 19 reminds us that God "speaks" continually through his creation; in the prophets we find oracles to the nations; John's Gospel, with its contextual use of *Logos*, surely appealed to non-Christians; etc. Thus there is a sense in which this world is drenched with God's speech, as Chrétien, in particular, has noted. However, in both Old and New Testaments God's word is given primarily for the covenant people, yet we bear in mind that covenant is inseparably related to God's purpose for the whole world.

95. M. Magrassi, *Praying the Bible: An Introduction to Lectio Divina*, trans. E. Hagman (Collegeville, MN: Liturgical Press, 1998), 4.

96. L. Newbigin, *The Sending of the Church—Three Bible Studies* (Edinburgh: Church of Scotland Board of World Mission and Unity, 1984), 131.

Christ promises to be present when we gather in his name so that "the Word is living when the speaker [Christ] is present and it is actually coming from his mouth."[97] The Catholic Constitution on the Sacred Liturgy rightly declares, "It is he himself who speaks when the Holy Scriptures are read in the church."[98] Similarly, we should notice that the extraordinary potential of the sermon, as Karl Barth in particular has pointed out, is that God will address *us* through the exposition:

> Proclamation is human speech in and by which God Himself speaks like a king through the mouth of his herald, and which is meant to be heard and accepted as speech in and by which God Himself speaks, and therefore heard and accepted in faith as divine decision concerning life and death, as divine judgment and pardon, eternal Law and eternal Gospel both together.[99]

Claritas scripturae teaches us that the large landmarks of Scripture are clear, but the metaphor of clarity simultaneously alerts us to the fact that much in Scripture is not clear and not least how Scripture is relevant for us today in all areas of life. This is a major reason why groups of Christians, all of whom are in holy orders, in full-time service of the Lord Christ, set apart those appropriately gifted to devote *their full time* to prayer and *the Word*. If we are to listen fully to God's address through his Word, then we need skilled preachers who increasingly lift the veil that for us remains over much of Scripture.

However, it is a mistake to think that preachers function only to increase our knowledge of the Bible. Speaking of the role of the Word and teaching in the church, Bavinck rightly insists, "This teaching, nevertheless, must not be understood in an intellectualist sense."[100] This would be to reduce faith and personal encounter with God to information. Karl Barth is right to link preaching and the nature of Scripture to *proclamation*. Scripture's character is kerygmatic; it is the message or announcement of the great king and as such is addressed to the very core of our being, what Old Testament Wisdom literature refers to as our heart. As kerygma, Scripture is not confined to one illocutionary force in its speech acts. Kerygma can take many forms:

---

97. Magrassi, *Praying the Bible*, 3.
98. Vatican II, *Sacrosanctum Concilium* 7 (1963), http://www.vatican.va/archive/hist_councils/ii_vatican_council/documents/vat-ii_const_19631204_sacrosanctum-concilium_en.html.
99. K. Barth, CD I/1:52.
100. H. Bavinck, *Reformed Dogmatics*, ed. J. Bolt, trans. J. Vriend, 4 vols. (Grand Rapids: Baker Academic, 2003–8), 4:419. He refers to such an approach as "nomism": "The nomism that runs from Judaism through Pelagianism and as far as modern rationalism is content with an external call, an intellectual, moral or aesthetic operation of the word, and in this connection considers a special supernatural operation of the Spirit superfluous" (456).

the telling of a story as in Jonah, the sermons of Moses in Deuteronomy, the Letters of the New Testament, the visionary form of Revelation, and so on. Undoubtedly, *a* function of Scripture as kerygma is to instruct and to provide information, but the *knowledge* that Scripture seeks to impart is far more than that. Scripture is *the* means by which God gives himself to us and draws us into his very life. Preaching is never there simply to illumine what we do not already know, although it may and should do that; it is primarily to enable us to encounter again and again the living God who has come to us in Christ. Doubtless preachers will need to lead us into the deep waters of texts like Romans 9–11, but so too will they need to bring us back to texts like John 3:16 and to immerse us again in the immense depths of God's love. As K. Barth declares,

> The concrete encounter of God and man to-day, whose actuality, of course, can be created only by the Word of God Himself, must find a counterpart in the human event of proclamation, i.e., the person called must be ready to make the promise given to the Church intelligible in his own words to the men of his own time. Calling, promise, exposition of Scripture, actuality—these are the decisive definitions of the concept of preaching.[101]

Clearly this entails a high view of Scripture and of preaching. And so it should. Dr. Martyn Lloyd-Jones, one of the great preachers of the twentieth century, commented that the sort of preaching he looks for is preaching that ushers us into the presence of God. Similarly, John Stott asserted that what we need in our pulpits is truth on fire. As Karl Barth rightly explains above, such encounter can be created only by God himself, and thus the hermeneutic involved will always be *pneumatic* and prayerful since it is the delight of the Spirit to use the Word to bring us to God. At the same time it helps enormously to be aware of what preaching is about. The sermon is not a lecture, a mistake that is not uncommon as pastors seek to deepen their preaching by turning the sermon into an extended, cerebral lesson. A lecture is qualified logically and directed primarily toward the head, philosophically speaking, whereas a sermon is qualified by faith and directed not firstly to the head but to the heart. The difference is tangible. "The business of the sermon is to bring hearers face to face with Jesus Christ as he really is."[102]

The Christian tradition holds word and sacrament closely together as *the* means of grace. This is especially true of the Eucharist, a common cause of

---

101. K. Barth, *CD* I/1:59.
102. L. Newbigin, *The Good Shepherd: Meditations on Christian Ministry in Today's World* (Oxford: Mowbray, 1977), 24.

division among Christians. Let me therefore quote a contemporary Catholic scholar on this issue. Kereszty, in his *Wedding Feast of the Lamb*, notes that historically, apart from Hippolytus's *Apostolic Tradition*, "all available documents attest that the liturgy of the word always had to precede the liturgy of the Eucharist."[103] The reason for this: "because our senses and our mind, left to their own natural resources, cannot appreciate Christ's sacramental presence, the eyes of faith must first be opened by listening to the Word of Christ. In this way our sense perception, supplemented by the light of faith, may discover Christ under the signs of bread and wine."[104] Kereszty goes on to argue, wrongly in my opinion, that the incarnate one cannot be as fully present to us embodied humans through his Word as he is through his bodily presence in the Mass.[105] This brings us to the differences between Protestants and Catholics, but we should not lose sight of the enormous common ground. For all orthodox Christians, the Word and the Eucharist are inseparable, with the Word leading naturally into the Eucharist. "In every tradition, the bread of the sacrament recalls the bread of the Word."[106] Intriguingly, Paul extends the notion of proclamation to the Eucharist in 1 Corinthians 11:26, "For whenever you eat this bread and drink this cup, you *proclaim* [καταγγέλλω] the Lord's death until he comes" (NIV). Proclamation and the attentive listening that accompanies it is about far more than the imparting of knowledge; it is about encounter and relationship, and thus it is entirely appropriate that it should be followed by participation in the body and blood—the very life—of Jesus. Such participation is a proclamation of the Lord's death both as an enacted word and as we become part of his death and keenly anticipate the messianic feast that lies ahead.

Acts 3:15 describes this Jesus, in whose life the Word and sacraments facilitate our participation, as the "Author of life." Similarly, Colossians 1:15–20 is eloquent in its insistence that the Christ who is the head of his body, the church, is the one from whom, through whom, and to whom are all things. Thus Bavinck rightly explains, in terms of the relationship between Word and world, that

103. R. A. Kereszty, *Wedding Feast of the Lamb: Eucharistic Theology from a Historical, Biblical, and Systematic Perspective* (Chicago: Hillenbrand Books, 2004), 179. F. Randolph (*Know Him in the Breaking of the Bread: A Guide to the Mass* [San Francisco: Ignatius, 1994]) similarly states, "Listening to the Word of God is vital; unless we have heard about Jesus, how can we love him? There may be only a brief whispered passage from the Gospel, or there may be a long, drawn-out sequence of readings, but in one way or other the message of Scripture must be proclaimed" (25).
104. Kereszty, *Wedding Feast*, 179.
105. Ibid., 180. While silence, as I will stress below, is very important, it is hard to see the value of bodily presence without verbal communication. The latter is as human as bodily presence.
106. Magrassi, *Praying the Bible*, 43.

Christ—even now—is prophet, priest, and king; and by his Word and Spirit he persuasively impacts the entire world. Because of him there radiates from everyone who believes in him a renewing and sanctifying influence upon the family, society, state, occupation, business, art, science, and so forth. The spiritual life is meant to refashion the natural and moral life in its full depth and scope according to the laws of God.[107]

"The church," says Bavinck, "is the communion, and hence also the mother, of believers. . . . It also exists on earth to be the holy circle within which Christ communicates all his benefits, also the benefit of regeneration."[108] And it is above all else through his Word that Christ communicates his benefits. "The kingship of Christ over his church consists in that by this word and Spirit he gathers and governs his own and protects and keeps them in the redemption acquired."[109] Listening to the Word, as we have understood it, involves personal transformation that has implications for all areas of one's life, *including* biblical interpretation!

One of the most damaging effects of modernity on the church has been the largely unnoticed privatization of religion so that what we do when we gather as ecclesia is reduced to a kind of leisure activity, with little or no consequences for our practice of biblical studies. Word has been separated from world, with fatal consequences. Bonhoeffer is one who with crystal clarity saw the inseparable relationship between the two; as the quote at the outset of this chapter indicates, he rightly asserts that church has essentially to do with "the whole man in his existence in the world with all its implications," and that surely includes biblical studies! In ecclesial worship the great drama of Scripture, the true story of the whole world, is enacted before us week in and week out so that it can become the basic narrative out of which we live. One cannot take such an approach to worship seriously and then adopt an alternative, secular metanarrative within which to practice one's study of the Bible. Indeed, it is in the ecclesia that we discover there is no neutral approach to Scripture; we either welcome the witness of the Spirit to and through Scripture, or we reject it.

Magrassi rightly asserts that "cultic [ecclesial] contemplation must be said to be superior to private contemplation."[110] Similarly, Chrétien says of prayer,

---

107. Bavinck, *Reformed Dogmatics*, 4:437.
108. Ibid., 447. Randolph evokes the catholicity of the church in his moving account of the Jesuit Walter Ciszek. While a prisoner in the Soviet Union, he managed to slip away and celebrate the Mass secretly, using a tree stump as an altar: "In so doing he was far from alone; he was one with millions of Catholics all over the world. The whole Church came into that forest; Christ was made present among a people who were unaware of his existence" (*Know Him*, 24).
109. Bavinck, *Reformed Dogmatics*, 4:372.
110. Magrassi, *Praying the Bible*, 2.

"Only the voice can fall silent, and only speech can stop talking. The withdrawal or suspension of the voice cannot come first, and vocal prayer is always presupposed.... It is the foundation of all the other forms of prayer, which suspend or interiorize the voice."[111] However, we noted above that the ecclesial context is the maximal but not exclusive context for reception of the Word. Again, this is clear from Deuteronomy 6:4–9. The goal of hearing the Word is that it should take possession of our hearts (6:6),[112] the innermost core of our being, from which life springs forth. "The oneness of God's Being demands the heart, the entire being of the faithful."[113] "The great spiritual gain yielded by this 'orthodox' attitude in Israel is that, in the moral field too, it meant the end of all temporizing because the heart is claimed entirely for the worship of the one Yahweh. Life in its entirety is focused on God."[114] For that to occur, exposure to the Word in the gathered community is insufficient. The Shema consequently stresses the need for the hearing of the gathered community to extend into the home, to accompany one's travel, to dominate both action and thought, public and private life, to be attended to as one goes to sleep and as one wakes up.

The family has been evocatively referred to as *the domestic church*. Even in today's differentiated society, the family remains as the most formative of environments, which is neglected or broken at our peril.[115] "Tocqueville strongly argued the positive social functions of love and marriage.... The family was central to his concern with 'habits of the heart,' for it is there that mores are first inculcated."[116] The home is where we spend most of our time, and thus it is not surprising that it is here above all other places that we are formed by the ethos and practices; it is here that the habits of the heart are formed day in and day out. In a creative and life-giving way, the home should, from the perspective of the Shema, be suffused with Scripture. Many of us have encountered distorted examples of this so that it can be hard to imagine what this might look like today. Link this with the challenges of marriage and family life in the individualistic West[117] and it becomes hard to see ways forward.

---

111. Chrétien, *Ark of Speech*, 37.
112. Moberly (*Old Testament Theology*, 24) argues that the reference of "these words" in v. 6 is to vv. 4–5. They may be the primary reference, but in the context of Deut. 6 and of Deuteronomy as a whole, they clearly refer to God's torah in its breadth.
113. T. C. Vriezen, *An Outline of Old Testament Theology* (Oxford: Blackwell, 1958), 323.
114. Ibid., 325.
115. Cf. G. Bachelard, *The Poetics of Space* (Boston: Beacon, 1964, 1994).
116. R. N. Bellah et al., *Habits of the Heart: Individualism and Commitment in American Life*, updated ed. (Berkeley: University of California Press, 2008), 85.
117. See, e.g., ibid., 85–112. Bellah and his coauthors helpfully explore the interface of family dynamics with cultural dynamics.

And yet, detailed attention to the home as a place of listening to the Word may be one of the most important keys to recovering the Word today. Small groups and Bible studies are rightly popular nowadays, but they pale into insignificance in comparison to the formative influence of the home. A focus on *listening* may again provide a key to such recovery. One danger of the Protestant tradition is to make a kind of preaching central in the home, a practice that often inoculates children *against* Christianity. A better way would be to shape the home such that it becomes an environment creatively conducive to listening to God. This would involve far more than practices of communal Bible reading after the meal or family devotions, valuable as these are. The home would have to become a barrier against the dromocratic (high-speed), individualistic culture of our day and be shaped as a place of renewal, relationship, and rest. Only as children are listened to and nurtured as human beings in their own right can we expect them to extend their experience of the covenant of family life to the covenant with God. Parents "are God's stewards in helping the development of people made in God's image."[118] A deep openness to God is utterly central to the *imago Dei* so that failure in this respect is serious. As Christ's love for the church is embodied in the daily *practices* of the family, an openness toward God will follow. "The cosmic care, love and patience with which God treats mankind is the basis on which the family is constructed."[119] Proclamation without plausible practice is fatal in the family and easily recognized as empty and hypocritical.

Exposure to Scripture is vital at every phase of a child's development, but so too is development of a receptive listening. Indeed, the home is *the* place where *lectio sacra*, or as it is more commonly known, lectio divina, is nurtured. Much more needs to be said about how this might happen in our day. A radical rethinking of the contemporary home and its practices will be required. Some of my friends have adopted the church calendar as the way in which to restructure the rhythm of their families. Ignatian spirituality provides important resources too, with its use of the imagination to enter into Scripture and its easy adaptability for children.[120]

Certainly today for most of us, liturgical reception of the Word will not suffice. Gone, it would appear, are the medieval days when the bells would

---

118. A. Storkey, *A Christian Social Perspective* (Downers Grove, IL: InterVarsity, 1979), 224.
119. Ibid.
120. See, e.g., D. Linn, S. F. Linn, and M. Linn, *Sleeping with Bread: Holding What Gives You Life* (Mahwah, NJ: Paulist Press, 1995). A key insight of this approach is the recognition that God is deeply at work in our daily lives and that there is no dichotomy between his written Word and such daily work. Any family can start to adopt Ignatian practices by asking two simple questions at the end of each day: What in my day was most life-giving? What in my day was most not life-giving?

call the faithful to morning and evening prayers apart from Sunday worship. Lectionaries, if followed, tend to be piecemeal so that large swaths of Scripture are never heard in church. In this context it is imperative that personal reading of Scripture is prioritized. At its best the evangelical tradition has led the way to a renewed daily acquaintance with the Bible, and it deserves full credit for this. However, speaking as an evangelical, it has not always been clear how to spend time nourishing the deepest parts of one's being with the Word; how to "read it as a Word that is present and puts me in dialogue with the God who is living and present; an ease in translating reading into prayer and using it to shed light on questions of existence in order to model my life on it."[121] Fortunately there is just such a tradition in the church, what is known as *lectio sacra*, or lectio divina.

There is a welcome renewal of interest in lectio divina today. One of the best works available is Magrassi's *Praying the Bible: An Introduction to Lectio Divina*. With de Lubac and many others, Magrassi draws on the tradition of the church to recover this practice.[122] Utterly central to lectio is the belief that it is in and through Scripture that we encounter the living Christ. Hence Magrassi's appropriate use of "sacramental" to describe the Bible.[123] Lectio is about "deep communion" between the author and reader of Scripture.[124] Scripture facilitates "the kiss of eternity."[125] "More precisely, when I go beyond the letter of Scripture to its spirit, I personally encounter the living Christ. He is present to explain his own Word, which is gradually revealed to the eyes of faith. Understanding the Bible is like having a conversation with him."[126] Lectio opens up a dialogue between the reader and God so that the universal dialogue of the liturgy becomes intensely personal.

Most of Magrassi's book is rightly taken up with evoking the reality of lectio. Method is confined to a final chapter. In essence, lectio is "prayerful reading" of the Bible.[127] It involves "loving, calm, reflective, personal poring over the text."[128] Guigo II (d. 1188) was the first to systematize the practice of lectio into four stages:

121. Magrassi, *Praying the Bible*, 13.
122. For an Orthodox perspective on lectio, see J. Breck, *Scripture in Tradition: The Bible and Its Interpretation in the Orthodox Church* (Crestwood, NY: St. Vladimir's Seminary Press, 2001), 67–86.
123. Magrassi, *Praying the Bible*, 35.
124. Ibid., 29.
125. Ibid., 24. This is William of Thierry's expression.
126. Ibid., 21–22.
127. J. Leclercq, *The Love of Learning and the Desire for God: A Study of Monastic Culture* (Bronx, NY: Fordham University Press, 1961), 73.
128. Ibid., 6.

1. *Reading.* This is the starting point, but it should be distinguished carefully from analytical exegesis. Application is always already in operation in lectio.[129] Rather, it is attentive, contemplative reading, much like taking a hard candy into one's mouth and slowly letting it circulate as one's tongue explores and savors its surface.

The normal practice of taking a small chunk of Scripture as the focus of meditation is not antithetical to an awareness of and immersion in the scriptural metanarrative.[130] Rightly understood, the church calendar enacts not just the events of Jesus's life but also the scriptural drama in its totality,[131] and lectio can easily mirror this. Magrassi helpfully outlines the shape of the calendar as follows:

a. Advent and Christmas season: Isaiah and the infancy stories in the Gospels.
b. Time after Epiphany: Pauline Epistles.
c. Sundays before Lent: Genesis, the first acts in the drama of Scripture.
d. Lent: Exodus, the Passover, entry into the promised land.
e. Passion time: Jeremiah, Second Isaiah, the Gospels' passion accounts, Hebrews.
f. Easter season: Acts—the life of the early church, Revelation, 1–2 Peter, 1–3 John, and James.
g. Time after Pentecost: the remaining historical, wisdom, and prophetic books.

This outline of the calendar shows how the metanarrative of Scripture can be foregrounded liturgically *and* in lectio; it would contribute enormously to the health of the church if this were done.[132] In chapter 3 I argue that a sense of the different acts in the drama of Scripture can complement the creeds as a rule of faith. This is certainly the case with lectio, in which one can chew on a small chunk of Scripture while aware of its position within the story of the Bible as a whole.

2. *Meditation.* Lectio is reading aimed at receiving the Word into the heart and not just or primarily into the head: "It presupposes that I am able to

---

129. On application, see the important work by A. Spears, "The Theological Hermeneutics of Homiletical Application and Ecclesiastes 7:23–29" (PhD diss., University of Liverpool, 2006).
130. It has been said that the (evangelical) church in recent years has recovered mysticism but failed to bring the Bible along with it. If this is the case, it need not and certainly should not be so.
131. I do think that, as with the catholic creeds, a better job could be done of this. See my comments in chap. 3 (below).
132. See C. G. Bartholomew and M. Goheen, *The Drama of Scripture: Finding Our Place in the Biblical Story* (Grand Rapids: Baker Academic, 2004).

create space in my heart for the Word of God to ring out."¹³³ The metaphor of eating is common in evoking the process of meditation. "The heart is the mouth in which the text is chewed—or as they prefer to say, ruminated."¹³⁴ Lesslie Newbigin has rightly alerted us to the fact that we need to *indwell* Scripture as the primary foundational story within which we live our lives. What is not always recognized is that Scripture will not become our homeland through cerebral knowledge alone. Sustained meditation flows out into the whole of one's life so that at any time of the day one finds Scripture rising up in one's consciousness and thereby facilitating ongoing "inner reading." Like many monks and nuns throughout history, we need to become "living concordances."¹³⁵

3. *Prayer*. Meditation leads naturally to prayer. Scripture is the medium by which God addresses us, and we respond in prayer. In his magisterial book on prayer, von Balthasar declares that God not only addresses us in Scripture but also teaches us how to respond!¹³⁶ Historically, it is the Psalter that the church has used in particular as the vehicle for responding to God. Even today many monks chant the entire Psalter every week.

4. *Contemplation*. Scripture witnesses to God, and the goal of lectio is appropriately contemplative communion with God. Lectio begins in silence as one stills oneself to read; it ends in silence too as one is present to God. Recall Habakkuk's exhortation in 2:20: "The LORD is in his holy temple; let all the earth be silent before him" (NIV). As Magrassi perceptively notes, "Contemplation is certainly the peak of this entire activity. It is not something superimposed from without but is like a delicious fruit that ripens on the tree of Bible reading."¹³⁷ "What matters is to hear him, gaze on him and remain under his great light."¹³⁸

There is a reciprocal relationship between liturgical reception of the Word and lectio divina as in the Shema. Liturgical proclamation should overflow into daily practices of lectio, and lectio likewise prepares us for liturgical proclamation. "The soul's doors must be opened to the One who makes himself lovingly available in his Word. . . . Received without preparation, without faith and love, the Bread of Life is no longer lifegiving. God's saving initiative is frustrated. God stops in front of doors that are shut."¹³⁹

---

133. Magrassi, *Praying the Bible*, 109. The development of interior space is an important theme in Christian spirituality.
134. Ibid., 109.
135. Ibid., 5.
136. H. U. von Balthasar, *Prayer* (San Francisco: Ignatius, 1986).
137. Magrassi, *Praying the Bible*, 116.
138. Ibid., 117; cf. the title of J.-L. Chrétien's *Sous le regard de la Bible* (Paris: Bayard, 2008); ET, *Under the Gaze of the Bible*, trans. J. M. Dunaway (Bronx, NY: Fordham University Press, 2015).
139. Magrassi, *Praying the Bible*, 5.

It goes without saying that the preacher will need to be steeped in lectio while preparing the Word for the congregation. As Augustine observed, "More important than any amount of grandeur of style to those of us who seek to be listened to with obedience is the life of the speaker."[140] The life of the preacher must daily be opened to formation through lectio. But what of the biblical scholar and exegete? How does biblical hermeneutics relate to liturgical proclamation and lectio divina? Hagman perceptively notices that "the Fathers, recognizing the Spirit as the author of Scripture, ask its readers to be men and women of the Spirit and friends of Christ, even *before* they are perfect exegetes."[141] Magrassi says, "In the presence of divine realities (such as the Word), what counts most is faith. It alone can lead us into the mystery. Everything else matters only if it is part of this atmosphere and functions within it."[142] The Catholic Church's *Starting Afresh in Christ* observes that

> every vocation to consecrated life is born in contemplation, from moments of intense communion and from a deep relationship of friendship with Christ, from the beauty and light . . . seen shining on his face, . . . Every vocation must constantly mature in this intimacy with Christ. . . . Every reality of consecrated life is born and is regenerated each day in the unending contemplation of the face of Christ.[143]

This is perhaps the most controversial aspect of this chapter. It is exceedingly rare to find liturgy and lectio linked integrally with biblical exegesis in theory, let alone in practice. In my library, as I glance through major books on theological interpretation and biblical hermeneutics, it is rare even to find a reference to prayer in their indexes. Amid the plethora of books and commentaries now emerging on theological interpretation, it is unknown to find a commentary that integrates lectio into interpretation. Must even theological interpretation be kept separate from liturgy and lectio as a kind of *corrective* to ecclesial interpretation?

As we noted at the outset of this chapter, this brings us to the root of contemporary challenges for biblical interpretation. It appears that the autonomy

---

140. Augustine, *On Christian Teaching* 4, trans. R. P. H. Green (Oxford: Oxford University Press, 1997), 151.
141. E. Hagman, "To the Reader," in Magrassi, *Praying the Bible*, vii–ix, esp. viii–ix, with added emphasis.
142. Magrassi, *Praying the Bible*, 24.
143. Congregation for Institutes of Consecrated Life and Societies of Apostolic Life, *Starting Afresh from Christ: A Renewed Commitment to Consecrated Life in the Third Millennium* (Sherbrooke, Quebec: Médiaspaul, 2002), 48.

of academic interpretation must be preserved at all costs, as a kind of sacred enclosure fundamental to the quest for truth.

The Love of Learning and the Desire for God

This is the title of Jean Leclercq's classic study of monastic culture. In his introduction Leclercq uses two twelfth-century writings to transition into his examination of monastic theology. The first is Peter Lombard's *Prologue on St. Paul*. Lombard's purpose is to obtain knowledge, and the method is that of the scholastic *quaestio*. "St. Paul's Epistles are subjected to the same type of investigation as might be applied to any other historical document.... Thus the purpose of the commentary and its Prologue is to resolve the problems which arise in objective history. This text . . . has little that is personal."[144]

The second example is St. Bernard's prologue to his *Sermons on the Canticle of Canticles*. The audience is monks and contemplatives, and the goal is to articulate *sapientiam loquimur*, words of wisdom. "This theology assumes on the part of the teacher, and on the part of his audience, a special way of life, a rigorous asceticism, or as they say today, a 'commitment.' Rather than speculative insights, it gives them a certain appreciation, of savoring and clinging to the truth and, what is everything, to the love of God."[145] Bernard's approach is oriented not toward learning but toward spirituality; God does the teaching, and prayer is constituent of this approach. One must go beyond the rational approach of theology so that it yields a deep attachment to God. The experience of God that results will bear fruit in poetry and hymn. The Song of Songs must be read so that it "accompanies and sustains the progress of faith, from grace to grace, from vocation, conversion to monastic life, until one's entrance into the life of the blessed.... For the Lord is there at the beginning. He is there at *every stage*, He is at the close, He is the End. The important word is no longer *quaeritur*, but *desideratur*; no longer *sciendum*, but *experiendum*."[146]

Clearly, from what we have said above, Bernard's approach is far more attractive than that of Lombard. The crucial question, however, is the relationship between them. What does it mean to read Scripture as one might read any other historical document? And what is objective history? In our post-post-Enlightenment era, it is far harder to justify such a reading of Scripture. Leclercq sees the biblical interpretation of the schoolmen as complementary to that of the monks, but I suspect that a nature-grace dichotomy is at work

---

144. Leclercq, *Love of Learning*, 3–4.
145. Ibid., 4.
146. Ibid., 5, with original emphasis.

in his otherwise superb scholarship. There is much debate about the extent to which the Thomistic nature-grace dichotomy stems from Thomas himself or represents a distorted development of his thought. However one resolves this contentious issue, many Thomists adopt a nature-grace distinction. The Catholic historian James Turner notes, for example, that the one lasting thing he and others learned from Thomas is that in scholarship "faith gives no *epistemological edge*."[147] Religious practice is one thing, but scholarship proceeds according to the agreed rules of the discipline. Apart from the challenge of the wild pluralism in the academy today, it is imperative to face up to the fact that the autonomy of scholarship is far from neutral. Buckley has rightly pointed out the fatal error made by Christians in early modernity in conceding the epistemological ground to secular scholarship; this move is indeed *At the Origins of Modern Atheism*.

If Scripture is the Word of God, then, as Karl Barth rightly observes, no one can stand before it as a spectator.[148] Jerome insisted that the Bible must be read and interpreted "in the light of the same Spirit by whom it was written."[149] Academic biblical exegesis is, in many ways, a different animal from the practice of lectio divina, but why might it not also be true of the highest levels of academic interpretation that "the Lord is there at the beginning. He is there at *every stage*, He is at the close, He is the End"? Why should prayer not suffuse academic exegesis just as it does lectio?

The reason, I suspect, is the secularization of biblical studies and the Western academy. But if ecclesial reception of the Word is primary, then the Christian biblical scholar works out of that primary reception, which ought to lead back into that reception, deepening the reception as it does so. Like the preacher, the biblical scholar's work ought to emerge out of sustained ecclesial reception and lectio divina and always be oriented toward attending to God's address. Christ's rule over his people by his Word does not cease when the biblical scholar leaves church, as though the obedience of faith is confined to the cultic sphere, whereas in the academy an entirely different worldview holds sway! The whole point of the Shema is that communal hearing of the Word proclaimed is to be translated into every area of our lives. Sadly, it has become common over the past 150 years for Christian scholars to inhabit two unrelated worlds: the world of the church, and the world of their study and lecture room. In the one, Christ is acknowledged; in the other, Christ is unwelcome, since in the latter domain so-called reason and neutrality reign.

---

147. M. A. Noll and J. Turner, *The Future of Christian Learning: An Evangelical and Catholic Dialogue*, ed. T. A. Howard (Grand Rapids: Brazos, 2008), 106, with original emphasis.

148. Magrassi, *Praying the Bible*, 31.

149. Jerome, *St. Jerome: Commentary on Galatians*, trans. A. Cain, FC (Washington, DC: Catholic University of America Press, 2010), 207.

This dichotomy is unsustainable and will never yield the sort of academic biblical interpretation that we so urgently need today.

We need a healthy integration of ecclesial and academic interpretation. Both should be rooted in a profound sense of Scripture as God's Word. Both should be rooted in the practice of lectio divina. Brevard Childs was once asked by a student how to become a better exegete. His reply: Become a deeper person! Exegetes need spiritual formation as much if not more than preachers, bearing in mind the dangers inherent in an academic approach to Scripture in our context of rampant secular humanism and hubris. Both should aim to facilitate the hearing of God's address today. Certainly they can raise critical questions of each other; that is what we expect. This is not a proposal for the complete subservience of academic interpretation to ecclesial understandings. What should happen is an ongoing, healthy dialogue between these partners in the greater task of attending to God's Word. But it is wrong—folly, in the biblical sense—to see academic interpretation as a corrective to ecclesial. This is to buy into a nature-grace dichotomy that is profoundly unbiblical. *Wise* biblical interpretation will hold Word and world (academic interpretation) together.

In one of the most popular books of the fifteenth century, *L'orloge de sapience* (The Hourglass of Wisdom), Lady Wisdom is the protagonist. The Master of Jean Rolin created a series of exquisite illuminations for it. In one, Wisdom sits on her throne, holding in her left arm the globe and in her right an open book.[150] This seems to me the right image: wisdom underlies and should inform both biblical interpretation and academic exegesis. And biblically, "The fear of the LORD is the beginning [both starting point and foundation] of wisdom" (Prov. 9:10).

The radicality of liturgy is, alas, easily underestimated today, as noted above. Hence Jean-Yves Lacoste's *Expérience et absolu* is a vital book for today.[151] It is a phenomenology of liturgy, although liturgy is defined broadly as "the logic that presides over the encounter between man and God writ large."[152] Lacoste's work is a rigorous piece of philosophy and repays careful study. Here we simply draw attention to his argument for the radical difference liturgy makes to human existence. In response to Heidegger, he asserts, "When we pray, we contest that being-in-the-world accounts entirely for our being; and we are proposing that a relation to the Absolute can have the first and last word on the question of who we are."[153] Liturgy initiates a situation in which someone other than the immanent possibilities of the world control our lives:

> But no intellection of liturgy is possible if we do not recognize in it the clearing in which the Absolute's eschatological claims over us are substituted for the world's historical claims—not,

---

150. See A. Manguel, *A History of Reading* (New York: Penguin, 2008), 220.

151. J.-Y. Lacoste, *Expérience et absolu: Questions disputées sur l'humanité de l'homme* (Paris: Presses Universitaires de France, 1994); ET, *Experience and the Absolute*.

152. Lacoste, *Experience and the Absolute*, 2.

153. Ibid., 44.

of course, by abolishing the facticity of the world, but by taking possession of the liturgical nonplace and enabling a certain overshadowing of our facticity that does not amount to an act of divertissement.[154]

Lacoste uses the wonderful expression "liturgical reason"[155] and insists that liturgy has implications for rationality:

> But if there is a place in experience for a worldly inchoation of the great eschatological peace whereby the world would no longer be interposed between man and God, and in which the heavens unambiguously sing to the glory of God, such that being-in-the-world organically unfolds into being-before-God, and that liturgy seems to pass for the ultimate dimension of our facticity, then such an inchoation would mark a rupture with the rationality presiding over our worldly existence, and could only have the character of a grace beyond the universal.[156]

Liturgy is thus not alien to creation but fits with it along the grain, as it were. In words reminiscent of another Catholic philosopher, Michel Henry,[157] Lacoste insists that, "Liturgy, understood in its broadest sense, is the most human mode in which we can exist in the world or on the earth."[158] Similarly Chrétien asserts, "That is why there is a life of prayer, 'a life,' says Claudel, 'which transports into the domain of the spirit the astonishingly complex, varied, ingenious and sometimes paradoxical activities of physiology,' for 'the Word must be made flesh in us.'"[159]

A remarkable recent example of lectio divina is Jean Vanier's rich commentary on John.[160] Intriguingly, like the monastic tradition that Leclercq focuses on, Vanier's exposition is in a semipoetic style very different from traditional commentary. Books like this are rare, but I see no reason why a renewed theological interpretation might not incorporate such an approach *as part of* a theological commentary. This would start to address the core problem that we discerned at the outset of this chapter and help us to root our biblical interpretation in listening.

---

154. Ibid., 61.
155. Ibid., 75–76.
156. Ibid., 65.
157. See M. Henry, *I Am the Truth: Toward a Philosophy of Christianity*, trans. S. Emanuel (Stanford, CA: Stanford University Press, 2003); idem, *Words of Christ*, trans. C. M. Gschwandtner, Interventions (Grand Rapids: Eerdmans, 2012).
158. Lacoste, *Experience and the Absolute*, 98.
159. Chrétien, *Ark of Speech*, 36.
160. J. Vanier, *Drawn into the Mystery of Jesus through the Gospel of John* (Ottawa: Novalis, 2004).

PART 2

Biblical Interpretation and Biblical Theology

3

The Story of Our World

The Bible—Old Testament and New Testament together—has a unity of its own; and that unity is to be found in the fact that the Bible tells the story of salvation—the story of God's covenant mercy. This explains what the Bible is. It is a record of God's revelation of Himself as a righteous God and a Saviour.

F. F. Bruce[1]

The Old Testament has been compared by Dr. Emil Brunner to the first part of a sentence and the New Testament to its second and concluding part. This comparison is all the more forceful if we think of a complex sentence in Dr. Brunner's native German tongue, where the sense of the whole cannot be comprehended until the last word is spoken.

F. F. Bruce[2]

The real question is not whether to do Biblical Theology or not, but rather what kind of Biblical Theology does one have.

Brevard Childs[3]

---

1. F. F. Bruce, *The Books and the Parchments: Some Chapters on the Transmission of the Bible*, 2nd ed. (London: Pickering & Inglis, 1963), 82.
2. Ibid., 87.
3. B. S. Childs, *BTIC* 95.

Introduction

A presupposition of listening to Scripture for God's address, as explored in chapter 2, is that the primary author of Scripture is God and that he speaks with a unified voice. As Childs asserts, "It is a basic Christian confession that all scripture bears testimony to Jesus Christ. In this sense, there is a single, unified voice in scripture. . . . The basic hermeneutical problem of the Bible, therefore, is not adequately formulated by using the terminology of unity and diversity."[4] The unity of Scripture has, however, been severely challenged by historical criticism and postmodernism so that many would think it irrecoverable today. Biblical theology is the discipline that attends to the unity of Scripture *on its own terms and using its own categories*, so to this subject we now turn.

The historical-critical challenge to the unity of Scripture is well known. In Pentateuchal studies, for example, despite the literary turn, JEDP continues to be the default mode for many or most Old Testament scholars. The effect of historical criticism on biblical theology has been stifling: "from around 1870 [when historical criticism took hold], for approximately a century, 'biblical theology,' in the sense of writing of works on the theology of OT and NT together, to all intents and purposes ceased to exist."[5]

What is less commonly noticed is that postmodernism represents an even greater challenge to the unity of Scripture. Even so constructive a postmodern philosopher as Paul Ricoeur insists, in his discussion of creation order, that "the theological field cannot be totalized."[6] He speaks of us as "having become strangers to this kind of totalizing thinking."[7] Within postmodernism there is a legitimate and welcome critique of the totalizing *of modernity*, but in context Ricoeur is reacting against holding together creation, justice, and salvation under the rubric of creation order. For Ricoeur, it is the enigma of God's justice, in particular, that shatters any such totalizing. In my view, by contrast, it is a biblical, dynamic understanding of creation order that secures the very possibility of justice in our world.[8] Chrétien articulates a far more helpful approach to totalizing, if we must use such language.[9] In his inimitable style, he writes,

> As long as the speech that sings the world is absent from the world, the world lacks nothing and everything. . . . Nothing is added to the world by the speech that magnifies it, and speech does not form a new world. And yet, everything is changed by the speech that expresses the totality: the world really does become a world when it comes into the light of speech. It is the same, unique world that is made new by having someone to recite its qualities. Song adds nothing and, if one may borrow an expression from colloquial language, it does not hype it up. It has the sobriety of the clear-eyed gaze. But *the totality shines as a*

---

4. B. S. Childs, *BTONT* 725.
5. C. H. H. Scobie, *TWOG* 18; cf. Childs, *BTONT* 719.
6. A. LaCocque and P. Ricoeur, *Thinking Biblically: Exegetical and Hermeneutical Studies*, trans. D. Pellauer (Chicago: University of Chicago Press, 1998), 60.
7. Ibid., 61.
8. See C. G. Bartholomew and B. Ashford, *The Doctrine of Creation* (Downers Grove, IL: IVP Academic, forthcoming).
9. See J.-L. Chrétien, *The Ark of Speech*, trans. A. Brown (New York: Routledge, 2004), 111–48.

totality, sends itself and addresses itself as totality, when it has a witness to welcome and receive it in his song.[10]

The speech of the world calls to us to respond: "We cannot sing the world unless the world itself sings already. But even a detailed enumeration of things does not make a world. It is by being sung that the world is properly a world, grasped in its unity. The world ceases to be a scattered vocabulary, it has become a poem, it has a meaning, it has an order.... We have our place and our role within it. We are associated with a liturgy."[11]

Chrétien quotes Moltmann with approval: "In the praise of creation the human being sings the cosmic liturgy, and through him the cosmos sings before its Creator the eternal song of creation."[12] Inherent to liturgy and thus a Christian perspective is the view of the world *in its totality* as creation, and biblical studies will need to pursue this clue despite the challenges of historical criticism and postmodernism. The view of the unity of creation by the Word is inseparably related to the unity of Scripture as God's Word. Few have seen this connection as clearly as Bonaventure:

> In the state of innocence man had a knowledge of created things and was impelled by their representations to praise God, to honour him and love him.... But when man had fallen and lost his knowledge, there was no one to lead man and his knowledge back to God. The book, in other words the world, was then as it were dead and effaced, which is why another book was necessary by which man was illuminated in order to interpret the metaphors of things. This book is the book of Scripture which brings out the resemblances, the properties and metaphors of things written in the book of the world, and reorders the whole world to the knowledge, praise and love of God.[13]

For humankind to be illumined by Scripture, a sense of it as a unified whole is essential. Postmodernism has subverted many aspects of modernity, but in biblical studies its historicism and wild pluralism has even less to contribute toward biblical theology than does historical criticism.

The Bible as the Unified Word of God

Reventlow asserts that the greatest challenge for biblical theology today is the relationship between the Testaments.[14] As de Lubac rightly says, however, in order to discern how the early church came to view the two Testaments as one book, the one Word, one has to go right back to the Christ event. How, he asks, did the early church come to graft[15] the New Testament onto the Old?

10. Ibid., 122, with added emphasis.
11. Ibid., 132, quoting P. Claudel, "Du sens figuré de l'Écriture," in *Introduction au livre de Ruth* (Paris: Desclée de Brouwer, 1938), 61.
12. J. Moltmann, *God in Creation: An Ecological Doctrine of Creation*, trans. M. Kohl (London: SCM, 1985), 71.
13. St. Bonaventure, *Collationes in Hexaëmeron* 13.12; quoted in Chrétien, *Ark of Speech*, 141.
14. H. G. Reventlow, *Problems of Biblical Theology in the Twentieth Century* (London: SCM, 1986).
15. "Graft" is de Lubac's word. If it implies adding something foreign to what is receiving the graft, it is an unfortunate word choice.

> Rather was it the consequence of the fact of the Incarnation on the conscience of some few Jews. In the end what was originally known by intuition was developed into a skillfully constructed theory; ... right from the beginning the essential was there, the synthesis was made, in the dazzling and confused light of revelation. *Novum testamentum in Vetere labet: Vetus nunc in Novo patet.* ... Very early, of course, separate traditions in the interpretation of scripture were established, different schools arose. ... But the same fundamental principle compelled the recognition of all. From the beginning "the harmonious agreement of the Law and the Prophets with the Testament delivered by the Lord" was the "rule of the Church."[16]

De Lubac here perceptively notes that central to Christian *faith* from its inception is an intuitive sense of the unity of the Testaments in Christ. Thus a view of the canon as a whole basically originates in the Christ event itself.

The Christian commitment to the unity of Scripture, centered *in* Christ, thus has its source in encounter *with* Christ. All faith, as it were, finds itself sooner or later on the Emmaus road, with the dawning recognition that Christ is the fulfillment of the Old Testament. As de Lubac declares, Christ is "Master both of the first Testament and of the second. He made them both for one another. He separates them, and he also unites them in himself."[17] Through the successive stages of redemptive history, God has "led his people to the feet of Someone."[18]

> Thus Jesus Christ effects the unity of Scripture because he is its end and its fullness. Everything in Scripture is related to him. And he is its unique Object. We could even say that he is the totality of its exegesis. ... He is the Head of the body of Scripture, just as he is the Head of the body of his Church. He is the Head of all sacred understanding, just as he is the Head of all the elect. He is the complete contents of Scripture, just as he contains it all in himself.[19]

Christ is both the exegesis of Scripture and its exegete. He explains it to us by his Spirit, and in explaining it he is himself explained.

---

16. Latin to English: "The New Testament in the Old lies concealed: the Old in the New is revealed." H. de Lubac, *Catholicism: A Study of the Corporate Destiny of Mankind*, trans. L. C. Sheppard (New York: Sheed & Ward, 1958), 88. H. de Lubac (*Scripture in the Tradition*, trans. L. O'Neill [New York: Crossroad, 2000]) says, "Within the very consciousness of Jesus—if we may cast a human glance into that sanctuary—the Old Testament was seen as the matrix of the New or as the instrument of its creation" (7).

17. De Lubac, *Scripture in the Tradition*, 103.

18. Ibid., 105, quoting C. Hauret, "Comment lire la Bible?," *La Table Ronde*, no. 107 (November 1956): 141.

19. De Lubac, *Scripture in the Tradition*, 105–6.

The journey to Emmaus from Jerusalem is found in Luke 24:13–35.[20] As scholars note, its narrative location is important. Tom Wright, for example, emphasizes the parallel between Luke 1–2 and Luke 24; the story of the twelve-year-old Jesus in the temple and the incognito Jesus on the road to Emmaus. "The tired, anxious couple in the Temple are matched by the sad, disappointed couple on the road."[21] The motifs of seeing and not seeing (24:15, 24, 31), of knowing but ironically not knowing (v. 18), and of being "slow in heart" (v. 25) are central to the text. The narrative revolves around the removal of such barriers to understanding Jesus and the Old Testament. Green says, "Possibility (vv 1–12) thus gives way to probability (vv 13–35), and probability to actuality (vv 36–49) and resolution (vv 50–53)—that is, to fresh understanding and obedience" so that Jesus's disciples are prepared to be "witnesses of these things" (v. 48), which they do in the book of Acts.[22] The motif of "necessity" is found in Luke 1–2 and in Luke 24, and "it reveals, to people who had not previously grasped the point, the story that Israel's scriptures had been telling all along."[23]

Central to the story is thus the identity of Jesus and how to read the Old Testament. In the reference in 24:27 to "Moses and all the prophets," Lim rightly sees that "the Lukan Jesus is interpreting texts."[24] The Emmaus road narrative shares similarities with accounts of encounter with God in Genesis but is distinct in its deliberation over Jesus's passion.[25] Numerous studies have foregrounded the parallels with Philip's encounter with the Ethiopian eunuch (Acts 8:26–40). Green rightly observes, "From the standpoint of the Lukan narrative, the key to making sense of the death of Jesus lies in construing it within the matrix of 'the scriptures' (vv 25–27, 32)."[26] Revelation comes "through a hermeneutical process of comprehending the purpose of God in the correlation of Jesus's career with the Scriptures of Israel. What has happened with Jesus can be understood only in the light of the Scriptures, yet the Scriptures themselves can be understood only in light of what has happened with Jesus. These two are mutually informing."[27] Similarly Nolland asserts of verse 27,

> The text reflects an early Christian conviction that the Scriptures witness pervasively to the Christ and, in particular, to the way in which the career of Jesus has unfolded. Such a view has not been generated inductively from a detailed study of the Old Testament. It is a more global phenomenon and involves a particular hermeneutical approach. . . .

---

20. See J. Nolland, *Luke 18:35–24:53*, WBC 35C (Dallas: Word, 1993), 1194–96, for the extensive bibliography related to this text. Also see A. M. Schwemer, "Der Auferstandene und die Emmausjünger," in *Auferstehung/Resurrection*, ed. F. Avemarie and H. Lichtenberger, WUNT 135 (Tübingen: Mohr-Siebeck, 2001), 95–117.

21. N. T. Wright, *The Resurrection of the Son of God*, vol. 3 of Christian Origins and the Question of God (London: SPCK, 2003), 651.

22. J. B. Green, *The Gospel of Luke*, NICNT (Grand Rapids: Eerdmans, 1997), 841.

23. Ibid., 651.

24. T. H. Lim, *The Formation of the Jewish Canon* (New Haven: Yale University Press, 2013), 163. On pp. 162–65 Lim argues that Luke's "OT" was tripartite (cf. Luke 24:44) but maintains that it is unclear whether the third part was closed. For Lim, Luke mentions the Psalms in 24:44 because he gives them a prominent place in his writings, and he asserts that there is no evidence that the Psalms represent the whole of the third division. It seems to me that including the Psalms in the Scriptures because one "gives them a prominent place" is not persuasive. The emphasis in 24:27 on "*all* the scriptures" appears to imply completeness. See C. A. Kimball, *Jesus' Exposition of the Old Testament in Luke's Gospel*, JSOTSup 94 (Sheffield: JSOT Press, 1994).

25. L. Legrand, "Christ the Fellow Traveller: The Emmaus Story in Luke 24:13–35," *ITS* 19 (1984): 33–34.

26. Green, *Gospel of Luke*, 843.

27. Ibid., 844.

The view is supported by exegesis of chosen texts that were seen to anticipate the shape of Jesus' career.[28]

Nolland, like many New Testament scholars, is cautious in affirming that the Old Testament does indeed witness pervasively to Jesus. The crucial question is the hermeneutical one: How does Jesus relate to the story of the Old Testament? In 24:27 we are told he "interpreted [διερμηνεύω] to them the things about himself in all the scriptures." If Luke 24 mirrors Luke 1–2, as Tom Wright suggests, it is hard not to connect διερμηνεύω in 24:27 with διήγησις (an orderly account) in Luke 1:1. As Jeffrey comments, "His discourse with them appears to have been not merely exposition but [also] detailed analysis according to first principles; the terms remind us of the detailed, patient ordering that has characterized Luke's own *diēgēsis*, his ordered narrative of all the critical elements in Jesus's life, death, and resurrection as he has learned them."[29] This suggests, contra Nolland, that Jesus did indeed "inductively" show them how the Old Testament bore witness to him in its totality. The problem for New Testament scholars today is that we find it hard to make sense of how the New Testament reads the Old Testament. It is here, I think, that N. T. Wright has made a seminal contribution with his emphasis on story.

Wright's unique contribution lies in explaining how Jesus shows them that he fulfills "all the Scriptures" (24:27) and not just chosen texts seen to anticipate Jesus's career.[30] As Moyise states, "Wright is able to say far more about Jesus fulfilling prophecy than most scholars because he does not focus on individual sayings but rather the broad contours of Israel's story."[31] Wright discerns a vital biblical echo of Genesis 3:7 in "their eyes were opened" in Luke 24:31. "This, Luke is saying, is the ultimate redemption; this is the meal which signifies that the long exile of the human race, not just of Israel, is over at last. This is the start of the new creation."[32]

> What Luke's whole oeuvre is designed to do at a large scale, to tell the story of Jesus and the early church so that its position at the climax of Israel's scriptural story can be fully understood and appreciated, Luke's Jesus enables the disciples to do close up. They are to understand the Bible in a whole new way, in the light of the events that have happened to him. And they are to make this fresh reading of scripture the source of their inner life of burning zeal (24.32) and their framework for understanding who Jesus was and is, who they are in relation to him, and what they must do as a result (24.45–48).[33]

Verse 35, with its dual emphasis on the journey *and* the meal, "assures the dual importance of both hermeneutical activity and participation in ongoing table fellowship with Jesus. The 'breaking of bread' refers to the meal itself and thus provides a bridge from table fellowship during Jesus' ministry to the celebrative meals characteristic of the early church in Acts (e.g., Acts 2:46)."[34] If Christ is the exegesis and exegete of Scripture, then *encounter with him* is fundamental to biblical interpretation. Such encounter is individual but becomes corporate as one becomes part of his community. This reminds us again of the priority of ecclesial reception in the interpretation of Scripture.

---

28. Nolland, *Luke 18:35–24:53*, 1205.
29. D. L. Jeffrey, *Luke*, Brazos Theological Commentary on the Bible (Grand Rapids: Brazos, 2012), 285.
30. For N. T. Wright's detailed defense of Jesus's hermeneutic, see *Jesus and the Victory of God*, vol. 2 of Christian Origins and the Question of God (London: SPCK, 1996), 477–653.
31. S. Moyise, *Jesus and Scripture* (London: SPCK, 2010), 104.
32. N. T. Wright, *Jesus and the Victory of God*, 652.
33. Ibid., 659–60.
34. Green, *Gospel of Luke*, 851.

The unity of Scripture is thus a basic and foundational Christian belief in the sense in which Alvin Plantinga defines basic beliefs.[35] Evidence for such a belief is *not* required *before* one is warranted in taking this belief as foundational and working from it in one's scholarship. In other words, faith in Christ and consequent belief in the unity of Scripture resist the classical foundationalist approach to knowledge. This is not to say there are not good reasons for believing in the unity of Scripture—there are!—but it *is* to assert that one may legitimately *start* from such a belief rather than seeing it as a possible crowning achievement of biblical scholarship. As Childs recognizes, the unity of the Testaments is primarily theological: "What binds the testaments together is their witness to the selfsame divine reality, to the subject matter, which undergirds both collections, and cannot be contained within the domesticating categories of 'religion.' Scripture . . . points beyond itself to the reality of God."[36]

It is important not to be anachronistic in our understanding of the early church's commitment to the unity of Scripture. We generally think of the New Testament books as gradually achieving equality with the Old Testament, but Frances Young points out that Christians adopted the codex form for New Testament scrolls long before the codex became the norm. This appears to imply that Christian books had a certain priority and that as the "Old Testament" was taken over, it was subordinated to the Christ event and its witnesses. "We are witnessing, it seems, not the gradual elevation of recent Christian books to the sacred status of the Jewish scriptures, but rather the relativising of those ancient scriptures. . . . They have become secondary to the Gospel of Christ."[37]

In her work *The Art of Performance*, Young stresses the importance of the Rule of Faith, or Canon of Truth, for furnishing the overarching story or extracanonical framework for interpreting the Scriptures. She argues that such creedal formulations must have provided the hermeneutical key to public reading and exposition of Scripture even before it was articulated by Irenaeus:

> The one-clause form gave Jesus Christ and the story of his life, death and resurrection primacy over the books which nevertheless testified to him; the two-clause form drew attention to the continuity between promise and fulfilment, and the revelation through Christ of God already known in the Jewish scriptures; the three-clause form reinforced the inspired nature of the words

---

35. See the discussion in C. G. Bartholomew and M. Goheen, *Christian Philosophy: A Systematic and Narrative Introduction* (Grand Rapids: Baker Academic, 2013), chap. 13.

36. Childs, *BTONT* 721.

37. F. Young, *Biblical Exegesis and the Formation of Christian Culture* (Peabody, MA: Hendrickson, 2002), 15.

which testified to the Word of God. All were ways of affirming *the unity of scripture* as testimony to the revelation of God in Christ.[38]

The creed and the Rule of Faith did not summarize the whole biblical narrative but provided the reading of the beginning and end, the focus of the plot and the relations between the main characters, thereby enabling the middle to be heard meaningfully in parts. "They provided the 'closure' which contemporary theory prefers to leave open."[39]

Some of the church fathers articulated the unity of the Bible in significant terms: Irenaeus wrote of the *hypothesis* of Scripture; Origen and Athanasius stressed the *skopus* of Scripture.[40] Peter Gorday characterizes patristic exegesis as emerging from a "real and vital wholeness." "This pattern is termed by the patristic writers an 'economy' since the wholeness of scripture is represented in a creedal pattern reciting the progress of salvation from creation to eschaton."[41] To reach a proper interpretation in grasping *the unitive mind* of Scripture was seen as essential.

Young describes the Rule of Faith as extracanonical, but it is important to stress, as Young herself does, that the church fathers saw it as emerging from Scripture, as thoroughly in line with Scripture, and not as a plot imposed on Scripture to order what is disordered. Bruce asserts that the Rule of Faith

> in the earlier Christian centuries . . . was a summary of Christian teaching, believed to reproduce what the apostles themselves taught, by which any system of doctrine offered for Christian acceptance, or any interpretation of biblical writings, was to be assessed. But when once the limits of holy scripture came to be agreed upon, holy scripture itself came to be regarded as the rule of faith.[42]

For our purposes it is intriguing to notice how a narrative biblical theology functions in ways closely parallel to the Rule of Faith. Paul Blowers says,

> The Rule, being a narrative construction, set forth the basic "dramatic" structure of a Christian vision of the world, posing as a hermeneutical frame of reference

---

38. Ibid., 18–19, with added emphasis.
39. Ibid., 21.
40. On Athanasius, see J. D. Ernest, *The Bible in Athanasius of Alexandria*, The Bible in Ancient Christianity 2 (Leiden: Brill, 2004). Here he comments that "Occasional anachronisms, pastiches that blend texts from various parts of the Bible, and similar features of his readings are signs that Athanasius finds one, coherent, over-arching metanarrative in the Bible" (356).
41. P. Gorday, *Principles of Patristic Exegesis: Romans 9–11 in Origen, John Chrysostom, and Augustine* (New York: E. Mellen, 1983), 35, 36.
42. F. F. Bruce, *The Canon of Scripture* (Downers Grove, IL: InterVarsity, 1988), 18, referring to Aquinas's statement that "canonical scripture alone is the rule of faith."

for the interpretation of Christian Scripture and Christian experience, and educing the first principles of Christian theological discourse and of a doctrinal substantiation of Christian faith.[43]

As such the Rule outlined the true story of the world and played a vital role in forming Christian identity: "The Rule in effect offers the believer a place in the story by commending a way of life framed by the narrative of creation, redemption in Jesus Christ, and new life in the Spirit. It immediately sets the believer's contemporary faith and future hope into the context of the broader transhistorical and trinitarian economy of salvation."[44]

I suggest that a narrative biblical theology is precisely a contemporary explication of the Rule of Faith, demonstrating its grounding in Scripture and providing invaluable help in reading parts of Scripture within *tota Scriptura*. Below I discuss the relationship between the Bible as narrative and as drama. Suffice it here to note that some such view of the Bible as a drama in six acts is very useful as a Rule of Faith, complementing the catholic creeds, which are indispensable yet tend to overlook the acts of the drama constituted by the major parts of the Old Testament.[45]

An effect of modern biblical scholarship, which works largely within a classical foundationalist framework,[46] has been to endlessly fragment Scripture so that nowadays even believing scholars are wary of articulating the unity of the Bible. It needs to be recognized just how far removed this is from the patristic concern with the unitive mind of Scripture. If anything, much modern biblical scholarship embraces the fragmented minds of Scripture! In recent decades very few biblical theologies have been published. However, biblical theology is essential. If, as Lesslie Newbigin says, "Christ is the clue to all that is,"[47] and if it is in Scripture that we find Christ, then it is crucial that we understand Scripture in its unified totality, since to do less would be to misunderstand Christ! Christ appointed the apostles as eyewitnesses to him, and essentially what we have in the New Testament is a collection of their authoritative witness.[48] As

---

43. P. M. Blowers, "The *Regula Fidei* and the Narrative Character of Early Christian Faith," *Pro Ecclesia* 6, no. 2 (1997): 199–228, esp. 202.

44. Ibid., 214.

45. The same could be said of the church calendar. It is vital but, as stated above, needs to be revised to take account of the entirety of the biblical story in a clear fashion.

46. See Bartholomew and Goheen, *Christian Philosophy*, chap. 13.

47. L. Newbigin, *The Light Has Come: An Exposition of the Fourth Gospel* (Grand Rapids: Eerdmans, 1982), 3. See also idem, *The Gospel in a Pluralist Society* (Grand Rapids: Eerdmans, 1989), 126; idem, *Truth and Authority in Modernity* (Valley Forge, PA: Trinity Press International, 1996), 52.

48. F. Watson (*Gospel Writing: A Canonical Perspective* [Grand Rapids: Eerdmans, 2013]), however, argues, "The older assumption that canonical gospels are apostolic whereas noncanonical ones are not has proved equally untenable" (610). See chap. 8 below.

with Christ, their witness assumes the authority of the Old Testament so that it is only through Scripture that we have reliable access to the Christ event. De Lubac sums up the relationship between the Testaments as follows:

> Thus the New Testament follows upon the Old, the Old is found once again in the New, and *both together make only one*; and, just as in God unity expands into trinity, and trinity then communes with itself in unity, the New Testament is expanded into the Old and the Old is condensed in the New: "*Atque ita fiet ut et Vetus testamentum constringatur in Novo, et Novum in Vetere dilatetur.*"[49]

It is worth pausing to reflect on the importance of biblical theology in this respect. *Everything depends on what we make of Jesus.* If Newbigin is right, as I think he is, that Christ is the clue to all that is, then to understand Scripture in its unity in Christ is essential *for understanding our world*: grasping Scripture has fundamental importance for *ontology* and *epistemology*, including biblical hermeneutics. This is not for a moment to suggest that grasping or being grasped by Scripture in its totality provides all the answers to all our questions, but it does insist that only thus will we find the key, *the* clue, to the universe. The responsibility, not least of the biblical scholar, is to pursue this clue with all the rigor one can muster.

For us it is vital to recognize that Newbigin's "all that is" *includes* biblical hermeneutics. If Christ is the exegesis and the exegete of Scripture, then biblical interpretation is clearly not exempt from similarly pursuing Christ as the clue *to the Bible and biblical interpretation.* In a stimulating chapter on "Reading the Bible," Catholic philosopher Robert Sokolowski makes the obvious but easily missed point that "the most fundamental intellectual requirement for understanding the Bible is that it be read in the light of the Christian distinction between God and the world. If that is not done, the salvation promised in the scriptures is almost bound to be distorted."[50] Sokolowski rightly states that the Bible does not provide us with this distinction in a metaphysical sense. Does this, he asks, mean that we have to go beyond Scripture to find the light under which to read it? He rightly answers "No." For him, "the Christian distinction between God and the world is most vividly asserted in the actions and events that present it, not primarily in the words that make it known."[51] In agreement with what we argued in chapter 2, Sokolowski declares that the distinction between God and the world is "the kind of thing that has to be

---

49. De Lubac, *Scripture in the Tradition*, 188, with added non-Latin emphasis.

50. R. Sokolowski, *The God of Faith and Reason: Foundations of Christian Theology* (Washington, DC: Catholic University of America Press, 1995), 122.

51. Ibid., 123.

lived before it can be stated."[52] The appropriate repetition of this distinction is the imitation of Christ in the Christian life.

> The need to imitate Christ . . . is not simply a matter of pious exhortation or moral excellence; it is based on the kinds of events that occurred in the life of Jesus, on the distinctions that were brought out in these events. It is based on the "nature" of the things made manifest in Christ. We cannot hear about these realities without, simultaneously, being called to imitate them and to involve ourselves with them.[53]

Christian Biblical Theology[54]

De Lubac rightly stresses the newness of the Christ event.[55] In terms of the relationship between the Testaments, he speaks of the Christian dialectic.[56] "Dialectic" may not be the best term,[57] but de Lubac's meaning is correct; Christ contrasts the relationships between the Testaments but also unites them.[58] There is discontinuity and continuity, and the Christ event is the key to the whole. Thus biblical theology must be sure not to subvert the radical newness of the Christ event.

However, the very newness and finality of the Christ event emerges in relation to God's work with Israel. The Christ event is above all *eschatological*, as the language of the kingdom of God/heaven indicates.[59] Jesus and the New Testament writers view history within a framework of two ages, this age and

---

52. Ibid.
53. Ibid., 124.
54. Readers should notice the comparable work in Jewish biblical theology. J. D. Levenson (*The Hebrew Bible, the Old Testament, and Historical Criticism: Jews and Christians in Biblical Studies* [Louisville: Westminster John Knox, 1993]) maintains that Jews generally do not practice biblical theology, but see I. Kalimi, ed., *Jewish Bible Theology: Perspectives and Case Studies* (Winona Lake, IN: Eisenbrauns, 2012).
55. De Lubac, *Scripture in the Tradition*, 159–229. Here cf. B. S. Childs, "The Canon in Recent Biblical Studies," in *Canon and Biblical Interpretation*, ed. Bartholomew et al., Scripture and Hermeneutics 7 (Grand Rapids: Zondervan, 2006): 33–57, who notes, "The gospel is neither simply an extension of the old covenant, nor is it to be interpreted merely as a commentary on the Jewish scriptures, but it is an explosion of God's good news" (45).
56. De Lubac, *Scripture in the Tradition*, 173–82.
57. In the history of philosophy, "dialectic" has multiple possible meanings. See P. A. Angeles, *Dictionary of Philosophy* (New York: Harper & Row, 1981), 61–62.
58. De Lubac, *Scripture in the Tradition*, 173.
59. An important work in this respect is A. König, *The Eclipse of Christ in Eschatology: Toward a Christ-Centered Approach* (Grand Rapids: Eerdmans, 1989). For a sense of ongoing debates about NT eschatology, see, e.g., J. G. van der Watt, ed., *Eschatology of the New Testament and Some Related Documents*, WUNT 2/315 (Tübingen: Mohr Siebeck, 2011).

the age that is to come. This view has its background in the Old Testament prophets who anticipate the "last days" and "the day of the LORD," when God's people will be redeemed and their enemies destroyed. According to the New Testament, with the coming of Jesus the last days, the day of the Lord, the kingdom of God—these have arrived.[60] However, a profound change is introduced: the *twofold consummation* of judgment and deliverance becomes a *two-stage consummation*.[61] The age to come has broken into history, and the redemption of the world has been achieved; yet the present is the time between the coming of the kingdom and its final consummation in deliverance and judgment. Ellis helpfully depicts the differences between the Platonist/gnostic, the Jewish, and the New Testament views as follows:[62]

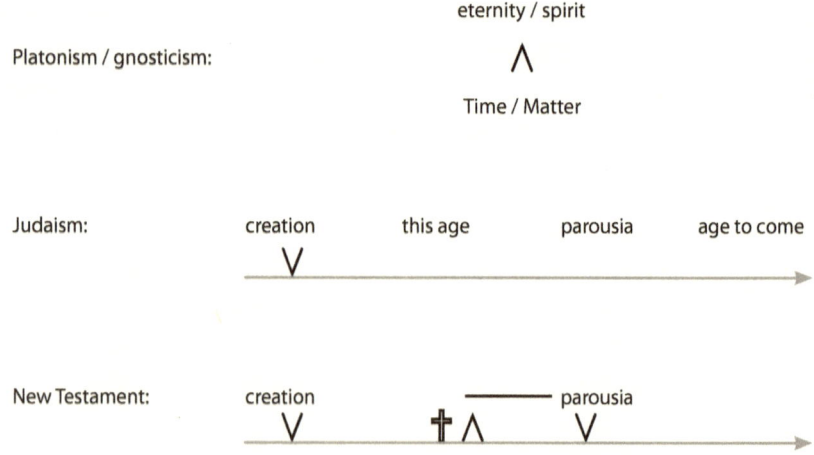

Platonism and gnosticism looked for redemption *from* time and matter in eternity and the realm of the spirit. Jewish thought hoped for redemption *within* time and history, initiated by the coming (*parousia*) of the Messiah, for bodily resurrection and triumph over their enemies in a renewed creation under the reign of God. As Ellis asserts,

> The New Testament's modification of Jewish apocalyptic rested upon the perception that in the mission, death, and resurrection of Jesus the Messiah, the

---

60. For an insightful analysis of the centrality of fulfillment in the Christ event, see J. McIntyre, *The Christian Doctrine of History* (London: Oliver & Boyd, 1957), 45–93.
61. E. E. Ellis, "The New Testament's Use of the Old Testament," in *Biblical Hermeneutics: A Comprehensive Introduction to Interpreting Scripture*, ed. B. Corley et al. (Nashville: B&H, 2002), 72–89, esp. 83.
62. Ibid., 83.

age to come, the future kingdom of God, had become present in hidden form in the midst of this present evil age, although its public manifestation awaited the parousia (P) of Jesus. Thus, in the words of Oscar Cullmann, for Jesus "the kingdom of God does not culminate a meaningless history, but a planned divine process" (233). Equally, for the New Testament writers faith in Jesus means faith in the story of Jesus, the story of God's redemptive activity in the history of Israel that finds its high point and fulfillment in Jesus.[63]

Ellis's connecting Jesus as *the eschaton* with the *story* of Jesus and the *narrative* of God's redemptive activity in the Old Testament is crucial. The newness and significance of the Christ event become evident in relation to the narrative of the Old Testament. The *end* that has come in Jesus makes sense only in relation to the beginning (creation) and all that follows, leading up to its fulfillment in Jesus.

Biblical theology aims to expose the unity of Scripture in terms of the Bible's own categories, in contrast to systematic theology, which reflects on God's revelation in terms of its own, systematic categories. A helpful analogy for biblical theology is to conceive of the Bible as a cathedral. A cathedral has a complex structure and many hidden rooms and passages, which often only the staff know about. It can be entered through many doors, and different entrances and rooms will provide different perspectives on the whole. So too with the Bible: there are many entrances into the project of biblical theology, and different approaches bring their own insights.[64] However, a cathedral has a main entrance from which one gains the most helpful perspective of the unified whole. A question for biblical theology is whether there is such a main entrance. I think there is. The center of biblical theology is Christ, and as we have seen, eschatology is central to understanding the Christ event. Such an eschatological approach pushes us in the direction of the *narrative* shape of Scripture, and in my view a *narrative* biblical theology should therefore be seen as primary, with other legitimate approaches subsumed under it. Narrative has received sustained attention in recent decades in various disciplines, and in what follows we will attend to such developments with a view to the light they cast on biblical theology.

The Impetus toward Narrative from Philosophy and Theology

Recent decades have seen a veritable explosion of interest in narrative, and this across a variety of disciplines. In philosophy, Paul Ricoeur, Alasdair

---

63. Ibid., 84. The reference to O. Cullmann is to his *Salvation in History*, trans. S. G. Sowers (New York: Harper & Row, 1967).
64. See C. G. Bartholomew et al., eds., *Out of Egypt: Biblical Theology and Biblical Interpretation*, SAHS 5 (Grand Rapids: Zondervan, 2004), 1–184.

MacIntyre, Charles Taylor, and others have taken up the theme of narrative with vigor. MacIntyre attends to the way in which all human life and thought is traditioned; he believes that our life decisions are shaped and ordered by our sense of how they fit within a larger story or tradition[65] and insists, "I can only answer the question 'What am I to do?' if I can answer the prior question, 'Of what story do I find myself a part?'"[66]

From the 1980s onward, narrative moved to center stage in Ricoeur's thought. He explores the way in which narrative is foundational to the world and how humans live in it. As Mark Wallace explains Ricoeur, "Everyone needs a story to live by in order to make sense of the pastiche of one's life. Without a narrative a person's life is merely a random sequence of unrelated events: birth and death are inscrutable, temporality is a terror and a burden, and suffering and loss remain mute and unintelligible."[67] The semantic innovation in narrative and metaphor originates from the productive imagination with its capacity to schematize. "The plot of a narrative . . . 'grasps together' and integrates into one whole and complete story multiple and scattered events, thereby schematizing the intelligible signification attached to the narrative taken as a whole."[68]

There is, according to Ricoeur, an "incipient 'configuring' or 'emplotting' process that is the experiential foundation of the human capacity to write literature and history."[69] Ricoeur notes that the "seeing as," which is the power of metaphor and of narrative, could be the revealer of a "being-as" on the deepest ontological level.[70] Ricoeur's hypothesis is that "between the activity of narrating a story and the temporal character of human experience, there exists a correlation that is not merely accidental but that presents a transcultural form of necessity. To put it another way, *time becomes human to the extent that it is articulated through a narrative mode, and narrative attains its full meaning when it becomes a condition of temporal existence.*"[71] Literature and history writing share a representative or *mimetic* function; in *Time and Narrative*, Ricoeur distinguishes three levels of mimesis. The incipient aspect

---

65. See A. C. MacIntyre, *After Virtue: A Study in Moral Theory*, 2nd ed. (Notre Dame, IN: University of Notre Dame Press, 1984), chap. 15.
66. Ibid., 216.
67. M. I. Wallace, introduction to *Figuring the Sacred: Religion, Narrative, and Imagination*, by P. Ricoeur (Minneapolis: Fortress, 1995), 1–34, esp. 11.
68. P. Ricoeur, *Time and Narrative*, trans. K. McLaughlin and D. Pellauer, 3 vols. (Chicago: University of Chicago Press, 1984–88; reprint, 1990), 1:x.
69. D. R. Stiver, *The Philosophy of Religious Language: Sign, Symbol and Story* (Oxford: Blackwell, 1996), 137.
70. Ricoeur, *Time and Narrative*, 1:xi.
71. Ibid., 52, with original emphasis.

is identified in level 1. Emplotment and thus mimesis is constructed on this preunderstanding.

Mimesis 1 refers to the fact that the composition of the plot of a narrative is grounded in a preunderstanding of the world of action, its meaningful structures, its symbolic resources, and its temporal character. It is a relation of presupposition *and* transformation.

> We may sum up this twofold relation between narrative understanding and practical understanding as follows. In passing from the paradigmatic order of action to the syntagmatic order of narrative, the terms of the semantics of action acquire integration and actuality. Actuality, because the terms, which had only a virtual signification in the paradigmatic order, that is, a pure capacity to be used, receive an actual [*effective*] signification thanks to the sequential interconnections the plot confers on the agents, their deeds, and their sufferings. Integration, because terms as heterogeneous as agents, motives, and circumstances are rendered compatible and work together in actual temporal wholes.[72]

Ricoeur is cautious about whether we can assert that the world itself has a narrative structure. He does assert that action can never be ethically neutral,[73] and in action he recognizes temporal structures that "call for narration."[74] "I shall not push my analysis of the temporal elements of action to the point where we could rightfully speak of a narrative structure, or at least of a prenarrative structure of temporal experience, as suggested by our ordinary way of talking about stories."[75] Ricoeur finds Heidegger's notion of temporality most helpful on this issue: "Narrative configurations and the most elaborated forms of temporality corresponding to them share the same foundation of within-time-ness."[76]

Mimesis 2 opens up the kingdom of the "as if" and has a mediating function deriving from the dynamic character of the configuring operation of emplotting. Plot mediates in three ways:[77]

1. It draws a diversity of events or incidents into a meaningful, intelligible story so that we can always ask of a story what its "thought" is.

---

72. Ibid., 56–57.
73. Ibid., 59.
74. Ibid.
75. Ibid., 59–60.
76. Ibid., 64. See also the discussion on pp. 60–64 and 85–86.
77. Ibid., 65–66.

2. Plot brings together a variety of factors such as agents, goals, interactions, means, fearful incidents, reversals, and so forth. Indeed, for Ricoeur, at the heart of plot is "concordant discordance."[78]
3. Plot mediates by its temporal characteristics in both a chronological or episodic sense[79] and by grasping together the incidents into a temporal whole.

Through its mediation between event and story, plot brings a solution to the paradox of temporality, which was foregrounded by Augustine. Following a story involves moving through the incidents and reversals toward the "conclusion" of the story. The conclusion provides an "end point" from which the story can be seen as a whole:

> To understand the story is to understand how and why the successive episodes led to this conclusion, which, far from being foreseeable, must finally be acceptable, as congruent with the episodes brought together by the story.
> It is this "followability" of a story that constitutes the poetic solution to the paradox of distention and intention. The fact that the story can be followed converts the paradox into a living dialectic.[80]

Mimesis 3. Mimesis 2 requires a third stage, which Ricoeur also sees as mimesis and which corresponds to what Gadamer terms "application."[81] Mimesis 3 relates to the intersection between the world of the text and that of the hearer/reader. The traversal from mimesis 1 to 3, via 2, is not, for Ricoeur, a vicious circle but an endless spiral. The act of reading schematizes emplotment. Following the insights of Roman Ingarden and Wolfgang Iser, who view the written work as a "sketch for reading," Ricoeur finds a significant role for the reader in interpretation; as a result a world is opened up in front of the text. For Ricoeur, this is akin to Gadamer's fusion of horizons.[82]

In theology, narrative has been appropriated in a variety of ways, such that one can distinguish between the following emphases:

1. An emphasis on Scripture as *the* story.
2. An understanding of the importance of *our* communal *story* for theology. All our lives are storied by virtue of the cultural contexts in which we live, and theology needs to take this cultural, communal context seriously.

---

78. Ibid., 66.
79. See ibid., 67–68, for how emplotment presents temporal features directly at odds with the episodic dimension.
80. Ibid., 67.
81. Ibid., 70.
82. Ibid., 77.

3. Each of our lives is individually a story, and thus *personal narrative* has theological implications.

Stiver discerns three major theological schools that have developed, each of which centers on one of the above three aspects.[83] The Yale school (1), associated with Frei and Lindbeck, emphasizes the narrative shape of Christianity as a particular religion and asserts that Christians should appropriate this narrative and its language and allow it to "absorb the world."[84] In comparable ways Stanley Hauerwas has stressed the importance of narrative for theological ethics.[85] The Chicago school (2), associated with Ricoeur and Tracy, is less interested in the particularity of the Christian narrative than in the philosophical and cultural relevance of narrative. This moves in the direction of general hermeneutics and ways of correlating theology with contemporary culture. The California school (3), associated with McClendon,[86] attends to the relationship between theology and personal narrative, thus developing the importance of biography and autobiography for theology today.

All three of these schools of thought have implications for narrative approaches to biblical theology. For our purposes, the Yale school is of particular interest, with its concern for the overarching Christian narrative. An example of work in this tradition is that of Stroup, *The Promise of Narrative Theology*. Stroup is excited about the possibility that narrative holds for a recovery of the gospel in the church. In the process of exploring the possibilities of a narrative theology, he pays considerable attention to narrative and the Bible. He recognizes the diversity of the Bible; much of it cannot be described as narrative.[87] Even those parts of the Bible that fit the genre of narrative differ in form, structure, and function.[88] Nevertheless he claims,

---

83. Stiver, *Philosophy of Religious Language*, chap. 7.

84. H. W. Frei (*The Eclipse of Biblical Narrative: A Study in Eighteenth and Nineteenth Century Hermeneutics* [New Haven: Yale University Press, 1974]) quotes Auerbach's striking contrast between Homer's *Odyssey* and the OT story:

> Far from seeking, like Homer, merely to make us forget our own reality for a few hours, it seeks to overcome our reality: we are to fit our own life into its world, feel ourselves to be elements in its structure of universal history. . . . Everything else that happens in the world can only be conceived as an element in this sequence; into it everything that is known about the world . . . must be fitted as an ingredient of the divine plan. (3)

85. See S. Hauerwas, *The Peaceable Kingdom: A Primer in Christian Ethics* (Notre Dame, IN: University of Notre Dame Press, 1983); S. Hauerwas and L. G. Jones, *Why Narrative? Readings in Narrative Theology* (Grand Rapids: Eerdmans, 1989).

86. J. W. McClendon Jr., *Biography as Theology: How Life Stories Can Remake Today's Theology* (Philadelphia: Fortress, 1983; reprint, Eugene, OR: Wipf & Stock, 2002).

87. G. W. Stroup, *The Promise of Narrative Theology: Recovering the Gospel in the Church* (Atlanta: John Knox, 1981), 80, 136–54.

88. Ibid., 137.

At the center of Scripture is a set of narratives and these narratives are the frame around which the whole of Scripture is constructed. Apart from these narratives the Prophets would not be intelligible, and without the frame of the Gospel narratives it would be difficult to understand the full meaning of the parables, epistles, creeds, and hymns of the New Testament.[89]

Stroup rightly notes that there are good reasons why narrative is such a primary genre in the Bible. At a philosophical and sociological level, the identity of a community or person requires the interpretation of historical experience, and narrative is the best genre for this. And since God's action is central to Christian faith, it is not surprising that much of the Bible takes the form of narrative. On this issue, Stroup explores Deuteronomy and Mark. He explains, "The Christian community gives expression to its identity by means of a narrative that begins, 'A wandering Aramean was my father' . . . culminates in the confession 'that Christ died for our sins in accordance with the scriptures' . . . and continues in the narrative history of the church through the ages as it witnesses to the coming kingdom of God."[90]

Stroup makes an admirable attempt to take the Bible seriously in his narrative theology. His work thereby foregrounds the fecundity of narrative for theological interpretation of the Bible as well as its complexity. Narrative figures prominently in the Bible; yet from Stroup's perspective, there is considerable diversity among biblical narratives, and there is much material that is not narrative. Indeed, in this respect there is a tension in Stroup's work: on the one hand, Scripture seems to range from the wandering Aramaean to the Christ and thus to have something of an overall narrative shape, while, on the other hand, Stroup confines himself to individual narratives. Stroup's work is thereby an impetus for closer examination of the Bible and narrative as a whole.

The Impetus toward Narrative from Practical Theology and Theological Ethics

Practical theology is concerned with lived experience, and so it is not surprising that practical theologians have attended to the Bible as narrative. Central to the interest in narrative among practical theologians is the recognition that human beings interpret and make sense of their world through a story. That is to speak of story, not in literary categories, but as the essential shape of a worldview. As the pastoral theologian Charles Gerkin says: "All things

89. Ibid., 145.
90. Ibid., 146.

human are in some way rooted in, or find their deepest structural framework in, a narrative or story of some kind."[91] Hence Gerkin wants to establish the practice of pastoral care on the solid foundation of a unified biblical narrative.

> This sense in which practical theological thinking is grounded in narrative is, of course, rooted in the faith that *the Bible provides us with an overarching narrative in which all other narratives of the world are nested*. The Bible is the story of God. The story of the world is first and foremost the story of God's activity in creating, sustaining, and redeeming the world to fulfill God's purposes for it. The story of the world is the story of God's promises for the world. It is also the story of the vicissitudes of God's gracious effort to fulfill those promises.[92]

Gerkin qualifies the statement above by recognizing the plurality of the biblical stories of God's activity that leads to tension between biblical themes. Nevertheless, he insists that "the stories of the Bible taken together disclose a way of seeing the world and human life in the world as always held within the 'plot' of God's intentional purposes and direction. Life in the world is life nested within that overarching narrative."[93] It is this narrative context in which pastoral theology must take place.

Similarly, Stanley Hauerwas wants to situate ethics in the context of the biblical story. The first task of ethics is not to articulate ethical standards but to "rightly envision the world" so that our life as a Christian community is consistent with the world as it exists.[94] To rightly understand the world, we must attend to the biblical story. For Hauerwas too, story is fundamentally a worldview category.

> My contention is that the narrative character of Christian convictions is neither incidental nor accidental to Christian belief. There is no more fundamental way to talk of God than in a story. The fact that we come to know God through the recounting of the story of Israel and the life of Jesus is decisive for our truthful understanding of the kind of God we worship as well as the world in which we exist.[95]

Like Gerkin, Hauerwas recognizes that this story is complex, with many different subplots and digressions. Nonetheless, it provides an overarching narrative that enables the Christian church to understand its ethical calling.

---

91. C. V. Gerkin, *Widening the Horizons: Pastoral Responses to a Fragmented Society* (Philadelphia: Westminster, 1986), 26.
92. Ibid., 48, with added emphasis.
93. Ibid., 49.
94. Hauerwas, *Peaceable Kingdom*, 29.
95. Ibid., 25.

In homiletics Greidanus and Goldsworthy underscore the importance of the biblical story for preaching: "Biblical theology involves the quest for the big picture, or the overview of biblical revelation.... If we allow the Bible to tell its own story, we find a coherent and meaningful whole.... If God has given us a single picture of reality, albeit full of texture and variety, a picture spanning the ages, then our preaching must reflect the reality that is thus presented."[96]

The quest for the big picture is important for two reasons. The first is *hermeneutical*: since the Bible is *progressive* revelation, it has an epochal structure. Greidanus rightly states that the interpreter must see the message of the text not only in its immediate historical-cultural context but "also in its broadest possible context, that is, Scripture's teaching regarding history as a whole." That is because "Scripture teaches one universal kingdom history that encompasses all of created reality: past, present, and future.... Its vision of history extends backward all the way to the beginning of time and forward all the way to the last day.... The biblical vision of history spans time from the first creation to the new creation, encompassing all of created reality."[97]

The second reason for stressing the whole story is *homiletical*: the preacher's task is to call God's people to live in the biblical story. Newbigin suggests that preaching must "challenge" the cultural story with the biblical story. Preaching calls God's people to indwell the biblical story: "Preaching is the announcing of news, the telling of a narrative. In a society that has a different story to tell about itself, preaching has to be firmly and unapologetically rooted in the real story."[98] Preaching in this way "can only happen when the Bible in its canonical wholeness recovers its place as Scripture."[99]

---

96. G. L. Goldsworthy, *Preaching the Whole Bible as Christian Scripture: The Application of Biblical Theology to Expository Preaching* (Downers Grove, IL: InterVarsity, 2000), 22.

97. S. Greidanus, *The Modern Preacher and the Ancient Text: Interpreting and Preaching Biblical Literature* (Grand Rapids: Eerdmans, 1988), 95.

98. In another place, L. Newbigin (*A Word in Season: Perspectives on Christian World Missions* [Grand Rapids: Eerdmans, 1994]) speaks of his personal Bible reading, but his words could easily be applied to his understanding of preaching:

> I more and more find the precious part of each day to be the thirty or forty minutes I spend each morning before breakfast with the Bible. All the rest of the day I am bombarded with the stories that the world is telling about itself. I am more and more skeptical about these stories. As I take time to immerse myself in the story that the Bible tells, my vision is cleared and I see things in another way. I see the day that lies ahead in its place in God's story. (204–5)

99. L. Newbigin, "Missions," in *Concise Encyclopedia of Preaching*, ed. W. H. Willimon and R. Lischer (Louisville: Westminster John Knox, 1995), 335–36, esp. 336.

The Impetus toward Narrative from Missiology: Missionary Encounter between Two Stories

Within missiology Newbigin is known for emphasizing the foundational importance of understanding the Bible as one story. His notion of a missionary encounter illustrates how much is at stake here. For Newbigin, a missionary encounter is the normal posture of every church in its culture when it is faithful to the gospel. All of human life is shaped by some story: "The way we understand human life depends on what conception we have of the human story. What is the real story of which my life story is a part?"[100] The only question is, *which* story? In contemporary Western culture there are "two quite different stories" on offer as the "real story" of the world: the humanist story that flows from the classical philosophy of Greece and Rome, and the story that is told in the Bible.[101] These stories offer two incompatible ways of viewing the world. The primary difference between them is the location of reliable truth. The biblical story locates truth in the story of God's deeds and words in history, centered in Jesus Christ; the classical humanist story finds truth in timeless ideas that can be accessed by human thought. In the West that missionary encounter takes place between the story of the Bible as it is embodied in the church and the cultural story of the West.[102]

For Newbigin both the biblical and the rationalist-humanist story have to do with *history*, an interpretation of what really happened. One story begins in our evolutionary past and sees history in terms of the progressive development of human mastery over nature by science and technology, which leads to a world of freedom and material prosperity. The other story begins with the creation of the world and ends with its renewal, leading through a narrow road marked by Israel, Jesus, and the church. God's work in Israel and in the church, and especially in Jesus, offers the clue to the meaning of history. The Bible tells the story of the coming of God's rule over the whole creation. These stories are not mere literature or linguistically constructed discourses. They interpret past history and look to the goal of history. Consequently these stories are claims to *universal* history.[103] They offer answers to the origin and

---

100. Newbigin, *Gospel in a Pluralist Society*, 15.
101. Ibid. See also L. Newbigin, *Proper Confidence: Faith, Doubt, and Certainty in Christian Discipleship* (Grand Rapids: Eerdmans, 1995), 2.
102. For an excellent discussion on this theme, see R. Bauckham, *Bible and Mission: Christian Witness in a Postmodern World* (Grand Rapids: Baker Academic, 2003), chap. 4. He speaks of witnessing to the worth of the biblical metanarrative over against the dominant metanarrative of global capitalism.
103. "Universal history" is the term Newbigin most often uses to point to the comprehensive scope of the biblical story. For disadvantages in the use of the term "universal history," see M. J.

destiny of the whole world, and they offer a clue to the meaning of world history and human life within it. The Bible is universal history: it sets forth a story of the whole world from its beginning to its end. It is the true story of the world, and all other stories are at best partial narratives, which must be understood within the context of the biblical story. Newbigin was challenged to see the Bible as universal history by Chaturvedi Badrinath, a Hindu scholar of world religions, who once said to him:

> I can't understand why you missionaries present the Bible to us in India as a book of religion. It is not a book of religion—and anyway we have plenty of books of religion in India. We don't need any more! I find in your Bible a unique interpretation of universal history, the history of the whole of creation and the history of the human race. And therefore a unique interpretation of the human person as a responsible actor in history. That is unique. There is nothing else in the whole religious literature of the world to put alongside it.[104]

As universal history, these stories make absolute and totalitarian claims on our lives.[105] They claim to understand the world as it really is and interpret the true meaning of history. Thus, the way we understand all of human life depends on what we believe to be the true story of the world. While the origin and authority of the humanist story is encapsulated in the phrase "I discovered," the biblical story finds its origin and authority in "God has spoken."[106]

A missionary encounter occurs when the church believes the Bible to be the true story of the world and thus embodies or "indwells"[107] the comprehensive claims of that story as a countercultural community over against the dominant cultural story. Since both stories make comprehensive and absolute claims, only one story can be *the* basic and foundational story for life. Newbigin charges that the Western church is in "an advanced case of syncretism" because it has allowed the biblical story to be accommodated into the more comprehensive Enlightenment story.[108]

Buss, "The Meaning of History," in *Theology as History*, ed. J. M. Robinson and J. B. Cobb (New York: Harper Books, 1967), 135–54.

104. L. Newbigin, *A Walk through the Bible* (Louisville: Westminster John Knox, 1999), 4. See also idem, *Gospel in a Pluralist Society*, 89.

105. In the words of G. Loughlin (*Telling God's Story: Bible, Church, and Narrative Theology* [Cambridge: Cambridge University Press, 1996]), the biblical story is "omnivorous": it seeks to overcome our reality (37).

106. Newbigin, *Gospel in a Pluralist Society*, 60.

107. Employing Michael Polanyi's terminology, Newbigin speaks of "indwelling" the biblical story. For more, see ibid., 33–38.

108. L. Newbigin, *The Other Side of 1984: Questions for the Churches* (Geneva: World Council of Churches, 1983), 23.

If the church is to be faithful to its missionary calling, it must recover the Bible as one true story: "I do not believe that we can speak effectively of the Gospel as a word addressed to our culture unless we recover a sense of the Scriptures as a canonical whole, as the story which provides the true context for our understanding of the meaning of our lives—both personal and public."[109] If the story of the Bible is fragmented into bits (historical-critical, devotional, systematic-theological, moral), it can easily be absorbed into the reigning story of culture. Newbigin's recognition of this, and thus his passion for the importance of seeing the Bible as one story, comes from his missionary experience. In India he saw how easy it was for the Bible to be absorbed into a more comprehensive and alien worldview. The Bible as one comprehensive story in contrast to the comprehensive worldview of Hinduism was a matter of life and death.

Part of Newbigin's call for a missionary encounter in the West was to challenge biblical scholars to equip the church by helping to recover the Bible as one story.[110] He believed that, while historical-critical scholarship had brought much insight into Scripture, it also had capitulated to the Enlightenment story as the controlling story. While it claimed to be objective and neutral, in truth much biblical scholarship was "a move from one confessional stance to another, a move from one creed to another."[111] Or as he put it elsewhere, "The Enlightenment did not (as it is sometimes supposed) simply free the scholar from the influence of 'dogma'; it [also] replaced one dogma by another."[112] The power of the Enlightenment story is such that it is difficult to convince modern biblical scholars "to recognize the creedal character of their approach."[113]

From the above, it is apparent that the impetus toward the recovery of the Bible as one story has been polyphonic—voices in philosophy, theology, ethics, and practical theology push us in this direction. Where is biblical studies in all of this?

---

109. L. Newbigin, "Response to 'Word of God?,' by John Coventry, SJ," *The Gospel and Our Culture Newsletter* 8 (1991): 2.

110. Newbigin's response was twofold. First, he sought to stir up discussion among biblical scholars. He approached George Caird, professor of the interpretation of Holy Scripture at Oxford. Caird told him: "You are asking for a total revolution in the way biblical scholars see their job." Nevertheless this initiative led to a group of younger biblical scholars beginning to discuss these issues. See L. Newbigin, *Unfinished Agenda: An Autobiography*, rev., exp. ed. (Edinburgh: St. Andrew Press, 1993), 249. Second, he himself wrote a number of papers challenging the unrecognized faith assumptions that shaped critical biblical scholarship.

111. Newbigin, *Proper Confidence*, 80.

112. Ibid.

113. L. Newbigin, "The Role of the Bible in Our Church," unpublished remarks given at a meeting of the United Reformed Forward Policy Group, April 17–18, 1985, 1.

Story and Biblical Theology

Story has a long history in biblical theology, and we cannot review it in detail here. Already Irenaeus worked with a narrative understanding of the Bible as a whole.[114] Central to Irenaeus's hermeneutic is the concept of "recapitulation." God's original intention for creation was dynamic: God intended to lead creation from its original state to final fulfillment. Hence, the incarnation is aimed not just at redeeming humanity but also at leading the creation to its intended fulfillment. Christ *recapitulates* in himself what has preceded him in human history and thereby overcomes sin and leads the whole of human history to its consummation. "Creation, the incarnation of Christ, redemption, and resurrection belong together as different parts of one all-embracing saving work of God."[115]

Farrow discerns three major elements in Irenaeus's doctrine of recapitulation, developed from Paul in Ephesians 1.[116]

1. Jesus is the ground of creation. Recapitulation's "first task is to signify that no realm whatever lies beyond the pale of his domain, that there are no autonomous times or spheres over which he is not the Lord—and because the Lord, also the redeemer."
2. Recapitulation reminds us where the problem in creation lies. For the gnostics redemption separates what is unnaturally united, whereas for Irenaeus redemption unites what is unnaturally separated through sin.
3. Recapitulation has a reduplicative force of transformation and headship. Christ's descent and ascent do not cancel but heal, restore, and consummate human existence.

The redemptive-historical approach to the Bible, stemming from Calvin and exemplified in Geerhardus Vos and Herman Ridderbos,[117] also works with

---

114. See M. A. Donovan, "Part Four: The One Story of Salvation," in *One Right Reading? A Guide to Irenaeus* (Collegeville, MN: Liturgical Press, 1997), 95–138. D. Farrow (*Ascension and Ecclesia: On the Significance of the Doctrine of the Ascension for Ecclesiology and Christian Cosmology* [Grand Rapids: Eerdmans, 1999]) notes that by attending to the creation-redemption nexus, Irenaeus launched systematic theology. Loughlin (*Telling God's Story*, xii) mentions Augustine, Aquinas, and Hamann as important figures in this narrative tradition.

115. A. Grillmeier, *Christ in the Christian Tradition*, vol. 1, *From the Apostolic Age to Chalcedon (451)*, trans. J. Bowden, 2nd ed. (London: Mowbrays, 1975), 101.

116. Ibid., 52–58.

117. A redemptive-historical school developed in the Netherlands from the late nineteenth century and reached its zenith in the twentieth century between the World Wars. This tradition is not broadly known but is rich in resources for biblical theology. A leader in this movement, B. Holwerda (in *Begonnen*; trans. and quoted by Sidney Greidanus, *Sola scriptura: Problems and Principles in Preaching Historical Texts* [Toronto: Wedge, 1970]), in 1940 summarized this redemptive-historical approach as follows:
   The Bible does not contain many histories but *one* history—the one history of God's constantly advancing revelation, the one history of God's ever progressing redemptive

an understanding of the Bible as one unfolding story, even though it precedes the contemporary stress on literature and narrative.[118]

In his work *The Concept of Biblical Theology*, Barr devotes a chapter to "story," in which he reports that from the 1960s onward, he and others have stressed the importance of story as a category in Old Testament studies. Story in this context is deliberately set against *history*, partly as a reaction to the emphasis on the acts of God in the Biblical Theology Movement (BTM). Story embraces material that is historical as well as that which includes myth and legend, and above all divine speech. Story focuses attention on the beginning, the progression, and the culmination as more important than the historical realities behind the text. Barr notes that G. Ernest Wright and others in the BTM had already indicated the importance of story in biblical theology, but he asserts that they made little of the actual story character of the Bible so that story functioned in their works more as an idea.[119]

Barr continues to see great value in approaching the Bible as story, as long as we don't set this against historical criticism. "That the story is a totality and to be read as such would seem to agree with the 'holistic' emphasis of many literary and canonical tendencies of today. But the fact that it is a totality does not mean that it has to be swallowed whole, uncritically."[120] Barr, as we will see below, defends taking the whole of the Bible as story. Making Genesis the starting point enables us to avoid past mistakes such as isolating the exodus from its broader narrative context. A story approach also connects with current understandings of communal and personal identity.

Childs is less positive toward story and biblical theology than is Barr. He discusses narrative under literary approaches to biblical theology. His major

---

work. And the various persons named in the Bible have all received their own peculiar place in this one history and have their peculiar meaning for this history. We must, therefore, try to understand all the accounts in their relation with each other, in their coherence with the centre of redemptive history, Jesus Christ. (41)

A parallel to the redemptive-historical movement is also found in the *Heisgeschichte* (salvation history) approach developed by J. C. K. von Hofmann (1810–77) at Erlangen University.

118. See, e.g., H. N. Ridderbos, *When the Time Had Fully Come: Studies in New Testament Theology* (Grand Rapids: Eerdmans, 1957; reprint, Jordan Station, ON: Paideia, 1982); idem, *Redemptive History and the New Testament Scriptures*, trans. H. de Jongste, rev. R. B. Gaffin, 2nd ed. (Phillipsburg, NJ: P&R, 1988); idem, *The Coming of the Kingdom*, trans. H. de Jongste (Phillipsburg, NJ: P&R, 1962); idem, *Paul: An Outline of His Theology*, trans. J. R. de Witt (Grand Rapids: Eerdmans, 1975).

119. It remains a relevant question as to the extent to which we can draw on the BTM in this respect today. See chap. 10, on history.

120. J. Barr, *The Concept of Biblical Theology: An Old Testament Perspective* (Minneapolis: Fortress, 1999), 352.

concern with narrative is that "the threat lies in divorcing the Bible when seen as literature from its theological reality to which scripture bears witness."[121] Barr, by comparison, finds a story approach to the Bible helpful theologically in that it alerts us to the Bible as the raw data of theological reflection. We will explore Childs's objection below. Barr's positive approach to story and biblical theology is helpful, even if one disagrees with him on the relation of the story to history. In my view there is room for a smorgasbord of ways of doing biblical theology, although (as argued above) the narrative shape of Scripture is fundamental and will need to be taken into account by all readings, even if it is not their central concern.

The fact remains, however, that there is little sign of this sort of biblical theology being written. For all the insights of older story approaches to biblical theology, things have moved on since then, and there would appear to be considerable scope for new work in this area if, as Barr asserts, story has a lot to offer biblical theology, not least in approaching the Bible as a whole. What would such an approach look like today? How can we appropriate the seminal insights of Ricoeur and so many others in terms of a contemporary narrative biblical theology?

Tom Wright and the Recovery of Story in Biblical Studies

> God who sent the Savior remains the creator; the New Testament can only speak of a new creation because God remains the creator.[122]

N. T. Wright believes there is much at stake in recognizing the Bible as one story. In fact, the theological authority of the biblical story is tied up with its overarching narrative form. He offers a rich metaphor to explicate this authority.[123] Imagine that a Shakespearean play is discovered for the first time, but its ending, most of the fifth act, is missing. The decision to stage the play is made. The first four acts and the remnant of act 5 are given to well-trained and experienced Shakespearean actors, who immerse themselves both in the first part of the play and in the culture and time of Shakespeare. They are told to work out the concluding act for themselves.

---

121. B. S. Childs, *BTONT* 723. For a response to Childs's concerns, see C. G. Bartholomew and M. W. Goheen, "Story and Biblical Theology," in *Out of Egypt: Biblical Theology and Biblical Interpretation*, ed. C. G. Bartholomew et al. SAHS 5 (Grand Rapids: Zondervan, 2004), 172–84. Intriguingly, in relation to canon Childs himself (*BTONT* 724) speaks of "the one story of God's purpose in Jesus Christ."

122. C. Westermann, *Genesis 1–11: A Commentary* (Minneapolis: Augsburg, 1984), 177.

123. N. T. Wright, *NTPG* 139–43.

This conclusion must be both consistent and innovative. It must be consistent with the first part of the play. The actors must immerse themselves in full sympathy in the unfinished drama. The first four acts would contain a cumulative forward movement that would demand that the play be concluded in a way consistent and fitting with that impetus. Yet an appropriate conclusion would not mean a simple repetition or imitation of the earlier acts. The actors would carry forward the logic of the play in a creative improvisation. Such an improvisation would be an authentic conclusion if it were coherent with the earlier acts.

This metaphor provides a specific analogy for how the biblical story might function authoritatively to shape the life of the believing community. Wright sees the biblical story as consisting of four acts—creation, fall, Israel, Jesus—plus the first scene of act 5, which narrates the beginning of the church's mission.[124] Furthermore, this fifth act offers hints at how the play is to end. Thus the church's life is lived out consistently with the forward impetus of the first acts and moving toward and anticipating the intended conclusion. The first scene of act 5, the church's story, begins to draw out and implement the significance of the first four acts, especially act 4. In new cultural situations, the church continues today to do the same in fresh and creative ways. This requires a patient examination and thorough immersion in what act 4 is all about, how act 4 is to be understood in light of acts 1–3, and how the first scene of act 5 faithfully carries forward the implications of act 4.

This divine drama, told in Scripture, "offers a story which is the story of the whole world. It is public truth."[125] Thus it is to be normative: it is to function as the controlling story[126] for the whole life of the Christian community. The biblical narrative is an authoritative worldview. A worldview expresses the deepest and most basic (yet often unconscious) beliefs through which human beings perceive reality. Worldviews operate at a presuppositional and precognitive level; they have to do with the ultimate concerns that grip people's lives. Worldviews function as a lens through which the whole world is seen, as a blueprint that gives direction for life, as a grid according to which people organize reality, and as a foundation that, though invisible, is vital in giving stability and structure to human life. The biblical and Western worldviews

---

124. C. G. Bartholomew and M. Goheen have argued for a six-act drama in *The Drama of Scripture: Finding Our Place in the Biblical Story* (Grand Rapids: Baker Academic, 2004).

125. N. T. Wright, *NTPG* 41–42.

126. N. T. Wright speaks of the biblical narrative as a "controlling story" (*NTPG* 42). His use is similar to N. Wolterstorff's notion of "control beliefs" (*Reason within the Bounds of Religion*, 2nd ed. [Grand Rapids: Eerdmans, 1999], chap. 1). Wolterstorff speaks in the context of scholarship. Control beliefs are the fundamental beliefs that function foundationally to guide our theoretical work. For Wright, a "controlling story" is the foundational story that gives shape and meaning to our lives.

come in the shape of a grand story, a "worldview-story."[127] Some worldview story will shape the life of a community. A culture is a community whose praxis and life are shaped by a controlling story. In the West, the Enlightenment and now its postmodern counterpart offer a public and comprehensive story that shapes Western culture.[128]

Attention needs to be given to the relationship between drama and narrative. In Wright's analogy the language slips easily from narrative to drama, as it does in Vanhoozer's *The Drama of Doctrine*.[129] Indeed, Vanhoozer uses drama in relation to a variety of referents: the gospel is "intrinsically *dramatic*";[130] the life of Jesus is a historical drama;[131] doctrines are life-shaping dramatic directions;[132] reading Scripture is dramatic;[133] the subject matter and the process of interpreting Scripture and theology are all dramatic;[134] "Scripture is a theo-dramatic criterion that indicates how to go on following Jesus Christ."[135] "Drama" is doing a lot of work in Vanhoozer's canonical-linguistic proposal, yet with the concomitant danger of blurring precision in the use of "drama" and "dramatic."

Clearly, in Aristotle's view[136] or that of contemporary theories of drama, Scripture is *not* a dramatic text. Pfister draws an important distinction between narrative and drama. Dramatic texts lack the mediating role of the fictional narrator and the fictional addressee. Dramatic texts "lack the fictional narrator as an overriding point of orientation."[137] Within biblical narrative the narrator plays a crucial role, as indicated, for example, by Sternberg's discussion of the omniscient narrator.[138] Narrative texts allow for a variety of arrangements of the time-space relationships, whereas in dramatic texts "it is the time-space continuum of the plot alone that determines the progress of the text within the individual scenic units"; "the invariable continuity and homogeneity of time and space within the chosen scenic unit is a condition of the medium of drama, and thus, finally, of the dramatic communication model."[139] Unlike a narrative text, a dramatic text utilizes acoustic and visual codes. In narrative texts dialogue is one of several formal elements, whereas in dramatic texts it is the basic mode of presentation. Pfister refers to the so-called fourth wall

---

127. N. T. Wright's term, as in *NTPG* 135. He uses this term to set off story as a comprehensive worldview from the various stories that express that worldview. The communal nature and narrative structure is important for Wright's understanding of worldview.

128. Ibid., 139.

129. Vanhoozer draws heavily on H. U. von Balthasar, *Theo-drama: Theological Dramatic Theory*, 4 vols. (San Francisco: Ignatius, 1988–94). See also idem, *The Glory of the Lord: A Theological Aesthetics*, 7 vols. (San Francisco: Ignatius, 1983–91; 2nd ed., 2009).

130. K. J. Vanhoozer, *The Drama of Doctrine: A Canonical-Linguistic Approach to Christian Theology* (Louisville: Westminster John Knox, 2005), 17, with original emphasis.

131. Ibid., 17.

132. Ibid., 18.

133. Ibid., 19.

134. Ibid., 21.

135. Ibid., 31.

136. Aristotle, *Poetics*. In his *Poetics*, "poetry" includes drama as well as lyric poetry, epic poetry, and the dithyramb.

137. M. Pfister, *The Theory and Analysis of Drama*, trans. J. Halliday (Cambridge: Cambridge University Press, 1988).

138. M. Sternberg, *The Poetics of Biblical Narrative: Ideological Literature and the Drama of Reading* (Bloomington: Indiana University Press, 1987), 12–13, 32–35, 41, 58–185, 411–15.

139. Pfister, *Theory and Analysis of Drama*, 5; cf. 201–2.

in the realist convention of drama: "A dramatic utterance is not addressed to the spectator any more than it is a statement by the author."[140]

What drama and narrative have in common, according to Pfister, is *story*. He, somewhat reductionistically, defines story as having three ingredients: one or more human or anthropomorphic subjects; a temporal dimension; and a spatial dimension.[141] I say "reductionistically" because I would include "plot" in the definition of "story," whereas Pfister distinguishes between "story" and "plot."[142] In my view Ricoeur is right in declaring, "With narrative, the semantic innovation lies in the inventing of another work of synthesis—a plot. By means of the plot, goals, causes, and chance are brought together within the temporal unity of a whole and complete action."[143] From this perspective, story is synonymous with narrative, so that drama becomes a subset of narrative or a different genre with much in common with narrative. The online *Free Dictionary* defines "drama" thus:

1.a. A prose or verse composition, especially one telling a serious story, that is intended for representation by actors impersonating the characters and performing the dialogue and action.
  b. A serious narrative work or program for television, radio, or the cinema.
2. Theatrical plays of a particular kind or period: *Elizabethan drama.*
3. The art or practice of writing or producing dramatic works.
4. A situation or succession of events in real life having the dramatic progression or emotional effect characteristic of a play: *the drama of the prisoner's escape and recapture.*
5. The quality or condition of being dramatic: *a summit meeting full of drama.*

Scripture is thus far more accurately defined as a narrative than as drama. Why then is the metaphorical juxtaposition of Scripture/drama so evocative and fruitful? First, we should notice that the metaphor works just as long as we "can perceive . . . the resistance of the words in their ordinary use and therefore their incompatibility at the level of a literal interpretation of the sentence."[144] Thus it is precisely because Scripture is *not* a dramatic text that the application of the metaphor "drama" to it is so evocative. In this way drama, as a metaphor, alerts us to the similarities *and* differences between Scripture and drama. In my view the juxtaposition of Scripture/drama is insightful in exploring the *unified* world opened up in front of the biblical text, as Ricoeur's mimesis 3. The acts in a drama are far more chronologically sequential than in many narratives, as is evident in Tom Wright's five acts and my and Goheen's six acts, and thus of great help in grasping the overarching shape of Scripture. Drama is more embodied, visceral, and immediate than narrative and thus helpfully evokes the connection between the biblical metanarrative and the rich texture of life as God has made it. Humans act out a drama, and the biblical story invites us to become participants in the Missio Dei. Simultaneously there are myriad differences between Scripture and drama. Scripture tells the true story of the world in which we are already participants; there is no audience, unless we take the angelic host into account, but they too are part of the drama! It would be highly unusual for an audience to act in a drama. Wright's dramatic analogy is telling here since he has to posit a missing act, which actors are called to improvise in order to make his analogy work.

In conclusion, it is better to retain the category of story/narrative for Scripture. "Drama" becomes useful, however, when explicating the unified world opened up in front of the biblical text.

140. Ibid., 4, quoting P. Szondi, *Theorie des modernen Dramas* (Frankfurt: Suhrkamp, 1956), 15.
141. Pfister, *Theory and Analysis of Drama*, 196.
142. See ibid., 197–98.
143. Ricoeur, *Time and Narrative*, 1:ix; cf. 1:149–68.
144. Ibid.

In the title of my and Goheen's *The Drama of Scripture*, therefore, much hinges on the appropriate understanding of the genitive "of"—of how we conceive of Scripture as a drama.

Both the biblical and the Western worldview stories claim to be public truth. The Christian community—including biblical scholarship—is faced with a clash of stories: since both are comprehensive and claim the whole of one's life, loyalty can be given to only one grand story. Wright is concerned that biblical scholarship often does not carry out its work under the authority of the controlling story of Scripture. Instead the Enlightenment, modernist, Western worldview story is the lens through which many scholars view the Bible.

When this happens, biblical scholarship becomes reductionistic: Scripture is reduced to only a literary or historical phenomenon. One passes beyond these reductionist readings of Scripture, Wright believes, by taking into account the worldview story of both the original writers and readers of the New Testament, and the worldview story of contemporary readers and interpreters. It is the worldview of the original writers that gives meaning to the events they narrate. Historical study is always a matter of event and interpretation, the outside happened-ness and inside meaning of an event. The earliest writers of the New Testament believed they were narrating actual events that possessed ultimate significance because God was acting in a climactic way in history. But the biblical authors and readers are not the only ones with a worldview: the modern reader coming to the Bible does not come as a neutral and objective observer but also with a particular worldview lens.

A worldview story is public and comprehensive: it offers a lens through which to view everything else, including what adherents of other worldviews are "really" up to. Biblical scholars, who may be unaware of their Western worldview lens,[145] or who have consciously embraced the Enlightenment vision as normative, look at the biblical texts and offer an account of what the biblical authors were "really" up to. The biblical authors believed that God was acting in the historical events they proclaimed. One must either

---

145. A Chinese proverb highlights the difficulty in seeing one's own cultural story and assumptions: "If you want to know about water, don't ask a fish." L. Newbigin tells of his experience prior to India, before the "immense power and rationality of the Vedantin's [Vedantic] vision of reality" (*The Light Has Come*, ix) enabled him to understand the formative power of Western culture on him:

> My confession of Jesus as Lord is conditioned by the culture of which I am a part. It is expressed in the language of the myth within which I live. Initially I am not aware of this as a myth. As long as I retain the innocence of a thoroughly Western man, unshaken by serious involvement in another culture, I am not aware of this myth. It is simply "how things are." ... No myth is seen as a myth by those who inhabit it: it is simply the way things are. ("Christ and Cultures," *SJT* 31 [1978]: 3)

believe those claims or reject them on the basis of other beliefs embodied in another story. If that story is the Enlightenment story, theological claims do not stand up well, and so they are dismissed. But accepting the authority of the Western story and dismissing the theological claims of the original writers would be abandoning the comprehensive and public claim of the biblical story. Enlightenment modernism then subsumes Christianity within it and makes the biblical story one more private religious option.[146]

It is possible, though, to work the other way around: to embrace the biblical story as the true and comprehensive story, and to understand Enlightenment modernism and its postmodern reaction from within the biblical story. Then the biblical story becomes the controlling story for biblical scholarship. This is how Wright wants to proceed. The task of biblical interpretation, then, will not be a matter of "purely literary" or "purely historical" study, divorced from worldview and theology. Rather, it will be "possible to join together the three enterprises of literary, historical, and theological study of the New Testament and to do so in particular by the use of the category of 'story.'"[147]

Theological interpretation will be as important as the literary or historical. Theology is concerned with claims about God embodied in a worldview: whether there is a God, his relation to the world, and whether God is acting to set the world right.[148] The theological beliefs of the biblical authors and the Bible's modern interpreters will be essential to biblical scholarship: "'Theology' highlights what we might call the god-dimension of a worldview. . . . As such it is a non-negotiable part of the study of literature and history, and hence of New Testament studies."[149]

The recovery of the Bible as one controlling story is important for Wright because that story provides the true worldview context for biblical scholarship, allowing all dimensions of the biblical text—theological, literary, and historical—to find full expression.

An important part of the recovery of the Bible as one story will be the work of Christian theology. For Wright, Christian theology is not the abstract arrangement of timeless truths or propositions in some overarching system. Rather, it is occupied with articulating the biblical story. Christian theology claims to be telling the true story about the creator and his world; it tells us what God is doing in history to restore his creation.[150] So Wright is interested

---

146. N. T. Wright, *NTPG* 137.
147. Ibid., 139.
148. Ibid., 127.
149. Ibid., 130–31.
150. For N. T. Wright's summary of the biblical story, see ibid., 132.

in "working in line with some recent studies in narrative theology."[151] Narrative theology, or telling the story, will be a necessary part of the church's task as it lives in act 5 of the biblical story: "The retelling of the story of the previous acts, as part of the required improvisation, is a necessary part of the task all through."[152] Israel retold the story of creation and sin. Jesus retold the story of Israel in his parables. The Gospel writers retold the story of Jesus. "This may suggest, from a new angle, that the task of history, including historical theology and theological history, is itself mandated upon the followers of Jesus from within the biblical story itself."[153] A narrative biblical theology has a vital role to play in making the church, including biblical scholars, aware of the grand story that ought to be shaping their whole lives.[154]

Conclusion

Andrew Walker challenges us to face the fact that "we are on the way to postmodernity, and already we are caught in an electronic field of blinding imagery and synthesized sounds. Where are our candles, smells, and electric bells? Where are our images of light and shade, our music of splendour, our divine dramas, the sacred dance? We have a story, but no one can see it. We tell the story, but no one can hear it."[155] The contention of this chapter, however, is that in biblical studies we do *not* tell the story! John Carroll perceptively warns, "The waning of Christianity as practised in the West is easy to explain. The Christian churches have comprehensively failed in their one central task—to retell their foundational story in a way that might speak to their times."[156] There is far too little energy directed toward telling the biblical story as a grand narrative. In practical theology, missiology, and ethics, there is a growing chorus of voices calling for such a reading of the Bible, and an answer to that call is long overdue in biblical theology. The objections to a narrative biblical theology do not stand up to critical scrutiny; while this is certainly not the only way to do biblical theology, it is an important

---

151. N. T. Wright also wants to distance himself from a narrative theological approach that doesn't take history seriously. He says: "Unlike most 'narrative theology,' however, I shall attempt to integrate this approach with a historical focus. And this combined approach grows out of the analysis offered above of worldviews and how they work" (ibid.).

152. Ibid., 142.

153. Ibid.

154. However, this approach is not popular among biblical scholars because of a number of criticisms that have been leveled against it. For a rebuttal of these critiques, see Bartholomew and Goheen, "Story and Biblical Theology."

155. A. Walker, *Telling the Story: Gospel, Mission and Culture* (London: SPCK, 1996), 197.

156. J. Carroll, *The Existential Jesus* (Berkeley: Counterpoint, 2007), 7.

approach. As Walker says, "In the act of telling the story, modern theologians cannot make people believe it. What they can do, however, is to stand up for the story, and learn again to tell it in the way it was meant to be told.... It is the Church's grand narrative, which is essential not only for its own identity but [also] for the salvation of the world."[157]

Clearly biblical studies has a central role to play in this area. Ironically the discipline that has most to offer in helping the church recover its story has to a large extent capitulated to the alternative grand narratives of modernity. The insights of missiology are thus particularly relevant to renewing biblical interpretation. The biblical scholar will always work out of some story of the world, and Christian biblical scholars have a responsibility to indwell the biblical story, to articulate it in their work, and to resist the pressure of conforming to alternative grand stories while working hard to retain the many, many insights of modern biblical studies. In my view, a narrative approach to biblical theology is the foundational and primary one. On this basis, however, a variety of approaches are possible, and it is to these that we turn in the following chapter. For now it is important to attend to the antidote that making narrative primary in biblical theology injects into the practice of biblical theology. The primacy of the biblical story allows us to develop diagnostic questions that *any* biblical theology must attend to, questions such as these:

1. Does the biblical theology of Old and/or New Testament in question take seriously the foundational *act of creation* in the narrative of Scripture? In terms of the biblical story, creation is utterly foundational to all that follows; yet in so much modern biblical study, there has been a reductionistic tendency to fail to make the connections with creation and its comprehensive range. This leads us to our second question.
2. Does the biblical theology in question attend to the fundamental relationship between creation and salvation/redemption in the Bible? This relationship is at the heart of the biblical narrative and yet continually goes unnoticed far too often in biblical studies. The great strength of Bill Dumbrell's *Covenant and Creation* is that, through detailed exegesis, it does precisely this,[158] as does the best, recent work on a missional hermeneutic.[159] This leads us to our third question.

157. Ibid., 53. In *Drama of Scripture* Mike Goheen and I endeavor to tell the story of the Bible at an accessible level.
158. Also cf. P. J. Gentry and S. J. Wellum, *Kingdom through Covenant: A Biblical-Theological Understanding of the Covenants* (Wheaton: Crossway, 2012).
159. Cf., e.g., M. Goheen, *A Light to the Nations: The Missional Church and the Biblical Story* (Grand Rapids: Baker Academic, 2011).

3. Is the biblical theology in question alert to the overarching themes of *covenant* and *kingdom* in Scripture? Both of these major, overarching themes focus attention on the Great King, and this brings us to our next question.
4. Does the biblical theology in question attend to the trinitarian God as the primary character rendered to us truly by the canon of Scripture? God's revelation is progressive. This leads us to the following two questions.
5. Does the biblical theology in question demonstrate awareness of the different stages or acts in the narrative of Scripture, do justice to their *discrete* integrity, and show their interrelationship?
6. Does the biblical theology in question locate the center of Scripture in the Christ event, which illuminates what comes before and what follows? From a narrative perspective, it is remarkable that discussion continues as to whether there is a center to the Bible, to the Old Testament, and to the New Testament. Clearly Yahweh is the center of the Old Testament, as is the same God who has come to us in Christ in the New Testament. It is the Christ event that opens out into the doctrine of the Trinity, and hence we have referred to "the trinitarian God" in question 4 above.
7. Finally, does the biblical theology in question open out onto the entirety of God's creation? Does it do justice to the *public* dimension of Scripture? This final question connects back into question 1 and the utterly comprehensive range of creation.

Doubtless there are many more questions that could be asked, but these are central ones to which any biblical theology or theology of part of the Bible will need to attend.

4

The Development of Biblical Theology

> Jesus thus does not come onto the terrain of a strange God, but into his own domain. . . . If the world was the work of another God, he himself would have appropriated the property of another. Then he would be a thief.
>
> A. Van de Beek[1]

Biblical theology is the attempt to grasp Scripture in its totality and according to its own categories, rather than imposing categories.[2] In the previous chapter I argued that primary importance should be given to a narrative biblical theology. This is the most obvious way in which Scripture is a unity and also does justice to the dynamic development of the Bible as well as indicating where *we* fit into the biblical metanarrative. With a narrative approach as the base, there is ample room for a variety of complementary approaches.

---

1. A. Van de Beek, *Een lichtkring om het kruis: Scheppingsleer in christologisch perspectief* (Zoetermeer: Meinema, 2014), 18, my translation.

2. For a discussion of the definition of biblical theology (BT), see J. Barr, *The Concept of Biblical Theology: An Old Testament Perspective* (Minneapolis: Fortress, 1999), chap. 1. My definition is akin to what Barr calls "pan-biblical theology" because it insists on relating BT to the whole of the Bible. This is not to deny the value of theologies of parts of the Bible but to argue that BT should always be oriented toward the whole. Indeed, if the biblical narrative is taken as foundational, then theologies of parts of the Bible will always proceed from and be oriented toward the whole.

In this chapter we will look briefly at the history of biblical theology, with particular attention to Gabler's inaugural lecture, which is often regarded as the origin of modern biblical theology. Then we will examine the Biblical Theology Movement (BTM), which is the major precursor to contemporary biblical theology. After that we will take note of the three major biblical theologies of recent years in light of the diagnostic questions we posed at the end of chapter 3, with a view to asking what sort of work needs to be done today.

The History of Biblical Theology

The origin of biblical theology is commonly traced back to Johann Gabler's inaugural address, "On the Proper Distinction between Biblical and Dogmatic Theology and the Specific Objectives of Each," given on March 30, 1787. Does this originating moment of biblical theology mean that it never existed before 1787? Barr argues that it is anachronistic to see Calvin and others as doing "biblical theology,"[3] while Childs insists that biblical theology has a history going back to the early church fathers. Certainly the church fathers were drenched in Scripture and wrestled with the relationship between the Testaments. Wilken tells of how in his research into the church fathers, he has been impressed by "the omnipresence of the Bible in early Christian writings. Early Christian thought is biblical, and one of the lasting accomplishments of the patristic period was to forge a way of thinking, scriptural in language and inspiration, that gave to the church and to Western civilization a unified and coherent interpretation of the Bible as a whole."[4] Wilken notices that "when they [the first Christian thinkers] took the Bible in hand, they were overwhelmed. It came upon them like a torrent leaping down the side of a mountain."[5] Clement's writings embody a "conceptual framework drawn from the Bible."[6] And Irenaeus, in his struggle with Marcion and the gnostics over the unity of the Bible, articulates the unity of the Bible as a single story:

> Two histories converge in the biblical account, the history of Israel and the life of Christ, but because they are also the history of God's actions in and for the world, they are part of a larger narrative that begins at creation and ends in a vision of a new, more splendid city in which the "Lord God will be their light."

---

3. Ibid., 3.
4. R. L. Wilken, *The Spirit of Early Christian Thought: Seeking the Face of God* (New Haven: Yale University Press, 2003), xvii.
5. Ibid., 53.
6. Ibid., 60.

The Bible begins, as it were, with the beginning and ends with an end that is no end, life with God, in Irenaeus's charming expression, a life in which one is "always conversing with God in new ways." Nothing falls outside of its scope.[7]

With Irenaeus's narrative approach to the Bible, we certainly have an incipient biblical theology.[8] The unity of the Testaments is affirmed—there is one God who called Abraham, spoke with Moses, sent the prophets, and is also the father of our Lord Jesus Christ[9]—and is articulated in terms of the story shape of the Bible as a whole. Furthermore, the story is explained in terms of the theme of renewal, or re-creation.[10]

Nevertheless, for all the common ground one finds with biblical theology in the church fathers, Aquinas, and the Reformers,[11] it remains true that before Gabler's time, theology and biblical theology were *undifferentiated*.[12] It is this differentiation that Gabler is associated with; provided that this delineation can be carefully distinguished from his rationalism and the endless fragmentation of the Bible to which historical criticism led, it is a helpful and legitimate distinction because it allows biblical theology, as distinct from systematic theology, to come into focus in its own right.

---

7. Ibid., 63.
8. See B. S. Childs, *BTONT* 30–33; C. H. H. Scobie, *TWOG* 10.
9. The issues Irenaeus wrestled with remain highly relevant today. The relationship between the OT and NT is perhaps the major issue in any BT. See H. G. Reventlow, *Problems of Biblical Theology in the Twentieth Century* (London: SCM, 1986), who devotes almost the entirety of his book to this issue. And Irenaeus's fight to affirm the identity of "the Lord" (Yahweh) with the God and Father of our Lord Jesus Christ remains foundational for the practice of a Christian BT. In response to salvation-historical readings of the Bible, Reventlow (ibid., 14) asserts that by itself the Christ event should not be regarded as a continuation of the Old Testament event, but only faith sees it thus. Such an assumption (by faith) seems to me to be an indispensable starting point for a Christian BT.
10. Wilken, *Spirit of Early Christian Thought*, 66. See C. E. Gunton, *Christ and Creation* (Eugene, OR: Wipf & Stock, 2005), for the importance of Irenaeus in discerning the shape of the Bible as a whole.
11. See Childs, *BTONT* 30–51; Scobie, *TWOG* 9–13. In an important work, P. A. Lillback ("The Binding of God: Calvin's Role in the Development of Covenant Theology" [PhD diss., Westminster Theological Seminary, 1985]) argues, "Calvin is the great architect of the Covenant Theology. He is not its inventor, since this honor must really fall to Zwingli. He is not the builder of the first popular model of covenant thought, since this distinction falls to Bullinger. Nevertheless, Calvin is the first of the early theologians to integrate the covenant concept into the entirety of his theological system" (496). In an appendix (499–527), Lillback provides a translation of Bullinger's 1534 "Of the One and Eternal Testimony or Covenant of God: A Brief Exposition by Henry Bullinger."
12. On the church fathers and BT, see G. Bray, "The Church Fathers and Biblical Theology," in *Out of Egypt: Biblical Theology and Biblical Interpretation*, ed. C. G. Bartholomew et al. (Grand Rapids: Zondervan, 2004), 23–40.

Gabler commences his inaugural lecture with his concern about the variety of views among Christians. One of the reasons he discerns for this is the failure to distinguish biblical theology from dogmatic theology. Gabler contrasts religion with theology: "Religion then, is every-day, transparently clear knowledge; but theology is subtle, learned knowledge, surrounded by a retinue of many disciplines, and by the same token derived not only from the sacred Scripture but also from elsewhere, especially from the domain of philosophy and history."[13] In this contrast, Gabler associates the Bible with religion. He argues, "There is truly a biblical theology, of historical origin, conveying what the holy writers felt about divine matters; on the other hand there is a dogmatic theology of didactic origin."[14] Biblical theology remains the same whereas dogmatics changes all the time.

Gabler's understanding of biblical theology is deeply rationalistic. There is much in the Bible that is culturally conditioned, and he insists that we need to separate the things in the Bible that refer to their own times from the "pure notions which divine providence wished to be characteristic of all times and places."[15] Thus we first need to collect the sacred ideas of the authors and then classify them, after which we should compare them with the universal ideas of reason. From this process biblical theology will appear!

Gabler was not original in making the distinction between biblical theology and dogmatics;[16] rather, he sought methodological clarity on the relationship between them. Gabler's whole approach is so colored by rationalism that one is tempted to dismiss him out of court, but this would be a mistake. His distinguishing of biblical theology from dogmatic theology is helpful and, I suggest, an important step in the differentiation of biblical theology in the "theological encyclopedia." For biblical theology to flourish as an entity in its own right, such a distinction is important, provided we can distinguish it from Gabler's rationalism.

The story of biblical theology since Gabler has often been told, and I will not repeat it here.[17] The rationalist scholar Georg Lorenz Bauer was the first to distinguish between Old Testament theology and New Testament theology, and

---

13. J. P. Gabler, "An Oration on the Proper Distinction between Biblical and Dogmatic Theology and the Specific Objectives of Each," in *Old Testament Theology: Flowering and Future*, ed. B. C. Ollenburger (Winona Lake, IN: Eisenbrauns, 1992), 493–502, esp. 495.

14. Ibid., 495.

15. Ibid., 496.

16. Childs, *BTONT* 4. The term "biblical theology" was first used in the seventeenth century. For the important *covenantal* contribution of J. Cocceius (1603–69), see Scobie, *TWOG* 13.

17. For a very useful overview, see Scobie, *TWOG* 13–45. This is not to say that the story of BT does not need to be retold. The way this story is told is never neutral: an urgent need of our time is the retelling of the story of biblical studies and BT, so that we can truly discern

soon the view arose that the discontinuities between the Testaments were so strong as to defy attempts to articulate their unity. Scholars started writing Old Testament and New Testament theologies, a trend that continues to this day,[18] so that, "from around 1870, for approximately a century, 'biblical theology,' in the sense of writing of works on the theology of Old Testament and New Testament together, to all intents and purposes ceased to exist."[19] Historical criticism is essentially the child of modernity; thus, unsurprisingly, biblical

---

what is at stake in the story. Such consciousness is a vital ingredient in any renewal of biblical interpretation.

18. In this volume I cannot attend to the many OT and NT theologies that have been written. Theologies of parts of the Bible or of one Testament are invaluable, especially if they work from the basis of Scripture as a unified whole. In practice this has generally not been the case. Important works in this genre continue to appear. In OT theology, notably B. S. Childs, *Old Testament Theology in a Canonical Context* (Minneapolis: Fortress, 1990); A. H. J. Gunneweg, *Biblische Theologie des Alten Testaments: Eine Religionsgeschichte Israels in biblisch-theologischer Sicht* (Stuttgart: Kohlhammer, 1993); H. D. Preuss, *Old Testament Theology*, trans. L. G. Perdue, 2 vols. (Louisville: Westminster John Knox, 1995–96); E. A. Martens, *God's Design: A Focus on Old Testament Theology*, 3rd ed. (N. Richland Hills, TX: Bibal, 1998); P. R. House, *Old Testament Theology* (Downers Grove, IL: IVP Academic, 1998); M. Nobile, *Teologia dell'Antico Testamento*, Logos: Corso di studi biblici 8.1 (Leumann [Torino]: Elle Di Ci, 1998); J. H. Sailhamer, *Introduction to Old Testament Theology: A Canonical Approach* (Grand Rapids: Zondervan, 1995); R. Rendtorff, *Theologie des Alten Testaments: Ein Kanonischer Entwurf*, 2 vols. (Neukirchen-Vluyn: Neukirchener, 1999–2001); E. S. Gerstenberger, *Theologies in the Old Testament*, trans. J. Bowden (London: T&T Clark, 2002); W. A. Brueggemann, *Theology of the Old Testament: Testimony, Dispute, Advocacy* (Minneapolis: Fortress, 2005); R. Routledge, *Old Testament Theology: A Thematic Approach* (Downers Grove, IL: IVP Academic, 2008); B. K. Waltke and C. Yu, *An Old Testament Theology: An Exegetical, Canonical, and Thematic Approach* (Grand Rapids: Zondervan, 2007); J. Goldingay, *Old Testament Theology*, 3 vols. (Downers Grove, IL: IVP Academic, 2003–9); J. W. Rogerson, *A Theology of the Old Testament: Cultural Memory, Communication, and Being Human* (Minneapolis: Fortress, 2010); J. Kessler, *Old Testament Theology: Divine Call and Human Response* (Waco: Baylor University Press, 2013); R. W. L. Moberly, *Old Testament Theology: Reading the Hebrew Bible as Christian Scripture* (Grand Rapids: Baker Academic, 2013).

In NT theology, notably H. Hübner, *Biblische Theologie des Neuen Testaments*, vol. 2 (Göttingen: Vandenhoeck & Ruprecht, 1993); G. B. Caird and L. D. Hurst, *New Testament Theology* (Oxford: Clarendon, 1995); P. Stuhlmacher, *Biblische Theologie des Neuen Testaments* (Göttingen: Vandenhoeck & Ruprecht, 1999); I. H. Marshall, *New Testament Theology: Many Witnesses, One Gospel* (Downers Grove, IL: IVP Academic, 2004); F. Thielman, *Theology of the New Testament: A Canonical and Synthetic Approach* (Grand Rapids: Zondervan, 2005); G. Segalla, *Teologia biblica del Nuovo Testamento: Tra memoria escatologica di Gesù e promessa del futuro regno di Dio*, Logos: Corso di studi biblici 8.2 (Leumann [Turin]: Elle Di Ci, 2006); T. R. Schreiner, *New Testament Theology: Magnifying God in Christ* (Grand Rapids: Baker Academic, 2008); U. Schnelle and M. E. Boring, *Theology of the New Testament* (Grand Rapids: Baker Academic, 2009); G. K. Beale, *A New Testament Biblical Theology: The Unfolding of the Old Testament in the New* (Grand Rapids: Baker Academic, 2011).

19. Scobie, *TWOG* 18. This assessment depends on whether one regards the BTM as having produced such works.

studies were deeply and largely unhelpfully affected by attempts to relate interpretation to the major secular philosophies of the day.[20] An assumption developed that biblical theology was anachronistic, as embodied in Hermann Gunkel's (1862–1932) statement that "the recently experienced phenomenon of Biblical Theology's being replaced by the history of Israelite religion is to be explained from the fact that the spirit of historical investigation has now taken the place of a traditional doctrine of inspiration."[21]

The scientific and historical revolutions drove the engine of modernity, and here we witness the demise of biblical theology related to a progressive view of history, along with the concomitant move from theology to religion.[22] The related stress on the diversity of Scripture that has been central to most historical criticism has haunted biblical theology to this day.

The Biblical Theology Movement

The more immediate context for contemporary efforts in biblical theology is the rise and demise of the so-called Biblical Theology Movement (BTM). Dates for this movement can be set with precision, from around the end of World War II to 1961, when publications by Gilkey and Barr are said to have sunk the BTM. The BTM was strongly Protestant, particularly American, and consciously oriented toward reading the Bible for the church, while acknowledging the legitimacy of historical criticism. The BTM was connected with the emergence of the neo-orthodoxy of Karl Barth, although it tended to be suspicious of Barth's supposed rejection of historical criticism. Indeed, Brunner rather than Barth was the greater influence on the BTM.

The BTM in the United States represented a meaningful attempt to break out of the impasse of the modernist/fundamentalist debate about the Bible that had plagued American churches and move toward a vibrant recovery of biblical theology. Its major emphases were these:[23]

1. A recovery of the Bible as a *theological* book. Historical criticism has a legitimate role to play, but it represents the start and not the end; it must lead us to hear God address us through his Word, and biblical theology is a major ingredient in this effort. G. Ernest Wright, one of the major representatives of the BTM, lamented the neglect of biblical theology and

---

20. Childs, *BTONT* 6. On philosophy and biblical interpretation, see chap. 9 below.
21. H. Gunkel, "Biblische Theologie und biblische Religionsgeschichte: I des AT," in *Religion in Geschichte und Gegenwart*, 2nd ed. (Tübingen, 1929), 3:1089–91; quoted in Childs, *BTONT* 6.
22. Cf. Scobie, *TWOG* 20–22.
23. Here I am leaning heavily on B. S. Child's classic *BTIC*, which tells the story of the BTM.

noted that it was difficult to find a leading graduate school where one could specialize in it.[24]

2. The BTM stressed *the unity of the Bible* as a whole and regarded it as vital that we overcome the chasm that had opened up between Old Testament and New Testament. G. E. Wright recognizes that "the scholarly study of the Old Testament has been separated from that of the New and from its moorings in the proclamation of the Church."[25] He diagnoses the condition of biblical interpretation in his day as a revival of Marcionism and argues strongly against this: "Surely, if the New Testament is not proclaimed as the fulfillment of the Old, if the Gospel as proclaimed by Jesus and by Paul is not the completion of the faith of Israel, then it must inevitably be a completion and fulfillment of something which we ourselves substitute—and that most certainly means a perversion of the Christian faith."[26] Wright himself articulates the unity of the Bible through a recitation of the great acts of God, finding their fulfillment in Jesus of Nazareth.

3. The BTM, as is evident from Wright's approach described in point 2 (above), made *God's revelation of himself in history* central to biblical theology. The pagan religions of the ancient Near East had no concept of history; from this angle, Israel was regarded as utterly unique: God reveals his being and will through his great acts, and particularly in the Old Testament through his redemption of the Israelites from Egypt.

4. The BTM laid great stress on *the distinctiveness of the biblical perspective*. It reacted strongly to the tendency among scholars to explain Israel's faith as part of an evolving history of religion. Israel's view of God and the world were quite unique in its ancient Near Eastern context, and this stemmed from God's revelation of himself to Israel.[27]

By 1961 the BTM, which manifested such energy and hope for a recovery of the Bible, was verging on collapse. What were the structural deficiencies that facilitated the demise of this great edifice? Childs argues that there were a host of unresolved problems in the BTM that eroded it from within and made it vulnerable to an attack from Barr and Gilkey from without. These include the following:

1. According to Childs, the BTM never resolved the issue of the Bible and its authority. Fundamentalism was rejected, but so too was Karl Barth's use of the Bible, which was regarded as not taking historical criticism sufficiently seriously. Problematically, no clear alternative emerged to either

24. Ibid., 36–37.
25. G. E. Wright, *God Who Acts: Biblical Theology as Recital* (London: SCM, 1952), 15.
26. Ibid., 17; cf. J. Bright, *The Authority of the Old Testament* (Nashville: Abingdon, 1967).
27. See, e.g., G. E. Wright, *The Old Testament against Its Environment* (London: SCM, 1950).

of these views. For all its emphasis on the Bible, the BTM failed to produce great commentaries and generally seemed to confine its use of the Bible to a few favorite books. Scobie states, "Perhaps the most surprising failing of the so-called Biblical Theology Movement, yet one that is seldom commented upon, was the fact that it did not produce a single major, scholarly volume of 'biblical theology.'"[28]

2. The emphases of the BTM were seldom translated into educational and curriculum policy in the seminaries. "Very infrequently did Biblical Theology become an integrating factor that provided a focus for the other disciplines."[29] This meant, inter alia, that changes in systematic theology and hermeneutics left biblical theology vulnerable and with little defense.

3. In the late 1950s and in the 1960s the church was feeling the need to respond to the modern world and the great diversity of challenges it represented, challenges that extended way beyond the institutional church. The BTM appeared to be sorely lacking in the face of these challenges: it had not given rise to a new style of preaching, and theological ethics seemed to be getting along quite well without it.

4. The BTM's emphasis on God's acts *in history* appeared to solve many problems, but this apparent success concealed some major cracks in its edifice, cracks that Barr and Gilkey exploited. The distinctiveness of Israel's perspective was also being questioned: scholars such as F. C. Cross demonstrated that Israel's neighbors were much closer to its views in all sorts of ways than the BTM proponents had allowed. We will explore Barr's and Gilkey's critiques in more detail below; suffice it here to recognize that their publications in 1961 were perceived as dealing a death blow to the BTM. Childs says of Barr's *Semantics*, "Seldom has one book brought down so much superstructure with such effectiveness."[30]

The consequent thrust of Child's *Biblical Theology in Crisis* (*BTIC*) is that biblical theology is in crisis, and a new paradigm is required. In *BTIC* and in his subsequent writings, Childs goes on to propose a *canonical* paradigm for biblical theology as the answer to this crisis. Barr argues, by contrast, that Childs overestimates the extent of the problem in order to set the stage for his new paradigm. Indeed, Barr denies that there really was/is a crisis of biblical theology, which has continued to flourish in all sorts of ways.[31] Rather, what

28. Scobie, *TWOG* 25.
29. Childs, *BTIC* 56.
30. Ibid., 72.
31. J. Barr, "The Theological Case against Biblical Theology," in *Canon, Theology, and Old Testament*, ed. G. M. Tucker, D. L. Petersen, and R. R. Wilson (Minneapolis: Fortress, 1988), 3–19, esp. 3–4.

happened was that biblical theology lost its power to assert itself over against other aspects of the "theological encyclopedia."

Either way, the arguments that facilitated the demise of the BTM bear close scrutiny. It is fascinating to look back *now* on the arguments that were perceived as fatally damaging for the BTM. Gilkey's 1961 article is titled "Cosmology, Ontology, and the Travail of Biblical Language." He argues that the BTM got caught between being half liberal and half modern, plus half biblical and half orthodox: "Its world view or cosmology is modern, while its theological language is biblical and orthodox."[32] In opposition to liberalism, the BTM asserted its belief in revelation through God's mighty acts, thereby understanding God's speech and acts literally and univocally. At the same time it held on to the modern belief in the causal continuum. As Gilkey explains, "This assumption of a causal order among phenomenal events, and therefore of the authority of the scientific interpretation of observable events, makes a great difference to the validity one assigns to biblical narratives and so to the way one understands their meaning."[33]

A modern understanding of causality means that most of the biblical events did not in fact happen; they instead become symbols: "We believe that the biblical people lived in the same causal continuum of space and time in which we live, and so one in which no divine wonders transpired and no divine voices were heard."[34] Gilkey probes the writings of the BTM on this issue and finds them riddled with contradictions. He argues that the implication of this tension for the BTM is that the Bible is really a book of great acts that the Hebrews believed God to have done, but which we know he in fact did not do. The result is that the mighty acts of God are reduced to God's "inward incitement of a religious response to an ordinary event within the space-time continuum,"[35] akin to Schleiermacher's emphasis on religious experience.

Gilkey argues that the BTM needs a more sophisticated view of language and a theological ontology. Hebrew recital must be distinguished from our recital; the biblical writers use language *univocally* whereas we know that we can only speak of God *analogically*. Furthermore we need to relate the biblical message to our understanding of the world: "For this reason, while the dependence of systematic and philosophical theology on biblical theology has long been recognized and is obvious, the dependence of an intelligible

---

32. L. Gilkey, "Cosmology, Ontology, and the Travail of Biblical Language," *JR* 41 (July 1961): 194–205, esp. 194.
33. Ibid., 195.
34. Ibid., 196.
35. Ibid., 201.

theology that is biblical on the cosmological and ontological inquiries of believing men, while now less universally accepted, is nonetheless real."[36]

Living as we do in the light of "postmodernism's" undermining of many aspects of modernity, it is remarkable to think how effective Gilkey's argument was. As with Bultmann and Barr and so much modern thought, there is an implicit assumption of the modern doctrine of historical progress.[37] The contemporary perspective is simply assumed and absolutized, without ever being argued for. However, it is now more apparent that Gilkey is assuming the particular perspective of modernity,[38] as well as misrepresenting the biblical and Christian tradition. Even within the Bible there is awareness that its language of God is not univocal, and certainly the Christian tradition[39] is well aware of the complexity of its language for and of God.[40]

Barr's critique of the BTM relates to two main areas: the concept of revelation and history central to the BTM,[41] and its misuse of word studies and the so-called Greek/Hebrew contrast in views of the world.[42] Barr's critique of the historical emphasis of the BTM is similar to that of Gilkey. He focuses on the

---

36. Ibid., 205.

37. See D. Bebbington, *Patterns in History: A Christian Perspective on Historical Thought* (Leicester, UK: Inter-Varsity, 1979; reprint, Leicester, UK: Apollos, 1990), 68–91, on the idea of progress.

38. P. L. Berger (*A Rumour of Angels: Modern Society and the Rediscovery of the Supernatural* [London: Allen Lane, 1970]) helpfully alerts us to the fact that

> it may be conceded that there is in the modern world a certain type of consciousness that has difficulties with the supernatural. The statement remains, however, on the level of socio-historical diagnosis. The diagnosed condition is not thereupon elevated to the status of an absolute criterion: the contemporary situation is not immune to relativizing analysis. We may say that contemporary consciousness is such and such; we are left with the question of whether we will assent to it. (46–47)

39. Already in Aquinas we find a careful distinction between univocal, equivocal, and analogical language. See, e.g., *Summa theologiae* 1.13.5.

40. See, e.g., M. S. Horton, *Covenant and Eschatology: The Divine Drama* (Louisville: Westminster John Knox, 2002), esp. chap. 2. William P. Alston and others have developed sustained critiques of Gilkey's view of God (not) acting in our world. William P. Alston, "Divine and Human Action," in *Divine and Human Action: Essays in the Metaphysics of Theism*, ed. T. V. Morris (Ithaca, NY: Cornell University Press, 1988), 257–80, esp. 258, argues that language of God may be partly univocal. William P. Alston's excellent "How to Think about Divine Action: Twenty-Five Years of Travail for Biblical Language," in *Divine Action: Studies Inspired by the Philosophical Theology of Austin Farrer*, ed. B. Hebblethwaite and E. Henderson (Edinburgh: T&T Clark, 1990), 51–70, is devoted entirely to a rebuttal of Gilkey's view of God's action as articulated in Gilkey's 1961 article. Alston also notes that, contra Gilkey, we need to distinguish univocal from literal language.

41. See J. Barr, "The Concepts of History and Revelation," in *Old and New in Interpretation: A Study of the Two Testaments*, 2nd ed. (London: SCM, 1982), 65–102.

42. See J. Barr, *The Semantics of Biblical Language* (London: SCM, 1982; reprint, Eugene, OR: Wipf & Stock, 2004).

antinomy, or "double talk,"[43] between the confession of God's acts in history, and on history as the result of critical examination of data. Barr furthermore finds that substantial parts of the Bible do not fit with an historical emphasis.

Barr's better-known critique is of the BTM's persistent failure to take modern semantics into account and thus to be guilty time and again of "illegitimate totality transfer," thereby wrongly reading meanings into words. Barr is critical of the tendency of the BTM to find the distinctive theological content of the Bible in its vocabulary, as exemplified, for example, in the Kittel-Friedrich *Theological Dictionary*. Barr devotes an entire book to the BTM's handling of the biblical words dealing with time.[44] According to Barr, Cullmann's theology of time in the Bible is illegitimate:[45]

> The whole case being argued is that the Bible has, and normally and constantly displays, a particular conception of time, which can be traced in its lexical stock and which forms an essential background or presupposition for the understanding of its theology. It is therefore naturally impossible to except any example of usage from full consideration on the grounds that it is "merely temporal" and not of theological significance.[46]

There was undoubtedly a need for Barr's critique of the understanding of how language worked in the BTM. Indeed, Barr mediated modern semantics à la Saussure into biblical studies, and his contribution in this area has been of lasting importance. However, Francis Watson has recently and rightly argued that Barr's critique of the BTM in this respect is not as devastating as is often suggested.[47] According to Watson, Barr builds his sweeping criticism on a narrow foundation and wrongly suggests that the errors are foundational to the entire project of the BTM. Watson reexamines Cullmann's work on time, a particular object of Barr's critique, and demonstrates how Cullmann is aware of the diverse ways in which the New Testament words for time are used, but consciously chooses to focus on those occasions that are theologically poignant. Such an approach is quite legitimate. Barr also criticizes Cullmann for his contrast between Hebrew and Greek thought. Cullmann contrasts the New Testament view of the resurrection with the "Greek" concept of immortality; as Watson shows, Cullmann is quite right on this matter.

---

43. See J. Barr, "Trends and Prospects in Biblical Theology," *JTS* 24 (1974): 265–82, esp. 267, for the language of double-talk.
44. J. Barr, *Biblical Words for Time*, 2nd ed. (London: SCM, 1969).
45. Ibid., chap. 3.
46. Ibid., 49.
47. F. Watson, *Text and Truth: Redefining Biblical Theology* (Grand Rapids: Eerdmans, 1997), 18–28.

From his analysis of Barr's critique of the BTM, Watson concludes, "There is little basis for his claim that 'biblical theology' as once practiced was fundamentally and irretrievably flawed. If biblical theology collapsed, it did not do so because of the overwhelming force of its critics' arguments."[48] Indeed, for Francis Watson, "There is, then, little or nothing in this piece of modern theological history to deter one from attempting to renew and to redefine biblical theology."[49]

What is clear from both Gilkey's and Barr's critiques of the BTM is that they stem from particular theological outlooks. The demise of the BTM is related to the radicalization of modern theology at the time, and Barr appeals to this "progress" as part of his critique. Indeed, a common element in Barr's armory is the appeal to progress. Thus, in his 1974 article on "Trends and Prospects in Biblical Theology," he argues contra the BTM's concern to see the Bible as a whole, that "*the tendency now* is to say that there is no one theology, either of the Old Testament or of the New, and still less of the entire Bible: rather, the Bible, and each Testament contains a number of quite different theologies, the theologies of different strata, different writers, and different periods."[50] Likewise in his work *The Bible in the Modern World*, Barr stresses that *nowadays* there is less enthusiasm for reading the Bible as a whole.[51]

This style of argument is found regularly in Barr's critique of the BTM,[52] and it is a style of argument that lays great weight on the theological trends of one's immediate context, thereby suggesting that theology has progressed toward this point. What is lacking in Barr's and Gilkey's approach is a healthy sense of plurality in theology and of the way in which different theological perspectives might relate to something like the BTM. Barr's approach is very much that of liberal theology, whereas Childs's is that of a scholar working in the Reformed, Barthian tradition, and these contexts orient them toward biblical theology and the BTM in quite different ways. Theological context makes a huge difference when it comes to (the very possibility of) biblical theology, and it helps to be aware of all the elements in the often-vitriolic debates around the subject.

Barr suggests, as noted above, that there never really was a crisis in biblical

---

48. Ibid., 24.
49. Ibid., 26.
50. Barr, "Trends and Prospects," 270, with added emphasis.
51. J. Barr, *The Bible in the Modern World: The Croall Lectures Given in New College, Edinburgh in November 1970* (London: SCM, 1973), 6.
52. F. Watson (*Text and Truth*, 23–24) also notes Barr's tendency to work out of a particular theological style that privileges the more radical spectrum in theology.

theology, but that Childs needed there to be one to justify his new canonical approach to the subject. This seems to me somewhat ingenuous in the light of the successful attacks by Barr on the BTM, but it does alert us to the fact that biblical theology was always more than the BTM. There were real problems with the BTM, as Childs indicates. Although these were not as serious as Barr and Gilkey suggest, it is important to recognize that the well-being of biblical theology does not stand or fall with the BTM. Within the evangelical tradition, for example, biblical theology continued to thrive despite the so-called death knell of the BTM in 1961. Scholars such as Herman Ridderbos, O. Palmer Robertson, George Eldon Ladd, Meredith Kline, Graeme Goldsworthy, Bill Dumbrell,[53] and others continued to take biblical theology seriously in the years following the demise of the BTM, with the result that a corpus of ongoing work in biblical theology is available from the evangelical stable.[54] We also recognize that there is a great deal of valuable material to be retrieved from the work of the BTM.[55] And since 1960 multiple works in Old Testament and New Testament theology, plus studies of the theology of parts of the Bible, have been published. What is noticeably lacking, however, are a plethora of attempts at a theology of the Bible *as a whole*. Recent decades have witnessed the appearance of only a handful of major biblical theologies.[56] If biblical theology is concerned with the Bible as a whole, then this may be more significant than the multitude of publications to which Barr refers; it may well indicate that biblical theology remains in a crisis.

    53. Goldsworthy and Dumbrell both worked for many years at Moore College in Sydney, Australia, where BT has been a core part of the curriculum for years, stemming from (Archbishop) Donald Robinson's innovative leadership.
    54. See, e.g., T. D. Alexander and B. S. Rosner, eds., *New Dictionary of Biblical Theology: Exploring the Unity and Diversity of Scripture* (Downers Grove, IL: InterVarsity, 2000).
    55. This includes commentaries such as G. E. Wright, *The Book of Isaiah* (Richmond: John Knox, 1964). G. E. Wright was working on the Anchor Bible commentary on Joshua when he died, and it was completed by Robert G. Boling.
    56. Apart from the three that we will focus on below, note should be made of W. J. Dumbrell, *The End of the Beginning: Revelation 21–22 and the Old Testament* (reprint, Eugene, OR: Wipf & Stock, 2001); W. Kaiser, *The Promise-Plan of God: A Biblical Theology of the Old and New Testaments* (Grand Rapids: Zondervan, 2008); T. R. Schreiner, *The King in His Beauty: A Biblical Theology of Old and New Testaments* (Grand Rapids: Baker Academic, 2013). S. Croatto is one of the few to have worked within the field of BT in Spanish. He was an Argentine who taught at ISEDET in Buenos Aires. Of particular relevance are his *Alianza y Experiencia Salvífica en la Biblia* [Covenant and the salvation experience in the Bible] (Buenos Aires: Paulinas, 1964); *Historia de la salvación* [History of salvation] (Buenos Aires: Paulinas, 7 eds., 1964–95); idem in Portuguese, *Historia da salvaçao* (Caxias do Sul, Brazil: Paulinas, 1967); and *Historia de salvación: La experiencia religiosa del pueblo de Dios* [History of salvation: The religious experience of the people of God] (Navarre, Spain: Verbo Divino, 1995; 2nd ed., 2000; also in Florida, Mexico, Uruguay).

Quo Vadis?

Childs discerns the following eight models for current biblical theology:[57]

1. Biblical theology organized according to the categories of dogmatics
2. Allegorical or typological approaches
3. A great-ideas or themes approach
4. A history-of-redemption approach
5. Literary approaches
6. The cultural-linguistic method
7. Sociological perspectives
8. Jewish biblical theology

In his work *The Hebrew Bible, the Old Testament, and Historical Criticism*, Jon Levenson has a chapter titled "Why Jews Are Not Interested in Biblical Theology."[58] Subsequent reactions have, however, demonstrated that Jewish scholars are indeed interested in biblical theology! Already in 1992 Childs commented quite correctly, "Jews continue to reflect theologically on the Bible in a variety of different and creative ways. Whether this reflection should be called Biblical Theology is actually a secondary issue. Far more important is this contribution both in terms of its own integrity as well as to a common theological use of the Bible."[59] Childs refers to the creative contributions of Martin Buber, Abraham Heschel, M. Goshen-Gottstein, E. E. Urbach, J. Neusner, M. Greenberg, Jon Levenson, A. Cooper, and M. Wyschrogrod. A host of other names should be added, such as Leo Strauss,[60] James Kugel,[61] Michael Walzer,[62] Leon R. Kass,[63] Eric Nelson,[64] Benjamin D. Sommer,[65] Yoram Hazony,[66] Len E. Goodman,[67] Alan Mittleman,[68] and so on. Suffice it to refer

---

57. Childs, *BTONT* 11–29. See E. W. Klink III and D. R. Lockett, *Understanding Biblical Theology: A Comparison of Theory and Practice* (Grand Rapids: Zondervan, 2012) for a different categorization.

58. J. D. Levenson, *The Hebrew Bible, the Old Testament, and Historical Criticism: Jews and Christians in Biblical Studies* (Louisville: Westminster John Knox, 1993), 33–61.

59. Childs, *BTONT* 25.

60. See in particular L. Strauss, "On the Interpretation of Genesis (1957)," in *Jewish Philosophy and the Crisis of Modernity: Essays and Lectures in Modern Jewish Thought* (Albany: State University of New York Press, 1997), 359–76.

61. Especially J. L. Kugel, *The Bible as It Was* (Cambridge, MA: Belknap, 1997).

62. See, e.g., M. Walzer, *Exodus and Revolution* (New York: Basic Books, 1985); idem, *In God's Shadow: Politics in the Hebrew Bible* (New Haven: Yale University Press, 2012).

63. L. R. Kass's *The Beginning of Wisdom: Reading Genesis* (Chicago: University of Chicago Press, 2003) is an extraordinary work.

64. E. Nelson, *The Hebrew Republic: Jewish Sources and the Transformation of European Political Thought* (Cambridge, MA: Harvard University Press, 2010).

65. B. D. Sommer, *The Bodies of God and the World of Ancient Israel* (Cambridge: Cambridge University Press, 2009).

66. See Y. Hazony, *The Philosophy of Hebrew Scripture* (Cambridge: Cambridge University Press, 2012).

67. See, e.g., L. E. Goodman, *Love Thy Neighbor as Thyself* (Oxford: Oxford University Press, 2008).

68. A. Mittleman, *Hope in a Democratic Age: Philosophy, Religion, and Political Theory* (New York: Oxford University Press, 2009).

to two recent publications that provide a sense of the current situation: Isaac Kalimi's edited volume, *Jewish Bible Theology: Perspectives and Case Studies*,[69] and Marvin A. Sweeney's *Tanak: A Theological and Critical Introduction to the Jewish Bible*.[70] There is a reservoir of wealth and insight in Jewish interpretation, and one of its great assets is the constant dialogue opened up between such readings and contemporary culture. It may surprise readers to see some of the names listed above since some of them are not biblical scholars, yet their work does justice in particular to our seventh criterion for biblical theology, that it attends to the *public dimension* of Scripture. Jewish scholars have also made an outstanding contribution to the Bible as literature, exemplified in the works of Robert Alter and Meir Sternberg.

Categories such as those of Childs (above) are useful as a guide, but in practice biblical theologies are often a mixtures of categories. Dumbrell's excellent *The End of the Beginning: Revelation 21–22 and the Old Testament*, for example, would primarily fit under a great-themes approach, but it is more than that. It would also fit with a typological approach, a redemptive-historical one, and a canonical one. Scholars such as Dumbrell have also learned much from literary approaches to the Bible. My affirmation of a narrative reading as foundational would fit primarily under a history-of-redemption approach, yet (as noted in chap. 3 above) it is one that has learned a great deal from the literary and canonical turns.

In the remainder of this chapter we will examine the three major biblical theologies of recent years and see how successful they are in relation to our seven diagnostic questions developed at the end of chapter 3 (above).

Brevard Childs's Canonical Biblical Theology

Childs interacts critically with each of the eight approaches above and then makes a new proposal for a canonical biblical theology.[71] He remains as committed as ever to his earlier view: "There is a need for a discipline that will attempt to retain and develop a picture of the whole, and that will have a responsibility to synthesize as well as analyze."[72] The canon is the proper context within which such biblical theology is to be done. "The Scriptures of the church are not archives of the past but a channel of life for the continuing church, through which God instructs and admonishes his people."[73] Biblical

---

69. I. Kalimi, ed., *Jewish Bible Theology: Perspectives and Case Studies* (Winona Lake, IN: Eisenbrauns, 2012).
70. M. A. Sweeney, *Tanak: A Theological and Critical Introduction to the Jewish Bible* (Minneapolis: Fortress, 2012). See also S. D. Sperling, ed., *Students of the Covenant: A History of Jewish Biblical Scholarship in North America* (Atlanta: Scholars Press, 1992).
71. This is an extension of Childs's earlier proposal in *BTIC*.
72. Ibid., 92.
73. Ibid., 99.

theology must take the different extent of the canon in Catholic compared with Protestant circles seriously, and it must "participate in the search for the Christian Bible."[74] Utterly central to biblical theology must be the question of the relationship between the two Testaments, and this needs to be carefully nuanced:

> At the heart of the problem of Biblical Theology lies the issue of doing full justice to the subtle canonical relationship of the two testaments within the one Christian Bible. On the one hand, the Christian canon asserts the continuing integrity of the OT witness. It must be heard on its own terms. . . . On the other hand, the NT makes its own witness. . . . The challenge of Biblical Theology is to engage in the continual activity of theological reflection which studies the canonical text in detailed exegesis, and seeks to do justice to the witness of both testaments in the light of its subject matter who is Jesus Christ.[75]

In *BTIC*, Childs uses the citations of the Old Testament in the New Testament as a major route into the biblical theology of both Testaments. But by the time of his *BTONT*, Childs is more wary of this approach, lest it undermine the discrete witness of the Old Testament.[76] The way in which the New Testament uses the Old need not exhaust the witness of the Old, and it is vital that we attend to the discrete witness of each Testament in its own right. Consequently, Childs organizes his *BTONT* according to the following sections:

- Discrete Witness of the Old Testament
- Discrete Witness of the New Testament
- Theological Reflection on the Christian Bible

In terms of biblical theology, it is this third section in Childs's work on "Theological Reflection" that is most relevant since here he draws the material together in relation to our seven diagnostic questions.

1. Childs takes seriously the foundational role of creation in the Bible. In his "Theological Reflection" his discussion of "God, the Creator" follows immediately after his first chapter on "The Identity of God."

2. Already in his discussion of "God, the Creator," Childs notes, in relation to Revelation 21:3 and other passages in the New Testament: "The

---

74. Childs, *BTONT*, 67.
75. Ibid., 78–79.
76. Ibid., 76.

theological point is that the scope of God's redemption includes the whole of his creation."[77]

3. Childs has chapters on both covenant and kingdom.[78] His exploration of covenant is a good example of his sustained attempt to hold historical criticism and his canonical approach together. Childs takes seriously the current view that covenant is a late idea in the life of Israel and argues that in the process of canonical formation the Deuteronomic formulation of covenant became normative, and hence the tradition of Israel was read through this lens. The application of covenant to the earliest traditions of Israel is thus a reinterpretation, but not necessarily against the substance of those traditions. Canonically, Childs identifies the covenant with Noah as the first one but does not make the connection, as does Dumbrell, back to Genesis 1 as the foundational covenantal text.[79] Childs's view of covenant thus lacks the comprehensive vision that we find in Dumbrell.

In his chapter "God's Kingdom and Rule," Childs notes that "no great theological work on the subject comparable, say, to that of Ritschl has appeared for almost a hundred years. In sum, it would seem that few subjects are in greater need of the contribution of Biblical Theology in seeking to overcome the present fragmentation in the understanding of God's kingship over the world."[80] As with his discussion of covenant, Childs spends much time on historical-critical issues, somewhat at the cost of developing his own constructive position. However, he is clear that "the New Testament can only be understood as the bringing to completion of the Old Testament promise of God's eschatological rule."[81] A brief discussion of the kingdom also recurs in Childs's chapter "The Shape of the Obedient Life: Ethics."[82]

4. Childs's first chapter in part 6 of his *BTONT* is titled "The Identity of God." At the end of this section he discusses and defends the validity of reading Scripture in the light of the fuller knowledge of God gained from the whole Bible; for Childs, the decisive issue is *how* such exegesis is performed.

---

77. Childs, *BTONT* 398.
78. Ibid., in part 6, chap. 3 is titled "Covenant, Election, People of God"; in part 6, chap. 9 is titled "God's Kingdom and Rule."
79. However, Childs follows Karl Barth in speaking of creation as "the inner and outer grounds of the covenant" (ibid., 372).
80. Ibid., 624; pp. 646–50 highlight, albeit critically, the importance of H.-J. Kraus's *Reich Gottes: Reich der Freiheit* (Neukirchen-Vluyn: Neukirchener Verlag, 1975), rev. as *Systematische Theologie im Kontext biblischer Geschichte und Eschatologie* (1983). Kraus's work makes the kingdom of God the center of his BT.
81. Childs, *BTONT* 650.
82. Ibid., 689–70.

It must not rival historical exegesis but must rather embody a hermeneutical circle in which the reader(s) move from the text to reality as well as from reality back to the text. Childs is clear that "both testaments point beyond themselves to the selfsame divine reality."[83]

5. It is to Childs that we owe the language and emphasis on the discrete witness of Old Testament and New Testament. His wide-ranging and detailed work in *BTONT* bears eloquent witness to this concern. At the same time he is quite clear that "it is incumbent upon Biblical Theology to move in its reflection from the Old Testament to the New and from the New to the Old Testament."[84]

6. In his typically nuanced fashion, Childs is clear that "both Old Testament and New Testament bear truthful witness to Jesus Christ in different ways, and that both of their witnesses are measured in the light of the reality of Christ himself."[85]

7. In the light of his critique of the BTM, it is not surprising to find Childs taking seriously the public implications of biblical theology. In his discussion of God as creator, he explores the connections with science, liberation theology, and ecology.[86] The final chapter in part 6 of Childs's *BTONT* is titled "The Shape of the Obedient Life: Ethics." Childs argues that a great deal of work remains to be done in this area: "The enterprise of theological reflection on both testaments in respect to ethics remains largely an undeveloped field, and calls for fresh and rigorous commitment from a new generation of scholars of the church who are trained in both Bible and theology."[87] The range of Childs's scholarship is so remarkable that it may be churlish to offer a critique, but it is in the area of the public dimensions of biblical theology that his work is weakest in terms of our seven diagnostic questions.

In relation to our seven questions, Childs passes with flying colors! In my opinion the public dimensions of biblical theology could be worked out more suggestively than he does, and there remains the difficult issue of how historical criticism, as currently practiced, fits with biblical theology. Intriguingly, it is in his chapter on "Reconciliation with God" where Childs has a discussion on the doctrine of reconciliation and the historical-critical method![88]

83. Ibid., 477.
84. Ibid., 650.
85. Ibid., 477.
86. Ibid., 405–11.
87. Ibid., 711.
88. Ibid., 524–26.

Charles H. Scobie's Thematic Biblical Theology

Scobie's massive *The Ways of Our God* (*TWOG*) was published in 2003, the result of years of work. Whereas Childs was primarily an Old Testament scholar, Scobie is a New Testament scholar. In the preface Scobie explains the tension he has lived between a historical-critical approach to the Bible and reading the Bible for the church. He thus proposes that we envisage biblical theology as an intermediate discipline, as a bridge discipline between historical study and the use of the Bible by the church.[89] "An intermediate BT [biblical theology] will assume and accept the findings of the historical-critical approach, but will seek to go beyond them and move from analysis to synthesis."[90] Such a BT will be:

- Canonical. Its subject matter will be the Christian Scriptures. Scobie rightly argues, "It is therefore *the Christ event that is decisive in determining both the canon of the OT and the canon of the NT.*"[91]
- Based on both the Old Testament and the New Testament. Old Testament theology must be a Christian discipline so that "the two disciplines of Tanakh theology and Old Testament / biblical theology could exist alongside one another, could engage in dialogue and learn from each other, but they could never coalesce."[92]
- Based on the content and structure of the Christian canon. As a New Testament scholar, Scobie is conscious of the extent to which the New Testament uses the LXX (Septuagint), and he argues that the LXX must be seen as part of the scriptural tradition.[93]
- Structured. For Scobie, "the most satisfactory approach is clearly the thematic one that seeks to construct an outline based as closely as possible on themes that arise from within the Bible itself. Within this option, it is the multithematic approach that holds most promise."[94]

Key themes must be traced through both Old and New Testaments, and Scobie finds the theme of *promise and fulfillment* as most helpful in terms of the Testaments' relationship.[95] He expands this into "proclamation—promise" for the Old Testament and "fulfillment—consummation" for the New. "The

---

89. Scobie, *TWOG* 46.
90. Ibid., 47, with original emphasis.
91. Ibid., 57. See chap. 8 (below) on canon.
92. Ibid., 60.
93. Ibid., 72.
94. Ibid., 87.
95. Ibid., 90.

pattern of proclamation/promise: fulfillment/consummation thus offers a structure for discussing the main themes of Scripture in a way that will reveal their inner canonical and theological dynamic rather than just their tradition-historical development."[96] Scobie arrives at his four main themes under the promise-fulfillment motif through an examination of the diverse themes that have been proposed and settles on the four shown below:

Old Testament		New Testament	
Proclamation	Promise	Fulfillment	Consummation
God's Order	A New Order	The New Order	The Final Consummation
God's Servants	A New Servant	The New Servant	The Final Consummation
God's People	A New People	The New People	The Final Consummation
God's Way	A New Way	The New Way	The Final Consummation

Scobie's is a rich and creative biblical theology, and readers are encouraged to explore it for themselves. For now we restrict ourselves to asking how it measures up to our seven diagnostic questions.

1. Scobie's *TWOG* certainly takes the foundational act of creation seriously, as his theme of "God's order" makes clear. Scobie has four chapters under "God's Order"; he begins with "The Living God," then moves on to "The Lord of Creation," followed by "The Lord of History." This order parallels Childs's move from the identity of God to God the creator. Scobie rightly states, "From a literary point of view, it is the created order that constitutes a grand 'envelope structure' for the whole of Scripture with the theme of creation / new creation enclosing everything else."[97]

2. Scobie is clear that Christ mediates a redemption that embraces all of creation: "Christ's death avails not just for individual believers but [also] for the whole of creation."[98] What is less helpful in Scobie's BT is that he distinguishes between *the historical order* and *the created order*.[99] Scobie rightly resists the tendency to make creation subservient to history and insists that "recognition must be given to the dialectic between creation and redemption. God is Creator and Sustainer as well as Redeemer, is active in nature as well as in history, and has a relation to all humankind as well as to Israel."[100] "The recognition of God's activity in the created order and the historical order is crucial for the understanding of biblical eschatology, . . . of what God promises to do in the future."[101]

96. Ibid., 93.
97. Ibid., 149.
98. Ibid., 174.
99. Ibid., 148; cf. 189–232.
100. Ibid., 94.
101. Ibid., 101.

However, he argues that creation order is based primarily on *cyclic time* whereas historical order is based on *linear time*.[102] Scobie is helpfully attentive to the story line of the Bible and thus far more sympathetic to a narrative BT than is Childs. He quotes Patrick with approval: "What is noteworthy about the Old Testament narrative is a drive toward a single, all-embracing story line and chronological framework."[103] However, when Scobie sets out the story line of the Old Testament, he begins with the patriarchs and not with creation![104] He asserts, "In this work a constant effort is made to *balance* God's activity in the *created order* and in the *historical order*."[105] But this is a false dichotomy. The dynamic order of history is part of creation and its order, and we need integration, not balance of two seemingly opposing motifs. The result is that Scobie's story line neither starts with creation nor ends clearly with new creation in his chapter on "The Lord of History."

3. Scobie is alert to the centrality of covenant and kingdom in the Bible. However, he deals with covenant under the theme of "God's People" and discerns four covenants in the Old Testament.[106] One is *in the created order*, and the other three (Abraham, Sinai, David) are in the historical order. Although at this point Scobie refers to Dumbrell more than once, he sees the Noachian covenant as in the created order but fails to make the connection back to Genesis 1 as the foundational covenantal text. The result is that Scobie tends to keep the focus of covenant on Israel and the church as the people of God. He does notice the "end of the story,"[107] but the integral link between covenant and creation is compromised.

Scobie rightly holds that the message of the kingdom is central to Jesus's ministry and says, "The Gospels, consistent with the rest of the NT, witness to what is most accurately termed *inaugurated eschatology*; God's reign has already dawned in the Christ event and is operative within human history, yet only at the final consummation will it ultimately triumph and be manifested in its fullness."[108] Mistakenly, in my view,[109] Scobie reiterates the common view that the kingdom refers primarily to God's reign and not his realm. In my view it refers to both, and the realm in view is the entire creation.

102. Ibid., 152–53.
103. D. Patrick, *The Rendering of God in the Old Testament* (Philadelphia: Fortress, 1981), 102; cited in Scobie, *TWOG* 191.
104. Scobie, *TWOG* 194.
105. Ibid., 230, with original emphasis.
106. Ibid., 473–74.
107. Ibid., 503.
108. Ibid., 130.
109. See C. G. Bartholomew, *Where Mortals Dwell: A Christian View of Place for Today* (Grand Rapids: Baker Academic, 2011).

4. Scobie begins his *TWOG* appropriately with "The Living God" and says that while it might be anachronistic to label the New Testament texts that speak of Father, Son, and Spirit as "trinitarian," they at least reflect a "triadic formula."[110]

5. Scobie's promise-fulfillment rubric means that he is closely attentive throughout to the progressive nature of biblical revelation and sensitive to the developments and shifts within Scripture as the story unfolds.

6. Scobie is cautious regarding the quest for a center to BT, but does state, "To assert, as many have, that God is the center of BT, . . . is to state the obvious."[111] "Christ is certainly a center, if not the center of the NT."[112]

7. A great strength of Scobie's BT is that he devotes considerable attention to ethics, under the heading of "God's Way," in the process bringing into focus a great array of ethical issues and making connections to contemporary life. However, he distinguishes between ethical norms *in the historical order* and then *in the created order* without exploring the intimate relationship between them.[113] Scobie follows Chris Wright in seeing the life of Israel as a paradigm for the nations, but in his discussion of "The Theological Basis of Ethics," there is no section on creation, and his biblical theology of ethics lacks O'Donovan's poignant insight that resurrection is the reaffirmation of creation.

Scobie's *TWOG* is a major contribution and deserves close attention. As with Childs, the relationship to historical criticism remains unresolved; it is, in my opinion, unhelpful to see biblical theology as a bridge between a historical-critical reading of the Bible and the church's use of the Bible. As we will see in our chapter on history, historical criticism is not a neutral, objective approach but needs to be rethought and recontextualized within a Christian perspective. It is far better to see Scobie's biblical theology as a bridge between a narrative reading of the Bible and systematic theology.

Feldmeier and Spieckermann: *God of the Living*

Feldmeier and Spieckermann's *God of the Living* is the major recent German biblical theology, published in 2011.[114] It is cowritten by an Old Testament scholar (Spieckermann) and a New Testament scholar (Feldmeier), and its

110. Scobie, *TWOG* 135.
111. Ibid., 94.
112. Ibid., 95.
113. Ibid., 747–57.
114. R. Feldmeier and H. Spieckermann, *Der Gott der Lebendigen: Eine biblische Gotteslehre* (Tübingen: Mohr Siebeck, 2011); ET, *God of the Living: A Biblical Theology* (Waco: Baylor University Press, 2011).

aim is clear: "This work seeks to present the Christian Bible's understanding of God as a coherent scheme."[115] This is a noticeably different approach than the two previous biblical theologies we have examined: it seeks to characterize the content of biblical theology in a doctrine of God.[116] The authors refer to the definition of God "in the mouth of Jesus,"[117] an interpretation that unites God as creator and savior from an eschatological perspective of "God of the Living." Importantly, the authors insist on an existential engagement with God as a prerequisite for doing this sort of work. God is the God of life and liberation, and such work as this is done because "those who have recognized God because God has recognized them want to transmit knowledge of God reliably."[118] "God is not an object accessible to our knowledge, but can be apprehended only as the one *by whom the knower has himself been apprehended* (see Phil. 3:12 [KJV])."[119] The result is that "scholarly exegesis must adhere to this intention of the biblical documents if it wants to take seriously the true objective of the texts beyond the circumstances in which the texts originated."[120] Knowledge of God stems from instruction by God himself, and a biblical doctrine of God makes the God of the Bible its theme, with a view to facilitating knowledge of God in the sense of Anselm's "faith seeking understanding."

In their opening chapter, Feldmeier and Spieckermann identify Deuteronomy and Ezekiel as well as Old Testament wisdom as primary sources for a doctrine of the knowledge of God. In the New Testament, knowledge of God is possible only in and through Jesus Christ. They take the historical-critical (Deuteronomy, e.g., reached its final form in the fifth century BC), history of religions, and literary approaches seriously but insist that to stop there would be to fall short of the claims of the Bible: "Human beings can appreciate their lives only when they recognize God as the source and savior of their lives and acknowledge God as Lord of their lives. God's words of promise and command are 'food' for true life.... Such sayings demand human obedience.... Whoever reads the texts and takes them to heart should live in this qualified sense."[121]

Feldmeier and Spieckermann rightly maintain that an approach to biblical theology through the doctrine of God opens out onto the world and human beings, indeed, on God in all his relatedness. They distinguish their

115. Feldmeier and Spieckermann, "Preface," in *God of the Living*.
116. Ibid., 1.
117. Ibid.
118. Ibid., 2.
119. Ibid., 2n3, with added emphasis.
120. Ibid., 2.
121. Ibid., 7.

approach from other types of biblical theology and Old Testament and New Testament theology. Given the historical-critical diversity of the Bible, their project "is defined by an interest in coming to the most consistent depiction possible of the various aspects of biblical discourse about God, portraying both commonalities and differences."[122] Using the doctrine of God as their center, they aim to focus on both Testaments equally. "The name YHWH not only appears at the center of the Old Testament but [also] is the center of the Old Testament."[123] In a discussion of Philippians 2:6–11, they assert, "This text states pointedly that the exalted Jesus participates in God's (omni-) potency and even, in a certain manner, takes God's place."[124] As with Scobie, they take the LXX seriously as central to New Testament Christianity. Like Childs, they aim to do justice to the discrete witness of both Testaments and argue that having a scholar of each Testament write together facilitates an appropriate exchange between the Testaments and allows the independence and convergence between the Testaments to come into focus.

Any BT must have an organizing structure, and Feldmeier and Spieckermann argue for a historical-genetic and a systematic one. Their biblical theology falls into two major parts, the first dealing with "God's Being" and the second with "God's Doing." Fundamental to the entire project is the desire for relationship with the "God of the Living." As with Childs and Scobie, they begin with the person of God, although, not surprisingly, their treatment is more extensive, ranging in each chapter across the Old Testament and the New.

As with the above two biblical theologies, readers are encouraged to take and read! Once again we will ask how Feldmeier and Spieckermann's work relates to our seven criteria.

1. Creation is dealt with in the first chapter of part 2 under "Word and Creation," a fine chapter in which the comprehensive range of creation is expounded.

2. Feldmeier and Spieckermann clearly articulate the link between creation and redemption. They note, for example, how the interweaving of creation and eschatology in the Old Testament and intertestamental material "became determinative for the New Testament."[125]

3. The treatment of the kingdom of God is clear and holistic: "At the center of Jesus' message stands the announcement of the emerging kingdom of God."[126] "Despite every distinction, they [God's adopted children] remain

122. Ibid., 9.
123. Ibid., 23.
124. Ibid., 45.
125. Ibid., 263.
126. Ibid., 66.

related to the old creation as the avant-garde of the redemption that will ultimately extend to the whole creation, which, for its part, will attain a share in the freedom of God's children."[127]

The treatment of covenant is less persuasive, caught as it is in historical criticism's view that covenant is a late idea in the history of Israel's religion. For Feldmeier and Spieckermann, "exegetical scholarship of the past century significantly overvalued the concept of the covenant."[128] Covenant theology belongs to the exilic and postexilic Deuteronomistic shaping of Deuteronomy. Nevertheless, as they unpack covenant in the Priestly narrative and its role in the Prophets, leading to the Last Supper as a covenant meal, a significant covenantal theology is foregrounded and has strong creational overtones.

4. Feldmeier and Spieckermann's biblical theology attends to God in particular, and their detailed examination of how God is perceived in the Old Testament and the New Testament and their interrelationship is profound. Akin to Scobie, they assert, "The Christological and ecclesiological dimensions of biblical monotheism sound the themes that led to the development of trinitarian dogma in the early church."[129]

5. As noted above, Feldmeier and Spieckermann go out of their way to do justice to the discrete witness of Old Testament and New Testament; these two components of every chapter ensure that continuities and discontinuities are attended to rigorously.

6. God and God in Christ are unequivocally identified as the center of biblical theology. The Christ event is clearly central, but surprisingly the fulfillment of the Old Testament in Christ is not nearly as strong as one might hope, perhaps because of the structure of the book and because of the desire to be evenhanded in the treatment of the Hebrew Bible / Old Testament and the New.

7. The potential for developing the public dimensions of Feldmeier and Spieckermann's biblical theology is everywhere present but not actually developed in this direction. This in itself is not necessarily a critique since their aim to present the doctrine of God is clearly articulated. However, the public dimension is evident in the very title of their book, *God of the Living*, and as they declare, "Biblical theology in the form of a doctrine of God is 'life science.'"[130]

Once again we encounter a rich biblical theology full of fascinating insights. What is distinctive about Feldmeier and Spieckermann's biblical theology is their insistence that to execute this type of work, one must be *apprehended by*

127. Ibid., 87; cf. 263-70.
128. Ibid., 447.
129. Ibid., 96.
130. Ibid., 1.

God. From this perspective, faith is a requirement for doing biblical theology. I am entirely in agreement with them in this respect. However, as with Childs and Scobie, their attempt continues to build a biblical theology on the basis of historical criticism, and in Feldmeier and Spieckermann's case, the history-of-religions approach as well as the literary approach. This inevitably raises the question of the status of historical criticism. Is it a neutral, objective discipline? Or does being apprehended by the living God affect the way we think about historicity and the critical approach to the Bible as it has developed in post-Enlightenment times? I would not for a moment want to deny the many, many contributions that historical criticism has made to biblical study; yet its philosophical foundations are located in the human autonomy and scientism of the post-Enlightenment era, even taking into account the great diversity amid historical criticism. As I will argue in chapter 10, on history, we need to recontextualize and rethink historical criticism on different foundations, foundations that stem from and are compatible with a Christian view of the world and of history.

Conclusion

Our examination of Childs, Scobie, and Feldmeier and Spieckermann should give us hope for a renewal of biblical theology. Despite the challenges of doing biblical theology at this time, these four authors have produced creative and rich works amid their diverse methodologies. In my view the project of biblical theology would be strengthened immeasurably if we could agree that the grand story of the Bible is fundamental, and that on this basis a host of complementary approaches can and should develop. Considerable work remains to be done!

PART 3

The Story of Biblical Interpretation

5

The Traditions within Which We Read

> And I believe in one catholic and apostolic church.
>
> Nicene Creed

> But what is this force, the influence of the Bible in world history? . . . And in face of this influence we can only be amazed, first that we are not excluded from it, that we can be aware of it in our own lives, and then that we are not alone in this experience, but can publicly share it with so many others both past and present, both far and near. It claims our whole attention to take this influence seriously, and gratefully to do justice to it.
>
> Karl Barth[1]

Introduction

Ecclesial reception of Scripture is *communal*: we read within the rich context of the body of Christ, of the one, catholic, and apostolic church. In Hebrews 11–12 we encounter the great cloud of witnesses who encourage us to run the race of faith with perseverance. Toward the conclusion of this section, the author exhorts his readers: "See that you do not refuse the one who is speaking" (12:25). The imperative "See" (Βλέπετε) is a second-person

---

1. K. Barth, *CD* III/3:203.

plural imperative. "The one who is speaking" (τὸν λαλοῦντα) is a present active participle, implying that God *keeps on speaking*.² We are called to attend to God's speech as part of the "city of the living God" (12:22) and as part of the "assembly of the firstborn" (12:23). Hebrews is intensely aware that the way in which God is speaking is inseparably connected with how he has spoken, not least in the Old Testament but preeminently in Christ. The assembly of the firstborn has bequeathed to us a vast legacy of biblical interpretation in commentaries, sermons, liturgies, in their lives, and so forth, and this tradition is a great resource to help us hear what God is saying today.

The importance of tradition for biblical interpretation is closely connected with the hermeneutical insight that we never read and interpret Scripture with a tabula rasa. A central and key insight of hermeneutics of the Gadamerian sort is that we the readers are as embedded in history as is the text. We bring our own *prejudices*—prejudgments—to the text, and we are heirs to a variety of traditions of biblical interpretation. Clearly the sort of "prejudgments" I have outlined in chapters 2 and 3 are largely foreign to mainstream contemporary biblical studies. It is thus important to excavate the history of biblical interpretation in order to understand how we have arrived at where we are today and to identify rich nodes in the tradition that we can return to in order to find creative ways forward. Hence the recent emphasis on *reception history* is most welcome as a crucial component in biblical hermeneutics.

The impetus in this direction has come in recent years from hermeneutics and from within theology. The best-known thinkers within hermeneutics are Roman Ingarden (1893–1970), Hans Robert Jauss (1921–97), Wolfgang Iser (1926–2007), and members of the Konstanz school of literary studies in Germany.³ We will start our journey through the history of biblical interpretation with Jauss's aesthetics of reception.⁴

---

2. On the centrality of speaking in Hebrews, see the important chapter by M. Barth, "The Old Testament in Hebrews: An Essay in Biblical Hermeneutics," in *Current Issues in New Testament Interpretation: Essays in Honor of Otto A. Piper*, ed. W. Klassen and G. F. Snyder (London: SCM, 1962), 53–78, where M. Barth argues evocatively, "Exegesis is for the author of Hebrews the hearing participation in the dialogue that goes on within God and between God and man" (64).

3. Founded by H. R. Jauss and W. Iser.

4. For an introduction to reception theory, see R. C. Holub, *Reception Theory: A Critical Introduction* (London: Routledge, 1984); Jauss and Iser are dealt with on 53–106. On Iser, see also E. Freund, *The Return of the Reader: Reader-Response Criticism* (London: Methuen, 1987), 134–51. On the Konstanz school, see R. C. Holub, "Reception Theory: School of Constance," in *The Cambridge History of Literary Criticism*, vol. 8, *From Formalism to Poststructuralism*, ed. R. Selden (Cambridge: Cambridge University Press, 1995), 319–46.

The Aesthetics of Reception

Hans Robert Jauss studied under Gadamer, whose influence is readily discernible in Jauss's *Rezeptionsästhetik*. This is evident in Jauss's *first thesis*[5] regarding a renewal of literary history: such a renewal demands the "removal of the prejudices of historical objectivism and the grounding of the traditional aesthetics of production and representation in an aesthetics of reception and influence."[6] Jauss associates historical objectivism with the positivist view of history and asserts that this approach neglects the artistic character as well as the particular historicity of literature.[7] A literary work is not an isolated object that provides the same view to each reader in each period. It is more akin to an orchestration that produces ever-new resonances among its readers, thereby bringing the text to a contemporary existence.[8] The literary text has a dialogical character,[9] which is why "philological understanding can exist only in a perpetual confrontation with the text, and cannot be allowed to be reduced to a knowledge of facts."[10]

Jauss's *second thesis* protects literary history from subjectivism.[11] The reception history of a literary work must work "within the objectifiable system of expectations that arise for each work in the historical moment of its appearance, from a pre-understanding of the genre, from the form and themes of already familiar works, and from the opposition between poetic and practical language."[12] Jauss speaks of the initial horizon of expectations of a literary text. No literary text, however new, arises in a vacuum, but through

---

5. The following theses come from Jauss's highly influential 1967 inaugural lecture at the new University of Constance. For the place of this lecture within the development of Jauss's thought, see O. Rush, *The Reception of Doctrine: An Appropriation of Hans Robert Jauss' Reception Aesthetics and Literary Hermeneutics*, Tesi Gregoriana, Serie Teologia 19 (Rome: Pontifical Gregorian University, 1997), chaps. 1–2.

6. H. R. Jauss, *Toward an Aesthetic of Reception*, trans. T. Bahti (Minneapolis: University of Minnesota Press, 1982), 20; on 29, Jauss says he is assuming Gadamer's critique of historical objectivism. However, he (on 30–31) is critical of Gadamer's elevation of the classical to the status of prototype. See also H. R. Jauss, *Question and Answer: Forms of Dialogic Understanding* (Minneapolis: University of Minnesota Press, 1989); idem, *Wege des Verstehens* (Munich: Wilhelm Fink, 1994). Relevant studies of Jauss and biblical hermeneutics include Rush, *The Reception of Doctrine*; H.-U. Gehring, *Schriftprinzip und Rezeptionsästhetik: Rezeption in Martin Luther's Predigt und bei Hans Robert Jauss* (Neukirchen-Vluyn: Neukirchener Verlag, 1999).

7. Jauss's stated aim is to restore history to the heart of literary studies.

8. Jauss, *Toward an Aesthetic*, 21.

9. See Jauss, *Question and Answer*.

10. Jauss, *Toward an Aesthetic*, 21.

11. Jauss (*Wege des Verstehens*, 11) insightfully describes the skepticism of postmodernism as the absolutization of *langue* in its view of language. In this respect, cf. F. de Saussure's influential distinction between *langue* (the systems of signs) and *parole* (the use of signs in speech acts).

12. Jauss, *Toward an Aesthetic*, 22.

various means it alerts its audience to a kind of reception. Such "paradigmatic isotopy" makes a description of reception possible,[13] and Jauss is quite clear that "the subjectivity of the interpretation . . . can be asked meaningfully only when one has first clarified which transsubjective horizon of understanding conditions the influence of the text."[14] Even if specific signals are lacking in the literary work, the disposition that the author anticipates from the readers can be ascertained through attention to the following points:

1. Familiar norms or the immanent poetics of the genre.[15]
2. The implicit relationship to familiar works in the literary-historical context. A similar insight is found in Kristeva's view of *intertextuality*.[16] For Kristeva, the notion of intertextuality replaces the concept of intersubjectivity since meaning is not transferred directly from writer to reader but is mediated by codes imparted to the writer and reader from other texts.[17] I am not sure that "replaces" is the right word;[18] "expands" is better since, with Jauss, it retains a chastened sense of authorial intention, but the insight that textual meaning is constrained by codes and genres from associated texts is surely correct.
3. The opposition between fiction and reality.[19]

Jauss's *third thesis* is that the horizon of expectation of a literary work allows one to ascertain its artistic character by the nature of its influence on a presupposed audience. The artistic character is determined by the

---

13. For Jauss's dismissal of the postmodern notion of textual play, see P. de Man, introduction to *Toward an Aesthetic*, by Jauss, vii–xxv, esp. xviii–xxii.
14. Jauss, *Toward an Aesthetic*, 23.
15. On genre, see Jauss, *Toward an Aesthetic*, 76–109. He states,
    Just as there is no act of verbal communication that is not related to a general, socially or situationally conditioned norm or convention, it is also unimaginable that a literary work set itself into an informational vacuum, without indicating a specific situation of understanding. To this extent, every work belongs to a genre—whereby I mean neither more nor less than that for each work a preconstituted horizon of expectations must be ready at hand . . . to orient the reader's (public's) understanding and to enable a qualifying reception. (79)
16. Rush says of Jauss's approach, "It is this intertextuality that is constitutive of the work itself" (*Reception of Doctrine*, 19).
17. J. Kristeva, *Desire in Language: A Semiotic Approach to Literature and Art* (New York: Columbia University Press, 1980), 69.
18. See A. C. Thiselton, *New Horizons in Hermeneutics* (Grand Rapids: Zondervan, 1992), 41. The literature on intertextuality is immense. For a good introduction, see M. Orr, *Intertextuality: Debates and Contexts* (Cambridge: Polity, 2003). For a sense of the author's view, see C. G. Bartholomew, "The Intertextuality of Ecclesiastes and the New Testament," in *Reading Ecclesiastes Intertextually*, ed. K. Dell and W. Kynes (London: T&T Clark, 2014), chap. 19.
19. Jauss, *Toward an Aesthetic*, 24.

distance between the horizon of expectations and the *horizontal change* demanded by the new work. To the degree that this distance decreases, a work approximates culinary or entertainment art. Masterworks are peculiarly vulnerable to such a decrease in their ongoing reception since their "obvious" value leads them "dangerously close to the irresistibly convincing and enjoyable 'culinary' art, so that it requires a special effort to read them 'against the grain' of the accustomed experience to catch sight of their artistic character once again."[20]

Jauss's *fourth thesis* is that a reconstruction of the horizon of expectation enables one to pose questions that the text answered and thereby to discern the difference between the former and contemporary understanding of a work. As Collingwood notes, "We can understand a text only when we have understood the question to which it is an answer."[21]

Jauss's *fifth thesis* is that an aesthetic of reception demands that one read a literary work in its "literary series" so as to discern its historical position and significance in that context of the experience of literature.

Jauss's *sixth thesis* is that in relation to diachrony and synchrony, it must be possible to take a synchronic cross-section in the reception of a literary work in an historical moment.

Finally, the *seventh thesis* asserts that reception history must take into account the social function of literature whereby the literary experience of the reader enters and forms one's understanding of the world and life in it.

Biblical Interpretation and Reception History

The relevance of Jauss's work to biblical interpretation is clear. The view that historical objectivism neglects the literary character of a text is easily demonstrated in historical criticism—the manifestation of such objectivism in biblical studies—which has far too often moved quickly to the identification of sources and that which lies behind the text while bypassing the unavoidable attention to the literary shape of the text *first*. Inevitably a view of the text as a whole is assumed, but this has too often been at an unconscious or unacceptably naive level. The sort of analysis typical of historical criticism has avoided that perpetual confrontation with the text that Jauss rightly notes is indispensable to philological understanding.

20. Ibid., 26.
21. As quoted in ibid., 29. In turn, R. G. Collingwood, *An Autobiography* (Oxford: Galaxy, 1970), 293–94, is referencing H.-G. Gadamer, *Truth and Method* (London: Sheed and Ward, 1989), 370. Gadamer's reference differs slightly from Jauss's; I have followed Gadamer.

Second, Jauss's approach resists the postmodern tendency to disempower the text and overempower the reader,[22] while taking the role of the reader in the production of meaning seriously. The literary and biblical text has an objective horizon of expectation, and reception history is built on this stable basis. The novelty of a text arises from its dependence on readers' expectations and on its transgression of these. This insight is profoundly helpful with biblical interpretation and is amply demonstrated, for example, in Tom Wright's work on the Gospels.[23] Third, Jauss's attention to the danger of masterworks being reduced to culinary work is profoundly insightful for biblical interpretation. Familiarity easily breeds contempt, and biblical literature requires the *defamiliarization* that reception history can often provide if we are to hear the Bible afresh today. Too often liberals and conservatives already know what Scripture says, and we thereby fail to listen again to these powerful texts.

Biblical texts were produced in history, and it is crucial to give attention to the questions they were seeking to answer before asking our own questions. This is particularly the case with difficult and obscure texts. A classic example is the creation narratives in Genesis 1 and 2. To hear them in all their power, we need to attend first to the questions they are seeking to answer before bringing our own twenty-first-century questions about evolution and science to bear on them. Historical and literary context is crucial for biblical interpretation; we will have more to say about this in chapter 9. Finally, it is vital that biblical reception history explore the transformative dimensions of the history of reception of the Bible both positively and negatively.

Jauss's *Wege des Verstehens* consists of three parts. Part A contains a defense of a literary hermeneutic. Part B presents examples of this hermeneutic in action. Part B is important for demonstrating,

---

22. Jauss's provocative inaugural was given in the same year that Derrida gave his hugely influential "La Difference" lecture at Yale, inaugurating poststructuralism. Jauss's inaugural lecture in 1967 at the University of Konstanz, titled "Literary History as a Challenge to Literary Theory," was highly influential in its call for a new approach to literary studies. The following years witnessed the development of his program, at times in vigorous debate with a diversity of dialogue partners. Jauss is rightly critical of the infinitely open-ended approach to interpretation of the postmoderns but also resists the single-meaning approach to literary texts. See Rush, *Reception of Doctrine*, 53–55. Similarly, as Holub (*Reception Theory*, 101) notes, Iser claims "that the text allows for different meanings, while restricting the possibilities." A comparable and fertile position is taken by U. Eco, *The Limits of Interpretation* (Bloomington: Indiana University Press, 1990), with his language of open and closed texts. Holub (*Reception Theory*, 59–63) criticizes Jauss for remaining within an objectivist model of the text. In my view, a Christian hermeneutic would defend a notion of *thick objectivity*, which takes into account the influence of the reader's "prejudices" *and* the objectivity of the text and its resistance to being turned into a wax nose.

23. See N. T. Wright, *NTPG*; etc.

as Jauss notes in his preface, that hermeneutics is not an esoteric discipline but the theory of a practice.[24] Jauss's first example in Part B is the book of Jonah, "a paradigm of the hermeneutic of the other."[25] At the outset Jauss poses the question as to what a literary hermeneutic can contribute to the true interpretation of such a text. He rightly states, "Aesthetic experience does not stand per se in opposition to religious experience."[26] Indeed, Jauss's rich exploration of Jonah demonstrates the value of his literary approach. I cannot here discuss his chapter in detail;[27] suffice it to identify the major contours of his thought and how his theses above are brought to bear on Jonah. For Jauss, Jonah confronts the modern, enlightened reader and the theologian with a whole bundle of otherness/strangeness, such as the insubordinate prophet, the repentance of the sailors, God's repentance about Nineveh, and so forth. Jauss proposes, following Odo Marquard, to pursue his reading of Jonah in two stages: first, to inquire after the question to which the text is the answer; and second, to inquire after the (contemporary) question to which the text was not produced as the answer. He later refers to the first as the "theological reconstruction" and the latter as the "literary application."[28] With this approach Jauss reveals his dialogical view of literary texts. He works through Jonah chapter by chapter, manifesting a true literary sensitivity for the narrative. Jonah's reception history demonstrates repeated attempts to smooth over its otherness. A motif he finds throughout the book is that between the great and the small: the great Yahweh and the small prophet, the great city of Nineveh and the single prophet, the small worm and the big shrub, and so on. Jauss concludes that in its original context Jonah is an "answer" to the questions "Which goal does God pursue with the nations? Which view belongs thereby to Israel?" He perceptively notices the irony in Jonah: while Jonah is the central character, the real focus is Israel, for whom the book holds up a mirror. Jauss works toward the answer to his second stage/question through a fascinating examination of part of the reception history of Jonah—some of which destroys the subtlety of the book—and through relating Jonah's extraordinary creativity to contemporary views of the novel. He concludes that Jonah's otherness resists the last resistance to the other found in the refusal by modern authorities to countenance the miraculous.

A great deal of work is emerging on the history of biblical interpretation,[29] but it is rare to find attention given to the horizons of expectation of the biblical texts.[30] Indeed, this is a controversial area but unavoidable. The way one tells the story of biblical interpretation will be profoundly affected by one's view of the Bible. We are approaching the Bible as Scripture, whose horizon of expectation is that it be received as such with full attention to its literary, historical, and kerygmatic dimensions. Thus our aim in this chapter is to

24. Jauss, *Wege des Verstehens*, 8.
25. Ibid., 85.
26. Ibid.
27. On Jonah, see C. G. Bartholomew and H. Thomas, *The Minor Prophets: A Theological Introduction* (Downers Grove, IL: IVP Academic, forthcoming).
28. Jauss, *Wege des Verstehens*, 96.
29. See, e.g., the 5 vols. of *A History of Biblical Interpretation*: thus far vol. 1, *The Ancient Period*, and vol. 2, *The Medieval through the Reformation Periods*, ed. A. J. Hauser and D. F. Watson (Grand Rapids: Eerdmans, 2003–9); H. Reventlow, *History of Biblical Interpretation*, 3 vols. (Leiden: Brill, 2010); the multivolume work edited by M. Saebø, *HB/OT*.
30. See the Yale Program in the History of the Book as a comparable example. A new series with Princeton University Press is also emerging, exploring the history of influential books. See, e.g., G. Marsden, *C. S. Lewis's "Mere Christianity": A Biography* (Princeton: Princeton University Press, 2011).

indicate major contours in the reception of the Bible as Scripture so as to equip contemporary interpreters to orientate themselves amid current trends.

Not surprisingly, reception history has taken hold within biblical studies. Within theology a major impetus was Gerhard Ebeling's "Church History as the History of the Exposition of Holy Scripture."[31] Central to Ebeling's approach was the complicated history of a self-interpreting and an interpreted Bible.[32] Ebeling's lecture was heard by many as a call for *Auslegungsgeschichte*, the history of the interpretation of the Bible. At the First Patristic Conference in Oxford in 1955, David Lerch and Lukas Vischer, two young church historians, outlined how such a new discipline might operate.[33] They argued that attention to reception history could illuminate exegesis and open up fresh exploration of largely unexplored material in the commentary literature of the tradition. "The history-of-exegesis material becomes a mirror of the mystery which the text itself is witnessing to."[34] Around this time two monograph series were started in Germany in this area, and since then reception history has moved increasingly to the foreground. Froehlich states:

> I have become convinced myself that historical "understanding" of a biblical text cannot stop with the elucidation of its prehistory and of its historical *Sitz im Leben*, with its focus on the intention of the author. Understanding must take into account the text's post-history as the paradigm of the text's own historicity, i.e., as the way in which the text itself can function as a source of human self-interpretation in a variety of contexts, and thus, through its historical interpretations, is participating in the shaping of life.[35]

Writing in 1991, Froehlich was less than impressed with the results in biblical interpretation thus far.[36] He is rightly critical of approaches that merely produce a modern catena and insightfully declares, "Without much more detailed study independent of the production of commentaries and without

---

31. G. Ebeling, "Church History as the History of the Exposition of Holy Scripture," first published as "Habilitation Lecture" in 1947; republished in *Wort Gottes und Tradition: Studien zu einer Hermeneutik der Konfessionen* (Göttingen: Vandenhoek & Ruprecht, 1964).

32. K. Froehlich, "Church History and the Bible," in *Biblical Hermeneutics in Historical Perspective: Studies in Honor of Karlfried Froehlich on His Sixtieth Birthday*, ed. M. S. Burrows and P. Rorem (Grand Rapids: Eerdmans, 1991), 1–15, esp. 8. This chapter is a reprint from *PSB* 1, no. 4 (1978): 213–24.

33. D. Lerch and L. Vischer, "Die Auslegungsgeschichte als notwendige theologische Aufgabe," *Studia patristica* 1 (1957): 414–19.

34. Ibid., 418n1.

35. Froehlich, "Church History and the Bible," 9.

36. See K. Froehlich, "Postscript," in Burrows and Rorem, *Biblical Hermeneutics*, 339–49. See Froehlich, "Church History and the Bible," 10, for his comments on B. S. Childs, *The Book of Exodus: A Critical, Theological Commentary* (Philadelphia: Westminster, 1974).

effective teamwork, similar single-handed enterprises have little chance of success, particularly when an exegete is doing the whole job."[37]

Inner-Biblical Exegesis and Intertextuality

The history of biblical interpretation begins in the Bible, not just in the New Testament reading of the Old, but also in the intertextuality prevalent in the Old itself. It is, however, not easy to define *intertextuality*.[38] William Irwin asserts that the term "has come to have almost as many meanings as users, from those faithful to Kristeva's original vision to those who simply use it as a stylish way of talking about allusion and influence."[39] It indeed probably was Julia Kristeva who introduced the term "intertextuality."[40] Intertextuality is a post-Saussurean development in studies of *semiotics* (the analysis of signs and sign systems) and textuality. Saussure[41] perceptively distinguished between the network of words and their interrelationship at any one time (*langue*) and the use of this network in a speech act (*parole*). Especially in the work of Barthes and Derrida, Saussure's semiotics is developed in a radical direction, in which accurate reference to the world as it is becomes impossible, texts become radically indeterminate, and authorial intention vanishes.[42] Thiselton observes, "Linguistic *method* has now become a linguistic *world-view*" in which intersubjectivity is replaced by intertextuality.[43]

However, as Raymond Tallis has rightly pointed out, Barthes's and Derrida's Saussure is *Not Saussure*.[44] Thiselton rightly recognizes, "It is not the case,

---

37. Froehlich, "Church History and the Bible," 10.
38. For a survey of approaches, see the introductory essay in M. Worton and J. Still, eds., *Intertextuality: Theories and Practices* (Manchester, UK: Manchester University Press, 1990).
39. W. Irwin, "Against Intertextuality," *Philosophy and Literature* 28, no. 2 (October 2004): 227–42, esp. 228.
40. See J. Kristeva, *Desire in Language*; idem, *Revolution in Poetic Language*, trans. M. Waller (New York: Columbia University Press, 1984). Kristeva states, "The term *inter-textuality* denotes this transposition of one (or several) sign system(s) into another; but since this term has often been understood in the banal sense of 'study of sources,' we prefer the term *transposition* because it specifies that the passage from one signifying system to another demands a new articulation of the thetic—of enunciative and denotative positionality" (*Desire in Language*, 59–60).
41. F. de Saussure, *Cours de linguistique générale* (Paris: Payot & Rivage, 1995). See Roy Harris, *Reading Saussure: A Critical Commentary on the "Cours de linguistique générale"* (London: Duckworth, 1987) for a critical commentary on Suassure's *Cours*.
42. For the details of these developments, see Thiselton, *New Horizons*, 55–141. On the various receptions of Saussure's work, see Roy Harris, *Saussure and His Interpreters* (Edinburgh: Edinburgh University Press, 2003).
43. Thiselton, *New Horizons*, 97.
44. R. Tallis, *Not Saussure: A Critique of Post-Saussurean Literary Theory*, 2nd ed. (Basingstoke, UK: Macmillan, 1995). Jauss, *Wege des Verstehens*, 11, insightfully evaluates the skepticism of postmodernism: "Solche Skepsis verabsolutiert Sprache als System (*langue*)."

in Saussure, that *parole* can be generated by a subjectless system, in isolation from the *constraints* on possibility imposed by the purposive *choices of the speaking subject*."[45] Saussure's approach has been extended in semiotics to cultural analysis[46] and to inter*text*uality, thereby focusing attention on the production of texts. Thiselton's critique of Barthes and Derrida is that they have turned semiotics into a worldview; I would rather say that they have recontextualized semiotics within *a different worldview*, based on an absolutization of a distorted view of language. Hermeneutics has focused on how we understand texts; semiotics has focused on the production of texts.[47] There is, however, no reason why these emphases should be mutually exclusive. At a deeper level, what is at stake is our philosophy of language. As Eco rightly explains, "A general semiotics is nothing else but a philosophy of language, and . . . the 'good' philosophies of language, from *Cratylus*[48] to *Philosophical Investigations*,[49] are concerned with all the semiotic questions."[50]

Especially with the impact of postmodernism on biblical studies it has—or at least, *should have*—become impossible to ignore language and how it works, which is philosophy of language. Faced with deconstructionist readings of biblical texts, for example, it is vital to be aware of the philosophy of language at work in such readings. Positively, philosophy of language can help one avoid the sort of errors that James Barr has exposed in word studies.[51] A further positive example is how we understand a dictionary. Dictionaries may seem straightforward, but this is far from the case. Eco, rightly in my view, rejects the historically dominant model for defining words of the Porphyrian tree, arguing instead for an *encyclopedic* model, with the encyclopedia understood as a netlike labyrinth: "The main feature of a net is that every point can be

---

45. Thiselton, *New Horizons*, 99. Roy Harris (*Saussure*, 188) concludes that Derrida's reading of Saussure "is nothing remotely resembling a close, sustained reading. It is a caricature of Saussure, drawn in order to prop up a philosophical thesis of dubious worth."

46. Claude Lévi-Strauss was the major figure in this respect. See, e.g., Lévi-Strauss, *Structural Anthropology* (New York: Basic Books, 1963).

47. Thiselton, *New Horizons*, 28.

48. A dialogue by Plato: *Cratylus*.

49. L. Wittgenstein, *Philosophical Investigations*, trans. G. E. M. Anscombe, first published in 1953 by Oxford, Blackwell.

50. U. Eco, *Semiotics and the Philosophy of Language* (Bloomington: Indiana University Press, 1984), 4. Eco has written a number of important works in this area, including *A Theory of Semiotics* (Bloomington: Indiana University Press, 1976); *The Role of the Reader: Explorations in the Semiotics of Texts* (Bloomington: Indiana University Press, 1979); and *Limits of Interpretation*.

51. J. Barr, *The Semantics of Biblical Language* (London: SCM, 1982; reprint, Eugene, OR: Wipf & Stock, 2004); idem, *Biblical Words for Time*, 2nd ed. (London: SCM, 1969). But see F. Watson, *Text and Truth: Redefining Biblical Theology* (Grand Rapids: Eerdmans, 1997), 18–28, for an important, critical engagement with Barr.

connected with every other point, and where the connections are not yet designed, they are, however, conceivable and designable."[52] The implication of such an approach is that meanings of words are not fixed but subject to continual change, so it is untenable to think of dictionaries as providing fixed definitions of words. Dictionaries, as Eco recognizes, remain useful tools, but "the dictionary-like arrangements we continuously provide are transitory and pragmatically useful hierarchical assessments of [the encyclopedia]. . . . *The encyclopedia is a semantic concept and the dictionary is a pragmatic device.*"[53]

Rightly understood, semiotics and intertextuality do not for a moment detract from the text as a human speech act, but they do alert us to the layers of meaning involved in a text. As Eco explains, "The so-called signifying chain produces texts which carry with them the recollection of the intertextuality which nourishes them."[54] Semiotics has produced a bewildering catena of technical jargon, and debate is ongoing. For our purposes we recognize that intertextuality covers a range of phenomena and must not be reduced to simplistic proof-texting through the discovery of similar vocabulary in texts. Detailed analysis of vocabulary is an indispensable part of intertextual analysis, but only in the context of the literary work in which such vocabulary occurs and with a keen sensitivity to what the author does with that vocabulary. Being aware that an author has certain codes and genres available to use can serve to deepen our understanding of a text and alert us to its complex interrelationship with other texts.

This is certainly the case with the Bible. Within the life of Israel, we would expect to find in its authoritative texts ongoing engagement with the tradition by which Israel was formed. "Indeed, the Bible is not merely a collection of books but a network of connections in which stories talk to poems and laws to prophecies."[55] According to Shinan and Zakovitch, "As these ancient thinkers wrote their texts, whether historical accounts or psalms, legal texts or narratives, they planted them firmly into the already growing canon, incorporating them into already-established contexts or appending them to existing texts, and, by doing so, they introduced new ideas and interpretations."[56]

Whereas Shinan and Zakovitch explore inner-biblical interpretation in relation to ancient traditions, Fishbane, in his *Biblical Interpretation in Ancient*

52. Eco, *Semiotics and the Philosophy of Language*, 81.
53. Ibid., 85, with original emphasis.
54. Ibid., 24.
55. A. Shinan and Y. Zakovitch, *From Gods to God: How the Bible Debunked, Suppressed, or Changed Ancient Myths and Legends*, trans. V. Zakovitch (Lincoln: University of Nebraska Press, 2012), 1.
56. Ibid., 3.

Israel, focuses exclusively on the phenomenon of *inner-biblical exegesis* in the Old Testament. His three major categories are legal exegesis, which seeks to fill out some perceived lack in the *traditum*; haggadic exegesis, which by contrast focuses on features of the *traditum* that are well known and seeks to draw out fuller meaning from them; and mantological exegesis, which attends to oracular material such as we find in the prophets. We cannot here discuss Fishbane's creative work in detail; suffice it to refer to one example that indicates the fecundity of his work.

Fishbane notes that Second Isaiah's concern with creation and his focus on the link between creation and redemption have long been recognized. Focusing on verses such as Isaiah 45:7, 18 in relation to Genesis 1:2; on 40:18, 25 and 46:5 in relation to Genesis 1:26; and on 40:28 in relation to Genesis 2:2–3, Fishbane argues that Second Isaiah has

> *exegetically reappropriated* Gen. 1:1–2:4a and transposed it into a new theological key. The underlying cognitive concern was not so much to undermine Gen. 1:1–2:4a as to maintain it in a newly understood way. As seen, this could not be completely achieved, for notions like a divine likeness in man or divine rest were not spiritualized but completely rejected.[57]

The extent to which Second Isaiah corrects Genesis 1:1–2:4a and rejects the *imago Dei* and the idea of divine rest is surely debatable.[58] For example, the focus in Isaiah 40:12–31 is on the transcendence of God, and in 40:18–20 "likeness" occurs not in relation to humankind but to idols. Nevertheless, the data that Fishbane foregrounds is important and opens up fertile directions of interpretation in all sorts of ways. For example, as we will see in chapter 11 (below), it is much debated whether the Old Testament teaches creation ex nihilo. Isaiah's haggadic interpretation of Genesis 1 certainly provides

---

57. M. A. Fishbane, *Biblical Interpretation in Ancient Israel* (Oxford: Oxford University Press, 2004), 326. Cf. B. D. Sommer, *A Prophet Reads Scripture: Allusion in Isaiah 40–66* (Stanford, CA: Stanford University Press, 1998), 142–48. Already in 1968 M. Weinfeld ("God the Creator in Genesis 1 and in the Prophecy of Second Isaiah," *Tarbiz* 37 [1968]: 105–32 [Hebrew]) argued that Second Isaiah rejected four central ideas in Gen. 1:1–2:4a. Even earlier, in 1895, H. Gunkel (*Creation and Chaos in the Primeval Era and the Eschaton: A Religio-historical Study of Genesis 1 and Revelation 12* [Grand Rapids: Eerdmans, 2006], Kindle loc. 502–3) noted, "But even leaving this out of consideration, it is apparent to us from Jewish literature, above all from Deutero-Isaiah, that the idea of chaos is not consistent with the idea of God as an independently working creator." Of Gen. 1's view of darkness, he declares, "The idea certainly does not stem from Jewish culture, of which the conception of God was much more consistent with the word of Deutero-Isa 45:7" (ibid., Kindle loc. 492–93).

58. C. Westermann (*Genesis 1–11: A Commentary* [Minneapolis: Augsburg, 1984]), e.g., rightly states, "The protest of Is 40:18f., that God is incomparable and that there is nothing like him, does not stand in contradiction to Gen. 1:26f" (158).

support for the view that at least some of the Old Testament writers were aware of the danger of reading Genesis 1:2 so as to see darkness (cf. Isa. 45:7) and chaos as rival powers to Yahweh.

Another good example is found in Levy's dramatic analysis of the intertextual echoes of the Shema in Proverbs 7:1–6.[59] What this sort of work demonstrates is the far more integrated nature of the Old Testament than historical criticism has led us to expect. As with the literary turn, the full implications of intertextuality still have to be appropriated in biblical studies.[60] Old Testament intertextuality extends to comparative ancient Near Eastern materials,[61] to the New Testament, and beyond into the history of reception. An example of ancient Near Eastern intertextuality is what Brevard Childs calls "broken myth."[62] The Old Testament uses the images of Rahab, Leviathan, and the Dragon from its cultural context but without the uncritical approach of myth, hence Childs's designation.

In biblical studies the major focus of intertextuality is on the relationship between the two Testaments. Intertextuality has yielded very close readings and literary comparisons in New Testament studies, some of which it is hard to believe were ever intended by the authors of those books, who functioned in an oral-literary culture. Walter Ong's *Orality and Literacy* is important in this respect, alerting us to the extent to which biblical literature functioned amid a literarily oral culture. As Ong notices, the sort of close readings one finds in much biblical interpretation nowadays presuppose the primarily literary culture that followed the invention of the printing press.[63] Intertextual studies of this nature are, I suggest, in danger of anachronism.

While vocabulary and citation will remain indispensable parts of biblical intertextuality, we need a broader and richer concept of the interrelationship of Old Testament and New Testament texts. N. T. Wright's use of *story* is, I think, an example of an approach that has opened up such a broader understanding.

---

59. S. Levy, *The Bible as Theatre* (Portland, OR: Sussex Academic, 2000), 135–42. See C. G. Bartholomew, "Hearing the Old Testament Wisdom Literature: The Wit of Many the Wisdom of One," in *Hearing the Old Testament: Listening for God's Address*, ed. C. G. Bartholomew and D. J. H. Beldman (Grand Rapid: Eerdmans, 2012), 325–26.

60. Intertextuality is related to tradition history, which remains valuable but speculative. The advantage of intertextuality is that it focuses on the texts as we have them, although interpreting intertextual data is far from a precise science!

61. See, e.g., Westermann, who says, "The question is now: what is the relationship of the biblical reflection on Creation in its broadest compass to a history of reflection on Creation stretching over thousands of years, as we meet it in the succession of Sumerian, Babylonian, and Assyrian texts?" (*Genesis 1–11*, 9).

62. B. S. Childs, *Myth and Reality in the Old Testament*, 2nd ed. (Eugene, OR: Wipf & Stock, 2009).

63. See chap. 11 below.

Wright's exploration of how the Old Testament and intertestamental narratives of Israel are dealt with in the New Testament[64] opens up rich veins of intertextual relationship between Old Testament and New.[65] Yet in the process intertextuality becomes far harder to pin down and to evaluate, but in my view that is a fair price to pay for the rich theological insights foregrounded. Intriguingly, intertextuality also connects us in a fresh way with premodern exegesis, in which scholars invariably drew on a vast knowledge of Scripture for their exegesis.

Patristic Exegesis

Study of the exegesis of the church fathers has exploded since World War II, and this welcome development shows no sign of slowing down.[66] All the church fathers engaged in spiritual exegesis, what we would call theological interpretation,[67] in that they share two common assumptions: (1) the historical sense is the foundation of all interpretation of Scripture, and (2) Scripture is to be related to the community of believers as the Word of God.[68] The important difference that emerges amid their extraordinary creativity is between typology and allegory, a debate that reemerged in the twentieth century. All the fathers affirmed typology, but the Antiochene school rejected allegory.

In *The Spirit of Early Christian Thought*, Robert Wilken has pointed out the extraordinary achievement of the church fathers. Any reception of their contribution, however critical, should recognize the enormity of the task they bore and their achievements in biblical interpretation, a legacy to which we are all in debt. Kannengiesser, for example, observes, "There is no doubt that its intimate link with allegory is a proper mark of patristic typology. By playing on both registers, the typological and the allegorical, the expositors of patristic exegesis succeeded in producing symphonic masterpieces of biblical interpretation."[69] We will have cause to critique the allegorism of much patristic exegesis, but this should not detract from its achievement. In often adverse circumstances, the church fathers were faced with the reception

---

64. Cf. also R. B. Hays, *The Faith of Jesus Christ: An Investigation of the Narrative Substructure of Galatians 3:1–4:11* (Chico, CA: Scholars Press, 1983); idem, *Echoes of Scripture in the Letters of Paul* (New Haven: Yale University Press, 1989).

65. See chap. 11 below.

66. An indispensable guide to patristic exegesis is the work by C. Kannengiesser, ed., *Handbook of Patristic Exegesis* [HPE], 2 vols., The Bible in Ancient Christianity (Leiden: Brill, 2004; 2 vols. in 1, 2006), with detailed bibliographies on all of these authors.

67. See C. G. Bartholomew and H. Thomas, eds., *Manifesto for Theological Interpretation* (Grand Rapids: Baker Academic, forthcoming).

68. T. Böhm, "Allegory and History," in Kannengiesser, HPE 1:224.

69. Kannengiesser, HPE 1:238.

and protection of the apostolic tradition, discerning the limits of the canon, dealing with the thorny issues of translation, pastoral responsibilities, and so forth. Translation, for example, played a central role in the development of biblical interpretation:

> From Hebrew to Greek, and from Greek to Latin, the message of the church rested entirely on the intimate metamorphosis of its discourse conditioned by the work of translators. If theories of interpreting sacred Scripture were developed later on by intellectually gifted leaders like Origen, Augustine and Jerome, it was first of all because of the constant struggle of earlier Christian generations which translated Scripture into their mother tongues.[70]

The Literal Meaning

For all the church fathers, the literal meaning of the text, the *littera*, was foundational and "in itself a spiritual exercise, because for them the materiality of the written text itself was filled with divine mysteries."[71] "Literal" should not necessarily be confused with literalism. Thus, for Antiochene interpreters such as Diodore of Tarsus metaphor is encompassed within the literal sense. In his commentary on Psalm 1, he explains one metaphor after another. Thus *hodos* (way) in Psalm 1:1b is the name the psalmist gives to behavior; in verse 3, "As the tree, . . . so may be the person"; "chaff" in verse 4 means the evanescent. In principle, allegory followed on from the literal sense even among its most ardent proponents, so that even if we are cautious of the allegorical approach of some church fathers—and a defender of allegory such as de Lubac readily acknowledges excesses—there remains a rich feast of interpretation among the fathers.

Spiritual Sense and Allegory

The origin of the distinction between history and allegory is philosophically conditioned.[72] Allegory had its origins among the Stoics and the Hellenistic grammarian Heraclitus. The Stoic philosopher Cornutus used etymology to "retrieve" philosophical wisdom from ancient mythology. His approach rested

---

70. Ibid., 1:196.
71. Ibid., 1:168.
72. See D. Obbink, "Early Greek Allegory," in *The Cambridge Companion to Allegory*, ed. R. Copeland and P. T. Struck (Cambridge: Cambridge University Press, 2010), 15–25; G. W. Most, "Hellenistic Allegory and Early Imperial Rhetoric," in Copeland and Struck, *Companion to Allegory*, 26–38; P. T. Struck, "Allegory and Ascent in Neoplatonism," in Copeland and Struck, *Companion to Allegory*, 57–70; D. Turner, "Allegory in Christian Late Antiquity," in Copeland and Struck, *Companion to Allegory*, 71–82.

on a natural view of language, according to which in primordial naming the essence of an object was contained in the word used to name it.[73] Through etymology Cornutus is able to show how ancient mythology fits with Stoic wisdom.

Plato's *Republic* offers extensive discussion of problems with the legends of the gods, recommending which stories should be told to children and which should not, without resorting to allegory. Heraclitus sought to defend the Homeric legends through allegorical interpretation of them. To do this, he separates Homer's narratives into two levels: a surface level of mythical poetry (the literal sense) and a deeper level of truth (the allegorical sense). Heraclitus believed that Homer intentionally composed his works in allegory, and in his reading he interweaves literal and allegorical, making use (inter alia) of etymology, with the primary aim of neutralizing offensive passages.[74]

Ancient thought also contained substantial resources for resisting allegory. Plato resists allegorization of the Homer epics in his *Republic*; in the *Cratylus*, Socrates's lengthy exploration of etymology runs aground and culminates in attention to the things themselves, the Forms. Both the non-Stoic dialogue partners in Cicero's *On the Nature of the Gods* and in the Stoic Seneca rejected allegorization. The Middle Platonist Plutarch (ca. AD 45–125) takes a mediating position in relation to interpretation of the ancient myths.[75] Rather than resorting to allegory, the Alexandrian textual critics edited the classics to conform to their own cultural standards.[76] "Consequently, the allegorical hermeneutic of Hellenistic Judaism and early Christianity was not an automatic outgrowth of pagan hermeneutical tradition."[77]

Allegorical interpretation took hold in the church very early. Many trace allegorical interpretation back to Paul: "The word which was first used by St. Paul, and which was generally used thereafter in the Latin tradition, to express this symbolic transposition was *allegory*."[78] There is, however, only one place in the New Testament in which "allegory" is used, and that is in Galatians 4:21–31. In verse 24 Paul comments, "Now this is an allegory." Aquinas uses this text as an opportunity to expound the four senses of Scripture.[79] It

---

73. The Stoics also articulated a propositional theory of meaning, but Cornutus's etymological approach relies on the natural approach to meaning.

74. See D. A. Dawson, *Allegorical Readers and Cultural Revision in Ancient Alexandria* (Berkeley: University of California Press, 1992), 42–52.

75. See ibid., 58–66.

76. Ibid., 66–71.

77. Ibid., 52.

78. H. de Lubac, *Scripture in the Tradition*, trans. L. O'Neill (New York: Crossroad, 2000), 12–13. De Lubac himself prefers the words "spiritual meaning."

79. Thomas Aquinas, *Commentary on Saint Paul's Epistle to the Galatians*, trans. F. R. Larcher (Albany, NY: Magi Books, 1966), 137–38.

is debatable whether Paul's treatment of the Hagar-Sarah story from Genesis is typological or allegorical.[80] Either way, as Bruce writes, "In the present 'allegory,' however, there is a forcible inversion of the analogy which is unparalleled elsewhere in Paul."[81] C. K. Barrett's proposal that Paul's opponents used the incident of the two sons to support their case and that Paul refutes it by inverting their argument has won wide support.[82] Clearly this text from Galatians should not be taken as typical of Paul's interpretation of the Old Testament, which is typological through and through. As Ellis rightly states, "Typological interpretation expresses most clearly the basic approach of earliest Christianity toward the Old Testament."[83] The word "typology" may be late,[84] but it helpfully distinguishes the Antiochene approach from that of the Alexandrian school, as we will see below.

Paul's contrast between letter and spirit (2 Cor. 3:6) is further adduced as evidence for a spiritual reading of the Old Testament, as is his use of Deuteronomy 25:4 in 1 Corinthians 9:8–9, and Hebrews' use of the Old Testament.[85] In chapter 14 (below) we will examine the use of the Old Testament in Hebrews. In 2 Corinthians 3 the focus is Paul's defense of his ministry and its context of the new covenant, compared with the old. The contrast between letter and spirit is an example of antithetic typology, but 2 Corinthians 3 also contains examples of synthetic typology and an emphasis on the continuity between Old and New Testaments. Barrett notes that 2 Corinthians 3:4–6 is controversial and remarks,

> It was certainly not Paul's intention to suggest that the Old Testament law was merely a human instrument; it was, on the contrary, spiritual, inspired by the Spirit of God (Rom. 7:14). But it was easy to misuse it—easy for the Jew to assume that, simply because he possessed it, he was himself superior to the

---

80. F. F. Bruce (*The Epistle to the Galatians: A Commentary on the Greek Text* [Exeter, UK: Paternoster, 1982], 217) views it as typology; R. N. Longenecker (*Galatians*, WBC 41 [Dallas: Word, 1990], 209) views it as allegory.

81. Bruce, *Galatians*, 218.

82. C. K. Barrett, "The Allegory of Abraham, Sarah, and Hagar in the Argument of Galatians," in *Rechtfertigung: Festschrift für Ernst Käsemann zum 70. Geburtstag*, ed. J. Friedrich, W. Pöhlmann, and P. Stuhlmacher (Tübingen: Mohr, 1976), 1–16; cf. Longenecker, *Galatians*, 207.

83. E. E. Ellis, *History and Interpretation in New Testament Perspective* (Leiden: Brill, 2001), 115; on 115–16, Ellis distinguishes between creation and covenant typology, and between synthetic and antithetic typology. The latter distinction relates to whether the OT type corresponds with or differs from the realities of the new age. On typology, see also L. Goppelt, *Typos: The Typological Interpretation of the Old Testament in the New*, trans. D. H. Madvig (Grand Rapids: Eerdmans, 1982).

84. De Lubac, *Scripture in the Tradition*, 15.

85. See ibid., 29, 44.

rest of mankind (Rom. 2:17ff.), easy to treat it, not as a divine gift (Rom. 9:4), but as an indication of human achievement.[86]

Thus letter and spirit are not, in my view, useful categories by which to generalize about the relationship between the two Testaments.[87]

The emergence of allegorical interpretation of the Bible in Alexandria can be traced through the Jewish thinkers Aristobulus, Aristeas, and in particular Philo; the gnostic Christian Valentinus; and the early church fathers Justin Martyr (ca. 100–165) and Clement of Alexandria (ca. 150–ca. 215).[88] In his reading of the Torah, Philo uses allegory to redescribe Hellenism within Judaism and to make Judaism measure up to the insights of Greek thought, which are anticipated by Moses.[89] Valentinus erases the border between text and allegory by using allegory to create his own compositions, rooted in his personal (gnostic) vision. Justin Martyr and Clement retain the border between text and allegory and used a Logos theology informed by Middle Platonist categories to interpret the Bible allegorically.

At this time Middle Platonism was pervasive in the Roman Empire. By the second century AD, it had replaced Stoicism as the dominant philosophy, yet embracing certain elements of Stoic ethics and physics. Middle Platonism was concerned with the relationship between the transcendent principle and the realm of becoming; it insisted that a mediating principle was required. Many Middle Platonists appropriated features of the Stoic *logos* (reason) to this mediating principle or element.

In John 1, Justin and Clement found grounds for connecting Jesus with the Logos, understood as the divine *voice* mediating God's truth. Typical of Platonism, this easily produced an upward pull rather than an eschatological one; it flattened out Scripture so that such interpreters had to resort to allegory to find the same divine truth throughout the Bible. Justin's reading of the Old Testament is more typological in that his great concern is to show

---

86. C. K. Barrett, *The Second Epistle to the Corinthians* (London: Continuum, 1973), 112–13.
87. On Paul's use of Deut. 25:4 in 1 Cor. 9:8–9, see the excellent discussion in A. C. Thiselton, *The First Epistle to the Corinthians: A Commentary on the Greek Text*, NIGTC (Grand Rapids: Eerdmans, 2000), 685–88.
88. See Dawson, *Allegorical Readers*.
89. Dawson (ibid., 76) notes that the modern concept of symbolic discourse as distinct from allegorical, a Romantic distinction, was not operative in the ancient world. For an example of Philo's allegorization of Gen. 22:3–4, see ibid., 83–84. Inter alia, this involves Philo taking "place" to be a homonym for "Word" and "God." He does not pursue the different possible nuances in "place" that would make realistic narrative sense. A natural philosophy of naming also underlies Philo's hermeneutic (ibid., 86). On Philo's reading of Gen. 1:1–5, see ibid., 130. For Philo, these verses describe the creation of the intelligible universe, which contains the pattern for the material creation.

how the Old Testament is fulfilled in Christ. With Clement, we observe the mix of typology and allegory that became typical of the Alexandrian school and many other fathers.

Prestige explains: "The Church was saved from abjuring rationalism by Clement of Alexandria. . . . Philosophy, he said, was 'the clear image of truth, a gift of God to the Greeks.'"[90] Clement's achievement in this respect is very important, and so is the use of philosophy in Augustine and Aquinas. One ignores the role of philosophy in biblical interpretation at one's peril; yet the question must be asked whether Clement was sufficiently critical in his openness to Greek thought. The proof of the pudding is ever in the eating, and we turn to several examples in Clement's writings.

Clement's practice of an etymological approach, which we observed among the Stoics, is evident in *Stromata* 1.5, as is his dependence on Philo:

> And Philo interprets Hagar to mean "sojourning." For it is said in connection with this, "Be not much with a strange woman." Sarah he interprets to mean "my princedom." He, then, who has received previous training is at liberty to approach to wisdom, which is supreme, from which grows up the race of Israel. These things show that that wisdom can be acquired through instruction, to which Abraham attained, passing from the contemplation of heavenly things to the faith and righteousness which are according to God. And Isaac is shown to mean "self-taught"; wherefore also he is discovered to be a type of Christ. He was the husband of one wife Rebecca, which they translate "Patience." And Jacob is said to have consorted with several, his name being interpreted "Exerciser." And exercises are engaged in by means of many and various dogmas. Whence, also, he who is really "endowed with the power of seeing" is called Israel, having much experience, and being fit for exercise.

In *Stromata* 5.6, Clement deals with the mystical meaning of the tabernacle and its furniture. Here is an example of his commentary:

> Now the high priest's robe is the symbol of the world of sense. The seven planets are represented by the five stones and the two carbuncles, for Saturn and the Moon. The former is southern, and moist, and earthy, and heavy; the latter aerial, whence she is called by some Artemis, as if Ærotomos (cutting the air); and the air is cloudy. And cooperating as they did in the production of things here below, those that by Divine Providence are set over the planets are rightly

---

90. G.-L. Prestige, *Fathers and Heretics: Six Studies in Dogmatic Faith with Prologue and Epilogue; Being the Bampton Lectures for 1940* (London: SPCK, 1977), 62. The references in Clement of Alexandria are to his *Stromata* 1.2 and 20.1. Select Clement at http://www.early christianwritings.com/.

represented as placed on the breast and shoulders; and by them was the work of creation, the first week. And the breast is the seat of the heart and soul.

Stromata 5.11 is headed, "Abstraction from Material Things Necessary in Order to Attain to the True Knowledge of God." In this section Clement discusses Genesis 22.

> Again: "Abraham, when he came to the place which God told him of on the third day, looking up, saw the place afar off." [Genesis 22:3–4.] For the first day is that which is constituted by the sight of good things; and the second is the soul's best desire; on the third, the mind perceives spiritual things, the eyes of the understanding being opened by the Teacher who rose on the third day. The three days may be the mystery of the seal, in which God is really believed. It is consequently afar off that he sees the place. For the region of God is hard to attain; which Plato called the region of ideas, having learned from Moses that it was a place which contained all things universally. But it is seen by Abraham afar off, rightly, because of his being in the realms of generation, and he is immediately initiated by the angel. Thence says the apostle: "Now we see as through a glass, but then face to face," by those sole pure and incorporeal applications of the intellect. In reasoning, it is possible to divine respecting God, if one attempt without any of the senses, by reason, to reach what is individual; and do not quit the sphere of existences, till, rising up to the things which transcend it, he apprehends by the intellect itself that which is good, moving in the very confines of the world of thought, according to Plato.

Several points are noteworthy here: the narrative is clearly read allegorically; the influence of Platonism is evident; and the effect of this reading is to focus attention on contemplation of the eternal, which is described as "intellectual." Such a reading detracts from and distorts the rich literary narrative of Genesis 22.[91]

Allegory was particularly used to make sense of the Old Testament from a Christian perspective. However, it is by no means limited to that text. Clement's work *Who Is the Rich Man That Shall Be Saved?* is an example of the allegorical reading of the New Testament. As he notes in chapter 5, "But well knowing that the Saviour teaches nothing in a merely human way, but teaches all things to His own with divine and mystic wisdom, we must not listen to His utterances carnally; but with due investigation and intelligence must search out and learn the meaning hidden in them."

Clement rejects the view that the rich young man is actually asked to abandon his wealth and property: "He does not, as some conceive off-hand, bid

---

91. See *Stromata* 7.18 for Clement's reading of the clean and unclean animals.

him throw away the substance he possessed, and abandon his property; but bids him banish from his soul his notions about wealth, his excitement and morbid feeling about it, the anxieties, which are the thorns of existence, which choke the seed of life."[92] The result is a perceptive reading of the apostolic tradition on wealth and property, but the potential for allegory to violate the plain sense of the narrative is clear. The Franciscan tradition, for example, would not exist if St. Francis had not read Matthew 19:21 literally.[93]

Origen (ca. 185–254) was an extraordinary figure. "He was the founder of biblical science, and, although not absolutely the first great biblical commentator, he first developed the principles which exposition was to follow and applied the fashion of methodical explanation on the widest possible scale."[94] When he was seventeen, persecution broke out in Alexandria, and his father was arrested. He wrote to his father, encouraging him to remain faithful to Christ and not to change his purpose on account of his family. His father was martyred. Amid persecution, Origen assumed the mantle of Christian philosophy in Alexandria and was successful in attracting many students. Some were martyred, and Origen was exemplary in visiting them in prison and attending their executions to give them their last kiss of peace.

The Bible was of fundamental importance to Origen, and he even took lessons in Hebrew from a Jewish tutor. At the same time he "claimed the widest liberty to drink at all the springs of Hellenic rationalism."[95] Origen's *Hexapla*, a colossal edition of the Old Testament arranged in six columns—presenting the unvocalized Hebrew, a vocalized transliteration in Greek characters, and four Greek versions in circulation—was a major achievement, which came to fill fifty volumes. The texts in the six columns were divided up into clauses so as to show with ease how different versions rendered the equivalent Hebrew phrase. "The work was an object-lesson not only of portentous industry but [also] of essentially sound method; and it was a wholly new venture."[96]

Origen wrote about his method of interpretation in his work *On First Principles*,[97] composed at the same time as he was writing his *Commentary on John*. Scripture is to be read as a whole since it is all part of God's revelation. He does not neglect the literal sense but places great import on the

---

92. Clement, *Who Is the Rich Man That Shall Be Saved?*, 10. Select Clement at http://www.earlychristianwritings.com/.
93. Pope Honorius III, The Bull on the Rule of the Friars Minor (November 29, 1223), to Francis of Assisi and his fellow friars (*Regula Bullata*), chap. 2, http://www.franciscan-archive.org/patriarcha/opera/regula-e.html.
94. Prestige, *Fathers and Heretics*, 43.
95. Ibid., 46.
96. Ibid., 54.
97. See Origen, *First Principles* (*De principiis*), chap. 4, http://www.newadvent.org/fathers/.

deeper meanings. On the Old Testament, he asks: "All the narrative portion, relating either to the marriages, or to the begetting of the children, or to battles of different kinds, or to any other histories whatever, what else can they be supposed to be, save the forms and figures of hidden and sacred things?"[98]

The same he asserts is true of the New Testament.[99] Thus a threefold manner of interpretation is recommended so that the reader can penetrate to the soul of Scripture:[100] the literal, the moral, and the spiritual. He does not apply this triad in a constrictive way; some texts contain no historical sense but only the spiritual one.[101] The historicity of Scripture is fundamental: "Let no one, however, entertain the suspicion that we do not believe any history in Scripture to be real."[102] Furthermore he says, "The passages which hold good in their historical acceptation are much more numerous than those which contain a purely spiritual meaning. Then, again, who would not maintain that the command to honour your father and your mother, that it may be well with you, is sufficient of itself without any spiritual meaning, and necessary for those who observe it?"[103]

The spiritual sense is of great import for Origen, and *allegory* is his method for discerning it.[104] Prestige claims that the allegorical method saved the Bible for the church because it enabled the Old Testament to be defended against Jewish critics and against educated Hellenists[105]—but at what cost? The Alexandrian tradition includes literal and typological interpretation and thus continues to offer a feast to the church today. However, the tension between the literal and the spiritual/allegorical is very often real, with the latter obscuring the former. The Platonic emphasis also results in subverting the doctrine of the creation in Scripture, turning the gravitational pull upward to the incorporeal.

Not all third-century exegesis was as strongly allegorical as that of Origen. Cyprian of Carthage's exegesis, for example, was thoroughly christological but lacked the fanciful allegorizing of Origen.[106] Nevertheless Origen's hermeneutic was very influential. For example, his influence underlies Gregory of Nyssa's (ca. 335–395) hermeneutic, as Fahey reports: "This movement

---

98. Ibid., 4.9.
99. Ibid., 4.10.
100. Ibid., 4.11.
101. Ibid., 4.12.
102. Ibid., 4.19.
103. Ibid.
104. See D. Boyarin, "Origen as Theorist of Allegory: Alexandrian Contexts," in Copeland and Struck, *Companion to Allegory*, 39–56.
105. Prestige, *Fathers and Heretics*, 59; see also 64–66.
106. See M. A. Fahey, *Cyprian and the Bible: A Study in Third-Century Exegesis*, Beiträge zur Geschichte der biblischen Hermeneutik 9 (Tübingen: Mohr, 1971), 48–49.

toward God is particularly founded in neoplatonism. It was assimilated in a Christian context by Gregory of Nyssa. The tendency of approximation towards the intelligible beyond the sensual is mediated by linguistic form: by using the language of difference one should ultimately be able to transcend the difference."[107] Another major example is Jerome. An example of this deleterious effect are Origen's and Jerome's readings of Ecclesiastes. It is read allegorically as teaching *contemptus mundi*, an interpretation that dominated for over a thousand years and frames the most popular spiritual classic of all times, Thomas à Kempis's *Imitation of Christ*. Jerome's reading was finally and rightly broken by the Lutheran Reformers, with their strong sense of creation and vocation in this world.

Yet crediting Origen with saving the Bible for the church would underestimate the contribution of the Antiochene school, which included such luminaries as Diodore, Theodore of Mopsuestia, Chrysostom, and Theodoret. In my opinion it is in this tradition that we find the most fruitful patristic resources for biblical interpretation. The Council of Nicaea in 325 provides a convenient mark for the start of the Antiochene school. In 326 Eustathius was deposed as bishop of Antioch by the Arians; he was the first to speak at Nicaea. His only surviving work, which attacks Origen's homily on the witch of Endor (1 Sam. 28), "was nevertheless a signature statement of Antioch's approach to biblical texts."[108]

Theodore of Mopsuestia (ca. 350–428)[109] joined a monastic community headed by Carterius and Diodore when he was about sixteen years old.[110] Diodore was "le véritable fondateur" of the Antiochene exegetical school[111] even if the scholar-priest Lucien (martyred in 312) was "l'initiateur" of the method of interpretation.[112] Diodore's pupils included John Chrysostom[113] (ca. 344–407) and Theodore. Later condemned, like Theodore, because of his association with Nestorius, sadly most of Diodore's commentaries have been lost. His only surviving manuscript is his *Commentary on the Psalms*.

---

107. Ibid., 223.

108. R. C. Hill, *Reading the Old Testament in Antioch*, Bible in Ancient Christianity 5 (Leiden: Brill, 2005), 3n7.

109. For a brief account of his life, see F. M. Young and A. Teal, *From Nicaea to Chalcedon: A Guide to the Literature and Its Background* (Grand Rapids: Baker Academic, 2010), 262–63. For an introduction to Theodore as exegete, see M. Simonetti, "Theodore of Mopsuestia (ca. 350–428)," in Kannengiesser, HPE 2:799–828.

110. On Diodore as exegete, see Kannengiesser, HPE 2:780–83.

111. Simonetti, "Theodore of Mopsuestia," 803.

112. J.-M. Olivier, *Diodori Tarsensis commentarii in Psalmos*, vol. 1, *Commentarius in Psalmos I-L*, CCSG 6 (Turnhout: Brepols, 1980), ciii.

113. On Chrysostom as exegete, see Kannengiesser, HPE 2:783–98.

Diodore was vigorously opposed to the allegorical approach. In a surviving fragment of his *Quaestiones* on the Octateuch, he declares, "We [in Antioch] far prefer τὸ ἱστορικόν to ἀλληγορία (as practiced in Alexandria)."[114] He says of his reading of the Psalter:

> We shall treat of it historically and literally and not stand in the way of a spiritual and more elevated insight. The historical sense, in fact, is not in opposition to the more elevated sense; on the contrary it proves to be the basis and foundation of the more elevated meanings. One thing alone is to be guarded against, however, never to let the discernment process be seen as an overthrow of the underlying sense, since this would no longer be discernment but allegory: what is arrived at in defiance of the content is not discernment but allegory.... Self-opinionated innovators in commenting on the divine Scripture, by contrast, who undermine and do violence to the historical sense, introduce allegory, not in the apostle's sense, but for their own vainglory making the readers substitute one thing for another—for example, by taking abyss as demons, a dragon as the devil, and the like (not to add folly to folly).[115]

Diodore's commentary on the Psalms is thus straightforward and literal. He begins by quoting 2 Timothy 3:16 and applies it to the Psalter, which "gives gentle and kindly instruction in righteousness to those willing to learn."[116] For Diodore, the Psalms provide moral and doctrinal instruction.[117] His emphasis on instruction is redolent of McCann's recent approach in *The Psalms as Torah*.

The Psalms are a vehicle for thanksgiving yet also a remedy to heal our wounds: "On encountering problems and troubles, we then come to our senses and apply ourselves when our wound of itself almost of its nature elicits the proper response."[118] In line with our privileging ecclesial reception of Scripture (see chap. 2 above), Diodore writes his commentary "in case the brethren at the time of singing the psalms be likely to be confused by the sentiments, or by failing to understand them give their minds to other pursuits. Instead, they should grasp the movement of thought and 'sing with understanding,' as the text says, from the depths of their mind and not superficially at the level of lips alone."[119]

---

114. R. C. Hill, Introduction to *Diodore of Tarsus: Commentary on Psalms 1–51* (Atlanta: SBL, 2005), xii.
115. Ibid., 4.
116. Ibid., 1.
117. Ibid., 2.
118. Ibid.
119. Ibid.

Diodore argues that Psalms 1 and 2 are not divided in the Hebrew, "being combined into one."[120] In this he anticipates the recent insight that 1 and 2 are together an introduction to the Psalter, but this is an approach he does not explore, reading them independently and Psalm 2 as christological. Intriguingly Diodore understands "law" (torah) in Psalm 1 as not only the written law but also the "innate natural law."[121] In Psalm 19 he says that the things of the visible creation "announce some pattern and cry aloud the order of the orderer and the folly of the notion of being self-made."[122] "The law of the LORD" in verse 7 "means that discerned in nature: what the written law does by teaching its intentions to those with a knowledge of writing, the law in nature does by teaching those with an understanding eye that there is a creator of visible realities."[123] Here one may quibble about parts of Diodore's exegesis, yet his recognition of the link between redemption and creation is perceptive and theologically fecund.[124]

In his *Catechetical Homilies*, Theodore says to prospective Christians, "Now is the time for me to say, 'Sing unto the Lord a new song, for he has done marvelous things.' Indeed a new song is required for new things, as we are dealing with the New Testament which God established for the human race through the Economy of our Lord Jesus Christ, when he abolished all old things and showed new things in their place."[125]

Theodore stresses the newness of the Christ event (chap. 3 above stresses its importance), and his awareness of eschatology and his doctrine of two ages "considerably modifies, if it does not quite remove, the then-current Platonic emphasis on escape from the world below to the world of spiritual realities in heaven! . . . Theodore also points to successive stages in the creative purposes of God, of a new creation anticipated in Christ and awaiting its final consummation."[126]

His sense of the overarching metanarrative of Scripture strengthens his emphasis on the concrete realities of the Bible; the Old Testament writings address their own situation; the New Testament proclaims a new, final act of God, which anticipates the consummation of God's purposes in the future. By

---

120. Ibid., 10.
121. Ibid., 5.
122. Ibid., 60.
123. Ibid., 62.
124. Cf. C. E. Gunton, in *Christ and Creation* (Eugene, OR: Wipf & Stock, 2005), using Irenaeus to foreground the vital theological link between redemption and creation. See also C. Seerveld, *Rainbows for a Fallen World: Aesthetic Life and Artistic Task* (Toronto: Tuppence, 2005).
125. Young and Teal, *From Nicaea to Chalcedon*, 261.
126. Ibid.

means of his doctrine of the two ages, Theodore criticized the tendency in his day to view the human person as a soul trapped in flesh by the fall. Instead, he drew attention to the Pauline distinction between humankind-in-Adam and humankind-in-Christ, between creation and new creation. As the image of God, Christ fulfills what Adam was meant to be.

For Theodore, the implication of his approach was that allegory was to be avoided[127] because it undermined this view of Scripture and, by finding Christ everywhere in the Old Testament, subverted the newness of the Christ event. Theodore affirmed typology but carefully distinguished a type from allegory: "For an allegory's meaning is derived not from within Scripture but from the imaginative speculations of the exegete."[128] Like the other Antiochenes, Theodore followed the canonical list of the Hebrew Bible rather than that of the LXX.[129] Theodore's literal-historical approach is quite clear in his extant commentaries. Theodore became bishop of Mopsuestia in 392, and his commentaries on the Bible were widely influential. Alas, his association with Nestorius resulted in his being condemned, and most of his writings—he appears to have commented on nearly all the books of the Bible—were destroyed. A limited number of his works remain extant in Syriac versions.[130]

Even as part of the Antiochene school, Theodore was an independent thinker. He argued that Job was based on a pagan story and excluded Song of Songs from the canon. Zaharopoulos notes of his work on Job, "For the first time in the history of the church a book of the Bible was expounded from the perspective of a critical method by a scholar."[131]

Augustine of Hippo[132]

Trained in rhetoric, "Augustine's creative contribution consisted in a deliberate synthesis of late antique rhetorical culture with the biblical hermeneutics already elaborated over several centuries inside the church community."[133] In

---

127. Theodore is less sympathetic to allegory than are Chrysostom and Theodoret, and he held a different view of the *imago Dei*. See F. G. McLeod, *The Roles of Christ's Humanity in Salvation: Insights from Theodore of Mopsuestia* (Washington, DC: Catholic University of America Press, 2005), 43.

128. Ibid., 49.

129. Ibid., 38.

130. Young and Teal, *From Nicaea to Chalcedon*, 263. See F. G. McLeod, *Theodore of Mopsuestia* (London: Routledge, 2009), for the most accessible current translation of his works.

131. D. Z. Zaharopoulos, *Theodore of Mopsuestia on the Bible* (New York: Paulist Press, 1989), 45–46.

132. For a useful overview of Augustine's biblical hermeneutic, see Kannengiesser, *HPE* 2:1149–1233.

133. Ibid., 2:1149.

his *De utilitate credenda*, Augustine (354–430) explains how to distinguish four senses of Scripture: historical (what happened), etiological (why it happened; *aetia* = cause), analogical (involving both Testaments), and allegorical (not literal but figurative). His major work on biblical interpretation is *De doctrina christiana*, started around 395, while he was writing his *Confessions*,[134] but only finished around 426/7, a few years before his death. This book explores the rules for interpreting Scripture, an approach that in the preface Augustine defends against those who appeal directly to the guidance of the Spirit and deplore human agency in helping one read Scripture. In the book Augustine's aim is to equip readers so that they can discover the truth *for themselves* in the Bible. Books 1–3 deal with the process of discovering the truth in Scripture, and book 4 is on presenting the discovered truth. Hermeneutics and homiletics are rightly held together.

Book 1 positions interpretation within the telos of Scripture:

> The fulfillment and end of the law . . . and all the divine scriptures is to love the thing which must be enjoyed and the thing which together with us can enjoy that thing. . . . So anyone who thinks that he has understood the divine scriptures or any part of them, but cannot by his understanding build up this double love of God and neighbor, has not yet succeeded in understanding them.[135]

Book 2 develops Augustine's hermeneutic from his understanding of *signs*.[136] A sign makes another thing come to mind; as written signs, Scripture is designed to make the things of God come to mind. "The aim of its readers is simply to find out the thoughts and wishes of those by whom it was written down and, through them, the will of God, which we believe these men followed as they spoke."[137] Thus fundamental to reading Scripture is approaching it via "the fear of the LORD" with a view toward learning his will.

Augustine positions interpretation (knowledge) within a six-part schema of ascent:

1. fear
2. holiness

---

134. Augustine has some 1,700 biblical references in his *Confessions*. On biblical hermeneutics and the *Confessions*, see Kannengiesser, HPE 2:1158–62.

135. Augustine, *DDC* (*De doctrina christiana*) 1.84–86, in Augustine, *On Christian Teaching*, trans. R. P. H. Green (Oxford: Oxford University Press, 1997).

136. See C. Kirwin, "Augustine's Philosophy of Language," in *Cambridge Companion to Augustine*, ed. E. Stump and N. Kretzmann (Cambridge: Cambridge University Press, 2001), 186–204. Augustine is influential in the history of semiotics.

137. Augustine, *DDC* 2.32. On the importance of authorial intention, see also ibid., 3.84.

3. **knowledge**
4. repentance
5. compassion
6. purification of the eye, by which God may be seen

The focus of interpretation seeking knowledge is the canon of Scripture.[138] "These are all the books in which those who fear God and are made docile by their holiness seek God's will."[139] One must first immerse oneself in the canonical books so as to become familiar with them. Then the clear passages should be studied, and only then the obscure ones. Meaning may be veiled by unknown or ambiguous signs. Language study is indispensable in clarifying texts: Latin speakers need Hebrew and Greek as well so they can have recourse to the originals.[140] It is intriguing, in light of his correspondence with Jerome, that Augustine stresses the importance of Hebrew.[141] Nevertheless he asserts that, "as far as the Old Testament is concerned, the authority of the Septuagint is supreme."[142]

In book 3 Augustine draws on his expertise in rhetoric to stress the importance of distinguishing between literal and figurative language in the Bible. We should not quickly conclude that the literal sense of a passage is problematic; if close consideration still leaves a passage unclear, we must read it in the light of the Rule of Faith.[143] Context, both literary and cultural, is also a vital element in interpreting a text. He establishes as a rule that, "generally speaking, . . . anything in the divine discourse that cannot be related either to good morals or to the true faith should be taken as figurative."[144]

By figurative, Augustine appears to refer to literary tropes such as irony, which he helpfully articulates. Book 2 concludes with his positive engagement with Tyconius's[145] *Book of Rules*.[146] Notable here is Tyconius's sixth rule, dealing with recapitulation: "Some passages are presented as if their contents follow in chronological order or in a continuous sequence, when in

138. For Augustine's contents of the canon, see ibid., 2.26–31.
139. Ibid., 2.30.
140. Ibid., 2.34.
141. See chap. 8 below.
142. Augustine, *DDC* 2.53.
143. Ibid., 3.3.
144. Ibid., 3.33.
145. Tyconius was an early pioneer in biblical hermeneutics. See H. Chadwick, "Tyconius and Augustine," in *Heresy and Orthodoxy in the Early Church*, ed. H. Chadwick (Aldershot, UK: Ashgate, 1991), 49–55.
146. On Augustine's engagement with Tyconius in *DDC*, see the essays in part 2 of *Augustine and the Bible*, ed. P. Bright (Notre Dame, IN: University of Notre Dame Press, 1999), 107–80.

fact the narrative covertly switches back to earlier matters which had been passed over." Genesis 2:8–9 is given as an example.[147]

De doctrina christiana is an extremely helpful introduction to biblical hermeneutics; noticeably absent are extreme examples of allegorization. Augustine's sophisticated hermeneutic indicates why his corpus of work on the Bible is so rich and helpful. Jeanrond argues that Augustine's influential hermeneutic represents a synthesis of the allegorical and literal approaches.[148] Nevertheless, as his six-part schema indicates and as some of his interpretation confirms, his neoplatonism regularly led him in the direction of unhelpful allegorization.

The gravitational pull of Platonism is always upward; for example, in his work *On the Morals of the Catholic Church* (*De moribus ecclesiae catholicae*), Augustine demonstrates a reading of Ecclesiastes similar to that of Origen and Jerome:

> To this New Testament authority, requiring us not to love anything in this world, . . . to this authority, then, if I seek for a parallel passage in the Old Testament, I find several; but there is one book of Solomon, called Ecclesiastes, which at great length brings all earthly things into utter contempt. The book begins thus: "Vanity of the vain, says the Preacher, vanity of the vain; all is vanity. What profit has a man of all his labor which he takes under the sun?" [Eccles. 1:2–3] If all these words are considered, weighed, and thoroughly examined, many things are found of essential importance to those who seek to flee from the world and to take shelter in God; but this requires time and our discourse hastens on to other topics. But, after this beginning, he goes on to show in detail that the vain are those who are deceived by things of this sort; and he calls this which deceives them vanity—not that God did not create those things, but because men choose to subject themselves by their sins to those things, which the divine law has made subject to them in well-doing. For when you consider things beneath yourself to be admirable and desirable, what is this but to be cheated and misled by unreal goods? The man, then, who is temperate in such mortal and transient things has his rule of life confirmed by both Testaments, that he should love none of these things, nor think them desirable for their own sakes, but should use them as far as is required for the purposes and duties of life, with the moderation of an employer instead of the ardor of a lover. These remarks on temperance

---

147. Augustine, *DDC* 3.123–25. Recapitulation goes back to Aristotle. Its significance in narrative analysis has been stressed by P. Ricoeur, "Narrative Time," *Critical Inquiry* 7/1 (1980): 169–90, e.g., and it has major implications for biblical interpretation.

148. W. G. Jeanrond, *Theological Hermeneutics: Development and Significance* (London: SCM, 1994), 22.

are few in proportion to the greatness of the theme, but perhaps too many in view of the task on hand.[149]

Wisdom is central to Augustine's thought, but it is a neoplatonic view of wisdom (*sapientia*), focused upward and carefully distinguished from earthly knowledge (*scientia*).[150] Not surprisingly, therefore, allegory plays a strong role in Augustine's reading of the Proverbs 31 woman, as we will see below.

The Problem with Allegory

Amid the renaissance of theological interpretation, scholars have naturally turned to the Christian tradition of biblical interpretation to find resources for today. This is as it should be, provided we do not absolutize certain stages of the tradition or ignore the very real progress made over the centuries, not least in modern times. This is not for a moment to uncritically espouse a modern doctrine of progress,[151] but it is to insist that the philosophical paradigms shaping different stages in the tradition need careful evaluation, and that progress *has been made* over the centuries and not least during the Reformation period. Across the range of ecclesiastical confessions, there is a tendency now for some scholars to defend the *quadriga* (see below) as a viable approach to biblical interpretation. The test for such reappropriation must be historical examination of the extent to which such fourfold readings allowed the Scriptures to be heard truly and powerfully in their contexts. Is, as de Lubac claimed, allegory the reading of the Old Testament from the perspective of the New? Or does it impose an unhelpful, neoplatonic framework on Scripture? The proof of the pudding will be in the eating, and we have already suggested above that in this task of interpretation, allegory does not deliver. Example after example could be foregrounded; suffice it to conclude this section with further examples.

Maximus the Confessor on Jonah

In my book on place, *Where Mortals Dwell*, I identify Maximus as a resource for recovering a theology of place. Such a positive assessment cannot be made of his reading of Jonah.[152] Maximus finds himself unable to make

---

149. Augustine, *On the Morals of the Catholic Church* 39, http://www.newadvent.org/fathers/.
150. See esp. Augustine, *De Trinitate* (e.g., book XII, chap. 4).
151. See D. Bebbington, *Patterns in History: A Christian Perspective on Historical Thought* (Leicester, UK: Inter-Varsity, 1979; reprint, Leicester, UK: Apollos, 1990), 68–91.
152. CCSG 22:187–241.

sense of the expression in Jonah 4:11, according to which many Ninevites "do not know their right hand from their left." He finds nothing edifying in the literal sense since he cannot imagine a man of sound mind who does not know his right hand from his left. Scripture lends itself to many meanings[153] by virtue of "the potency of the Hebrew language,"[154] so the interpreter must therefore find the appropriate spiritual reading. For Maximus the myriad Ninevites turns out to be the church, which has abandoned vainglory in its achievements (the right hand) and intemperance in shameful passions (the left hand)! A strong Platonic tendency manifests itself in his explication that a person who knows neither the right nor left hand is one who has "gone beyond the principles of time and nature and passed over to the magnificence of eternal and noetic realities."[155] "Such a mind, having been drawn toward God and away from all created beings, knows none of the *logoi* [reasons] of the things from which it has withdrawn; in its ineffable vision it knows only that Logos whom it approaches by grace."[156]

Typology runs rampant in his reading, facilitated (inter alia) by eight translations of Jonah's name. Jonah becomes a type of Adam, of our shared humanity, of Christ, of prophetic grace, and of the ungrateful Jews, who are jealous of God's grace. Joppa is a figure of paradise, and humankind is always fleeing Joppa, as does Jonah! As Adam, when he sinned, was tossed from paradise into this world, so our human nature is dragged down into the sea of sin and borne along in the chaos of material things. The whale is the devil. The cattle and oxen symbolize different categories of sinners.

> In turn we may interpret the *king* of that *city*, or soul, as the mind [νοῦς] and its captains as the soul's innate faculties. The *men*, then, signify impassioned thoughts, the *cattle* movements of the concupiscible faculty in relation to the body, the *oxen* covetous functions of the irascible faculty toward material objects, and the *sheep* the attempts of the senses to grasp sensible objects without intelligent reflection.[157]

And so it continues!

---

153. In *Ambigua* 37 (PG 91:1293A–1296D), Maximus identifies ten progressive means of discerning the spiritual meaning of things in Scripture. See P. M. Blowers, "The World in the Mirror of Holy Scripture: Maximus the Confessor's Short Hermeneutical Treatise in *Ambiguum ad Joannem 37*," in *In Dominico Eloquio—In Lordly Eloquence: Essays on Patristic Exegesis in Honor of Robert Louis Wilken*, ed. P. M. Blowers et al. (Grand Rapids: Eerdmans, 2002), 408–26.
154. Note Maximus's awareness of the LXX as a *translation*.
155. Maximus the Confessor, *On the Cosmic Mystery of Jesus Christ*, Popular Patristics 25 (Crestwood, NY: St. Vladimir's Seminary Press, 2003), 156.
156. Ibid., 158.
157. Ibid., 155.

It is hard to see how this is a helpful development from the literal sense of Jonah. In Maximus's hands the text becomes a wax nose, which can be twisted in a host of directions simultaneously while obscuring the powerful narrative of the book. Far from such allegory unlocking the spiritual depths of this text, it obscures them in a way that a rich, narrative reading would not. This type of allegory is eisegesis, not exegesis.

Augustine and the Proverbs 31 Woman

Edmund Hill rightly observes that "Augustine . . . treats the valiant woman throughout as a figure of the Church, and so is involved all the time in an allegorical interpretation of the text."[158] The literal sense is not altogether lost but is utterly subordinated to the identification of the woman with the church. The Spirit is at work with the joys it has conceived from God, and Augustine asks his audience to provide his sermon "with a nest among you" to receive the Word.[159]

The woman is the church, and the precious stones (Prov. 31:10) are the saints. The "wool and flax" of verse 13 are respectively something of the flesh (public) and something of the spirit (private). Integrality between the two is essential in the Christian life. Augustine's Latin version reads verse 22 as "She has made double cloaks for her husband," and he reads the double cloaks as confession of Christ as both God and man. On verse 24, Augustine asks why the woman sells the linen garments. He argues that the sale is gratuitous; she sells them for nothing, and he relates her garments to the waters of Isaiah 55:1, which are bought without money.

Clearly this is a strong allegorization of the ending of Proverbs. It obscures this passage, which is a powerful climax to the book of Proverbs, with its vision of wisdom incarnate in the earthly life of this valiant woman. The details mentioned above have no basis in the literal sense of the text and are controlled only by Augustine's theology and imagination. The great danger of neoplatonism is its lack of a robust view of creation and history; thus it is not by chance that such passages embodying a rich doctrine of creation are allegorized to refer to the church and "spiritual" matters. If this is what is advocated by allegorization, then it cannot help us today in opening up the Scriptures as the Word of God.

In my opinion Daniélou is thus right in arguing for a careful distinction between typology and allegory.[160] This may be a recent distinction, but it has

---

158. Augustine, *Sermons on the Old Testament, 20–50*, part 3 in *The Works of Saint Augustine: A Translation for the 21st Century*, trans. and annotated by E. Hill (Hyde Park, NY: New City, 1990), 2:201–2.

159. Ibid., 37.1.

160. See J. Daniélou, *From Shadows to Reality: Studies in the Biblical Typology of the Fathers* (Westminster, MD: Newman, 1960).

its basis in the difference between the Alexandrian and Antiochene schools. Typology emerges from the relationship between the two Testaments and centers in Christ as the fulfillment of the Old Testament. Allegory emerges from a flattening of the Scriptures into an atemporal whole, in which the same truth is to be found throughout. In this it reveals the vertical dualism of Platonism rather than the eschatological vision of Scripture, in which the new age has already broken into the old.

Medieval Biblical Interpretation

It is impossible to adduce a specific date for the beginning of the Middle Ages, but 529 lends itself as a date of symbolic significance for biblical interpretation. In this year the Christian emperor Justinian closed the Platonic academy in Athens, and St. Benedict established Monte Cassino, the first Benedictine abbey. "Here, then, we find something very much like a visible boundary where a dying and a new-born age touch one another."[161] Augustine operated completely within the *Imperium Romanum*, but in the Middle Ages the Vandals penetrated this ancient world from the north. "In terms of place, as well, the center of intellectual life shifted."[162] Instead of Athens, Antioch, Alexandria, and Carthage, the center now shifts to the court of Theodoric (Ravenna, Verona, Paris), the court of Charlemagne, and the cities of Canterbury, Paris, Oxford, and Cologne. Here Boethius is a symbolic figure.[163] He turned his attention to the new elements of the population and the transmission of the great body of existing thought. Central to Boethius's work is the relationship between faith and reason, a theme that would become ever more important as the Middle Ages developed.

Augustine is thus at the overlap of the border between the ancient and medieval worlds.[164] Not surprisingly, his work *De doctrina christiana* was very influential; indeed, it was the foundational document for medieval interpretation. There is significant continuity between patristic and medieval exegesis. Scripture was understood to be the living Word of the risen Christ, and especially in early medieval exegesis—roughly from Gregory I (pope, 590–604) to the twelfth century—it was assumed that Scripture could be understood correctly only by those who were living its realities. Scripture

---

161. J. Pieper, *Scholasticism: Personalities and Problems of Medieval Philosophy* (South Bend, IN: St. Augustine's Press, 2001), 17.
162. Ibid., 21.
163. Ibid., 25–34.
164. See R. A. Norris Jr., "Augustine and the Close of the Ancient Period," in Hauser and Watson, *History of Biblical Interpretation*, 1:380–408.

was understood as a unity, and it was read as an extended and continuing story that encompassed those living in the medieval period.[165] This did not mean that the individuality of books was ignored; Athanasius, for example, had attended to both the differences between books and their unity as one Scripture, and such an awareness continued on.[166]

Early Medieval Interpretation

Biblical interpretation took place in three major contexts in this period: in the liturgy as homilies, in the monastic context, and in the schools. Homilies focused on the lectionary readings, an effect of which was to attend to connections between passages rather than a passage in its literary context. "This process of interpreting passages in relation to one another was founded on, and continued to promote, the assumption that all the Scriptures were essentially one."[167] The assumption of the unity of Scripture is healthy, but it is not hard to see how this, combined with the allegorical method, would enhance the flattening of the text (to which we referred above). Within the monasteries, liturgy dominated, with the Psalms front and center. *Lectio sacra* was carefully cultivated in the monasteries, and attention given to the moral level of interpretation in particular, so as to enhance the spirituality of the monks. As the early medieval period developed, interpretation was more and more practiced in the schools. It was here that the scholastic approach would be honed and developed in a direction different and more academic than the practice of the monasteries.

The patristic legacy served as both resource and norm for medieval interpretation, not least in relation to the method of fourfold interpretation.[168] The four are commonly listed as the literal sense (what happened), the allegorical sense (what one ought to believe), the moral sense (what one ought to do), and the anagogical sense (what one must strive for). Justification for the fourfold method (quadriga) of interpretation was found in the major Latin fathers. In the preface to his commentary on the Psalms, Cassiodorus lists them, and Augustine provides brief definitions of each in his *De utilitate credendi* and in his *De Genesi ad litteram*.[169]

---

165. M. A. Mayeski, "Early Medieval Exegesis: Gregory I to the Twelfth Century," in Hauser and Watson, *History of Biblical Interpretation*, 2:87.

166. See J. D. Ernest, *The Bible in Athanasius of Alexandria*, The Bible in Ancient Christianity 2 (Leiden: Brill, 2004).

167. Mayeski, "Early Medieval Exegesis," 91.

168. See H. de Lubac, *Exégèse médiévale: Les quatre sens de l'Écriture*, part 2.1–2 (Paris: Aubier, 1961–64).

169. In section 2.5 of his *Unfinished Literal Commentary on Genesis* in Augustine, *On Genesis*, trans. E. Hill (Hyde Park, NY: New City, 2002), 116, he states:

In the latter he declares:

> All divine scripture is twofold, . . . which are also said to be the two testaments. In all the holy books, however, one ought to note what eternal realities are there suggested, what deeds are recounted, what future events foretold, what actions commanded or advised. So then, in accounts of things done, what one asks is whether they are all to be taken as only having a figurative meaning, or whether they are also to be asserted and defended as a faithful account of what actually happened. No Christian, I mean, will have the nerve to say that they should not be taken in a figurative sense, if he pays attention to what the apostle says: *All these things, however, happened among them in figure* [1 Cor. 10:11], and to his commending that is written in Genesis, *And they shall be two in one flesh* [Gen. 2:24], *as a great sacrament in Christ and in the Church* (Eph 5:32).[170]

As Hill notes of this passage, Augustine's real twofold concern is with that between the figurative and the literal. "His giving priority to the figurative or spiritual meaning is in line with the practice of most of the Fathers, from Origen onward, but is the exact opposite, of course, of contemporary exegetical orthodoxy today—and indeed of the line Augustine is taking in this work."[171] We have mentioned above how helpful *De doctrina christiana* is in using rhetoric to develop a sophisticated approach to the literary nature of Scripture. The problem with allegory, however, is that it too easily obscures and distorts the plain sense of Scripture, and the potential for this is evident in the above quote from Augustine. Augustine asserts that the figurative/allegorical meaning is always present, but the literal may not be. Priority is given to the figurative sense and to the discovery of eternal realities. Yet under the influence of Plotinus and his neoplatonism, "eternal realities" easily becomes not the two ages of the two Testaments but a vertical focus on the incorporeal realm. The rough ground[172] of Scripture then becomes flattened out so that the eternal realities are equally discoverable throughout the Bible. This legacy was not

---

Four ways of expounding the law have been laid down by some scripture commentators, which can be named in words derived from Greek, while they need further definition and explanation in plain Latin; they are the way of history, the way of allegory, the way of analogy, the way of aetiology. History is when things done by God or man are recounted; allegory when they are understood as being said figuratively; analogy, when the harmony of the old and new covenants is being demonstrated; aetiology, when the causes of the things that have been said and done are presented.

170. Augustine, *The Literal Meaning of Genesis 1.1*, in Hill, *On Genesis*, 168, with original emphasis.

171. Augustine, in Hill, *On Genesis*, 168n1.

172. Here I allude here to the late Wittgenstein's return to the rough ground—his words—of ordinary language after his earlier embrace of logical positivism.

helpful in the medieval period: "Medieval exegetes were unanimous in their conviction that the extended sense (however they may have subdivided it) was the superior meaning, and determining it was the exegete's primary task."[173]

Gregory the Great (540–604)

As a monk, diplomat, scholar, and bishop of Rome, Gregory I is the first of the early medieval exegetes and a fountainhead for subsequent interpretation. While papal *apocrisiarius* (legate) in Constantinople, Gregory began his *Expositio in Librum Job, sive Moralium libri xxv* in response to requests from monks in Constantinople.[174] Gregory consistently explained the process of interpreting Scripture according to multiple senses even as he modeled this approach. His *Magna moralia* on Job provides us with a good insight into his hermeneutic.

Gregory divides his commentary into historical, allegorical, and moral sections. He alerts the reader to the fact that

> there are some parts, which we go through in a historical exposition, some we trace out in allegory upon an investigation of the typical meaning, some we open in the lessons of moral teaching alone, allegorically conveyed, while there are some few which, with more particular care, we search out in all these ways together, exploring them in a threefold method. For first, we lay the historical foundations; next, by pursuing the typical sense, we erect a fabric of the mind to be a stronghold of faith; and moreover as the last step, by the grace of moral instruction, we, as it were, clothe the edifice with an overcast of colouring.... Yet it sometimes happens that we neglect to interpret the plain words of the historical account, that we may not be too long in coming to the hidden senses, and sometimes they cannot be understood according to the letter, because when taken superficially, they convey no sort of instruction to the reader, but only engender error; for here, for instance, ... under the pressure of calamities he exclaims, *So that my soul chooseth strangling, and death rather than life.* [Job 7:15] Now who that is in his right senses could believe that a man of so high praise, who in a word, we know, received from the Judge of that which is within the reward of the virtue of patience, settled amidst his afflictions to finish his life by strangling?[175]

Gregory takes the literal/historical sense seriously but prefers the spiritual senses, as is evident in the above quote. Similarly on Job 28:12–15, he asserts:

173. Mayeski, "Early Medieval Exegesis," 93.
174. Gregory I also wrote on Ezekiel, possibly on the Song of Songs, as well as the *Cura Pastoralis* (ca. 590).
175. Gregory the Great, *Magna moralia* 1.3.

"But the holy man being full of mystical ideas sends us on for the making out other things, so that we should look for not wisdom created, but Wisdom creating; for except in those words we search the secret depths of allegory, surely those things that follow are utterly deserving of disregard, if they be estimated according to the historical narration alone."[176]

The poem in Job 28 is a wonderful passage dealing with the source of wisdom. However, Gregory falsely sets "wisdom created" against "wisdom creating." The genius of Old Testament wisdom is that "The LORD by wisdom founded the earth" (Prov. 3:19), thereby holding inseparably together wisdom's source in God and its embodiment in the creation (cf. Prov. 8:22–31).

Gregory's approach to Job 7:15 is typical of his commentary as a whole and indicates the extent to which his theology controls his interpretation, even at the literal level. Since Gregory finds it unimaginable that Job would stoop to such depths in his experience, he finds a way to mute the agony and directness of Job in his response to his sufferings. Thus he quite remarkably reads Job's laments as the expression of a godly desire for the things above in comparison with transitory, earthly life.

> When the minds of the elect perceive that all things transitory are nought, they seek out which be the things for which they were created, and whereas nothing suffices to the satisfying them out of God, thought itself, being wearied in them by the effort of the search, finds rest in the hope and contemplation of its Creator, longs to have a place among the citizens above; and each one of them, while yet in the body an inhabitant of the world, in mind already soars beyond the world, bewails the weariness of exile which he endures, and with the ceaseless incitements of love urges himself on to the country on high.[177]

In chapter 3, Job curses the day he was born. Gregory asks, "What then is it to curse the day of his birth, but to say plainly, 'May the day of change perish, and the light of eternity burst forth?'"[178]

All the above examples indicate the extent to which Gregory's theology, shaped by neoplatonism, influences his reading of Job even at the literal level. The gravitational pull is always upward, toward the eternal and unchangeable. In Old Testament wisdom books like Job, this inevitably distorts the reading, since it must subvert the strong doctrine of creation in such books. It is not surprising, therefore, that Gregory finds the further levels of meaning most attractive since it is there that one penetrates to the spiritual meaning of the text.

176. Ibid., 18.61.
177. Ibid., 3.34.
178. Ibid., 4.4.

In his allegorical level of interpretation of Job, Gregory understands Job to represent both Christ and the church. Etymology and allegory run riot in his interpretation. Job's seven sons (1:2) represent the apostles going forth to preach the gospel. His three daughters are the weaker multitude of the faithful. The seven thousand sheep represent some men's perfect innocence; the three thousand camels the crooked defectiveness of gentiles coming to fullness of faith. The east (1:3) represents our redeemer, who is the "greatest" because he is both God and man. Such allegory is also central to Gregory's moral interpretation.

And so it continues. Such fanciful interpretation detracts from the literary text before us, and it is very difficult to see how this style of interpretation could be a model for us today. As with Augustine and Maximus (above), this sort of allegorization stems from a neoplatonic theology and is an obstacle to hearing the true spiritual sense present in the plain meaning of the text.

Gregory's influence was huge, and his style of interpretation dominates the early medieval period. Bede (673–735) wrote commentaries on Mark, Luke, Acts, the General Epistles, and Revelation, as well as on various Old Testament books and sections. His hermeneutic is thoroughly patristic, and he normally divides his commentaries and homilies into two parts: historical and mystical. However, Bede attends more closely than Gregory to the literal/historical meaning of the text, and he also has an interest in textual criticism, demonstrated most clearly in his *Retractions* on Acts. De Lubac regards Bede as the first to develop a fully articulated account of the fourfold sense of Scripture.[179] His massive three-volume work on the Jewish sanctuaries is unique among patristic works: *De tabernaculo* on the tabernacle in Exodus 24:12–30:31, his *De templo* on Solomon's temple in 1 Kings 5:1–7:51, and his *In Ezram et Neemiam* on the postexilic construction of the second temple.[180] *On Ezra and Nehemiah* is the first and only extant, complete commentary on Ezra-Nehemiah in the Middle Ages.[181] "Indeed, the variety of exegetical problems addressed in *On Ezra and Nehemiah*, from considering variant readings to explaining the history and topography to unfolding the allegory, reveal Bede to be a versatile exegete, sensitive to the multifaceted exigencies of scriptural interpretation."[182]

---

179. H. de Lubac, *Medieval Exegesis: The Four Senses of Scripture* (Grand Rapids: Eerdmans, 2000), 1:91–93.

180. See Liverpool University Press's Translated Texts for Historians: Bede, *On the Tabernacle*, trans. A. G. Holder (1994); *On the Temple*, trans. S. Connolly (1996); *On Ezra and Nehemiah*, trans. S. DeGregorio (2006).

181. S. DeGregorio, introduction to *Bede: On Ezra and Nehemiah*, xv. Bede's commentary on Tobit is also the first sustained commentary on this book: in *Bede: A Biblical Miscellany*, trans. W. T. Foley and A. G. Holder, Translated Texts for Historians (Liverpool: Liverpool University Press, 1999), 53–79. Bede reads Tobit as an allegory of Christ and the church.

182. DeGregorio, introduction to *Bede: On Ezra and Nehemiah*, xxi–xxii. On the content of Bede's commentary, see xxv–xxxvi.

Carolingian Schools

The Carolingian schools flourished in the period during which Charlemagne and his descendents ruled a united Francia (ca. 785–850). These schools did not produce the sort of memorable exegesis that came from Gregory and Bede, yet their exegesis was formative and foundational for subsequent interpretation. With his *Admonitio generalis*, published in 789, Charlemagne sought to establish schools throughout the empire, thereby laying the basis for major intellectual advances and the emergence of scholasticism.

Alcuin of Northumberland (fl. 785) developed the structure of the curriculum for the schools in his *De vere philosophia*. His program of the liberal arts emerged from his neoplatonic speculation about knowledge. "He transforms Augustine, insisting that it is through Scripture that we grasp the underlying nature of knowledge, not the other way around. . . . Biblical exegesis became, then, the hermeneutical key by which all knowledge was accurately situated and understood, not just the appropriate teleology for a liberal education."[183] Alcuin stressed grammar and dialectic in relation to exegesis and thereby promoted the historical/literal sense. His translation of the pseudo-Augustinian *De decem categoriis* revived interest in Aristotle's logic and was influential on the school of Auxerre (scholars at the monastery of Auxerre, ca. 835–893), which applied the "old logic" fruitfully to biblical studies.

The archbishop of Mainz, Rabanus Maurus (ca. 780–856), developed a major initiative in biblical education in order to evangelize and deepen the faith in his diocese. In the process he wrote commentaries on most of the books of the Bible. Inter alia, he developed Bede's work on 1 and 2 Kings. Mayeski reports:

> Carolingian scholars laid down the major lines along which medieval exegesis would further develop: an assumption that the historical/literal meaning of the text was only a foundation to its more important spiritual meaning, an emphasis on grammar and dialectic as the tools used to unlock all levels of scriptural meaning, the critical use of the patristic sources vis-à-vis the contemporary questions, and consultation with Jewish scholars.[184]

School Glosses and Scholasticism

By the middle of the eleventh century, two significant trends emerged in the schools: the development of the *Glossa ordinaria*, whose origin Smalley

---

183. Mayeski, "Early Medieval Exegesis," 98. See J. Marenbon, *From the Circle of Alcuin to the School of Auxerre: Logic, Theology, and Philosophy in the Early Middle Ages* (Cambridge: Cambridge University Press, 1981).

184. Mayeski, "Early Medieval Exegesis," 100.

traces to Berengar of Tours (d. 1088), Drogo of Paris, and Lanfranc of Bec[185] (d. 1089),[186] and the directing of exegesis toward theology under philosophical influence. The gloss was a school text that consisted of a manuscript with lecturer's notes written in the margins or between lines. Exegetes developed their appropriation of Boethian dialectic into a tool to speculate about the shape of the natural world. They began to distinguish between two different worlds behind natural phenomena: spiritual realities of which natural phenomena were a symbol, and the logical aspects of the natural order. Biblical exegesis could illuminate the first, but the latter required theological speculation. This separation set the stage for scholasticism and was to have dire consequences for biblical interpretation and theology. The *quaestio* part continued to develop and eventually became separated from the text it was commenting on, becoming a compilation in its own right, with its own glosses. Thus was born Peter Lombard's (1100–1160) *Book of the Sentences*, which became the primary text for theological study, replacing the combined tool of biblical text and commentary.

Victorines

The Victorines refers to several generations of scholars at the Abbey of St. Victor, founded in 1110 at Paris. Hugh (1096–1141), Richard (d. 1173), and Andrew (d. 1175) of St. Victor sought to return biblical interpretation to its roots in *lectio sacra*. Intriguingly, in the process they placed great emphasis on the historical/literal sense of Scripture. Hugh clearly states that the intended meaning of the author must guide the exegete even in selecting from patristic writings.[187] Andrew demonstrated almost no interest in the spiritual sense and provides the most thorough historical exegesis of the early medieval period.

The Cistercian School

This school represents a full flowering of *lectio sacra* with such luminaries as Bernard of Clairvaux (1090–1153), Aelred of Rievaulx (1109–67), Isaac of Stella (ca. 1100–1178), and William of Thierry (ca. 1075/80–1148). In his brilliant work *The Love of Learning and the Desire for God*, Jean Leclercq

---

185. Lanfranc's work on the Pauline Epistles was original in his search for the dialectical structure of his argument. See M. Gibson, "Lanfranc's Commentary on the Pauline Epistles," *JTS* 22 (1971): 86–112.

186. See B. Smalley, *The Study of the Bible in the Middle Ages*, 3rd ed. (Oxford: Blackwell, 1983); cf. K. Walsh and D. Wood, eds., *The Bible in the Medieval World: Essays in Memory of Beryl Smalley*, Studies in Church History, Subsidia 4 (Oxford: Blackwell, 1985).

187. Smalley, *Bible in the Middle Ages*, 94–95.

examines these exegetes as an example of monastic interpretation in comparison to that of the schools.

Scholasticism[188]

Scholasticism flourished in the emergent universities—by 1500 at least seventy-five had been founded—although it was also embodied in a multitude of widely dispersed schools. Scholasticism was "above all an unprecedented process of learning, a scholarly enterprise of enormous proportions that went on for several centuries."[189] The Bible and Peter Lombard's *Four Books of Sentences* were the standard textbooks in theology faculties. Biblical study was central to scholasticism; when John Colet lectured on Paul's Epistles in Oxford and then in St. Paul's Cathedral, and when Luther lectured on the Bible at the University of Wittenberg, both in the sixteenth century, it was the content of their lectures that was innovative and not the fact that they lectured on the Bible.[190] The *Ordinary Gloss* exercised a major influence, and many other forms of biblical commentary appeared. In the early thirteenth century the running commentary, or *postilla*, made its appearance and was used by the greatest scholastic commentators, such as Bonaventure and Aquinas.[191]

Tradition dominated medieval interpretation of Scripture, and so it is not surprising that allegorical interpretation characterizes much medieval exegesis, in which the fourfold meaning was maintained.[192] However, just as the early Christians were influenced by secular methods in their reading of Scripture, so too were theologians in the Middle Ages; toward the end of the Middle Ages, this led to a renewed interest in the literal sense. Ocker argues that "in Scholasticism, divine revelation was increasingly associated with the Bible's

---

188. For an excellent introduction to scholasticism, see Pieper, *Scholasticism*.
189. Ibid., 23.
190. C. Ocker, "Scholastic Interpretation of the Bible," in Hauser and Watson, *History of Biblical Interpretation*, 2:256.
191. On the significance of the *postilla*, see C. Ocker, *Biblical Poetics before Humanism and Reformation* (Cambridge: Cambridge University Press, 2002), 12–13; on the development of exegetical tools at the Dominican school, see M. M. Mulchahey, *"First the Bow Is Bent in Study": Dominican Education before 1350* (Toronto: Pontifical Institute of Medieval Studies, 1998), 485–526.
192. On the interpretation of the Bible in the Middle Ages, see G. W. H. Lampe, ed., *The Cambridge History of the Bible*, vol. 2, *The West from the Fathers to the Reformation* (Cambridge: Cambridge University Press, 1969); Smalley, *Bible in the Middle Ages*; H. Brinkmann, *Mittelalterliche Hermeneutik* (Tübingen: Niemeyer, 1980); J. K. Farge, *Orthodoxy and Reform in Early Reformation France: The Faculty of Theology of Paris, 1500–1543* (Leiden: Brill, 1985). On the fourfold meaning see Ocker, "Scholastic Interpretation," 264–66.

literal sense, without really historicizing the literal sense. The ambition was to recognize the past in the present, and vice versa, while reading."[193]

Smalley, for example, points out that for theologians in the medieval schools, the rediscovery of Aristotle's *Politics* led to a renewed interest in politics and ethics,[194] and thus to a fresh examination of the Old Testament Wisdom literature, which shared these interests.[195] The result was an increased output of commentaries on all the wisdom books in the thirteenth century. The neoplatonic influence mediated by Augustine and Jerome privileged the spiritual reading, yet the influence of the rediscovery of Aristotle favored the literal reading.[196]

Bonaventure

The renewed emphasis on the literal meaning is evident in Bonaventure's (1221–74) exegesis. Karris notes that "the major reason for the contemporaneity of Bonaventure's interpretations is that they are rooted in the literal sense."[197] There are three works in which Bonaventure systematically articulates his approach to Scripture: his *Breviloquium*, the *De reductione atrium ad theologiam*, and the *Collationes in Hexameron*.[198] Scripture emerged through the work of the trinitarian God, and "Faith in Christ is the light, portal, and foundation of the proper understanding of the Scriptures."[199] Importantly, Bonaventure situates Scripture in relation to creation; since the fall, the book of Scripture became necessary so that humankind can discern the proper order of things in creation and thus be led to glorify and praise God. As is common among the scholastics, neoplatonic influence on Bonaventure is evident in his stress on *exitus* and *reditus*; everything emanates from God and returns to God. Knowledge is acquired through contemplation of the threefold Word: the *Verbum increatum*, through whom all is created; the *Verbum incarnatum*, through whom everything is restored; and the *Verbum inspiratum*, through whom all

---

193. Ocker, "Scholastic Interpretation," 271.
194. Smalley, *Bible in the Middle Ages*, xxxi. Cf. B. Smalley, *Medieval Exegesis of Wisdom Literature: Essays by Beryl Smalley*, ed. R. E. Murphy (Atlanta: Scholars Press, 1986).
195. See Smalley, *Bible in the Middle Ages*, 308–28.
196. See Ocker, "Scholastic Interpretation," 266–67, who claims that Aquinas's philosophy of language strengthened the focus on the literal sense. On Aquinas's philosophy of language, see Y. Delegue, *Les machines du sens: Fragments d'une sémiologie médiévale* (Paris: Archives du Commentaire, 1987).
197. R. J. Karris, introduction to *St. Bonaventure's Commentary on the Gospel of Luke, Chapters 1–8*, trans. R. J. Karris with notes, Works of St. Bonaventure 8.1 (St. Bonaventure, NY: Franciscan Institute Publications, 2001), viii.
198. See T. Reist, *Saint Bonaventure as a Biblical Commentator: A Translation and Analysis of His Commentary on Luke XVIII, 34–XIX, 42* (Lanham, MD: University Press of America, 1985), 29–46.
199. Ibid., 31.

things are revealed. Although Bonaventure affirms and practices the fourfold meaning of Scripture, he insists on the literal as foundational: "For him the literal sense of Scripture is decisive.... This literal meaning is the only way Scripture may be used as an 'authority' to ground theological arguments."[200]

Bonaventure's work is saturated with Scripture, and he uses the image of a zither to illuminate his approach. Scripture is like a single zither, and harmony is produced by the working of the strings in union with one another. "In brief, in his commentary on St. Luke's Gospel, Bonaventure is playing a single zither and plucking on hundreds of biblical strings at the same time."[201]

Bonaventure's lengthy commentary on Luke was written during his time in Paris in 1248–50, when he was responsible for offering literal commentary on the Bible. Robert Karris, himself a Lukan expert, has written extensively on Bonaventure and not least in comparison to contemporary interpretation of Luke.[202] On Luke 8:22–25, Jesus's stilling of the storm, Karris shows that Bonaventure's reading is original; unlike Ambrose, Bede, and Hugh of St. Cher, Bonaventure focuses extensively on the literal interpretation. Karris then compares Bonaventure's reading to those of four contemporary scholars: Joel Green, C. F. Evans, Joseph Fitzmyer, and John Nolland.[203] Karris finds Bonaventure's reading to fit well with all four and to be particularly close to that of Nolland. Bonaventure is "contemporary" in his use of the Old Testament to illuminate the passage.

In his postil on Ecclesiastes, Bonaventure exploits the possibilities in the literal sense that Guerric had opened up as a result of the growing influence of Aristotle.[204] He reads Ecclesiastes as teaching contempt for the world, but makes more use of speculative philosophy to do so. Bonaventure expounds his favorite theme: wisdom as the means to sanctification. He discusses contempt of the world; in an effort to explain how the world can be regarded as vanity, he compares the world to a wedding ring. The wife must regard the ring as nothing relative to her love for her husband, and our attitude to the world must be the same.

In my opinion it is this renewed attention to the literal sense that facilitated the production of the finest commentaries of the medieval era. This is evident in the writings of the colossus of the medieval era, Thomas Aquinas.

---

200. D. Monti, "Bonaventure's Use of 'The Divine Word' in Academic Theology," in *That Others May Know and Love: Essays in Honor of Zachary Hayes, OFM, Franciscan, Educator, Scholar*, ed. M. F. Cusato and F. E. Coughlin (New York: Franciscan Institute, 1997), 87.

201. Karris, introduction to *St. Bonaventure's Commentary*, xxii.

202. R. J. Karris, *Prayer and the New Testament* (New York: Crossroad, 2000); idem, "Luke 8:26–39: Jesus, the Pigs, and Human Transformation," *New Theological Review* 4, no. 3 (1991): 39–51; idem, "Bonaventure and Talbert on Luke 8:26–39: Christology, Discipleship, and Evangelization," *Perspectives in Religious Studies* 28 (2001): 57–66.

203. Karris, introduction to *St. Bonaventure's Commentary*, xxvii–xxxii.

204. See Smalley, *Bible in the Middle Ages*, 292–308.

Thomas Aquinas

Aquinas wrote several commentaries on biblical books,[205] but his commitment to Scripture extends way beyond such works. Scripture permeates his works. Martin Hubert counted 38,000 citations in Thomas's *Summa theologiae* and *Summa contra Gentiles*; of these, 25,000 come from the Bible, 8,000 from Christian authors, and 4,300 of those from pagan authors are from Aristotle![206] Étienne Gilson rightly states, "For Thomas all of theology was a commentary on Scripture; he drew no conclusion without justifying it by some word of Sacred Scripture, which is the Word of God."[207]

In the Old Testament, Thomas favored Isaiah and the Wisdom literature, and in the New Testament he favored Paul and John. His commentary on Job is one of his most developed and polished such works. It is a fine commentary and remains well worth reading.

Thomas sees the dispute among Job's friends as akin to a medieval disputation finally determined by God himself. He is creative and persuasive in his construal of their arguments and dialogue. Intriguingly, while Thomas is sympathetic to much of what Elihu, the fourth friend, says, he holds that Elihu is presumptuous. He argues that the first question of God's speech, "Who is this that darkens counsel by words without knowledge?" (Job 38:2), is addressed to Elihu rather than to Job!

For Thomas, the major theme of Job and of the dispute among the friends is God's providence:

> The affliction of just men is what seems especially to impugn divine providence in human affairs. For although it seems irrational and contrary to providence at first glance that good things sometimes happen to evil men, nevertheless this can be excused in one way or another by divine compassion. But that the just are afflicted without cause seems to undermine totally the foundation of providence. Thus the varied and grave afflictions of a specific just man called Job, perfect in every virtue, are proposed as a kind of theme for the question intended for discussion.[208]

The friends assume what we nowadays refer to as a rigid doctrine of the act-consequence structure. Job, however, understands that providence allows

---

205. See T. G. Weinandy, D. A. Keating, and J. P. Yocum, eds., *Aquinas on Scripture: An Introduction to His Biblical Commentaries* (London: T&T Clark, 2005).
206. Cited by J.-P. Torrell, *Aquinas's "Summa": Background, Structure, and Reception* (Washington, DC: Catholic University of America Press, 2005), 72.
207. Cited in ibid., 73, without reference.
208. Thomas Aquinas, *Commentary on the Book of Job*, prologue, available at http://dhspriory.org/thomas/SSJob.htm#0.

the worst adversities to befall a virtuous person. With similar insights to those we find in St. John of the Cross, Thomas asserts that it is those closer to God who are likely to be afflicted the most. This side of eternity we remain beset by sin, and God uses suffering like medicine to prepare us for life with him. "Medicine" is a recurring metaphor in Thomas's commentary. For example, he comments,

> Just like a doctor does not heal the plea of the sick man who asks him to take the bitter medicine away (if the doctor does not remove the remedy he knows to be health inducing, he nevertheless hears the actual advantage of the plea of the patient because he induces the health, which the sick person greatly desires), God does not take away trials from a man set down in the midst of trial, although he prays for mercy, because he knows that trials are useful to final salvation. Thus, although God truly heeds him, nevertheless the man who set down in the midst of miseries does not believe that he is heard.[209]

Thomas's reading of Job is nuanced and theologically perceptive. Indeed, I think that his interpretation is theologically and pastorally superior to that of Calvin.[210] Today it is controversial as to whether the book of Job, let alone Thomas's reading of it, has anything to offer to a theology of suffering. To the faithful it does, and philosophically Eleonore Stump rightly argues that Thomas's reading "must be recognized as a rich, sophisticated account and well worth attending to."[211]

The distance between a work such as Aquinas's on Job and the commentaries of the Reformers is short and yet worlds apart. The Renaissance greatly enhanced the critical tools available to biblical scholars, and the Reformation shattered the unity of the church while ushering in an unprecedented renewal of biblical interpretation. In chapter 7 (below) we will explore the history of biblical interpretation in the Reformation and post-Reformation periods. It remains to take account of early and medieval Jewish interpretation, which we will do in the next chapter. As one works on patristic and medieval exegesis, one is regularly struck by comments that this scholar and that scholar engaged in dialogue with Jewish interpreters. Much is to be gained from an examination of Jewish biblical interpretation.

---

209. Ibid., chap. 9, Third Lesson.
210. For my reading of Job, see C. G Bartholomew and R. O'Dowd, *Old Testament Wisdom Literature: A Theological Introduction* (Downers Grove, IL: IVP Academic, 2011); Craig Bartholomew, *When You Want to Yell at God: The Book of Job* (Bellingham, WA: Lexham, 2014).
211. E. Stump, "Biblical Commentary and Philosophy," in *Cambridge Companion to Aquinas*, ed. N. Kretzmann and E. Stump (Cambridge: Cambridge University Press, 1993), 252–68, esp. 264.

6

Early and Medieval Jewish Biblical Interpretation

> Yet my close reading of current studies of the use of the Old Testament in the New has led me to concur with those working in the field of Jewish studies . . . who claim that the Jewish nature of early Christianity is often insufficiently acknowledged by New Testament commentators, who are all too often unaware of significant developments in Jewish studies which could be relevant to their work.
>
> Susan Docherty[1]

Introduction

Few of us Christian scholars have been trained in Jewish interpretation, but this field has become one of growing fascination for me and offers a vital contribution to biblical and especially Hebrew Bible / Old Testament interpretation. The Hebrew Bible so clearly relates to all of life, and a particular contribution of Jewish interpretation is in rigorously exploring the public dimensions of faith and Scripture. Martin Buber exemplifies this in his comment,

---

I am glad to acknowledge the substantial help of Justin Orr with this chapter.

1. S. E. Docherty, *The Use of the Old Testament in Hebrews: A Case Study in Early Jewish Bible Interpretation*, WUNT 2/260 (Tübingen: Mohr Siebeck, 2009), 201–2.

One should beware altogether of understanding the conversation with God—the conversation of which I had to speak in this book and almost all of my later books—as something that occurs merely apart from or above the everyday. God's address to man penetrates the events in all our lives and all the events in the world around us, everything biographical and everything historical, and turns it into instruction, into demands for you and me.[2]

Jesus is a Jew, and so the Hebrew Bible and Jewish studies also form an indispensable background to the New Testament. On this issue, a great disservice was done to New Testament studies when scholars overemphasized *the criterion of dissimilarity* for discovering authentic Jesus material. Dissimilarity is important as *a* criterion. Géza Vermès, for example, notes that the "imagery of eating a man's body and especially drinking his blood, . . . even after allowance is made for metaphorical language, strikes a totally foreign note in a Palestinian Jewish cultural setting (cf. John 6.52[–53])."[3] However, dissimilarity becomes a problem when emphasized at the expense of similarity. Joachim Jeremias's exceptional work exemplifies the rich rewards of taking Jesus's Jewish context seriously. He declares that the criterion of dissimilarity is a "serious source of error" because "all the cases in which Jesus takes up already available material, whether apocalyptic ideas or Jewish proverbs or language current in his environment, slip through the net, as do the cases in which the early church handed down words of Jesus unaltered, as e.g. *'Abbā* as a mode of addressing God."[4]

Early Jewish interpretation can be divided into the following periods:

1. The five centuries from the start of the fourth century BC until the first century AD. The literature of this period includes the Second Temple literature, which is of vital importance for New Testament studies:

> Jews, Jesus of Nazareth and his disciples breathed this religious and cultural environment and spoke its idiom. They received their Bible from the Jewish community and as it was interpreted by this community. Indeed, the very early church was a messianic movement within the bosom of Judaism, and fundamental aspects of its early history are intelligible only when viewed against

---

2. M. Buber, *I and Thou*, trans. W. Kaufmann (Edinburgh: T&T Clark, 1970), 182.
3. G. Vermès, *The Religion of Jesus the Jew* (Fortress: Minneapolis, 1993), 16.
4. J. Jeremias, *New Testament Theology*, trans. J. Bowden (London: SCM, 1971), 2. Cf. idem, *Abba: Studien zur neutestamentlichen Theologie und Zeitgeschichte* (Göttingen: Vandenhoeck & Ruprecht, 1966). K. E. Bailey's work provides fertile examples of the importance of the NT's Jewish background. See, e.g., his *Jacob and the Prodigal: How Jesus Retold Israel's Story* (Downers Grove, IL: InterVarsity, 2003).

the rejection of its messianic views and expectations by the vast majority of contemporary Jews.[5]

In recent decades the importance of this literature as background to the New Testament has increasingly been foregrounded.

2. The destruction of the temple in AD 70 was a watershed for Judaism and Jewish interpretation. With the catastrophic destruction of the temple, Judaism was forced to "reinvent" itself, and the rabbis emerged to fill the vacuum of leadership. By the Middle Ages, rabbinic Judaism had become the dominant form of Judaism and continues to be so today. After AD 70, Judaism begins at Yavneh (Jamnia) with Yohanan/ai ben Zakkai. It can be divided into the following periods:

a. The period of the Tannaim, in the first and second centuries AD
b. The period of the Amoraim, from the third to the fifth centuries

Central to Judaism after AD 70 was a regaining of what was lost at Sinai; hence the emphasis on the oral tradition stemming from Sinai and the consequent emergence of the Mishnah and Talmuds in these periods.

c. The period of the Geonim, from the seventh to the thirteenth centuries
d. The period of the Rishonim, from the eleventh to the sixteenth centuries

A development of great importance was the origin of Jewish biblical commentaries and, more precisely, *peshat* (*pěšaṭ*, literal)[6] exegesis in the medieval era. This generated a rich tradition of Jewish commentary writing that is still being excavated today.

Early Jewish Interpretation

Second Temple Literature

Even a superficial survey of all the literature of this period is impossible in a short chapter of this sort. Fortunately, there are a number of good

---

5. G. W. E. Nickelsburg, *Jewish Literature between the Bible and the Mishnah* (Minneapolis: Augsburg, 2009), 2.
6. The definition of *peshat* exegesis in this context is contested. S. Garfinkel ("Clearing *Peshat* and *Derash*," in Saebø, *HB/OT* 1.2 [2000]: 129–34) argues against equating *peshat* exegesis with "literal"; rather, "*peshat* interpretations acknowledge the historical, linguistic, and literary contexts of a phrase, verse, or pericope" (131).

introductions to the literature available.⁷ Focusing on the literature alone, however, brings danger of an atomistic approach,⁸ whereas what we need is a sense of the period and the ways in which the Hebrew Bible was read during this time. We need "more thoroughgoing interpretations which attempt to do justice to the underlying structures of belief and aspiration, and above all to the symbolic world which gave meaning to Jewish life."⁹ It is within such an understanding that we can trace the major types of Old Testament interpretation. Neusner observes that at the time of Jesus, "the most certain testimony of all to the enduring covenant was the Temple, which stood as the nexus between Jew and God. Its services bore witness to Israel's enduring loyalty to the covenant and the commandments of Sinai. They [first-century Jews] saw Jerusalem with the eye of faith, and that vision transformed the city."¹⁰

In terms of its history, the major sources for the intertestamental period are the works of Josephus; 1–4 Maccabees; the later rabbinic literature, which nevertheless contains important earlier material; the Apocrypha and Pseudepigrapha; the Dead Sea Scrolls (DSS); the Targums; and so forth. The Hebrew Bible is central to intertestamental Judaism, and many of the apocryphal and pseudepigraphical works and the DSS consist of readings of Hebrew Bible texts to discern their meaning for new generations. "The grids of interpretation thus offered constitute the key variations in the first-century Jewish worldview. This worldview was expressed in stories told and retold, symbols acted out and lived out, agendas taken up, tasks attempted, and (in a few cases) books written."¹¹

N. T. Wright refers to "stories told and retold." Géza Vermès, in 1961, was the first to identify a group of late Second Temple works as part of a genre he labeled "The Rewritten Bible,"¹² a genre that relates closely to Wright's approach to intertestamental interpretation. Vermès's original list included Josephus's *Antiquities*, *Jubilees*, the *Liber antiquitatum biblicarum* of Pseudo-Philo, and the *Genesis Apocryphon*. Vermès's approach depends

---

7. See, e.g., Nickelsburg, *Jewish Literature*; M. Henze, ed., *A Companion to Biblical Interpretation in Early Judaism* (Grand Rapids: Eerdmans, 2012); J. J. Collins and D. C. Harlow, eds., *Early Judaism: A Comprehensive Overview* (Grand Rapids: Eerdmans, 2012); S. J. D. Cohen, *From the Maccabees to the Mishnah*, 2nd ed. (Louisville: Westminster John Knox, 2006); and the many books by Jacob Neusner.
8. See N. T. Wright, *NTPG* 150.
9. Ibid., 149.
10. J. Neusner, *Judaism in the Beginning of Christianity* (Philadelphia: Fortress, 1984), Kindle loc. 121–22.
11. N. T. Wright, *NTPG* 152.
12. G. Vermès, *Scripture and Tradition in Judaism*, Studia Post-Biblica 4 (Leiden: Brill, 1961), 67–126.

on books being recognized as canonical; yet Crawford, for example, argues that the terms "Bible" and "canon" are anachronistic in the Second Temple period.[13] Among others, Alexander, Brooke, Tov, and Crawford have sought to explore the category of rewritten Scripture with greater precision.[14] Crawford prefers "rewritten scriptural texts" or "Rewritten Scripture" and argues that this category or group of texts is "characterized by a close adherence to a recognizably and already authoritative base text (narrative or legal) and a recognizable degree of scribal intervention into that base text for the purpose of exegesis."[15] Crawford identifies a spectrum of texts within this definition, with 4QCommentary on Genesis A (4Q252) embodying the transition at the end of the Second Temple period toward "citation plus comment," the form that dominates later Jewish and Christian commentary.[16]

Second Temple Judaism's story is one of suffering, tension, and tragedy. Persian rule enabled some of the Israelites to return to Judea and to rebuild the temple, the period with which Ezra, Nehemiah, Haggai, and Zechariah deal. The Persians were generous overlords but nevertheless overlords, a pattern central to the Second Temple period. Alexander the Great conquered Palestine in 332 BC and inaugurated a period of Hellenism, in which Greek influence was felt everywhere. "Any idea of a hidden curtain between Judaism and Hellenism, in the sense of a geographical line at which it might be said that the one stopped and the other began, must be completely rejected."[17] The LXX translation is an indication of the spread of Greek as a lingua franca. The subsequent overlords, Egypt in the third century BC and Syria in the second century, complicate the ethos but do not detract from the pervasive Hellenism. Overlordship challenged Judaism's political identity, while Hellenism challenged its cultural and religious identity. Should Jews assimilate or remain distinctive, and if distinctive, how?

Under Syrian rule, Antiochus Epiphanes's desecration of the temple on December 25, 167 BC, forced the issue of identity to the fore. Some refused

---

13. S. W. Crawford, *Rewriting Scripture in Second Temple Times* (Grand Rapids: Eerdmans, 2008), 10.

14. P. S. Alexander, "Retelling the Old Testament," in *It Is Written: Scripture Citing Scripture*, ed. D. A. Carson and H. G. M. Williamson (Cambridge: Cambridge University Press, 1988), 99–121; E. Tov, "Rewritten Bible Composition and Biblical Manuscripts, with Special Attention to the Samaritan Pentateuch," *Dead Sea Discoveries* 5 (1998): 334–54; M. J. Bernstein, "'Rewritten Bible': A Generic Category Which Has Outlived Its Usefulness?," *Textus* 22 (2005): 169–96; G. J. Brooke, "Rewritten Bible," in *Encyclopedia of the Dead Sea Scrolls*, ed. L. H. Schiffman and J. C. VanderKam (Oxford: Oxford University Press, 2000), 2:777–81; idem, *Reading the Dead Sea Scrolls: Essays in Method* (Atlanta: SBL, 2013), 51–65, 115–35.

15. Crawford, *Rewriting Scripture*, 12–13.

16. Ibid., 130.

17. N. T. Wright, *NTPG* 153.

to submit to Antiochus's actions and died rather than submit. Others who escaped looked to Yahweh to act in a new and decisive way to vanquish his enemies. Judas Maccabeus and his companions organized a revolt and drove out Antiochus, so that three years to the day after its desecration, the temple was reconsecrated (December 25, 164 BC). This victory became formative for Judaism and was seen as comparable to the great events of Israel's history. However, the ambiguity of the years that followed created the same sort of puzzle as had the "return from exile." God had acted, but it seemed as though another great intervention must still come. The ambiguous years following the revolt evoked different responses among Jews, and it was this pluriform response that created the pluriform Judaism in Jesus's day.

It was during the third to second/first centuries BC that the Septuagint (LXX) came into existence. The need for such a translation is directly related to the hellenization of the Roman world, a context in which fewer and fewer Jews spoke and read Hebrew and Aramaic. The *Letter of Aristeas* connects the translation of the Pentateuch into Greek with Alexandria, a Greek-speaking city in which the Jewish population soon forgot their Palestinian vernacular. "And the internal evidence of the Septuagint suggests that this Greek version of the Old Testament was made in the first instance to meet the requirements of the Jewish population of Alexandria, and not to grace the royal library."[18] As with the Pax Romana, so too the LXX was of great missional import. Although it was initially done for the Jews, at the same time it made the Hebrew Bible available to the Greek-speaking gentile world.[19] "The Septuagint had thus, in the providence of God, a great and honourable part to play in preparing the world for the Gospel."[20] "As soon as the gospel was carried into the Greek-speaking world, the Septuagint came into its own as the sacred text to which the preachers appealed."[21] "'Greek Judaism,' it has been said, 'with the Septuagint had ploughed the furrows for the gospel seed in the Western world,' but it was the Christian preachers who sowed the seed."[22] To a large extent the LXX became the Bible of the early church; this meant that ready at hand was a Greek theological vocabulary that did not need to be invented from scratch: "The New Testament writers often use Septuagint terms or

---

18. F. F. Bruce, *The Books and the Parchments: Some Chapters on the Transmission of the Bible*, 2nd ed. (London: Pickering & Inglis, 1971), 148.

19. Ibid., 161.

20. Ibid., 162; cf. T. Rajak, *Translation and Survival: The Greek Bible of the Ancient Jewish Diaspora* (Oxford: Oxford University Press, 2011); T. Law, *When God Spoke Greek* (Oxford: Oxford University Press, 2013).

21. F. F. Bruce, *The Canon of Scripture* (Downers Grove, IL: InterVarsity, 1988), 49.

22. Ibid.

phrases that were not in common usage in the first century (e.g., *pasa sarx*, 'all flesh,' in Luke 3:6)."[23]

The early Greek translations of the Hebrew Bible are of vital importance for biblical study. They represent a Hebrew text/s a thousand years older than our MT manuscripts and thus are an important source for textual criticism.[24] Here an example is Genesis 4:8, in which the MT does not tell us what Cain said to Abel. The LXX and Samaritan versions supply "Let us go into the field," which is followed by English translations.[25] To a significant extent the early church and the writers of the New Testament depended on Greek versions of the Hebrew Bible, and one needs to be aware of this filter when studying the New Testament. In Philippians 2:10 Paul uses the phrase "every knee shall bow" to refer to Jesus's exaltation, the same Greek phrase that occurs in Isaiah 45:23 LXX. Paul thus uses vocabulary from the Greek version of Isaiah 45:23 to evoke that passage in order to express the divinity of Jesus.[26] The New Testament writers quote the early Greek some one hundred times, sometimes drawing conclusions that are not immediately obvious from the MT. In the period following New Testament times, the church fathers and councils used the early Greek translations, and exegetical debates centered on the Greek Hebrew Bible. This inevitably opened the door to the influence of Greek philosophy, a natural but ambivalent development.

As with the DSS, study of the early Greek versions is still in development, and critical versions of some have still to be published.[27] We recognize that the LXX is not a uniform translation of the Hebrew Bible into Greek. Indeed, if the term LXX is used to refer to the oldest Greek translation, then, strictly speaking, this applies only to the Pentateuch, which was translated in the third century BC. The remaining books were translated in different places by different people in the following two centuries. "The reader is cautioned, therefore, that there really is no such thing as *the* Septuagint. One must pay particular care to the context in which the term is used, even by the same writer."[28] Most scholars now reserve the term Old Greek (OG) to designate a text that represents the original translation of a book. Critical editions for many books are now available and continue to be published in the Göttingen Septuaginta series. McLay notes that the need for critical editions of all books of the LXX is the most important issue in LXX research.[29] A second major issue in LXX research is the evaluation of translation technique,[30] the process by which a Greek translator worked to translate a Hebrew text into Greek.[31] Translation inevitably involves interpretation, but as Longenecker rightly observes, it "is an overstatement of the facts" to hold "that the LXX should be looked on as a theological commentary, as has sometimes been suggested, and thereby used as a primary source for a knowledge of the hermeneutical procedures of the day."[32]

---

23. K. H. Jobes and M. Silva, *Invitation to the Septuagint* (Grand Rapids: Baker Academic, 2000), 23.

24. The literature on textual criticism is immense and growing. An indispensable resource is E. Tov's home page: www.emanueltov.info.

25. For this and other examples, see Bruce, *Books and the Parchments*, 157–58. On Gen. 4:1–8 in the LXX, see Jobes and Silva, *Septuagint*, 206–15.

26. Jobes and Silva, *Septuagint*, 23–24; cf. ibid., 201–4.

27. On the history of Septuagintal studies, see ibid., 239–57.

28. Ibid., 32.

29. R. T. McLay, *The Use of the Septuagint in New Testament Research* (Grand Rapids: Eerdmans, 2003), 13.

30. Cf. Jobes and Silva, *Septuagint*, 114–17.

31. McLay, *Use of the Septuagint*, 13–14.

32. R. N. Longenecker, *Biblical Exegesis in the Apostolic Period*, 2nd ed. (Grand Rapids: Eerdmans, 1999), 8. For work being done in this area, see Jobes and Silva, *Septuagint*; E. Tov, *Textual Criticism of the Hebrew Bible* (Minneapolis: Fortress, 1992), 121–54; E. Tov, *The Text-Critical Use of the Septuagint in Biblical Research* (Jerusalem: Simor, 1981); N. F. Marcos,

An example of the importance of the OG in New Testament interpretation is found in the citation of Amos 9:11–12 in Acts 15:16–18:[33] Amos 9:11–12 (NIV) reads:

> [11] "In that day
>   "I will restore David's fallen shelter—
>   I will repair its broken walls
>   and restore its ruins—
>   and will rebuild it as it used to be,
> [12] **so that they may possess the remnant of Edom**
>   and all the nations that bear my name,"
>   declares the LORD, who will do these things.

Acts 15:15–18 (NIV) reads:

> [15] The words of the prophets are in agreement with this, as it is written:
> [16] "'After this I will return
>   and rebuild David's fallen tent.
>   Its ruins I will rebuild,
>   and I will restore it,
> [17] **that the rest of mankind may seek the Lord,**
>   even all the Gentiles who bear my name,
>   says the Lord, who does these things'—
> [18] things known from long ago.

As McLay notes, this passage is a good example because it illustrates the complexities of the use of the Greek Jewish Scriptures in the New Testament.[34] A comparison of the OG and the MT of

---

The Septuagint in Context: Introduction to the Greek Versions of the Bible, trans. W. G. E. Watson (Leiden: Brill, 2000); L. Greenspoon, "Hebrew into Greek: Interpretation in, by, and of the Septuagint," in *The Ancient Period*, vol. 1 of *History of Biblical Interpretation*, ed. A. J. Hauser and D. F. Watson (Grand Rapids: Eerdmans, 2003), 80–113; idem, "It's All Greek to Me: The Septuagint in Modern English Translations of the Hebrew Bible," in *7th Congress of the International Organization for Septuagintal and Cognate Studies*, ed. C. Cox, SCS 31 (Atlanta: Scholars Press, 1991), 1–21; idem, "The Use and Abuse of the Term 'LXX' and Related Terminology in Recent Scholarship," BIOSCS 20 (1987): 21–29; J. Cook, ed., *Septuagint and Reception: Essays Prepared for the Association for the Study of the Septuagint in South Africa*, VTSup 127 (Leiden: Brill, 2009); G. Veltri, *Libraries, Translations and Canonic Texts: The Septuagint, Aquila and Ben Sira in the Jewish and Christian Traditions*, JSJSup 109 (Leiden: Brill, 2006); A. Schenker, ed., *The Earliest Text of the Hebrew Bible: The Relationship between the Masoretic Text and the Hebrew Base of the Septuagint Revisited*, Septuagint and Cognate Studies (Leiden: Brill, 2003); M. Popovic, ed., *Authoritative Scriptures in Ancient Judaism* (Leiden: Brill, 2010).

33. Cf. Jobes and Silva, *Septuagint*, 194–95; for a detailed discussion, see McLay, *Use of the Septuagint*, chap. 1. Cf. J. A. Meek's useful chapter in his *The Gentile Mission in Old Testament Citations in Acts: Text, Hermeneutic, and Purpose* (London: T&T Clark, 2008), 56–94; S. Nägele, *Laubhütte Davids und Wolkensohn: Eine auslegungsgeschichtliche Studie zu Amos 9,11 in der jüdischen und christlichen Exegese*, AGJU 24 (Leiden: Brill, 1995). For a comparable discussion of Heb. 11:21 citing Gen. 47:31, see M. Silva, "The New Testament Use of the Old Testament: Text Form and Authority," in *Scripture and Truth*, ed. D. A. Carson and J. D. Woodbridge (Leicester, UK: Inter-Varsity, 1983), 147–65.

34. See McLay, *Use of the Septuagint*, chap. 1, for the texts as well as for the translations of the originals.

Amos 9:11–12 shows that the Greek is, for the most part, a faithful translation of a Hebrew text that was similar to the text preserved in the MT. There is thus a direct relationship between the Greek and the Hebrew. The most significant differences between the OG and the Hebrew are the portions of text in bold above. Here the New Testament follows the OG rather than the MT. Where did this translation come from? McLay asserts that by comparison with the militaristic tone of the Hebrew, the OG says that the renewal of the Davidic kingdom will catalyze the remainder of humanity so that they turn to Israel's God.[35] McLay explores the various possibilities and concludes that the OG translator produced a translation influenced by his theology, although it is questionable whether this was intentional.[36] In Acts 15 Luke uses the OG, but there are changes introduced independent of both the LXX and MT. "We do not know whether the author was aware of the reading of the MT, but the OG text allowed the passage to be reinterpreted and applied as a proof text to vindicate the mission to the Gentiles and their inclusion in God's people."[37]

"After this I will return" is a clear departure from the OG, but it is not a translation of the Hebrew text. How do we account for such differences? Did the New Testament writers quote their sources directly or from memory? The latter would be a way to explain how the New Testament authors sometimes blended several quotations. McLay suggests that the similar themes and vocabulary regarding the kingdom of David in 2 Samuel 7:13, 16 are probably responsible for the author's choice of vocabulary.[38] While Acts 15:16 departs quite significantly from Amos 9:11 in the OG, Acts 15:17 is almost identical to Amos in the OG. This makes it unlikely that the differences between Acts and the OG result from a different OG or Hebrew text. McLay concludes that the differences in Acts 15 alert us to the freedom the New Testament writers exercised in handling their sources when employing a citation.[39] "We have argued above that the writer of Acts capitalized on the theology of the OG reading and reinterpreted it in the light of the Christ event. This accounts for the addition of the Lord, but also for the omission of just as in the days of old from the quotation."[40] Acts has retained most of the text from the OG of Amos 9:11–12, but the writer has also acted as an author, reinterpreting the Scriptures for his readers.

An important question is whether this creativity involves a misreading of the Hebrew. In Amos, 9:11–12 are a unit within the epilogue.[41] McLay is right about the militaristic ethos, especially in relation to the subjugation of Edom. In the Hebrew, 9:11 has its complexities, and it is probably best to understand the *wĕ* at the start of verse 12b as epexegetic or emphatic, with "all the nations" being the subject of the verb *yîrĕšû* (they will possess).[42] Thus in Amos 9:12 MT, universal redemption in the Abrahamic sense of "all nations will be blessed" (cf. Gen. 12:1–3) is in view as much as in Acts 15 and the OG. Bruce rightly comments, "But the LXX version must represent a variant Hebrew text which has disappeared; and even the Masoretic text would have served James's purpose (if not with the same explicitness), since it predicts that the house of David will regain its sovereignty over the gentile nations formerly ruled by it—a prediction fulfilled and surpassed by the gentiles yielding their allegiance to Christ as Lord."[43] Bruce thus differs from McLay in positing a variant Hebrew text, but his theological point is correct. Indeed, his theological point

---

35. Ibid., 21.
36. Ibid., 23.
37. Ibid., 24.
38. Ibid., 26–27.
39. Ibid., 28.
40. Ibid., 29.
41. See F. I. Andersen and D. N. Freedman, *Amos: A New Translation with Introduction and Commentary*, AB 24A (New York: Doubleday, 1989).
42. Ibid., 918.
43. Bruce, *Books and the Parchments*, 151. Yet in his *Canon of Scripture* Bruce comments, "Here the Septuagint translators themselves had gone a long way towards spiritualizing and universalizing an oracle which originally spoke of national revival and expansion" (53).

is strengthened if we read Amos 9:12 as suggested above. It remains intriguing how a translation for the Jews produced the reading in OG.

Textual criticism is in a state of flux and development, and we do well to remember a few key points about it. First, the ongoing work on the DSS and the LXX reminds us of the importance of ancient language study for biblical interpretation. Sadly, we live in a day when less or no linguistic study is required of seminarians and scholars of religion at the very time when more is needed! Second, we need to remember that, as Silva comments, "with regard to the bulk of Scripture, we know what the autographs said. To be more specific: the possibility of textual variation hardly ever affects those passages that are claimed by some to teach error or falsehood."[44]

As mentioned above, Neusner argues that *the temple* was the great symbol of first-century Judaism, and that the different groupings can be located in relation to it. The Essenes abandoned it, regarding it as impure and its calendar as erroneous. The Pharisees thought that the priests should conduct themselves in accordance with the oral tradition they believed God had revealed to Moses at Sinai, passed on from Moses to the prophets, and the prophets to sages, down to their own group. The Sadducees won over the main body of officiating priests and wealthier Jews. They were thus very closely connected to the temple, although wary of the "Second Torah" espoused by the Pharisees.[45] With the destruction of the temple in AD 70 their ranks were decimated.

The Pharisees began as a religious/political pressure group at the time of the Maccabees and attained their greatest power under the Hasmoneans.[46] They focused strongly on purity, and particularly on purity in relation to the temple. Under Roman rule their agenda remained the same: "to purify Israel by summoning her to return to the true ancestral traditions; to restore Israel to her independent theocratic status; and to be, as a pressure group, in the vanguard of such movements by the study and practice of Torah."[47] In the first century we find Hillel and his followers arguing against revolution and for a retreat into Torah study, whereas Shammai and his followers were more in favor of revolution. The Pharisees were devout; they prayed the Shema and the Shemoneh Esreh (*Šĕmōneh 'eśreh*, Eighteen Benedictions = Amidah), and these prayers are not escapist. The Benedictions include the bringing of a redeemer to Israel, the resurrection of the dead, the gathering of dispersed Israel, and the vanquishing of Israel's enemies. Their belief in resurrection

---

44. Silva, "New Testament Use of the Old Testament," 147.
45. In his writings, J. Neusner makes much of the "dual Torah," written and oral, as central to Judaism. Both forms are said to issue from Moses and Sinai, but this raises the issue of the historicity of Sinai. In his *A Midrash Reader* (Minneapolis: Fortress, 1990), 3, he refers to "the myth of divine revelation to Moses at Sinai."
46. On the Essenes, Pharisees, and Sadducees in/and the DSS, see J. C. VanderKam, *The Dead Sea Scrolls and the Bible* (Grand Rapids: Eerdmans, 2012), 96–117.
47. N. T. Wright, *NTPG* 189.

was not just speculation about life after death but related to a restored Israel. This was probably why the Sadducees rejected this belief, since it threatened their tenuous hold on power.[48]

The Essenes came into existence sometime in the second century BC. Their withdrawal was probably a response to the ambiguities following the Maccabean revolt. They saw themselves as the true heirs of Judaism, the true Israel. They studied the Hebrew Scriptures with all the focus on the present and immediate future. Israel had not really returned from exile, and the state of mainstream Judaism was seen as the problem. However, Yahweh had begun to act in assembling their group and would soon act decisively. Most experts believe that the authors of the DSS were members of the larger Essene movement.[49] Not surprisingly, eschatology/apocalyptic is a major feature of the DSS.[50] They did not think the world would end when God acted, but that Yahweh would act within history to establish them as his people, in his land, and occupying his temple.

The discovery of the DSS has been a major event in the history of biblical interpretation.[51] Its significance is particularly felt in the field of Hebrew Bible *textual criticism*. Among the more than 900 manuscripts that editors of the DSS have identified, approximately 200 to 210 are copies of one or more Hebrew Bible books.[52] These copies of biblical books precede the earliest copies of the MT by a thousand years and are several hundred years earlier than most ancient Greek codices. As VanderKam rightly declares, "There is no guarantee that older is better, but the ancient copies offer unique comparative evidence, allowing one to test whether the more recent (MT, LXX, etc.) and the more ancient copies (the scrolls from the Qumran caves) are the same, almost the same, or quite different in their readings and to draw conclusions from the results."[53]

Waltke states, "To restore the original text of ancient documents, such as the OT Scriptures, is the task of textual criticism. The critic must know both the tendencies of scribes and the history and character of the sources bearing witness to the documents."[54] Believers certainly have a vested interest in the original text of the Hebrew Bible books, but some contemporary scholarship

---

48. Ibid., 200.
49. VanderKam, *Dead Sea Scrolls and the Bible*, 96.
50. The literature on the DSS is vast. For an introduction, see Nickelsburg, *Jewish Literature*, 126–45. See also H. Stegemann, *The Library of Qumran: On the Essenes, Qumran, John the Baptist, and Jesus* (Grand Rapids: Eerdmans, 1998); J. Magness, *The Archaeology of Qumran and the Dead Sea Scrolls* (Grand Rapids: Eerdmans, 2002); G. J. Brooke, *Reading the Dead Sea Scrolls: Essays in Method* (Atlanta: SBL, 2013); VanderKam, *Dead Sea Scrolls and the Bible*; L. H. Schiffman and J. C. VanderKam, eds., *Encyclopedia of the Dead Sea Scrolls*, 2 vols. (Oxford: Oxford University Press, 2000).
51. See J. J. Collins, *The Dead Sea Scrolls: A Biography* (Princeton: Princeton University Press, 2012).
52. VanderKam, *Dead Sea Scrolls and the Bible*, 1.
53. Ibid., 7.
54. B. K. Waltke, "The Textual Criticism of the Old Testament," in *Biblical Criticism: Historical, Literary, and Textual*, ed. R. K. Harrison et al. (Grand Rapids: Zondervan, 1978), 47–78, esp. 47.

has suggested that the fluidity of the Hebrew Bible text goes all the way back.[55] However, such a conclusion is unwarranted. Tov, for example, writes that

> the biblical books in their final and canonical edition... are the objective of textual criticism. From this point of view it seems that the opinion of de Lagarde,[56] who posited an *Urtext* for all the biblical books, is acceptable, even if several details of his view are not plausible. Our description corresponds, therefore, with the accepted view in research of one original text, albeit in a more moderate formulation, for it takes into account the possibility of earlier, written stages.[57]

Waltke concludes, "Our stance toward the MT is based on cautious confidence. It must be shown rather than assumed to be in error; the burden of proof rests on the critic."[58]

Clearly the DSS have major implications for Hebrew Bible textual criticism. But how do they help with interpretation, important as is the establishment of a stable text as close to the original as possible? Many examples could be given, but I confine myself to an example from the Hebrew Bible and one from the New.[59] First, an example from Isaiah: according to the United Bible Society's Greek New Testament, there are more than four hundred quotations, paraphrases, or allusions to Isaiah in the New Testament. These are more or less evenly distributed across the book(s).[60] Diverse as Second Temple messianism was, there is nothing in it to indicate a crucified Messiah. Hence Paul speaks in Galatians 5:11 and 1 Corinthians 1:23 of the "scandal" of Christ having been crucified. A challenge to the early Christians was how to account for Jesus being the Messiah and being crucified. Inter alia, they turned to the Hebrew Bible for insight, and they found a major resource in the servant song of Isaiah 52:13–53:12.[61] However, for some

---

55. See, e.g., S. Weitzman, *Solomon: The Lure of Wisdom* (New Haven: Yale University Press, 2011).

56. P. A. de Lagarde (1827–91) is regarded as the father of modern Septuagintal textual criticism. See Jobes and Silva, *Septuagint*, 242–45.

57. Tov, *Textual Criticism of the Hebrew Bible*, 189. See also idem, "Post-Modern Textual Criticism?," in *Greek Scripture and the Rabbis*, ed. T. M. Law and A. Salvesen (Leuven: Peeters, 2012), 1–18. For the history of textual criticism and the work that underlies the new *Biblia Hebraica Quinta*, see D. Barthélemy, *Studies in the Text of the Old Testament: An Introduction to the Hebrew Old Testament Text Project*, trans. S. Lind, Textual Criticism and the Translator 3 (Winona Lake, IN: Eisenbrauns, 2012). Also cf. G. D. Martin, *Multiple Originals: New Approaches to Hebrew Bible Textual Criticism* (Atlanta: SBL, 2010), which on pp. 205–48 contains a fascinating discussion of textual criticism and the Decalogue. Notably lacking in this discussion, important as it is, is the extent to which context and theology account for the differences between the Exodus and Deuteronomy versions of the Decalogue, and especially in relation to the Sabbath commandment. W. Dumbrell (*Covenant and Creation: A Theology of Old Testament Covenants* [Nashville: Nelson, 1984]) perceptively notes, e.g., that

> two such different applications of the fourth commandment have often been thought to be contradictory. They are in fact complementary, since it is the Exodus redemption which makes the new life in the land, and thus the Edenic values recaptured, possible. Israel in Canaan is a microcosm of mankind as blessed, an illustration of what is intended for the whole world. (122–23)

58. B. K. Waltke and M. P. O'Connor, *An Introduction to Biblical Hebrew Syntax* (Winona Lake, IN: Eisenbrauns, 1990), 28.

59. For a useful introduction to the DSS and Christianity, see Collins, *Dead Sea Scrolls*, 96–138.

60. B. S. Childs, *The Struggle to Understand Isaiah as Christian Scripture* (Grand Rapids: Eerdmans, 2004), 5.

61. As noted by C. H. Dodd, *According to the Scriptures: The Sub-Structure of New Testament Theology* (London: Nisbet, 1952), 126–27; Joachim Jeremias, Christian Mauer, plus many others.

time now the individual identity of the servant in this passage, and "his" resurrection, have been questioned. For some forty years the arguments of Orlinsky and Whybray have held sway against finding resurrection in this text.[62] In a fascinating and accessible work, John Barry has revisited this issue of *The Resurrected Servant in Isaiah*.[63] Barry's book is worth reading in its entirety. He makes use of participatory reference discourse analysis to show that the individual servant is in view in Isaiah 52–53 and that this servant is distinguished from Israel. Making use of the Isaiah scrolls among the DSS, Barry argues that "the most probable *Urtext* behind Isa 53:11a is 'he will see light'"[64] and that this strengthens the view that the servant will die vicariously *and rise again*. The MT omits "light," whereas the DSS and the LXX include it.[65] Barry's argument is complex and wide ranging and, as he himself notes, such an argument can only be judged probable. For our purposes it embodies close textual work in drawing on the DSS to indicate that the New Testament uses of Isaiah 52–53 may indeed be an accurate reading of Isaiah at this point.

We have, second, already noted the importance of the DSS as background for the New Testament.[66] An immense amount has been written about Jewish messianism, and this is an area in which the DSS make a major contribution. One of the first scrolls to be discovered was 1QS, a well-preserved copy of the *Rule of the Community*, and it contains a statement that encapsulates the group's messianic expectations: "They [the men of holiness] shall depart from none of the counsels of the Law to walk in all the stubbornness of their hearts, but shall be ruled by the primitive precepts in which the men of the Community were first instructed until there shall come the Prophet and the Messiahs of Aaron and Israel."[67] The DSS appear to provide information about two messiahs, one priestly and the other nonpriestly, who would come in the last days and for the final conflict. Their presence would indicate the end of the present age. In the New Testament there is only one Messiah, Jesus, and he is of the Davidic line. However, in Hebrews the Messiah does indeed take on overtly priestly roles.

Most of the chief priests and aristocracy belonged to the party known as the *Sadducees*. They were conservative, opposed to the Pharisees, believed in free will, had little time for laws other than those in the Hebrew Bible, and denied the doctrine of the resurrection, as explained above.

Joan Taylor concludes, "Overall, among scholars of diverse backgrounds there is now a much greater awareness of Second Temple Judaism in all its rich *variety*, but still with a strong sense of internal cohesion founded on the *concept* of the Temple, the Law of Moses, and tradition."[68] Kugel says that if one steps back and surveys the diverse literature of Second Temple Judaism

---

62. H. M. Orlinsky, *The So-Called "Servant of the Lord" and "Suffering Servant" in Second Isaiah*, VTSup 14 (Leiden: Brill, 1977); R. N. Whybray, *Thanksgiving for a Liberated Prophet: An Interpretation of Isaiah, Chapter 53*, JSOTSup 4 (Sheffield: University of Sheffield Press, 1978).

63. J. Barry, *The Resurrected Servant in Isaiah* (Colorado Springs: Biblica, 2010).

64. Ibid., 105.

65. On the LXX of Isa. 52:13–53:12, see Jobes and Silva, *Septuagint*, 215–27.

66. See, e.g., VanderKam, *Dead Sea Scrolls and the Bible*, 118–66.

67. See 1QS 9.9–11.

68. J. E. Taylor, *The Essenes, the Scrolls, and the Dead Sea* (Oxford: Oxford University Press, 2012), 17.

from a distance, four common assumptions emerge about how Scripture was to be read:[69]

   a. The Bible is a cryptic document whose meaning is often hidden, and thus it requires careful interpretation.
   b. The Bible is a book of lessons whose words are aimed at people today.
   c. The Bible is perfectly consistent; it is free of error and contradictions.
   d. Every word of Scripture comes from God.

Tom Wright summarizes Israel's worldview in the Second Temple period as follows:[70]

   1. Who are we? We are Israel, Yahweh's chosen people.
   2. Where are we? We are in the holy land, focused on the temple, but, paradoxically we remain in exile.
   3. What is wrong? We have the wrong rulers.
   4. What is the solution? Yahweh must act to establish his rule through the right officials, and until then we must remain faithful.

The differences among the main groups in first-century Judaism can be plotted in relation to this analysis. The chief priests would have altered points 2–4: they were in the temple, and all was in order, but the problem was the recalcitrance of the other Jewish groups, who must therefore be kept in place. The Essenes would have modified point 4: Yahweh has acted in establishing the Essenes as the vanguard of his coming action.

This approach to the Second Temple period literature is illuminating and helpful. Yet there is far more to early Jewish exegesis than such a narrative approach.[71] However, as Kugel states,

> Retelling, it should be said, was actually the preferred form of biblical commentary in this period. That is, instead of citing a particular verse and explaining its meaning . . . Second Temple writers preferred to retell the text, substituting for a problematic word or phrase one that would be understood by all readers. . . . This form of writing (*Jubilees* is only one example) has been termed the "Rewritten Bible," but it was almost never a rewriting for rewriting's sake; by

---

69. J. L. Kugel, "The Beginnings of Biblical Interpretation," in Henze, *Companion to Biblical Interpretation*, 13–15.
70. N. T. Wright, *NTPG* 243.
71. See VanderKam, *Dead Sea Scrolls and the Bible*, 25–48; parts 2–8 in Henze, *Companion to Biblical Interpretation*.

retelling the text in their own words, commentators were able to explain things and eliminate any perceived inconsistencies or problems.[72]

Such an approach enables us to read the literature against its context and to see the emerging methods of exegesis as parts of the ongoing attempts to interpret the Hebrew Bible for the times and, inter alia, to do so through telling and retelling the Old Testament story. Wright helpfully distinguishes between retellings of the Hebrew Bible story as a whole, and smaller stories that focus on one part of the larger story.

There is ample precedent for telling and retelling the story of Israel in the Hebrew Bible. "As the biblical tradition grew and developed, the stories it contained, and the single story which holds them all together, grew with it, and the different elements interacted upon one another in a multitude of ways."[73] Chronicles is one of the most obvious examples of this. Scott Hahn, in his important work on Chronicles, explains, "More than a summary or overview, Chronicles is a theological and liturgical interpretation of Israel's history that answers key questions: Who are we? How did we get here? What must we do, and why?"[74]

The story of the Hebrew Bible was inevitably read in the Second Temple context as a story in search of a conclusion. Josephus's retelling of the story in the first century AD in his *Antiquities* provides an ending that subverts the narrative grammar of the rest: Yahweh sides with the Romans, Jerusalem is destroyed, and Judaism dispersed.[75]

Sirach (Ecclesiasticus) provides a different retelling of Israel's story in chapters 44–50, written around the start of the second century BC. Sirach 44 begins with the famous words, "Let us now sing the praises of famous men, our ancestors in their generations." Next 44:1–15 gives a reference in verse 2 to the Lord's "majesty from the beginning," and then it enumerates the different types of famous men in the history of Israel, including leaders, the wise, and prophets. The descendents of the great ones "stand by the covenants" (44:12). The whole section is an account of such of Israel's ancestors as a non-Jewish reader might admire,[76] but it is also a telling of Israel's story, with sections on the patriarchs, Moses, Aaron, Joshua, the judges, and others. It is fascinating to observe how the story is told, and the ending in 50:1–21 is

---

72. Kugel, "Beginnings of Biblical Interpretation," 3–23, 11.
73. N. T. Wright, *NTPG* 216; cf. M. A. Fishbane, *Biblical Interpretation in Ancient Israel* (Oxford: Oxford University Press, 2004), 380–440.
74. S. W. Hahn, *The Kingdom of God as Liturgical Empire: A Theological Commentary on 1–2 Chronicles* (Grand Rapids: Baker Academic, 2012).
75. N. T. Wright, *NTPG* 217.
76. This clearly affects the telling of the story. Sirach 46:11–12, e.g., describes the judges as those whose "hearts did not fall into idolatry."

highly significant. Chapter 50 concludes this section with a glowing portrait of Simon, the high priest who held office in 219–196 BC. "The message is clear: Israel's story finds its perfect conclusion in the splendid and ordered worship of her god in the Temple."[77] The theology of Sirach 24 fits with this, with Wisdom being "established in Zion" (v. 10).

Sirach was written before the temple was desecrated by Antiochus Epiphanes, and clearly Sirach's type of retelling of the story, serene and triumphant, would no longer fit in that new context. First Maccabees begins with a positive description of Alexander the Great's conquests and then moves on to the key element in the plot, the rise of that "sinful root" Antiochus Epiphanes (1:10). In a straightforward way, 1 Maccabees tells the events that unfolded after the desecration of the temple; "His purpose is to defend the legitimacy of the Hasmonean high-priestly dynasty by showing how the family of Mattathias delivered the Jews from the persecution, reimposed the rule of the Torah, and brought the nation to an era of peace and political independence."[78] So, for example, Mattathias's murder of a Jew coming to offer a sacrifice on an altar in Modein (2:23–26) is compared to the actions of Phinehas in Numbers 25:6–12. In 2 Maccabees there is a more overt theological linking of the triumphs of the Maccabees to the story of Israel. Nickelsburg notes of 1 Maccabees that the author "has proclaimed the gospel according to the Hasmoneans,"[79] and N. T. Wright notes of 1–2 Maccabees that "they hijacked the story-line of Israel's future hope, and claimed that this hope had been achieved through them."[80]

Jubilees—written in the first half of the second century BC—is an elaboration of Genesis 1–Exodus 12.[81] The stories of the patriarchs are retold with the eye on Israel's future. Only as Israel remains faithful to the covenant will Israel's story reach its appropriate conclusion. *Wisdom of Solomon* 10–19 covers the same terrain but from the perspective of Wisdom.[82] The story is full of hints as to how its hearers should live in the light of the narrative: above all, it teaches that paganism akin to that of Egypt and Canaan should be avoided.

77. N. T. Wright, *NTPG* 217.
78. Nickelsburg, *Jewish Literature*, 114.
79. Ibid., 117.
80. N. T. Wright, *NTPG* 217.
81. See Nickelsburg, *Jewish Literature*, 73–80; J. van Ruiten, *Primaeval History Interpreted: The Rewriting of Genesis 1–11 in the Book of Jubilees*, JSJSup 66 (Leiden: Brill, 2000); idem, "Biblical Interpretation in the Book of Jubilees: The Case of the Early Abram (Jub. 11:14–12:15)," in Henze, *Companion to Biblical Interpretation*, 121–56; M. Segal, *The Book of Jubilees: Rewritten Bible, Redaction, Ideology and Theology*, JSJSup 117 (Leiden: Brill, 2007).
82. The book's date is contested.

Clearly the Jews of the Second Temple period were well able to conceive of the story of Israel as a whole and deeply concerned to look for its proper conclusion.[83] Second Temple literature also provides many examples of the telling of smaller stories.

Susanna, *Bel and the Dragon*, and *Tobit* were probably written before Antiochus Epiphanes's desecration of the temple. *Susanna* is a story of persecution and vindication amid the Babylonian exile. She is cast in the role of the righteous person, sentenced to death because of her obedience to God, rescued by Daniel, the savior figure sent by God, and vindicated of the charges against her. Throughout Susanna's innocence and piety are contrasted with the wickedness of the elders. *Bel and the Dragon* contains a pair of episodes dealing with Daniel in Babylon and his vindication through his faithful resistance to idolatry. As is common in Jewish polemics against idolatry, the term "living God" recurs in this work. This work exhibits a number of significant parallels to Isaiah 45–46.[84]

The last historical event mentioned in *Tobit* is the rebuilding of the temple (515 BC), and presumably the author wrote before the persecution of the Jews by Antiochus Epiphanes (167 BC). Intriguingly, the narrative is set among the exiles from northern Israel in Nineveh, with Assyria as the dominant power. Bauckham concludes, "There is therefore no serious obstacle here to concluding that the book was written largely for the benefit of exiles of the northern tribes, who lived in Adiabene and especially in Media, by an author living somewhere in the eastern diaspora other than Media."[85]

Whereas Tobit used to go faithfully to Jerusalem from the north for the festivals, he acknowledges the apostasy of the north in their worship of the calf erected by Jeroboam. Indeed, Auneau evocatively describes Tobit as "the Decalogue in action."[86] The narrative of Tobit revolves around his life in exile; his sufferings, and those of Sarah, who was beset by a demon; God's faithfulness amid their suffering; the marriage of Tobias, Tobit's son, to Sarah; and the role of the angel Raphael in releasing Sarah from her demon. Piety includes almsgiving, ensuring burial of Jews, prayer, and keeping the food laws—central motifs. Intriguingly, there is a reference to the prophecies of Nahum about Nineveh (14:4), and before Tobias dies he hears of the destruction of Nineveh (14:15). Central to Tobit is the hope for

---

83. For a list of summary tellings of the story of Israel, see N. T. Wright, *NTPG* 218n10.
84. Nickelsburg, *Jewish Literature*, 27.
85. R. Bauckham, "Tobit as a Parable for the Exiles of Northern Israel," in *The Jewish World around the New Testament: Collected Essays I*, WUNT 233 (Tübingen: Mohr Siebeck, 2008), 459.
86. J. Auneau, *Écrits didactiques: Le Livre de Tobie; Les Psaumes et les autres Écrits*, Petite bibliothèque des sciences bibliques Ancien Testament 5 (Tournai: Desclée, 1990), 353–66, esp. 364.

the restoration of the nation Israel. As Bauckham argues, "Tobit's story is a parable of Israel's story from exile to restoration.... The overall shape of Tobit's story models that of Israel."[87]

The Epistle of Jeremiah takes its cue from Jeremiah 10:2–15 and the prophet's letter in chapter 29. The author alleges this to be another letter that Jeremiah wrote to the exiles in Babylon. The work is a diatribe against the gods of the gentiles as idols and "not gods." A refrain recurs in the work (as in v. 23):

> From this you will know that they are not gods;
> so do not fear them.

Second Temple literature is vast and a major resource both for interpretation of the Hebrew Bible and for the background to the New Testament. Study of the individual documents is indispensable, but as we have seen, a narrative approach such as that of Wright is illuminating in terms of the Hebrew Bible as an unfolding story and the multiple ways in which this story and its parts were read and reread in the Second Temple period.

The Period of the Tannaim and the Amoraim

Silver draws attention to a striking contrast between early Christian writings and Jewish ones:

> As far as we know, after the generations of Philo and Josephus—for perhaps seven centuries[88]—no sage wrote or signed a book, be it history, apologetic, or code.... None of the literature of the period—Mishnah, Tosefta, Talmudim, halachic Midrashim, and so on—were books in the sense of material presented by a single author on a predetermined theme; rather, these are simply collections of formulas and memorized notes which emerged over several generations, collected and set down as guides to action rather than as shaped literature.... But the sages were not idle. One of the paradoxes of Jewish history is that at the very moment when Hebrew scrolls were being transformed into Scripture, another body of teachings [that] Jews would also call Torah were being organized. This other body of teachings, the Mishnah and its later commentaries, the two Gemaras (Palestinian and Babylonian), came to be known as the Talmud and in a surprisingly short time replaced the *Tanakh* as the primary source book to which Jews turned for knowledge about doctrine and duty.[89]

---

87. Bauckham, "Tobit as a Parable," 434.
88. A very useful source for the literature of this period is E. Ben-Eliyahu et al., *Handbook of Jewish Literature from Late Antiquity, 135–700 CE* (Oxford: Oxford University Press, 2012).
89. D. J. Silver, *The Story of Scripture: From Oral Tradition to the Written Word* (New York: Basic Books, 1990), 174–75.

Tannaim (Aramaic *tannā'îm* = repeaters [of the law]; those who study) were the early rabbinic scholars responsible[90] for the Mishnah, *Pirqe Aboth*, Tosefta, and other tractates found in the Babylonian and Palestinian Talmuds. The Amoraim (speakers, expounders) were rabbinic scholars living in Palestine and Babylon from the third century to the sixth century AD. They were responsible for the Talmudic writings and haggadic midrashim.

The Mishnah is the body of rabbinic teachings attributed to the Tannaim and compiled about AD 200. It is a "philosophical law code, covering topics of both a theoretical and practical character."[91] "So the Mishnah indeed is, and therefore is meant as, a legal code, a schoolbook, and a corpus of tradition."[92] Although they drew heavily on the Hebrew Bible, they do not foreground this relationship, and thus the Mishnah contains little exegesis. The Mishnah is the basic halakic text, dealing with the regulation of conduct, in contrast with haggadah, which deals with ethical and theological issues. Jacob Neusner characterizes Mishnah thus:

> This language does not speak of sacred symbols but of pots and pans, of menstruation and dead creeping things; of ordinary water which, because of the circumstance of its collection and location, possesses extraordinary power; of the commonplace corpse and ubiquitous diseased person; of genitalia and excrement, toilet seats, and the flux of penises; of stems of pomegranates and stalks of leeks; of rain and earth and wood, metal, glass, and hide. This language is filled with words for neutral things of humble existence. It does not speak of holy things and is not symbolic in its substance. This language speaks of ordinary things, of things which everyone must have known. But because of the peculiar and particular way in which it is formed and formalized, this same language not only adheres to an aesthetic theory but [also] expresses a deeply embedded ontology and methodology of the sacred, specifically of the sacred within the secular, and of the capacity for regulation, therefore for sanctification, within the ordinary: All things in order, all things then hallowed by God who orders all things, so said the priests' creation tale.[93]

The commentaries of the Babylonian and Palestinian *Talmuds* are based on the Mishnah and Tosefta. The *Tosefta* is a body of rabbinic writings recording rabbinic discussions of various topics based on the Mishnah and

---

90. For the key rabbis of the five generations, see Ben-Eliyahu et al., *Handbook of Jewish Literature*, xxiii–xxiv.

91. J. Neusner, *Introduction to Rabbinic Literature*, Anchor Bible Reference Library (New York: Doubleday, 1994), 98.

92. J. Neusner, *The Mishnah: An Introduction* (1989; reprint, Lanham, MD: Rowman & Littlefield, 2004), 39.

93. Ibid., 39.

the Hebrew Bible. Tosefta literally means "supplement": it was supplemental to the Mishnah. The editorial work for the Babylonian Talmud took place around AD 500–600, and that for the Palestinian Talmud around AD 400–450.

The *Targums* were Aramaic translations of the Hebrew Bible produced by early rabbis for public reading of the Hebrew Bible in the synagogue. By the first century AD, Aramaic had become the vernacular of Jewish communities in Palestine, Syria, Mesopotamia, and elsewhere. They are not always literal and often contain interpretation. As they conclude their study of halakah in *Targum Jonathan to the Prophets*, Smolar and Aberbach rightly explain, "It cannot be sufficiently emphasized that the central purpose of the Aramaic translation of Biblical texts was not to provide an accurate rendering for the benefit of scholars, but to instruct the masses with an up-to-date version of the Scriptures, one which perforce had to agree with current laws and customs. Inevitably, accuracy and historical truth had to be sacrificed on the altar of halachic orthodoxy."[94]

As translation and interpretations, the Targums are of obvious interest to Old Testament biblical scholars. For example, there are thirteen occurrences of the phrase "Father in Heaven." Distribution is uneven, and only in Exodus 1:19 do all three representatives of the *Palestinian Targum* contain it.[95]

Of more immediate interest for the history of biblical interpretation are the *midrashim*, a distinctive form of rabbinic literature. "Midrash" can mean several things. The word "midrash" comes from the root *dāraš*, meaning "search" in Hebrew, and here it refers to the same thing as "interpretation" or "exegesis" in English. "Midrash" also stands for a compilation of such interpretations, as in *Midrash Rabbah*, which covers compilations of midrash for the Pentateuch and the Five Scrolls (Ruth, Esther, Lamentations, Song of Songs, Ecclesiastes), biblical books that were read in the synagogue liturgy. Finally, "midrash" may refer to the particular approach to interpretation of Judaic sages. Our concern here is with the midrash compilations that reached closure in the formative age of Judaism, that is, the first seven centuries AD, the time in which the Mishnah (ca. 200), the Talmud of the Land of Israel (ca. 400), and the Talmud of Babylonia (ca. 600) were written.[96]

Their explicit reference to the canonical text differentiates the midrash compilations from other Jewish literature like the Mishnah. Indeed, Neusner

---

94. L. Smolar and M. Aberbach, *Studies in Targum Jonathan to the Prophets*; [bound with] P. Churgin, *Targum Jonathan to the Prophets* (New York: Ktav, 1983), 61.

95. See M. McNamara, *Targum and Testament: Aramaic Paraphrases of the Hebrew Bible*, 2nd ed. (Grand Rapids: Eerdmans, 2010), 177–86.

96. For the literature, see Ben-Eliyahu et al., *Jewish Literature from Late Antiquity*, 61–95.

argues that a motivation for the midrashim was to show that the sort of material found in the Mishnah was indeed biblical.⁹⁷ *Sifra (Sipra)* on Leviticus and *Sifre (Sipre)* on Numbers and Deuteronomy, two of the earliest midrashic collections, were composed to demonstrate that logic unaided by reference to Scripture would distort one's understanding of God's will.⁹⁸

This foregrounds an issue of ongoing importance in Jewish and Christian biblical interpretation: the role of "unaided reason." Judaism has a strong emphasis on study and the role of reason. At the same time early Judaism produced a mystical literature with lasting influence.⁹⁹ Neusner argues that "the most distinctive and paramount trait of Judaism as it has been known for the past two thousand years is the conviction that the primary mode of the service of God (not the sole mode, but the paramount one) is the study of Torah."¹⁰⁰ As does Aquinas, Neusner locates the image of God in the mind and reason. "When man uses his mind, he is acting like God."¹⁰¹ "All reality comes under the discipline of the critical intellect; all is capable of sanctification."¹⁰² In their work *The Intellectual Foundations of Christian and Jewish Discourse*, Chilton and Neusner state, "Our thesis is that at their deepest foundations, Christianity and Rabbinic Judaism take their place wholly within Greek philosophical modes of articulating contradictory propositions and proposing explicit arguments and evidence to show that one is right, the other wrong."¹⁰³

> Our argument is that, from their first writings, Paul's letters and the Mishnah, through their climactic statements out of late antiquity, Augustine's *City of God* and the Talmud of Babylonia, Christianity and Judaism undertook their generative and formative thought wholly within, completely at home in, the Greek philosophical milieu, so far as that intellectual world required the explicit articulation of dispute and validation through rigorous argument of one position over the other, contradictory one.¹⁰⁴

---

97. J. Neusner, *Midrash in Context: Exegesis in Formative Judaism* (Philadelphia: Fortress, 1983).

98. Cf. Neusner, *Midrash Reader*, 36–48.

99. The major work on this was done by Gershom Scholem in the twentieth century. See J. Dan, *Gershom Scholem and the Mystical Dimension of Jewish History*, trans. N. Ambercrombie (New York: New York University Press, 1987). For the twentieth century, see J. J. Cohen, *Major Philosophers of Jewish Prayer in the Twentieth Century* (Bronx, NY: Fordham University Press, 2000).

100. J. Neusner, *Glory of God Is Intelligence: Four Lectures on the Role of Intellect in Judaism* (Salt Lake City: Religious Studies Center, Brigham Young University, 1978), Kindle loc. 131–32.

101. Ibid., Kindle loc. 139–40. In my view this is a reductive view of the *imago Dei*.

102. Ibid., Kindle loc. 195.

103. B. Chilton and J. Neusner, *The Intellectual Foundations of Christian and Jewish Discourse: The Philosophy of Religious Argument* (New York: Routledge, 1997), cited via Kindle ed.

104. Ibid., Kindle ed.

In my view this is a misreading of Paul and Augustine and the best of the early Christian tradition. Under the label of "evidentialism," some Christians today continue to espouse such a view, but it is far better to see reason as operating within the bounds of religion, as Wolterstorff, in contrast to Kant, has argued.[105] This raises the issue of what we read Scripture for; is it for a relationship with God that includes cognitive elements? Or do we read for cognition, with the relational element secondary?

In his *A Midrash Reader*, Neusner claims that "the ancient rabbis read Scripture as God's personal letter to them"[106] and that in the midrash compilations we find models for our study of and response to Scripture. "They show us choices we may not have known we had. And once we see how they read Scripture, we can do no less."[107] The midrashim arose in rabbinic academies where rabbis trained other rabbis; hence arose the style of collating rabbinic views in relation to texts and parts of texts. The Tannaitic midrashim are largely halakic; the homiletic midrashim contain a number of synagogue sermons and exemplify the desire to demonstrate the unity of the canon into a seamless whole as God's one Word.

An example of the importance of these early Jewish works for New Testament interpretation is the relationship between the Passover and the Last Supper.[108] In his *Jesus and the Jewish Roots of the Eucharist*, Brant Pitre draws on the DSS, the works of Josephus, the Mishnah, the Babylonian Talmud, and the Passover midrashim[109] to excavate the Jewish background to the Last Supper in the practice of the Passover.[110] The result is rich and illuminating. The Hebrew Bible itself does not provide us with much detail about the practice of the Passover meal;[111] furthermore, between

105. N. Wolterstorff, *Reason within the Bounds of Religion*, 2nd ed. (Grand Rapids: Eerdmans, 1999); cf. C. G. Bartholomew and M. Goheen, *Christian Philosophy: A Systematic and Narrative Introduction* (Grand Rapids: Baker Academic, 2013).
106. Neusner, *Midrash Reader*, 1.
107. Ibid.
108. For many critical details, see J. Jeremias, *The Eucharistic Words of Jesus*, trans. N. Perrin (Philadelphia: Fortress, 1966), who sets out evidence for the Last Supper being a Passover meal; I. H. Marshall, *Last Supper and Lord's Supper* (Carlisle, UK: Paternoster, 1980), who on 75 concludes, "Jesus held a Passover meal earlier than the official Jewish date . . . as the result of calendar differences among the Jews." Cf. N. T. Wright, *Jesus and the Victory of God*, vol. 2 of Christian Origins and the Question of God (London: SPCK, 1996), 555-59; on 556-57, following John's chronology, he suggests that Jesus deliberately celebrated a quasi-Passover meal a day ahead of the regular night.
109. Cf. also N. N. Glatzer, ed., *The Schocken Passover Haggadah* (New York: Schocken, 1953).
110. B. Pitre, *Jesus and the Jewish Roots of the Eucharist: Unlocking the Secrets of the Last Supper* (New York: Doubleday, 2011), draws on Jeremias, *Eucharistic Words*; S. McKnight, *Jesus and His Death: Historiography, the Historical Jesus, and Atonement Theory* (Waco: Baylor University Press, 2005); I. H. Marshall, *Last Supper*; D. Daube, *The New Testament and Rabbinic Judaism* (Peabody, MA: Hendrickson, 1995); etc. For a synopsis of the accounts of the Last Supper, see I. H. Marshall, *Last Supper*, 180-81.
111. Cf. Pitre, *Jewish Roots*, 50-58; R. de Vaux, *Ancient Israel: Its Life and Institutions* (New York: McGraw-Hill, 1961; reprint, Grand Rapids: Eerdmans, 1997), 484-93.

the exodus and the time of Jesus, it developed and changed. In order to grasp the full significance of the Last Supper as a Passover meal, the early Jewish works discussed above are indispensable. Josephus reports, for example, that in one year the number of lambs sacrificed for the Passover was 256,500.[112] Many Westerners have never witnessed a single animal slaughtered, but for Jews in Jesus's day, it would be impossible to forget how much blood was shed on the Passover. Some Jewish traditions connected the Passover to the coming of the Messiah and the dawn of the new age.[113] Jeremias insists that the Last Supper must be seen in conjunction with the many meals Jesus engaged in: "Like the rest of them, it is an *antedonation* of the *consummation* (Luke 22.16; Mark 14.25)."[114] Tom Wright points out that the Last Supper must be held together with Jesus's temple action; both symbolize Jesus's intention to replace the temple system with *himself*: "Jesus deliberately drew on to himself the whole tradition of Jewish expectation and hope.... The final meal ... gained its significance from his own entire life and agenda, and from the events which, he knew, would shortly come to pass. It was Jesus' chosen way of investing those imminent events with the significance he believed they would carry."[115]

The Mishnah and the Tosefta provide detailed descriptions of the sequence of the Passover meal. It was arranged around four cups of wine, with the following sequence:[116]

- The meal was preceded by several hours of fasting.
- Shortly before nightfall the father would gather his household at a large table.
- The meal began with the pouring and mixing of the first cup of wine, followed by a formal blessing over the cup and the feast day; the cup was shared.
- Then the food was brought to the table: unleavened bread, bitter herbs, a bowl of sauce, and the roasted Passover lamb.
- A preliminary course of the herbs and sauce was then eaten.
- Then the second cup was mixed but not drunk until after the explanation of the Passover.
- The son would ask, "Why is this night different from other nights?" The father would explain the significance of the meal and its symbolism.
- In a response of gratitude, the participants would sing Psalms 113–14.
- Then the third cup would be mixed, signaling the actual start of the meal.
- After the meal another blessing would be said over the third cup.
- Finally Psalms 115–18 were sung, after which the fourth cup of wine was drunk.

Jesus connects the meal with his impending death and its significance. According to Luke 22:15, Jesus eagerly desires to eat "this Passover" with his disciples before his passion. Then in Luke 22:16 Jesus says, "I will not eat it until it is fulfilled in the kingdom of God." Jeremias takes this to mean that Jesus desired to eat the Passover but abstained from it. However, as many have noticed, this is unlikely, and the addition of "again" by some ancient authorities likely gets at the correct meaning.[117] In Luke 22:18 Jesus asserts, "From now on I will not drink of the fruit of the vine until the kingdom of God comes." Although we cannot be certain, a fascinating suggestion is that Jesus deliberately did not drink of the traditional fourth cup at the Last Supper. The cup of the "new covenant" is the third cup, and Daube argues that Jesus's reference not to drink again of the fruit of the vine (cf. Matt. 26:29; Mark 14:25) is a reference to the fourth cup.[118] Pitre thus argues that the reference to "this cup" in Gethsemane (Matt.

---

112. Josephus, *Jewish War* 6.423–27.
113. Pitre, *Jewish Roots*, 66–68.
114. Jeremias, *New Testament Theology*, 290.
115. N. T. Wright, *Jesus and the Victory of God*, 558.
116. Pitre, *Jewish Roots*, 149–58; J. B. Green, *The Gospel of Luke*, NICNT (Grand Rapids: Eerdmans, 1997), 758; I. H. Marshall, *Last Supper*, 179.
117. Cf. I. H. Marshall, *Last Supper*, 81–82.
118. Daube, *New Testament and Rabbinic Judaism*, 330–31; cf. Pitre, *Jewish Roots*, 158–63.

26:36–46) is the fourth cup, the final cup to complete the Passover. On the way to be crucified, Jesus was offered wine but notably refused it (Matt. 27:31–36). At the very end, however, Jesus did drink wine, according to Matthew (27:48), Mark (15:36), and John (19:23–30). According to John 19:30, "When Jesus had received the wine, he said 'It is finished.'" Now the Passover is complete and the new exodus achieved because Jesus has drunk the final cup of the Passover.

Methods of Jewish Exegesis

In the first century four major methods of Jewish interpretation can be identified: literal, midrashic, pesher, and allegorical. There is no doubt that Judaism often read the Hebrew Bible according to its plain meaning. Since the fourth century AD, the term *peshat* (*pěšaṭ*) was used to distinguish literal from other forms of interpretation. Midrashic exegesis in the Babylonian Talmud, for example, is clearly distinguished from literal interpretation in that it seeks to penetrate into the spirit of the Scriptures and thereby to discern what may not be obvious. The Talmud attributes the seven basic rules of rabbinic exegesis to Hillel. Hillel was a near contemporary of Jesus. The dates commonly assigned to him are around 50 BC to around AD 10. Some of his teachings, moreover, are close to the teachings of Jesus.[119]

Here are the seven *middoth*, norms for interpretation:

1. *Qal wa-homer*: what applies in a less important case will certainly apply in a more important one.
2. *Gezerah shawah*: verbal analogy from one verse to another.
3. *Binyan 'ab mikathub 'ehad*: building up a principle from one text, which can then be applied to other texts.
4. *Binyan 'ab mishene kethubim*: building up a principle from two texts, which can then be applied to other texts.
5. *Kelal upherat*: a general principle may be restricted by another reverse or conversely a particular rule may be extended into a principle.
6. *Kayoze' bo bemaqom 'aher*: a difficulty in one place may be resolved by comparing it with another that has points of general similarity.
7. *Dabar halamed me-'inyano*: a meaning established by its context.

Early in the second century AD, Rabbi Akiba developed Hillel's *middoth* into thirteen rules, and much later Rabbi Eliezer ben Jose ha-Galili formed them into thirty-two rules. Some of Hillel's *middoth* are common sense, but others are open to abuse. As they were further expanded, rabbinic efforts developed into "an atomistic exegesis, which interprets sentences, clauses, phrases, and

---

119. Neusner, *Judaism in the Beginning of Christianity*, Kindle loc. 719–20.

even single words independently of the context of the historical occasion, as divine oracles; combines them with other similarly detached utterances; and makes large use of analogy of expressions, often by purely verbal association."[120]

Pesher interpretation is used for the interpretation in the material found at Qumran, the DSS.[121] We have already discussed how the Essenes reinterpreted the story of Israel. In his early study of Qumran exegesis, Brownlee distinguished thirteen characteristics of their hermeneutic.[122] Not surprisingly, his first one is that "everything the ancient prophet wrote has a *veiled, eschatological meaning*" related to the role of the Qumran community. This eschatological dimension distinguishes Qumran interpretation from rabbinic. Brownlee's second characteristic is "*forced or abnormal construction of the biblical text*," but this rests on deviations from the MT and is thus harder to demonstrate in the current state of textual criticism. In his remaining eleven characteristics, Brownlee shows that Qumran exegesis is very similar to *midrash*. Hence some characterize Qumranic exegesis as *pesher-midrash*. This is useful as long as one remembers the centrality of the eschatological dimension in their interpretation, ever seeking the mystery in the text and its fulfillment among themselves.

Philo was the most prominent Jewish *allegorist* of the first century.[123] He used Greek philosophical categories to present the truth of the Torah for his contemporaries and to vindicate it before the court of Hellenistic philosophy. As we saw in chapter 5, Greek thought offered two ways to contemporize Homer; Philo chose the allegorical route. "Philo usually treated the Old Testament as a body of symbols given by God for man's spiritual and moral benefit, which must be understood other than in a literal and historical fashion. The *prima facie* meaning must normally be pushed aside, even counted as offensive, to make room for the intended spiritual meaning underlying the obvious."[124] Philo is certainly representative of a trend in Hellenistic Jewish exegesis.[125] As we noticed in chapter 5, Philo was influential on certain church fathers although, not surprisingly, Theodore of Mopsuestia strongly opposed his approach and influence.

---

120. G. F. Moore, *Judaism in the First Centuries of the Christian Era: The Age of the Tannaim*, 3 vols. (Cambridge, MA: Harvard University Press, 1927–30), 1:248.

121. For primary DSS texts related to the Bible, see M. Abegg Jr., P. Flint, and E. Ulrich, *The Dead Sea Scrolls Bible: The Oldest Known Bible Translated for the First Time in English* (San Francisco: HarperSanFrancisco, 1999).

122. W. H. Brownlee, "Biblical Interpretation among the Sectaries of the Dead Sea Scrolls," *BA* 14 (1951): 60–62.

123. See P. Borgen, "Philo of Alexandria as Exegete," in Hauser and Watson, *History of Biblical Interpretation*, 1:114–43.

124. Longenecker, *Biblical Exegesis*, 31.

125. Ibid., 32.

Early Jewish interpretation remains an important resource, but its midrashic tendencies limit its potential for contemporary use.[126] Medieval Jewish interpretation is mixed and in many cases still unexplored territory, yet well worth exploring, not least because of the recovery and development of *peshat* interpretation in a major way.

Medieval Jewish Interpretation

Medieval Jewish interpretation encompasses the period of the *Geonim*, from the middle of the sixth to the middle of the eleventh centuries, and the period of the *Rishonim*, from the eleventh to the sixteenth centuries.[127] The *Geonim*[128] (pride or splendor) were the presidents of the two great Babylonian, Talmudic Academies of Sura and Pumbedita, in the Abbasid Caliphate. They were the generally accepted spiritual leaders of the Jewish community worldwide in the early medieval era. The Geonim played a prominent and decisive role in the transmission and teaching of Torah and Jewish law. A responsibility of the Gaon was to respond to questions from the Jewish Diaspora, and in the early part of the Geonic period their literary work was restricted to the *responsum*, responses to queries mainly in the area of talmudic exegesis and Jewish law (halakah).[129] Biblical study and commentary became prominent only in the tenure of Saadiah (AD 928–942) and his followers. Brody reports, "Geonic

---

126. Naturally, views differ in this respect. See, e.g., M. Fishbane, ed., *The Midrashic Imagination: Jewish Exegesis, Thought, and History* (Albany: State University of New York Press, 1993). For a fascinating exploration of midrash for today, see S. E. Sasso, *God's Echo: Exploring Scripture with Midrash* (Brewster, MA: Paraclete, 2007).

127. Our treatment is inevitably highly selective. M. Saebø, *HB/OT* 1.2 (2000), is a significant resource; see esp. chaps. 25, 31–32. Readers should also be aware of volumes on individual biblical books, such as B. D. Walfish, *Esther in Medieval Garb: Jewish Interpretation of the Book of Esther in the Middle Ages* (Albany: State University of New York Press, 1993); U. Simon, *Four Approaches to the Book of Psalms: From Saadiah Gaon to Abraham Ibn Ezra* (Albany: State University of New York Press, 1991); J. Kalman, "With Friends Like These: Turning Points in the Jewish Exegesis of the Biblical Book of Job" (PhD diss., McGill University, 2005); I. Kalimi, *An Ancient Israelite Historian: Studies in the Chronicler, His Time, Place and Writing*, Studia Semitica Neerlandica 46 (Assen: Van Gorcum, 2006); idem, *The Retelling of Chronicles in Jewish Tradition and Literature: A Historical Journey* (Winona Lake, IN: Eisenbrauns, 2009); R. A. Parry and H. A. Thomas, eds., *Great Is Thy Faithfulness? Reading Lamentations as Sacred Scripture* (Eugene, OR: Pickwick, 2011); etc.

128. For bibliographical references, see R. Brody, "The Geonim of Babylonia as Biblical Exegetes," in Saebø, *HB/OT* 1.2 (2000): 74–88.

129. N. Roth ("Rabbis," in *Medieval Jewish Civilization: An Encyclopedia*, ed. N. Roth, Routledge Encyclopedias of the Middle Ages 7 [New York: Routledge, 2007]) states, "Responsa [answers] constitute for the modern historian perhaps the most important source material for an understanding of medieval Jewish life. Vast numbers of responsa have survived from the *geonim*" (556).

exegesis in general may be characterized as more disciplined and less fanciful than earlier rabbinic exegesis, and more concerned with a close, systematic reading of the biblical text, in which attention is devoted both to the smallest textual units and to the integrity of larger narratives."[130]

The *Rishonim* (the first ones) were the leading rabbis who lived during approximately the eleventh to the fifteenth centuries. For our purposes, prominent Rishonim include the following. The first three were members of the French school.

- Rashi (1040–1105)[131]

- Joseph Kara (1050–1125). Kara further developed Rashi's emphasis on the plain sense of the text, stating unequivocally, "Whosoever is ignorant of the plain meaning of the biblical text, preferring the homiletical interpretation, resembles a person who has been washed away by a flowing river, is drowning in the depths of the water and grasps at whatever he can to save himself; while if he heeded the word of the Lord he would investigate the explanations and the plain meaning."[132]

- Rashbam (1080–1160)

- Abraham ibn Ezra (1089–1164) was forced to leave Muslim Spain at the age of fifty, when he moved to Italy.[133] He describes his *peshat* hermeneutic as satisfying "meticulous philology ('the cords of grammar') and strict rational plausibility ('eye of reason')."[134]

- David Qimhi (Radak) (ca. 1105–70) of Provence. Mordechai Cohen appraises Radak's hermeneutic: "Although he rejects many rabbinic readings as *derash*, he subtly absorbs others into his *peshat* exegesis; and at the same time that he champions the Spanish *peshat* method, we can discern midrashic principles in his exegetical thinking."[135]

---

130. Brody, "Geonim of Babylonia," 87.
131. A. Grossman, *Rashi* (Portland, OR: Littman Library of Jewish Civilization, 2012); E. Wiesel, *Rashi*, Jewish Encounters (New York: Schocken Books, 2012); M. I. Gruber, *Rashi's Commentary on the Psalms* (Philadelphia: Jewish Publication Society, 2008).
132. Quoted in A. Grossman, "The School of Literal Jewish Exegesis in Northern France," in Saebø, *HB/OT* 1.2 (2000): 321–71, esp. 351.
133. I. Lancaster, *Deconstructing the Bible: Abraham ibn Ezra's Introduction to the Torah*, Routledge Jewish Studies Series (New York: Routledge, 2003).
134. U. Simon, "Jewish Exegesis in Spain and Provence and in the East in the Twelfth and Thirteenth Centuries: Abraham Ibn Ezra," in Saebø, *HB/OT* 1.2 (2000): 377–87, esp. 378.
135. M. Cohen, "The Qimhi Family," in Saebø, *HB/OT* 1.2 (2000): 388–415, esp. 398. Also see F. Talmage, *David Kimhi: The Man and His Commentaries* (Cambridge, MA: Harvard University Press, 1975); idem, ed., *The Commentaries on Proverbs of the Kimhi Family* [Hebrew] (Jerusalem: Magnes, 1990).

- Maimonides (1135/8–1204). A Spanish North African, Maimonides wrested with the relationship between religion and philosophy, and in the introduction to his *Guide for the Perplexed*, he sets forth the principles of his midrashic allegorical hermeneutic.[136]
- Nahmanides (Ramban) (1194–1270). A Spanish Jew, Elman says of his *Commentary on the Pentateuch*, "The result is a highly nuanced, often open-ended, multileveled interpretation of the Pentateuch, in which literal, moral, and legalistic exegesis, and eschatological and mystical interpretation all find their place."[137]
- Isaac Abarbanel (Abravanel) (1437–1508/9), born in Lisbon but spent his later years in Italy. He was an exegete[138] whose output is estimated at twelve thousand pages of biblical commentary.[139] Roth says, "Abravanel's greatest originality certainly lay in his biblical commentaries. If he was by no means the first or the only Spanish Jewish author to cite non-Jewish, even Christian, theological sources, he was apparently the first to provide systematic introductions to each book of the Bible on which he commented, analyzing the content of each."[140] While in many ways traditional, in his exegesis he also drew on Renaissance humanism to explore questions about the human origins of the Hebrew Bible. A distinctive of Abarbanel's exegesis was his practice of raising questions *before* explaining a pericope in order to "highlight issues, spark debate, and broaden the inquiry."[141] Intriguingly, in the monumental, multivolume *The Commentators' Bible: The JPS Miqra'ot Gedolot*, translated, edited, and annotated by Michael Carasik, virtually each page contains one or more of Abarbanel's questions. Their Socratic style remains provocative and stimulating. For example, on Exodus 20 the following questions from Abarbanel are included:
  - Why is there such a mixture of positive and negative commandments?

---

136. See S. Klein-Braslavy, "The Philosophical Exegesis," in Saebø, *HB/OT* 1.2 (2000): 302–20, esp. 311–20 on Maimonides.

137. Y. Elman, "Moses ben Nahman/Nahmanides (Ramban)," in Saebø, *HB/OT* 1.2 (2000): 416–32, esp. 418. Cf. N. Caputo, *Nahmanides in Medieval Catalonia: History, Community, and Messianism* (Notre Dame, IN: University of Notre Dame Press, 2008).

138. See E. Lawee, "Isaac Abarbanel: From Medieval to Renaissance Jewish Biblical Scholarship," in Saebø, *HB/OT* 2 (2008): 190–214. From the sixteenth to the eighteenth centuries, Abarbanel was much studied by Christian exegetes, most notably by Richard Simon (1638–1712), an early Roman Catholic critic.

139. Lawee, "Isaac Abarbanel," 194.

140. N. Roth, "Abravanel Family," in Roth, *Medieval Jewish Civilization*, Kindle loc. 960–62.

141. Lawee, "Isaac Abarbanel," 195.

- Why are the commandments written in this order?
- How can a just God "visit the guilt of the parents upon the children"?
- Why is "your neighbor" mentioned in the commandments against false witness and coveting but not in the others, for example, "You shall not murder your neighbor"?[142]

As noted above, a major development in this period was the emergence of *peshat* exegesis and a great number of commentaries in this style. There is ongoing debate about how and why this significant shift occurred, but many relate it to Karaite[143] exegesis[144] and exegesis in northern France.[145] *Merriam-Webster's Dictionary* defines Karaism as "a Jewish doctrine originating in Baghdad in the eighth century that rejects rabbinism and talmudism and bases its tenets on Scripture alone." Since the demise of the Eastern Bloc, some sixteen thousand Karaite manuscripts in Soviet collections have become available. Daniel Frank argues, "It was unquestionably the Karaites who moved biblical exegesis to center stage. Abandoning Rabbinic midrash while championing philology, they perfected a new form. The Biblical commentary was born in the Islamic East."[146] This may be overstated and needs to be correlated with the explosion of Jewish commentary writing in northern France in the eleventh century. During 1070–1170 at least ten commentaries on Job were written by French Jews.[147] Three factors are generally related to this dramatic development:[148] Spanish-Jewish influence,[149] the twelfth-century renaissance

142. M. Carasik, ed., *The Commentators' Bible: The JPS Miqra'ot Gedolot: Exodus* (Philadelphia: Jewish Publication Society, 2005), 155, 157, 162. The *Miqra'ot Gedolot* includes the most prominent Jewish medieval commentators—Rashi, Rashbam, Ibn Ezra, Nahmanides—as well as selected comments from other commentators of that time. It is a major and welcome resource. See also N. Grunhaus, *The Challenge of Received Tradition: Dilemmas of Interpretation in Radak's Biblical Commentaries* (Oxford: Oxford University Press, 2012).
143. See M. Polliack, ed., *Karaite Judaism: A Guide to Its History and Literary Sources*, Handbook of Oriental Studies: Section 1, The Near and Middle East 73 (Leiden: Brill, 2003).
144. See D. Frank, "Karaite Exegesis," in Saebø, *HB/OT* 1.2 (2000): 110–28; M. Polliack, "Major Trends in Karaite Biblical Exegesis in the Tenth and Eleventh Centuries," in Polliack, *Karaite Judaism*, 363–413.
145. See Grossman, "The School of Literal Jewish Exegesis in Northern France," 321–71.
146. D. Frank, *Search Scripture Well: Karaite Exegesis and the Origins of the Jewish Bible Commentary in the Islamic East* (Leiden: Brill, 2004), 257.
147. See Grossman, "Literal Jewish Exegesis."
148. See ibid., 326–31.
149. See A. Sáenz-Badillos, "Early Hebraists in Spain: Menaḥem ben Saruq and Dunash ben Labraṭ," in Saebø, *HB/OT* 1/2 (2000): 96–109; chap. 31, "The Flourishing Era of Jewish Exegesis in Spain," in Saebø, *HB/OT* 1.2 (2000): 261–320; chap. 33, "Jewish Exegesis in Spain and Provence, and in the East, in the Twelfth and Thirteenth Centuries," in Saebø, *HB/OT* 1.2 (2000): 372–466.

in Christian Europe, and polemics between Jews and Christians.[150] Debate continues about which was the major influence.[151]

This period "begins" with the Genoic academies of Babylonia. *Saadiah Gaon* (882–942) was head of the influential academy of Sura, the first major Jewish philosopher of the medieval era and perhaps the greatest figure of this period. His life is filled with a number of "firsts" in areas such as halakah, philosophy, exegesis, Hebrew grammar, liturgy, and poetry. He provided one of the first Arabic translations of the Old Testament and wrote a number of commentaries on Old Testament books, which influenced subsequent medieval Jewish exegesis.[152] As with many medieval Jewish commentators, his interpretation is closely connected to his philosophy so that his commentaries are a hybrid of linguistic analysis and philosophy.[153]

Saadiah's reading of Job is fascinating. As Eisen notes, Saadiah "very much appreciates the major exegetical difficulties in the Book of Job and . . . he displays considerable originality in his solutions to those difficulties."[154] He is also original in choosing Job rather than Abraham as the exemplar of divine trials.[155] Saadiah argues that Job is an historical figure and a righteous gentile who lived during the period of the exodus. Satan is a human person, an acquaintance of Job who leads a band of his companions to slander Job by arguing that his righteousness is the result of his wealth and large family. God tests Job to demonstrate to his contemporaries that his faith is genuine

150. This view was proposed by Izhak F. Bauer, says Grossman, "Literal Jewish Exegesis," 325. Cf. G. Stemberger, "Elements of Biblical Interpretation in Medieval Jewish-Christian Disputation," in Saebø, *HB/OT* 1.2 (2000): 578–90; Stemberger states, "The growing tendency of Jewish medieval exegesis to abandon popular midrashic interpretations in favor of the *peshat* is due to several reasons, not the least important one being the renewed Jewish-Christian disputation" (582).

151. See J. Kalman, "Medieval Jewish Biblical Commentaries and the State of *Parshanut* Studies," *Religion Compass* 2, no. 5 (2008): 820–34. This is a very useful article, with a full bibliography.

152. To date there is no comprehensive study of Saadiah's commentaries or hermeneutic. For his work on Job, see R. Eisen, *The Book of Job in Medieval Jewish Philosophy* (New York: Oxford University Press, 2004), 17–41; L. E. Goodman, ed., *The Book of Theodicy: Translation and Commentary on the Book of Job by Saadiah ben Joseph al-Fayyūmī*, Yale Judaica Series 25 (New Haven: Yale University Press, 1988). See also the fine essay by A. Mittleman, "The Job of Judaism and the Job of Kant," *HTR* 102, no. 1 (2009): 25–50. For this entire discussion of Job, see also Kalman, "With Friends Like These." On the *Testament of Job*, see M. Wisse, *Scripture between Identity and Creativity: A Hermeneutical Theory Building upon Four Interpretations of Job*, Ars Disputandi: Supplement Series 1 (Utrecht: Ars Disputandi, 2003), 35–49; in addition, this work focuses on Calvin, Orlando di Lasso, and Gustavo Gutiérrez.

153. Eisen, *Book of Job*.
154. Ibid., 36.
155. Ibid., 39.

and to give him the opportunity to earn reward now and in the afterlife. The dialogue between Job and his friends embodies two viewpoints: that of Job, who is convinced that God is just but has caused him to suffer arbitrarily; and that of the friends, who believe Job's suffering must be punishment for sin. Only Elihu correctly suggests that Job's suffering is a test. That the divine speeches do not address Job's suffering is a part of the trial; if God were to explain the suffering, it would derail its purpose, which is to manifest Job's righteousness to others.

For Saadiah, Job is a symbol of Israel even though a gentile. In this respect Saadiah's typological/symbolic exegesis is noteworthy. For example, he reads the garden of Eden as a symbol of the temple, the laws given to Adam as representative of the Torah, the snake in the garden as symbolic of the false prophets, and the exile from Eden as prefiguring the exile from the land.[156] Such work anticipates some of the seminal insights of modern scholars. Gordon Wenham has noticed the sanctuary symbolism in Genesis 2–4,[157] and the relationship between God's instructions to Adam, the order of creation, and torah is a vital biblical-theological insight. The centrality of the exile motif is another important pattern in the Hebrew Bible.

A breakthrough for literal interpretation came with the northern French school of medieval Jewish thought, as we mentioned above. This school included such luminaries as Rashi (1040–1105), Rashi's grandson Rashbam (1080–1160), Rashbam's student Eliezer of Beaugency (mid-twelfth century), and Joseph ben Isaac Bekhor Shor (mid- to late twelfth century). *Rashi* was influential in the development of *peshat* exegesis, which abandoned midrashic exegesis in favor of interpreting biblical texts according to context.[158] He wrote commentaries on virtually every book of the Old Testament.[159] We should also recognize Rashi's significant appropriation by Nicholas of Lyra, who was "the most consummate exegete of his time and may be called the greatest after Jerome."[160] Nicholas's works are saturated with wide-ranging Jewish knowledge and, significantly, he insisted on the literal sense as utterly foundational.[161]

---

156. Ibid., 35.

157. G. Wenham, "Sanctuary Symbolism in the Garden of Eden Story," *Proceedings of the 9th World Congress of Jewish Studies* 9 (1986): 19–25.

158. See B. J. Gelles, Peshat *and Derash* in the Exegesis of Rashi (Leiden: Brill, 1981).

159. See, e.g., A. Berliner, ed., *Rashi: The Commentary of Solomon B. Isaac on the Torah* [Hebrew], 2nd ed. (Frankfurt: Kauffmann, 1905); Gruber, *Rashi's Commentary on Psalms*.

160. H. Hailperin, *Rashi and the Christian Scholars* (Pittsburgh: University of Pittsburgh Press, 1963), 252.

161. Ibid., 257.

Rashbam (ca. 1085–1155) interprets according to the principle that the text has only one single meaning.[162] The strength of his conviction on this matter is seen in his willingness to go against tradition in insisting that Exodus 13:9 is metaphoric language and not the first reference to tefillin. Rashbam displays great sensitivity, for example, to the literary nature of Ecclesiastes[163] and was the first to realize that Qohelet was set within a framework; 1:1–2 and the last seven verses were written by those who edited the book. Rashbam locates the essence of the argument of Ecclesiastes in 1:2–11. Ecclesiastes here contrasts the transience of human life with the permanence of nature, thus showing the latter's advantage. None of the experiments in Ecclesiastes are successful in dispelling this melancholy; the only adequate response is to live in conformity to traditional values, to enjoy life calmly while resigned to providence. Present mysteries will be rectified in the future life.

Eliezer of Beaugency was Rashbam's principal disciple. "Eliezer's devotion to the *peshat* and almost complete neglect of rabbinic midrash are as complete as that of his master."[164] His commentaries on Isaiah, Ezekiel, and the Book of the Twelve are extant.[165] Eliezer is important for recognizing the role of redactors in the formation of Old Testament books.[166] Joseph Bekhor Shor, like other northern French commentators, is sensitive to the literary aspects of Old Testament books. Importantly, he is sensitive to Hebrew parallelism, which he apparently learned from Rashbam.[167]

Maimonides (1138–1204), with his *Guide for the Perplexed*, set the agenda for Jewish medieval philosophy, and his influence is apparent, for example, on all subsequent medieval Jewish readings of Job.[168] Maimonides was born in Spain, which had succeeded Babylonia as the most prominent center of Jewish learning by the mid-tenth century. As a young man he moved to Egypt, where he spent the rest of his life. In Maimonides's time the major challenge was

---

162. Rashbam's commentary on Job was discovered in full in the 1930s. See S. Japhet, "Rashbam's Commentary on Job—The History of Its Discovery [Hebrew]," *Tarbiz* 66 (1996): 5–39. Japhet edited and published it in 2000 as *The Commentary of Rabbi Samuel Ben Meier (Rashbam) on the Book of Job* [Hebrew] (Jerusalem: Magnes, 2000).

163. See S. Japhet and R. B. Salters, eds., *The Commentary of R. Samuel Ben Meir Rashbam on Qoheleth* (Jerusalem: Magnes; Leiden: Brill, 1985).

164. Robert A. Harris, "Medieval Jewish Biblical Exegesis," in *The Medieval through the Reformation Periods*, vol. 2 of *A History of Biblical Interpretation*, ed. A. J. Hauser and D. F. Watson (Grand Rapids: Eerdmans, 2009), 141–71, esp. 149.

165. See Robert A. Harris, "The Literary Hermeneutic of Rabbi Eliezer of Beaugency" (PhD diss., Jewish Theological Seminary, 1997).

166. Robert A. Harris, "Medieval Jewish Biblical Exegesis," 149–50.

167. Ibid., 150–51.

168. See Eisen, *Book of Job*. For M. Maimonides on Job, see his *Guide of the Perplexed* 3.22–23, trans. S. Pines (Chicago: University of Chicago Press, 2010).

no longer Islamic thought, as with Saadiah, but rediscovered Aristotelianism. Maimonides became the most prominent expert in Aristotle's philosophy and sought to reinterpret Judaism in light of it. His esoteric style and his insistence that biblical books whose plain sense presents philosophical difficulties, such as Job, must be read allegorically—these features make it a challenge to discern his readings accurately.

For Maimonides, only humans experience *providence*,[169] the theme of Job. He reads Job as fiction and as a parable: "Uz" can mean "reflect" or "meditate," and it is as though Scripture were saying to us, "Reflect on this parable!" The Job we encounter in the opening chapters possesses *moral* but not *intellectual* perfection, and his intellectual deficiencies were responsible for his distorted view of providence. Job knew God only by authority and not through philosophical speculation, and thus he thought that happiness consisted of material blessings. Only when he gained knowledge did he find peace and true happiness. Satan is a symbol: "According to Maimonides, the divine beings represent the generative forces of nature, Satan is symbolic of privation, and Job suffers because of privation but is unaware that this is the cause of his troubles because of his intellectual deficiencies."[170]

The discussion between Job and the friends is a philosophical debate. Job represents the Aristotelian view that there is only general providence and no individual providence. Eliphaz argues for the view that Job is being punished for his sins. Bildad claims that Job is being tested so he can earn greater reward in the life to come. Zophar takes the view that Job's suffering is due to God's arbitrary will, and therefore inquiring after its meaning is futile. Elihu and God provide the correct view of providence.[171] Elihu tells Job that nature consists of benevolent and harmful forces; eventually the forces of privation will win out as humans inevitably die. The divine speeches add that God's providence is beyond human knowledge. In fact, the limit of human knowledge with respect to providence is the point of the book. One can guard oneself from suffering only psychologically and not physically. "This psychological immunity from suffering is achieved when Job perfects his intellect, contemplates God, and detaches himself from the material concerns of the world so that he is entirely caught up with the pleasure of focusing all his thoughts on the Deity."[172]

A Spanish contemporary of Maimonides was *Abraham Ibn Ezra*. Forced to leave Spain around 1140, he eventually moved to other parts of Europe,

---

169. For Maimonides's views of providence see his *Guide* 3.17–18, 51; Eisen, *Book of Job*, 45–48.
170. Eisen, *Book of Job*, 55; see 49–55, on the difficulties of interpreting Maimonides at this point.
171. See ibid., 56–67.
172. Ibid., 57.

where he wrote most of his commentaries.[173] He was committed to *peshat* and disparaged midrashic exegesis. His style of exegesis is evident in his commentary on Hosea, for example, which remains a useful resource today.[174] Ibn Ezra hinted at the possibility of post-Mosaica in the Torah, a position made famous by Spinoza (himself of Sephardic Jewish descent) in his *Politico-Theological Treatise* (1670).

Conclusion

There are many, many more significant Jewish exegetes that we could explore but for the limits of space.[175] Exegetes like *Gersonides*[176] (1288–1344), Albo (1380–1440), Meir Arama (ca. 1460–1545), Ovadiah Seforno (ca. 1475–1550),[177] and others. Clearly ancient and medieval Jewish interpretation is of major importance for biblical interpretation today. Second Temple Judaism is of inestimable value for early readings of the Old Testament as well as of critical importance as background to the New Testament. Midrashic exegesis shares the limits of patristic allegory, but in the returns to the plain sense of the text, we find rich pickings. In terms of theological interpretation, this is particularly so since, unlike so many modern biblical scholars, Jewish interpreters take the Old Testament seriously as Scripture.

Note should also be taken of the major interaction with the Old Testament by Jewish *philosophers*.[178] As a result of the long shadow of Karl Barth in the contemporary recovery of theological interpretation, many see no need to take philosophy seriously. As we will see in chapter 9 (below), this is a mistake. Yet

---

173. M. Friedlander, ed., *Essays on the Writings of Abraham Ibn Ezra* (London: Society of Hebrew Literature/Trübner, 1877; reprint, 1964); A. Ibn Ezra, *The Commentary of Ibn Ezra on Isaiah*, ed. M. Friedlander, 4 vols. (London: Society of Hebrew Literature / Trübner, 1873–77); U. Simon, "Abraham Ibn Ezra," in Saebø, *HB/OT* 1.2 (2000): 377–87.

174. A. Ibn Ezra, *The Commentary of Rabbi Abraham Ibn Ezra on Hosea*, ed. and trans. A. Lipshitz (New York: Sepher-Hermon, 1988). See also idem, *Abraham Ibn Ezra's Commentary on the First Book of the Psalms*, trans. H. N. Strickman (Brighton, MA: Academic Studies, 2009); idem, *Abraham Ibn Ezra's Commentary on the Second Book of Psalms*, trans. H. N. Strickman (Brighton, MA: Academic Studies, 2009).

175. And not just the key interpreters; see M. Saperstein, *Jewish Preaching, 1200–1800: An Anthology* (New Haven: Yale University Press: 1989).

176. For Gersonides's work on Job, see Eisen, *Book of Job*, 143–73; see also idem, *Gersonides on Providence, Covenant, and the Chosen People: A Study in Medieval Philosophy and Biblical Commentary* (Albany: State University of New York Press, 1995).

177. The latter three all wrote on Job. Kalman reports, "In summary, as is evident, the need to defend God was met by most medieval exegetes who chose to find fault in Job" ("Medieval Jewish Biblical Commentaries," 833). On p. 832 Kalman states that Job received significant attention from Jewish mystics, but work remains to be done in excavating this work.

178. Eisen, *Book of Job*, is an excellent resource in this respect.

a crucial issue is the type of philosophy that informs and is in dialogue with exegesis. Maimonides's Aristotelianism, for example, had a largely negative influence on his exegesis, in my view. We see a more helpful approach amid the contemporary renaissance in Christian philosophers, with leading figures like Alvin Plantinga, Nicholas Wolterstorff, and Eleonore Stump engaging seriously with Scripture.[179] Abarbanel's life straddles the shift from the medieval period to modernity, the subject of our next chapter.

---

179. Both A. Plantinga (*Warranted Christian Belief* [Oxford: Oxford University Press, 2000]) and E. Stump (*Wandering in Darkness: Narrative and the Problem of Suffering* [Oxford: Oxford University Press, 2010]) attend to Job in relation to theodicy, the major interest of Jewish medieval philosophers, as we have seen. In his book *Justice: Rights and Wrongs* (Princeton: Princeton University Press, 2008), N. Wolterstorff begins by engaging the biblical tradition.

7

Renaissance, Reformation, and Modernity

Characteristic of Calvin's hermeneutics was that it made possible a fully theological exegesis of the Old Testament. . . . More than Luther, however, Calvin also uses a salvation-historical framework with respect to law and gospel, which leads to a different accentuation. The real contrast has to do not with law and gospel but with an understanding of the law with or without the Spirit.

Willem van't Spijker[1]

Just as old or bleary-eyed men and those with weak vision, if you thrust before them a most beautiful volume, even if they recognize it to be some sort of writing, yet can scarcely construe two words, but with the aid of spectacles will begin to read distinctly; so Scripture, gathering up the otherwise confused knowledge of God in our minds, having dispersed our dullness, clearly shows us the true God.

John Calvin[2]

---

1. W. van't Spijker, *Calvin: A Brief Guide to His Life and Thought*, trans. Lyle D. Bierma (Louisville: Westminster John Knox, 2009), 134.
2. J. Calvin, *Institutes of the Christian Religion*, ed. J. T. McNeill, trans. F. L. Battles, LCC 20–21 (Philadelphia: Westminster, 1960), 2:70.

Introduction: The Renaissance

"Renaissance" means "rebirth" in French and points to the (re)discovery of the world and the changing views of what it means to be human in a period of extraordinary vitality, from about 1400 to about 1530. In retrospect we can see that the Renaissance was a *threshold period* in which new things were interwoven with medieval tradition. The emergence of the universities in the twelfth century and the rediscovery of Aristotle set the context for a burst of energy in all areas of life.[3]

In terms of philosophy three major traditions characterized the Renaissance. *Humanism* emerged in Italy at the end of the thirteenth century. Its distinctive emphasis was the study of the classical Greek and Latin writers. The humanists devised rules for interpreting these texts and promoted imitation of the Roman authors for rhetoric and writing. They professed disdain for the study of logic and natural philosophy, so much the concern of the scholastics. Indeed, a reaction to scholasticism is characteristic of Renaissance thought. But they were by no means antireligious. The *rediscovered Plato*, or more accurately *neoplatonism*, was like a magnet in this setting. Petrarcus's program led to the translation of some of Plato's dialogues by the early humanists, and this was strengthened when infused with Byzantine neoplatonism. The third major strain of Renaissance philosophy was the *humanistic Aristotelianism* of thinkers like Pomponazzi and Zabarella, a type of philosophical exclusivism. Aristotelianism first appeared in Italy in the late thirteenth century. Significantly, although in Paris Aristotelianism was closely bound up positively or negatively with theology, there were no such constraints in Italian universities, where Aristotelianism was elaborated well into the Renaissance.

> But where Ficino and the Platonists went back to the Hellenistic world and the religious philosophies of Alexandria, the naturalistic humanism, initiated by Pomponazzi and culminating in Zabarella, built on the long tradition of Italian Aristotelianism an original philosophy in accord with the spirit of the emerging natural science and strikingly anticipatory of Spinoza.[4]

Unlike Thomas, as it developed this approach did not hesitate to follow Aristotle where it disagreed with the Christian faith. Thus John of Jandun, who

---

3. See P. Johnson, *The Renaissance: A Short History* (London: Phoenix, 2000).
4. P. O. Kristeller and J. H. Randall Jr., introduction to *The Renaissance Philosophy of Man*, ed. E. Cassirer, P. O. Kristeller, and J. H. Randall Jr. (Chicago: University of Chicago Press, 1948), 9.

taught in Paris during the first twenty years of the fourteenth century, accepted Christian doctrine as true but continued developing rational interpretations of Aristotle that contradicted Christian doctrine. Pietro Pomponazzi of Mantua's (1465-1525) work[5] indicates a growing intent to sever relations between philosophy and theology.

This increasingly naturalistic and scientific philosophy was strongly opposed by the humanists: "Thus the two great philosophic rivals in early sixteenth-century Italy are a naturalistic and an imaginative and religious humanism, with the former widespread and rapidly increasing in strength."[6] The former turned out to be very influential: the rationalists of the sixteenth century inspired the free thinkers of the seventeenth, especially in France. Galileo owes little to Platonism but much to the critical Aristotelianism of the Italian universities. Spinoza and Leibniz demonstrate the continuing influence of Italian Aristotelianism in the mid-seventeenth century.

Central to the Renaissance was the rediscovery of Greek and Roman antiquity with the cry of *Ad fontes*, "Back to the sources." As a threshold period, Christianity remained dominant during the Renaissance, and leading lights such as Petrarch, Valla, and Pico took Christianity with the utmost seriousness, even as they struggled to integrate their faith with their passion for the new learning. Inevitably the new spirit affected biblical studies.[7] *Ad fontes* meant reaching behind the Vulgate to the Hebrew and Greek texts and behind medieval commentators to the church fathers.

Although the Renaissance originated largely in Italy, printing was a German invention. The first best seller in this new world was Thomas à Kempis's *The Imitation of Christ*, which went through ninety-nine editions from 1471 to 1500. Apart from the Bible, it remains the most influential writing in Christian spirituality. A renewed interest in the study of Greek and Hebrew[8] emerged with major consequences for biblical studies, inter alia leading to Desiderius Erasmus's new version of the Greek New Testament.[9] Monasteries were scoured for ancient manuscripts; every attempt was made to recover

---

5. See ibid., 114-40.
6. Ibid., 11.
7. See the essays in part A of M. Saebø, *HB/OT* 2 (2008).
8. Despite some misgivings. See E. Rummel, "The Renaissance Humanists," in *The Medieval through the Reformation Periods*, vol. 2 of *A History of Biblical Interpretation*, ed. A. J. Hauser and D. F. Watson (Grand Rapids: Eerdmans, 2009), 280-98, esp. 282-83.
9. See E. Rummel, "The Textual and Hermeneutic Work of Desiderius Erasmus of Rotterdam," in Saebø, *HB/OT* 2 (2008): 215-30. Rummel explains that John Colet "was instrumental in focusing Erasmus's interest on the scriptural text and in shaping his *philosophia Christi*, a philosophy that called for the imitation of Christ in one's life" (216-17). "Digestion" and "transformation" are central images in Erasmus's biblical hermeneutic.

the literature and art of the ancient world, and this was abetted by imports from Constantinople. The first complete Hebrew Bible (the Soncino Bible) was published in 1488. Erasmus collated Greek and Latin manuscripts for his edition of the New Testament, published in 1516; it contained extensive notes on textual and editorial decisions. Harbison notices just how remarkable was this renewal of interest in the ancient languages:

> By 1500 a good Latinist could find as many jobs open to him as a psychologist today; a mediocre Graecist could find students eager to pay him almost anywhere in Europe; and any sort of Hebraist at all could cause a stir by hanging out his scholarly shingle. In the hottest part of Paris summer a young Italian Humanist, Aleander, announced a series of lectures on a third-rate Roman poet, Ausonius. Two thousand people turned out for the first lecture and listened for two hours and a half—according to the lecturer, with no sign of fatigue. On the third day, all the seats were taken at eleven o'clock although the lecture did not begin until one. It is a famous story not because it was unusual, but because it was fairly typical of the Humanist and his audience during the classical revival.[10]

The center of learning moved from the monasteries to the princely courts and to the universities. A new sense of history and of anachronism developed, which raised the question of the relationship between contemporary Christianity and the apostolic age.[11]

In 1497 the Englishman John Colet,[12] who had spent four years in Italy studying how to interpret ancient texts, gave, at the age of thirty, a sensational series of lectures at Oxford on Paul's Letter to the Romans in which he abandoned the scholastic approach and read Romans against its historical background.[13] Erasmus (ca. 1466–1536) not only published his Greek New Testament but also editions of Jerome, Augustine, Tertullian, Basil, Cyprian, Arnobius, Hilary, Ambrose, Origen, and John Chrysostom. By the mid-sixteenth century critical editions of all the major patristic authors were in print. The biblical text and the church fathers were available for scrutiny as never before, and both played a key role in the Reformation.

Clearly the seeds of the Reformation were laid in the Renaissance. *Ad fontes* was of seminal importance and biblically would come to fruition in the rich exegetical labors of the Reformation period. Christianity remained

---

10. E. H. Harbison, *The Christian Scholar in the Age of the Reformation* (Grand Rapids: Eerdmans, 1983), 33–34.
11. Ibid., 35–38.
12. See ibid., 55–67.
13. J. Colet, *An Exposition of St. Paul's Epistle to the Romans* (London: Bell & Daldy, 1873), via openlibrary.org.

prevalent in the Renaissance, and yet the seeds of secular humanism were already present, particularly in the humanistic Aristotelianism. Thus the humanism "born again" in the fourteenth century was not to claim the status of "the light of the world" until the Enlightenment of the eighteenth century. Aquinas's two stories were coming apart: the natural world, the *saeculum*, was becoming separated from the realm of grace, and also becoming the principal focus of scholarly interest. In itself, this renewed delight in God's good creation was undoubtedly a healthy development, but increasingly it would come at the cost of diminishing or even denying God's involvement and authority in this world.

The Reformation

The Reformation, for all the criticisms leveled against it, represents a massive recovery of Scripture for the church, an achievement that continues to resonate and shape biblical hermeneutics today. Raeder observes, for example, that "Luther's entire work can be understood as a comprehensive, many-faceted interpretation of the Bible."[14] Building on the humanist rediscovery[15] of ancient languages, texts, and rhetoric,[16] Reformational exegesis represented the triumph of literal interpretation over allegorical interpretation and theological speculation.[17] Both Luther and Calvin came to say a firm "No" to

14. S. Raeder, "The Exegetical and Hermeneutical Work of Martin Luther," in Saebø, *HB/OT* 2 (2008): 363–406, esp. 365. Luther's output was immense, as is the literature on his biblical work. Raeder contains a full bibliography plus a useful overview of Luther's work.

15. Some scholars, such as W. Maurer, *Der junge Melanchthon zwischen Humanismus und Reformation* (Göttingen: Vandenhoeck & Ruprecht, 1996), see humanism and the Reformation as antithetical, whereas others, such as P. O. Kristeller and M. Mooney, *Renaissance Thought and Its Sources* (New York: Columbia University Press, 1979), see the Reformers as building on humanist methodologies. The relationship is complex, as was the Renaissance, but in terms of method the Reformers are hugely and rightly indebted to the humanists.

16. For the significance of rhetoric in Melanchthon's exegesis, see T. J. Wengert, "Biblical Interpretation in the Works of Philip Melanchthon," in Hauser and Watson, *History of Biblical Interpretation*, 2:321, reporting, "Melanchthon was the first Christian exegete to organize and analyze Romans thoroughly on the basis of standard rules of rhetoric." See T. J. Wengert, "Philip Melanchthon's 1522 Annotations on Romans and the Lutheran Origins of Rhetoric Criticism," in *Philip Melanchthon, Speaker of the Reformation: Wittenberg's Other Reformer* (Burlington, VT: Ashgate, 2010), reprinted from *Biblical Interpretation in the Era of the Reformation: Essays Presented to David Steinmetz in Honor of His Sixtieth Birthday*, edited by R. A. Muller and J. L. Thompson (Grand Rapids: Eerdmans, 1996), 118–40; T. J. Wengert and M. P. Graham, eds., *Philip Melanchthon (1497–1560) and the Commentary* (Sheffield: Sheffield Academic, 1997).

17. K. Mueller-Vollmer (ed., *Herder Today: Contributions from the International Herder Conference, Nov. 5–8, 1987, Stanford, California* [Berlin: de Gruyter, 1990], 2) and J. Grondin (*Introduction to Philosophical Hermeneutics* [New Haven: Yale University Press, 1995], 42–44) both regard Illyricus as the most important Protestant theorist of biblical interpretation.

allegorical interpretation.[18] Luther reported: "When I was a monk, I was an expert in allegories. I allegorized everything. Afterwards through the Epistle to the Romans I came to some knowledge of Christ. There I saw that allegories were not what Christ meant but what Christ was."[19] After 1517 Luther ceased to use allegory and insisted on "one simple solid sense" in exegesis. He acknowledged the presence of allegories in the Bible but only where the author intended them.

Calvin[20] does not make much mention of the letter-spirit distinction so prominent in previous exegesis and has little time for allegory.[21] He embraces typology and prefers the "plain" or "natural" sense of the biblical text. However,

> on closer inspection it becomes clear that Calvin's understanding of the "plain" sense was not woodenly literal. Indeed, many of the meanings that earlier commentators had ascribed to one or another of the so-called spiritual senses seemed to Calvin to be in fact the plain and natural sense of the letter itself. ... Perhaps it would therefore be more accurate to say that Calvin stood for a principled reduction of "spiritual" readings of the text rather than a total and unconditional rejection of them. Indeed, by modern standards, Calvin adhered to what can only be regarded as a generous reading of the "plain sense" of the text.[22]

Indeed, it is vital to recognize that for the Reformers the plain sense was the *spiritual* sense![23] Neither Luther nor Calvin thought that one could just read Scripture "objectively" in the modern sense.

For Calvin, it was vital that the reader participate in the realities to which Scripture witnesses, and Luther declared, "Experience is necessary for the understanding of the Word. It is not merely to be repeated or known, but to be believed and felt."[24] "Many speculate wisely but nobody is wise in Scrip-

---

18. For Zwingli on the quadriga, see W. P. Stephens, *The Theology of Huldrych Zwingli* (Oxford: Clarendon, 1988), 73–77. For Zwingli, the natural sense is the spiritual sense.

19. Quoted in R. M. Grant with D. Tracy, *A Short History of the Interpretation of the Bible*, 2nd ed., reprint (Eugene, OR: Wipf & Stock, 2001), 94.

20. On Calvin's hermeneutics, see T. F. Torrance, *The Hermeneutics of John Calvin* (Edinburgh: Scottish Academic Press, 1988); R. W. Holder, *John Calvin and the Grounding of Interpretation: Calvin's First Commentaries* (Leiden: Brill, 2005).

21. For a nuanced statement of his view, see D. L. Puckett, *John Calvin's Exegesis of the Old Testament* (Louisville: Westminster John Knox, 1995), 106–13.

22. D. C. Steinmetz, "John Calvin as Interpreter of the Bible," in *Calvin and the Bible*, ed. D. K. McKim (Cambridge: Cambridge University Press, 2006), 285.

23. Cf. R. A. Muller, "Biblical Interpretation in the Era of the Reformation: The View from the Middle Ages," in *Biblical Interpretation in the Era of the Reformation: Essays Presented to David C. Steinmetz in Honor of His Sixtieth Birthday*, ed. R. A. Muller and J. L. Thompson (Grand Rapids: Eerdmans, 1996), 3–22.

24. Luther, WA 5:108.

ture and understands it if he does not fear the Lord. And he who fears more, understands more. For 'the fear of the Lord is the beginning of wisdom.'"[25] In 1518 Luther wrote to his friend Georg Spalatin:

> It is absolutely certain that one cannot enter into the Scripture by study or innate intelligence. Therefore your first task is to begin with prayer. You must ask that the Lord in his great mercy grant you a true understanding of his words, should it please him to accomplish anything through you for his glory and not for your glory or that of any other man. For there is no one who can teach the divine words except he who is their author. . . . You must therefore completely despair of your own diligence and intelligence and rely solely on the infusion of the Spirit. Believe me, for I have had experience in this matter.[26]

Luther's *Christum treibet* principle[27] is well known: "Christ is the point in the circle from which the whole circle is drawn."[28] Christ is found wrapped "in the swaddling cloths of Scripture."[29] Both Luther[30] and Calvin asserted *the clarity of Scripture*, but neither claimed that apart from the work of the Spirit. In his debate with Erasmus about free will, Luther appealed to two forms of Scripture's clarity: external in relation to ministry, and internal in relation to the understanding of the heart.[31] Both are the works of the Spirit, but external clarity is entailed because of God's choice to express himself in human words.[32] The Bible is not infinitely pliable. Calvin asserts that in order for God's truth to remain forever in the world, he engraved it, as it were, on "public tablets."[33] "Scripture adorns with unmistakable marks and tokens the one true God."[34] Calvin insists that Word and Spirit be held together:

> For by a kind of mutual bond the Lord has joined together the certainty of his Word and of his Spirit so that the perfect religion of the Word may abide in our

---

25. WA 4:519.3–4.
26. WA BR 1:133.31–39; *Luther's Works*, vol. 48, *Letters I* (Philadelphia: Fortress, 1963), 53–54.
27. See M. D. Thompson, "Biblical Interpretation in the Works of Martin Luther," in Hauser and Watson, *History of Biblical Interpretation*, 2:304–6.
28. Erlangen edition of *Luther's Works* [German] (1826–57, revised later), 46:338–39.
29. Luther, WA DB 8:12.1–8.
30. See F. Beisser, *"Claritas scripturae" bei Martin Luther*, Forschungen zur Kirchen- und Dogmengeschichte 18 (Göttingen: Vandenhoeck & Ruprecht, 1966); B. Rothen, *Die Klarheit der Schrift*, vol. 1, *Martin Luther: Die wiederentdeckten Grundlagen* (Göttingen: Vandenhoeck & Ruprecht, 1990).
31. WA 18:609.4–5.
32. For H. Zwingli, see his "Of the Clarity and Certainty of the Word of God," in *Zwingli and Bullinger*, ed. G. W. Bromiley (London: SCM, 1953), 49–58.
33. Calvin, *Institutes of the Christian Religion* 6.2.
34. Ibid.

minds when the Spirit who causes us to contemplate God's face, shines; and that we in turn may embrace the Spirit with no fear of being deceived when we recognize him in his own image, namely, in the Word.[35]

The Reformers' concentration on the literal sense was not new. I noted in chapter 5, for example, that in my view Thomas's literal reading of Job is superior to that of Calvin's.[36] What was new was the Reformers' view of the authority of Scripture and its relation to tradition and theology. Doctrine was to emerge from Scripture and to be subject to it: Luther asserted, "This is the golden age of theology. It cannot rise higher, because we have come so far as to sit in judgment on all the doctors of the church and test them by the judgment of the apostles and prophets."[37] *Sola scriptura* meant that interpretation became a critical issue in the life of the church, as did (biblical) theology. This did not, however, mean neglecting tradition. Luther and Calvin[38] engaged seriously with the church fathers.

The close interface between theology and exegesis in the writings of the Reformers is important, not least in our day, when too much theology has become separated from exegesis, and too much exegesis is disconnected from theology. Even when Scripture is taken seriously in theology nowadays, we generally think in terms of a move from Scripture to doctrine, which then easily takes on a life of its own[39] and often functions as more authoritative than Scripture. Calvin, on the contrary, sees doctrine rightly as a guide to engaging Scripture more deeply.[40] In his 1559 preface to his *Institutes*, he declares, "It has been my purpose in this labor to prepare and instruct candidates in sacred theology for the reading of the divine Word, in order that they may be able both to have easy access to it and advance in it without stumbling."[41]

---

35. Ibid., 1.9.3. For Zwingli on this issue, see Stephens, *Theology of Huldrych Zwingli*, 59–64.

36. For a discussion of Calvin's sermons on Job (he did not write a commentary on this book), see S. Schreiner, "Calvin as an Interpreter of Job," in *Calvin and the Bible*, ed. D. K. McKim (Cambridge: Cambridge University Press, 2006), 53–84; D. Thomas, *Proclaiming the Incomprehensible God: Calvin's Teaching on Job* (Fearn, UK: Mentor, 2004). Calvin finds his champion in Elihu!

37. Luther, WA TR 1:108.

38. B. Pitkin, "John Calvin and the Interpretation of the Bible," in Hauser and Watson, *History of Biblical Interpretation*, 2:349–50, esp. 346–49; A. N. S. Lane, *John Calvin: Student of the Church Fathers* (Grand Rapids: Baker, 1999); D. C. Steinmetz, *Calvin in Context*, 2nd ed. (Oxford: Oxford University Press, 2010), 122–56.

39. This move parallels modern science, in which the royal road to truth is abstraction and theory.

40. See Pitkin, "John Calvin and the Interpretation," 349–50.

41. Calvin, *Institutes*, p. 4. See F. Wendel, *Calvin: Origins and Development of His Religious Thought* (Grand Rapids: Baker Books, 2002), 144–49. On the purpose of the *Institutes*, see R. C. Zachman, *John Calvin as Teacher, Pastor, and Theologian: The Shape of His Writings and Thought* (Grand Rapids: Baker Academic, 2006), 55–76.

We should recognize the different theological frameworks among the Reformers and their implications for exegesis. Luther's law-grace contrast and two-kingdoms approach is, in my opinion, less helpful than that of Calvin.[42] Melanchthon, like Luther, made justification too central to the biblical message. He saw it as the heart of Romans and saw Romans as the key to the main themes of Scripture.[43] The center of Calvin's theology is harder to determine because of his constant attempt to let his theology be shaped by Scripture. Wendel comments, "It would be better, we think, to confess that Calvin's is not a closed system elaborated around a central idea, but that it draws together, one after another, a whole series of Biblical ideas, some of which can only with difficulty be logically reconciled."[44]

The new Reformed theology that emerged was often revolutionary in its interpretation. Take Ecclesiastes, for example. Neither Calvin nor Zwingli wrote on Ecclesiastes, but the Lutheran Reformers Luther, Melanchthon, and Brenz did so. Luther and Calvin rediscovered a robust doctrine of creation manifested, for example, in Luther's doctrine of *vocatio*, whereby every vocation was sacred and of equal value. This lens enabled the Lutheran Reformers to break the back of Jerome's reading of Ecclesiastes as promoting *contemptus mundi*—the reading that frames Thomas à Kempis's *Imitation of Christ* and held sway for a thousand years—and to see it rather as life affirming. Charles Taylor recognizes the significance of the Reformers' recovery of *the ordinary* in a delightful chapter titled "God Loveth Adverbs," in his monumental *Sources of the Self*. The recovery of creation reoriented theology horizontally and eschatologically in a way that not even Aquinas's engagement with Aristotle made possible. In this regard, Calvin's central image[45] for Scripture is that of a pair of spectacles:

> Just as old or bleary-eyed men and those with weak vision, if you thrust before them a most beautiful volume, even if they recognize it to be some sort of writing, yet can scarcely construe two words, but with the aid of spectacles will begin to read distinctly; so Scripture, gathering up the otherwise confused knowledge of God in our minds, having dispersed our dullness, clearly shows us the true God.[46]

---

42. Melanchthon is important in the Lutheran tradition for his development of a third function of the law, as a guide in the life of the believer. See Wengert, "Interpretation in the Works of Philip Melanchthon," 334.

43. Ibid., 325.

44. Wendel, *Calvin: Origins and Development*, 358.

45. For a wider analysis, see R. C. Zachman, *Image and Word in the Theology of John Calvin* (Notre Dame, IN: University of Notre Dame Press, 2009), 25–54.

46. Calvin, *Institutes* 1.6.1.

In a footnote Lewis Battles rightly states, "This simile . . . is probably Calvin's decisive utterance on the role of Scripture as related to the revelation of the Creator in creation."[47] Human life in all its dimensions achieved a new importance, and biblical interpretation was—potentially at least—opened out in the direction of all of life.

The proof of the pudding is always in the eating, and recent decades have witnessed a welcome focus on Calvin's *practice* of interpretation in his commentaries, sermons, and other writings.[48] Generations of pastors and scholars continue to find his work stimulating, and no less a theologian than Karl Barth was significantly influenced by Calvin, as we will see below. His characteristic *lucid brevity* may detract from his work for some readers, but it also means that his thought is readily available with minimal effort, at least in terms of his commentaries.

The Era of Protestant Orthodoxy, 1565–1700

The post-Reformation period has often been written off as a time of Protestant scholasticism and mere proof-texting from the Bible. Richard Muller and others have shown this not to be the case. As Muller notes, "Rather than a turn away from Renaissance and Reformation developments, the post-Reformation era should be seen as a time of intensification of Protestant interest in the original languages of the text to the inclusion of cognate Semitic languages in the curriculum of major universities."[49] The production of a series of polyglot Bibles in this period bears witness to the intense textual labors. In terms of biblical hermeneutics, major works were Matthias Flacius Illyricus's *Clavis scripturae sacrae* (1567), William Whitaker's *Disputation on Holy Scripture* (1588), Andreas Rivetus's *Isagoge in Novum Testamentum* (1616), Johannes Drusius's *Ad voces Ebreas N. T. commentarius duplex* (1606), John Weemes's *Christian Synagogue* (1623), Salomon Glassius's *Philologia sacra* (1626), Benjamin Keach's *Tropologia: A Key to Open Scripture Metaphors* (1682), as well as many of the essays in *Critici sacri* (9 vols., starting in 1660).

Matthias Flacius Illyricus was professor of Hebrew at Wittenberg (1544–49), professor at the University of Jena (1557–61), and thereafter spent fourteen

---

47. Ibid., 70n1.
48. See, e.g., the multiple works by T. H. L. Parker, including *Calvin's Old Testament Commentaries* (Edinburgh: T&T Clark, 1993) and *Calvin's New Testament Commentaries*, 2nd ed. (Edinburgh: T&T Clark, 1993); McKim, *Calvin and the Bible*; Steinmetz, *Calvin in Context*; Puckett, *John Calvin's Exegesis*.
49. R. Muller, "Biblical Interpretation in the 16th & 17th Centuries," in *Historical Handbook of Major Biblical Interpreters*, ed. D. K. McKim (Downers Grove, IL: InterVarsity, 1998), 139.

years in exile. While at Jena and in exile, he immersed himself in biblical hermeneutics and exegesis. His work in this area climaxed in the publication of his *Clavis scripturae sacrae*, described by Dilthey as "the origin of hermeneutics." The *Clavis* is divided into two parts: part 1 is a biblical dictionary that includes philological analysis and theological exposition of biblical concepts. Flacius avoided the intrusion of philosophical principles and patristic references in the attempt to allow Scripture to interpret Scripture.

Part 2 consists of seven treatises on hermeneutics. The first provides definitions and tools for the interpretation of Scripture as well as introductory information for the study of different parts of the Bible. The second provides rules for the proper interpretation of Scripture as established in the writings of the first three centuries. Treatises 3 and 4 deal with grammar and tropes in the Bible. Treatise 5 has been called "the first approach to evaluating biblical styles" since it includes a comparison of Johannine style with Pauline style. Treatise 6 contains academic addresses on the study of Scripture plus short reports on biblical geography, Hebrew vowels, and other topics. Treatise 7 deals with issues under dispute with Roman Catholics.

Flacius was mentored by Luther and was a friend of Melanchthon, so not surprisingly he saw the center of Scripture as Christ, and his hermeneutic centered in Luther's view of justification. Eschatology is central since the Old Testament is fulfilled in Christ (in the NT). The analogy of faith should guide biblical interpretation, and such exegesis should lead to trust in Christ. On this issue, the law/gospel distinction is crucial for Flacius. God's Word is one but was given in two Testaments and three covenants: those with Adam, Moses, and Christ. "Adam's covenant (reaffirmed with Abraham) was confirmed and completed by the covenant in and through Christ."[50] The work of the Spirit is essential to true interpretation. Flacius's early humanist training influenced him deeply, and he argued that the entire array of disciplines can help illumine the biblical text.

"Flacius argued that the literal and the spiritual sense of the biblical text dare not be separated, for the nature of Scripture and its usage in the lives of God's people are inseparable. . . . Christ continues his ministry in the preaching of his word as recorded in Scripture."[51] Similarly, Whitaker and Rivetus stressed the literal sense while including figures and types within the literal sense. Glassius's work on principles of interpretation is known for his use of classical rhetoric to identify the range of rhetorical figures in the Bible. He argues for a double sense of Scripture, literal and spiritual, but insisted

50. R. Kolb, "Flacius Illyricus, Matthias," in McKim, *Historical Handbook*, 192.
51. Ibid., 194.

that the spiritual sense be located in the New Testament fulfillment of Old Testament promise.

In his *Clavis*, Flacius outlined a simple method for interpreting a biblical text. One should begin with grammatical interpretation and then focus on the intention of the author, including the purpose of the larger composition in which the text is found. Finally, the use of the text in the life of the church must be established.

The Protestant exegetical tradition of the sixteenth and seventeenth centuries produced an astonishing array of textual, linguistic, and hermeneutical works and commentaries on the Bible. As we see an emerging renaissance of theological interpretation in our day, this is a resource that largely remains to be excavated.[52] For example, consider the interpretation of Hosea 6:7. Most contemporary interpreters read "at Adam" and understand "Adam" as a place name, although there is no agreement on what events *at* Adam are referred to.[53] As far as I know, none of the Protestant interpreters in this era explores such an interpretation. Indeed, "the text indicated, as virtually all of the patristic and medieval commentators concluded, a prelapsarian covenant made by God with Adam and broken in the fall."[54] However, there is among Protestant exegetes an extensive debate over whether "Adam" in Hosea 6:7 is generic or specific.[55]

Whatever we make of Hosea 6:7, Protestant exegetes of this period have much to offer in terms of a theology of covenant and thus insight for biblical theology. Apart from Hosea 6:7, Bill Dumbrell in his *Covenant and Creation* has demonstrated persuasively that the primary and foundational covenantal text is Genesis 1–3. This is established and discussed among exegetes of this era and remains a resource to be reexcavated. Muller concludes:

> In sum, the Protestant exegetical tradition of the sixteenth and seventeenth centuries evidences a fairly continuous and highly variegated development.

---

52. On exegetes and their commentaries, including major Catholic works, see Muller, "Interpretation in the 16th & 17th Centuries," 140–51. Much of this work remains untranslated.

53. See, e.g., J. A. Dearman, *The Book of Hosea* (Grand Rapids: Eerdmans, 2010), 197–98. L. E. McComiskey, "Hosea," in *The Minor Prophets: An Exegetical and Expository Commentary*, ed. L. E. McComiskey (Grand Rapids: Baker, 1992), 1–238, esp. 95, is an exception.

54. R. Muller, *Post-Reformation Reformed Dogmatics: The Rise and Development of Reformed Orthodoxy, ca. 1520 to ca. 1725*, 2nd ed. (Grand Rapids: Baker Academic, 2003), 2:437. This tradition is summed up in the massive commentary of the seventeenth-century Jesuit, Cornelius à Lapide, *Commentarius*, who on Hos. 6:7 cites for confirmation Jerome, Cyril, Rupert of Deutz, Hugh of St. Victor, and Nicolas of Lyra. A. Ibn Ezra (*The Commentary of Rabbi Abraham Ibn Ezra on Hosea*, ed. and trans. A. Lipshitz [New York: Sepher-Hermon, 1988]) understands the reference generically: "*like* [ordinary] *men have transgressed the covenant*" (66, with original emphasis).

55. See Muller, *Post-Reformation*, 436–41.

In theological content and in their use of textual, philological, homiletical and dogmatic styles, the commentaries of the seventeenth-century exegetes follow the models and the substance of their sixteenth-century predecessors. Notable developments in approach include the increasing Protestant interest in Judaica and in the so-called oriental languages, namely, the cognate languages of the ancient Near East plus Ethiopic and Persian. Immersion in textual and philological study was characteristic of the era of orthodoxy. It also produced, in such authors as [Louis] Cappel, [Hugo] Grotius and [Richard] Simon, the first stirrings of what would become the historical-critical method.[56]

The Counter-Reformation

The Council of Trent (1545–63)[57] clearly had to attend to the role of Scripture in response to the Reformation.[58] Skarsaune states, "In Trent the Roman Catholic Church, for the first time, met challenges to its doctrine by meeting the challengers on common ground: the interpretation of Scripture."[59] Partially in reference to John 20:30—"Jesus performed many other signs in the presence of his disciples, which are not recorded in this book" (NIV)—the Council of Trent affirmed the Bible with seventy-three books as one part of revelation and the apostolic traditions as the other.[60] "Trent's texts leave open whether the traditions only interpret Scripture or whether they also add doctrines and practices beyond Scripture."[61] Right interpretation is judged by the Magisterium of the Church.[62] There was no prohibition on laity reading Scripture, but this was restricted and controlled. A new catechism was published in October 1566.

56. Muller, "Interpretation in the 16th and 17th Centuries," 151.
57. See G. Bedouelle, *La réforme du catholicisme, 1480–1620* (Paris: Cerf, 1989); R. Bireley, *The Refashioning of Catholicism, 1450–1700* (London: Macmillan, 1999); J. W. O'Malley, *Trent and All That: Renaming Catholicism in the Early Modern Era* (Cambridge, MA: Harvard University Press, 2000); idem, *Trent: What Happened at the Council* (Cambridge, MA: Harvard University Press, 2013); idem, *Catholicism in Early Modern History: A Guide to Research*, Reformation Guides to Research 2 (St. Louis: Center for Reformation Studies, 1988); H. Jedin, *A History of the Council of Trent*, trans. E. Graf (London: Nelson, 1949), 52–124.
58. Cf. J. Wicks, "Catholic Old Testament Interpretation in the Reformation and Early Confessional Eras," in Saebø, *HB/OT* 2 (2008): 617–68, esp. 624–32.
59. O. Skarsaune, "From the Reform Councils to the Counter-Reformation: The Council as Interpreter of Scripture," in Saebø, *HB/OT* 2 (2008): 319–28.
60. See O'Malley, *Trent: What Happened*, 97–98.
61. Wicks, "Catholic Old Testament Interpretation," 626.
62. See O'Malley, *Trent: What Happened*, 283–85, for "The Tridentine Profession of Faith," which declares: "I likewise accept Holy Scripture according to the sense that Holy Mother Church has held and does hold, to whom it belongs to judge the true meaning and interpretation of the Sacred Scriptures. I shall never accept or interpret them otherwise than according to the unanimous consent of the Fathers" (283).

The Jesuits made biblical study a specialty, and one of their number, Cornelius à Lapide, commented on the whole Bible apart from Job and the Psalms.⁶³ The complete edition of his work, published again and again in the eighteenth century, comprised eleven huge folio volumes. À Lapide prioritized the literal sense. A French Benedictine, Augustin Calmet, published a *Literal Commentary on All the Books of the Old and the New Testaments* (1710–16). This nonpolemical work includes Jewish and Protestant perspectives. Richard Simon's (1638–1712) work signaled a birth of "critical" exegesis in the Catholic Church and beyond.⁶⁴ Simon questioned the Mosaic origin of parts of the Pentateuch.

Space prohibits any detailed exploration of the works of this period, but note must be made of Ignatius of Loyola's *Spiritual Exercises*.⁶⁵ Intriguingly, Erasmus, Calvin, and Ignatius studied at the same college in France and under the same principal, but at different times! Ignatius's writings and practices are a milestone in the development of lectio divina, an approach that is rightly being revitalized among evangelicals today.

The Rise of Modern Biblical Interpretation: Humanism Becomes the Light of the World

In the course of our narrative of the history of biblical interpretation thus far, it is clear that exegesis never operated apart from the influence of philosophy and theology. This insight is particularly important as we come to the rise of modern biblical criticism, still the most immediate context in which we practice biblical interpretation today. As Scholder perceptively observes, "One can say with some justification that the beginnings of biblical criticism are initially far more a philosophical than a theological problem . . . in dealing with these questions. . . . The church historian finds himself or herself transported into the largely uncharted area which lies between philosophy and theology."⁶⁶

The roots of modern criticism go far back into the Reformation and the Counter-Reformation, beyond that into the Renaissance and so on. However, something new appeared with the rise of modern philosophy, science, and the consequent historical revolution, developments with radical implications for biblical interpretation. Philosophy was closely connected with the emergent

---

63. See P. Gilbert, "The Catholic Counterpart to the Protestant Orthodoxy," in Saebø, *HB/OT* 2 (2008): 758–73, esp. 764–67.

64. See R. Simon, *A Critical History of the Old Testament* (London: Davis, 1678); idem, *A Critical History of the New Testament* (London: Taylor, 1689).

65. See J. W. O'Malley, *The First Jesuits* (Cambridge, MA: Harvard University Press, 1995).

66. K. Scholder, *The Birth of Modern Critical Theology: Origins and Problems of Biblical Criticism in the Seventeenth Century* (London: SCM, 1990), 5–6.

science; figures such as Descartes, Kant, and Hegel transformed the philosophical landscape with implications for every academic discipline.

As we will see, the early modern critical biblical scholars acknowledged the formative influence of the new philosophies on their work, but a crucial change came with Julius Wellhausen, who argued that philosophy followed on from biblical criticism but did not precede it. Karl Barth, a very different figure from Wellhausen, has ironically had a similar effect. Barth is the colossus standing behind the recovery of theological interpretation today, but part of his legacy is a profound suspicion of philosophy, with the result that many proponents of theological interpretation continue to ignore the formative influence of philosophy on the discipline of biblical interpretation.

Despite the ravaging of modernity by so-called postmodernity,[67] the narrative of modernity as one of *progress* remains deeply rooted in Western culture,[68] and it is still far too easy to accept such a narrative uncritically in biblical studies today. The way we tell the story of the emergence of modern biblical criticism is, however, *never neutral*. For example, in volume 4 of his *History of Biblical Interpretation*, when Reventlow comes to deal with Wilhelm de Wette, the father of modern biblical criticism, the chapter is headed "Biblical Studies as a Science." Implicit in such a heading is that it was not a science or truly critical before this era! Our narrative thus far reveals that this is quite incorrect, but so deeply is the modern narrative embedded in our consciousness that we need to become sensitized as to what baggage we are accepting when we periodize biblical studies with terms like *precritical* and *critical*, *premodern* and *modern*. This is *not* for a moment to deny the genuine progress made by modern biblical criticism or to propose a return to patristic exegesis, for example, but it is to insist that modern (and postmodern) biblical criticism operates within philosophical paradigm/s and that these require close inspection before being adopted as the "objective" way forward. Scholder and Reventlow have stressed the importance of examining the development of the historical-critical method in its historical and cultural context. The main figures of the development are well known, but "up until now it has not been described in context."[69] Exploring this context will involve examining its philosophical-hermeneutical elements closely, as Scholder recognizes in his

---

67. See C. G. Bartholomew and M. Goheen, *Christian Philosophy: A Systematic and Narrative Introduction* (Grand Rapids: Baker Academic, 2013), chap. 11.

68. Mary Hesse ("How to Be Postmodern without Being a Feminist," *The Monist* 77/4 [1994]: 445–61) notes that Western liberalism remains so much the background of postmodernism that it is barely noticed.

69. Scholder, *Birth of Modern Critical Theology*, 1; cf. H. G. Reventlow, *The Authority of the Bible and the Rise of the Modern World* (London: SCM, 1984), 2–3.

assertion that investigation of this area will result in the theologian finding himself or herself "transported into the largely uncharted area which lies between philosophy and theology."[70]

The Development and Nature of the Historical-Critical Method

Modern biblical criticism has come to be called historical criticism, which is fine as long as we remain alert to the diversity within this "family." "Historical" and "critical" both identify key elements of the historical-critical method of biblical interpretation. *Critical* signifies the subjection of the biblical tradition to examination on the basis of the modern worldview. As Scholder points out, this was clearly understood by F. C. Baur, who in a discussion with a colleague at Jena, Karl Hase, asserted that "in the end only that view can prevail which brings unity, connection and rational consistency to our world-view, our understanding of the history of the Gospel, our whole consciousness."[71] Scholder comments: "'Unity, connection and rational consistency': that means, quite simply, honest exegesis—honest to the degree that in principle it must be carried on with a concern for the understanding of reality 'which has been gained by the spirit in modern times.'"[72] *Historical* indicates that it is particularly the Enlightenment historical method that is applied to the Bible by the historical-critical method, especially as it came to maturity in the nineteenth century.[73]

In this section our approach will be as follows. First, we will briefly outline the development of the historical-critical method, with a detailed focus on de Wette and Wellhausen. Then we will examine Edgar Krentz's explication of the method as an example of a proponent of historical criticism.

The Origins of the Historical-Critical Method

Rogerson describes Germany as the home of the historical-critical method,[74] and indeed, it was in nineteenth-century Germany that the historical-critical

---

70. Scholder, *Birth of Modern Critical Theology*, 5–6.
71. Ibid., 2–3. For a discussion of Baur's hermeneutic, see R. A. Harrisville and W. Sundberg, *The Bible in Modern Culture: Theology and Historical-Critical Method from Spinoza to Käsemann* (Grand Rapids: Eerdmans, 1995), 111–30.
72. Scholder, *Birth of Modern Critical Theology*, 2–3.
73. Cf. E. W. Nicholson, *Interpreting the Old Testament: A Century of the Oriel Professorship* (Oxford: Clarendon, 1981). E. Krentz (*The Historical-Critical Method* [London: SPCK, 1975]) comments that "historical criticism . . . introduced into biblical interpretation a new method based on a secular understanding of history" (1).
74. J. W. Rogerson, *Old Testament Criticism in the Nineteenth Century: England and Germany* (London: SPCK, 1984), ix.

method reached maturity. However, before the second half of the eighteenth century, Germany had hardly been touched by critical theology, whereas a century earlier orthodoxy was forced onto the defensive in all other Western European countries.[75] Thus, if the mature adulthood of the historical-critical method is to be found in Germany, this is not true of its early and adolescent years; generally they are found elsewhere.

Exactly how far back one goes to discover the roots of the historical-critical method is debatable.[76] However, the emergence of the modern worldview and the rejection of a synthesis of nature with grace[77] were things new and unprecedented in their scale. Consequently, it seems wise to follow Krentz and Scholder in focusing analysis on the seventeenth and following centuries as we trace the rise of the historical-critical method.[78] Renaissance rediscovery of antiquity and the development of the printing press were crucial ingredients in the recipe for modernity. But, as Toulmin's distinction between the two origins of the modern world indicates,[79] it was a particular approach to and use of antiquity that produced the modern worldview, not just rediscovery of antiquity.

This particular approach emerged through the emancipation of reason from "all constraints" in philosophy and its penetration of science and history. The scientific and historical revolutions of the Enlightenment gave birth to the historical-critical method. It was Descartes who emancipated reason, and "like a young stallion locked up in stables for winter set free in spring pasture, it galloped far and wide with a wild and virile exuberance. The main shackle to be cast off was that of religion. . . . Out of the scientific explosion the decisive blow against religion was struck by history, which now replaced myth."[80] The changes that came about in the seventeenth century and became focused on the Bible in the historical-critical method began with philosophy (Descartes), exploded in the ongoing scientific revolution (Newton), and developed in history, from where they were focused hermeneutically on the Bible. Alan Richardson expresses this most clearly:

75. Scholder, *Birth of Modern Critical Theology*, 4–5.
76. See the important work by S. W. Hahn and B. Wiker, *Politicizing the Bible: The Roots of Historical Criticism and the Secularization of Scripture 1300–1700* (New York: Herder and Herder, 2013).
77. See W. Windelband, *A History of Philosophy* (London: Macmillan, 1901), 310–51.
78. Reventlow (*Authority of the Bible*, 3) locates the starting point of historical-critical theology in late medieval spiritualism.
79. S. Toulmin, *Cosmopolis: The Hidden Agenda of Modernity* (New York: Free Press, 1990; reprint, Chicago: University of Chicago Press, 1992).
80. J. Carroll, *Humanism: The Wreck of Western Culture* (London: Fontana, 1993), 120.

The thought of our own times has been shaped by the two great intellectual revolutions of the modern period—the scientific revolution of the sixteenth and seventeenth centuries, and the revolution in historical method which was the great achievement of the nineteenth century. The two revolutions are not indeed separate and distinct things; perhaps we should think rather of one great reorientation of the human mind, which began with the Renaissance and is still continuing. It began with the rise of what we today call the natural sciences; and by the nineteenth century it had embraced the sphere of history and what are now called the human sciences.[81]

Shifts in historiography are harder to identify than scientific ones, with the result that the changes in historiography are regularly subordinated to the scientific revolution. "That is certainly a mistake; for which insight in the end changed our understanding of reality more deeply is a completely open question."[82] As early as the mid-seventeenth century Isaac de la Peyrère in his *Praeadamitae* (*Man before Adam*, on Rom. 5:12–14) raised the question of how the nations and their religion could be reconciled with the Bible. "There is no more impressive evidence than this remarkable book of what a profound problem the old view of history had already become by the middle of the seventeenth century. With it—almost a century before Voltaire—the development of the new universal-historical conception of world history begins."[83]

The medieval view of history did not collapse overnight; historical consciousness was slowly restructured between 1550 and 1650. Jean Bodin's *Methodus ad facilem historiarum cognitionem* produced the first criticism of Melanchthon's picture of history.[84] Bodin critiqued the scheme of the four monarchies of Daniel, pled for the notion of human progress, made chronology the presupposition of all historical understanding, and maintained that the question of whether time is eternal must be decided not by tradition but by compelling arguments. "The more marked consideration of political realities, the extension of perspective beyond the limits of the West, the demands for compelling arguments even where tradition has long decided—all this points to the beginning of an emancipation from a purely biblical-theological understanding of the world and the history of nations."[85]

81. A. Richardson, "The Rise of Modern Biblical Scholarship and Recent Discussion of the Authority of the Bible," in *The Cambridge History of the Bible*, vol. 3, *The West from the Reformation to the Present Day*, ed. S. L. Greenslade (Cambridge: Cambridge University Press, 1975), 295.
82. Scholder, *Birth of Modern Critical Theology*, 65.
83. Ibid., 67.
84. No fewer than 12 editions of this text were published up to 1650.
85. Scholder, *Birth of Modern Critical Theology*, 75.

The result was a shift similar to that in philosophy and science. History gradually became autonomous from theology. The Scriptures were treated more and more as ordinary historical documents. "The process of objectification had begun."[86]

The eighteenth century was the heyday of the Enlightenment. The critical approach toward the Bible was consolidated in deism,[87] but the triumph of abstract reason restrained the move toward a fully historical approach to the Bible. However, already in the seventeenth century Spinoza had argued for a historical approach to the Bible.[88] Now through the labors of scholars such as Turrentinus, Wetzstein, Ernesti, Astruc, Semler, Eichhorn, Gabler, and Michaelis[89] there was a slow but steady move toward a more historical interpretation of the Bible. A particularly significant figure in the latter half of the seventeenth century was Semler. He was the first German Protestant theologian to approach the Bible through the history of religions and to insist on a critical rather than a dogmatic reading of it. The interpreter must seek to discover what the original author meant by the text.[90] Keil likewise stressed that an interpreter must think the author's thoughts after him without judging them. The exegete should establish only the facts. "The standard for subsequent commentaries was formulated."[91]

By the end of the eighteenth century in Germany, most Old Testament professors were either neologists (skeptical biblical scholars) or rationalists. Semler and Michaelis were the founders of neologism. Brought up as Pietists, they abandoned Pietism through the influence of Spinoza and deism. As the eighteenth century moved into the nineteenth, neologism was increasingly replaced by rationalism and supranaturalism, both responses to the Kantianism that penetrated most of the theological faculties in the 1790s.[92] Source criticism of the Pentateuch was advanced through the labors

---

86. Krentz, *Historical-Critical Method*, 16.
87. Ibid., 16–17; cf. Reventlow, *Authority of the Bible*, 289–410.
88. See J. S. Preus, "A Hidden Opponent in Spinoza's *Tractatus*," *HTR* 88, no. 3 (1995): 361–88.
89. On Michaelis, see M. C. Legaspi, *The Death of Scripture and the Rise of Biblical Studies* (Oxford: Oxford University Press, 2010), who states, "The most fundamental question that one can address to Michaelis's biblical project is whether the Bible—given its particular shape, contents, and afterlife—can be fully comprehended in cultural categories" (160). J. G. Hamann launched a devastating attack on Michaelis in "Aesthetica in nuce" (1762, http://gutenberg.spiegel.de/buch/aesthetica-in-nuce-1624/1), in his *Writings on Philosophy and Language*, trans. and ed. K. Haynes (Cambridge: Cambridge University Press, 2007), 61–95.
90. W. G. Jeanrond, *Theological Hermeneutics: Development and Significance* (London: SCM, 1994), 39.
91. Krentz, *Historical-Critical Method*, 19.
92. Rogerson, *Old Testament Criticism*, 16–18.

of Eichhorn in particular, but there was no radical reconstruction of the history of Israel.[93]

The historical thought of the Enlightenment, as we explained above, was more philosophical than historical. The eighteenth century fostered an understanding of history dominated by the idea of progress.[94] This philosophy of history continued on into the nineteenth century, but it was being displaced by German historicism and Hegelian philosophy. Historicism refers to the sort of historical thought that dominated Germany from the rise of Romanticism at the end of the eighteenth century, down to the mid-twentieth century. It represents a reaction to the idea of progress and is characterized by a belief that all cultures are molded by history, a privileging of intuition as the means whereby we understand groups other than our own, and a denial of history as linear.[95]

Barthold G. Niebuhr's *Römische Geschichte* (1811–12) was a major early historicist work. According to Krentz, two questions dominated his method: What is the evidence? What is the value of the evidence? In this way Niebuhr sought to separate poetry from truth in his sources and to reconstruct what happened in a more believable narrative.[96] As Collingwood points out, the classic example of this is Niebuhr's treatment of Livy.[97] Niebuhr argues that much of what was taken for early Roman history is patriotic fiction of a later period, and that even the earliest stratum is not sober fact but a national epic of the ancient Roman people. Behind the epic, Niebuhr detects the historical reality of early Rome, a society of peasant farmers.[98] As Bebbington makes clear, Niebuhr's approach was more nuanced than Krentz suggests.[99]

Leopold von Ranke, another historicist, concentrated on collecting the facts of history—commitment to detail being a characteristic of this school—but also sought the unity of history. The historian must penetrate to the inwardness of events. Every moment in history is equidistant from God. This approach assumed some sensible idea or divine presence moving through all history, whether it was Hegel's spirit, von Ranke's governing God, Droysen's ethical progress, or Humboldt's pantheistic truth. After 1850, historical inquiry became

---

93. Ibid., 19–27.
94. D. W. Bebbington, *Patterns in History: A Christian Perspective on Historical Thought* (Leicester, UK: Inter-Varsity, 1979; reprint, Leicester, UK: Apollos, 1990), 68–91.
95. Ibid., 92–94. Cf. F. C. Beiser, *The German Historicist Tradition* (New York: Oxford University Press, 2012).
96. Krentz, *Historical-Critical Method*, 22.
97. R. G. Collingwood, *The Idea of History* (Oxford: Oxford University Press, 1946), 130.
98. Collingwood notes that this method goes back via Herder to Vico, and that by the mid-nineteenth century it was the common property of all competent historians, at least in Germany (ibid., 130).
99. Bebbington, *Patterns in History*, 106.

more immanentist, a turn well represented by Eduard Meyer,[100] for whom the historian should describe happenings and not seek laws and general ideas.

It was during the early nineteenth century that the turning point for critical study of the Old Testament occurred.[101]

W. M. L. de Wette (1780–1849): Founder of Modern Biblical Criticism

Wilhelm de Wette was the first to use a critical methodology to articulate a view of Israel's history quite different from that implied in the Old Testament.[102] Because of his doctorate on Deuteronomy, his seventh-century BC dating of it, and his association of the promulgation of Deuteronomy with the reign of King Josiah, de Wette is most well known as an Old Testament critic. However, de Wette wrote substantially on the Old Testament, the New Testament, and Christian theology. He stands therefore at the origin of biblical criticism as a whole.

De Wette grew up in a Protestant family and studied at the University of Jena, where his illustrious teachers included Fichte, Schelling, Hegel, and Griesbach. For de Wette, however, the major challenge to his faith came from Kant. In 1798, the year before de Wette came to Jena, Kant published his *Der Streit der Fakultäten*, in which he outlines an understanding of religion within the bounds of reason alone.[103] As Rogerson says,

> However illustrious his Jena teachers were, the greatest initial impact that was made upon de Wette came from the philosophy of Kant. Indeed, for the remainder of his life, de Wette remained, intellectually, a sort of Kantian; and he spent many years of his life trying to reconcile his intellectual acceptance of Kant with his aesthetic and almost mystical instinct for religion.[104]

Just how influential Kant was on de Wette is apparent from de Wette's semi-autobiographical novel *Theodore*, in which he describes Kant's influence on him as follows:[105]

---

100. Krentz, *Historical-Critical Method*, 24.
101. Rogerson, *Old Testament Criticism*, 28–49.
102. Ibid., 28–29. On de Wette and biblical criticism, see also T. A. Howard, *Religion and the Rise of Historicism: W. M. L. de Wette, Jacob Burckhardt, and the Theological Origins of Nineteenth-Century Historical Consciousness* (Cambridge: Cambridge University Press, 2000).
103. Earlier I. Kant published *Religion within the Limits of Reason Alone* (1793), trans. T. M. Greene and H. H. Hudson (New York: Harper & Row, 1960), in which he develops the view of religion also expressed in *Der Streit der Fakultäten* (1798; Hamburg: Felix Meiner, 2005).
104. J. W. Rogerson, *W. M. L. de Wette, Founder of Modern Biblical Criticism: An Intellectual Biography* (Sheffield: Sheffield Academic Press, 1992), 27.
105. Cf. Rogerson, *W. M. L. de Wette*, 27–30, for a description of the content of a lecture that Kant gave at the University of Jena the year before de Wette arrived there. This lecture gives one an insight into the view of religion that Kant was expounding at this time.

> Theodore heard at the same time some lectures on morals from a Kantian philosopher, through which a completely new world was opened up to him. The notions of the self-sufficiency of reason in its law-giving, of the freedom of the will through which he was elevated above nature and fate, . . . all these notions gripped him powerfully, and filled him with a high self-awareness. Those shadowy ideas about the love of God and Christ, about the new birth, about the rule of God's grace in the human mind, . . . these he translated now into this new philosophical language, and so they appeared to him clearer and more certain.[106]

Kant's view had radical implications for religion and biblical interpretation. There is no agreed interpretation of the Bible, but a religion of reason can yield this, because it gets at universal truths of reason. Religion is reduced to morality, and Christian theology is adjusted accordingly. The contingent truths of history cannot be revelatory since revelation is disclosed through reason. Schelling helped de Wette to develop a critique of Kant's overprivileging of philosophy as final arbiter in all disciplines. For Schelling, God as the Absolute was primary, and reason was a part of the Absolute by which the individual could perceive the Absolute in the particular. Religion is the contemplation of the Absolute as it is manifested in nature, history, and art. Schelling regarded mythology positively because it is an attempt to grasp the Absolute. Schelling's understanding of mythology profoundly influenced de Wette's approach to the Bible, especially to the Old Testament.

In his dissertation (submitted 1804) and in his *Auffo[r]derung zum Studium der hebräischen Sprache und Literatur* (1805), de Wette developed a portrait of the history of Israelite religion differing radically from that of the Old Testament itself, a portrait that formed the basis for development of critical scholarship in the nineteenth and twentieth centuries. But whence did de Wette get this portrait? From reading the text, from reading it in a way not constricted by theories of unity of authorship, but also, says Rogerson, by reading the Old Testament through the grid of a certain view of religion, regarding it as developing from a simple to a complex phenomenon, a view that de Wette probably got from Schelling's *Philosophie der Kunst*. The *Aufforderung* contains a devastating attack on the historicity of the Old Testament, motivated by de Wette's view of religion and mythology. From Kant, de Wette had learned, and learned well, that the contingent truths of history cannot be revelatory. Probably from Karl Philipp Moritz's *Die Götterlehre* (1791), de Wette learned that myths were never history but poetry, and although myths were fantasy, they could contain sublime ideas.

---

106. Quoted by Rogerson, *Old Testament Criticism*, 37.

Thus the pentateuchal stories are generally of no value for the historian but of great value for the theologian because of their witness to religion. The Pentateuch "is a product of the religious poetry of the Israelite people, which reflects their spirit [*Geist*], way of thought, love of the nation, philosophy of religion."[107] Similarly, in his 1811 commentary on the Psalms, de Wette argues that in many cases it is impossible to determine the historical contexts of many biblical psalms, but this does not matter because what is important is religion expressed in poetic form.[108]

One is struck by the profound influence of philosophical and theological issues on de Wette's thought. According to Rogerson:

> De Wette was convinced that biblical interpretation and theology were concerned with reality, and that *reality could only be understood with the help of philosophy*. In this he was surely right. Implicit in Christian belief are claims about the nature of reality, about the sort of world in which we live and about the sort of things human beings are. Although philosophy in a broad sense does not seek to provide answers to these questions, it does offer critiques of attempted answers, it exposes contradictions and tautologies and offers conceptual frameworks for deeper reflection. Those who claim to have no philosophy are simply unaware of their philosophical presuppositions.
>
> In using philosophy so unashamedly in his biblical interpretation, theology and ethics, de Wette was standing in an honourable tradition reaching back through Protestant scholasticism to Aquinas and the church of those centuries that produced the classical creeds of Christian orthodoxy. This was one reason why de Wette rejected such orthodoxy, believing that it was based upon inadequate philosophy. . . . We cannot fault de Wette's sincerity in making his views about the nature of reality affect his biblical interpretation and his theology.[109]

Three ways in which de Wette is of major significance for our narrative are as follows:

1. De Wette recognized that human perspectives or worldviews are unified, and he saw the unavoidable connections between one's view of reason and history and religion, thus one's philosophy, and how one reads the Bible. Here de Wette has much to teach us. Modernity has been characterized by an explosion in knowledge and a strong differentiation into disciplinary and subdisciplinary areas. An effect of this is that scholars take longer and

---

107. Quoted in Rogerson, *W. M. L. de Wette*, 55.
108. See Theodore Parker's comment that de Wette is a rationalist and mystic at the same time, via ibid., 66.
109. Ibid., 267, 268, with added emphasis.

longer to specialize in less and less. There is little time and often no encouragement for scholars to descend into the subtexts of their disciplines and so connect with the larger issues that impact their scholarship. De Wette's work is a reminder that, like it or not, our view of the world and our understanding of reason, religion, language, and so forth will shape the way we work with the Bible. The great merit of de Wette is his consciousness of these influences.

2. De Wette recognized the *fundamental role of philosophy* in academic analysis. De Wette saw, as it were, that philosophical scaffolding is always in place when academic construction is being done, even if scholars are not aware of it: always an epistemology is assumed, always some ontology is taken for granted, always some view of the human person is in mind. De Wette is remarkably contemporary with regard to this, for he was alert to the philosophical subtext of his work, yet many contemporary scholars seem blissfully unaware of philosophy behind their own work. As Thiselton observes, biblical scholars tend to remain philosophically illiterate and thus to be destined to work within outworn paradigms.[110] De Wette's work is a salutary reminder of *all* the ingredients involved in biblical interpretation.

3. De Wette believed that the true philosophy was that done in the Kantian/Schelling/Friesian tradition, and his life's work is devoted to rethinking religion and the Bible and theology within that framework. Especially in our late modern time, this commitment to Kantian philosophy is controversial. But, whatever one thinks of de Wette's Kantianism, his candor is refreshing, as is his quest for integration of his philosophy with his scholarship and his theology.

Scholars continue to work with philosophical paradigms shaping their work, but generally they ignore these paradigms, with the result that they are hidden from view and their scholarship has the appearance of neutral, objective analysis. De Wette's openness about his paradigm enables one to get a look at the total picture that makes up his work, and this puts the reader in a position to examine and evaluate his work in its totality.

---

110. A. C. Thiselton, "Communicative Action and Promise in Interdisciplinary, Biblical, and Theological Hermeneutics," in *The Promise of Hermeneutics*, by R. Lundin, C. Walhout, and A. C. Thiselton (Grand Rapids: Eerdmans, 1999), 133–239. Thiselton states,
> Curiously, the limits of scientific method to explain all of reality seem to be appreciated more readily in the philosophy of religion than in biblical studies. Views and methods that students in philosophy of religion recognize as "positivist," "reductionist," or even "materialist" are often embraced quite uncritically in issues of judgement about, e.g., acts of God in biblical narrative. In place of the more rigorous and judicious exploration of these issues in philosophical theology, biblical studies seems too readily to become polarized. (ibid., 137)

Rogerson agrees with de Wette that philosophy is unavoidable in theoretical analysis. But then Rogerson makes some extraordinary moves! He asserts that Christian belief implies certain philosophical positions. And then, on *this* basis, de Wette is commended for adopting a *Kantian* framework and fitting religion within it! Does Christian belief imply the framework of Kant's secular city, so that we then search for a place for religion within the limits of reason? The assumption that Kant's philosophy is compatible with Christian belief is not an unusual view, as the image of Kant as the "philosopher of Protestantism" reminds us.[111] There is a strong tradition in liberal Protestant theology of Kant's philosophy as a mediator between faith and modern culture. However, as Beiser[112] shows, even in Kant's day his views were very controversial, and the issues of theology and God in relation to Kant's theology were fiercely debated. A figure we need to recover in the story of philosophy is Hamann, a contemporary and fierce critic of Kant, after his conversion to Christianity.[113]

In recent decades Kant's anthropology has come in for strong criticism from liberation and feminist theologians and from postliberals,[114] reminding us at the very least that "the Cartesian-Kantian model of the self is historically contingent, rather than the indispensable conceptual device for properly framing the issue of faith and transcendence."[115] It is true that evaluation of Kant as a "Christian thinker" remains controversial today.[116] Personally, I think Michalson is right to argue that Kant's immanentism and view of human autonomy subvert theism so that Kant, as much as Hegel, should be understood as facilitating the transformations in European culture that we associate with the rise of atheism rather than being foundational for a mediating theology.[117] From this perspective, Kant is a key figure on the Luther-Kant-Feuerbach-Marx trajectory, and one of whom, as Buckley warns in his explorations of the origins of atheism, Christian thinkers should be cautious![118] The implications for theology and biblical interpretation are clear:

111. G. E. Michalson Jr., *Kant and the Problem of God* (Oxford: Blackwell, 1999), 1.
112. F. C. Beiser, *The Fate of Reason: German Philosophy from Kant to Fichte* (Cambridge, MA: Harvard University Press, 1993).
113. See ibid.; J. R. Betz, *After Enlightenment: The Post-secular Vision of J. G. Hamann* (Oxford: Blackwell, 2012).
114. Michalson, *Kant and the Problem*, 128-32.
115. Ibid., 136.
116. For different perspectives on Kant and Christianity, see works by M. Westphal, N. Wolterstorff, A. W. Wood, G. E. Michalson Jr., A. Plantinga, et al.
117. Michalson, *Kant and the Problem*, 127.
118. M. J. Buckley, *At the Origins of Modern Atheism* (New Haven: Yale University Press, 1987), which rightly states:
> The atheism evolved in the eighteenth century was thus not to be denied by the strategies elaborated in the revolutions of Kant and Schleiermacher: it was only to be transposed

The consistent subordination of divine transcendence to the demands of autonomous rationality strongly suggests that Kant's own thought ... is moving in a non-theistic direction rather than in a direction with obviously constructive possibilities for theology.... The religious feature may remain present, but that is not where the real life is, any more than the twitching body of a beheaded reptile indicates real life. As a result, Kant's own example is hardly a comforting model for those committed to holding divine transcendence and a modern sensibility in proper balance. In his case, the balancing act cannot be sustained; his particular way of endorsing modernity is finally too self-aggrandizing.[119]

One may—which I do not!—wish to argue that Kant is a helpful mediating figure for biblical interpretation between faith and modern culture, but then the case has to be argued, not assumed. As J. D. Caputo perceptively notes, "So what you think about modernity lies at the root of many of the arguments you hear about philosophy and theology."[120] Rogerson rightly declares that de Wette's lasting "achievement" was to apply historical criticism to the Bible so as to produce a history radically different from that of the Bible itself. Nicholson notices the indebtedness of Reuss, George, Vatke, and crucially Wellhausen to de Wette.[121] What tends to be forgotten is de Wette's indebtedness to Kant in moving Old Testament scholarship in this direction in the first place.

Gesenius, Gramberg, and George developed de Wette's reconstruction of the history of Israel.[122] Vatke published his *Biblical Theology* in 1835 (in German). In the critical interpretation of the Old Testament, he was mainly guided by de Wette and Gesenius, but his work is deeply influenced by Hegel. Under the influence of contemporary philosophical trends and secular historical research, biblical criticism refined its techniques. Schleiermacher had given historical criticism a positive place in his analysis of understanding, and his prestige gave respectability to the use of historical method in biblical studies, which now came to be increasingly practiced at German universities,

---

into a different key. Argue god as the presupposition or as the corollary of nature; eventually natural philosophy would dispose of god. Argue god as the presupposition or as the corollary of human nature; eventually the denial of god would become an absolute necessity for human existence. (322–33)

119. Michalson, *Kant and the Problem*, 137.

120. J. D. Caputo, *Philosophy and Theology* (Nashville: Abingdon, 2006), 11. For a trenchant, accessible critique of Descartes and Kant, see ibid., 21–34.

121. E. W. Nicholson, *The Pentateuch in the Twentieth Century: The Legacy of Julius Wellhausen* (Oxford: Oxford University Press, 1998), 4.

122. Rogerson, *Old Testament Criticism*, 50–68. He mentions but does not explore the philosophical influences on all three.

where the Old Testament was studied on a large scale.[123] The *Biblia Hebraica* soon appeared, and in 1829 Heinrich Meyer produced the first volume of his *Critical and Exegetical Commentary*. For Meyer, exegesis was to be free of dogmatic and party spirit, not captive to any "ism," and the exegete should simply determine what the author said. By the end of the century, the International Critical Commentary and the *Handkommentar* were also in production. By this time even the conservative scholars used the historical method to determine the facts. They differed only in their attempt to keep revelation close to the facts.[124]

In terms of historical criticism and New Testament studies, the work of Ferdinand Christian Baur (1792–1860) had far-reaching consequences. Baur was raised in a pastor's home, trained at the seminary of the University of Tübingen, and served as a pastor in 1814–26. At seminary he espoused the rationalism of the day, but the turning point for him came when he read Schleiermacher's *The Christian Faith*. Shortly after reading this, in a letter to his brother of July 26, 1823, Bauer stated that, "according to Schleiermacher, the primary source of Christianity lies in the religious self-consciousness, out of whose development the principal doctrines of Christianity are to be obtained."[125] Baur embraced this view and argued that the universal, religious sense of dependence manifested itself in a variety of religions and myths, all resulting from a process of divine education within history. Far more than Schleiermacher, Baur proved willing to apply his antisupernatural approach consistently to the New Testament.[126]

Using Hegel's evolutionary paradigm, Baur articulated a comprehensive explanation of the development of early Christianity via a split between a gentile Christianity represented by Paul and a Jewish Christianity represented by Peter. This bitter conflict and its ultimate resolution within the emerging Catholic church dominate the New Testament and drove the development of the early church until the end of the second century. In his *Paulus* (1845), Baur argued that the Pauline Letters could not be reconciled with the accounts in Acts; the latter book cannot be accepted as historically trustworthy and dates from the mid-second century. Based on his historical work, Baur concluded that only Romans, Galatians, and 1 and 2 Corinthians were genuinely Pauline.

As Scott Hafemann explains:

123. Ibid., 138.
124. Cf. Krentz, *Historical-Critical Method*, 27–28.
125. Quoted in H. Harris, *The Tübingen School: A Historical and Theological Investigation of the School of F. C. Baur* (Grand Rapids: Baker, 1990), 148.
126. See S. Neill, *The Interpretation of the New Testament, 1861–1961* (Oxford: Oxford University Press, 1964), 19–28.

With the rise of Baur, a purely historical and critical investigation of the Bible established itself as orthodoxy within the world of scholarship. Ever since Baur all interpretations of the New Testament have had to pass the test of historical probability in a way not enforced prior to the nineteenth century, even for those who accept the reality of divine intervention and the authority of Scripture.[127]

H. Harris argues that no single event changed biblical scholarship as much as the appearance of the Tübingen school.[128]

Probably the most significant Old Testament figure of the nineteenth century was Wellhausen. His documentary hypothesis (for the origins of the Pentateuch) became the virtual consensus, as did his understanding of the history of Israel. Wellhausen's *decontextualization* of Old Testament research is a good example of Toulmin's characterization of modernity; decontextualization became ever stronger in Old Testament studies. Indeed, up to the present, it is rare to find biblical scholars who find it necessary to grapple with these broader issues in their research. Sadly, we would be most surprised to find a contemporary Old Testament scholar, like Vatke, starting a book with a chapter on the nature of religion!

Julius Wellhausen (1844–1918): A Watershed

The most thorough recent study of Wellhausen and German philosophy is Perlitt's (1965) *Vatke und Wellhausen*. Perlitt recounts the similarities of Wellhausen to Vatke but also their differences. For example, Wellhausen, unlike Vatke, does not see postexilic Judaism as a positive development,[129] whereas a Hegelian view of history would push one in this direction. And in his finding of a secure starting point for the history of Israel in the formation of Israel as a people, Wellhausen follows the organic-development method of the historical school *and* Hegel and Vatke.[130] Likewise with his view of progress, Perlitt points out that Wellhausen does not need Hegel or evolutionism: "The concept of development stretching from Lessing via Herder, Goethe, Schleiermacher, and idealistic philosophy to de Wette, Ranke, and Wellhausen has, of course, a specific, common foundation and colouring in its application to history."[131] Perlitt later argues that Wellhausen's view of Israel's development is akin to

---

127. S. J. Hafemann, "Baur, F(erdinand) C(hristian) (1792–1860)," in McKim, *Historical Handbook*, 289.
128. H. Harris, *Tübingen School*, 1.
129. L. Perlitt, *Vatke und Wellhausen*, BZAW 94 (Berlin: Töpelmann, 1965), 177.
130. Ibid., 172.
131. Ibid., 178–79.

Renaissance, Reformation, and Modernity

"historicism's individualising concept of development," of which Herder is a prime example.[132] The relationship of Wellhausen to the philosophies of his day is complex, and such areas of overlap with Vatke and Hegel do not demonstrate strong dependence.

Perlitt states, furthermore, that Wellhausen, like the Dutch critic Kuenen, firmly rejected the imposition of alien philosophies on the Bible: Wellhausen and Kuenen "agree completely at least in the rejection of pre- and alien philosophical determination."[133] In contrast to Vatke, Wellhausen began his work with philological and text-critical analysis of the biblical text. "Thus Wellhausen proceeded in a methodologically secure way from literary analysis to historical criticism."[134]

Wellhausen was aware that history writing is never a neutral, totally objective enterprise. However, despite this awareness, Wellhausen's response to Strauss's *Leben Jesu* manifests where his real sympathies lie with respect to philosophical influence on biblical study. Wellhausen wrote:

> Because Strauss showed and acknowledged himself to be a child of Hegel in his concept of myth, his book was judged simply as an extension of so-called Hegelianism. Biblical criticism, however, did not in general develop under the influence of philosophical ideas. . . . Philosophy does not precede, but follows [biblical criticism], in that it seeks to evaluate and to systematise that which it has not itself produced. The authors—who were friends—of the two great theological works of 1835 [Strauss's *Life of Jesus* and Vatke's *Biblical Theology*, both in German] were certainly Hegelian. But that which is of scholarly significance in them does not come from Hegel. As Vatke is the disciple of, and the one who brings to completion the work of, de Wette, so Strauss completes the work of the old rationalists. The true value of the *Life of Jesus* lies not in the philosophical introduction and concluding section, but in the main part which in terms of its extent exceeds the others by far.[135]

Perlitt and Rogerson notice how this statement exemplifies Wellhausen's view of philosophy and biblical study. "Where Wellhausen positions his own work in this clear distinction between biblical criticism (as science) and philosophy (as an interpretation which follows criticism and merely systematizes

---

132. Ibid., 185. On the key role of "development" in nineteenth-century historiography, see M. Mandelbaum, *History, Man, and Reason. A Study in Nineteenth-Century Thought* (Baltimore: Johns Hopkins University Press, 1971).
133. Perlitt, *Vatke und Wellhausen*, 160.
134. Ibid., 168.
135. Quoted in ibid., 204.

it), can after all not be doubted."¹³⁶ "One must rather proceed from particular impulses which arise from the exegesis."¹³⁷

With this statement we see the extent to which Wellhausen differed from Vatke and many of his predecessors. Their extensive treatments of the nature of religion indicate a strong awareness of the influence of philosophical questions on their work. Wellhausen has a different view of the relationship between Old Testament exegesis and philosophy. It is a view in which exegesis is relatively uncontaminated by philosophy; Old Testament research uncovers the facts, and philosophy can follow the facts but should not precede them!

Rogerson is alert to philosophical influence on biblical studies, and he acknowledges that biblical criticism has been more influenced by philosophy than Wellhausen allows. However, he quotes from Wellhausen's discussion of Strauss's *Leben Jesu*, and then in agreement with Wellhausen, Rogerson argues:

> If biblical criticism is defined as the investigation of the literary processes which brought the books of the Bible to their extant form, together with a critical evaluation of the history and culture of ancient Israel and Judea so as to interpret biblical material in its original historical and cultural setting, *it is difficult to see how philosophy, even defined very broadly, can affect such investigations. Surely, the reconstruction of the history of Israel, or of the apostolic period, involves the use of an historical method unaffected by philosophy.* Further, the conclusion, based upon the alteration of the divine names and other criteria in the "Flood" narrative of Genesis 6–9, that this narrative is a combination of two originally separate written accounts, is something else that in *no way depends upon philosophy.* . . . *I am happy to agree that in many of its technical procedures, biblical criticism is not affected by philosophy.*¹³⁸

Wellhausen—plus Rogerson and so many others!—have thereby adopted a radically different understanding than de Wette and Vatke of how philosophy relates to biblical criticism. For de Wette, biblical interpretation is shaped by one's view of religion and one's philosophy. For Wellhausen and for Rogerson, philosophy follows on from biblical interpretation and scholarship. The effect is dramatic! In one fell swoop, as it were, what Toulmin calls the standard account of modernity is entrenched in biblical criticism, thereby obscuring the tradition/s in which this style of biblical interpretation is embedded. The

136. Ibid.
137. Ibid., 205.
138. J. W. Rogerson, "Philosophy and the Rise of Biblical Criticism: England and Germany," in *England and Germany: Studies in Theological Diplomacy*, ed. W. Sykes (Frankfurt: Peter Lang, 1982), 63, with added emphasis.

observation of the text by Wellhausen and his followers now becomes objective and scientific, (relatively) unadulterated by philosophical perspectives.

The effect of this approach to biblical study is in a positivist direction, in the sense that historical criticism is now understood to uncover the facts of Israel's history, and to be scientific, objective, and neutral in this regard. And since Wellhausen, this view has come to dominate Old Testament studies. James Barr has been very influential on Old Testament studies and in a recent publication, despite the emergence of postmodernism, he can still assert:

> *The typical biblical scholarship of modern times has been rather little touched by philosophy*—certainly much less than it has been touched by theology. Going back to the last century, one remembers Vatke and his Hegelianism, and it has long been customary to accuse Wellhausen of the same thing though the accusation has long been proved to be an empty one. And after that we do have an influence of philosophy, but mostly on the theological use of the Bible rather than on biblical scholarship in the narrower sense.[139]

This approach won the day in modern liberal and, to a significant extent, evangelical biblical studies. A common epistemological starting point was assumed, the difference generally being the conclusions reached. Thus there is some truth in James Barr's critique of evangelicalism in his *Fundamentalism* that one generally knows which conclusions evangelicals are going to reach. Nowadays this common epistemological starting point often manifests itself in the noble guise of "going where the truth takes you" as if the questions you ask and your epistemology and unavoidable religious starting point have no influence on the "truth" arrived at. Rogerson does grapple with the broader philosophical issues, and he acknowledges that biblical criticism has been far more influenced by philosophy than Wellhausen allows, but he too removes the heart of historical criticism from philosophical influence.

The problem of the relationship between faith and historical knowledge became acute toward the end of the nineteenth century, with the emergence of the history of religions school, which sought to explain the Bible in terms of its surrounding cultures. Gunkel was the key Old Testament figure in the history of religions school. "Its basic outlook was positivistic. The Bible, firmly anchored in its own world, was interpreted as an amalgam of various borrowed motifs, and became a book strange to modern men."[140]

---

139. J. Barr, *History and Ideology in the Old Testament: Biblical Studies at the End of a Millennium* (Oxford: Oxford University Press, 2005), 26–27, with added emphasis.
140. Krentz, *Historical-Critical Method*, 28; cf. H. F. Hahn, *The Old Testament in Modern Research* (Philadelphia: Fortress, 1966), 83–118.

With Germany at the forefront, by the end of the nineteenth century historical criticism dominated Protestantism on the continent. England and America embraced the historical-critical method much later than Germany, but by the end of the nineteenth century its success there was also ensured. As Krentz points out,

> It is difficult to overestimate the significance the nineteenth century has for biblical interpretation. It made historical criticism *the* approved method of interpretation. The result was a revolution of viewpoint in evaluating the Bible. The Scriptures were, so to speak, *secularized*. . . . The Bible was no longer the criterion for the writing of history; rather history had become the criterion for understanding the Bible. . . . The Bible stood before criticism as defendant before judge. The criticism was largely positivist in orientation, immanentist in its explanations, and incapable of appreciating the category of revelation.[141]

From one angle the whole of twentieth-century theology can be seen as an attempt to relate modernity and faith.[142] World War I called historicism and evolutionary thought into question, inter alia generating a strong reaction to the straitjacket of positivism in biblical interpretation. Karl Barth called for theological interpretation while also finding a place for historical criticism. Krentz captures the tension of biblical interpretation in Barth and the twentieth century: "By the end of the Second World War historical criticism was firmly established, not to be dislodged by any attack. But the dangers of historicism to faith were also clear. The central problem of the relation of faith and historical method was posed as strongly as ever."[143] Throughout the twentieth century there have been strong reactions to the historical-critical method in Old Testament studies. These reactions will be our concern below.

Krentz's Articulation of the Historical-Critical Method

It is apparent from the above that historical method in modernity is diverse. Different historical methods handled the Old Testament differently, so it seems impossible to pin down *the* historical-critical method in biblical interpretation. Krentz recognizes this ambiguity: "Today historical criticism is taken for granted. . . . Yet it is anything but clear just what we mean when

---

141. Krentz, *Historical-Critical Method*, 30, with added emphasis.
142. Cf. H. Zahrnt, *The Question of God: Protestant Theology in the Twentieth Century* (London: Collins, 1969).
143. Krentz, *Historical-Critical Method*, 32.

we use the phrase *historical method*."[144] The effect of modernity, however, has been to decontextualize the method and to promote the assumption that there is one historical-critical method.[145] Thus even Krentz, who recognizes this problem, does not face it but quotes Wilckens with approval and then follows his advice: "The only scientifically responsible interpretation of the Bible is that investigation of the biblical texts that, with a methodologically consistent use of historical understanding in the present state of its art, seeks via reconstruction to recognize and describe the meaning these texts have had in the context of the tradition and history of early Christianity."[146]

For Krentz, history is systematic (analytical) knowledge of the past.[147] The historical-critical method in biblical interpretation "produces history in the modern sense, for it consciously and critically investigates biblical documents to write a narrative of the history they reveal."[148] The modern historian, like the historical-critical biblical scholar, seeks to explain what happened and why. History involves interpretation, and the biblical scholar must explain how the diversity of thought arose in Israel. His first task is to hear the text on its own terms: "This basic respect for the historical integrity of a text is inherent in all criticism."[149] The text has hermeneutical autonomy, and the exegete must go where the text leads. Thus "the critical biblical scholar will not only question the texts, but [also question] himself—his methods, his conclusions, and his presuppositions—and the others who share in the same task."[150] His work is his own judgment, and yet he submits to the text: "where that text deals with the profundities of man, that calls for a submission to the autonomy of the text that calls the historian forth for judgment and knowledge of himself. Then history performs its humane (or in the case of the biblical texts) its theological function."[151]

144. Ibid., 33.
145. This tendency is recognized in a fascinating article by J. McIntyre, "Historical Criticism in a 'History-Centered Value System,'" in *Language, Theology, and the Bible: Essays in Honour of James Barr*, ed. S. E. Balentine and J. Barton (Oxford: Clarendon, 1994), 370–84. His opening sentence is as follows: "One circumstance which, more than any others, has controlled the discussion of the relation of faith to history, has been the assumption, held by both the theologians and the historical critics with whom they have been debating, that historical criticism is a single, and fairly simply identifiable, entity."
146. Wilckens, "Über die Bedeutung historischer Kritik in der modernen Bibelexegese," *Wass heisst Auslegung der Heiligen Schrift?* (Regensburg: Friedrich Pustet, 1966), 133, quoted by Krentz, *Historical-Critical Method*, 33.
147. Krentz, *Historical-Critical Method*, 34.
148. Ibid., 35.
149. Ibid., 39.
150. Ibid., 53–54.
151. Ibid., 54.

Krentz argues that historical criticism is conservative in its privileging of the text and refusal to privilege traditional interpretations.[152] The historian listens to the text and interrogates it in order to assess it as a testimony to history. All the linguistic tools available are used to determine the meaning of the text for its original hearers. "Concern for literary figures . . . [is] used by the historian to judge the historical usefulness of material, not to achieve a literary appreciation of it *per se*."[153] Historical method evaluates its sources to determine what really happened and what the significance of those events is. It does not exclude specifically Christian goals for the critical interpretation of the Bible because the historian also seeks to understand himself through a study of the past.[154] However, "the differences between biblical scholarship and secular history derive from the major source, the Bible, and not the methods used. Biblical scholars use the methods of secular history on the Bible to discover truth and explain what happened. The methods are secular. The procedures may be modified to fit the Bible, but are not essentially changed."[155] Krentz lists the following as the main methods of historical-critical interpretation of the Bible: textual criticism, philological study, literary criticism, form criticism, redaction criticism, historical criticism, and perhaps *Sachkritik* (critical assessment of the text).[156]

With regard to presuppositions, Krentz acknowledges that "historical method is anything but a carefully defined and agreed on set of axioms and presuppositions."[157] Troeltsch's 1898 essay articulated the principles of historical criticism and continues to haunt theology. According to Troeltsch, there are three principles of historical method: first, the principle of methodological doubt; second, the principle of analogy; third, the principle of correlation. Troeltsch recognized that the third principle rules out miracle and salvation history, but it is inescapable. By the principle of analogy and correlation, Christianity loses its uniqueness. All current historiography affirms Troeltsch's first principle. The second one is generally affirmed, although a "problem arises when this uniformity is raised to a universal principle that makes some evidence inadmissible."[158] The third principle is very complex. Historicism allowed only causation that is not transcendental or theological; although historicist and positivist philosophies of history are presently in

152. Ibid., 39.
153. Ibid., 44.
154. Ibid., 41.
155. Ibid., 48.
156. Ibid., 49–54.
157. Ibid., 61.
158. Ibid., 57.

demise, this does not mean that a theological interpretation of history is being rehabilitated.[159]

Despite contemporary disagreements about the nature of historiography, theology cannot, according to Krentz, return to a precritical age: "Christian theologians . . . can in the present only seek to use historical criticism in the service of the Gospel."[160] Historical criticism does not pose a threat to Scripture because it is congruent with its object, the Bible. The Bible is an ancient text, and historical criticism positions the Bible in our history and "makes the 'full brightness and impact of Christian ideas' shine out."[161] To refuse to use historical criticism would be docetic and a denial of faith in Jesus as the Lord of history.

How does faith relate to this method of biblical interpretation? For Krentz, it is a mistake to think that there is a sacred method of interpretation: "A method does not have faith or unbelief; there are only believing or unbelieving interpreters. As little as there are sacred engineering and architecture used in the construction of a church building, so little is there a sacred method of interpreting a text."[162] However, there are real tensions between secular historical method and faith. Within the Christian community, the ideal is biblical interpretation in the service of the gospel. Within historical study, the aim is verifiable fact in a significant narrative. A number of proposals for dealing with this tension have been made.[163] For Krentz the tension

> can be resolved only in the person of the interpreter living in the community of faith, who combines dedication to historical truth with the recognition of his own humanity and need for forgiveness. Historical research, like all of man's efforts, is also perverted by sin. But in the community of scholarship that lives in the fellowship of the people of God, the errors that arise from human frailty can be corrected and sin forgiven by God's grace. Then biblical criticism will grow together with faith into the full measure of the stature of Christ, his Gospel, his Word, and his Holy Scripture.[164]

In the course of the twentieth century, a variety of additional reading strategies were added to the typical historical-critical ones, including such approaches as anthropological, sociological, psychological, liberationist,

159. Ibid., 58–61.
160. Ibid., 61; see 63–67 for his list of ten positive results of the historical-critical method, making it worthwhile.
161. Ibid., 61.
162. Ibid., 68.
163. Cf. ibid., 67–72.
164. Ibid., 72.

rhetorical, and so forth. This diversity would explode once postmodernism connected with biblical interpretation, as we will see below.

Conservative Responses

Note should be taken of conservative responses to historical criticism as it emerged. Not surprisingly, this was often reactive or embodied in a withdrawal into an unintellectual piety, but this was not always the case. In Germany a prominent critic of historical criticism was the Lutheran churchman Ernst Wilhelm Hengstenberg (1802-69). Although somewhat isolationist in his ecclesiology, his exegetical works were widely influential; several translated into English include his *Dissertations on the Genuineness of the Pentateuch*. No less a contemporary scholar than Gordon Wenham has found resources in Hengstenberg's work for rethinking the critical approach to Deuteronomy.[165]

In North America a formidable conservative approach to the Bible emerged in the Princeton and then Westminster schools, with such luminaries as Dick Wilson, Ned Stonehouse, and E. J. Young. In Toronto a more thorough *Introduction to the Old Testament* than that of Young was produced by R. K. Harrison, a sign of evangelical scholarship beginning to catch up with mainstream scholarship.

Nineteenth-century evangelicalism in the English-speaking world was largely unprepared for the scientific and biblical challenges of its day. After the 1870s evangelicalism tended to retreat into a reactive pietism, and it was only in the middle of the twentieth century that this really changed. In terms of biblical studies, the establishment of Tyndale House in Cambridge was significant, and it has gone on to make a major contribution to biblical studies, albeit predominantly in a historical mode.

In terms of the triumph of historical criticism for most of the twentieth century, an important difference between Old Testament and New Testament studies is noteworthy. Stephen Neill and Tom Wright have written a magisterial history of New Testament studies over the past 150 years, and I will not repeat their narrative here.[166] It is noteworthy that under the influence of historical criticism, New Testament studies were far less radicalized than Old Testament studies, with moderate, rigorous New Testament study continuing throughout the modern period.

165. G. J. Wenham, "The Date of Deuteronomy: Linch-Pin of Old Testament Criticism, Part One," *Themelios* 10, no. 3 (April 1985): 15-20.
166. S. Neill and N. T. Wright, *The Interpretation of the New Testament, 1861-1986* (Oxford: Oxford University Press, 1988).

The reason for this, I suggest, is that there was no comparable figure to Wellhausen in New Testament studies (although Baur may be a contender), and even while his work was triumphing in Old Testament studies, moderate, high-caliber, critical but believing work was being done on the New Testament in Cambridge by Westcott (1825–1901), Hort (1828–92) and Lightfoot (1828–89). C. L. Church reviews the scene:

> At that critical point when British scholarship was in transition between a complacent, precritical stance to a guarded acceptance of critical methodology, if not conclusions, Lightfoot, Westcott and Hort took the Tübingen challenge seriously. By careful use of historical-critical methods in their commentaries and other works, they showed that more conservative answers could be given to the questions Baur had raised. Lightfoot's unique contribution was his work in patristics; Westcott's, his *History of the Canon of the New Testament*; Hort's, his *Judaistic Christianity*.[167]

All three in this Cambridge trio were devout churchmen: they saw themselves as sharing the faith of the apostolic church.[168] As Westcott's "first and greatest" qualification for the interpretation of the Bible, C. K. Barrett ranks his "conviction that in handling the Bible he was handling the Word of God, and his readiness, or rather his determination, to hear, faithfully and obediently, whatever should be spoken through the written word."[169] In New Testament studies the line can be traced from this Cambridge trio to twentieth-century New Testament scholars such as the Australian Leon Morris, Ralph Martin, Donald Guthrie, F. F. Bruce, C. K. Barrett, and to myriad contemporary scholars including such luminaries as Don Carson, James Dunn, Richard Bauckham, Ben Witherington, and N. T. Wright.

Certainly in British scholarship there was no comparable trio in Old Testament studies, and it was much later—through the work of Derek Kidner and especially scholars such as Gordon Wenham, John Goldingay, Walter Moberly, and their students—that a comparable believing presence was established in Old Testament scholarship. John Goldingay's doctorate was in the area of Old Testament theology,[170] and a related but earlier and mainly American movement, now largely forgotten, was that of the Biblical Theology Movement (BTM, 1945–61). See chapter 4 (above) for our discussion of the BTM and its retrieval as a source for today.

---

167. C. L. Church, "Westcott, B. F., and F. J. A. Hort," in McKim, *Historical Handbook*, 393.
168. Neill and Wright, *Interpretation of the New Testament*, 10.
169. C. K. Barrett, *Westcott as Commentator* (Cambridge: Cambridge University Press, 1959), 2–3.
170. J. Goldingay, *Theological Diversity and the Authority of the Old Testament* (Grand Rapids: Eerdmans, 1987).

Karl Barth (1886–1968)

Within evangelical circles two tendencies have militated against taking Karl Barth seriously as an exegete. First, there has been a tendency to see Barth as heterodox and thus an enemy of orthodoxy. Cornelius Van Til's philosophical and theological critique of Barth exemplifies this trend.[171] Second, biblical scholars tend to see Barth as a theologian and not as an important exegete.

However, exegesis is utterly central to the *Church Dogmatics* (*CD*). What Barth says of Calvin's *Institutes* is true of the *CD*: it is a web of exegesis![172] The *Registerband* of *CD* identifies some fifteen thousand biblical references and two thousand-plus pieces of detailed exegetical discussion of biblical texts. Thus, when he is dealing with the doctrine of creation, Barth has more than one hundred pages discussing Genesis 1 and 2, a treatment that includes detailed exegetical considerations on par with the most rigorous commentary. Two examples from his exegesis might be mentioned to underline this point. Hasel, Wenham, Stek, and others have rightly pointed out that the creation stories in Genesis are inter alia a polemic against worldviews present in the ancient Near East.[173] This poignant insight, which is crucial for a theological understanding of Genesis, is already well developed in Barth's work on Genesis 1 and 2. Second, recent years have witnessed considerable debate about animal rights and Scripture. In the context of the creation of the beasts on the same day as humankind in Genesis 1, Barth has a wonderful discussion of animals and their connection with humankind, in which he ranges throughout Scripture, drawing in verses like Jonah 4:11.

The truth is that *CD* and Barth's other works are an exegetical resource that has been sadly neglected by biblical scholars. But what of the claim that Barth is an enemy of theological orthodoxy? Might this not support keeping him at arm's length? There is certainly room for theological critique of Barth, but what must be understood is Barth's theologically conservative reaction to the liberalism of his day, and his recovery of the Bible as Scripture, involving at its core a reappropriation of the Reformed tradition and of Calvin in particular.

Barth's recovery of the Reformed tradition was so damaging to liberalism because he had been one of them. However, as a young pastor he found that liberalism was bankrupt in the aftermath of World War I when it came to addressing his congregation in the European context. Berkouwer says of Barth and Thurneysen,

---

171. C. Van Til, *Karl Barth and Evangelicalism* (Philadelphia: P&R, 1964).
172. K. Barth, *The Theology of John Calvin*, trans. G. W. Bromiley (Grand Rapids: Eerdmans, 1995), 393.
173. Cf. G. J. Wenham, *Genesis 1–15*, WBC 1 (Waco: Word, 1987).

But ultimately and most importantly, it was the Bible which saved them from utter despair. "We read the Bible anew, with far fewer presuppositions than before." They heard again the message concerning the forgiveness of sins and the proclamation of the kingdom which is not of men but which comes from God Himself. "From this meeting and confrontation with the Bible in the midst of the need of the time Karl Barth's *Römerbrief* was born." They found again actual answers to the problems with which the times confronted them. They did not find an answer that remained distant from the reality in which they found themselves, but they discovered a *message* of God that was close as life to them.[174]

It was Calvin in particular on whom Barth drew as he sought to recover the Bible as the Word of God and as he sought to develop a truly biblical theology.[175] In his lectures on Calvin,[176] Barth recognizes the unique contribution of Calvin as an expositor of Scripture to the Reformation: "Scripture did not play quite the same part in Reformed Protestantism as in Lutheranism. Its dignity here was one of principle as it never was in Lutheranism, no matter how highly the latter regarded it."[177] The big issue for Reformed Protestantism was "how to give God, the true God, the glory, how to do it here and now,"[178] and against the backdrop of medieval Catholicism, its answer was to look to the Bible as the final norm in faith and life.

God is known through Scripture; hence the vital importance of exposition. "The relation to the Bible is a living one. The spring does not flow of itself. It has to be tapped. Its waters have to be drawn. The answer is not already there; we have to ask what it is."[179] Here as elsewhere, Barth acknowledges the need to take the written character of Scripture seriously: "We must study it, for it is here or nowhere that we shall find its divinity."[180] This makes historical study of Scripture imperative although such study must never be only historical. Exegesis must finally aim at opening up the mind of Scripture: "The Word ought to be exposed in the words."[181] The work of the Spirit is fundamental to this process because "God is not just the theme but also the

---

174. G. C. Berkouwer, *The Triumph of Grace in the Theology of Karl Barth* (Grand Rapids: Eerdmans, 1956), 44–45.
175. See K. Barth, *Theology of John Calvin*, 393, on Calvin's importance for Barth's study of Romans and for the preface to the 1921 edition of Karl Barth's *Romans*.
176. Published as K. Barth, *The Theology of John Calvin*.
177. Ibid., 386.
178. Ibid., 387.
179. Ibid., 388.
180. K. Barth, *CD* I/2:463.
181. K. Barth, *The Epistle to the Romans*, trans. E. C. Hoskyns from the 6th German ed. (London: Oxford University Press, 1933), 8.

Lord of biblical truth."[182] Such a process demands hard, objective study of Scripture. Barth rightly invokes the metaphor of listening for this activity: "Listening, even if on the premise of secret identity with the one who speaks, is the task of the exegete."[183]

Barth identifies three characteristics of Calvin's exegesis that he finds exemplary. First, there is the extraordinary *objectivity of his exegesis*. At times Calvin does engage in eisegesis—"if we read nothing into the Bible, we will also read nothing out of it"![184]—but his exegesis is always characterized by a concern to stay close to the text and to do justice to what is actually there. The example Barth gives of Calvin's eisegesis is that Calvin assumes the unity of the message of the Bible when he reads it: though Scripture is polyphonic, the diverse voices are all seeking to say the same thing.[185]

Second, there is the *uniformity* of Calvin's exegesis. By this, Barth refers to Calvin's concern to attend to individual books in their literary totality and to the whole of Scripture: "If in principle it is seen to be right to listen to the Bible, then we should listen to the whole Bible."[186] In his commentary work, for example, he is always concerned to expound the whole of a book and not just the parts that have been influential.[187] Calvin's premise of the verbal inspiration of the Bible did not prevent him from critically examining the trustworthiness of the Bible, but it did give "him a consistent zeal to track down the content of the whole Bible, a zeal incidentally that would also stand historical investigation of the Bible in good stead."[188]

The third characteristic of Calvin's exegesis is its *relevance*. By relevance, Barth is not thinking of application to the cultural and historical context, but the sense that this is God's Word addressing us. Calvin is at pains to attend to the particularity of texts, but at the same time he is busy with a living dialogue across the centuries. Barth gives the example that when Calvin expounds Paul, "We believe Calvin the more readily because he is not deliberately trying to make us believe but simply setting out what he finds in Paul, yet not, of course, without being able or even trying to hide the fact that he himself believes it. This quiet kinship between the apostle and the exegete speaks for itself."[189]

---

182. K. Barth, *Theology of John Calvin*, 389.
183. Ibid.
184. Ibid., 390.
185. Ibid., 393: "It is in its relation to the practical goal of systematics, though without prejudice to its own significance, that the importance of Calvin's exegesis finally lies."
186. Ibid., 391.
187. Ibid., noting that verbal inspiration is in the background here.
188. Ibid.
189. Ibid., 392.

In the preface to the second edition of his Romans commentary, Barth defends himself against the accusation that he is an enemy of historical criticism. He denies this but insists that historical criticism must be in the service of genuine understanding and interpretation:

> By genuine understanding and interpretation, I mean that creative energy which Luther exercised with intuitive certainty in his exegesis; which underlies the systematic interpretation of Calvin.... For example, place the work of Jülicher side by side with that of Calvin: how energetically Calvin, having first established what stands in the text, sets himself to re-think the whole material and to wrestle with it, till the walls which separate the sixteenth century from the first become transparent! Paul speaks, and the man of the sixteenth century hears.... If a man persuades himself that Calvin's method can be dismissed with the old-fashioned motto "The Compulsion of Inspiration," he betrays himself as one who has never worked upon the interpretation of Scripture.[190]

There are some differences between Calvin and Barth. Calvin wrote far more commentaries than did Barth and less theology. But just as Calvin's commentaries are concerned with the theology of the text, so Barth's dogmatics takes the above characteristics of Calvin's exegesis with the utmost seriousness. It should thus be clear why Calvin and Barth represent the sort of historical bloodline that urgently needs transfusing into the present. If the Bible is to be recovered for the church as God's Word, then Calvin and Barth, in my opinion, represent the type of biblical interpretation that we need to appropriate for our day. This will not mean simple repetition of Calvin and/or Barth; whether we agree with Barth's reading of Calvin or not, Barth's work alerts us to the way in which a tradition has to be developed and appropriated afresh in a new historical context. Nevertheless, Calvin and Barth's exegesis pulsates with concerns that biblical interpretation must recover if it is to assist the church in hearing God's address. Emphases such as these are greatly needed:

- A deep commitment to the Bible as God's Word.

Both Calvin and Barth recognize that if we wish to glorify God here and now, we must listen to Scripture for his address. As Barth declares, "We are tied to these texts. And we can only ask about revelation when we surrender to the expectation and recollection attested in these texts."[191] "Death usually

---

190. K. Barth, *Romans*, 7.
191. K. Barth, *CD* I/2:492.

reigns in the church when it is thought that this acknowledgement [of the priority of the Bible] should not be made."[192] Even in circles where the authority of Scripture is taken with the utmost seriousness, academic interpretation of the Bible has often failed to have as its goal to hear God's address.[193] Barth is at pains to defend historical criticism, but always insists that it must serve the large goal of listening to Scripture to hear God speak. The problem for Barth is that so much historical criticism stops far short of this goal. Sadly, this has also been true of much orthodox biblical scholarship.

- A refusal to separate biblical study from Christian faith and theology.

Calvin and Barth know nothing of the chasm that has appeared between biblical interpretation and theology in the contemporary academy. Both Calvin and Barth recognize that it is only in faith that one sees Scripture for what it truly is: the Word of God. It is as part of the church that one reads the Bible as Scripture, and as Barth says, "The door of the Bible texts can be opened only from within."[194] One of the great characteristics of Barth's *CD* is that even as his conceptual framework takes hold, he does more and not less exegesis. It is as though the doctrinal framework stimulates rather than—as in too many contemporary theologies—suppresses exegesis.

- A commitment to rigorous scholarship, both historical and theological, in the service of exegesis, but always in the service of listening to the whole of the Bible—*tota Scriptura*—as the word of God.

As Childs insists, we need a hermeneutic in which "the final task of exegesis is to seek to hear the Word of God, which means that the witness of Moses and Jeremiah, of Paul and John, must become a vehicle for another Word. The exegete must come to wrestle with the kerygmatic substance which brought into being the witness."[195] Barth asserts the principle of *tota Scriptura* as follows: "An exposition is trustworthy to the extent that it not only expounds the text in front of it, but implicitly at least expounds all other texts, to the extent that it at any rate clears the way for the exposition of all other texts."[196]

---

192. Ibid., 502.
193. See E. H. Peterson, *Working the Angles: The Shape of Pastoral Integrity* (Grand Rapids: Eerdmans, 1987), chap. 4, for an important discussion of how the contemporary church has lost a capacity to listen.
194. K. Barth, *CD* I/2:533.
195. B. S. Childs, "Interpretation in Faith: The Theological Responsibility of an Old Testament Commentary," *Int* 18 (1964): 432–49, esp. 443.
196. K. Barth, *CD* I/2:485.

A good example of the way in which a reading of a text makes the rest of Scripture resonate, as it were, is Barth's rich reading of Genesis 1:24–25.[197] Barth explores the creation of the animals on the same day as humankind and the consequent links between them. Writing long before the current emphasis on animal rights, Barth explores this text:

> Man's salvation and perdition, his joy and sorrow, will be reflected in the weal and woe of this animal environment and company. Not as an independent partner of the covenant, but as an attendant, the animal will participate with man (the independent partner) in the covenant, sharing both the promise and the curse which shadows the promise. Full of forebodings, but also full of confidence, it will wait with man for its fulfilment, breathing freely again when this has taken place provisionally and will take place definitively.[198]

In the small-print exegetical discussion that follows this section, what is remarkable is the way Barth ranges across Scripture, thereby demonstrating just how fertile an exegetical principle *analogia Scriptura* can be. Barth notices that this linking of animal and humankind is a familiar thought in both Testaments, as exemplified in Psalm 36:6, in which the LORD is praised because he preserves both man and beast. He leads a fascinating tour of passages ranging among Isaiah 43:20–21; Hosea 2:18; Ezekiel 34; Jonah 3:8; 4:11; Mark 1:13; and so on.

Barth's caution about philosophy in theology is well known.[199] Indeed, in the contemporary renewal of theological interpretation, a legacy from Barth is that many of its best proponents are deeply cautious of "the hermeneutic detour." There are scholars such as Anthony Thiselton whose two major volumes on hermeneutics bear ample witness to his belief that philosophical hermeneutics has a great deal to offer biblical (and theological) interpretation. But scholars such as Francis Watson and John Webster, and many of the Yale school, are far more reticent about the help that general hermeneutics can provide. Watson and Webster plead for a regional theological hermeneutic for biblical interpretation, a hermeneutic that stems from Christian doctrine and is for theological interpretation. What Barth does not explore is what Alvin Plantinga calls "positive Christian philosophy," which might be particularly

---

197. See K. Barth, *CD* III/1:176–81. I cannot repeat all the details of Barth's exegesis, and the reader is strongly encouraged to read these pages directly from Barth.

198. K. Barth, *CD* III/1:178.

199. For a nuanced account of K. Barth's view of philosophy and theology, see K. Oakes, *Karl Barth on Theology and Philosophy* (New York: Oxford University Press, 2012). Oakes concludes: "Barth never settled on an exact and well-defined account of theology and philosophy. . . . Barth wrote in a welter of ways about this relationship" (ibid., 245).

helpful in bringing philosophy captive to Christ (2 Cor. 10:4-5) so that it might more readily help exegesis in comparison to more alien philosophies. Barth is open to ways in which a theological hermeneutic might provide insights for general hermeneutics;[200] he fails, however, to take sufficiently seriously the insights that hermeneutics might provide for exegesis.

Graham Ward and others have suggested that there may be strong links between Barth and postmoderns such as Derrida.[201] This suggestion founders when one looks closely at Barth's understanding of exegesis and his actual exegesis. Barth is quite clear, for example, that

> in demanding a historical appreciation of the Bible, it must also require—and self-evidently of every reader of the Bible—that his understanding of it should be based on what is said in the Bible and therefore on God's revelation. It cannot, therefore, be conceded that side by side with this there is another legitimate understanding of the Bible, that, e.g., in its own way it is right and possible when we hear and expound the Bible not to go beyond the humanity as such which is expressed in it.... It does not speak of itself, but of God's revelation, and no honest and unprejudiced reader of the Bible can ignore this historical definiteness of the word.[202]

Here, as elsewhere, Barth adopts an approach to interpretation much like that of Childs's canonical hermeneutic, in which he argues for determinate interpretation that interprets for God's revelation; like Childs, Barth is not prepared to see this as one among a smorgasbord of hermeneutic possibilities. Barth and Calvin's emphasis on the literal sense of Scripture[203] is contrary to the postmodern tendency to play with texts and to tease out as many meanings as possible. Barth, very much in the spirit of Calvin, is adamant that "in exegesis, too—and especially in exegesis—there is only one truth."[204] Barth says of Calvin that he "hated what he called on one occasion the pleasurable playing about with every possible interpretation of the text that we can hardly avoid when it comes to Revelation, and wherever he could he avoided leaving us with two or more meanings.... Each passage has its own truth. Each is self-grounded. Each must be expounded in its own context."[205] Such an orientation to exegesis is poles apart from that of Derrida and other postmoderns.

200. For an example, see K. Barth, *CD* I/2:465-66, 471.
201. Graham Ward, *Barth, Derrida, and the Language of Theology* (Cambridge: Cambridge University Press, 1995).
202. K. Barth, *CD* I/2:468.
203. See K. Greene-McCreight, *Ad Litteram: How Augustine, Calvin, and Barth Read the "Plain Sense"* (New York: Peter Lang, 1999).
204. K. Barth, *CD* I/2:470.
205. K. Barth, *Theology of John Calvin*, 390.

The ongoing influence of Barth should not be underestimated. I still recall hearing Brevard Childs in Cambridge, at a Scripture and Hermeneutics Seminar, telling us the story of his journey as a biblical scholar. Inter alia, he described the formative influence of sitting under Barth. Barth's influence on Childs was, in my view, *the* motivating factor for his lifelong project of recovering the Bible as canon. Similarly the work of Frei, Lindbeck, Seitz, and many others is at least indirectly indebted to Karl Barth.

The Literary Turn

A helpful way to grasp the shape of biblical studies in the twentieth and twenty-first centuries is to think in terms of a *series of turns*, bearing in mind that a new turn does not eradicate the previous one. The twentieth century was dominated by the *historical* turn initiated by de Wette and Wellhausen. In the 1970s this was challenged by the literary turn.

At the end of the nineteenth century and the start of the twentieth, positivism was the dominant philosophy in Europe. In literary studies this manifested itself in a concern with questions of genesis, context, and authorial intent. What such an approach neglected was the *literary text* itself, and this neglect is paralleled in historical criticism's concern with questions of origin and what lies behind the text, and consequent neglect of the (unavoidable) literary shape of the text itself. Alter and Kermode perceptively assess such historical criticism:

> This "scientific" criticism was of great cultural and doctrinal importance; but, as we have said, it diverted attention from biblical narrative, poetry, and prophecy as literature, treating them instead as more or less distorted historical records. The characteristic move was to infer the existence of some book that preceded the one we have—the lost documents that were combined to make Genesis as it has come down to us, the lost Aramaic Gospel, the lost "sayings-source" used by Matthew and Luke, and so on. The effect of this practice was curious: one spoke of the existing books primarily as evidence of what must once have been available in an original closer to what actually happened. That was their real value—as substitutes for what had unfortunately been lost.[206]

In literary studies New Criticism[207] developed in response to this neglect of the literary text, and somewhat later the literary turn developed in biblical

---

206. R. Alter and F. Kermode, *The Literary Guide to the Bible* (Cambridge, MA: Harvard University Press, 1999), 3.
207. See C. G. Bartholomew, *Reading Ecclesiastes: Old Testament Exegesis and Hermeneutical Theory* (Rome: Pontificio Istituto Biblico, 1998).

studies to fill the parallel gap. Alter and Kermode rightly identify Erich Auerbach's remarkable *Mimesis* (1946; ET, 1953) as a landmark in this literary turn. The literary turn in biblical studies has been traced from the growing awareness of the limitations of the historical-critical method through canon criticism[208] and New Criticism (including Muilenburg's rhetorical criticism) to the narratology of Alter, Berlin, and Sternberg[209] and parallel developments in New Testament studies.

In 1981, Alter was able to write that "over the last few years, there has been growing interest in literary approaches among the younger generation of biblical scholars . . . but, while useful explications of particular texts have begun to appear, there have been as yet no major works of criticism, and certainly no satisfying overview of the poetics of the Hebrew Bible."[210] Alter's *The Art of Biblical Narrative* is such an overview, but Sternberg's *The Poetics of Biblical Narrative* is the major work on Old Testament narrative. Gunn rightly noted that "Sternberg's recent book on poetics moves such a narratology into a whole new dimension of discrimination and sophistication and will be fundamental to the emerging generation of narrative critics."[211]

The literary turn has radical implications for historical criticism. What was a doublet, thereby signaling a source, is now an example of careful, artistic repetition. Some have practiced literary analysis of the Bible without concerning themselves much with historical issues.[212] But clearly the historical turn is not unaffected by the literary turn. Sternberg, Tom Wright,[213] Thiselton,[214] and others rightly argue for a careful integration of the historical and literary dimensions of the Bible, as well as the ideological or theological.

For Sternberg, seeing narrative technique as part of the text itself means taking the historical construction of the text seriously if one is going to come

---

208. J. Barton (*Reading the Old Testament: Method in Biblical Study*, 2nd ed. [London: Darton, Longman & Todd, 1996]) notes the similarities between New Criticism and Childs's canonical approach, but Childs insists that his is a theological hermeneutic.

209. D. M. Gunn, "New Directions in the Study of Biblical Hebrew Narrative," *JSOT* 39 (1987): 65–75.

210. R. Alter, *The Art of Biblical Narrative* (New York: Basic Books, 1981), 15.

211. Gunn, "New Directions," 68.

212. This is a real danger in our postmodern context. As N. T. Wright, *NTPG* 13, points out, "While history and theology work at their stormy relationship, there is always a danger, particularly in postmodernism, that literary study will get on by itself, without impinging on, or being affected by, either of the others."

213. Ibid., the whole work.

214. A. C. Thiselton, "On Models and Methods: A Conversation with Robert Morgan," in *The Bible in Three Dimensions: Essays in Celebration of Forty Years of Biblical Studies in the University of Sheffield*, ed. D. J. A. Clines, S. E. Fowl, and S. E. Porter, JSOTSup 87 (Sheffield: JSOT Press, 1990), 337–56.

to grips with the functional purpose of biblical narrative. Sternberg is highly critical of the tendency to categorize Old Testament narratives as fiction. Fiction and history cannot, in Sternberg's view, be distinguished by form but only in terms of overall purpose. When the Old Testament narratives are assessed by this criterion, "the product is neither fiction nor historicized fiction nor fictionalized history, but historiography pure and uncompromising."[215] In Sternberg's view, everything points in this direction. The Israelite obsession with memory of the past, that memory's significance for the present, and Israel's uniqueness in this respect in the ancient Near East—these factors all confirm that the Old Testament narratives are making a strong historical truth claim. "Were the narrative written or read as fiction, then God would turn from the lord of history into a creature of the imagination, with the most disastrous results."[216] Certainly Sternberg's approach is contested! But it indicates well the way in which the literary turn complicates the historical turn.

The substance of Sternberg's theory of biblical narratology is found in the first three chapters of his *Poetics*. The remaining chapters flesh out this theory in exegetical examples. Sternberg defines poetics as "the systematic working or study of literature as such."[217] It is important to Sternberg that biblical narrative is a work of literature so that in a poetics such as his, the discipline and its object come together. He stresses this in opposition to biblical scholars who see "literary approaches" to the Bible as the conscious imposition of alien categories on the Old Testament text. For Sternberg, the authors of the biblical narratives have used narrative techniques to convey their message, and poetics is a study of *these* techniques. Consequently, at the very outset of his *Poetics* he indicates his understanding of narrative as *functional discourse* and sees poetics as research into how this discourse functions.[218] Sternberg's opening paragraph is a ringing affirmation of communication as the context within which narrative interpretation takes place.[219] "Biblical narrative is oriented to an addressee and regulated by a purpose or set of purposes involving the addressee. Hence our primary business as readers is to make purposive sense of it." Recognition of the genre of the text alone is insufficient: "Unless firmly anchored in the relations between narrator and audience, therefore, formalism degenerates into a new mode of atomism."[220]

---

215. M. Sternberg, *The Poetics of Biblical Narrative: Ideological Literature and the Drama of Reading* (Bloomington: Indiana University Press, 1987), 35.
216. Ibid., 32.
217. Ibid., 2.
218. In this sense Sternberg's poetics represents a sort of textual realism far removed from the pluralism and indeterminacy of postmodernism.
219. Ibid., 1.
220. Ibid., 2.

Sternberg regards the discernment of *objectified or embodied intention* as crucial: "Such intention fulfils a crucial role, for communication presupposes a speaker who resorts to certain linguistic and structural tools in order to produce certain effects on the addressee; the discourse accordingly supplies a network of clues to the speaker's intention."[221]

Taking authorial intention seriously means that source criticism and narratology should not be set against each other. This is especially so considering the gap in sociocultural context between our time and that of the origin of the biblical narratives. We can never fully bridge this gap, but this does not mean we cannot try. In fact, this is the only alternative: "Once the choice turns out to lie between reconstructing the author's intention and licensing the reader's invention, there is no doubt where most of us stand."[222] The historicity of the text cannot be avoided; at the very least all scholars acknowledge that the language and its meaning require historical reconstruction. Yet the nature of the source criticism we engage in needs careful attention, and Sternberg is very critical of much that has been called source criticism. There is an inevitable tension between source and discourse, but Sternberg appeals for a closer partnership between the two; indeed, he maintains that the two cannot but work together, and neither has the primacy over the other.

Frequently it is falsely assumed that the Bible as a religious text is in antithesis to the Bible as literature. For Sternberg, this is a false antithesis. In the ancient world highly poetic and literary material was regularly highly ideological and attended to for instruction. "The question is how rather than whether the literary coexists with the social, the doctrinal, the philosophical."[223] Representation is never to be set against evaluation, although the extent to which these aspects dominate in any piece of literature will vary. Only if the Bible were ideological in an extreme form of didactic would taking it seriously as literature be inadmissible. However, "if biblical narrative is didactic, then it has chosen the strangest way to go about its business. For the narrator breaks every law in the didacticist's decalogue. Anything like preaching from the narrative pulpit is conspicuous for its absence."[224] Narrative is the means whereby the Bible presents its message; the two, narrative technique and message, are not to be set against each other.

So now it is time we stopped seeing the techniques of narrative as *literary* techniques. "What determines literariness is not the mere presence but the

---

221. Ibid., 9.
222. Ibid., 10.
223. Ibid., 35.
224. Ibid., 37–38.

dominance of the poetic function, the control it exerts over all the rest."²²⁵ Narrative techniques are as much the prerogative of the historical-biblical narratives as of fictional texts, and the presence of these techniques must not be seen as compromising the texts' ideological nature.

So how does the aesthetic aspect relate to the ideological in biblical narrative? "Biblical narrative emerges as a complex, because multifunctional, discourse. Functionally speaking, it is regulated by a set of three principles: ideological, historiographic, and aesthetic."²²⁶ The ideological is particularly prominent in the law sections of the Pentateuch and in prophetic moralizing, for example. The historiographic is prominent in the names of places, people, and etiologies. The aesthetic is in high profile in the narratives. The relation of these three principles is one of coordination and tense complementarity. Sternberg sums up the point at which the three merge as "the drama of reading." "They join forces to originate a strategy of telling that casts reading as a drama, interpretation as an ordeal that enacts and distinguishes the human predicament."²²⁷ The ideological principle is seen in the foolproof aspect of the narratives; the aesthetic is seen in the exposition of biblical doctrine in a narrative that has built into it the cognitive antithesis between God and humanity.

Sternberg stresses the need not to impose a poetics on the biblical narratives but to work so as to allow the biblical poetics to emerge:

> In practice as well as in methodology, the gravest danger to the literary approaches lurks in their imposition of models that do not fit the Bible, nor indeed . . . literature in general. . . . In most of the theoretical work I have done, on narrative and other subjects, the Bible has proved a corrective to widely held doctrines about literary structure and analysis, often a pointer to the formation of alternatives.²²⁸

Sternberg's work is in a class of its own, and it will be in the center of discussion of biblical narrative for a long time to come.

At its best the literary turn has proved remarkably fruitful in biblical interpretation ranging from Alter's work to Clines's study on *The Theme of the Pentateuch*, Wenham's work on Genesis, Van Leeuwen's study on Proverbs, Joel Green's work on *Luke*, and so forth, as well as myriad articles and studies of parts of biblical books. There is no part of the study of the Bible that has not benefited in some way from literary analysis.

225. Ibid., 40.
226. Ibid., 41.
227. Ibid., 46.
228. Ibid., 56–57.

Closely related to this is the recovery of *intertextuality* and the many ways in which it has opened up the network of connections between biblical texts. Fishbane's work in particular but also Sailhamer's has been significant in this area in Old Testament studies, spawning some highly creative works on intertextuality, although not always focusing sufficiently on the indispensable historical formation of texts, as noted by Sternberg above. No one has warned so strongly against the danger and limits of treating the Bible solely as literature as has George Steiner in his review of *The Literary Guide to the Bible*.[229] This reminds us again that an urgent need is a hermeneutic that integrates the historical, literary, and kerygmatic dimensions of biblical texts, a matter to which we attend in following chapters.

The Postmodern Turn

So-called postmodernism began in literary studies and was then extended to a critique of Western culture as a whole in the 1980s. It has impacted biblical studies from both these places. Christopher Norris argues that "literary theory, through its colonizing drive into other disciplines, bids fair to reverse that entire movement of progressive or enlightened critique which has sought to establish adequate protocols for the discrimination of truth from falsehood, of factual from fictive or historical from mythic modes of utterance."[230] Whether we agree with Norris's articulation of the dangers of postmodernism or not, the postmodern debate has questioned central assumptions of modernity, including its notions of history, and it was inevitable that such questioning would eventually threaten the dominance of that quintessentially modern method in biblical studies: historical criticism.

Interwoven with this is the fact that since the literary turn in biblical studies, biblical scholars have kept an eye on developments in literary studies and the door open to importing their methods. Thus it is no surprise that literary theory's colonizing drive should find a receptive audience in biblical studies. By the late 1960s, New Criticism was being replaced by structuralism, and then came the poststructuralist developments, and it was only a matter of time before Fish, Rorty, Derrida, Barthes, Foucault, and the like were being applied in Old Testament studies.[231]

---

229. G. Steiner, review of *The Literary Guide to the Bible*, by R. Alter and F. Kermode, *The New Yorker*, January 11, 1988, 94–98.

230. C. Norris, *Truth and the Ethics of Criticism* (Manchester, UK: Manchester University Press, 1994), 114.

231. See, e.g., A. K. M. Adams, ed., *Handbook of Postmodern Biblical Interpretation* (St. Louis: Chalice, 2000).

The contours of the postmodern landscape are not always easily identifiable. Postmodernism is nearly synonymous with diversity and pluralism, and one needs to take care not to impose contours on diverse positions. Thus Rorty is to be distinguished from Derrida, and Derrida from Baudrillard, and so on. Nevertheless, it is clear that in its more extreme forms, postmodernism constitutes a radical challenge to biblical studies, whether historical or literary. With its wild pluralism, its view of texts as radically indeterminate, and its suspicion of getting behind texts, much postmodernism renders the historical-critical enterprise deeply problematic. If "the past is not discovered or found, . . . but created and represented by the historian as a text, which in turn is consumed by the reader,"[232] where does this leave the enterprise of historical criticism?

The depth of the postmodern challenge in this respect should be recognized. Postmodernism questions the foundational assumptions of modernity so that its challenge to an enterprise like historical criticism is not always immediately obvious but at a deep, *philosophical* level. As long as the standard narrative of modernity as rational progress was assumed, historical criticism did not need to worry too much about its philosophical presuppositions. Indeed, to this day the myth continues to be entertained that historical criticism has no philosophical presuppositions. But postmodernism queries such objective neutrality and insists that particular epistemologies and views of history underlie the practice of historical criticism. If such views are to be maintained, then their basis must be argued for: the basis cannot just be assumed.[233]

It is particularly via postmodern views of history that historical criticism and any view of the biblical narratives as accurately representing what happened are challenged. Munslow, in his *Deconstructing History*, discerns three current options in historiography: first, reconstructionism; second, constructionism; and third, deconstructionism. Reconstructionism believes that the more carefully we write history, the closer we will get to what actually happened. Constructionism refers to the approaches to history that invoke general laws, Marxism being the most well-known example. Munslow gathers postmodern approaches together under the label of "deconstructionism," and this includes authors such as Hayden White and Keith Jenkins. Such approaches stress the fact that history writing is always an example of literary production, with all the attendant complexities that brings.

Central to postmodern debates about history is the question of the extent to which history can accurately represent the past through narrative.

---

232. A. Munslow, *Deconstructing History* (London: Routledge, 1997), 178.

233. J. D. Levenson's *The Hebrew Bible, the Old Testament, and Historical Criticism: Jews and Christians in Biblical Studies* (Louisville: Westminster John Knox, 1993) is an important text in terms of the current status of historical criticism.

Scholars point to the unavoidable interpretative and hermeneutical element in all history writing, and many draw radical conclusions therefrom.[234] This postmodern emphasis on the linguistic and narrative nature of history raises profound questions about historiography, whether one agrees with the likes of Hayden White or not. What kind of knowledge production is history writing? History always brings a narrative grid to bear on its telling of the past, and Munslow, for example, suggests that "history is best viewed epistemologically as a form of literature producing knowledge as much by its aesthetic or narrative structure as by any other criteria."[235] History is a form of narrative, and as such is part of the historical process: "All such narratives make over events and explain why they happened, but are overlaid by the assumptions held by the historian about the forces influencing the nature of causality."[236]

Postmodernism has penetrated deeply into biblical studies, and there is hardly an area where some postmodern approach is not available. The postmodern turn *problematizes* the literary and historical turn in biblical studies. Indeed, its strength lies in problematizing, not in offering constructive ways forward. This has had two effects:

1. It came so soon on the heels of the literary turn that the latter was problematized before it had been fully appropriated in biblical studies.
2. The inability of postmodern approaches to offer constructive ways forward has meant that historical criticism lingers as a kind of default mode for many scholars.

In my view postmodernism is now in decline, and the question is, what will emerge now? A positive development, which we come to below, is the renaissance of theological interpretation, but it needs to be a mode of interpretation that is not just one more method on the smorgasbord. To accomplish this, it will itself need to come to grips with the turns that precede it even as it reaches back behind historical criticism to retrieve healthy modes of theological interpretation. In my view an urgent need is to further the engagement of the literary turn with historical criticism and to begin the consequent rethinking of what lies behind the biblical text, even as we direct our energies to the world opened up in front of the text. The strength of historical criticism is its rigorous attention to the data of the text; its weakness is the hermeneutic with which it handles this data.

---

234. To taste the radicality of this, see F. S. Burnett, "Historiography," in A. K. M. Adams, *Postmodern Biblical Interpretation*, 106–12.
235. Munslow, *Deconstructing History*, 5.
236. Ibid., 10.

Take Old Testament law, for example. It is ridiculous to suggest that there was no development in Old Testament law since this would violate all we know about how law develops as a society matures. Historical criticism has fingered the data on this matter and alerted us to the important differences between the collections of Old Testament law. But, in the light of the literary turn, we need to be at work constructing better hypotheses about the development of Old Testament law than JEDP.

Amid Contemporary Pluralism: A Theological Turn?

In his inaugural lecture at Oxford University, John Barton mentioned the crisis in Old Testament studies and that an emerging response is to call for a *religious* hermeneutic.[237] Barton is suspicious of this move and argues for a recovery of Enlightenment values as the center of Old Testament studies. Barton is right in noticing that an increasing number of scholars are arguing, in response to the postmodern turn, that we need a *theological* hermeneutic in biblical studies, and nowadays works in what is fuzzily called theological interpretation are springing up all over the place. The minority renewal I refer to is a broad church umbrella, including such scholars as Stephen Fowl, Tom Wright, Brevard Childs, Christopher Seitz, Walter Brueggemann, Walter Moberly, John Webster, Francis Watson, Kevin Vanhoozer, Francis Martin, the Scripture and Hermeneutics Seminar, and others.

It would be an unfortunate mistake to suppose that historical criticism produced no theological interpretation; von Rad's theological readings of Old Testament traditions and sources and his classic *The Wisdom of Israel* belie any such view. However, such works are the exception rather than the rule, and theological interpretation has emerged partially out of frustration with historical-critical scholarship. Karl Barth, Childs's canonical approach, and Yale's postliberal theology are major ingredients in this renewed interest in theological interpretation. Childs has long argued that the goal of the interpretation of Christian Scripture must be to understand both Testaments as witness to the selfsame divine reality: the God and Father of Jesus Christ. Although this theological turn is now gathering momentum in response to the pluralism and nihilistic direction of (some) postmodernism, Childs's extensive corpus has played a major role in laying the foundation for a theological, canonical hermeneutic in biblical studies. The theological turn is in its early days in biblical studies. Inevitably, as with Childs, a theological turn will involve going back to premodern

---

237. J. Barton, *The Future of Old Testament Study* (Oxford: Clarendon, 1993).

readings of biblical texts and finding traditions that can be reappropriated and developed in our day.

There are (at least) two elements to this theological turn. One aspect is that of simply getting on with reading the Bible theologically. Thus scholars such as Christopher Seitz invoke the plain sense of Scripture, allow a limited role for historical (canonical-historical) criticism, and get on with interpretation in relation to the church and Christian doctrine.[238] In his *Text, Church, and World: Biblical Interpretation in Theological Perspective*, Francis Watson argues for a theological hermeneutic in biblical interpretation, but he is quite clear that

> the goal is a theological hermeneutic within which an exegesis oriented primarily towards theological issues can come into being. This is therefore *not an exercise in general hermeneutics*. . . . The hermeneutic or interpretative paradigm towards which the following chapters move is a theological rather than a literary one, and the idea that a literary perspective is, as such, already "theological" seems to me to be without foundation.[239]

A somewhat different approach is to argue that we need a theology of history (and literature, etc.) to fund biblical interpretation. Neill and Tom Wright identify this need:

> Similarly, there has, alas, been little progress in the areas of a theology of history, or of New Testament ecclesiology. It is an exciting idea, as was mooted in the first edition of this work, that "An understanding of history which is incompatible with a Christian doctrine of revelation is bound to land the New Testament scholar in grave perplexities; a true theological understanding of history would not of itself solve any New Testament problems, but it would, so to speak, hold the ring within which a solution can be found." But where are the scholars sufficiently familiar with actual history-writing, sufficiently at home in philosophy and the history of ideas, and sufficiently committed to the study of the New Testament, to undertake the task?[240]

Wright himself makes considerable progress in this direction in his *The New Testament and the People of God*.[241] Kevin Vanhoozer argues that "the

---

238. C. R. Seitz, *Word without End: The Old Testament as Abiding Theological Witness* (Grand Rapids: Eerdmans, 1998).

239. F. Watson, *Text, Church, and World: Biblical Interpretation in Theological Perspective* (Grand Rapids: Eerdmans, 1994) 1, with added emphasis.

240. Neill and Wright, *Interpretation of the New Testament*, 366.

241. Not uncontroversially, of course. See, inter alia, C. C. Newman, ed., *Jesus and the Restoration of Israel: A Critical Assessment of N. T. Wright's "Jesus and the Victory of God"* (Downers Grove, IL: InterVarsity, 1999). In terms of a theology of history, W. Pannenberg's work remains very

best general hermeneutics is a trinitarian hermeneutics. Yes, the Bible should be interpreted 'like any other book'; but *every* book should be interpreted with norms that we derive and establish from Trinitarian theology."[242] Clearly there are different emphases among proponents of theological interpretation. Whatever the precise view, theological interpretation undoubtedly impacts how we think about literature, history, and biblical interpretation.

Thus, as we advance the cause of theological interpretation in our attempt to renew biblical interpretation, it is important to think carefully about *the relation* between the theological turn and the other three turns—namely, the historical, the literary, and the postmodern. There is also the *vital* question of how these turns relate to more fundamental philosophical or paradigm shifts. Indeed, the postmodern turn, as we noticed, forces the depth issue of philosophical presuppositions to the surface. In a different context, Botha comments, "The question I found intriguing was whether these 'turns' were representative of fundamental philosophical or epistemological revolutions, gestalt shifts, 'metaphoric revolutions' in the history and philosophy of science, or whether they were in fact no more than manifestations and variations of one overall epistemological root metaphor or basic metaphor, characteristic of the epistemology of the twentieth century."[243]

In this way a model of turns helps us to start to get at the variety of factors involved in any attempt to reassess biblical interpretation today. There are complex archaeological layers to modern biblical interpretation. In my opinion an example of work that seeks to take these multiple dimensions seriously is Tom Wright's major New Testament project on Christian Origins and the Question of God. We may not agree with every detail of his execution of the project, but it is to his credit that he has attended to the philosophical, literary, historical, and theological dimensions of reading the New Testament today. Nothing less will suffice for a full-blown recovery of theological interpretation today.

Conclusion: An Invitation to the Feast

In his foreword to Thomas Oden's *Requiem*, which he heads "An Invitation to the Feast," Richard John Neuhaus says,

---

important (e.g., *Revelation as History* [New York: Macmillan, 1969]). See also A. C. Thiselton, *The Two Horizons: New Testament Hermeneutics and Philosophical Description with Special Reference to Heidegger, Bultmann, Gadamer, and Wittgenstein* (Grand Rapids: Eerdmans, 1980), 74–84.

242. K. J. Vanhoozer, *Is There a Meaning in This Text? The Bible, the Reader, and the Morality of Literary Knowledge* (Grand Rapids: Zondervan, 1998), 456.

243. M. E. Botha, "Understanding Our Age: Philosophy at a Turning Point of the 'Turns'?— The Endless Search for Elusive Universal," *TCW* 30, no. 2 (1994): 16–31, esp. 16.

More and more "young fogeys" like Oden are discovering the truth that is "ever ancient, ever new" (Augustine). It is called the catholic faith, and it is a feast to which he invites us. It is a movable feast, still developing under the guidance of the Spirit. Oden is like cinema's "Auntie Mame," who observed that life is a banquet and most poor slobs are starving to death. Origen, Irenaeus, Cyril of Alexandria, Thomas Aquinas, Teresa of Avila, Martin Luther, John Calvin, John Wesley—the names fall trippingly from Oden's tongue like a gourmet surveying a most spectacular table. Here are arguments you can sink your teeth into, conceptual flights of intoxicating complexity, and truths to die for. Far from the table, over there, way over there, is American theological education, where prodigal academics feed starving students on the dry husks of their clever unbelief.[244]

One need only reflect on our narrative of the history of biblical interpretation to realize just how absolutely central is the Bible to this feast of the catholic faith. And yet one can so easily replace "American theological education" with "academic biblical interpretation" in the above quote: such is the barren wilderness of so much that goes under the name of biblical studies nowadays. Even in our years of wild pluralism and tolerance of a great diversity of readings of the Bible, this does not necessarily mean that interpretation of the Bible as Christian Scripture is welcome.[245] Theological interpretation is fine in seminaries but not in the academy.

And in our seminaries, where one is more likely to find a concern with the Bible as Scripture, good academic work in the service of profound interpretation of the Bible as Scripture is rare. There has been an (understandable) tendency for orthodox scholars to fight the battle for Scripture where opponents have attacked. Thus a huge amount of Christian energy has been devoted to historical issues during the twentieth century—far less, alas, to interpretation of the Bible as God's address.

I learned from the Canadian aesthetician Calvin Seerveld that practicing Christian scholarship today will often mean going back in history in one's discipline until one finds a healthy tradition, which one can then transfuse into the present.[246] Theological interpretation has a growing number but

---

244. R. J. Neuhaus, foreword to *Requiem: A Lament in Three Movements*, by T. Oden (Nashville: Abingdon, 1995), 9–12, esp. 10.

245. An OT scholar like Philip R. Davies can still argue that interpretation of the Bible as canonical Scripture is inappropriate to the academy, where the "discourse of the academy should dominate." See C. G. Bartholomew, "Warranted Biblical Interpretation: Alvin Plantinga's 'Two (or More) Kinds of Scripture Scholarship,'" in *"Behind" the Text: History and Biblical Interpretation*, ed. C. G. Bartholomew et al., Scripture and Hermeneutics 4 (Grand Rapids: Zondervan, 2003), 58–78.

246. See C. Seerveld, *Rainbows for the Fallen World: Aesthetic Life and Artistic Task* (Toronto: Tuppence, 2005), where he encourages Christian artists to "distill a fruitful Christian

still few healthy, contemporary examples, whether we look to theology or biblical studies. Frederick Dale Bruner's two-volume work on Matthew, *The Christbook* and *The Churchbook*, stands out as a rich exception. Childs, who is himself another great exception to this rule in biblical studies, notes, for example, that although "scripture functions toward sanctification," there has been little attention during the reign of historical criticism to reading the Bible as a whole for ethics. In this respect Oliver O'Donovan's work is in a class of its own,[247] combining exegesis and theology in a style reminiscent of Karl Barth. Theological interpretation is thus in urgent need of Seerveld's strategy; my hope is that these three chapters on the history of biblical interpretation will alert readers to fecund sources for such a bloodline for theological interpretation today, as well as highlighting where work needs to be done.

For those of us committed to Christian/theological interpretation of the Bible, we are heirs to an extraordinary tradition, truly a feast. It is a feast, however, that has been seriously contaminated in modernity and late modernity. No less a philosopher than Gadamer declared, "Enlightenment critique is primarily directed against the religious tradition of Christianity—i.e., the Bible. . . . This is the real radicality of the modern Enlightenment compared to all other movements of enlightenment: it must assert itself against the Bible and dogmatic interpretations of it."[248] This prejudice is evident for all to see in biblical studies today.

How then should we proceed?

1. We should continue to engage the mainstream, both in terms of learning from it and engaging it critically. This is no call for withdrawal from the debates of our age. A major task for us is to reengage historical criticism and to recontextualize its insights in a healthier paradigm.

2. We must, however, move beyond engaging with where others set the agenda, move to attending to agendas arising from the gospel itself, agendas that may be crucial for both church and world *today*, yet in which mainstream scholarship may have no interest. Alvin Plantinga's inaugural lecture at Notre Dame ought to be compulsory reading for all of us with its call to boldness, courage, and integrity. Examples that come to mind are Richard

---

art historical tradition in your own blood and pioneer its contribution in our day" (197). Note also 182–91, encouraging and vital comments about Christian work as a minority culture. Gordon Wenham's use of Hengstenberg in pentateuchal criticism is a good example of this; see Wenham, "The Date of Deuteronomy," 15–20.

247. See esp. O. O'Donovan, *Resurrection and Moral Order: An Outline for Evangelical Ethics* (Grand Rapids: Eerdmans, 1986); idem, *The Desire of the Nations: Rediscovering the Roots of Political Theology* (Cambridge: Cambridge University Press, 1996).

248. H.-G. Gadamer, *Truth and Method* (New York: Seabury, 1975), 272.

Bauckham's work on the Gospels and eyewitness testimony and his edited volume *The Gospels for all Christians*, as well as the highly creative project on the New Testament that Tom Wright is engaged in. In an earlier chapter I have indicated the fundamental importance of biblical theology for biblical interpretation. And yet there are few signs of a resurgence of biblical theology comparable to the heyday of von Rad, Eichrodt, Vriezen, Vos, and, more recently, Childs and Scobie. We need major, rigorous work done on the internal unity of Scripture as a whole.

3. Very few of us have been trained for the tasks at hand, and we need to face this directly. If the renascent theological interpretation is to fulfill its potential, then practitioners and emerging scholars will need to acquire the needed skills. With foreign language skills in steady demise, both ancient and contemporary, we will need to recover them. We will need to explore the story of biblical interpretation in depth, working out the key turning points and how to orient ourselves in relation to them, identifying streams from which we can most fruitfully resource a recovery of theological interpretation, and so on. Philosophical and theological expertise will be indispensable. And so too will be a sense of where we are in Western culture at present so that our work can be done at that crossroads between the biblical story and our cultural stories, the place of true mission, which Newbigin describes as a place of painful tension.

4. Biblical interpretation must make its goal attending to the address of God *for all of our life*. The most rigorous exegesis must be practiced in the spirit of listening, and this must always be in the service of listening for God's address. Such careful listening will confirm that "the Author of life" has a word to say for all of life as he has made it. Theological interpretation cannot restrict itself to church doctrine; it has to help us hear God's address for all of life: politics, economics, family life and sexuality, business, art, sport, and on and on.

5. Finally, I return to my point in chapter 2 that ecclesial reception of the Bible is primary, and the test of academic theological interpretation will be whether it deepens ecclesial reception. Healthy biblical interpretation of the utmost rigor in the service of the Lord Christ can add immeasurably to the messianic feast. It can arise from lectio divina, return there continually, and again and again find itself in the presence of the living Christ.

8

Canon

> I make no apology for taking revelation seriously.
> Thomas F. Torrance[1]

> We must begin Christian theology with Jesus Christ the man from Nazareth who was and is the Word of God incarnate because, as T. F. Torrance consistently recognized, he is an ultimate; he is *the ultimate* for Christian thinking and acting.
> Paul D. Molnar[2]

Introduction

In recent decades canon has again become a controversial issue in biblical studies, with a considerable amount at stake. Thiselton rightly urges, "We must either grasp the nettle of canonical approaches or give up the enterprise of seeking to build Christian theology upon biblical foundations."[3] Gordon Spykman asserts:

---

1. T. F. Torrance, *Space, Time, and Resurrection* (Grand Rapids: Eerdmans, 1976), 1.
2. P. D. Molnar, *Incarnation and Resurrection: Toward a Contemporary Understanding* (Grand Rapids: Eerdmans, 2007), 321.
3. A. C. Thiselton, introduction to *Canon and Biblical Interpretation*, ed. C. G. Bartholomew et al., Scripture and Hermeneutics 7 (Grand Rapids: Zondervan, 2006), 3.

Epistemologically, therefore, it all comes down to Scripture. This book is the indispensable guide for our knowledge of the way of salvation. It confronts us with the Word incarnate in Jesus Christ. It is also the hermeneutic key for our knowledge of the enduring norms of God's creational Word in its holding power for our life together in the world. . . . Only in the light of that redeeming and liberating Word in its lingual form can we gain insight into the meaning of created reality.[4]

Already in 1975, David Dungan argued that major new developments with respect to the canon were beckoning: "I see six areas of intense activity which will sooner or later precipitate a massive series of changes regarding the shape and content of the Bible which should rival for creativity the Reformation period, if not the second through fifth centuries."[5] Dungan's predictions have been right, at least insofar as foundational questions are now being asked about the canon in almost every area. The seven questions with which Lee McDonald concludes his work *The Biblical Canon* demonstrate unequivocally what is at stake in "The Canon Debate."[6]

1. Is the church correct in seeing the need for a closed canon of Scripture? Is the notion of a biblical canon Christian?
2. Has the present biblical canon legitimized oppression?
3. Does a closed canon restrict the work of the Spirit in the church?
4. Should the church be committed to an Old Testament canon where Jesus and his disciples were not so limited?
5. If we continue to uphold apostolicity as a criterion for inclusion in the canon, should we continue to include 2 Peter, the Pastorals, and other nonapostolic New Testament literature in the canon?
6. Should we bind the modern church to a canon that emerged out of the historical circumstances of the second to fifth centuries AD?

---

4. G. J. Spykman, *Reformational Theology: A New Paradigm for Doing Dogmatics* (Grand Rapids: Eerdmans, 1992), 87. For a very different perspective, see W. J. Abraham, *Canon and Criterion in Christian Theology: From the Fathers to Feminism* (Oxford: Oxford University Press, 2002). Central to Abraham's work is a clear distinction between means of grace and epistemic criteria. He seeks a view of canon that privileges the former. In my view, this is a false dichotomy since the grace yielded by Scripture is pregnant with epistemological significance.

5. D. L. Dungan, "The New Testament Canon in Recent Study," *Int* 29 (1975): 339–51. Dungan's six areas are (1) the criteria for the NT canon in light of reappraisal of texts such as the *Gospel of Thomas*; (2) the effect of the Qumran discoveries; (3) LXX studies and the reappraisal of the MT; (4) the collation of the some 6,000 manuscripts of the Christian Bible; (5) the ecumenical movement; and (6) research related to the Jewish and Greco-Roman background to the NT.

6. L. M. McDonald, *The Biblical Canon: Its Origin, Transmission, and Authority*, 3rd ed. (Peabody, MA: Hendrickson, 2007), 426–29; cf. L. M. McDonald and James A. Sanders, eds., *The Canon Debate* (Peabody, MA: Hendrickson, 2002).

7. If the Spirit inspired only the written documents of the first century, does that same Spirit not continue to speak today about contemporary issues?

McDonald hastens to add that he is not for rejecting the present canon in favor of another closed canon, and he also stresses that no alternative ancient documents are on the whole more reliable for the church's faith. However, in the light of the questions posed, one gathers the feeling that the horse may already be out of the barn, so to speak!

The Journey to Here

When I was a student at Oxford in the 1990s, Roger Beckwith was finishing off his major work *The Old Testament Canon of the New Testament Church and Its Background in Early Judaism*. As is often noted, it remains *the* major recent work on the canon although from the outset it has generated controversy. There has probably never been a time in the history of the church during which the precise limits of the canon have not been controversial, but McDonald's questions indicate a far more radical dimension to the contemporary debate. His questions 2, 3, and 7 are, in my opinion, relatively easily dealt with. Clearly the Bible *has been* used to legitimate oppression. Growing up in apartheid South Africa, I know only too well how the Bible can be used to legitimate racism and oppression of the worst sort. Yet it is an entirely different question as to whether such use is faithful to Scripture. Regarding question 3, it is hard to see why a Scripture inspired by the Spirit should restrict the work of the Spirit. Theologians who are orthodox rightly associate the Spirit in particular with the work of creation, and the canon itself points us in this direction. The more important question is the epistemological one: how do we know when the Spirit is at work? Orthodox Christianity appeals to Scripture as the criterion. So with question 7: no Christian that I know would deny that the Spirit continues to speak to the church on these issues; instead, believers argue that the Spirit speaks *in accord with Scripture.*

Questions 1, 4, 5, and 6 indicate just how foundational the current debate is. Historically, the church has debated the extent of the canon, but now the issue is raised of whether the very notion of a biblical canon is Christian. Question 4 emerges from the majority view, at least among those writing on canon today, that the Old Testament canon was closed, for both Jews and Christians, only significantly *after* the time of Jesus and his disciples. Thus it is argued that Jesus himself viewed the Old Testament canon as open. Question 5 relates to the early church criterion of apostolicity. We now know, or so it is argued, that books like 2 Peter, the Pastoral Epistles, and others were not written by apostles or their close associates, and so the church got it wrong on these books in terms of the criterion of apostolicity.

How have we arrived at this situation? From the mid-1960s to the 1990s, canon was a major focus in biblical studies. This renewal of interest was sparked by several factors such as the study of the Dead Sea Scrolls; a renewed emphasis on the diversity in Hellenistic Judaism, requiring a rethinking of G. F. Moore's portrayal of normative Judaism;[7] renewed attention to the noncanonical, apocryphal, and pseudepigraphic literature, enhanced by the discovery of the gnostic papyri; and fresh attention to the Septuagint, Targums, and midrashim. Woven into this was an emphasis on a history of religions approach as the right way to study the development of the canon in comparison with a theological orientation.

In 1957 A. C. Sundberg published his *The Old Testament of the Early Church*, in which he argued for a distinction between Scripture and canon, a distinction that was widely accepted.[8] Within the English-speaking world, this distinction marked the start of a new phase in study of the canon, focused primarily on the *historical* process that resulted in the canon of the Jewish and Christian Bibles. We need to understand what "historical" means in this context. With respect to the canon of the New Testament, the older view of Zahn and Westcott was that the major force in the development of the New Testament was theological. However, as Childs notes, this "major emphasis shifted to historical reconstructions of extrinsic forces as decisive."[9] The traditional criteria for canonicity (apostolicity, catholicity, orthodoxy) were marginalized and seen as lacking historical evidence, so increasingly canonization was studied according to categories from comparative history of religions. The focus became describing the historical process of canonization according to the neutral, scientific approaches of religious phenomenology. Gamble's conclusion to his review of the canonization process of the New Testament is indicative of the direction in canon studies that has resulted from this approach: "The scope of the canon is . . . indebted to a wide range

---

7. G. F. Moore, *Judaism in the First Centuries of the Christian Era: The Age of the Tannaim*, 3 vols. (Cambridge, MA: Harvard University Press, 1927–30).

8. E. Ulrich, "The Notion and Definition of Canon," in McDonald and Sanders, *Canon Debate*, 21–35.

9. B. S. Childs, "The Canon in Recent Biblical Studies: Reflections on an Era," in *Canon and Biblical Interpretation*, ed. Bartholomew et al., Scripture and Hermeneutics 7 [Grand Rapids: Zondervan, 2006]: 33–57, esp. 37.

of contingent historical factors and from a historical standpoint is largely fortuitous."[10]

A common emphasis in the newer approach is attention to the relationship between canon and *community*. Sanders is the major exponent of this approach, and his model has become dominant in academic circles in America.[11] Canon surely is inextricably linked to the Christian community, but as Childs rightly states, "This anthropocentric, sociological interpretation of canon for a community is a modern, oblique history-of-religions reading of its role."[12] Community response is seen as at the heart of the formation of a canon, and canon functions as the means for a community to create and *adapt* its Scriptures to meet its changing needs. Canon is characterized by a dialectic between stability and adaptability. It provides stability in the community's life by meeting its needs, but because the historical and the social context of the community changes, the community adapts the canon and opens the stable forms to allow for new challenges and needs. Sanders finds a classic example of this in the Hellenistic period, when the Jewish canon had begun to stabilize. However, the canon could not meet the community's needs in the new religious crises, and thus the techniques of midrash were developed to reinterpret its canon into new forms.[13]

Sanders hereby reinterprets the traditional Christian view of the canon as an established apostolic rule of faith, making it into a flexible paradigm by which faith can continually be adjusted to the changing circumstances of modernity. Childs rightly declares that, theologically, Sanders shares the deepest theological commitments of Protestant theological liberalism in the nineteenth and twentieth centuries. Instead of canon being seen as the church's response to a divine initiative, grounded in the Christ event, it is reduced to a sociopolitical attempt by the community of faith at self-definition. The role of the Spirit in constantly renewing the church through

---

10. H. Y. Gamble, *The New Testament Canon: Its Making and Meaning* (Philadelphia: Fortress, 1985), 83.

11. J. A. Sanders, *Torah and Canon* (Philadelphia: Fortress, 1972); idem, "Adaptable for Life: The Nature and Function of Canon," in *Magnalia Dei: The Mighty Acts of God; Essays on the Bible and Archaeology in Memory of G. Ernest Wright*, ed. F. M. Cross et al. (New York: Doubleday, 1976), 531–60; idem, *Canon and Community: A Guide to Canonical Criticism*, Guides to Biblical Study (Philadelphia: Fortress, 1984). See also D. M. Carr, "Canonization in the Context of Community: An Outline of the Formation of the Tanakh and the Christian Bible," in *A Gift of God in Due Season: Essays on Scripture and Community in Honor of James A. Sanders*, ed. R. D. Weis and D. M. Carr, JSOTSup 225 (Sheffield: Sheffield Academic Press, 1996), 22–64.

12. Childs, "Canon in Recent Biblical Studies," in Bartholomew et al., *Canon and Biblical Interpretation*, 39.

13. For a critique of this view of midrash, see B. S. Childs, "Critiques of Recent Intertextual Canonical Interpretation," *ZAW* (2003): 173–84.

the inspired Scriptures is replaced with an exercise in human imagination and ingenuity.

A parallel debate about the canon went on in German circles.[14] German scholarship dominated the canon debate in the nineteenth century, and discussion continued throughout the 1950s; especially significant are the works by Bauer and von Campenhausen. A period of silence followed, punctuated by Käsemann's *Das Neue Testament als Kanon* in 1970. By the 1980s, German interest in the newer approaches in the English world appeared, led in part by Rendtorff,[15] and followed by Dohmen and others.[16] The German debate is important not least because of its differences with the English one. The confessional context was far stronger,[17] and the relationship of canon to biblical theology was taken seriously without marginalizing a history of religions approach. As Dohmen noted, "The canon in its significance for Biblical Theology can hardly be overestimated."[18] Not surprisingly the issue of the Old Testament and the Jewish Bible featured largely in German discussions. Lohfink argued for the continuity of Old and New Testaments,[19] and Zenger went so far as to assert that the New Testament is a commentary on the Jewish Scriptures.[20] More recently Dohmen has argued that the canon can be understood only in a faith community and has resorted to reception history in this regard.[21] Childs summarizes the German debate as follows:

> A survey of the role of canon within the German-speaking academy brought to light a very different focus from that of the English-speaking world. By remaining primarily church-oriented, it was able to wrestle with the modern task of biblical interpretation from a canonical perspective in a far profounder theological manner and to break open many new intellectual frontiers. Yet, ironically, the challenge of modernity has also, in the end, pushed the German

---

14. See Childs, "Canon in Recent Biblical Studies," in Bartholomew et al., *Canon and Biblical Formation*, 43–53. The editors of *The Canon Debate* assert that they tried to include all the main players in the debate, but no key German figures are contributors.

15. R. Rendtorff, *Canon and Theology: Overtures to an Old Testament Theology*, trans. and ed. M. Kohl (Philadelphia: Fortress, 1993).

16. C. Dohmen and M. Oeming, *Biblischer Kanon, warum und wozu? Eine Kanontheologie*, Quaestiones disputatae 137 (Freiburg: Herder, 1992); C. Dohmen and T. Söding, eds., *Eine Bible—zwei Testamente: Positionen biblischer Theologie* (Paderborn: Schöningh, 1995).

17. Largely due to Roman Catholic involvement.

18. C. Dohmen, "Probleme und Chancen biblischer Theologie aus alttestamentlicher Sicht," in Dohmen and Söding, eds.*, Eine Bible—zwei Testamente*, 15.

19. N. Lohfink, *Der niemals gekündigte Bund: Exegetische Gedanken zum christlich-jüdischen Dialog* (Freiburg: Herder, 1989).

20. E. Zenger, *Einleitung in das Alte Testament*, 3rd ed. (Stuttgart: Kohlhammer, 1998).

21. C. Dohmen and G. Stemberger, *Hermeneutik der Jüdischen Bibel und des Alten Testaments* (Stuttgart: Kohlhammer, 1996), 133–213.

debate into some of the same areas which occupied the English-speaking academy from the outset.[22]

Canon and Christology

As the new decisive form which that community of reciprocity has taken with the incarnation of God's Word in Jesus Christ, the Christian Church is essentially and necessarily bound up with the unique self-revelation of God in Jesus Christ which, in communicable form, is handed on to us in the apostolic Scripture of the New Testament.[23]

After his review of the new debate about canon in the English-speaking world, Childs asks, "Whatever has happened to traditional, orthodox Christian theology within this embrace of modernity?"[24] A moot question. The answer, I think, is that theology has been marginalized from the debate so that one is left, as it were, with "unbelief seeking understanding." Indeed, the extent to which theological reflection is omitted or marginalized is noticeable in many of the recent books on canon. John Webster identifies four aspects to current explorations of the canon:[25]

1. Critical-historical approaches in which the development of the canon is seen, for example, as the church's response to the threat posed by Marcion. The effect of such an approach is to desacralize the canon and to view canonization as an arbitrary process.
2. Religious history and comparative approaches in which a history of religions approach is applied to the development of the canon.[26]
3. Sociopolitical theories in which the link is made between the canon as poetics, which equates to politics, which equates to power.
4. Postmodern approaches in which all the weight is on acts of reading.[27]

Webster rightly notices the negative effect on our understanding of canonicity once it is transplanted out of its native soil, the saving economy of the triune God.[28]

---

22. Childs, "Canon in Recent Biblical Studies," in Bartholomew, *Canon and Biblical Formation*, 51. See ibid., 51–53, for his more detailed assessment of the German debate.
23. Torrance, *Space, Time, and Resurrection*, 2.
24. Childs, "Canon in Recent Biblical Studies," in Bartholomew et al., *Canon and Biblical Interpretation*, 43.
25. J. Webster, *Word and Church: Essays in Christian Dogmatics* (New York: T&T Clark, 2001), 11–17.
26. For multiple references, see ibid., 12n2.
27. M. C. Taylor, *Erring: A Postmodern A/theology*, 8th ed. (Chicago: University of Chicago Press, 2010).
28. Webster, *Word and Church*, 9; cf. Torrance, *Space, Time, and Resurrection*, 2–3.

The force of these approaches is to turn canon into *a product* rather than what it is, *a norm*. Indeed, our view of the canon will overwhelmingly be shaped by our view of Jesus. René Girard refers to the ending of a piece of literature as the "temple of truth."[29] If this is true of endings in general, how much more is it true of the Christ event? The Christ event is portrayed in the New Testament as God's final and complete word: the fulfillment of history, of God's purposes with Israel, and that around which everything revolves (cf. Heb. 1:1–4).

In the early church[30] the tradition arose of referring to the Old *Testament* and the New *Testament*. "Testament" here means covenant, and this nomenclature is profoundly insightful since the literature of both Old Testament and New Testament stems from two major covenants, Sinai and the new covenant. "Each of these covenants—the ancient covenant of Sinai and the new covenant inaugurated by Jesus—launched a great spiritual movement. Each of these movements gave rise to a special body of literature, and these bodies of literature came to be known in the Christian church as 'the books of the ancient covenant' and 'the books of the new covenant.'"[31] Indeed, the Old Testament and the New Testament can be seen as the deposit of God's work in these two covenants.

In his stimulating and neglected *Cult and Canon*, Östborn queries the tendency to see Old Testament canon formation as taking place in periods of demise in the life of Israel. Instead, he looks to times of vitality and stability. But if one does not believe in the Sinai event or the Christ event, then one is left without any explosions of revelation and naturally has to resort to "firm" historical data according to secular historiographical criteria indicating precisely when or even if the canon was closed. Hence the modern debate about a closed canon is just that, a *modern* debate.

I suggest that one reason we do not find the sort of modern debate among the ancients is that they believed in—and many experienced—the Sinai event and the Christ event and their aftereffects. The modern debate focuses on the terminus ad quem for the canon, whether it be that of the Old Testament or the New, but for Israel and the church, canonicity is directed toward the founding events, and hence they think in terms of a terminus a quo. They

---

29. R. Girard, *Deceit, Desire, and the Novel: Self and Other in Literary Structure*, trans. Y. Freccero (Baltimore: Johns Hopkins University Press, 1965), 307–8.

30. These titles are attested at the end of the second century, almost simultaneously in both Greek and Latin; in Greek in works of Clement of Alexandria (*Stromata* 1.9; 3.11; 4.21; 5.13), and in Latin in works of Tertullian (*Against Marcion* 4.1; *Against Praxeas* 15).

31. F. F. Bruce, *The Canon of Scripture* (Downers Grove, IL: InterVarsity, 1988), 21; cf. G. Östborn, *Cult and Canon: A Study in the Canonization of the Old Testament*, Uppsala Universitets Årsskrift 10 (Uppsala: Almqvist & Wiksell, 1950), 76–80.

have no doubt about Yahweh's activity at Sinai and in Christ: this action is so definitive and authoritative that the formal documents emerging from these events assume that authority. If, for example, as we suggest below in line with Östborn, the cultus was the place in the Old Testament era where the authoritative writings were preserved, then they would quite naturally share in the holiness of the temple. There would be no question about the authority of God's presence and God's Word literally located in the temple.

The new covenant fulfills the old and is understandable only in relationship to it. In this sense a redemptive-historical approach is helpful. However, the danger with such an approach is that it fails to take account of the radical newness of the Christ event. Thus, as T. F. Torrance rightly points out, despite the continuity between the covenants, the message of the New Testament can be understood only "with a profound revolution in the tradition of Judaism in which basic categories of thought have to be creatively reconstructed."[32] For Torrance, the resurrection is akin to the creation in the beginning,[33] and the Christ event was "quite unexpected" from the human perspective.[34] "It was not just a miracle within the creation, but a deed so decisively new that it affected the whole of creation and the whole of the future."[35]

In terms of *adaptability* as a criterion advocated by Sanders and McDonald, doubtless there is some truth to this, but as Torrance perceptively observes:

> The incarnation and the resurrection of Jesus Christ . . . forced themselves upon the minds of Christians from their own empirical and theoretical ground in sharp antithesis to what they had believed about God and in genuine conflict with the framework of secular thought or the world view of their age. That God himself had become man was an offence to the Jew and folly to the Greek; that Jesus Christ rose from the dead was deemed to be utterly incredible. Yet the incarnation and the resurrection forced themselves upon the mind of the Church against the grain of people's convictions, as ultimate events bearing their own intrinsic but shattering claims in the self-evidencing reality and transcendent rationality of God himself, and they took root within the Church only through a seismic restructuring of religious and intellectual belief.[36]

Thus, insofar as adaptability is a criterion, cultural *resistance* is a far stronger one. Any criterion of adaptability would have to be subsumed under the

---

32. Torrance, *Space, Time, and Resurrection*, 30. See also in this respect N. T. Wright, *Jesus and the Victory of God*, vol. 2, *Christian Origins and the Question of God* (London: SPCK, 1996).
33. Bruce, *Canon of Scripture*, 31.
34. Ibid., 33–34.
35. Ibid., 36.
36. Torrance, *Space, Time, and Resurrection*, 17.

authority of the Christ event, which was—and should be—viewed as self-authenticating. Belief in the incarnation and resurrection would clearly imply that the Christ event fits with the grain of the universe, since it is from him, through him, and to him; yet believers would have a hermeneutic of trust toward Christ and one of suspicion toward themselves on this issue. The problem with the current understanding of adaptability is that it works with a hermeneutic of trust in us and our—politically correct—culture, lacking an appropriate suspicion of ourselves and lacking a trust in Christ.

Christ is indeed *the* temple of truth and the clue to all that is, including the canon. There are important analogies between Christ's appointment of twelve apostles[37] and the twelve tribes of Israel, except that now the Twelve are the foundation for a people of God drawn from all nations. *Apostolicity* was pervasively and rightly regarded as a key criterion for canonicity in the early church since the apostles were appointed to be with Jesus for the three years of his public ministry and thus to bear authoritative testimony to him especially after his death, resurrection, and ascension. First John 1:1–3 is crystal clear on this:

> We declare to you what was from the beginning, what we have heard, what we have seen with our own eyes, what we have looked at and touched with our hands, concerning the word of life—this life was revealed, and we have seen it and testify to it, and declare to you the eternal life that was with the Father and was revealed to us—we declare to you what we have seen and heard so that you also may have fellowship with us; and truly our fellowship is with the Father and with his Son Jesus Christ.

The testimony of John is grounded in the eyewitness experience of the apostles, and this experience has led him to understand the Christ event within the economy of God, the very soil in which John Webster rightly asserts canon should be located, as a *consequential* doctrine.

Childs thus rightly notes the lack of an adequate Christology in too much of the modern debate about the canon. The church has always confessed the Old Testament to be part of Scripture, but the newness of the Christ event must not be forgotten; the gospel was "an explosion of God's good news."[38] Ridderbos perceptively declares:

---

37. On the historicity of the Twelve as a group formed by Jesus, see J. P. Meier, *A Marginal Jew: Rethinking the Historical Jesus* (New York: Doubleday, 2001), 3:98–106. See also R. Bauckham, *Jesus and the Eyewitnesses: The Gospels as Eyewitness Testimony* (Grand Rapids: Eerdmans, 2006), 93–112.

38. Childs, "Canon in Recent Biblical Studies," in Bartholomew et al., *Canon and Biblical Interpretation*, 53.

The key to the solution of the whole problem of canonization and the authority of the New Testament Scriptures is the recognition of its Christological basis. Jesus Christ is not only the canon Himself, in which God comes to the world, but He also lays down the canon and gives it a concrete, historical shape in the authority of the apostles, in their witness and tradition. And he guarantees the connection between this authoritative institution and the Church: On this rock I will build my Church.[39]

The development of the canon is generally conceived of in stages: often the Law, then the Prophets, then the Writings, then, at various points, the New Testament, with the New Testament gradually coming to be placed on par with the Old Testament. *Chronologically*, at least in terms of origins, there is obviously truth to this, but *theologically and historically* a very different interpretation of the emergence of the Christian Bible is possible.

The Austrian statistician Franz Graf-Stuhlhofer[40] has used statistical analysis to explore the intensity of citations and use of biblical books in the early church, with a view to shifting the focus to *how often* they cite the New Testament and other works. What emerges from his analysis is surprising and clear: from the apostolic fathers onward, the Synoptic Gospels (esp. Matthew), John, and the major Pauline Epistles are cited far more often than one would predict if the whole of the New Testament were equally canonical. The rest of the New Testament is quoted far less frequently. Of books scarcely cited, most of them were later declared to be noncanonical.[41]

What is fascinating from Stuhlhofer's analysis is that astonishingly early the core of the New Testament was already being treated as the main authoritative source for Christians. There was little controversy about the Synoptics, John, or the major Pauline Epistles. There are few references to these books as *graphē*, but proportionate to size they are referred to *more* than the Old Testament by most writers from the apostolic fathers onward. It is only in the third century that citations of Old Testament and New Testament start to level out. "This is perhaps the really surprising conclusion to which Stuhlhofer's statistics lead: that the core of the New Testament mattered more to the Church of the first two centuries than the Old, if we are to judge by its

---

39. H. Ridderbos, *When the Time Had Fully Come: Studies in New Testament Theology* (Grand Rapids: Eerdmans, 1957; reprint, Jordon Station, ON: Paideia, 1957), 87.

40. F. Graf-Stuhlhofer, *Der Gebrauch der Bibel von Jesus bis Euseb: Eine statistische Untersuchung zur Kanongeschichte* (Wuppertal: Brockhaus, 1988).

41. (Graf-)Stuhlhofer (ibid.) proposes a three-phase development of the NT canon: (1) very early the central core was treated as authoritative; (2) the reference to OT and NT levels out, and NT books in the second class are more frequently cited; (3) only in the fourth century do the fringes of the canon become clear and firm.

actual *use* of the texts."⁴² Thus in the apostolic fathers the New Testament is used the following times more often than the Old Testament:

Shepherd of Hermas	5.5
2 Clement	5.5
Ignatius	5 to 50
Didache	12
Polycarp	27

What are we to make of this evidence? In my opinion what is required is a nuanced view of *time*. In terms of chronological *and* narrative time, the New Testament follows on from the Old. However, in terms of the early church the *kairos* moment was the Christ event. Thus, not surprisingly, in Acts 2:42 the first converts—who were Jews!—devoted themselves not to the Old Testament but to "the apostles' teaching," to the authoritative testimony about Jesus. This is not to set the apostles' teaching above the Old Testament, but it is to make the obvious point that the first converts were converted to Jesus. Naturally the apostles' teaching would include the manifold ways in which Jesus fulfilled the authoritative Old Testament, but it would be madness to keep one's attention focused there when Yahweh's final act and word was present in their midst. As Cyprian declared in the third century AD:

> There are many things that God spoke through the prophets, his servants, which he wants us to hear. But *how much more* would he have us hear those which the Son spoke, to which the Word of God, who was in the prophets, bears witness through his own voice; now not simply ordering that the way of his coming be made ready, but coming himself, showing us and opening to us the way, so that we who previously were wandering, blind, and reckless in the shadow of death, should be illuminated by the light of grace on the journey of life and keep to the way with the Lord as our leader and guide.⁴³

Once again, this pushes us back to the Christ event as that from which canonicity stems rather than a secular historical approach that is trying to

---

42. J. Barton, *Holy Writings, Sacred Text: The Canon in Early Christianity* (Louisville: Westminster John Knox, 1997), 18.

43. Cyprian, *On the Lord's Prayer* 1, in Tertullian, Cyprian, and Origen, *On the Lord's Prayer*, Popular Patristics 29 (Crestwood, NY: St. Vladimir's Seminary Press, 2004), with added emphasis. On Cyprian's hermeneutic, see M. A. Fahey, *Cyprian and the Bible: A Study in Third-Century Exegesis*, who writes (on 48), however, that Cyprian lacks a clear sense of the progressiveness of revelation and tends to treat the Bible as "Parole presque intemporelle [almost timeless Word]." As we saw in chap. 5 (above), this kind of flattening of Scripture is a result of an allegorical hermeneutic.

determine when the canon was finally closed. It is not that the latter question is unimportant, and doubtless a variety of circumstances impressed on the early church the need to discern and declare the limits of the canon, but the process was one of recognizing intrinsic authority related back to the Christ and his apostles rather than imposing authority on texts.

The Old Testament Canon and Cultus

In chapter 2 we argued for the priority of listening in our approach to Scripture and located the primary context for such listening in the *ekklēsia*. Intriguingly, this emphasis is also illuminating when it comes to the canon of the Old Testament. In previous chapters I have suggested that the canon is helpfully conceived of as the deposit of God's dealings with Israel and preeminently his activity in Jesus of Nazareth. Yet such a metaphor might be taken to mean that the Old Testament is merely the national literature of Israel. It does form part of this literature, but I have more in mind with the metaphor of "deposit" than Israel's national literature.

In the Old Testament, Israel is God's elect nation, through whom he pursues his purposes for his entire creation. The name *Yahweh* evokes God's special relationship with Israel, and the Old Testament covenants alert us unequivocally to Yahweh's authority in Israel as *the* Great King who has taken Israel as his vassal nation. Throughout the Old Testament, God is portrayed as communicating with people and in particular with Israel, through Moses, through the prophets, through the wise, *and* through the priests.

As we know, many today think that even if there is a God, he does not speak. Thus David Clines, for example, simply asserts that he would be surprised if any scholar nowadays believes that God spoke the ten words (the Decalogue).[44] It is astonishing that such a distinguished Old Testament scholar could manifest such blindness to the pluralism in Old Testament studies: after all, there are thousands of Jewish, Christian, and Muslim scholars—to say nothing of nonscholars—who do indeed believe that God speaks, has spoken, and has uttered a version of the ten words to Israel at Sinai.

Throughout the Old Testament there are indications of writing accompanying God's speech. Clearly, for Israel, if Yahweh has spoken, then his words are and remain authoritative: hence comes the motifs of the tablets of the ten words being stored in the ark, and so forth. Canonical scholars such as Beckwith and

---

44. D. J. A. Clines, "The Ten Commandments: Reading from Left to Right," in *Words Remembered, Texts Renewed: Essays in Honour of John F. A. Sawyer*, ed. J. Davies, G. Harvey, and W. Watson (Sheffield: Sheffield Academic Press, 1995), 97–112.

Dempster draw attention to such motifs, but they are rarely taken seriously by mainstream scholars presumably because they regard much of the Old Testament as historically unreliable. Although the historical-critical reconstructions of the Old Testament have been severely savaged by the literary turn, the "assured results" of historical criticism seem still to provide a fallback position for many Old Testament specialists. To an extent this is understandable; historical critics are close readers of the Hebrew text, and the data they have uncovered cannot and should not be ignored. However, the literary turn has challenged us over what to make of such data foundationally, and we urgently need new critical work to be done on the history of the Old Testament and its literature, work reckoning with the context of different frameworks that take the literary turn seriously. Having said this, it seems to me that even in the current state of our discipline, the literary turn makes it much harder than it was in the past to simply ignore the references to Old Testament documents and the cultus. Such motifs are pervasive in the Old Testament, and even if they are historically untrustworthy in their contexts, they still alert us to a strong tendency to connect cultus and authoritative writings in the life of Israel.

We noted above that God spoke not only through Moses, the prophets, and the wise, but also through *the priests*. Understandably revelation is not normally associated with the priests because in a basic way their role in relation to God's speech was secondary. For our purposes, however, precisely herein lies their importance. The ark and the temple are literally the place where Yahweh dwells among his people. Not surprisingly, the presence of the Holy One requires a diplomatic corps to mediate the relationship between Yahweh and his people. The covenant relationship is established at Sinai, but the ongoing relationship is a challenge, as eloquently witnessed to by the Old Testament. God spoke through Moses and would continue to speak through his prophets, but once he had spoken, where was one to go to hear his word for Israel again and again? The answer is the temple, where God lived amid his people. Little wonder, then, that when the priesthood is consecrated in Leviticus 8–10, a twofold role is assigned to the priests: they are to distinguish between the holy and the common, between the unclean and the clean, and they are *to teach* the people of Israel all the statutes that Yahweh has spoken to them through Moses (Lev. 10:10–11; cf. Deut. 33:10).

Scott Hahn points out that the Levitical economy emerges in response to the golden calf incident—what the tree was for Adam, the calf was for Israel[45]—as

---

45. S. W. Hahn, *Kinship by Covenant: A Canonical Approach to the Fulfillment of God's Saving Promises* (New Haven: Yale University Press, 2009), 174. In this respect, Hahn footnotes R. Scroggs, *The Last Adam: A Study in Pauline Anthropology* (Philadelphia: Fortress, 1966), 53.

a "remedial response to their hard-heartedness."⁴⁶ "To use an architectural metaphor, the whole Levitical economy was a scaffolding erected around the House of Israel in order to repair it. The divine architect was free to use the Levitical priesthood for as long as it took to restore the House of Israel fully to the covenant."⁴⁷ The seriousness of the priestly role should be recognized; failure to practice the distinctions referred to in Leviticus 10:10 could be a matter of life and death, as could the failure to know and attend to God's torah. In Hahn's words, the Levites are to ensure that a "holy secularity" prevails among the Israelites.⁴⁸

The priesthood performed this role through maintaining the cultus and through teaching Yahweh's torah to the Israelites. Torah should not here be limited to law since law in the Pentateuch always comes embedded in narrative. "Illustrative of the relationship between a cultic narrative and the Canon is, furthermore, their obligation of being propagated. It is the duty of members of the cult to make the contents of the cultic story known to others."⁴⁹ Through sacrifice the priests enacted God's presence amid his people, and through instruction they reoriented the people in relation to God's Word. "What cult ultimately aims at in serving and promoting is life itself. It is always striving to bridge death and life. For this purpose it also utilizes the word expressed in cult. In my opinion, such a word may also be the Old Testament as a whole, even though we may not definitely be able to claim that everything in the Old Testament was read in the Temple service of Israel."⁵⁰ Consequently it is natural to expect that the cultus would be the repository of God's word written. "From the very fact that the OT Canon constitutes a collection of holy writings belonging to the cultic assembly of Israel, it must be held to be a religious canon."⁵¹

It is to H. E. Ryle that we owe the influential theory of a three-stage development of the Old Testament.⁵² Admitting the paucity of external evidence, Ryle asserted that "Scripture must tell its own tale."⁵³ For Ryle, the tripartite division of the Hebrew Bible reflects an ancient tradition of the linear development of the Old Testament through three successive stages. He argued that the Law was canonized under Ezra sometime in the mid-fifth century,

---

46. S. W. Hahn, *Kinship by Covenant*, 167.
47. Ibid.
48. Ibid., 174.
49. Östborn, *Cult and Canon*, 103.
50. Ibid., 107–8.
51. Ibid., 20.
52. H. E. Ryle, *The Canon of the Old Testament: An Essay on the Gradual Growth and Formation of the Hebrew Canon of Scripture*, 2nd ed. (London: Macmillan, 1925).
53. Ibid., 9.

before the schism between Jews and Samaritans in 432 BC. The Prophets were canonized by the end of the third century BC, before the composition of Ecclesiasticus (= Ben-Sira, or Sirach) in approximately 180 BC. The Writings received canonical standing by AD 100, perhaps at the rabbinical council in Jamnia in AD 90. In his theory, Ryle conceives of canon as nationally observed, officially authoritative, and literarily delimited. Canonization is thus an a posteriori judgment by official Israel. A book only became truly canonical when its subcollection became canonical.

Ryle's approach remains influential today but has been severely criticized.[54] The significance of Jamnia in terms of closing the Old Testament canon has been shown to lack any evidence.[55] Furthermore, Ryle's approach is far too tidy and his definition of canon too narrow, laying all the weight (as it does) on the terminus ad quem. Bruce rightly judges his theory thus: "For all its attractiveness, this account is completely hypothetical: there is no evidence for it, either in the Old Testament itself or elsewhere."[56] While the tripartite division of the Old Testament may be of relatively little help in terms of understanding the process of canonization, it is of help in terms of a literary approach to the Old Testament.

We need to admit how little we know about the process by which the Old Testament books reached their final forms and were then divided into three sections. As Kalin states, "The gaps in our knowledge are so severe that all of us are driven to speculation and conjecture. Perhaps in our natural and important attempts to say something, we all pretend to know more than the available evidence gives us a right to know."[57] Lacking external evidence, Ryle is correct to recognize that Scripture must tell its own story, but scholars remain seriously divided about the story it tells. Historical criticism remains a dominant paradigm in canon studies, which continue to work with its assured results despite the fact that the literary turn and intertextual studies have raised foundational questions about nearly every assured result. Thus the Deuteronomistic history, the non-Mosaic origin of most, if not all, of Exodus–Deuteronomy, the source of 3 Isaiah, and so forth—these issues are formative in most studies of the Old Testament canon even though theories

---

54. S. G. Dempster ("Torah, Torah, Torah: The Emergence of the Tripartite Canon," in *Exploring the Origins of the Bible: Canon Formation in Historical, Literary, and Theological Perspective*, ed. C. Evans and E. Tov [Grand Rapids: Baker Academic, 2008], 88n4) reports that a majority of scholars continue to hold to a slight modification of Ryle's view.

55. S. Z. Leiman, *The Canonization of the Hebrew Scripture: The Talmudic and Midrashic Evidence* (Hamden, CT: Archon, 1976).

56. Bruce, *Canon of Scripture*, 36.

57. E. Kalin, "How Did the Canon Come to Us? A Response to the Leiman Hypothesis," *Concordia Theological Monthly* 4 (1997): 52.

such as that of the Deuteronomistic history are just that: theories, without substantial evidence.[58]

We urgently need alternative historical reconstructions of the Old Testament that take into account the literary turn and are informed by a theology of history. Such approaches would take the data uncovered by historical critics seriously but would attend closely to how we interpret this data. For example, the differences between the law codes in the Pentateuch cannot just be smoothed over as if they do not exist, but what we do with their differences remains an open question. Theology cannot be kept out of this investigation: theology will make a major difference as to whether we view Sinai as historical and take Yahweh's revelation to Israel through Moses and the prophets with utmost seriousness. Taking these elements seriously will reorient us toward the authoritative origins of the Old Testament canon and incline us to approach "canonization" as the formal recognition of the authority of the Old Testament rather than its belated origin. James Barr asserts:

> The men of the Bible were, as we now see it, engaged in the process out of which our Bible in the end would emerge, but they themselves had no Bible: at that time, clearly, the Bible as we know it was not yet there. A scripture in the sense of an already existing defined and delimited, written guide for the religion did not yet exist. In the time of (say) the prophet Isaiah there was as yet no scripture, and he never speaks of there being one.[59]

Central to such a view is the question of revelation. For Israel, Yahweh was *the* authority, and thus his speech and records of his speech were canonical in the sense of being binding, delimited, and authoritative. As Lee McDonald states, "In a very real sense, Israel had a canon when the tradition of Moses receiving the Torah on Sinai was accepted into the community."[60] Yet the question is the nature of this "tradition" and whether it had its origins in an actual covenant at Sinai made with Yahweh. If we take the historicity of Sinai seriously, then at the outset of its formation Israel already had a body of authoritative writing, even if that only consisted of the two tablets of the Decalogue.[61] Furthermore, the prophets clearly presuppose authoritative torah on which their messages depend, and the true prophet is clearly regarded as a

---

58. See C. G. Bartholomew, "Hermeneutics," in *Dictionary of the Old Testament: Historical Books*, ed. B. T. Arnold and H. G. M. Williamson (Downers Grove, IL: IVP Academic, 2005).
59. J. Barr, *Holy Scripture: Canon, Authority, Criticism* (Oxford: Clarendon, 1983), 1.
60. L. M. McDonald, *The Formation of the Christian Biblical Canon*, rev., exp. ed. (Peabody, MA: Hendrickson, 1996), 20.
61. A. Phillips (*Ancient Israel's Criminal Law: A New Approach to the Decalogue* [Oxford: Blackwell, 1970]) states of the Decalogue, "It was in fact a conscious creation at a specific point

messenger of Yahweh. Thus, once we take Yahweh's involvement with Israel seriously, we will stop looking primarily for a terminus ad quem but rather see canonical writings as emerging from the outset. As Bruce perceptively declares, "But, as later with the New Testament, so with the Old Testament it is probable that, when the canon was 'closed' in due course by competent authority, this simply meant that official recognition was given to a situation already obtaining in the practice of the worshipping community."[62]

Having said this, attention to the terminus ad quem for the Old Testament canon remains important. About much of this, we simply cannot be sure and thus need to work, as Bruce says, in terms of *probability*. Clearly Old Testament books were edited and updated from time to time. A challenge is to discern how comprehensive the reshaping was and by whom this editing was done. The close connection between canon and cultus may again be insightful here. If the sacred writings were held in the cultus, then their primary use would have been liturgical, and it is perhaps to the priests that one must look for updating and shaping. Thus Östborn suggests, "Presumably, it is most correct to take the compilation of the Tetrateuch as a product of the activity of priests belonging to the first Temple."[63]

Association with the temple would mean that any kind of freewheeling adaptation would have been out of the question. In terms of adaptation, Chapman perceptively declares, "Israel had no 'interest' in a canon which would only affirm its present beliefs and practices."[64]

Mired in the mists of the past as is the history of the Old Testament canon, an important question is that of the latest date by which it was closed. There is no agreement about this among scholars, but suffice it to report here that there is considerable evidence to support closure well before the time of Jesus and the apostles. Ecclesiasticus was written by Ben-Sira, who was active in the first part of the second century BC. Around 132 BC his grandson translated Ecclesiasticus into Greek, and in the prologue he describes his grandfather as a student of "the Law itself, the Prophecies, and the rest of the books." It is highly likely, but not certain, that we have here a reference to the Law, the Prophets, and the Writings,[65] and the grandson is clear that his grandfather knew of this tripartite corpus.

---

in time, being the stipulations of the covenant entered into at Sinai resultant on the exodus from Egypt" (153).

62. Bruce, *Canon of Scripture*, 42.

63. Östborn, *Cult and Canon*, 83.

64. S. B. Chapman, *The Law and the Prophets: A Study in Old Testament Canon Formation* (Tübingen: Mohr Siebeck, 2000), 284.

65. See Bruce, *Canon of Scripture*, 31; E. E. Ellis, *The Old Testament in Early Christianity: Canon and Interpretation in the Light of Modern Research* (Tübingen: Mohr, 1991), 39–40;

Josephus wrote in the last decade of the first century AD and identifies twenty-two books as constituting the Old Testament canon, a tripartite ordering that probably correlated with the Hebrew Bible as we have it today, with the possible exception of one book.[66] From Josephus's perspective, this is no new canon but one long recognized.

There is considerable evidence that Chronicles was the final book of the Writings and thus of the Old Testament. This is intriguing since chronologically the narrative of Ezra-Nehemiah follows on from that of Chronicles.[67] Whatever the reason for this, there is evidence that Jesus knew of Chronicles as the final book of the Old Testament. In Luke 11:50–51 Jesus refers to "the blood of all the prophets shed since the foundation of the world, from the blood of Abel to the blood of Zechariah." Abel is known as the first martyr in the Old Testament (Gen. 4:8), and Zechariah is most probably the son of Jehoida who was stoned to death in the temple because of his prophetic critique (2 Chron. 24:20–22). *Canonically* speaking, Zechariah was the last prophet to die as a martyr, so that Jesus here refers to the Old Testament canon in its totality. Many of the details of the formation of the Old Testament canon elude us, but there is no reason to doubt that it was closed well before the time of Jesus.

The Criteria for the New Testament Canon

The criteria for canonicity used by the early church stem directly from the Christ event, namely, apostolicity and antiquity, orthodoxy and catholicity. The concern for genuine continuity with the teaching of the apostles is well documented elsewhere, and so we will not discuss the multiple sources here. Suffice it to take note of one or two authors to indicate just how strong this concern was among the church fathers.

Clement is clear that "the apostles received the gospel for us from the Lord Jesus Christ; Jesus the Christ was sent forth from God. So then Christ is from God, and the apostles are from Christ."[68] In his *Prescription against Heretics*, Tertullian again and again affirms the importance of the apostolic

---

R. T. Beckwith, *The Old Testament Canon of the New Testament Church and Its Background in Early Judaism* (Grand Rapids: Eerdmans, 1986), 110–11.

66. See Beckwith, *Old Testament Canon*, 78–80; Bruce, *Canon of Scripture*, 32–34.

67. On the order of books in the Writings, cf. Sara Japhet, *I and II Chronicles: A Commentary*. Old Testament Library (London: SCM, 1993); S. W. Hahn, *The Kingdom of God as Liturgical Empire: A Theological Commentary on 1–2 Chronicles* (Grand Rapids: Baker Academic, 2012), as well as Steven Cole, Stephen G. Dempster, and others.

68. See *1 Clement* 42.1–2, in M. W. Holmes, ed., *The Apostolic Fathers: Greek Texts and English Translations*, updated ed. (Grand Rapids: Baker Books, 1999).

testimony.[69] In this work he quotes and refers to a significant range of the New Testament writings; thus he amply illustrates Barton's point that the earlier church fathers refer more to documents that came to be included in the New Testament than to the Old Testament. Such an emphasis flows directly from his theology: "Our authorities are the Lord's apostles, and they in turn chose to introduce nothing on their own authority. They faithfully passed on to the nations the teaching which they had received from Christ. So we should anathematize even an angel from heaven if he were to preach a different gospel."[70]

Tertullian provides an explication of the *regula fidei* (Rule of Faith) in chapter 13, which has a clear narrative shape that correlates with Scripture as a whole. "Faith is established in the Rule. . . . To know nothing against the Rule is to know everything."[71] While on earth Jesus declared what he was, what he had been, and how he fulfilled his Father's will and his ethic for humankind. "He declared all this either openly to the people or privately to the disciples, twelve of whom he had specially attached to his person and destined to be the teachers of the nations."[72] "For no one knows the Father save the Son and he to whom the Son has revealed him, nor is the Son known to have revealed him to any but the apostles whom he sent to preach—and of course to preach what he revealed to them."[73]

Antiquity is an important criterion for Tertullian. Of the heretics he discusses, he reports, "There are still people living who remember them,"[74] demonstrating a historiographic interest similar to that referred to by Bauckham. By contrast, the churches can trace their origins to the apostles and their preaching. In the cities where the apostles founded churches, "the authentic letters of the apostles are still recited, bringing the voice and face of each one of them to mind."[75] Thus apostolic doctrine and succession become two standards (*utramque formam*)[76] for discerning truth from error. Tertullian eloquently evokes the blessing of the church, on which the apostles poured their teaching and blood:

> She knows one Lord God, Creator of the universe, and Christ Jesus, born of the Virgin Mary, Son of God the Creator, and the resurrection of the flesh; she

---

69. See S. L. Greenslade, ed., *Early Latin Theology: Selections from Tertullian, Cyprian, Ambrose, and Jerome*, LCC 5 (Philadelphia: Westminster, 1956), 65–73, for material from Irenaeus's *Against Heresies* very close to Tertullian's thought.
70. Tertullian, *Prescription against Heretics* 6.
71. Ibid., chap. 14.
72. Ibid., chap. 20.
73. Ibid., chap. 21.
74. Ibid., chap. 30.
75. Ibid., chap. 36.
76. Ibid., chap. 32.

unites the Law and the Prophets[77] with the writings of the evangelists and the apostles; from that source she drinks her faith, and that faith she seals with water, clothes with the Holy Spirit, feeds with the eucharist, encourages to martyrdom; and against the teaching she receives no one.[78]

The logic behind the criterion of apostolicity and antiquity is the unique nature of the apostles and their associates as eyewitnesses of the Christ event. It was commonplace to discern Peter's witness behind Mark's Gospel, to see Matthew as one of the Twelve, Luke as Paul's companion and the author as well of Acts, and John as the son of Zebedee. Thus Irenaeus, for example, having stressed the apostolic source of the truth of the gospel, writes:

> Thus Matthew, among the Hebrews, produced a written gospel in their language, while Peter and Paul were preaching at Rome and founding the Church. After their departure, Mark, the disciple and interpreter of Peter, himself handed on to us in writing what Peter had preached. Luke, the companion of Paul, set down in a book the gospel preached by him. Afterwards John also, the disciple of the Lord, "which also leaned on his breast," himself published the gospel during his stay at Ephesus in Asia.[79]

Modern critical scholarship has subjected these views to critical scrutiny, and in the process major questions have been raised about every aspect of the New Testament. In the process, the reality of eyewitness testimony has been radically questioned and several Pauline epistles and 2 Peter regarded as pseudonymous. Clearly, if these views are correct, then they have serious implications for the early church's approach to canonicity.

In a single chapter it is not possible even to begin to examine the vagaries of New Testament scholarship over the past 150 years.[80] Suffice it to recognize some of the rigorous work that has recently emerged supporting the centrality of eyewitness testimony in the New Testament. Probably the most significant work in this area is Bauckham's *Jesus and the Eyewitnesses*. He argues that the Gospels

> embody the testimony of the eyewitnesses, not of course without editing and interpretation, but in a way that is substantially faithful to how the eyewitnesses

---

77. Tertullian cites the Writings as well, so clearly for him the Law and the Prophets includes them.
78. Ibid., chap. 36.
79. Greenslade, *Early Latin Theology*, 67.
80. See esp. S. Neill and N. T. Wright, *The Interpretation of the New Testament, 1861–1986* (Oxford: Oxford University Press, 1988).

themselves told it, since the Evangelists were in more or less direct contact with eyewitnesses, not removed from them by a long process of anonymous transmission of the traditions. In the case of one of the Gospels, that of John, I conclude, very unfashionably, that an eyewitness wrote it.[81]

Bauckham revisits Papias's *Fragments*[82] and makes the important point that while Papias wrote his sadly no-longer-extant five-volume *Expositions of the Sayings of the Lord* (perhaps) early in the second century, he speaks about an *earlier* time in his life, precisely that period during which the Gospels of Matthew, Luke, and John were most likely being written.[83] Papias's expressed preference for "a living and surviving voice" over "information from books" has often been misunderstood; Papias is using a proverb to assert that what is preferable to books is not oral tradition but access to those who were active participants in the events and still alive.[84]

Bauckham examines both the internal and external evidence for eyewitness testimony being embodied in the Gospels. His study of the personal names (onomastics) in the Gospels supports the view that many of these names demonstrate the eyewitness source of the stories in which they are found.[85]

Bauckham also draws attention to the fact that there is a stress in the Gospels on eyewitnesses who were present for *the whole* of Jesus's public ministry. In Acts 1:21–26 a requirement of the replacement for Judas is that he be "one of the men who accompanied us during all the time that the Lord Jesus went in and out among us, beginning from the baptism of John until the day when he was taken up from us." Only such a person can be a "witness with us to his resurrection." Intriguingly, two men are nominated, but only Matthias chosen, indicating the presence of more than the apostles who witnessed the breadth of Jesus's ministry from John's baptizing to the ascension. In the summary of Peter's sermon in Acts 10:36–42, we again find the emphasis on the message of the gospel *beginning* in Galilee after the baptizing activity of John. In John 15:26–27, a passage about the Spirit who will witness concerning Jesus, the disciples are told that "You also are to testify because you have been with me *from the beginning*." Similarly Luke 1:2 notes that his account is taken from those who "*from the beginning* were eyewitnesses."[86] All this

---

81. Bauckham, *Jesus and the Eyewitnesses*, 6.
82. See M. W. Holmes, ed., *The Apostolic Fathers in English*, 3rd ed. (Grand Rapids: Baker Academic, 2006), 556–95.
83. Bauckham, *Jesus and the Eyewitnesses*, 14.
84. Ibid., 21–30.
85. Ibid., 67–84.
86. Ibid., 121–22, arguing that the beginning Luke refers to is not the events of Luke 1–2 but the ministry of John the Baptist.

indicates that there was a real concern not only for eyewitness testimony but also for eyewitness testimony that covered the whole of Jesus's public ministry.

Papias reports, "And the Elder used to say this: 'Mark, having become Peter's interpreter, wrote down accurately everything he remembered, though not in order, of the things either said or done by Christ.'"[87] The evidence for Petrine testimony underlying Mark's Gospel is well documented, but Bauckham also foregrounds a Petrine inclusio in Mark presumably to indicate Peter as the main eyewitness underlying the Gospel (Mark 1:16–18; 16:7).[88] Through use of the inclusio of eyewitness testimony, Mark tells the story of Jesus predominantly although not exclusively from Peter's perspective. Bauckham identifies multiple literary techniques used by Mark to present Peter's perspective or witness.[89]

A remarkable aspect of Bauckham's work is his defense of the Gospel of John as written by an eyewitness of Jesus, taking seriously the testimony of Papias[90] and of John 21:24–25.[91] Bauckham's conclusion is that John was written by an eyewitness, but by John the elder, not John the son of Zebedee.[92] Bauckham argues that "John's Gospel thus uses the *inclusio* of eyewitness testimony in order to privilege the witness of the Beloved Disciple, which this Gospel embodies. It does so, however, not simply by ignoring the Petrine *inclusio* of Mark's Gospel, but by enclosing a Petrine *inclusio* within its *inclusio* of the Beloved Disciple."[93] Bauckham identifies Andrew's companion in John 1:35–42 as the Beloved Disciple, who appears before Peter (cf. John 1:40–42). In 1:38 Jesus turns and sees them *following*, and in 21:20 Peter turns and sees the Beloved Disciple *following*. Andrew and the Beloved Disciple *remained* with Jesus (1:39), and in 21:22 the Beloved Disciple is the one who will *remain*. All of this suggests that the author of John and his readers knew Mark's Gospel. "But, the Fourth Gospel implies, Peter has not said the last word about Jesus or the most perceptive word."[94]

A further element in apostolicity and antiquity in relation to the Gospels lies in the reconsideration of the common assumption that they were written for particular communities—the Johannine, Matthean, and so forth—and that discernment of this community and its beliefs is vital in interpreting the Gospels. This is connected with the process of tradition we envisage between

---

87. "Fragments of Papias," in Holmes, ed., *Apostolic Fathers in English* (2006), 308–19, sections 3, 15. See Bauckham, *Jesus and the Eyewitnesses*, 202–39.
88. Bauckham, *Jesus and the Eyewitnesses*, 124–27.
89. Ibid., 155–81.
90. Ibid., 412–37; on the testimony of Polysocrates and Irenaeus, see 438–71.
91. Ibid., 358–83.
92. For a list of works that defend John the son of Zebedee as the author, see ibid., 413n2.
93. Ibid., 129.
94. Ibid.

the Christ event and the writing of the Gospels. Bauckham rightly distinguishes between historical tradition and anonymous oral tradition; in a recent volume he and several others have successfully debunked the uncritical assumption that the Gospels were written for individual communities. Doubtless the authors were parts of one or several such communities, but it is far more likely that they reduced their testimony to writing for the sake of the larger church; thus the Gospels were written *for all Christians*.[95]

Bauckham follows Samuel S. Byrskog[96] in arguing that the Gospels share with ancient historians a preference for involved *testimony*; they preferred the eyewitnesses who were socially involved or had been actively involved in the events reported. In terms of the type of committed testimony we find in the Gospels, Bauckham compares it to the testimony of Holocaust victims. In comparison to the horror of the testimony of Holocaust victims, "it is wonder that would be lost were we deprived of the Gospel testimonies that evoke the theophanic character of the history of Jesus."[97]

> Reading the Gospels as eyewitness testimony differs therefore from attempts at historical reconstruction behind the texts. It takes the Gospels seriously as they are; it acknowledges the uniqueness of what we can know only in testimonial form. It honors the form of historiography they are. From a historiographic perspective, radical suspicion of testimony is a kind of epistemological suicide.[98]

All of this is to say that the early church's insistence of apostolicity as a criterion is far from obsolete today.[99] There remains the question of the rest of the New Testament. Here the importance of Acts must not be underestimated. Paul's Letters were authoritative because of his recognition as an apostle to the gentiles. The bringing together of the Pauline and General Epistles into one book was facilitated by Acts. As Bruce notes, "Acts had thereafter to play a part of its own, and an important part it proved to be. 'A canon which comprised only the four Gospels and the Pauline Epistles,' said Harnack, 'would have been at best an edifice of two wings without the central

---

95. R. Bauckham, ed., *The Gospels for All Christians: Rethinking the Gospel Audiences* (Grand Rapids: Eerdmans, 1997). All the contributions to this important volume repay a close reading.

96. S. S. Byrskog, *Story as History—History as Story: The Gospel Tradition in the Context of Ancient Oral History* (Tübingen: Mohr Siebeck, 2000).

97. Bauckham, *Jesus and the Eyewitnesses*, 500; cf. N. T. Wright, *NTPG*; C. S. Evans, *The Historical Christ and the Jesus of Faith: The Incarnational Narrative as History* (Oxford: Oxford University Press, 1996).

98. Bauckham, *Jesus and the Eyewitnesses*, 506.

99. Contra F. Watson, *Gospel Writing: A Canonical Perspective* (Grand Rapids: Eerdmans, 2013).

structure, and therefore incomplete and uninhabitable.'"[100] Acts forms part 2 of Luke's Gospel and shares its commitment to eyewitness testimony, part of which would have come from Luke himself, as the "we" passages indicate (Acts 16:10–17; 20:5–15; 21:1–18; 27:1–28).

Questions remain about some of Paul's Letters and some of the General Epistles. Historical-critical questions about the authenticity of some of the letters have raised the issue of *pseudonymity*, and we noted (above) McDonald's questions on this question. If some of the letters were pseudonymous, such as the Pastorals and 2 Peter, for example, and the early church mistook them for authentic, how should we regard them if we continue to take apostolicity as a criterion?

This is an important question but hardly a crucial one. The status of pseudonymity and pseudonymous literature in the ancient world is contested, and the early church applied other criteria such as *catholicity* when it came to books like Hebrews and 2 Peter, about which they had some questions. However, the seriousness with which the early church took apostolicity makes it highly unlikely that pseudonymity would not have been an issue for it.[101] Indeed there are, as Ellis points out, recorded cases of documents being rejected by church leaders once it was discovered that they were pseudonymous. As Ellis explains, "While certain ancient writings were composed—as school exercises and otherwise—in the name of an ancient master with no intention to deceive, apostolic pseudepigrapha are not analogous to them. For they were produced in a community where the apostles' teaching had a unique 'Word of God' authority and where its content and even the identity of true apostles were subject to continuing dispute."[102]

The Old Testament, the Septuagint, and the Apocrypha

It is one thing to conclude that the Old Testament canon was closed well before the time of Jesus and the apostles; it is another to decide on the status of the Apocrypha. The Septuagint (LXX) included the apocryphal books, and because the early church largely adopted the Old Greek translation, many of them also tended to regard the Apocrypha as canonical. This was the subject of debate between Augustine and Jerome.[103] Augustine asserts, "The Greek

---

100. Bruce, *Canon of Scripture*, 133.
101. See E. E. Ellis, *History and Interpretation in New Testament Perspective* (Leiden: Brill, 2001), 17–29.
102. Ibid., 28. On the Pastorals, see ibid., 65–83.
103. For their correspondence on this issue, see J. W. Trigg, *Biblical Interpretation* (Wilmington, DE: M. Glazier, 1988), 250–95.

Septuagint is certainly definitive, seeing how it has been used so widely and was the version used by the Apostles."[104] For Augustine, we should see this translation as "definitively authoritative."[105]

The point of contention between Augustine and Jerome was twofold: first, Jerome resorted to the Hebrew text for his translation of the Old Testament into Latin, and Augustine found this disturbing because it could undermine the faith of the believers by raising questions about the LXX. Second, Jerome followed Jewish tradition in regarding the Hebrew Old Testament as authoritative, thus excluding the apocryphal books, which he regarded as edificatory but not inspired.

As is well known, the Reformers followed Jerome on this, and the Roman Catholics followed Augustine. It is unlikely that we will solve this issue in this volume! In favor of the Reformed position, we reason that if Jesus and the apostles regarded the Apocrypha as inspired it is remarkable, as Seitz has noted, that the New Testament "rarely—probably never—quotes from a so-called apocryphal book as if this were on par with other Greek language versions of the more restricted Hebrew canon."[106] Jude 9 probably comes from the *Testament of Moses*,[107] which is no longer extant and not part of the Apocrypha. Furthermore, even Augustine clearly acknowledges that the LXX is a translation of the Hebrew; he just happens to think it is the definitive one!

Suffice it here to state that what could go a long way toward healthy ecumenicity is the inclusion of the apocryphal books in Protestant Bibles, albeit clearly designated as for edification and not on par with the inspired books. If this seems radical, it should be remembered that Luther's Bible did this, and so did the initial version of the King James Bible.

Textual Criticism and the Disappearing Text

In this chapter we have argued the case for maintaining the biblical canon as we have it, bearing in mind the difference—but *substantial* overlap—between Protestant, Catholic, and (Eastern, Syrian, Ethiopian) Orthodox lists. A new challenge that has recently emerged is provided by textual criticism. Just how radical this challenge has become is well represented by Weitzman's introductory comments to his book on Solomon:

104. Ibid., 272.
105. Ibid., 259.
106. C. R. Seitz, "The Canonical Approach and Theological Interpretation," in Bartholomew et al., *Canon and Biblical Interpretation*, 58–110, 93, esp. 90–95.
107. See R. Bauckham, *Jude, 2 Peter*, WBC 50 (Waco: Word, 1983), 65–76.

One of the goals of secular biblical scholarship, a project known as text-criticism, is to try to construct from these different versions the content of the original biblical text before it was altered by changes introduced over the course of its transmission. The goal has proven elusive, however, and what text-critics have found instead is that there is no such thing as an original biblical text. It is fluid as far back as we can trace it.[108]

Clearly, if this is the case, it presents an enormous challenge to any notion of biblical authority, vested as it is in a stable canon. As Beckwith rightly declares, "With no canon there is no Bible. . . . With no *text* there is no Bible."[109] On this issue readers are referred to our discussion of textual criticism in chapter 6.

Conclusion

The limits of the canon and its authority can never be proved. What we have demonstrated in this chapter, however, is that there are good reasons for resisting the radical approaches to canon being promoted nowadays. The theological dimension of this debate is *unavoidable*, and in our case everything hinges ultimately on what we make of Jesus and his authority—as reflected in the quotes at the outset of this chapter. Taking Sinai and the Christ event seriously reorients one's view of canon from an obsession with the terminus ad quem to a reverse focus on the terminus a quo, the originating events. This does not in any way remove the untidy historical data related to the "closing" of the canon but points toward a—sometimes messy—discernment of what is authoritative rather than a granting of canonical authority. The New Testament canon was formally closed in the fourth and fifth centuries AD but, as we have seen, the core of the New Testament was seen as authoritative remarkably early, and with time it remained for the early church to work out which books were genuinely apostolic and catholic.

We are now in a position to return to McDonald's questions referred to above and to answer those left unanswered. Regarding his first question, yes, the church is correct in seeing the need for a closed canon of Scripture, and the notion of a biblical canon is profoundly Christian. Regarding his fourth question, we have argued that the Old Testament canon was closed well before the time of Jesus, and the church should similarly be committed to a closed Old Testament canon. Regarding his fifth question, we should continue to uphold apostolicity, with catholicity, as a criterion for the New Testament,

---

108. S. Weitzman, *Solomon: The Lure of Wisdom* (New Haven: Yale University Press, 2011), xv.
109. Beckwith, *Old Testament Canon*, 5.

and we should maintain 2 Peter and the Pastorals in the canon. Regarding his sixth question, we should indeed bind the modern church to a canon that emerged out of the historical circumstances of the first century (and the second?), even though it was only closed in the fourth to fifth centuries.

Thus far in this chapter we have not invoked the Spirit but have rather sought to articulate the logic and historicity of the development of the canon. Christians, however, rightly connect the work of the Spirit with the emergence of the canon amid the vagaries of history, as does Paul in 2 Timothy (3:16–17). As Ridderbos declares, "The Spirit of God is the teacher and guide of the apostles. But his work is not to be understood apart from the witness of the apostles. He takes care of their witness. And that is why his witness becomes their witness."[110]

---

110. Ridderbos, *When the Time Had Fully Come*, 85.

PART 4

Biblical Interpretation and the Academic Disciplines

9

Philosophy and Hermeneutics

Speak, that I may see you!—This wish was fulfilled by creation, which is a speech to creatures through creatures; for day unto day utters speech, and night unto night shows knowledge. Its watchword traverses every clime to the end of the world, and its voice can be heard in every dialect.

Johann Georg Hamann[1]

All the colors of this most beautiful world grow pale once you extinguish its light, the firstborn of creation.

Johann Georg Hamann[2]

The historical critique of Scripture that emerges fully in the eighteenth century has its dogmatic base, as our brief look at Spinoza has shown, in the Enlightenment's faith in reason.

H.-G. Gadamer[3]

---

1. J. G. Hamann, *Writings on Philosophy and Language*, trans. and ed. K. Haynes (Cambridge: Cambridge University Press, 2007), 65.
2. Ibid., 78.
3. H.-G. Gadamer, *Truth and Method,* 2nd ed. (London: Sheed and Ward, 1989), 182.

Enlightenment critique is primarily directed against the religious tradition of Christianity—i.e., the Bible. . . . This is the real radicality of the modern Enlightenment compared to all other movements of enlightenment: it must assert itself against the Bible and dogmatic interpretations of it.

H.-G. Gadamer[4]

Introduction

Philosophical hermeneutics is a twentieth-century development. Hans-Georg Gadamer (1900–2002), whose life straddled the twentieth century, is the major figure in modern philosophical hermeneutics. In 1960 at the age of sixty, he published his magnum opus *Truth and Method*, *the* central text in hermeneutical theory. When Gadamer published *Truth and Method*, "hermeneutics" was little known. Gadamer's original title for the book was *Foundations of a Philosophical Hermeneutic*, but when presented with the manuscript, his publisher responded, "Hermeneutics . . . what on earth is that?"[5] And so, at the advice of his publisher, the obscure word was demoted to the subtitle.

So influential have Gadamer and his successors been that nowadays hermeneutics is common coin, not least in biblical studies. No one has done more than Anthony Thiselton to promote the awareness and relevance of hermeneutics in biblical studies,[6] and yet the value of philosophical hermeneutics for biblical studies remains controversial, not least among proponents of theological interpretation. The suspicion of general hermeneutics relates back, at least partially, to Karl Barth's suspicion of philosophy. Theological interpretation, it is argued, should be forged from theological concepts and has no major need of philosophy. With this view goes the argument that biblical studies requires a *regional* theological hermeneutic and not a general one. A host of issues enter into the discussion at this point. Suffice it here to recognize that, like it or not, philosophy does have a major influence on biblical interpretation, as argued in detail in this volume and elsewhere.

Take *philosophy of language*, for example. Every exegete is constantly at work with words and their meanings, with Hebrew and Aramaic and Greek,

---

4. Ibid., 272.
5. J. Grondin, *Hans-Georg Gadamer: A Biography* (New Haven: Yale University Press, 2003), 5.
6. See A. C. Thiselton, *The Two Horizons: New Testament Hermeneutics and Philosophical Description with Special Reference to Heidegger, Bultmann, Gadamer, and Wittgenstein* (Grand Rapids: Eerdmans, 1980); idem, *New Horizons in Hermeneutics* (Grand Rapids: Zondervan, 1992); idem, *The Hermeneutics of Doctrine* (Grand Rapids: Eerdmans, 2007); idem, *Thiselton on Hermeneutics: Collected Works and New Essays* (Grand Rapids: Eerdmans, 2006); etc.

and with translation. Philosophy of language shapes all these endeavors, from the nature of a dictionary/lexicon,[7] to the views of language shaping translation and current modes of interpretation, not least those of postmodernism.

James Barr's critique of biblical scholars' understanding of words rests on Ferdinand de Saussure's work and that of modern linguistics.[8] Thiselton, Francis Watson, Vanhoozer, and Wolterstorff have all in different ways drawn on speech-act theory to forge creative ways forward for biblical interpretation. A view of language is *always* at work in biblical interpretation, and *a* contribution of philosophy of language is to make that conscious so that we can see what is at stake in particular readings and the options available. Nowhere is this clearer than in the postmodern readings that have proliferated in biblical studies over the past thirty years. Philosophy of language is utterly central to postmodernism; unless we have a good grasp of the views of language being brought to bear on Scripture, we will be disadvantaged in our evaluations of such readings.

As a branch of philosophy, hermeneutics is concerned with understanding, and not least with the understanding of texts. As we saw in our chapters on the history of biblical interpretation, there is a discussion of biblical hermeneutics that much precedes the twentieth century. Prior to the twentieth century, however, hermeneutics was understood as rules for biblical interpretation.[9] In response to (inter alia) modern scientism and the disasters it unleashed on the twentieth century, *philosophical* hermeneutics arose with a focus on understanding across the disciplines, even as it resisted and questioned the universality of "scientific" explanation; biblical hermeneutics has become a subdiscipline of this larger enterprise. Thus, intriguingly from our perspective, hermeneutics has moved from

rules for biblical interpretation
→ a hermeneutics of understanding
→ biblical hermeneutics.

7. Dictionaries are by no means so straightforward as they seem. See, e.g., W. J. Ong, "The Word in Chains," in *In the Human Grain: Further Explorations in Contemporary Culture*, ed. W. J. Ong (New York: MacMillan, 1967), 52–59. F. Schleiermacher (*The Hermeneutics Reader: Texts of the German Tradition from the Enlightenment to the Present*, ed. K. Mueller-Vollmer [New York: Continuum, 1988], 88–90) already recognizes this; e.g., he states: "The various instances cited in the dictionary should be regarded merely as a reasonable selection. . . . But a word is never isolated, even when it occurs by itself, for its determination is not derived from itself, but from its context" (89).

8. J. Barr, *The Semantics of Biblical Language* (London: SCM, 1982; reprint, Eugene, OR: Wipf & Stock, 2004); idem, *Biblical Words for Time*, 2nd ed. (London: SCM, 1969).

9. On the etymology and history of "hermeneutics" and its cognates, see G. Ebeling, "Hermeneutik," in *Religion in Geschichte und Gegenwart: Handwörterbuch für Theologie und Religionswissenschaft*, ed. H. D. Betz et al., 4th ed. (Tübingen: Mohr Siebeck, 2008), 243–62.

The central insight of hermeneutics for textual interpretation is that the text being interpreted is as much embedded in history *as is* the reader/s. In my classroom experience, I find that students still struggle to grasp this insight. If you ask them what the challenges are of interpreting an ancient text, generally all the problems identified lie with *the text*, embedded in ancient history as it is. Generally they fail to identify the fact that the interpreter/s is/are as embedded in history as the text! And yet this is an inescapable fact, which feminism, postmodernism, sociocritical approaches, and many other methods of interpretation available nowadays have drawn to our attention again and again.

This insight enables one to see how compelling the postmodern relativism of interpretation is if one holds to a historicist view of history. But it also indicates that biblical scholars cannot and should not ignore philosophical hermeneutics. Amid its dangers lie pearls of insight for interpretation, as we will demonstrate below.

Modern Hermeneutical Theory

Introduction

There are three major periods in the history of Western hermeneutics:[10] (1) classical Greek literary theory and philosophy; (2) Jewish and Christian theories of biblical interpretation; and (3) theories of modernity. *Post*modernity might suggest a further period, but these developments are better seen as part of (late) modernity.

Greek philosophy is the major source from which Western philosophy is derived, as the Greek revival in the Renaissance and Enlightenment demonstrates. Regarding textual hermeneutics, the Greek contribution arose from the need, in ancient Greek society, to determine the meaning of literary texts, especially of Homer. Indeed, as Jeanrond points out, "Homeric criticism may be called the cradle of literary theory: it offered a scope, a terminology and a methodology for all future literary criticism in the West."[11] In this context two distinct methods of reading developed, allegorical interpretation[12] and

---

10. W. G. Jeanrond, *Theological Hermeneutics: Development and Significance* (London: SCM, 1994), 13.
11. Ibid., 13–14.
12. Allegorical interpretation became dominant among Stoics in order to yield a philosophically acceptable meaning for the myths of Greek popular religion. Philo of Alexandria popularized the same method in interpretation of the OT for similar reasons. See J. Grondin, *Introduction to Philosophical Hermeneutics* (New Haven: Yale University Press, 1995), 23–32.

grammatical interpretation, both of which played a dominant role in early Christian interpretation.[13] Christian interpretation took place within a theistic, communal perspective with a trust in the contextual framework of tradition.[14] This trust hardened into a rigid control in the Middle Ages,[15] but before this in interpretation there was a careful balance between tradition and Scripture.[16]

Mueller-Vollmer discerns four streams that flow together into modern hermeneutics.[17] They are (1) the hermeneutics of the Reformers, (2) the resurgence of interest in Greek and Roman classical texts and the resultant philological developments, (3) the development of a special hermeneutics of jurisprudence resulting from renewed interest in Roman law, and finally (4) the influence of Enlightenment philosophy.

The Reformers' advocacy of the perspicuity and self-sufficiency of Scripture necessitated close attention to methods of interpretation to support these claims. As noted in chapter 7, the most important Protestant theorist in this area was Matthias Flacius Illyricus, with his *Clavis scripturae sacrae* (1567).[18] During the Renaissance there was a revival of interest in philology, and philological criticism was an important source of subsequent theories of interpretation. Starting in the twelfth century in Italy, there was a renewal of interest in Roman law involving, inter alia, the attempt to elucidate the Code of Justinian (AD 533). Constantius Rogerius (1463) introduced a fourfold distinction of forms of legal exegesis, a distinction that remained influential into the nineteenth century. The German jurist Johannes von Felde (1689) sought to determine principles of interpretation that would be valid for all classes of texts, literary and legal. With the desire of Enlightenment philosophers to establish all knowledge on a systematic and scientific base, hermeneutics became a province of philosophy, seen as part of logic. In this way *general hermeneutics* came into being, and although the major twentieth-century philosophers of hermeneutics

---

13. For an overview of Jewish hermeneutics see Jeanrond, *Theological Hermeneutics*, 15–17; and R. Loewe, "Jewish Exegesis," in *A Dictionary of Biblical Interpretation*, ed. R. J. Coggins and J. C. Houlden (London: SCM, 1990), 346–54.

14. See Thiselton, *New Horizons in Hermeneutics*, 145–73, for discussion of the nature of tradition in premodern Christian interpretation. This communal emphasis of premodern Christian interpretation has a parallel in postmodern trends, as Thiselton points out, in contrast to the individualism of modernity. A difference is that premodern Christians generally respected and trusted their corporate values and beliefs, but postmodern thinkers often think these corporate values need to be unmasked.

15. Jeanrond, *Theological Hermeneutics*, 26.

16. Jeanrond argues that Augustine's hermeneutic is a model of such balance (ibid., 22–26). See Grondin, *Philosophical Hermeneutics*, 32–39, on the contemporary importance of Augustine's hermeneutics. Heidegger and Gadamer revert to Augustine.

17. Mueller-Vollmer, *Hermeneutics Reader*, 1–5.

18. See our discussion of this in chap. 7 (above).

would construe the discipline very differently, they still tended to follow their eighteenth-century forebears in seeing hermeneutics as part of philosophy.

The latter move was particularly significant since it was only as philosophers focused on hermeneutical problems that general hermeneutics emerged as a discipline in its own right. Certainly for biblical hermeneutics the philosophical paradigm shift that modernity entailed was fraught with significance since it effectively called into question the role of Christian tradition in interpretation, as is particularly clear in the hermeneutics of Spinoza and Kant, in which human autonomy is central.

In the seventeenth century an initial universal hermeneutics was developed by Dannhauer, Meier, and Chladenius along rationalist lines.[19] However, Kant's critique of reason "dissolved the rationalism to which Dannhauer, Spinoza, Chladenius, and Meier owed their allegiance"; in Kant's "distinction between phenomena and things in themselves lies one of the secret roots of Romanticism and the emergence of hermeneutics."[20] The Romantic hermeneutics of Schleiermacher made room for religion, but very much within the emerging paradigm of modernity and still in an ahistorical way. Droysen and Dilthey were key thinkers in setting in motion a focus on the historical dimension of hermeneutics,[21] which is developed by Heidegger and brought to fruition by Gadamer, who in the process has thoroughly resurrected the notion of tradition and prejudice in hermeneutics. And Gadamer is *the* central figure of philosophical hermeneutics in the twentieth century.

We cannot review this history in detail and shall confine ourselves to examining the crucial Enlightenment figures of Spinoza and Kant, with particular reference to the role they assign religion epistemologically. We will then move on via Hamann, Herder, Kierkegaard, Schleiermacher, and Heidegger to Gadamer and the main reactions to his hermeneutics.

Spinoza (1632-77)

In contemporary texts on biblical hermeneutics, little attention is given to Spinoza.[22] Christopher Norris, by contrast, insists that Spinoza is of major

---

19. See Grondin, *Philosophical Hermeneutics*, 45-62. Note that Johann Conrad Dannhauer preceded Schleiermacher in universalizing hermeneutics.
20. Ibid., 64.
21. See ibid., 76-90.
22. In his two volumes *The Two Horizons* and *New Horizons in Hermeneutics*, Thiselton has only six references to Spinoza. Jeanrond, *Theological Hermeneutics*, has one brief reference. Most remarkably, H. Graf Reventlow (*The Authority of the Bible and the Rise of the Modern World* [London: SCM, 1984]) has no reference to Spinoza whatsoever in his nearly 700 pages on the authority of the Bible and the rise of the modern world! However, he does discuss Spinoza

significance not just for scriptural interpretation but also because he anticipates and gives a helpful perspective on many of the issues that concern literary theorists today.[23] Spinoza's Jewish background and his conflict with his Jewish coreligionists and Dutch Calvinism ensured that he gave sustained attention to religion and the interpretation of Scripture, and particularly the Old Testament. This combination makes him particularly interesting with respect to philosophy and Old Testament hermeneutics.

According to Spinoza, the world is understandable by reason, and falsity is the result of privation of knowledge resulting from inadequate ideas. Adequate ideas are universal ideas that are logically connected with other ideas. The key to successful human life, according to Spinoza, is the development of adequate ideas. Democratic society, which protects freedom of inquiry, is the best political context for such ideas to develop, and Spinoza is concerned to undermine anything that subverts adequate ideas and tolerance. Thus it is not surprising that his detailed consideration of Scripture and its proper interpretation occurs in his *Tractatus Theologico-politicus*. Spinoza was well aware that concepts of reason, religion, and scriptural interpretation have immense implications for society.

Spinoza's scriptural hermeneutic is shaped by his philosophy, although he does insist that "the Bible must not be accommodated to reason, nor reason to the Bible."[24] He rightly makes the point that a high view of Scripture should result in a method of interpretation that ensures it is Scripture that is heard and not just our prejudices and traditions. For Spinoza, this is particularly important since Scripture often contains what cannot be known to reason, but only by revelation. Spinoza aims to read Scripture in a fresh and impartial

---

in *History of Biblical Interpretation*, vol. 4, *From the Enlightenment to the Twentieth Century* (Atlanta: SBL, 2009–10). R. M. Grant with D. Tracy, *A Short History of the Interpretation of the Bible*, 2nd ed. (Eugene, OR: Wipf & Stock, 2001), devotes four pages to Spinoza and states, "Spinoza's method is very much like that followed in modern introductions to the Bible. It is clear and rational. It avoids all the theological questions involved in the interpretation of scripture; for scripture has no authority over the interpreter's mind" (108). An important exception is the useful chapter on Spinoza in R. A. Harrisville and W. Sundberg, *The Bible in Modern Culture: Theology and Historical-Critical Method from Spinoza to Käsemann* (Grand Rapids: Eerdmans, 1995), 32–48. See also L. Strauss, *The Early Writings (1921–1932)*, trans. and ed. Michael Zank (Albany: State University of New York Press, 2002), 139–200; idem, *Jewish Philosophy and the Crisis of Modernity: Essays and Lectures in Modern Jewish Thought* (Albany: State University of New York Press, 1997), 181–233.

23. C. Norris, in his remarkably interesting *Spinoza and the Origins of Modern Critical Theory* (The Bucknell Lectures in Literary Theory [Oxford: Blackwell, 1991]), shows how Spinoza continues to influence current debates in literary theory; he helps us to gain a perspective on the postmodern turn.

24. B. de Spinoza, *A Theologico-political Treatise and a Political Treatise* (Mineola, NY: Dover, 2004), 195.

manner and argues for a literal reading by means of natural reason. A major element of such an approach is the historical dimension of scriptural texts: "The universal rule, then, in interpreting Scripture is to accept nothing as an authoritative Scriptural statement which we do not perceive very clearly when we examine it in the light of its history."[25] Spinoza eschews the sort of allegorization undertaken by Maimonides, which seeks through subtle means to secure agreement between Scripture and reason. Meaning and truth must be clearly distinguished,[26] and scriptural meaning must be judged by reason.

There is a tension here since while on the one hand Spinoza acknowledges that Scripture regularly contains what can be known only by revelation, on the other hand he is opposed to submitting reason to Scripture. Much of this tension is defused by his distinguishing between the word of God and Scripture[27] and by his categorization of much of the Old Testament historical and prophetic material as imaginary and adjusted to the masses. Spinoza prefers the New Testament to the Old, since it contains more intelligible argument. Furthermore, Spinoza distinguishes between theology and philosophy by arguing that although Scripture contains a small core of ideas, "the sphere of theology is piety and obedience," whereas "the sphere of reason is . . . truth and wisdom."[28] "Philosophy has no end in view save truth: faith, as we have abundantly proved, looks for nothing but obedience and piety."[29] The practical limits of theology are made quite clear in Spinoza's statement that "theology tells us nothing else, enjoins on us no command save obedience, and has neither the will nor the power to oppose reason: she defines the dogmas of faith . . . only in so far as they may be necessary for obedience, and leaves reason to determine their precise truth: for reason is the light of the mind, and without her all things are dreams and phantoms."[30]

Although Spinoza maintains that "the Bible leaves reason absolutely free"[31] and argues that reason should not be submitted to Scripture or vice versa, in practice his philosophy determines the understanding of scriptural ideas, as his treatment of the Old Testament theme of election makes clear, for example. By "the help of God," Spinoza understands the fixed order of

---

25. Ibid., 101.
26. See C. Norris, *Spinoza and the Origins*, 194–202, for a critique of Kermode's appropriation of Spinoza as one who blurs the distinction between meaning and truth, thereby generating a plurality of meanings. See Harrisville and Sundberg, *Bible in Modern Culture*, 265–66, for the long-term influence of this distinction on historical criticism.
27. Spinoza, *Theologico-political Treatise*, 169–70.
28. Ibid., 194.
29. Ibid., 189.
30. Ibid., 194, 195.
31. Ibid., 9.

nature; since no one can do anything except by this order, "it follows that no one can choose a plan of life for himself, or accomplish any work save by God's vocation choosing him for the work or the plan of life in question, rather than any other."[32]

Spinoza's hermeneutic is an important early opponent of the orthodox model, which subjugated critical reason to religious or doctrinal truth. In practice, he reverses this relationship, making the meaning of Scripture accountable to the bar of critical reason. Although a rationalist, Spinoza's historical emphasis anticipates many elements of the historical-critical method of biblical interpretation that would develop in nineteenth-century Germany.[33] Already at the end of the seventeenth century, Spinoza is stressing the need to reevaluate traditional authors of biblical books and their contexts of origin. For example, he rejects Mosaic authorship of the Pentateuch and argues that Ezra is the author of the larger narrative of the history of the Jews, from their beginning down to the destruction of Jerusalem.[34] And he insists that these types of historical questions are crucial for a correct understanding of the Old Testament. Finally, it is refreshing to notice Spinoza's keen awareness that a critical issue in the debate over the interpretation of Scripture is that of the relationship between faith and reason, theology and philosophy. It is rare to find biblical scholars addressing this issue nowadays, but it is a foundational issue that shapes the direction any biblical hermeneutic takes.

Kant

A. W. Wood has declared: "No thinker ever placed greater emphasis on reason's boundaries than Kant; at the same time, none has ever been bolder in asserting its unqualified title to govern our lives."[35]

The issue of the relationship between faith and reason was central to German philosophy in the second half of the eighteenth century.[36] Enlightenment

---

32. Ibid., 45.
33. See J. S. Preus, "A Hidden Opponent in Spinoza's *Tractatus*," HTR 88, no. 3 (1995): 361–88, for a useful analysis of the difference between Ludwig (Lodewijk) Meyer's philosophical hermeneutic and Spinoza's historical one. Preus comments, "Spinoza's definitive substitution of history for philosophy as the categorical matrix for biblical interpretation makes the *Treatise* paradigmatic in the sense of an exemplary work that systematically formulates a new historical, critical, and comparative approach to the Bible" (367).
34. At an elementary level, Spinoza thus anticipates debates such as that over the Deuteronomistic history.
35. A. W. Wood, "Rational Theology, Moral Faith, and Religion," in *The Cambridge Companion to Kant*, ed. P. Guyer (Cambridge: Cambridge University Press, 1992), 414.
36. See the excellent work by F. C. Beiser, *The Fate of Reason: German Philosophy from Kant to Fichte* (Cambridge, MA: Harvard University Press, 1993).

rationalism received strong opposition from the Pietists, who saw rationalism as a threat to faith; in the 1740s and 1750s their opposition received new impetus through the writings of Crusius. The effect of this controversy was that the rationalists seemed to be faced with the dilemma of either a rational skepticism or an irrational fideism. The main task of Kant's philosophy in the 1750s was to provide a new foundation for metaphysics in the light of Crusius's criticisms; although Kant later became skeptical about the possibility of metaphysics, the question of the vindication of reason remained central to his mature philosophy. Kant sought to secure reason through a synthesis of the best insights of rationalism and empiricism.[37]

For Kant, the human mind is the ultimate source of meaning, and understanding; objective reality can be known only as it conforms to the structures of the knowing mind. In this way Kant acknowledges both the value and limitations of reason. The world can never be known as it is in itself, but only through the point of view by which it is perceived. "The world is as we think it, and we think it as it is."[38] Kant's Copernican revolution consisted in making our cognitive capacities primary over nature.

As the quote (above) from Wood indicates, if Kant stressed the limitations of reason, he also stressed its autonomy. In his view, rationalism is too ambitious, and he compares it to the builders of the tower of Babel.[39] However, the desire for autonomy that motivates the project is quite right; what is required is a more modest plan. We need to ask what can be built with the labor and materials available to us. O'Neill explains, "Kant represents attempts to ground practices of reason as a matter of proceeding with the 'materials' and 'labor power' that our daily practice of defective reasoning has made available to us, and rebuilding these in ways that reduce dangers of collapse or paralysis in thought or action."[40]

Kant proposes that we think of reason as a discipline that rejects external authorities, is reflexive in that it involves self-discipline, and is lawlike.[41] In terms of the relationship between reason and faith/religion, the character of reason as negative in the sense of rejecting external authorities is particularly significant. For Kant, autonomy is a fundamental characteristic of reason: "Reason is indeed the basis of enlightenment, but enlightenment is no more

---

37. R. Scruton, *Kant* (Oxford: Oxford University Press, 1982), 11–21, indicates that Leibniz (1646–1716) and Hume (1711–76) form the particular background to Kant's thought in his *Critique of Pure Reason*. Scruton (*Kant*, 38) maintains that one might call Kant's synthesis an attempt to give a fully enriched account of the objectivity of the physical world.
38. Scruton, *Kant*, 23.
39. O. O'Neill, "Vindicating Reason," in Guyer, *Companion to Kant*, 280–308, esp. 289–90.
40. Ibid., 291–92.
41. See ibid., 280–308, for a very useful discussion of Kant's mature view of reason.

than autonomy in thinking and acting—that is, of thought and action that are lawful yet assume no lawgiver."[42] Judgment is possible with phenomenal objects alone, and not the noumenal. The latter can be used only negatively in order to demarcate the limits of experience. This limitation arises from the fact that in a rational system, all attempts to embrace the noumenal world will ultimately fail since they always end in irresolvable contradictions or antinomies.

Religion is made subservient to morality in Kant's scheme, which defines religion as "the cognition of all duties as divine commands."[43] Kant was opposed to religious ceremonies and regarded creeds as an imposition on our inner freedom of thought. Morality leads to religion, and we can be justified practically in holding religious propositions, but religious beliefs are necessary only insofar as they support our sense of morality. Religious tutelage is strongly rejected by Kant; as Scruton puts it, "Kant's writings on religion exhibit one of the first attempts at the systematic demystification of theology."[44] Worship of God is translated into veneration of morality, and faith is turned into certainty of practical reason. "The object of esteem is not the Supreme Being, but the supreme attribute of rationality."[45] In this way Kant's philosophy epitomizes the move from providence to progress.[46]

Alvin Plantinga argues that Kant's understanding of reality represents turning a Christian perspective on its head, especially if taken to its logical conclusion in what Plantinga calls "creative anti-realism."[47] From a Christian perspective, God's knowledge is creative; from a Kantian perspective, our knowledge is creative. Plantinga suggests that it is an easy step from the view that we are responsible for the way the world is to the postmodern view that we do not all live in the same world. Thus Plantinga suggests that the creative antirealism of postmodernity has its roots in Kantian idealism and that this tendency is profoundly unchristian.[48]

42. Ibid., 299.
43. See A. W. Wood, "Rational Theology, Moral Faith," 406–8.
44. Scruton, *Kant*, 78.
45. Ibid.
46. For the description of modernity as a move from providence to progress, see D. Lyon, *Postmodernity*, Concepts in the Social Sciences (Buckingham, UK: Open University Press, 1994), 5.
47. A. Plantinga, "Christian Philosophy at the End of the 20th Century," in *Christian Philosophy at the Close of the Twentieth Century: Assessment and Perspective*, ed. S. Griffioen and B. M. Balk (Kampen, Netherlands: Kok, 1995), 30–37.
48. Compare this with the suggestion by C. Norris ("Criticism," in *Encyclopedia of Literature and Criticism*, ed. M. Coyle et al. [London: Routledge, 1990], 27–65) that postmodern indeterminacy has its roots in Christian readings of the Old Testament. For a Christian philosopher's analysis of Kant very different from that of Alvin Plantinga, see M. Westphal, "Christian Philosophers and the Copernican Revolution," *Christian Perspectives on Religious Knowledge*, ed. C. S. Evans and M. Westphal (Grand Rapids: Eerdmans, 1993), 161–79.

Kant's idealism does take account of human finitude, but his insistence on human autonomy makes it difficult to reconcile his account of reason with a Christian perspective. In the latter sense, he reinforces the essential Enlightenment belief in the authority of reason. The extent to which this is at odds with a view of Christianity as public truth is well captured by the title of Wolterstorff's *Reason within the Bounds of Religion*.[49] Gruenler is right that "the biblical interpreter who accepts the Kantian dichotomy will confine religious experience to the domain of personal, transcendental faith (which cannot be touched by historical criticism) and confine the historical-critical method to analysis of natural cause and effect without recourse to matters of faith or supernatural revelation."[50]

The subjective realm of the transcendental ego is reserved as the one area of freedom where God can be experienced, but only subjectively, so that "encounter with God will be confined to the subjective realm, while the Bible will be subjected to naturalistic criticism according to the rational canons of purely historical research."[51] Such a shift is evident in Kant's own readings of Scripture,[52] and it is amply supported by de Wette and other Old Testament theologians who were deeply indebted to Kant.[53]

Kant shares with Spinoza an emphasis on human autonomy, but his articulation of the limits of reason undermined the rationalist presupposition that the mind could penetrate the logical construction of the world. As Grondin points out, this problematizing of *rational* access to the world dissolved the rationalism of Dannhauer and Spinoza and opened the door to the subjectivism of Romanticism, in which, along Greek lines, the unity of the whole is discovered through "intuition."[54]

The Romantic Tradition

Romanticism emerged fully in the late eighteenth and early nineteenth centuries and has not ceased to be a powerful force in Western culture. It is a common

---

49. N. Wolterstorff, *Reason within the Bounds of Religion*, 2nd ed. (Grand Rapids: Eerdmans, 1999).

50. R. G. Gruenler, *Meaning and Understanding: The Philosophical Framework for Biblical Interpretation*, Foundations of Contemporary Interpretation 2 (Grand Rapids: Zondervan, 1991), 38.

51. Ibid., 40.

52. See, e.g., A. Edgar, "Kant's Two Interpretations of Genesis," *Literature and Theology* 6, no. 3 (1992): 280–90.

53. For the major influence of Kant on de Wette, the father of OT criticism, see J. Rogerson, *W. M. L. de Wette, Founder of Modern Biblical Criticism: An Intellectual Biography*, JSOTSup 126 (Sheffield: Sheffield Academic, 1992), 26–32.

54. Grondin, *Philosophical Hermeneutics*, 63–72.

emphasis in Romanticism that "it is through our feelings that we get to the deepest moral and, indeed, cosmic truths."[55] Herder offered a picture of nature like a great current of sympathy, running through all things: "See the whole of nature, behold the great analogy of creation. Everything feels itself and its like, life reverberates to life."[56] The human being is the creature who can become conscious of this and bring it to expression; hence Charles Taylor's categorization of the Romantic self as *the expressive self*. Romanticism is a reaction to the rationalism and idealism of the Enlightenment, but it is vital to realize that on these matters Romanticism remains largely within the *humanist vision*. It is a reaction within the contours of the Enlightenment vision rather than a move beyond it. While often opposed to institutional religion, Romanticism tended to be far more open to the divine, albeit increasingly in a pantheistic sense.[57]

Tarnas rightly states that the reaction of Romanticism led to a divided worldview in the West:

> Because both temperaments were deeply and simultaneously expressive of Western attitudes and yet were largely incompatible, a complex bifurcation of the Western outlook resulted. With the modern psyche affected by the Romantic sensibility and in some sense identified with it, yet with the truth claims of science so formidable, modern man experienced in effect an intractable division between his mind and his soul.[58]

The major philosophers of the Romantic tradition are not often attended to in relation to biblical hermeneutics. This is a mistake. As we will see below, in different ways they attended closely to religion and the Bible and have much to offer for hermeneutics today.

Johann Georg Hamann (1730–88)

According to Johann Georg Hamann, "All the colors of this most beautiful world grow pale once you extinguish its light, the firstborn of creation."[59] Although well known in Germany, where he was referred to as "the Wizard of the North," Hamann has until recently been widely ignored in the

---

55. C. Taylor, *Sources of the Self: The Making of the Modern Identity* (Cambridge: Cambridge University Press, 1989), 371.
56. Ibid., 369.
57. For a good introduction to early Romanticism, see F. C. Beiser, *The Romantic Imperative: The Concept of Early German Romanticism* (Cambridge, MA: Harvard University Press, 2003).
58. R. Tarnas, *The Passion of the Western Mind: Understanding the Ideas That Have Shaped Our World View* (New York: Ballentine, 1993), 375.
59. Hamann, *Writings on Philosophy and Language*, 78.

Anglo-American world. The great twentieth-century missiologist Hendrik Kraemer described Hamann as "probably the most profound Christian thinker of the eighteenth century,"[60] and yet, even in Christian circles, his work is hardly known. Hamann was a contemporary and acquaintance of Kant, and he was one of Kant's earliest critics and respondents. Kant and Hamann lived only a few miles apart in Königsberg. Hamann was part of the Enlightenment circle until his radical conversion while on diplomatic service in London. Between March and July after his conversion, he prepared his *London Writings*, which contain a commentary on the Bible.

Hamann initiated the highly influential *Sturm und Drang* (Storm and Stress) movement through his dialogue with Kant. When he returned to Germany from London, now converted, he eventually left the house of Berens, for which he had been working. However, Berens continued to make every attempt to reconvert Hamann to the view of the Enlightenment, enlisting Kant's help in the process! Hamann wrote a letter to Kant after their first meeting, which marks the start of the *Sturm und Drang* movement. It also, most probably, introduced Kant to Hume![61] In his correspondence, Hamann stresses faith as providing a special and indispensable kind of knowledge. Negatively, faith alerts us to the limits of reason: "Our own existence, and the existence of all things outside us, must be believed and cannot in any way be demonstrated." Hamann thus questioned the universal applicability of the principle of sufficient reason: "It would be *irrational* to universalize the principle of sufficient reason since this would be to ask for reasons in cases where none can be given. So if reason demands the right to criticize all our beliefs—to determine whether they have sufficient reasons—it transcends its proper limits and turns into its opposite, unreason."[62]

In 1762 Hamann published his *Aesthetica in nuce*, which became the Bible for the aesthetics of *Sturm und Drang* and for the epistemology of the Romantics. His stand against classicism and rationalism was revolutionary. The *Aesthetica* is a remarkable piece of work, not least for its pervasive use of Scripture. In it Hamann articulates a rich doctrine of creation as fundamental to reason and life: "The more vividly this idea of the image of the invisible GOD dwells in our heart, the more able we are to see and taste his lovingkindness in creatures, observe it and grasp it with our hands."[63]

Hamann helped to arrange a publisher for Kant's *Critique of Pure Reason*. In the process he obtained the proofs before it was published and wrote the

---

60. H. Kraemer, *The Christian Message in a Non-Christian World* (London: Edinburgh House, 1938), 117.
61. See M. Redmond, "The Hamann-Hume Connection," *Religious Studies* 23 (1987): 95–107.
62. Beiser, *Fate of Reason*, 28.
63. Hamann, *Writings on Philosophy and Language*, 79.

first critical review. According to Betz, it "remains to this day perhaps the most incisive critique of the *Critique*."[64] The result was Hamann's *Metacritique*, which can be seen as the starting point of post-Kantian philosophy. For Hamann, reason is not a faculty; it is particular and embodied in language. The insistence of the interwovenness of reason and language and the priority of faith enabled Hamann to question the universality of reason.

Hamann's writings are literary, notoriously dense and contextual, and thus hard reading. As Betz points out, his style is "above all a function of his self-understanding as a Christian author and, specifically, of his mimetic witness to the Word of God: the Johannine logos which 'shines in the darkness.'"[65] His style stems from his theology and his conversion, which alerted him to the real enlightenment that the "darkness" cannot grasp. His style enacts his belief that true enlightenment comes by way of Socratic ignorance, by humility, and by recognizing that the mysteries of faith lie beyond reason's grasp.[66] As he said in a late reflection on his authorship: "Not smoke from lightning, but from smoke to LIGHT."[67] Central to Hamann's philosophy are several views:

1. Reason is not autonomous but is governed by the subconscious. Reason is inseparable from language, and like language it is not universal but relative to a particular culture. As Beiser notes,

   > Although it is not as well known, Hamann's critique of reason was just as influential as Kant's. Its criticism of the purism of reason proved to be especially important for post-Kantian thought. Herder, Schlegel, and Hegel all accepted Hamann's advice to see reason in its embodiment, in its specific social and historical context. Indeed, the emphasis upon the social and historical dimension of reason, which is so important for post-Kantian thought, can trace its origins back to Hamann.[68]

2. The "naturalism" of modern science is unsustainable in its attempts to explain everything by mechanical laws without reference to God. Hamann disputes the distinction between natural and supernatural, which is at the heart of modern science's attempt to free itself from theology and metaphysics.

---

64. J. R. Betz, "Reading 'Sibylline Leaves': J. G. Hamann in the History of Ideas," *Journal of the History of Ideas* 70, no. 1 (2009): 103; see idem, "Enlightenment Revisited: Hamann as the First and Best Critic of Kant's Philosophy," *Modern Theology* 20 (2004): 291–301; idem, *After Enlightenment: The Post-secular Vision of J. G. Hamann* (Oxford: Blackwell, 2009), 230–57.

65. Betz, "Reading 'Sibylline Leaves,'" 101.

66. Fortunately more of Hamann's writings are now available in English, most recently in Cambridge Texts in the History of Philosophy.

67. Quoted and translated by Betz, "Reading 'Sibylline Leaves,'" 101.

68. Beiser, *Fate of Reason*, 18.

3. The Enlightenment's faith in human autonomy is irrational. "Nature and history are the two great commentaries on the divine word."[69]
4. Self-consciousness is decidedly not self-illuminating. We have no privileged access to ourselves.
5. Reason is not the sovereign royal road to truth: "It is the greatest contradiction and misuse of our reason if it wants to reveal. A philosopher who, to please his reason, puts the divine word out of vision is like those Jews who more stubbornly denied the New Testament the more they hung on to the old."[70]

Betz summarizes Hamann's influence as follows:

To Kant he introduced the thought of Hume, forcing Kant to undertake a more critical assessment of reason's limits; to Herder (and Hegel) he imparted a profound appreciation for reason's historical-linguistic embodiment; to Goethe he pointed the way beyond French classicism to a distinctly German literature; to Jacobi he confirmed that reason without faith cannot sustain itself and leads to nihilism; to Hegel and Schelling he signaled new and grander possibilities for philosophy by way of his understanding of nature and history in terms of divine kenosis; to Schelling, in particular, he pointed the way toward Schelling's late positive philosophies of mythology and revelation; and to Kierkegaard he presented a model of pseudonymous Christian authorship in an age of unbelief, not to mention the original forms of such "Kierkegaardian" doctrines as the "paradox," the "teleological suspension of the ethical," "indirect communication," and "the infinite difference between God and human beings."[71]

In terms of biblical interpretation and hermeneutics, Hamann is a resource we need to recover. His faith remained utterly central to his life's work after his conversion. "For, once the Bible with its merciful nearness of God had given him conquest of the deadly dissociation of the philosophers, had given him 'marriage' with God, the world, others, and himself, it became his a priori. So he could write, 'Another *Dos moi pou stō* I do not recognize or know than his word.'"[72] There must be very few philosophers whose work is justifiably published with an extensive Scripture index, as in Hamann's *Writings on Philosophy and Language*.

69. Ibid., 21.
70. Ibid., 22.
71. Betz, "Reading 'Sibylline Leaves,'" 118.
72. R. Harrisville and M. C. Mattes, "Translators' Epilogue," in *A Contemporary in Dissent: Johann Georg Hamann as a Radical Enlightener*, ed. O. Bayer (Grand Rapids: Eerdmans, 2011), 218. The Greek is from Archimedes: *Dos moi pou stō*, "Give me [a place] where I may stand, [and I will move the earth]."

For Hamann, Scripture is of fundamental importance epistemologically: "All the perceptions of nature are dreams, visions, riddles, which have their clear meanings and their obscure sense. The book of nature and the book of history are no more than ciphers, hidden signs which have need of the key which the Bible offers and which is the object of their inspiration."[73] Hamann's stress on nature *and* history is noteworthy: for him, the Old Testament is the primer by which one learns to spell history, and nature is disclosed by the Bible. Nature like history is a "sealed book, a concealed witness, a riddle that cannot be solved, without plowing with another heifer than our reason."[74]

Hamann was certainly not an exegete in the classical sense.[75] Nevertheless questions dealing with the canon and how Scripture was to be read occupied him his whole life. For him, the importance of the Bible lay in its witness to Christ, and it has relevance to all of life, including the most rigorous philosophy. Here Hamann is a model for what faith seeking understanding might look like in Christian, contextual scholarship in which Scripture is fully engaged. His critique of reason has resonances in postmodernism, but his faith resists the relativistic side of postmodernism: "Hamann concedes no totalizing approach to reason, and yet creation itself as God's continual and constant address to us provides a meaningful context for life and vocation."[76]

Johann Gottfried Herder (1744–1803)

In a chapter like this we cannot in any detail explore the riches of the thought of Herder,[77] Jacobi,[78] nor many others. Müller-Sievers argues that "Herder is indeed the pivotal figure in the transition from Hamann's '*Gott als Schriftsteller*' to the '*Schriftsteller als Gott*.'"[79] Overall there is truth in this, but the

---

73. Quoted by Harrisville and Mattes, "Translators' Epilogue," 218.
74. From Hamann's essay "Socratic Memorabilia" (1759), via G. G. Dickson, *Johann Georg Hamann's Relational Metacriticism* (Berlin: de Gruyter, 1995), 383; J. G. Hamann, *Sämtliche Werke*, ed. J. Nadler (Vienna: Herder, 1950), 2:64.11–13.
75. The closest Hamann gets to reflecting on hermeneutics is in his "Biblische Betrachtungen eines Christen," in *Londoner Schriften*, ed. O. Bayer and B. Weissenborn (Munich: C. H. Beck, 1993), 65–104.
76. Harrisville and Mattes, "Translators' Epilogue," 221. For a balanced critique of postmodernism's appropriation of the early Romantics, see Beiser, *Romantic Imperative*.
77. See the useful chapter on Herder in F. C. Beiser, *The German Historicist Tradition* (Oxford: Oxford University Press, 2011), 98–166.
78. On Jacobi, see F. H. Jacobi, *The Main Philosophical Writings and the Novel "Allwill,"* trans. G. di Giovanni, McGill-Queen's Studies in the History of Ideas (Montreal: McGill-Queen's University Press, 1994); Beiser, *Fate of Reason*.
79. H. Müller-Sievers, "'Gott als Schriftsteller': Herder and the Hermeneutic Tradition," in *Herder Today: Contributions from the International Herder Conference, Nov. 5–8, 1987, Stanford, California*, ed. K. Mueller-Vollmer (New York: de Gruyter, 1990), 319–30, esp. 329.

picture is more nuanced. Throughout his life Herder retained his faith, but he changed positions in terms of how he related to the Enlightenment tradition. Theology was of prime importance for Herder, and early in his career he was influenced by the new historical school of biblical interpretation begun by Jakob Baumgarten (1706–57) and continued by Ernest, Michaelis, and Semler.[80] Intriguingly, Herder states that the implication of this new approach for theology is "to determine dogmatics through hermeneutics."[81]

What is less well known is that throughout the 1770s Herder returned to a more orthodox faith, which received Hamann's approval:[82]

> Alone, disappointed and isolated, Herder was thrown back upon himself; and, inspired by the Countess Maria's example, he began to return to his own religious roots for comfort and support. It was also during these years that he read Pascal, whose defense of religion against the rationalism of his day greatly impressed him. The net result was that Herder grew more skeptical, even hostile, toward the *Aufklärung*, especially its intolerance toward religion.[83]

Herder characterized the period that ensued in the words "Heaven and the hermit's cell always go together."[84]

Beiser observes that the most remarkable sign of this shift in Herder was his approach to the Old Testament. Previously Herder had discerned in Genesis 1:2–3 a structure with a strange symmetry, which he represented in the form of a hexagon, with a point in the middle. Now he became fascinated with this symbol, and he found himself agreeing with Hamann that creation is the language of God. His new ideas were published in the first part of his *Älteste Urkunde des menschlichen Geschlechts*. In it he repudiates his older work on Genesis, now seeing that the biblical criticism he had embraced was "heading toward the abyss."[85] He opposed any division between nature and revelation and warned against rationalistic interpretations of the Bible. Herder's reconversion also had a major effect on his philosophy of history, as evidenced in his 1774 work *Auch eine Philosophie der Geschichte zur Bildung*

---

80. See J. G. Herder, "Nachricht von einem neuen Erläuterer der H. Dreieinigkeit," in *Sämtliche Werke*, ed. B. Suphan, C. Redlich, and R. Stein (Berlin: Weidmann, 1877), 1:28–42. On Herder and biblical interpretation, see M. Saebø, *HB/OT* 2 (2008): 1041–50.

81. Herder, "Dreieinigkeit," 33, quoted by Beiser, *German Historicist Tradition*, 111.

82. See Beiser, *German Historicist Tradition*, 127–32.

83. Ibid., 128.

84. From Herder's October 17, 1772, letter to Merck, via Beiser, *German Historicist Tradition*, 128.

85. Beiser, *German Historicist Tradition*, 129. Herder's full title: *Christiani Zacchaei Telonarchae Prolegomena über die neueste Auslegung der ältesten Urkunde des menschlichen Geschlechts: In zweyen Antwortschreiben an Apollonium Philosophum* (1774).

der Menschheit. He rejected both the skeptical view of history as meaningless and the optimistic view that its meaning was found in the present, arguing instead that the meaning of history comes from providence, whose ends are inaccessible to reason. This book welds together the major themes of the historicist tradition into a major attack on Enlightenment historiography.[86]

It was during this period of his reconversion that Herder wrote his work on the Song of Songs as well as some two volumes of letters on his plans for a seminary.[87] Herder's interest in the Song of Songs began in 1761, and his work on it was finally published in 1778. Baildam explains that "it was Hamann's fusion of revelation and poetry and exaltation of the primitive which exerted the most decisive influence on him and prepared the way for his future work, especially on the Song of Songs."[88] Herder attended to the Song as Hebrew poetry and strongly opposed allegorization of it. Translation is central to his interpretation,[89] and he reads it as an evocation of pure erotic love.[90]

Hamann's response is significant: "Yet that same evening I managed to obtain *Lieder der Liebe* for which my desire had become so insurmountable that I had to do my utmost to quieten it. Of all your writings, none has provided me with such a delightful evening and made such an impression upon me as this."[91] Baildam notes that a study waits to be done on the fascination with the Song among Herder and his contemporaries: Hamann (1762), Hase (1765), Jacobi (1771), Goethe (1775), Pufendorf (1776), Lessing (1777), Gleim (1779), Kleuker (1780), Döderlein (1780), and Hufnagel (1784).[92]

In later years Herder returned to the more positive approach to Enlightenment ideas he had previously held, largely through the influence of Lessing.[93] Lessing anonymously published parts of a posthumous work by H. S. Reimarus that articulated a radical deism and a critique of orthodox Christianity. In our chapter on history and biblical interpretation, we noticed the radical implications of Lessing's philosophy for the Bible. Herder was deeply influenced by Lessing, and through Lessing he was influenced by Spinoza, but

---

86. See Beiser, *German Historicist Tradition*, 132–42.

87. I am indebted for the latter information to Calvin Seerveld, "Overlooked Herder, and the Performative Nature of שיר השירים as Biblical Wisdom Literature," *STR* 4/2 (2013): 197–222.

88. J. D. Baildam, *Paradisal Love: Johann Gottfried Herder and the Song of Songs*, JSOTSup 298 (Sheffield: Sheffield Academic, 1999), 59.

89. Ibid., 214–93.

90. On Herder's reading of the Song, see Seerveld, "Overlooked Herder." For a discussion of the Song, see A. LaCocque and P. Ricoeur, *Thinking Biblically: Exegetical and Hermeneutical Studies*, trans. D. Pellauer (Chicago: University of Chicago Press, 1998), 235–303.

91. Hamann quoted in Baildam, *Paradisal Love*, 294.

92. Ibid., 304.

93. See Beiser, *German Historicist Tradition*, 142–48.

Herder never went as far as Lessing in terms of history and revelation. "For Herder, however, the fundamental source of faith came from history, from the testimony of the Bible, because reason alone could never provide a sufficient justification for characteristic Christian doctrine."[94]

Hermeneutically Herder, in my opinion, is not nearly as helpful as Hamann. Nevertheless his work provides an acute insight into the struggle of the early Romantics to relate faith to the doctrines of the Enlightenment.

Søren Kierkegaard (1813–55)

Kierkegaard was born and spent most of his life in Copenhagen. His many books were mainly published in print runs of 500, which never sold out before his premature death at age 42. It was only at the beginning of the twentieth century that "he exploded upon the European intellectual scene like a long-delayed time bomb, and his influence since then has been incalculable."[95]

In his short life Kierkegaard produced an astonishing corpus of highly creative writings, many under intriguing pseudonyms such as Johannes Climacus and Johannes de Silentio, and written from diverse perspectives. Genuinely Christian philosophy is, in my view, *missional*, and this was consciously the case with Kierkegaard. The Denmark in which he lived was one of *Christendom*; it was assumed that because one was a respectable Dane, one must be a Christian. Kierkegaard consciously saw himself as a missionary called to "reintroduce Christianity into Christendom."[96] Hence comes the style in many of his major works of pseudonymity or indirect communication. Kierkegaard aspired to be a modern-day Socrates who pushed his readers to personally appropriate truth. For Kierkegaard, truth involves the whole person—"truth is subjectivity"—and he wrote as he did to prod and push readers into personally engaging with existence and faith.[97]

An effect of Kierkegaard's indirect method of communication is that he has been read in many different ways: as an irrationalist, as postmodern, as the father of existentialism. It is difficult nowadays for Western intellectuals to take Christian faith seriously, and yet this is at the heart of Kierkegaard's

---

94. Ibid., 146.

95. C. S. Evans, *Kierkegaard: An Introduction* (Cambridge: Cambridge University Press, 2009), 1.

96. S. Kierkegaard, *Kierkegaard's Journals and Papers*, trans. and ed. H. V. Hong and E. H. Hong, vol. 6 (Bloomington: Indiana University Press, 1978), entry 6271.70–71.

97. See S. Kierkegaard, *The Point of View for My Work as an Author: A Report to History and Related Writings*, trans. W. Lowrie and B. Nelson (New York: Harper & Row, 1962); C. S. Evans, *Kierkegaard*, 24–45.

philosophy. He is a profoundly Christian philosopher and still is deeply relevant today. For our purposes, a major characteristic of his philosophy is his rich and creative engagement with Scripture. Kierkegaard's devotional writings—he called them "upbuilding" or Christian discourses—are the easiest way into his corpus. Published under his own name, unlike his pseudonymous philosophical writings, they are rich expositions of Scripture. In his "Understanding the Gift," a reflection on James 1:17, he asks, "These words are so consoling and soothing, but how many have there been who really understood how to suck the rich nourishment of comfort from them, or who really understood how to take them to heart?"[98] Postmodern philosophers[99] have put the theme of "the gift" back on philosophical agendas, but here is biblical, reflective, deep contemplation that biblical scholars would do well to emulate.

What is truly remarkable is not only that Kierkegaard published devotional works and philosophical ones, but also that his Christianity and engagement with Scripture permeate both genres. As with Hamann, if we are looking for models as to how Scripture might engage scholarship, Kierkegaard stands out in this respect. His engagement with Scripture is inseparably related to his philosophy.

Central to Kierkegaard's philosophy is his concern with human existence as it is lived.[100] Thus he stressed inwardness and human subjectivity;[101] this is not an irrational move but his way of alerting us to the fact that a self is not just something I am but also something I must become. The unfinished self shapes itself through its choices; every decision we make is also a decision about the type of people we want to be. Kierkegaard affirms human freedom and responsibility but rejects the disengaged, disinterested self that we have witnessed emerging in modern philosophy. We make choices because of our desire and passions, and thus any understanding of human existence must extend beyond reason to include our emotional lives. "Subjectivity or inwardness are simply Kierkegaardian terms for this affective dimension of human life that must take center stage if we are to understand human existence."[102] For Kierkegaard, the human self is inherently relational: it is relational with regard to itself (it must "relate itself to itself"), relational with regard to others, and relational preeminently with respect to God.

---

98. S. Kierkegaard, *Spiritual Writings: Gift, Creation, Love; Selections from the Upbuilding Discourses*, trans. G. Pattison (New York: Harper Perennial, 2010), 5.

99. See Jacques Derrida, Jean-Luc Marion, et al.

100. A major theme, e.g., in S. Kierkegaard, *Fear and Trembling: Repetition*, trans. H. V. Hong and E. H. Hong (Princeton: Princeton University Press, 1983).

101. See C. S. Evans, *Subjectivity and Religious Belief: An Historical, Critical Study* (Washington, DC: University Press of America, 1982).

102. Ibid., 22.

For Kierkegaard, human lives can be categorized as aesthetic, ethical, or religious. He describes these as both *stages* and *spheres*. Becoming fully human is not automatic, and humans can become stuck in one stage or sphere. However, the norm is for humans to develop from one stage to the next. Such progression does not obliterate the previous stage; it remains but is recontextualized in a larger framework. The stages are not intended as a psychologically watertight theory but as a kind of conceptual map that depicts the possibilities of human existence.

The common factor in the aesthetic sphere is concern for "the immediate," for spontaneous sensations central to conscious human existence. The aesthete is concerned with personal desires and lives in and for the moment. Kierkegaard recognizes a continuum of aesthetic life, from the immediate aesthete to the highly reflective aesthete. An isolated individualism is characteristic of the latter. Boredom is the great evil to be avoided, and the imagination is to be used to keep boredom at bay. In *Either/Or* the character "A" refers to this as rotation of crops: commitments must be avoided, one's environment and enthusiasms must be carefully controlled, and one must relish the arbitrary in search of the interesting.

The problem for the aesthete is that immediacy is hard to sustain, and the ethical insists on inserting itself amid the quest for the interesting. While the aesthetic life reduces to a series of moments, central to the ethical is a quest for a unified self, for identity, for a self that endures over time. The bulk of volume 2 of *Either/Or* is a critique of the aesthetic by one "Judge William" and a plea for the ethical. Against the aesthete, Judge William vigorously defends marriage; it is what enables love to endure. Judge William stresses the conscious becoming of a self as the heart of the difference between the aesthetic and the ethical: "the aesthetic in a person is that by which he immediately is what he is; the ethical is that by which he becomes what he becomes."[103] Choice is central to the ethical, hence the title *Either/Or*.

The sort of morality defended by Judge William is much the same as that of Johannes de Silentio in *Fear and Trembling*. It is Hegel's *Sittlichkeit*, or social morality, according to which one is ethical by fulfilling one's social responsibilities. For Hegel, the state is in some sense divine; not surprisingly, Kierkegaard finds this view of the ethical seriously incomplete.

In his (very long) *Concluding Unscientific Postscript*, Kierkegaard distinguishes between Religiousness A and B. The former is characteristic of a religious attitude in general and is not uniquely Christian. In this work, Climacus

---

103. S. Kierkegaard, *Either/Or*, ed. and trans. H. V. Hong and E. H. Hong (Princeton: Princeton University Press, 1987), 2:178.

declares, "I, Johannes Climacus, born in this city and now thirty years old, a quite ordinary human being just like anyone else, assume that for me, as much as for a serving maid and a professor, there awaits a highest good called an eternal happiness. I have heard that Christianity contracts to provide one with that good. And now I ask how do I enter into relation with this doctrine."[104]

This question is pursued by Climacus for hundreds of pages. It becomes clear that the ethical presupposes the religious: it "is the God-relationship that makes a human into a human being."[105] There is a universal dimension of human being, but humans are also individuals, each tasked with becoming themselves. The religious person recognizes that oneself is in some way broken and needs to be made whole again. Religion thus involves resignation (rather than Hegel's mediation), a letting go of created goods, and a recognition of dependence on God.

Religiousness A is one of immanence; that of B is one of transcendence. B is Christian faith and involves God's revelation of himself as gift to the individual, thereby transforming the whole person, including the emotions and reason. Kierkegaard is highly critical of an evidentialism thinking that reason or historical arguments can produce faith. He is not opposed to either but has a strong view of the *limits* of both when it comes to faith. This is captured in his controversial description of the incarnation as "absolute paradox." That the eternal should become temporal is not, for Kierkegaard, a *logical* contradiction but an event that confronts reason with its boundaries. "It is the boundary or limit of reason, and when reason attempts to comprehend this limit, it finds itself enmeshed in apparent contradictions."[106] At the same time reason finds its fulfillment in the incarnation. For Kierkegaard, there is no neutral ground when it comes to the incarnation: we respond with faith or denial.

In reaction to Hegel, Kierkegaard was wary of systems. Hence he rarely sets out his views systematically. We can, however, extrapolate his *epistemology* from his writings, and it is surprisingly relevant to today. Kierkegaard adamantly opposes what has come to be called *classical foundationalism*, an epistemology still dominant today. Classical foundationalism makes two major claims:

1. Genuine, warranted knowledge must be based on a foundation of truths known with a high degree of certainty.
2. Such certainty is achieved only by setting aside emotions and subjective attitudes so that one relies on reason alone.

104. S. Kierkegaard, *Concluding Unscientific Postscript*, ed. A. Hanney, Cambridge Texts in the History of Philosophy (Cambridge: Cambridge University Press, 2009), Kindle loc. 16–17.
105. Ibid., Kindle loc. 205.
106. Evans, *Subjectivity and Religious Belief*, 156.

Evans is right to note of Kierkegaard that "his whole outlook is a challenge to this classical foundationalist picture."[107] We are human, and the sort of absolute certainty sought by classical foundationalism is simply not available to us. And "truth is subjectivity!" Having the truth means being fully caught up in living life as it was intended to be. This is not to deny the importance of propositional truth, but it is to assert that subjective truth is equally important. We know the truth by living it, and the world opens up to us as we pursue the clue that is Christ. Evans notes the affinities between Kierkegaard's epistemology and that of virtue ethicists and *externalist* epistemology. Virtue ethicists have stressed the role of the cultivation of certain virtues in the knower, and externalist epistemology stresses that knowledge is a matter of being rightly related to the external world.

A distinguishing mark of Kierkegaard's Christian philosophy is his engagement with the Bible,[108] and not only in his more theological works such as *Training in Christianity*, but also in his major philosophical works. In its title, *Fear and Trembling* alludes to multiple biblical references; Kierkegaard in its opening section develops a wonderfully creative reflection on different ways in which the Genesis 22 narrative of Abraham's being called to sacrifice Isaac might have worked out. In his *Repetition*, Kierkegaard has a remarkable reflection on how "he" reads Job:[109]

> If I did not have Job! . . . I do not read him as one reads another book, with the eyes, but I lay the book, as it were, on my heart and read it with the eyes of the heart, in a clairvoyance interpreting the specific points in most diverse ways. . . . I take book to bed at night with me. Every word by him is food and clothing and healing for my wretched soul. . . . Have you really read Job? . . . Nowhere in the world has the passion of anguish found such expression. . . . At night I can have all the lights burning, the whole house illuminated. Then I stand up and read in a loud voice, almost shouting, some passage by him. . . . Although I have read the book again and again, each word remains new to me.

---

107. Ibid., 56.

108. See L. C. Barrett and J. Stewart, eds., *Kierkegaard and the Bible*, tome 1, *The Old Testament*; and tome 2, *The New Testament* (Farnham: Ashgate, 2010); J. Pons, *Stealing a Gift: Kierkegaard's Pseudonyms and the Bible* (Bronx, NY: Fordham University Press, 2004).

109. For Kierkegaard's reading of Job, see T. H. Polk's *The Biblical Kierkegaard: Reading by the Rule of Faith* (Macon, GA: Mercer University Press, 1997), 153–200, a useful chapter in which he contrasts metaphysical readings (S. T. Davis, ed., *Encountering Evil: Live Options in Theodicy* [Edinburgh: T&T Clark, 2001]) and sociological readings (Peter Berger, James Crenshaw) with that of Kierkegaard, whose reading Polk (*Biblical Kierkegaard*, 154) styles as a "proto 'post-critical' model and guide."

... Like an inebriate, I imbibe all the intoxication of passion little by little, until by this prolonged sipping I become almost unconscious in drunkenness.[110]

Even amid the remarkable renaissance of Christian philosophy in North America today, it is rare to find deep engagement with Scripture. Unsurprisingly, Kierkegaard's reading of Scripture is often "subjective" and engaged, as befits his philosophy. In this regard his work is reminiscent of that of Hamann.[111]

Kierkegaard's achievements were remarkable, and his legacy has still to be fully appropriated. His sense of mission to his culture is notable and exemplary in the depth with which he pursued it. One wonders what an equivalent sense of mission might look like philosophically in our late-modern day. As we move on to track the emergence of modern philosophical hermeneutics, it is worth pausing to note the fecundity of thinkers like Hamann, Herder, and Kierkegaard. We will not find anything like their engagement with Scripture while hermeneutics emerges in its own right as a philosophical discipline. Christians concerned with theological hermeneutics and with the relationship of Scripture to all academic disciplines will need to excavate these thinkers and transfuse their insights into a tradition of biblical hermeneutics for today.

Friedrich Schleiermacher (1768–1834)

Schleiermacher's significance lies in the synthesis he developed between religion and human autonomy, doing so in a context that increasingly saw religion as irrelevant.[112] Religious reality is to be understood, according to Schleiermacher, through an analysis of human consciousness focused on feeling and intuition.[113] In this way Schleiermacher developed a Romanticist interpretation of religion that fits with the Enlightenment insistence on human autonomy. Reardon points out:

110. Kierkegaard, *Fear and Trembling*, 204.
111. Major work remains to be done on Kierkegaard's use of Scripture. Inter alia, see Polk, *Biblical Kierkegaard*.
112. For a useful discussion of this, see H. Vander Goot, "The Modern Settlement: Religion and Culture in the Early Schleiermacher," in *Hearing and Doing: Philosophical Essays Dedicated to H. Evan Runner*, ed. J. Kraay and A. Tol (Toronto: Wedge, 1979), 173–97. He points out that Schleiermacher's *Reden* (3 editions, 1799, 1806, 1831) "effected a resolution of the problem of the relation of culture and religion, or reason and faith, that became widely acceptable to Christians in the nineteenth century" (ibid., 177). B. M. G. Reardon, *Religion in the Age of Romanticism* (Cambridge: Cambridge University Press, 1985), and Vander Goot stress Schleiermacher's indebtedness to Kant and in particular to Spinoza.
113. Schleiermacher's understanding of religion and Christianity is more complex than this brief description. See Reardon, *Age of Romanticism*, 29–58.

Overall the impression he leaves in the mind of the reader is that of a theology subtly transformed into a philosophy of idealist monism. . . . The traditional landmarks are all there: revelation, the Bible, the articles of faith, the church. Yet all show up in a perspective new and somehow altered. . . . The viewpoint has shifted, that is, from a theocentrism to an anthropocentrism, so that what really has happened, one begins to suspect, is that Christian dogmatics has been covertly translated into a philosophy of the religious consciousness, for which a variety of elements have been drawn upon.[114]

In line with Romanticism,[115] Schleiermacher recognized the limits of reason in achieving understanding. Authors were understood as creators, and their productions as works of art, so that understanding involved reliving and rethinking the thoughts and feelings of an author.[116] Thus Schleiermacher speaks of interpretation as an art: "Hermeneutics deals only with the art of understanding, and not with the presentation of what has been understood."[117] Schleiermacher compares the process to that of getting to know a friend.

The transcendental turn to Schleiermacher's hermeneutics is significant. "For Schleiermacher, hermeneutics was . . . above all concerned with illuminating the conditions for the possibility of understanding and its modes of interpretation."[118] This universalization of hermeneutics was not new;[119] Schleiermacher's original contribution lay in his "universalization of misunderstanding," whereby he stressed that understanding needs to proceed *kunstgemäss* at every point.[120] He distinguishes between a less rigorous approach, assuming that understanding occurs as a matter of course, and a more rigorous approach, assuming that misunderstanding routinely occurs: "and so understanding must be willed and sought at every point."[121] This transcendental turn has received increasing attention among twentieth-century philosophers, and it is here that Schleiermacher's major influence lies. "The pervasiveness of total misunderstanding

---

114. Ibid., 57–58. Reardon points out that the Romantic understanding of religion, with its subjectivizing tendency, marks the start of "that process of immanentizing religious reality which was characteristic of the nineteenth century in general and which, despite the neo-orthodox reaction, has continued through the present century as well" (ibid., 10).

115. On the nature of Romanticism, see ibid., 1–28; for the diverse influences on Schleiermacher, cf. Thiselton, *New Horizons in Hermeneutics*, 209–16.

116. Reardon (*Age of Romanticism*, 8) points out that it was in the personal imagination that the Romantics located the real creative principle.

117. Schleiermacher, in Mueller-Vollmer, *Hermeneutics Reader*, 73. See Schleiermacher, *Hermeneutics and Criticism: And Other Writings*, trans. A. Bowie (Cambridge: Cambridge University Press, 1998).

118. Mueller-Vollmer, *Hermeneutics Reader*, 9.

119. See Grondin, *Philosophical Hermeneutics*, 50.

120. Cf. ibid., 63–75.

121. Schleiermacher, in Mueller-Vollmer, *Hermeneutics Reader*, 81–82.

has not disappeared. In fact, through authors like Nietzsche it has become an inescapable part of our intellectual universe."[122] For biblical hermeneutics the implication of this approach needs to be recognized. In the light of Schleiermacher's hermeneutic, it would be hard to affirm ecclesial reception of the Bible as primary since this is where the less rigorous interpretation and thus misunderstanding would reign. The expert thus becomes the one to uncover the truth of a text, a view that is all too familiar in the academy today.

Understanding a text involves reexperiencing the mental processes of the author. Schleiermacher discerns two aspects to such understanding: a grammatical aspect and a psychological or technical aspect.[123] The first concerns the understanding of an expression solely in terms of its relationship to the language of which it is a part. The second concerns the expression as part of the author's life-process and involves the comparative and the divinatory method.[124] As Thiselton points out, "Schleiermacher therefore explicitly raised for the first time a question which remains of permanent importance for hermeneutics: can we interpret the meaning of texts purely with reference to their language, or purely with reference to their author's intention, *or does textual meaning reside somehow in the inter-relation or inter-action between both?*"[125]

With Schleiermacher, we are also well on the way to a developed understanding of the *hermeneutical circle*.[126] The process of understanding must begin with a preliminary attempt to understand the whole; only then can one apply oneself to the details. This spiral moves between the grammatical and psychological, between the general and the particular, and between the divinatory and comparative. Schleiermacher believes that through this process it is possible to understand a text *better than its author*; indeed, this is the task of interpretation.

Schleiermacher's focus of hermeneutics on the process of understanding is to be welcomed, but in his approach there is a tendency to make the real focus of interpretation the author's thoughts and experience that lie behind the text rather than the text itself.[127] The divinatory aspect of interpretation is related to Schleiermacher's Romantic tendency to focus on human subjectivity as the key to understanding reality, so that the intuition of the reader is privileged as the means of interpretation, and the subjective experience behind the text

---

122. J. Grondin, *Sources of Hermeneutics* (Albany: State University of New York Press, 1995), 9. Derrida's work seems to me to exemplify understanding as misunderstanding.
   123. See the extracts from Schleiermacher in Mueller-Vollmer, *Hermeneutics Reader*.
   124. For Schleiermacher's explanation of the divinatory and comparative, see ibid., 96.
   125. Thiselton, *New Horizons in Hermeneutics*, 206, with original emphasis.
   126. Already Friedrich August Wolf and Friedrich Ast had developed this idea.
   127. Grondin, *Philosophical Hermeneutics*, 71–72.

becomes the focus of interpretation. This is evident in Schleiermacher's approach to Scripture, which is seen as a symbolic account of religious consciousness. Such experience is the crucial element and can be reproduced because it is in our consciousness as well. Thus Scripture is only a mausoleum, a monument that a great spirit who once was there is there no longer.

Schleiermacher's reading of Scripture through the grid of his analysis of religious consciousness alerts us to the extent to which his understanding of religion operates within the modern worldview. He takes biblical interpretation with the utmost seriousness and has much to say about it in his *Hermeneutics and Criticism*. Thus he affirms historical interpretation of the Bible but argues that it deals only with the grammatical side of interpretation and needs to be supplemented by the psychological. He argues for a positive approach to a text that assumes its coherence: "We may assume that the author is at fault only when our overview of the text uncovers evidence that the author is careless and imprecise, or confused and without talent."[128] However, his perspective on reality is Kantian in starting with an analysis of reality as we experience it, and then finding room in this for religion. Hence comes Thielicke's description of his theology as "Cartesian."[129] Thus, although Schleiermacher makes room for religion, it is very much within the bounds of human autonomy.

Palmer correctly alerts us to the atemporal dimension in Schleiermacher's hermeneutic.[130] Dilthey sought to introduce a critique of historical reason through his development of the psychological emphasis in Schleiermacher's hermeneutic.[131] This historical turn in hermeneutics is of great significance for biblical hermeneutics, for it was nineteenth-century *historical* philosophy that shaped the historical-critical method.[132] In the process Dilthey aimed at securing a different epistemology for the humanities from the sciences, whereas Heidegger was far more radical in calling attention to the temporality of being.[133]

---

128. Schleiermacher, in Mueller-Vollmer, *Hermeneutics Reader*, 88.

129. See H. Thielicke, *The Evangelical Faith: The Relation of Theology to Modern Thought Forms* (Edinburgh: T&T Clark, 1974), 1:38–45; for a critical assessment of Thielicke's view, cf. Thiselton, *New Horizons in Hermeneutics*, 230–33. Overall, I think Thielicke is correct.

130. R. E. Palmer, *Hermeneutics: Interpretation Theory in Schleiermacher, Dilthey, Heidegger, and Gadamer* (Evanston, IL: Northwestern University Press, 1988), 75.

131. For a brief discussion of this development in hermeneutics, see J. Bleicher, *Contemporary Hermeneutics: Hermeneutics as Method, Philosophy, and Critique* (London: Routledge & Kegan Paul, 1980), 16–26.

132. Cf. E. W. Nicholson, *Interpreting the Old Testament: A Century of the Oriel Professorship* (Oxford: Clarendon, 1981), 16. On historicism and hermeneutics, see Grondin, *Philosophical Hermeneutics*, 76–90.

133. In this respect, Heidegger built on Dilthey's historical hermeneutic. For a discussion of Dilthey's view of history and hermeneutics, see Grondin, *Philosophical Hermeneutics*, 84–90; T. Plantinga, "Dilthey's Philosophy of the History of Philosophy," in Kraay and Tol, *Hearing*

Martin Heidegger (1889-1976)

Heidegger's philosophy[134] is strongly ontological, and his epistemology is rooted in his ontology of *Dasein*. *Sein* can only be investigated if one begins with *Dasein*, which does not have a viewpoint outside history. In this sense "the phenomenology of *Dasein* is a hermeneutic."[135] This approach allowed Heidegger to rethink the subject-object relationship in knowing along historical lines, and it is here that his most significant hermeneutical contribution lies.[136] "Worldhood" refers to that whole in which the human person finds himself or herself immersed. It is ontological and a priori, given along with Dasein and prior to all conceptualizing. To conceive of objects as merely "present-at-hand" involves secondary conceptualization. The primary relationship of humans to objects is as "ready-to-hand." This contrasts with the Cartesian scientific orientation, which makes secondary conceptualization primary.[137]

Understanding is related to interpretation in that interpretation is not the acquiring of information about what is understood but the working out of the possibilities projected in understanding. What is understood has the structure of something *as* something. Interpretation is grounded in a "fore-having" (*Vorhabe*). "An interpretation is never a presuppositionless apprehending of something presented to us."[138] When this *as* (type of) structure becomes explicit, the object has become meaningful for us. Interpretation thus inevitably involves the hermeneutical circle: "Any interpretation which is to contribute understanding, must already have understood what is to be interpreted."[139]

In this way Heidegger opened the way for the recognition of the radical historicity of hermeneutics; indeed, in his view the question of Being can only be asked *within time*. Gadamer says of Heidegger: "But the concept of substance is in fact inadequate for historical being and knowledge; *Heidegger* was the first to make generally known the radical challenge of thought implicit in this inadequacy. He was the first to liberate Dilthey's philosophical

---

and Doing, 199-214; and idem, *Historical Understanding in the Thought of Wilhelm Dilthey* (Toronto: University of Toronto Press, 1980).

134. Here we focus on Heidegger's philosophy as represented by *Being and Time* (see next note). For the significance of this work and later developments in his philosophy for hermeneutics, see J. D. Caputo, *Radical Hermeneutics: Repetition, Deconstruction, and the Hermeneutic Project* (Bloomington: Indiana University Press, 1987).

135. M. Heidegger, *Being and Time* (Oxford: Blackwell, 1962), 62.

136. Speaking of the tension between objectivity and prejudice, Thiselton comments, "Heidegger has paid closer attention to the two-sidedness of this problem than perhaps any other thinker" (*Two Horizons*, 27).

137. Cf. ibid., 157-61, 187-91.

138. Heidegger, *Being and Time*, 191-92.

139. Ibid., 194-95.

intention."[140] This historicity of the interpreter has radical implications for hermeneutics and is central to Gadamer's hermeneutic.

Hans-Georg Gadamer (1900–2002)

Gadamer ascribes primary importance to understanding and insists on the historical nature of understanding itself: "Heidegger entered into the problems of historical hermeneutics and critique only in order to explicate the fore-structure of understanding for the purposes of ontology. Our question, by contrast, is how hermeneutics once freed from the ontological obstructions of the scientific concept of objectivity, can do justice to the historicity of understanding."[141]

Schleiermacher understood hermeneutics as the means to overcome the historical distance between the interpreter and the object of his interpretation. For Gadamer, however, "any interpretations of the past, whether they were performed by an historian, philosopher, linguist, or literary scholar, are as much a creature of the interpreter's own time and place as the phenomenon under investigation was of its own time and period in history."[142]

Part 1 of Gadamer's *Truth and Method* is concerned with the question of truth as it emerges in the understanding of art. Gadamer argues that experience and not abstraction is the key to understanding art. He attacks the Enlightenment exaltation of theoretical reason, as articulated by Descartes in particular, and appeals to Aristotle's notion of practical knowledge and the *sensus communis*. This has significance for hermeneutics in general; hermeneutics must be understood so as to do justice to the experience of art.

In part 2 of *Truth and Method,* Gadamer analyzes the hermeneutic tradition stemming from Schleiermacher and develops his own historical approach. In contrast to Enlightenment attitudes, Gadamer sees all interpretation as always guided by its own prejudice.[143] This prejudice is not just negative, and it cannot be simply discarded: "Using Heidegger, Gadamer rejects the Enlightenment prejudice against one's having presuppositions and working prejudgements, and the concomitant Enlightenment emasculation of tradition—as if one who does not question the prejudices of his own age is therefore a model knower."[144] The Enlightenment manifests a prejudice against prejudice, whereas Gadamer refuses to set reason in opposition to tradition. Indeed, understanding takes

---

140. H.-G. Gadamer, *Truth and Method* (New York: Seabury, 1975), 242–43.
141. Ibid., 265.
142. Mueller-Vollmer, *Hermeneutics Reader*, 38.
143. Gadamer, *Truth and Method*, 265–85.
144. C. Seerveld, "Review of *Truth and Method*, by H.-G. Gadamer," *Criticism* 36, no. 4 (1978): 488.

place as an event within a tradition. In contrast to existential thinking, Gadamer tries to locate meaning in the larger context of the community, as his view of tradition demonstrates.

In the light of the historicity of all interpretation, how is understanding possible? Certainly for Gadamer, the historicity of all interpretation makes Schleiermacher's aim of reconstructing the original world of the text impossible. What makes understanding possible is *Wirkungsgeschichte* (reception history/theory). This refers to the overriding historical continuum and cultural tradition of which both interpreter and historical object are part. Thus hermeneutics aims at prejudgments that will foster a fusion of the past with the present, thus facilitating the miracle of understanding, the sharing of a common meaning by temporally distant consciousnesses. In this fusing of horizons, distance and critical tension are never completely obliterated; indeed, the hermeneutic task is to foreground the tensions. Nevertheless interpretation always involves application.

Interpretation proceeds through a dialectical process of question and answer. Gadamer is against trying once and for all to fix the meaning of a text. Our interpretation is only one actualization of the historical potential of a text, so that correct interpretation will be characterized by unending dialogue. Knowledge is inherently dialectical, and we humans *are* conversations. The interpreter is to melt into the continuing, enlarging, ever-interacting history of tradition, or risk hubris.

This does not mean that the interpreter is free to simply dominate the text with imposed meanings. The good interpreter lets the text speak and convince the receiving interpreter.

> One could say that Gadamer is pointing out the philosophical reason why so much literary criticism . . . and critical analysis of "the other's" scholarship is judgmental rape of the text, when it should be a love affair, if hermeneutical activity is meant to be humane. Interpretation in the humanities went wrong, and remains obstinately wrongheaded, for Gadamer when it tried to understand art, literature, and research in the cultural sciences as if it were dissecting bugs and smashing atoms.[145]

In part 3 of *Truth and Method*, Gadamer offers a draft for an ontology of language-in-action. He proposes an ontology in which all understanding rests in language itself and seeks to systematically explore the universal conditions for just interpretation that will not presume that interpretation can be ahistorical.

145. Ibid.

Since Gadamer's approach, no other really groundbreaking hermeneutical innovations have appeared, but his hermeneutics has generated numerous debates. Indeed, Gadamer is a pivotal figure between modern and postmodern paradigms of thinking. Thiselton draws attention

> to Gadamer's role in focusing for hermeneutics, and addressing, a cluster of metacritical questions concerning the *basis* of understanding and of our possible relation to truth. Gadamer's distinctive way of addressing these questions not only constitutes a point of transition towards a new paradigm of hermeneutical theory; it also places him firmly on the boundary-line between modern and post-modern thought.[146]

According to Thiselton, the focus on metacritical issues that one finds in Gadamer emerges from three directions: first, the problem of radical historical finitude; second, the problem of the constitutive role of language in understanding; and third, the unease that has beset academic disciplines as they submit what have been regarded as foundations for their methods to reappraisal.[147]

In the remainder of this chapter, we will trace the postmodern turn and then examine the main ways in which Gadamer has been appropriated in contemporary hermeneutics.

Postmodernity / Late Modernity

Gadamer is appropriated by Habermas, who wants to get the project of modernity back on track; by a postmodernist pragmatist like Rorty;[148] and by Ricoeur. We will briefly explore the nature of the postmodern turn before examining the different ways in which Habermas, Rorty, and Ricoeur develop Gadamer's thought. The specifically "postmodern" debate began as a reaction to modernism in the arts in the 1960s and was extended to a critique of Western culture in its entirety in the 1980s, as philosophers joined the debate in earnest. There are cultural, social (late capitalism), and philosophical elements to the "postmodern condition." Philosophically, postmodernity involves a foundational crisis in the project of modernity. A marked pluralism characterizes epistemology, ontology, and anthropology as the modern "consensus" is increasingly questioned. This pluralism has major implications for hermeneutics,

---

146. Thiselton, *New Horizons in Hermeneutics*, 314, with original emphasis.
147. Ibid., 318.
148. I have found G. Warnke, *Gadamer: Hermeneutics, Tradition, and Reason* (Stanford, CA: Stanford University Press, 1987), particularly useful in explaining Habermas's and Rorty's reactions to Gadamer.

as the writings of Rorty, Derrida, Foucault, and Lyotard demonstrate. The relativistic extremes of the postmodern debate, exemplified by Baudrillard and Lyotard, are however only one stream in the contemporary philosophical scenario. Habermas, Ricoeur, C. Norris, and many others explore many of the same issues, but from a perspective of refining the project of modernity.

The philosophical diversity of the postmodern turn has been powerfully experienced in biblical hermeneutics, as in virtually all disciplines. Within biblical studies this influence has generally been mediated through literary theory, which over the past decades has itself come to exercise a powerful influence far beyond its disciplinary boundaries.[149] The turn to literary theory is related to the crisis in the nature of philosophy as it has been practiced in the Western tradition.

The effect of the literary turn, especially in biblical hermeneutics, should not be underestimated. It provides the most radical challenge to traditional models that has yet arisen. The very possibility of determinate and true readings of texts has been called into question by much postmodern literary theory. Author, reader, and text, along with their interrelationships, have come under fresh scrutiny, and a variety of positions have developed. Hirsch maintains that textual meaning is inseparable from authorial intention;[150] Barthes, Foucault, and others have pronounced the author dead.[151] Burke has declared the return of the author![152] The reader and the reader's role in the construction of meaning have received close attention, with a whole variety of proposals made.[153]

The nature of textuality itself has become highly problematic. New Criticism focused literary theory on the text itself; as a result of structuralism,

149. Cf. C. Norris's reference to literary theory's colonizing drive into other disciplines, in *Truth and the Ethics of Criticism* (Manchester, UK: Manchester University Press, 1994). In the process of this colonizing activity, the boundary between philosophy and literary theory has been blurred, so that literary conferences have often become predominantly philosophical. This blurring serves as a reminder that in reality literary theory has mediated and actively promoted the influence of certain philosophies rather than literary theory per se being the origin of the postmodern "literary" turn. This is important because, as Thiselton says, "If there is any area at all in theology and biblical studies where attention to method and to theory is crucial, it is here" (*Two Horizons*, 472).

150. E. D. Hirsch, *Validity in Interpretation* (New Haven: Yale University Press, 1967). See Grondin, *Philosophical Hermeneutics*, 125–29.

151. R. Barthes, "The Death of an Author," in *Modern Criticism and Theory*, ed. D. Lodge (London: Longman, 1988), 167–71; M. Foucault, "What Is an Author?," in *The Foucault Reader*, ed. P. Rabinow (New York: Pantheon, 1984), 101–20.

152. S. Burke, *The Death and Return of the Author: Criticism and Subjectivity* (Edinburgh: Edinburgh University Press, 1992).

153. Cf. S. R. Suleiman, "Introduction: Varieties of Audience-Oriented Criticism," in *The Reader in the Text: Essays on Audience and Interpretation*, ed. S. R. Suleiman and I. Crosman (Princeton: Princeton University Press, 1980), 3–45; E. Freund, *The Return of the Reader: Reader-Response Criticism* (London: Methuen, 1987); and R. C. Holub, *Reception Theory: A Critical Introduction; New Accents* (London: Routledge, 1984).

deconstruction, and poststructuralism, the nature of textuality has come under close scrutiny. Up until recently the classical-humanist paradigm of textuality had dominated the history of biblical interpretation. According to this tradition, texts are stretches of language that express the thoughts of their authors and refer to the extralinguistic world. Texts were seen as mediating interpersonal communication. The new approaches have called every aspect of this tradition into question.

Ricoeur

Paul Ricoeur wistfully writes, "Beyond the desert of criticism, we wish to be called again."[154]

Ricoeur is particularly significant for his understanding of interpretation as a semantic event, positing the fusion of text and interpreter through the interplay of metaphor and symbol, in a reading along the lines of a second naïveté.[155] In contrast to Gadamer, Ricoeur seeks to bring together *explanation* and *understanding*.[156] For Gadamer, in Ricoeur's view, the two collapse into each other so that there tends to be no space for critical testings of understandings. For Ricoeur, "explanation" embodies a hermeneutic of suspicion: the willingness to expose and to abolish idols, which are mere projections of the human will. Ricoeur is critical of the Enlightenment insofar as it locates meaning in the subject. He professes

> a permanent mistrust of the pretensions of the subject in posing itself as the foundation of its own meaning. The reflective philosophy to which I appeal is at the outset opposed to any philosophy of the Cartesian type.... The understanding of the self is always indirect and proceeds from the interpretation of signs given outside me in culture and history.... The self of self-understanding is a gift of understanding itself and of the invitation from the meaning inscribed in the text.[157]

---

154. P. Ricoeur, *The Symbolism of Evil* (Boston: Beacon Press, 1969), 349.

155. The range of Ricoeur's work is staggering, and it is impossible to do justice to the breadth and development of his thought in this section. S. H. Clark, *Paul Ricoeur* (London: Routledge, 1990), gives a helpful survey of Ricoeur's thought; I have also found J. Fodor's *Christian Hermeneutics: Paul Ricoeur and the Refiguring of Theology* (Oxford: Oxford University Press, 1995) and K. J. Vanhoozer's *Biblical Narrative in the Philosophy of Paul Ricoeur: A Study in Hermeneutics and Philosophy* (Cambridge: Cambridge University Press, 1990) helpful in terms of Ricoeur's approach to and significance for biblical hermeneutics.

156. On this issue, see P. Ricoeur, *Hermeneutics and the Human Sciences*, trans. and ed. J. B. Thompson (Cambridge: Cambridge University Press, 1981), 145–64.

157. P. Ricoeur, preface to *Hermeneutic Phenomenology: The Philosophy of Paul Ricoeur*, by D. Ihde (Evanston, IL: Northwestern University Press, 1971), xv. Note here the phenomenological

However, Ricoeur has no desire to be premodern. We cannot, nor should we, try to escape the lessons of the masters of suspicion, Nietzsche, Marx, and Freud. Hence "explanation" is an imperative part of interpretation.[158] However, explanation alone is inadequate: "to smash the idols is also to let symbols speak."[159] An effect of Cartesian epistemology is that Western civilization has lost a sensitivity to symbolic language.[160] Secularization has led to an estrangement from the kerygmatic situation; hence we need to move beyond suspicion to recover this sensitivity: "Myth's literal function must be suspended, but its symbolic function must be affirmed."[161] "Understanding" entails a willingness to listen with openness to symbols and to indirect language in such a way that we experience being called again.

In his later writings Ricoeur focuses particularly on metaphor and narrative. Unlike conceptual language, which reflects already-perceived actualities, metaphors create possible ways of seeing. Ricoeur develops a theory of metaphor in which the basic unit is the sentence, and in which metaphor makes new connections through the use of creative imagination. His more innovative and influential contribution emerges in the way he connects metaphor with narrative. For Ricoeur, the synthesis of the heterogeneous brings narrative close to metaphor. Narrative orders scattered sequential experiences and events into a coherent structure of human time. This refigured world becomes revelatory and transformative. Narrative constructs a world of the possible, which the reader is invited to indwell and explore.

There is good reason for the positive appropriation of Ricoeur by theologians.[162] Ricoeur's positive stance toward symbol makes him open to religious experience. Although Ricoeur retains a commitment to the autonomy of "responsible thought,"[163] he also wants to secure a fundamental place for

---

rootage of Ricoeur's philosophy: cf. L. S. Mudge, "Paul Ricoeur on Biblical Interpretation," in Ricoeur's *Essays on Biblical Interpretation*, edited and introduced by L. S. Mudge (Philadelphia: Fortress, 1980), 9–15.

158. For a concise statement of Ricoeur's insistence on demystification in interpretation, see P. Ricoeur, "The Critique of Religion," in *The Philosophy of Paul Ricoeur: An Anthology of His Work*, ed. C. E. Reagan and D. Stewart (Boston: Beacon, 1978), 212–22.

159. Ibid., 219.

160. Mudge, "Ricoeur on Biblical Interpretation," 4.

161. Ibid., 8.

162. Fodor and Vanhoozer are two such examples. Fodor (*Christian Hermeneutics*) appropriates Ricoeur's philosophy for the development of an adequate understanding of reference in theological statements. Vanhoozer (*Narrative in the Philosophy of Paul Ricoeur*) appropriates Ricoeur to explore how biblical narrative functions.

163. Ricoeur, *Essays on Biblical Interpretation*, 156. Fodor repeatedly refers to Ricoeur's concern to keep theology and philosophy distinct and to preserve the autonomy of philosophy. Hans Frei's insistence on a theological hermeneutic forms an interesting comparison with Ricoeur. See Fodor, *Christian Hermeneutics*, 258–330.

religion and theology. Not only has Ricoeur written extensively about literary theoretical and hermeneutical issues;[164] he has also specifically focused on biblical interpretation.[165]

Remarkably, Ricoeur specifically addresses the issue of a hermeneutic of Scripture as revelation.[166] He recognizes that revelation is the first and last word for faith and seeks to develop a hermeneutic of revelation that overcomes the opposition between an authoritative understanding of revelation and an autonomous view of reason. He rightly insists that such a hermeneutic must focus on the originating level of revelation as confession of faith rather than on the derived propositional levels. Scripture contains an ensemble of genres of discourse: prophetic, narrative, prescriptive, wisdom, and hymnic. Ricoeur focuses his attention on the "last" text, meaning the final form, and understands the Bible as a whole as testimony. Testimony generates revelatory discourse, and Ricoeur explores just how a revelatory text comes to be. Central to Ricoeur's notion of Scripture is its capacity to poetically disclose an alternative world and thereby to name God for us:

> Apprehended as a whole, the Bible forms one large living intertext where its constitutive heterogeneous elements are allowed to work on one another, simultaneously displacing their respective meanings but also mutually drawing upon their overall dynamism. These various modes of biblical discourse . . . are not merely juxtaposed with the result that the meaning of the Bible is cumulative. . . . Rather, a veritable augmentation of meaning occurs by virtue of these intertextual dynamics.[167]

Clearly Ricoeur's metacritical hermeneutic phenomenology is of great significance for biblical hermeneutics, as theologians and biblical scholars are starting to realize. Not only has Ricoeur addressed virtually every major theoretical issue in literary criticism but his irenic approach also mediates the interests of Gadamer and Habermas, redirecting hermeneutics away from Derridean extremes.[168] Ricoeur shares a central ontological concern with

---

164. P. Ricoeur's *Interpretation Theory: Discourse and the Surplus of Meaning* (Fort Worth: Texas Christian University Press, 1976) is a concise statement of his theory of interpretation.

165. Cf. Ricoeur, *Essays on Biblical Interpretation*, and note that his Sarum lectures, "Time and Narrative in the Bible: Toward a Narrative Theology," Oxford University, 1980, have still to be published.

166. Ricoeur, *Essays on Biblical Interpretation*, 73–118.

167. Fodor, *Christian Hermeneutics*, 252.

168. On the relationship between Gadamer, Habermas, and Ricoeur, see Clark, *Paul Ricoeur*, 110–15. Clark suggests that Ricoeur's provision of a *modus vivendi* with structuralism may indicate that Anglo-American literary theory has been unhelpfully distracted from the main issues by the French intellectual debate centered on poststructuralism (ibid., 110).

Gadamer, but his hermeneutics is focused on the written text and contains a clearer critical moment. As we will see below, however, the insistence on the autonomy of philosophy creates problems of its own, and in this respect I find Gadamer more helpful than Ricoeur.

Sociocritical Hermeneutics: Habermas

Habermas has used Gadamer's understanding of the hermeneutic process to clarify the conditions of social-scientific knowledge. In opposition to positivism in the social sciences, Habermas used Gadamer to stress that it is not possible to create a neutral language since all understanding is historically situated. However, Habermas has strongly criticized Gadamer's understanding of hermeneutics as a fusion of horizons leading to consensus because, in Habermas's view, it fails to take account of the possibility of systematic distortion in the communication process.[169] This has led to an ongoing debate between Habermas and Gadamer,[170] which has highlighted the metacritical (or lack thereof) dimension of Gadamer's hermeneutic. Habermas is deeply concerned that our understanding of "understanding" be able to account for the complexity and deeply entrenched nature of *ideologies*.

Habermas affirms from Gadamer the idea of the "immanent connection between understanding and application," and he illustrates this with the

---

169. W. G. Jeanrond (*Text and Interpretation as Categories of Theological Thinking* [Dublin: Gill & Macmillan, 1988], 8–37) focuses on this issue in relation to textual interpretation time and again. C. Norris (*Spinoza and the Origins*) says of Gadamer's hermeneutic that
    this version of the hermeneutic paradigm ends up in a prison-house of its own elaborate devising where there is no longer any role for the values of truth and falsehood, since everything is decided by preemptive appeal to beliefs that hold good for us (or our own "interpretive community"), and which therefore operate to screen out any evidence that doesn't fit in with the prevalent consensus-view. (201)
Norris describes this type of approach as "the hermeneutic hall of mirrors" (230). Thiselton (*Two Horizons*, 326) is more optimistic that Gadamer's hermeneutic has the resources for the maintenance of critical distance in interpretation.

170. See T. McCarthy, "Rationality and Relativism: Habermas' 'Overcoming' of Hermeneutics," in *Habermas: Critical Debates*, ed. J. B. Thompson and D. Held (London: Macmillan, 1982), 57–78; A. How, *The Habermas-Gadamer Debate and the Nature of the Social: Back to Bedrock* (Aldershot, UK: Avebury, 1995); H. J. Silverman, ed., *Gadamer and Hermeneutics* (London: Routledge, 1991), 151–77; D. Teigas, J. Habermas, and H.-G. Gadamer, *Knowledge and Hermeneutic Understanding: The Habermas-Gadamer Debate and the Nature of the Social* (Lewisburg, PA: Bucknell University Press, 1995); A. Harrington, *Hermeneutic Dialogue and Social Science: A Critique of Gadamer and Habermas* (New York: Routledge, 2001); P. Ricoeur, "Ethics and Culture: Habermas and Gadamer in Dialogue," *Philosophy Today* 17 (1973): 153–65; N. Adams, *Habermas and Theology* (Cambridge: Cambridge University Press, 2006), 61–65.

interpretation of Scripture: "In a sermon, the interpretation of the Bible, like the interpretation of positive law in adjudication, serves at the same time as an interpretation of the application of the facts in a given situation. Their practical life-relationship to the self-understanding of those addressed, the congregation or the legal community, is not added to the interpretation afterward. Rather, the interpretation is realised in its application."[171] Habermas agrees with Gadamer's critique of *scientism*[172] but thinks that Gadamer's approach to tradition does not do adequate justice to the "methodological distancing" that characterizes reflective thinking.[173]

Habermas describes Gadamer's approach as a linguistic idealism that needs a reference system outside itself to analyze systems of power and domination in society. Habermas uses the analogy of psychoanalytic theory to show how such a reference system would work in relation to the hermeneutic process. Gadamer denies that one can escape the hermeneutical process in this way and stresses that Habermas's account of the rational structure of communication is itself traditioned.[174] Habermas acknowledges this but maintains that this does not necessarily imply that a universalistic concept of rationality is fictitious. Indeed, Habermas suggests that Gadamer overemphasizes what "we" can learn from "the author" in the process of understanding; this needs to be balanced by a sense of what the author could learn from "us." "Gadamer fails to recognize the power of reflection that unfolds in *Verstehen*."[175]

In his earlier work Habermas responded to his critics with his project of universal pragmatics, in which he sought to establish that the possibility of ideal speech is implied in the structure of language. Any act of raising validity claims thus implies the possibility of unrestrained communication, so that the communicative practice of everyday life assumes the possibility of discourse in which speakers examine arguments in idealized conditions. In appealing to reasons, speakers assume that their claims could be substantiated through rational discourse alone. Thus communication in general points to something like Habermas's ideal-speech situation. However, Habermas's philosophy of the ideal-speech situation reached its most mature presentation in the 1970s,

171. J. Habermas, *On the Logic of the Social Sciences* (Cambridge: Polity, 1994), 162.
172. N. Adams defines scientism as "the belief that scientific method gives the observer a wholly detached perspective on the matter under investigation together with a methodology that yields statements that are independent of any interest held by the investigator" (*Habermas and Theology*, 61–62).
173. Habermas, *Logic of the Social Sciences*, 167.
174. For a summary of the debate between Gadamer and Habermas, see Warnke, *Gadamer*, 107–38.
175. Habermas, *Logic of the Social Sciences*, 168.

after which he abandoned the concept but not the centrality of reasoned debate and argumentation.[176]

In terms of the debate about modernity, Habermas has reacted strongly to the postmodern notion of its end, proposing instead that we think of modernity as an unfinished project.[177] Modernity is in crisis, but the answer is to get it back on track, not to abandon it. Habermas acknowledges the problem of logocentrism and foundationalist understandings of rationality, but he still argues that, politically, a privileging of rationality is indispensable. Problems have developed in modernity because theoretical, practical, and aesthetic reason have become separated from one another, and capitalist modernization has resulted in theoretical reason dominating the other two modes. The structures of language itself offer a way out of this impasse. Habermas elaborates on this with his philosophy of intersubjectivity revolving around communication and consensus. "Progress comes about by untiring attempts to achieve an ever more enlightened consensus on the basis of reasoned debate, not by way of a permanent crisis that refuses to resolve itself."[178]

Theology has been an interest of Habermas since early in his career, and in recent years he has focused more strongly on the role of religion in the public arena.[179] A major and laudable concern of Habermas is peaceful argumentation among diverse traditions, leading to consensus for public life. In this area he sees the role of religion positively and negatively. On the positive side, he urges that "the Christian churches must meet the challenges of globalization by appropriating their own normative potential more radically."[180] In an interview in 1999 Habermas states:

> For the normative self-understanding of modernity, Christianity has functioned as more than just a precursor or catalyst. Universalistic egalitarianism, from which sprang the ideals of freedom and a collective life in solidarity, the autonomous conduct of life and emancipation, the individual morality of conscience, human rights and democracy, is the direct legacy of the Judaic ethic of justice and the Christian ethic of love. This legacy, substantially unchanged, has been the object of a continual critical reappropriation and reinterpretation. Up to this very day there is no alternative to it. And in light of the current challenges

---

176. N. Adams (*Habermas and Theology*, 47) claims this is often not noted in theological literature.
177. See J. Habermas, *The Philosophical Discourse of Modernity: Twelve Lectures* (Cambridge: Polity, 1987); and R. J. Bernstein, *Habermas and Modernity* (Cambridge: Polity, 1985).
178. J. W. Bertens, *The Idea of the Postmodern: A History* (London: Routledge, 1995), 117.
179. See, e.g., J. Habermas, *Religion and Rationality: Essays on Reason, God, and Modernity* (Cambridge: Polity, 2002).
180. Ibid., 149.

of a post-national constellation, we must draw sustenance now, as in the past, from this substance. Everything else is idle postmodern talk.[181]

This sounds very positive, yet it is vital to explore what Habermas means by this.[182] Habermas argues that Christianity played an important role in fulfilling initial conditions for the rise of a secularized society, "which then, in turn, demanded a cognitive restructuring of the forms of religious faith and Church praxis."[183] This restructuring led to a reflexive mode of faith enabled by the development of Christian faith through the medium of philosophy. "Thus modern faith becomes reflexive. Only through self-criticism can it stabilize the inclusive attitude that it assumes within a universe of discourse *delimited* by secular knowledge and *shared* with other religions."[184] Habermas labels *fundamentalist* those movements that persist in advocating the exclusivity of premodern religious attitudes: "modern conditions are compatible only with a strict, Kantian form of universalism."[185] Such fundamentalism is a false answer to our epistemological situation, which "demands insight into the inevitability of religious tolerance and imposes on the faithful the burden of having to endure the secularization of knowledge and the pluralism of world pictures regardless of the religious truths they hold."[186]

Habermas sees the need to co-opt the religions in order to provide *the motivation* for a public ethic but is ambivalent toward religions as particular traditions and practices. "He wants to prise apart the worldview-unifying forces from the ethically binding forces."[187] In practice this entails religions submitting to the rational conditions of Kantian universalism, a situation that, as we argued in chapter 7, on the history of interpretation, eviscerated the Christian dimension in biblical interpretation.

Within theology and biblical studies, Habermas's work has been appropriated in a variety of ways.[188] It is particularly relevant to approaches to the

---

181. Ibid., 148–49.
182. A very useful work on Habermas is N. Adams, *Habermas and Theology*.
183. Habermas, *Religion and Rationality*, 150.
184. Ibid.
185. Ibid., 151. For Habermas's view of universalism, see N. Adams, *Habermas and Theology*, 92–105.
186. Habermas, *Religion and Rationality*, 151.
187. N. Adams notes that "in much of his work Habermas is not really interested in religion or theology as practices or living traditions, but sees them as powerful, sometimes dangerous, sometimes inspiring ancestors to modern self-consciousness" (*Habermas and Theology*, 13).
188. See esp. H. Düringer, *Universale Vernunft und partikularer Glaube: Eine theologische Auswertung des Werkes von Jürgen Habermas* (Leuven: Peeters, 1999); also N. Adams, *Habermas and Theology*, esp. 182–202. In a dialogue, J. Habermas and J. Ratzinger, *The Dialectics of Secularization: On Reason and Religion* (San Francisco: Ignatius, 2006), address such important

text that seek to get beneath its surface function in order to expose its role as an instrument of power, domination, or social manipulation. Habermas's type of hermeneutic is distinct from the pragmatism of Rorty in that it seeks to establish a metacritical or universal dimension distinct from the texts or traditions in question, on the basis of which their power functions can be exposed. Thus, while it shares in the postmodern critique of positivism, it does not abandon the search for universals.

Within Old Testament studies, Habermas has been appropriated by John Rogerson in his work on Old Testament ethics and theology.[189] Rogerson finds Habermas's theory of communicative interaction illuminating in terms of the development of Israel as a society and in terms of the problems we face today.[190] He attends in particular to our need to live in interdependence as constitutive of what it means to be human. Rogerson also draws on Habermas's discourse ethics, with its distinction between imposed ethics and an ethics of consent. In his *Erläuterung zur Diskursethik*, Habermas discusses Bernard Gert's modern statement of the Decalogue.[191] For Habermas, obligations cannot be imposed: they must be justified and accepted by consent. Rogerson explores this in relation to the Old Testament and concludes in relation to adultery, for example, that "discourse ethics would require that the interests of all parties affected by adultery were considered, and its rightness or wrongness would be an agreed decision that was in the interest of all parties."[192] According to Rogerson, "Passages such as Gen. 18:22–33 show that within the Old Testament there are conflicting ethical strands, some of which assert moral obligations or find no difficulty in the notion of corporate responsibility, others of which imply that what is just in a given situation is to be established by dialogue, taking into account the interests of individuals."[193]

At stake here, as with Habermas's philosophy, is the view of religion and tradition in operation. Divine command is a strong element of biblical ethics stemming from the character of God, and a tendency to include God as an ethical dialogue partner on par with the other partners goes counter to the

---

contemporary questions as these: Is a public culture of reason and ordered liberty possible in our postmetaphysical age? Is philosophy permanently cut adrift from its grounding in being and anthropology? Does this decline of rationality signal an opportunity or a deep crisis for religion itself?

189. See J. W. Rogerson, *Theory and Practice in Old Testament Ethics*, JSOTSup 405 (London: T&T Clark, 2004); idem, *A Theology of the Old Testament: Cultural Memory, Communication, and Being Human* (Minneapolis: Fortress, 2010).

190. Rogerson, *Theory and Practice*, 50–59.

191. J. Habermas, *Erläuterung zur Diskursethik* (Frankfurt: Suhrkamp, 1991), 171–76.

192. Rogerson, *Theory and Practice*, 63.

193. Ibid., 64.

biblical testimony. The real danger is of the biblical testimony being subsumed under Habermas's secularized understanding of rationality. Awareness of one's tradition as a tradition does relativize it to an extent, but the indwelling of a tradition is inevitable. Habermas is operating in a tradition of German thought just as much as the Christian operates in a particular tradition. The inevitability of being traditioned has been well argued by Alasdair MacIntyre.

Working in the postliberal theological tradition, Nicholas Adams perceptively notes, in regard to Habermas's attempt to transcend narrative with reason,[194] that "against Habermas, any attempt to transcend this [Christian] tradition, which simultaneously receives revelation and refuses to 'comprehend' it, is not just an ethical position but the abolition of the Christian tradition. It would acknowledge a higher authority than the one who is revealed as unintelligible yet known in Jesus Christ."[195]

N. Adams rightly asserts that "Christians should own their traditions to the extent that they are faithful to God's promise. It is not a matter of choosing Habermas or Gadamer, but of spelling out what kinds of distance from tradition are appropriate, and of placing the authority of traditions under a greater authority."[196] Trinitarian theology both embraces tradition and places its claims under judgment.[197] Thus trinitarian faith produces its *own* version of critical distance—"To the extent that traditions do faithfully anticipate God's reign, at least as far as finite humans can tell, the distance narrows"[198]—and one that cannot be surrendered to Habermas's secularized ethic.

Habermas's work is important in alerting us to the need to recover biblical and theological work that contributes to the common matters of our cultures. Biblical interpretation in particular has been weak in these areas, and we will attend to such issues in chapter 13. The crucial question is *how* Christian biblical scholarship can and should make such a contribution. N. Adams finds an answer in the Scriptural Reasoning project that is developing with scholars such as David Ford and Peter Ochs.[199] As will be discussed in a later chapter (13), I think this is an important initiative yet one with limited potential for serious public engagement. In biblical studies the *Christian* tradition should be allowed to come to full fruition, with a strong sense of the public dimensions of life; this, coupled with a robust philosophy of culture

---

194. On narrative and argument, see N. Adams, *Habermas and Theology*, 203–33.
195. Ibid., 219.
196. Ibid., 206, which refers to Kierkegaard's *Fear and Trembling* as exemplary in this respect.
197. N. Lash, *Believing Three Ways in One God: A Reading of the Apostles' Creed* (Notre Dame, IN: University of Notre Dame Press, 1993).
198. N. Adams, *Habermas and Theology*, 206.
199. Ibid., 234–55; D. F. Ford and C. C. Pecknold, *The Promise of Scriptural Reasoning* (Oxford: Blackwell, 2006).

and pluralism, would enable it to be in a position for serious dialogue with other traditions and to promote practices that enhance the flourishing of what we have in common.

Sociopragmatic Hermeneutics: Rorty

Rorty uses Gadamer to support his project of overcoming what he sees as the false distinctions between all forms of knowledge, between natural and human sciences, and also between these and creative enterprises in general.[200] The value of hermeneutics, according to this view, is how it shows that all knowledge is traditioned and that the idea of the accurate *representation* of reality, which underlies the Western concern with epistemology, is a myth. All forms of knowledge are closer to making than to finding and have this in common with creative enterprises in general. Consequently, the legitimation obsession of Western epistemology is irrelevant and wedded to an outmoded metaphysic.

According to Rorty, we ought not to think of science as progressing toward a more accurate description of reality as it is; different scientific paradigms are better thought of as ways of coping. Here Rorty stresses Gadamer's notion of *Wirkungsgeschichte*, whereas Habermas and Apel stress the dialogical element in Gadamer's hermeneutic.[201] The idea of ever-interacting history appears to fit with Rorty's pragmatism, in which one is not interested so much in what happened in history or what is out there, but in what we can use for our own purposes.[202] In place of the epistemological concerns of the Western tradition, Rorty proposes the goal of "edification." He sees this as the equivalent of Gadamer's *Bildung*. Rather than trying to justify our beliefs, we should foster conversations in which we are exposed to, and can explore, other options and thus find better ways of coping.

Rorty denies that his approach is relativistic or irrational. He openly acknowledges that it cannot be philosophically legitimated but insists that its

---

200. See Warnke, *Gadamer*, 156–66. Warnke's chap. 5 is a useful critique of Rorty's appropriation of Gadamer. See also C. Norris, *Contest of Faculties: Philosophy and Theory after Deconstruction* (London: Methuen, 1985).

201. See K.-O. Apel's essay in Mueller-Vollmer, *Hermeneutics Reader*, 333–35.

202. On comparing Richard Rorty with Hayden White, K. Jenkins, *On "What Is History?": From Carr and Elton to Rorty and White* (London: Routledge, 1995), says:

> Like Rorty, White has no time for the idea that we know what history really is, therefore freeing it up to be whatever we want it to be, a history that, for White, is useful for his own notion of utopia. This is not to say—yet again—that the actuality of the past did not exist exactly as it did, but it does mean that White thinks it can be (as it always has been) used as people desire. (132)

merits become clear from its practical advantages. We cannot escape being traditioned; we can only defend our commitments by continuing to think and explain them as important to have until shown otherwise. Rorty thus develops Gadamer's notion that there can be no determinate criteria of interpretation along thoroughly pragmatic lines. For Rorty, hermeneutics is a way of coping, not a way of knowing.

Similarly, Rorty has expounded a pragmatic version of postmodernity, which Bertens describes as fitting between Lyotard and Habermas.[203] What is required is not a new quest for legitimation but a detheoreticized sense of community. From such a position one could accept Habermas's privileging of undistorted communication without needing to ground it in a theory of communicative competence. Thus for Rorty postmodern bourgeois liberalism is "the Hegelian attempt to defend the institutions and practices of the rich North Atlantic democracies without using [the traditional Kantian] buttresses."[204]

For such postmodern liberalism, morality is stripped of its transcendent grounding and becomes equivalent to loyalty to a society. Rational behavior is simply behavior that conforms to that of other members of a society. This implies a modest understanding of the self as a network of beliefs and desires, with nothing behind it, and the necessity of an ungrounded communitarian solidarity. As Rorty explains, liberals disown cruelty, but liberal ironists (i.e., like himself), while they too disown cruelty, give no reason for not being cruel! Bertens rightly critiques Rorty's pragmatic postmodernism for his easy and imaginary optimism.[205]

Clearly pragmatism does not offer a way forward for the sort of biblical hermeneutic we have in mind in this volume. It would leave biblical studies at the mercy of contemporary trends and vulnerable to the critique that O'Donovan rightly makes of historicism: there are no ultimate norms, and one ends up simply siding with one part of contemporary culture against another. Yet it is important to be aware of just how pervasive pragmatism is in North American culture today, and not least in biblical studies, in which each practitioner does what is right in their own eyes. A casualty of postmodernism in biblical studies is the notion of *truth*, whereas a theological hermeneutic will make its goal to be truthful interpretation of Scripture.

This survey alerts us to the complex factors that have shaped the discipline of hermeneutics and the diversity of approaches that have developed. Issues

---

203. Bertens, *Idea of the Postmodern*, 141.
204. R. Rorty, "Postmodernist Bourgeois Liberalism," *Journal of Philosophy* 80, no. 10 (1983): 584–85.
205. C. Norris, *What's Wrong with Postmodernism?* (London: Harvester Wheatsheaf, 1990), 1–48.

like one's view of reason and the human person, one's view of history and tradition, one's philosophy of language, one's understanding of religion—all these influence the shape of the hermeneutic one adopts. And there is no consensus on any of these issues. In the context of modernity, the relative philosophic stability allowed a tacit set of philosophical presuppositions to be easily taken for granted. That is no longer possible today since some of the basic assumptions of modernity have been problematized in the context of the postmodern turn.

This lack of consensus should not detract from the decisive importance of philosophical hermeneutics for biblical interpretation. From our discussion of Spinoza and Kant, it is especially clear that philosophical hermeneutics has decisive implications for biblical hermeneutics. Enlightenment rationalism and idealism, which exempted religious prejudice from the interpretive process and insisted that Scripture should be read in terms of the modern worldview, resulted in very different ways to read Scripture. The important work of Hamann, Herder, and Kierkegaard alerts us unequivocally to the fact that we can draw on alternative resources for a contemporary hermeneutics. Gadamer, furthermore, reverses much of the sting of Enlightenment rationalism and idealism in his call for prejudice to be appropriated positively as part of the hermeneutic process. And Ricoeur argues that Christians will require a hermeneutic of revelation for the interpretation of Scripture.

Thus there is a plurality of philosophical hermeneutical approaches, and different ones will result in one approaching and interpreting the Bible differently. The issues that hermeneutics raises are unavoidable in interpretation; to simply ignore them will result in a naive practice of exegesis that unconsciously and thus uncritically enacts answers to the questions hermeneutics raises. In my opinion we need to draw on the tradition of Hamann, Herder, Kierkegaard, Gadamer, and Ricoeur to articulate the contours of a Christian hermeneutic for today. If Hamann is right that "all the colors of this most beautiful world grow pale once you extinguish its light, the firstborn of creation,"[206] then our response needs to be a hermeneutic articulated consciously in the light of the firstborn of creation, drawing on the best insights in the rich history of hermeneutics. As Milbank perceptively urges, "If Derrida can give a gnostic hermeneutic of the human text in the light of the gnostic logos, then we should have the confidence to give a Christian hermeneutic in the light of the real one."[207]

206. Hamann, *Writings on Philosophy and Language*, 78.
207. J. Milbank, *The Word Made Strange: Theology, Language, Culture* (Oxford: Blackwell, 1999), 79.

An Augustinian Hermeneutic

What shape might such a hermeneutic take? It is impossible to map out such a hermeneutic in detail here. It must suffice to articulate the main contours.

1. With Gadamer and Alasdair MacIntyre,[208] this hermeneutic would insist that all understanding and knowledge is *traditioned*. Contra MacIntyre, it would argue that the *Augustinian tradition* of faith seeking understanding rather than the Aristotelian-Thomistic tradition is the most biblical and fertile tradition for today.

2. Contra Ricoeur and so much modern philosophy, it would resist the pervasive doctrine of the autonomy of philosophy. Instead, such a hermeneutic would use all the resources of faith and the Christian tradition to map out the contours of a hermeneutic for today. Within philosophy, major work has been done by philosophers such as Alvin Plantinga, Nicholas Wolterstorff, and Stephen Evans in what might appropriately be called the Augustinian tradition.[209] Theology and philosophy would work together to explore the contours of a Christian hermeneutic for today.

3. As with Hamann and Kierkegaard, such a hermeneutic would be integrally informed by a view of this world as *creation*, which is read aright only in the light of faith.[210] The difference this makes should not be underestimated. The world *as creation* resists the absolutization of history in the current forms of postmodern historicism, in which history is seen as adrift amid flux and change, as well as resisting the absolutization of language, which is a danger of Gadamer's approach and central to Derrida's deconstruction.

What remains is a great challenge to articulate the view/s of history and language and reason that approaching this world as creation yields. Alvin Plantinga has done important work on *rationality* from such a perspective, but far less contemporary work is available on history and language. In our chapter on history and biblical interpretation, we explored some of the contours a theology of history might assume. In terms of language, Tom Wright alerts us to the challenge we face:

> Protests, then, against the postmodern readings of the Bible are likely to be ineffectual. Unless, that is, those who care about serious reading of the gospels set about exploring ways in which to articulate a better epistemology, leading

---

208. A. MacIntyre, *Whose Justice? Which Rationality?* (Notre Dame, IN: University of Notre Dame Press, 1988).

209. See A. Plantinga, "Augustinian Christian Philosophy," in *The Augustinian Tradition*, ed. G. B. Matthews (Berkeley: University of California Press, 1999), 1–26.

210. On an appropriate epistemology, see O. O'Donovan, *Resurrection and Moral Order: An Outline for Evangelical Ethics* (Grand Rapids: Eerdmans, 1986).

to a better account of what happens when a text is being read, a better account of what happens when a *sacred* text is being read. . . . *There is a sense . . . in which this demands a full theory of language. We need to understand, better than we commonly do, how language works.*[211]

Having taught philosophy of language for several years, I am aware of the complexity involved in this area. In my essay "Before Babel and after Pentecost," I drew on Scripture plus the evocative work of George Steiner and others to give an indication of the shape that a Christian view of language might take.[212] From Scripture I concluded:

a. Humans and language (and reason) are creaturely and thus part of God's ordered creation. Language is something that humans "do" and is a meaningful activity. The capacity for language is a central element in being a human creature. An *ethics* of language flows out of this, just as with one another we are not free to do what we like with texts but have a responsibility to understand them truthfully.
b. In a fallen world, language can be seriously misdirected by humans, as epitomized by Babel. Scripture draws our attention to what *we do* with language as potentially problematic; this is in contrast with some types of postmodernism, which appear to find the problem inherent in the good structure of language.
c. Language can be redirected redemptively. Pentecost is the great example of this, where the God-given diversity of languages is used to tell forth the gospel.
d. Believers have a responsibility to listen, and then to speak and write the truth in love.[213]

In terms of the development of a *theology/philosophy of language*, I proposed that it must do justice to the following:

a. Language as fundamentally good, a gift of God. A Christian perspective must, for example, take account of the capacity for words to be a means whereby humans give themselves to each other at the deepest level, as

---

211. N. T. Wright, *NTPG* 61–63, with added emphasis.
212. C. G. Bartholomew, "Before Babel and after Pentecost: Language, Literature and Biblical Interpretation," in *After Pentecost: Language and Biblical Interpretation*, ed. C. G. Bartholomew, C. Greene, and K. Möller, Scripture and Hermeneutics 2 (Grand Rapids: Zondervan, 2001).
213. For a useful discussion of the Christian ethics of truth telling, see D. Bonhoeffer, *Ethics* (New York: Macmillan, 1955), 363–72; and J. H. Burtness, *Shaping the Future: The Ethics of Dietrich Bonhoeffer* (Philadelphia: Fortress, 1985), 121–66.

in Jesus's words in the Eucharist, "This is my body." Augustine rightly speaks of words as "those precious cups of meaning."
b. Language as world disclosing and constituting, but not finally world creating.[214] The following incident that Timothy Radcliffe describes is an insightful example of the world-disclosing potential of words: "A Dominican sister from Taiwan told of a girl carrying the burden of a child on her back. Someone said to her: 'Little girl, you are carrying a heavy weight.' She replied, 'I am not carrying a weight; I am carrying my brother.'"[215] As Charles Taylor points out, there are some phenomena central to human life—such as feelings, relations, and political equality—that are partly constituted by language.[216] Such an approach differs from a postmodern tendency to see human life as a linguistic construct. The latter perspective absolutizes language and is in danger of idolatry; hence the creative and constitutive power of language needs to be distinguished from language as creative in an ultimate sense.
c. The capacity of language to disclose, to refer, *and* to communicate. We need understandings of language that open up these diverse and yet not mutually exclusive functions of language. I suspect this also relates to our need for understandings of language that explore language as one mode of being in a world made up of many diverse dimensions.
d. Our everyday use of language. Schleiermacher and so much postmodernism seems radically out of sync with this, but a Christian view of language must do justice to the way in which language functions quite happily much of the time.[217]
e. Language as capable of being misdirected, and our responsibility *not* to participate in such misdirection. Ethics should be a priority in our understanding and use of language.

This approach provides clues that Christian work in language needs to take seriously, but they need to be worked out in detail as theology and philosophy draw on the rich resources that are already available, resources such as

214. I have found Charles Taylor's discussion of language as constitutive most helpful; see his "Theories of Meaning," in *Human Agency and Language: Philosophical Papers* (Cambridge: Cambridge University Press, 1985), 248–92, esp. 270–73. Ricoeur's work in his three-volume *Time and Narrative* is a major contribution in this area.

215. T. Radcliffe, *Sing a New Song: The Christian Vocation* (Springfield, IL: Templegate, 1999), 18–19.

216. Ibid.

217. For a useful discussion of this point, see N. Wolterstorff, "The Importance of Hermeneutics for a Christian Worldview," in *Disciplining Hermeneutics: Interpretation in Christian Perspective*, ed. R. Lundin (Grand Rapids: Eerdmans, 199), 25–47.

speech-act theory, relevance theory, politeness theory, the burgeoning work on metaphor and language, and so forth.

4. The embeddedness of the reader/s in history needs to be affirmed as articulated by modern hermeneutics. But the view of *history* assumed in saying this requires close attention. If history is just flux and change, then relativism is the logical consequence. If, however, history is subject to God's dynamic order for creation, then there is much greater reason for optimism about right readings of ancient texts, although the complexity involved is rightly foregrounded. The Old Testament and New Testament are ancient Hebrew and Greek texts, and no matter how often we confess the clarity of Scripture, we cannot and should not evade the challenges in understanding, translating, and interpreting such texts.

5. We should take seriously Habermas's and Ricoeur's emphasis on ideology. The history of the church is littered with the abuse of Scripture to support oppressive ideologies. However, the critical distance required should be sought not in a secularized rationality à la Habermas, but in the sort of trinitarian distance so well articulated by N. Adams and discussed above.

6. It is obvious from the above how fruitful such work would be for biblical hermeneutics. In this sense biblical hermeneutics has much to learn from general hermeneutics. At the same time Scripture is not just another text; it will have its regional hermeneutical distinctives as well as its unique contributions to a general hermeneutic as expressed above.

Philosophy of Language and Biblical Interpretation

Amid the years of training required in biblical studies, students and scholars are understandably reluctant to be told that they also need some understanding of hermeneutics and philosophy. Thus it behooves us to show by example the difference that attention to philosophy can make in biblical interpretation. Hundreds of examples could be chosen. Later, in chapter 11 on literature and the Bible, for example, we will see just how illuminating Tom Wright's use of structuralism is in relation to the Gospels.

Issues of language are *always* already at work in interpretation and cannot be avoided. However, that does not mean that we are necessarily conscious of them. Exegetes often work unconsciously with certain views of language, and there is great benefit to be gained from becoming more conscious of what views of language are at work in exegesis and interpretation. To illustrate this point, I will discuss one example from the interpretation of Leviticus. Leviticus may seem an obscure example to choose, but if we want to know how language affects actual exegesis, then it is actual exegesis that we will have to explore, with particular examples.

The example in Leviticus that I will discuss came up in one of our regular biblical studies seminars when I was at the University of Gloucestershire, through a presentation by one of our doctoral students.[218] In other words, it is not untypical of the sort of thing a doctoral student in biblical studies might encounter.

In his major commentary on Leviticus,[219] Jacob Milgrom argues that in the Old Testament cultic texts the Hebrew verb אשם (*'āšām*) is best translated as "to feel guilty."[220] Milgrom asserts that this translation is highly significant: "The critical importance of this new rendering is that it necessitates an overhaul of every cultic passage in which the verb *'āšām* occurs without an object."[221] Milgrom gives six examples of such passages. One of them is Leviticus 5:17, which the NRSV translates thus: "If any of you sin without knowing it, doing any of the things that by the LORD's commandments ought not to be done, you *have incurred guilt*, and are subject to punishment."[222] NIV similarly translates *'āšām* as "they *are guilty*." However, Milgrom translates this verse differently: "If, however, a person errs by violating any of the LORD's prohibitive commandments without knowing it and he *feels guilt*, he shall bear his responsibility."[223] The other verses Milgrom refers to are Leviticus 4:27–28; 5:2–4; 5:5; 5:23a (6:4 ET); Numbers 5:6b–7.

It is moot how much hangs on deciding how to translate *'āšām* at these points. For our purposes, it is important to recognize that these discussions are the bread-and-butter issues biblical scholars deal with every day. And what do bear scrutiny are the arguments Milgrom marshals in favor of this translation. I cannot here discuss these in detail, but essentially they go as follows.

---

218. I am grateful to Jay Sklar for drawing my attention to this issue and for his help with some of the details in this discussion.

219. D. N. Freedman (preface to *Pomegranates and Golden Bells: Studies in Biblical, Jewish, and Near Eastern Ritual, Law, and Literature in Honor of Jacob Milgrom*, ed. D. P. Wright et al. (Winona Lake, IN: Eisenbrauns, 1995), ix–xi) says of Milgrom's first volume on Leviticus that "this magisterial undertaking has already established itself as a classic, the standard by which all future works must be judged, and a standing challenge to scholars in coming generations" (ix). I do not wish to detract from Milgrom's achievement in my analysis of a small part of his work. I merely wish to demonstrate how, in often surprising ways, issues of language are present in scholarship of even this caliber, and that we could all benefit from taking them more seriously.

220. J. Milgrom, *Leviticus 1–16: A New Translation with Introduction and Commentary*, AB 3 (New York: Doubleday, 1991), 343. N. Kiuchi (*The Purification Offering in the Priestly Literature: Its Meaning and Function* [Sheffield: Sheffield Academic, 1987]), by comparison, argues that we should understand *'āšām* as meaning "to realize one's guilt."

221. Milgrom, *Leviticus 1–16*, 343.

222. The rendering of *'āšām* in English is italicized in the translations cited.

223. Ibid., 319.

First, Milgrom argues that 'āšām is a consequential verb in the Old Testament cultic texts. That is, whereas in some parts of the Old Testament 'āšām refers to being culpable, in the priestly material it refers to the consequences of guilt. For the sake of the argument, let us concede this point. Milgrom says that there is also a psychological component to the consequential 'āšām in Leviticus. Immediately having said this, he continues, "The ancients did not distinguish between emotional and physical suffering; the same language describes pangs of conscience and physical pains,"[224] in support of which he states that in the penitential psalms it is hard to know whether the penitent is suffering emotionally or physically. The reason for this, according to Milgrom, is that unexplainable suffering may be regarded as the result of sin; hence the penitent is most concerned to discover the offense that caused the plight. "Thus it is logical to expect that a language that, as observed, will express the consequential syndrome of sin-punishment by a single word will also have at least one root in its lexicon to express another consequential relationship, that which exists between sin-punishment and guilt feelings. This root, I submit, is אשם."[225]

Second, Milgrom asserts that while nonlegal texts use metaphorical language to describe the feelings of guilt,[226] legal and cultic texts eschew metaphor so that in Leviticus a precise term would be needed to "pinpoint the existence of guilt."[227] This is the verb 'āšām!

Another prong in Milgrom's argument is that of "redundancy." In Leviticus 5:17 'āšām cannot, in his view, be translated as "incurring guilt" or "is guilty" because the contiguous "shall bear his responsibility" would make it tautologous.[228]

What is important for our purposes is that clearly some understanding/s of how language works is influencing Milgrom's decision to translate 'āšām as "to feel guilty." That is inevitable, but the question is, how helpful is his view of language? We could ask:

- Is it true that the ancients did not distinguish between emotional and physical suffering?
- Why would we expect Hebrew to have a root that expresses the connection between sin and the feeling of guilt?
- Do legal texts avoid metaphorical language in their need for precision?

224. Ibid., 342.
225. Ibid., 343.
226. E.g., "David's heart smote him" (KJV: 1 Sam. 24:5; 2 Sam. 24:10); "a stumbling [offense] of the heart" (1 Sam. 25:31 KJV); "my kidneys have whipped me" (Ps. 16:7, my trans.).
227. Milgrom, *Leviticus 1–16*, 343.
228. Ibid.

- Is metaphorical language imprecise?
- Is Milgrom right about redundancy in the texts he refers to?
- How would different answers to the above help with the translation of *'āšām*?

We could discuss these issues at length! Suffice it here to note that much of Milgrom's case rests on inadequate views of language. That similar vocabulary might be used for physical and emotional suffering does not mean that the ancients were unable to distinguish conceptually between them. Such an argument buys into the very logicogrammatical parallelism that Barr refuted. Long ago Barr exposed the weakness of the Biblical Theology Movement (BTM) in its suggestion that the vocabulary of the language of a people is closely related to how the people think. As Barr says of the BTM,

> All this can be summarized by saying that where linguistic evidence has been used in the Greek-Hebrew contrast it has not been adequately protected against, or indeed has positively presupposed, the idea of a logico-grammatical parallelism, a doctrine which can be traced from Aristotle though scholasticism, and which gained some of its plausibility from the predominant position of Latin and the corresponding attempt to force the forms of other languages into the moulds of Latin grammar.[229]

A case could be made that the ancients understood only too well the psychosomatic connections between physical and mental and emotional pain, yet in the Psalms it is clear that these different sufferings are not collapsed into one category.

Similarly, I cannot imagine why we should expect there to be a root in Hebrew expressing the consequential link between sin and the experience of guilt. Milgrom's logic is hard to follow at this point, but it seems to rest on the same logicogrammatical parallelism that Barr critiques.

Third, legal texts do differ in their use of language from, say, poetic texts, where metaphor abounds. Compare, for example, Psalm 42 with Leviticus 6:1–7. But the difference is one of degree and not one of the presence versus the absence of metaphor. There is perhaps also a difference in kind and function of metaphor. In the priestly literature there *are* central metaphors such as clean/unclean and holy/unholy that structure the entire discourse. In the early chapters of Leviticus, there are other common metaphors such as "without blemish" and "pleasing odor." Then there are other important metaphors in later chapters of Leviticus:

---

229. Barr, *Semantics of Biblical Language*, 43.

- 18:6–23 uses "uncover" for sexual intercourse.
- 18:25, "The land became defiled; . . . the land vomited out its inhabitants."
- 18:29, "cut off": "Whoever commits any of these abominations shall be cut off from their people."
- 18:30, "Keep my charge . . . not to defile yourselves."
- 25:1, "The land shall observe a sabbath."

An expression like "cut off" is clearly metaphorical and imprecise in terms of the precise penalty envisaged, as the scholarly discussion of just what is involved indicates.[230] It is a central clause expressing the penalty for very serious crimes. It is clear that "cut off" means that God will act decisively and probably through premature death, but it is never clear how God will achieve this or when.[231] The metaphor is very clear and yet is an open-ended expression. Perhaps legal language avoids being metaphorical in the same way as poetry, but clearly it is metaphorical in its own way. It must also be borne in mind that a text like Leviticus is more than a legal text; it is also educative material. And it can be argued that in educational material metaphors play a crucial role.[232]

Milgrom's view of metaphor appears to be the popular one of metaphor being ornamental and avoided by scientific texts. However, it is wrong to think that metaphorical language is necessarily imprecise and that scientific texts eschew metaphor.[233] Considerable work has been done in recent decades on vagueness, ambiguity, metaphor, and literal language.[234] Some studies of metaphor have argued that all language is metaphorical, albeit in different ways.[235] Certainly a more refined view of language is required to handle the

---

230. See, e.g., D. J. Wold, "The Karet Penalty in P: Rationale and Cases," *SBL Seminar Papers* (1979): 1–45.

231. Jay Sklar has helpfully alerted me to the considerable body of literature on the subject of being "cut off." It is not possible to interact with that literature here. My limited goal is to demonstrate that identifying "cut off" as a metaphor is an important part of understanding its function.

232. H. G. Petrie and R. S. Oshlag, "Metaphor and Learning," in *Metaphor and Thought*, ed. A. Ortony, 2nd ed. (Cambridge: Cambridge University Press, 1993), 579–609.

233. See, e.g., M. E. Botha, *Metaphor and Its Moorings: Studies in the Grounding of Metaphorical Meaning* (Bern: Peter Lang, 2007).

234. See, e.g., I. Scheffler, *Beyond the Letter: A Philosophical Inquiry into Ambiguity, Vagueness, and Metaphor in Language* (London: Routledge, 1979); G. Lakoff and M. Johnson, *Metaphors We Live By* (Chicago: University of Chicago Press, 1980); idem, *Philosophy in the Flesh: The Embodied Mind and Its Challenge to Western Thought* (New York: Basic Books, 1999); P. Ricoeur, *The Rule of Metaphor: Multi-Disciplinary Studies of the Creation of Meaning in Language* (Toronto: University of Toronto Press, 1977); J. M. Soskice, *Metaphor and Religious Language* (Oxford: Oxford University Press, 1985).

235. M. B. Hesse, "The Cognitive Claims of Metaphor," *Journal of Speculative Philosophy* 2 (1988): 1–16; here he says, "I am going to argue here for a radically different theory, which

data Milgrom is dealing with. If, for example, Milgrom is right about the consequential use of *'āšām* in Leviticus, might it not be the case that *'āšām* is being used somewhat differently from its normal usage precisely in order to evoke the range of consequences associated with being guilty of sin? Thus the term could be precise—the state or experience of guilt—and deliberately *encompassing* in terms of the effects at the same time! Feeling guilty would be one manifestation of the state of guilt, but perhaps the text deliberately refers to the experience in its totality without specifying the precise means.[236]

One is also surprised to encounter Milgrom's arguments about redundancy. In the study of the Psalms and the Pentateuch, redundancy has been repeatedly exposed as not truly redundant and thus as an inadequate argument.[237] However, it may be that redundancy is far less common in legal texts, in which case this might support Milgrom's case. Nevertheless this would still depend on the precise relationship between "become guilty" and "subject to punishment." Might it not be that this verse stresses that the lack of awareness at the time of the deed does not mean that one escapes the responsibilities of guilt?

No doubt the debate about how to translate *'āšām* in Leviticus will continue. But I hope it is clear that the debate ought *not* to continue uninformed by linguistic insight. How we conceive the relationship between language and thought, how we think about metaphor and literal language, what we make of redundancy in texts—these and myriad other issues of language inevitably shape our reading of the Bible right down to the detail of how we translate *'āšām*.

I shall call the *network* theory of meaning, and for a related thesis that 'all language is metaphorical'" (1).

236. This would support the standard translation of *'āšām* as "to be guilty" or "to become guilty."

237. See, e.g., M. Sternberg, *The Poetics of Biblical Narrative: Ideological Literature and the Drama of Reading* (Bloomington: Indiana University Press, 1987).

10

History

> The rejection of this historical mediation of truth and salvation has its roots, we have argued, in the devaluation of the realm of space and time in Greek thought, and has been allowed to flourish in the Christian theological tradition because of a neglect of the doctrine of creation. The soteriological consequence of this rejection of history is that, forsaking dependence upon what has taken place in Jesus, the individual finds within himself the resources of wisdom and insight to work out his own salvation.
>
> Murray Rae[1]

Introduction

Earlier we flagged Stephen Neill's point that New Testament studies urgently requires a *theology of history*, not that this will solve all the historical problems of the New Testament, but that it will provide the ring *within which solutions may be found*. In the past century a great deal of work has been done on the history of the Bible but without any emerging consensus. If anything, views today are more polarized than ever before.

---

1. M. Rae, "Creation and Promise: Towards a Theology of History," in *"Behind" the Text: History and Biblical Interpretation*, ed. C. G. Bartholomew et al. (Grand Rapids: Zondervan, 2003), 295.

In chapter 8 we explored Richard Bauckham's masterful work on Jesus and eyewitness testimony in the Gospels. And yet, juxtaposed with this we have a literary critic like Frank Kermode arguing that the New Testament accounts are "free narrative invention," "fictions inserted into a history-like record on later consideration of what ought properly to have occurred."[2] Kermode is not alone in holding such views: for some, the literary turn in which Kermode played a significant role confirms the history-like but in fact fictional nature of much of the narrative of the New Testament.

In terms of ancient Israel, recent decades have witnessed the emergence of a body of work questioning the historicity of almost every aspect of the Old Testament. Whitelam has gone as far as to declare the death of "biblical history."[3] For Whitelam, for example, the archaeological data do not even support the existence of a large, powerful Iron Age state founded by David. The people of Israel in the Old Testament are a literary and theological construct, so that there is little evidence that this biblical "Israel" existed other than as a literary fiction.[4] The parallel with Kermode's view of the New Testament is noteworthy.

Over the past century our knowledge of the ancient Near East and the context of the New Testament has increased dramatically, and yet scholars remain hopelessly divided about the historicity of both Old and New Testaments. It is common to find even Christian biblical scholars divided between maximalists and minimalists in relation to the historicity of the Bible. Clearly ever closer attention to the data alone will not solve this issue. Anthony Frendo, for example, set out to write about the emergence of ancient Israel but soon realized that "the real crux of the problem of the emergence of ancient Israel lay not so much in adducing some new datum or in drawing up a solid synthesis of the puzzle, but in the various presuppositions (often diametrically opposed) with which scholars approached the subject."[5] Thus, as Provan, Long, and Longman point out, "showing that biblical history is alive and well . . . must involve, rather, a discussion of all the fundamental issues of epistemology and of procedure . . . in relation to what is commonly referred to as 'critical method.'"[6] What is clear,

---

2. F. Kermode, "Deciphering the Big Book," a review of *The Birth of the Messiah*, by Raymond E. Brown, *New York Review of Books* 25, no. 11 (June 29, 1978): 39–42.

3. K. Whitelam, *The Invention of Ancient Israel: The Silencing of Palestinian History* (London: Routledge, 1996), 69.

4. Ibid., 23.

5. A. J. Frendo, *Pre-Exilic Israel, the Hebrew Bible, and Archaeology* (London: T&T Clark, 2011), ix.

6. I. W. Provan, V. P. Long, and T. Longman III, *A Biblical History of Israel* (Louisville: Westminster John Knox, 2003), 34.

especially in the light of the radically secular approaches now being applied to the Bible, is that one's view of history profoundly shapes one's approach to the historicity of the Bible.

Hence the fecundity of Neill's point; much will depend on the circle within which we approach historical issues. We need to recognize that some such ring will *always be in play* since it is impossible to attend to historical issues without some idea of the nature of history, criteria for assessment of historical reliability, the different options in philosophy of history both historically and now, and so forth. Postmodern readings of the Bible, presupposing a view of history as unordered flux and change, are as much committed to a particular view of history as the historical critic is committed to "neutral, objective, scientific" scholarship, with its notion of historical, scientific progress, while the Christian scholar is committed to a Christian view of history.

In biblical studies it would be a great help if we could resort to the practice of the early historical critics who would declare their views of history and religion so that they are in the foreground when one is assessing such work. As we noticed in our discussion of the rise of modern biblical studies in chapter 7, Wellhausen played a profoundly unhelpful role in this issue by seeking to erase such tradition and to insist that philosophy follows biblical studies but does not precede it.[7] As Alasdair MacIntyre in particular has shown, all scholarship is traditioned,[8] and honesty and rigor require that we own the traditions in which we work and make them clear to our readers. I do not assume that all my readers will agree with this. Postmodernism has made this view much harder to refute, but the dialogue between two major, contemporary Christian historians, Mark Noll and James Turner, reveals how stubborn the resistance can be. Both are historians at Notre Dame: Noll insists that our faith does shape our historical work, but Turner is adamant that when it comes to history, "faith gives no *epistemological* edge."[9] This, Turner argues, is one thing that we have learned from Thomas Aquinas. As I hope to show, such a view is untenable, and rejection of the formative power of a Christian view simply results in one adopting alternative views. History is utterly central to the Christian faith; and the Bible and the gospel invite us to take a position on this issue.

---

7. See C. Seerveld, "Footprints in the Snow," *Philosophia Reformata* 56 (1991): 1–34.

8. A. C. MacIntyre, *Whose Justice? Which Rationality?* (Notre Dame, IN: University of Notre Dame Press, 1988).

9. M. A. Noll and J. Turner, *The Future of Christian Learning: An Evangelical and Catholic Dialogue*, ed. T. A. Howard (Grand Rapids: Brazos, 2008), 106, with original emphasis. The dialogue is well worth reading.

History and the History of Biblical Interpretation

The Christ event did not occur in a culture ready to embrace the categories it brought with it, namely, the irruption of the kingdom of God into history, triggering the eschaton.[10] In chapter 3 we noticed just how central eschatology, and thus history, is to the New Testament. Within the Jewish tradition such categories *were* available, and thus it is not surprising, as we will see in chapter 11, that after his Hellenistic prologue, Luke resorts to Semitic idioms as he starts to tell the story of Jesus. In conflict with Judaism, however, there was the issue of the relationship *between events*, namely, the Christ event and the Old Testament. In conflict with Greek thought, there was the question of whether individual events could ever hold absolute significance.

As has often been observed, Luke-Acts is crucial in terms of laying out the historical framework of the early church.[11] But this was no easy task. Deeply rooted in Greek thought is the Platonic and neoplatonic view that the concrete world of everyday reality is one of flux and change, so that truth can never be derived from history.[12] Truth must be sought in the unchangeable realm of the Forms and Ideas or rooted ultimately in the One; only in this way can it be secured. Against this backdrop, John 1:14, "And the Word became flesh and lived among us," was scandalous in Greek ears, leading the early church father Tertullian to say, "I believe because it is absurd."

This radical contradiction between the world of the New Testament[13] and neoplatonism belies Sanders's notion, as noted in chapter 8, of the church constantly adjusting its faith and narratives to the times. This is not to deny that it was tempted in this direction. One of the great dangers of allegory among the church fathers was to flatten the historical development of the biblical story in favor of a "vertical" reading, which found the same truth throughout the Bible.[14] "St Irenaeus was the first to discover and propound without ambiguity the basis of a definitive solution."[15] His "offense" was to take time and thus history seriously as a constitutive element in the formation of the truth about the world. The two Testaments

---

10. As rightly noted by Thomas Torrance, Jean Daniélou, et al.

11. For a useful bibliographical survey, see J. B. Green and M. C. McKeever, *Luke-Acts and New Testament Historiography* (Grand Rapids: Baker, 1994).

12. See, e.g., Plato's parable of the cave in his *Republic*, book 7.

13. See, e.g., J. Daniélou, *The Lord of History: Reflections on the Inner Meaning of History*, trans. Nigel Abercrombie (Cleveland: World, 1968), 1–3.

14. See chap. 5 above.

15. Daniélou, *Lord of History*, 5. See Irenaeus of Lyons, *On the Apostolic Preaching*, trans. J. Behr, Popular Patristics 17 (Crestwood, NY: St. Vladimir's Seminary Press, 1997).

belong to one overarching scheme from creation to that end which is no end, but indicate two stages in its fulfillment, with a move from type to reality.

Herodotus (ca. 484–425 BC) is often and understandably viewed as the father of history.[16] By adopting the word *historia* to describe his work and the spirit in which he undertook his investigation, Herodotus ushered in a literary revolution. Earlier Heraclitus had used *historia* to denote philosophical inquiry; by using this word, Herodotus distances himself from the mere chronicle and narrative of what Cochrane calls "logography" (legendary stories) and raises history to the level of a science. As he states, his work embraced the study of fact, value, and causation. This freed Herodotus up to explore a great range of disciplines in his work. His cosmology is spatial, temporal, and material. As material it generates its own ebb and flow according to the law of compensation (τίσις), which is both eternal and comprehensive.[17] Indeed, under Herodotus history became a proper object of study, not because change and flux were denied, but because arbitrariness was denied.[18] However, τίσις ineluctably led to pessimism:

> The acceptance of this conclusion must necessarily breed a profound and ineradicable pessimism. In Herodotus such pessimism is everywhere apparent, but it finds no more dramatic or apposite expression than in the words which he puts into the mouth of a Persian grandee at the Theban dinner-party given on the eve of Plataea. "That which is destined to come to pass as a consequence of divine activity, . . . it is impossible for man to avert. . . . Of all the sorrows which afflict mankind, the bitterest is this, that one should have consciousness of much, but control over nothing."[19]

In subsequent classical historiography, serious attempts were made to avoid the conclusions reached by Herodotus. Of these, that by Thucydides was the

---

16. Herodotus, *The Histories*, ed. J. M. Marincola, trans. A. de Selincourt, rev. ed. (New York: Penguin, 2003); cf. J. T. Roberts, *Herodotus: A Very Short Introduction* (Oxford: Oxford University Press, 2011), who states (Kindle loc. 293–94), "To the groundbreaking Herodotus, then, the Roman man of letters Cicero gave the title *pater historiae*, 'Father of History.'" Note should also be taken of the work of Herodotus's predecessor, Hecataeus of Miletus, ca. 550–476 BC. See also N. Luraghi, ed., *The Historian's Craft in the Age of Herodotus* (New York: Oxford University Press, 2001); C. Dewald and J. Marincola, eds., *The Cambridge Companion to Herodotus* (Cambridge: Cambridge University Press, 2013); E. Foster and D. Lateiner, eds., *Thucydides and Herodotus* (Oxford: Oxford University Press, 2012); etc.

17. See C. N. Cochrane, *Christianity and Classical Culture: A Study of Thought and Action from Augustus to Augustine* (Oxford: Oxford University Press, 1957), 456–69.

18. Rae, "Creation and Promise," 269.

19. Cochrane, *Christianity and Classical Culture*, 468.

most significant.[20] He saw the weakness of his predecessors' work as its impregnation with myth. The way forward was to distinguish between primary and secondary causes, then focus exclusively on the latter, which are alone capable of observation and verification. History thus becomes focused on what humans do and say. For Thucydides, the state was of particular importance, with its combined wisdom and power intended to create an environment conducive to the moral and economic foundations for human happiness. However, what Thucydides had to face was the intervention of forces outside the state's control.[21] "For the story he has to tell is that of human reason defeated and crushed by the forces of irrationality."[22]

For the early Christians, the failure of classical historiography resulted from its failure to discern the true "cause" of human being and motivation. It thus posited the *logos* of Christ rather than that of classicism as *the* principle of understanding. As Cochrane tells the story, it took time for the full potential of Christianity to be worked out historically, with major progress made by Athanasius, culminating in the work of Augustine. What was foreshadowed in Athanasius's *De incarnatione* received fulfilment in Augustine's *City of God*. "But the divergence between Christianity and Classicism was in no respect more conspicuously or emphatically displayed than with regard to history; in a very real sense indeed it marked the crux of the issue between the two."[23]

Augustine's work on biblical hermeneutics was very significant, as explained in chapter 5. Scripture reveals the means whereby we obtain a just and happy life; as prophecy, the biblical history reveals the values that *scientia* by itself cannot uncover. The values are those of Christian insight, or *sapientia*:

> The recognition of *sapientia* as an instrument for historical interpretation involves implications of the utmost importance. To begin with, it is equally opposed to the conception of history whether as science or art. Christian historiography thus denies as purely supposititious the artistic and philosophic assumption that "nature" consists of a closed system of "necessary" physical laws.[24]

20. See C. N. Cochrane, *Thucydides and the Science of History* (London: Oxford University Press, 1929).
21. Rae writes, "For all his interest in history, Thucydides's recourse to the concept of universal and eternal law meant that he did not finally break free from the ahistorical conception of truth and meaning which we have seen in Greek thought" ("Creation and Promise," 269).
22. Cochrane, *Christianity and Classical Culture*, 473.
23. Ibid., 456.
24. Ibid., 478.

Augustine's rejection of "fortune," so dominant a motif in pagan thought, was "a matter of sheer intellectual and moral necessity."[25] Everything must be referred to divine providence, including the matter of chance: "What we call the fortuitous (*casum*) is nothing but that, the reason and cause of which is concealed from our view."[26] This analysis of fortuity enabled Augustine to do justice to the insights in the pagan concept of τύχη, or *fortuna*, claiming that the individual historical event is unique and thus unpredictable. Unlike pagan thought, for Augustine this does not indicate the intervention of an arbitrary cosmic force, but in relation to providence it is an essential part of the *necessitas rerum* (the necessity of things). "In substituting the embodied for the disembodied *logos*, Christian historiography claims to establish a concrete principle of interpretation in lieu of the barren ideologies of Classicism."[27]

This means history in relation to *personality*, thereby fulfilling classicism's desire for a basis for humanism, but one that is neither anthropocentric nor anthropomorphic. "The discovery of personality was, at the same time, the discovery of history."[28] For Christians, this clue was to be found, however, in the revelation of Christ, who is the true *logos* or account of being and movement in the universe. "Trinitarian Christianity thus pointed to an interpretation of history purely and simply in terms of the will of God."[29] The Christian neither seeks to read truth, beauty, and goodness into nature nor to "conserve" them in the face of a meaningless universe, but to discover them there. Christianity is not the opponent of science but its basis.

Augustine was vehemently opposed to cyclical views of history.[30] Human history does not consist in repetitive patterns but in a steady, albeit uneven, advance toward an ultimate goal. As Ambrose pointed out, time, space, matter, and form are "not gods, but gifts";[31] they present themselves as opportunity. In this way Augustine gave expression to the Christian view of history as *providence*.

The New Testament thus contains rich potential for a Christian view of history. What should not be forgotten, however, are the roots of such a view of history in the Old Testament. In an essay titled "Biblical Time," Ricoeur

25. Ibid., 479.
26. Augustine, *The Retractions* 1.1–2, FC 60 (Washington, DC: Catholic University of America Press, 1968).
27. Cochrane, *Christianity and Classical Culture*, 480.
28. Ibid., 456.
29. Ibid.
30. See Augustine, *City of God* 12.14, where he argues that we should not read the cyclical emphasis in Eccles. 1 in support of such views.
31. Quoted in Cochrane, *Christianity and Classical Culture*, 484.

explores the way in which the different genres of the Old Testament interact with one another in generating a biblical view of time, if there is such a thing. However, he concludes from this that "the project of a merely narrative theology is a chimera."[32] In my opinion, however, it is precisely a narrative biblical theology of the Bible that helps develop a biblical view of time and history. The genres apart from narrative in the Old Testament are canonically all connected into the grand story it tells, so that narrative holds the key to a biblical perspective of history. As Herrera explains,

> The foundational charter of the philosophy of history is found in one biblical verse: "God, at the beginning of time, created heaven and earth." ... This text, as traditionally interpreted, shattered the pagan conception of an eternal universe parceled out in an infinity of cycles. That view was voiced by Berossus, the Babylonian astrologer, who maintained that the universe passes through a number of Great Years with each cosmic cycle reproducing that which had preceded it. The doctrine of creation entailing linear time opened a vast horizon of novel events that took history beyond the limits of the ancient chroniclers. Even Herodotus ... was imprisoned in a circle.[33]

Similarly Smit stresses the importance of creation in his articulation of a Christian philosophy of history:

> When I maintain that *God is the meaning of history*, I mean to say that history has meaning in that it is totally, in all its elements and phenomena, in all its subjects and objects, *related to, oriented to* God. He has created the world in relation to himself.... That means for history not only fullness of meaning but also freedom, since for its meaning it is not dependent on the historical process, nor on the autonomous person.[34]

A philosopher of history who has paid significant attention to the Old Testament is Eric Voegelin. He argues that the structure of order in which we live has its source in divine revelation. The first volume in his Order and History series, *Israel and Revolution*,[35] reflects on Israel's reception of revelation in the context of the ancient Near Eastern world and on the resulting

---

32. P. Ricoeur, "Biblical Time," in *Figuring the Sacred: Religion, Narrative, and Imagination* (Philadelphia: Fortress, 1995), 179.

33. R. A. Herrera, *Reasons for Our Rhymes: An Inquiry into the Philosophy of History* (Grand Rapids: Eerdmans, 2001), 13.

34. M. C. Smit, *Toward a Christian Conception of History*, ed. H. D. Morton and H. Van Dyke (Lanham, MD: University Press of America, 2002), 325.

35. E. Voegelin, *Order and History*, vol. 1, *Israel and Revolution*, The Collected Works of Eric Voegelin 14 (Columbia: University of Missouri Press, 2001).

breakthrough in historical consciousness.[36] Voegelin argues that in the ancient Near East, humankind existed in a cosmological civilization whose symbolization expressed "the mythical participation of society in the divine being that orders the cosmos." In these civilizations there was a movement toward understanding the transcendence of the divine over against society, especially in the Memphite theology[37] and the reform of Akhenaton[38] in Egypt. History is a drama in which humanity is an actor, and the mystery of history is illumined when some aspect of the total experience of humankind is sharpened in human consciousness, thereby providing a vantage point for a clearer awareness of existential participation in the divine order of being. When this happened in Israel, a new type of person appeared on the world-political scene: such persons lived and acted politically vis-à-vis God, the transcendent author and source of the divine order in creation and history. The breaking in of divine reality found its optimum clarity in the Bible, where history is structured by crucial events such as the exodus and the incarnation.[39]

Through the exodus, Israel was liberated for a new life in historical form since the exodus heightened awareness of the gap between the immanent and the transcendent God. Moses led "an exodus from cosmological civilization," and a new type of society was born, living in immediacy under the kingdom of God. History became "the inner form" of Israel's existence, by comparison with other ancient Near Eastern civilizations, which existed in the form of cosmological myth. For Voegelin, without Israel there would be no history but only the recurring rhythms of cosmological civilization.

This breakthrough was difficult to maintain, and Voegelin sees the emergence of monarchy in Israel as the great derailment of the project, indicating a reentry into cosmological civilization. If it were not for the prophets, this movement would have been irreversible. For example, Second Isaiah envisions Israel's exodus from itself to penetrate all humankind with God's revelation (the Ecumenic Age).

The unique view of history in the Old Testament was a central theme of the Biblical Theology Movement (BTM).[40] Frankfort and his coauthors concur with this view.[41] For Israel, history was a comprehensive reality of the highest

36. Voegelin's critique of Wellhausen should be noted; see ibid., 192–200, esp. 202–5.
37. For the texts, see M. Lichtheim, *Ancient Egyptian Literature: A Book of Readings*, vol. 1, *The Old and Middle Kingdoms* (Berkeley: University of California Press, 1973), 49–55.
38. For the texts, see idem, vol. 2, *The New Kingdom* (1976), 47–55.
39. On the significance of the incarnation, see M. Henry, "Eric Voegelin on the Incarnate Christ," *Modern Age* 50, no. 4 (2008): 332–44.
40. See G. E. Wright, *God Who Acts: Biblical Theology as Recital* (London: SCM, 1952).
41. See also S. Moscati, *The Face of the Ancient Orient: A Panorama of Near Eastern Civilizations in Pre-Classical Times* (Chicago: Quadrangle, 1960), 235–81, and esp. 328–31.

importance. It has meaning: "Hebrew history was primarily a philosophy of history,"[42] and such a view of history had never been known among the great civilizations that preceded Israel. As the ruler of history, God is shaping events toward his purpose for history so that history is, in this sense, a story of progress.

Such views were sharply criticized by James Barr, who has more recently argued that the dominant form of Israel's traditions is story, which is history-like. Albrekston attempted to show that testimonies to divine activity in history were not unique to the Old Testament.[43] However, as B. W. Anderson declares, the real issue is the semantic field, the pattern of events within which such statements are made.[44] Anderson concludes, "Voegelin is right, I believe, in saying that Israel's knowledge of God brought about a sense of history which was a novelty in a cultural environment dominated by a mythical view of reality."[45]

This implication of the opening salvo of the biblical story becomes even clearer when the whole canon of Scripture is taken into account. While Cullmann's discussion of Greek thought about history as cyclical may be questionable at points,[46] his articulation of the significance of the Christ event for a biblical view of time and history remains insightful. Cullmann asserts, "The New Testament writings for the first time give to all revelation an essential anchorage in time; here for the first time the line is consistently carried through in its central significance for salvation and faith. Thus it is not as if we had to do with a Jewish survival; rather, that which is intimated in Judaism is here completely carried out."[47]

This is not to suggest that the Bible or the church fathers developed a comprehensive philosophy of history. David Bebbington's useful introduction, *Patterns in History: A Christian Perspective on Historical Thought*, demonstrates that it has taken centuries for Christians to develop the potential of the Bible for history and that inevitably Christian views have been developed in dialogue with and formed by the philosophies of the day. What I am arguing for is that Scripture contains a particular view of history, which continues

---

42. H. Frankfort et al., *The Intellectual Adventure of Ancient Man: An Essay on Speculative Thought in the Ancient Near East* (Chicago: University of Chicago Press, 1946), 322; also see 318–25.

43. B. Albrektson, *History and the Gods: An Essay on the Idea of Historical Events as Divine Manifestations in the Ancient Near East and in Israel* (Lund: Gleerup, 1967; reprint, Winona Lake, IN: Eisenbrauns, 2011).

44. B. W. Anderson, "Politics and the Transcendent: Voegelin's Philosophical and Theological Exposition of the Old Testament in the Context of the Ancient Near East," in *Eric Voegelin's Search for Order in History*, ed. S. A. McKnight (Lanham, MD: University Press of America, 1978), 71.

45. Ibid.

46. Ricoeur, "Biblical Time," 167–69. But cf. Herrera, *Reasons for Our Rhymes*, chap. 1.

47. O. Cullmann, *Christ and Time: The Primitive Christian Conception of Time and History*, 3rd, rev. ed. (London: SCM, 1967), 38.

to have the potential to be systematized into a theory of history for today. Modernity and postmodernism have made that a challenge, to say the least, and in the process have brought us back into a situation in terms of history similar to that of the Greeks and Romans.

Descartes (1596–1650), as is well known, sought certainty in the *cogito* (I think, [therefore I am]). This marks a major shift from starting with ontology to starting with epistemology; the source for truth in Descartes, as in so much modern thought, is rooted in the human subject. Just as the Greek rooting of truth in the realm of forms marginalized history, so too does the immanentism of Cartesianism. Thus Descartes declares:

> Fictitious narratives lead us to imagine the possibility of many events that are impossible; and even the most faithful histories, if they do not wholly misrepresent matters, or exaggerate their importance to render the account of them more worthy of perusal, omit, at least, almost always the meanest and least striking of the attendant circumstances; hence it happens that *the remainder does not represent the truth*, and that such as regulate their conduct by examples drawn from this source, are apt to fall into the extravagances of the knight-errants of romance, and to entertain projects that exceed their powers.[48]

As is clear from this quote, Cartesian doubt extends to history and history writing. It cannot be trusted to secure the certainty of truth that humans need.

Similarly in Spinoza (1632–77) the role of historical narrative is denigrated in relation to the quest for truth. In his *Tractatus*, in the section on the divine law, he says that divine law

> *does not depend on the truth of any historical narrative whatsoever*, for inasmuch as this natural Divine law is comprehended solely by the consideration of human nature, it is plain that we can conceive it as existing as well in Adam as in any other man, as well in a man living among his fellows, as in a man who lives by himself.
>
> *The truth of a historical narrative, however assured, cannot give us the knowledge nor consequently the love of God*, for love of God springs from knowledge of Him, and knowledge of Him should be derived from general ideas, in themselves certain and known, so that the truth of a historical narrative is very far from being a necessary requisite for our attaining our highest good.
>
> Still, though the truth of histories cannot give us the knowledge and love of God, I do not deny that reading them is very useful with a view to life in

---

48. R. Descartes, *Discourse on the Method of Rightly Conducting the Reason and Seeking the Truth in the Sciences*. Available at https:/ebooks.adelaide.edu.au/d/descartes/rene/d44dm/ with added emphasis.

the world, for the more we have observed and known of men's customs and circumstances, which are best revealed by their actions, the more warily we shall be able to order our lives among them, and so far as reason dictates to adapt our actions to their dispositions.[49]

Spinoza is an important forerunner of the historical-critical method, and in his discussion of how to read the Bible he explains his approach:

> I call passages clear or obscure according as their meaning is inferred easily or with difficulty in relation to the context, not according as their truth is perceived easily or the reverse by reason. We are at work *not on the truth of passages, but solely on their meaning*. We must take especial care, when we are in search of the meaning of a text, not to be led away by our reason in so far as it is founded on principles of natural knowledge (to say nothing of prejudices): in order not to confound the meaning of a passage with its truth, we must examine it solely by means of the signification of the words, or by a reason acknowledging no foundation but Scripture.[50]

For Spinoza, "the Divine origin of Scripture must consist solely in its teaching true virtue."[51]

This denigration of history as a source of truth can be tracked through Leibniz, Lessing, and Kant. Lessing (1729–81) shared with Kant a profound distrust of history as a vehicle of truth. He asserted, "Contingent truths of history can never become the necessary truths of reason."[52] "This, this is the broad and ugly ditch which I cannot get across, no matter how often and earnestly I have tried to make the leap."[53] Michalson points out that Lessing actually identified three different ditches and not just one![54] The first is *the temporal gap* separating the present from the revelatory events of the distant past. The second is the metaphysical gap between historical truths and religious truths. The third is the existential gap that separates a modern, autonomous, and secular "believer" from a message that appears historically doubtful and probably incredible too. The second gap reveals Lessing's

---

49. B. de Spinoza, *The Chief Works of Benedict de Spinoza*, translated from Latin and introduced by R. H. M. Elwes, vol. 1, *Introduction; Tractatus Theologico-politicus; Tractatus Politicus*, rev. ed. (London: George Bell & Sons, 1891), 61, with added emphasis.
50. Ibid., chap. 7, with added emphasis.
51. Ibid.
52. G. E. Lessing, *Philosophical and Theological Writings*, Cambridge Texts in the History of Philosophy (Cambridge: Cambridge University Press, 2005), 85.
53. Ibid., 87.
54. G. E. Michalson Jr., *Lessing's "Ugly Ditch": A Study of Theology and History* (University Park: Pennsylvania State University Press, 1985), 1–14.

rationalist predilection in matters of religion and thus "reveals both the artificiality and the dispensability of Lessing's concern about the temporal ditch. If, ultimately, a rational principle is in religious control, then nothing important really depends upon any form of factual inquiry, historical or otherwise."[55]

> For Lessing, Jesus is important only to the extent that he embodies or somehow brings to expression truths that are not contingent upon historical appearances. Thus, the contingency-necessity distinction not only informs Lessing's view of historical truth, but it [also] underwrites any truly religious interest he might have in Jesus: with respect to history, the contingency side of the distinction plays the determining role; with respect to Christology, the notion of necessary truth is decisive.[56]

Michalson draws attention to the importance of how Lessing's view frames the debate about theology of history, and he rightly asserts:

> The very employment of ditch imagery in the discussion of faith and history is itself the chief symptom of the disease. The deeper issue, really, is not even that we suffer the disease of confusion, but that we are unaware that we suffer from it. . . . The wrong topic, as the reader will quickly learn, is historical criticism and the procedures of historical research as they relate to Christian faith. The right topic, by contrast, is historical revelation. In other words, the wrong topic is wrong partly because it reflects the concerns of the secular, academic sensibility, while the right topic is right because it is what animates and sustains the worshiping community.[57]

Kant (1724–1804) argues for a religion of reason and is equally critical of the potential of historical narrative to provide truth.[58] We do not need an empirical example to furnish the idea of a morally well-pleasing person to God; as an archetype this idea is already present in our reason.[59] Of the historical element of Scripture, Kant notes that "the final purpose even of reading these holy scriptures, or of investigating their content, is to make men better; *the historical element, which contributes nothing to this end, is something which is in itself quite indifferent, and we can do with it what we like.*"[60]

55. Ibid., 11.
56. Ibid., 12.
57. Ibid., viii–ix.
58. See G. E. Michalson Jr., *The Historical Dimension of a Rational Faith: The Role of History in Kant's Religious Thought* (Washington, DC: University Press of America, 1977).
59. I. Kant, *Religion within the Limits of Reason Alone*, trans. T. M. Greene and H. H. Hudson (New York: Harper & Row, 1960), 56.
60. Ibid., 102, with added emphasis.

There are many other similar statements in this work by Kant, but in the light of the profound influence Kant had on de Wette, the father of modern biblical criticism,[61] it is worth pausing to consider the implications of Kant's rational religion. In his *Prolegomena to the History of Israel*, Wellhausen describes de Wette as "the epoch making pioneer of historical criticism in this field."[62] Kant grew up in a Christian home, and while at the University of Königsberg he attended Schultz's lectures on dogmatics. Apart from these lectures, Kant took little interest in theology, and when he came to write his *Religion within the Limits of Reason Alone*, he turned to his old catechism from his youth to refresh his memory.[63] Clearly Kant's view of the Bible and its historical narratives—we can do what we like with them!—is *not* derived from careful study of the narratives but stems from his idealistic philosophy. Thus it is quite ridiculous to argue that the influence of philosophy on modern biblical criticism is minimal or nonexistent. Here we see its power to frame an approach to Scripture, and clearly it is far from neutral or objective, *unless* one embraces Kant's philosophy. It is hard to see how a Christian could go along with Kant, bearing in mind the biblical stress on God's revelation in and through history. Alvin Plantinga traces postmodernism's "creative idealism" back to Kant: in much postmodern reading of Scripture, it is not hard to see Kant's dictum that we can do what we like with the historical narratives of Scripture coming home to roost, as it were.

Inevitably history bounced back on the philosophical agenda of modernity and not least in Hegel's (1770–1831) thought.[64] Right-wing Hegelians in particular sought to argue that Hegel's philosophy was consistent with Lutheran orthodoxy, but clearly his philosophy of *Geist* (spirit) working itself out through history via thesis, antithesis, and synthesis is a far cry from the biblical view of history.[65] Beiser reports, "Although Hegel attempts to reinstate the traditional idea of providence, he also gives it an entirely immanent or this-worldly meaning."[66] God does not exist apart from history; indeed, God realizes himself only through history, as far as one can know, and thus our efforts are necessary for the realization of the divine nature.

As Rae notes of Hegel, "In principle, therefore, the truth may be learned without reference to history. In Hegel and Marx, the great modern interpreters

---

61. See chap. 7 above.
62. J. Wellhausen, *Prolegomena to the History of Israel*, Cambridge Library Collection (Cambridge: Cambridge University Press, 2013), 4.
63. T. M. Greene, "The Historical Context and Religious Significance of Kant's Religion," in Kant, *Religion within the Limits of Reason Alone*, xxx.
64. For a good introduction to Hegel's view of history, see F. C. Beiser, *Hegel* (London: Routledge, 2005), 261–81.
65. See Rae, "Creation and Promise," 276–77.
66. Beiser, *Hegel*, 271.

of history, we find the modern rejection of the decisiveness of the moment in full cry."[67] As is well known, D. F. Strauss (1808–74) applied Hegel's philosophy of history to the New Testament. In his *Life of Jesus Critically Examined*, Strauss argues that much of the New Testament historical narrative is not history but myth; it contains timeless religious truth but clothed in unhistorical myth.

It is to Søren Kierkegaard's (1813–55) credit that he recognizes what is at stake for Christianity in these developments.[68] The challenge of such views of history is well expressed on the title page of Kierkegaard's *Philosophical Fragments*:

> Is an historical point of departure
> possible for an eternal consciousness; how can
> such a point of departure have any other
> than a merely historical interest;
> is it possible to base an eternal happiness
> upon historical knowledge?

Like many of Kierkegaard's works, *Philosophical Fragments* is highly creative; it is pseudonymous, akin to a drama and a dialogue, involves a thought experiment, and so forth. Regarding the challenge of the modern views of history we have been looking at, its importance is, in my view, comparable to that of Augustine's *City of God*. We cannot here explore the shape of Kierkegaard's argument in detail; suffice it to quote Thulstrup's admirable summary of the work:

> It is now evident that the questions on the title-page have been answered: there can be an historical point of departure for an eternal consciousness and this can have more than a merely historical interest if it is the unique historical fact, the Christ-revelation, the Moment in time when the eternal miraculously breaks into the temporal; but one cannot base an eternal happiness on merely historical knowledge, for it can be based only upon Faith.[69]

Kierkegaard thus affirms the vital importance of history for revelation and truth; in this he sets Christianity against idealism, whether of the Kantian or Hegelian sort. In relation to history, Kierkegaard perceptively distinguishes between two types of *belief* (Danish *Tro*). Historical events fall in the category

---

67. Rae, "Creation and Promise," 277.
68. Michalson (*Lessing's "Ugly Ditch,"* 61–92) has a significantly different reading of *Philosophical Fragments* from mine. He argues, "Kierkegaard's point is not that historical knowledge *potentially* stands in a positive relation to faith, but in fact does not because of an epistemological shortcoming; he means to show that historical knowledge stands in *no* relation to faith" (92). In my view, this is a misreading; Kierkegaard does see historical knowledge as potentially standing in a positive relation to faith, but historical evidence by itself will not produce faith: the work of the Spirit is required.
69. N. Thulstrup, "Commentator's Introduction," in *Philosophical Fragments*, by S. Kierkegaard (Princeton: Princeton University Press, 1962), lxxxiii.

of time, and as such the organ for their apprehension is *belief*. Kierkegaard rightly declares that even if we were to receive accurate historical testimony about the Christ event, this in itself would not be adequate for faith. The capacity for faith and thus for grasping the full dimensions of the Christ event is a gift of God, so that *in this sense* the contemporary disciple is on par with the disciples who actually accompanied and saw and heard Jesus.

As we noticed in chapter 7, these emerging views of history, and not least those of Kant and Hegel, profoundly influenced the history of biblical interpretation. It was in Germany in the second half of the nineteenth century that modern biblical criticism truly emerged, and this development was fundamentally shaped by the current views of history. Palmer correctly alerts us to the atemporal dimension in Schleiermacher's (1768–1834) hermeneutic.[70] Dilthey (1833–1911) sought to introduce a critique of historical reason through his development of the psychological emphasis in Schleiermacher's hermeneutic.[71] This historical turn in hermeneutics is of great significance for biblical hermeneutics, for as Nicholson explains, it was nineteenth-century *historical* philosophy that shaped the historical-critical method.

> To a remarkable extent, indeed to a greater extent than has often been realized or acknowledged, it was this historical thinking that provided the basis of biblical hermeneutics in the nineteenth century, and more than the theologians and biblical scholars themselves, it was the leading figures of the German historical school—Barthold Gustav Niebuhr, Wilhelm von Humboldt, Leopold von Ranke, Johan Gustav Droysen, Theodor Mommsen, and others—who created the interpretive framework and provided the method.[72]

It clearly becomes important, then, to get some idea of the sort of views of history promoted by these figures.[73] *Von Humboldt* (1767–1835)[74] stresses the creative role of the historian in connecting and placing in a larger whole

---

70. R. E. Palmer, *Hermeneutics: Interpretation Theory in Schleiermacher, Dilthey, Heidegger, and Gadamer* (Evanston, IL: Northwestern University Press, 1988), 75. Schleiermacher's view of God and the world is more nuanced than this suggests, but overall I think Palmer is correct.

71. For a brief discussion of this development in hermeneutics, see J. Bleicher, *Contemporary Hermeneutics: Hermeneutics as Method, Philosophy, and Critique* (London: Routledge & Kegan Paul, 1980), 16–26.

72. E. W. Nicholson, *Interpreting the Old Testament: A Century of the Oriel Professorship* (Oxford: Clarendon, 1981), 16. On historicism and hermeneutics, see J. Grondin, *Introduction to Philosophical Hermeneutics* (New Haven: Yale University Press, 1995), 76–90.

73. For Droysen (1808–84), see K. Mueller-Vollmer, ed., *The Hermeneutics Reader: Texts of the German Tradition from the Enlightenment to the Present* (New York: Continuum, 1988), 118–31. Above all else, Droysen stresses moral forces in historical interpretation, as well as the role of the imagination.

74. See W. von Humboldt, "On the Task of the Historian," in Mueller-Vollmer, *Hermeneutics Reader*, 105–18.

the fragmented pieces resulting from his research. In history the historian, like the poet, uses intuition and imagination that yet is subordinated to experience. The historian must strive for "the necessary"; he must keep the ideas of history's laws fixed in his mind so that he can discern their trace in his investigations. Von Humboldt asserts that history "strives toward the picture of human destiny in full truth, living fullness, and pure clarity," and he emphasizes "ideas" that "rule and control world history in all its aspects."[75] These must guide the historian and be the focus of his research. "It goes without saying, of course, that these ideas arise from the profusion of events itself, or, to be more precise, arise in the mind through a consideration of these events which is undertaken with a true historical sense."[76]

Ranke (1795–1886) did not believe that general theories could cut across time and space. Reacting against Hegel, he asserted, "I can therefore understand by the 'leading ideas' only the ruling tendencies in every century. These tendencies can only be described, but in the last analysis they cannot be subsumed under one concept."[77] This lack of emphasis on unifying theories or themes led some to denigrate his "mindless empiricism." In the nineteenth century, Ranke's work was very popular, and his ideas about historical practice gradually became dominant in Western historiography.[78]

While Ranke's method remains influential in the practice of history, his broader ideas of historiography and empiricism are now regarded as outdated and no longer credible. They held sway among historians until the mid-twentieth century, when they were challenged by E. H. Carr and Fernand Braudel. Carr, for example, opposed Ranke's ideas of empiricism as naive, boring, and outmoded, saying that historians did not merely report facts: they choose which facts they use. Commenting on the legacy of Ranke's dictum that historians should represent the past *"wie es eigentlich gewesen"* (as it really was), Walter Benjamin scathingly wrote that it represented "the strongest narcotic of the [nineteenth] century."[79]

75. Ibid., 107, 115.
76. Ibid., 111.
77. L. von Ranke, *The Theory and Practice of History*, ed. G. G. Iggers (London: Routledge, 2011), 22.
78. On the triumph of historicism, see F. C. Beiser, *The German Historicist Tradition* (Oxford: Oxford University Press, 2011).
79. However, it is important to read von Ranke himself: his views have often been misrepresented. See von Ranke, *Theory and Practice of History*. "The purpose of the present volume is in part to correct the image of Ranke as a narrow and fact-oriented historian hostile to theory" (xiii). According to Iggers *eigentlich* should be translated as "essentially," so that it is not factuality but a concern with the essential that renders an account historical (xiv).

From this brief examination of von Humboldt and Ranke, it should be very clear that they held to specific views of history that, certainly today, cannot be assumed as true or taken for granted. If, as Nicholson says, this was the soil in which historical criticism developed, then clearly both the soil and the plant—historical criticism—have to be reassessed in the light of more recent developments in philosophy of history as well as in the light of their religious commitments.

The emergence of modern biblical criticism is deeply influenced by the philosophies of its day. For example, *Gabler's* 1787 Altdorf inaugural is widely regarded as also the inaugural of biblical theology as a modern, independent discipline.[80] In relation to Gabler's inaugural, Reventlow comments rightly, "In distinguishing between the doctrinal views of the writers of sacred scripture and the rational 'philosophy' of contemporary dogmatic theologians, this formulation is redolent of the atmosphere of the Enlightenment; its sole concern is with universal truths, so that 'biblical theology remained a preparation for dogmatics.'"[81] Gabler was important in his understanding of biblical theology as a historical discipline, and this emphasis soon led to the separation of biblical theology into Old Testament theology and New Testament theology. Initially, as with de Wette, for example, this separation was under the rubric of biblical theology, but soon separate works started to appear. Crucially, then, Reventlow explains, "Future developments were characterized rather by *a move from any conscious philosophy of history* in the name of historical positivism and evolutionism."[82] In this connection Reventlow refers to Kuenen and Wellhausen.

After World War I, Reventlow discusses the influence of Gunkel's history of religions school. The chief influence on this school is Herder! Reventlow also notices Schleiermacher's formative influence on Gunkel in the latter's view that the aim of exegesis is neither the thoughts nor feelings of the author, but his personality. W. Robertson Smith is also dependent on Schleiermacher's hermeneutic, according to Reventlow. Within the prophets this approach manifested itself as a concern to identify the authentic words of the prophet as distinct from later accretions. Brett argues persuasively that this approach to the prophets is connected with *Romantic idealism* in historiography.[83]

Ernst Troeltsch (1865–1923) rightly recognized that the real problem with the historical-critical method is that it is "based on assumptions quite

---

80. See chap. 4 above.
81. H. G. Reventlow, *Problems of Old Testament Theology in the Twentieth Century* (Philadelphia: Fortress, 1985), 4.
82. Ibid., 4.
83. M. G. Brett, *Biblical Criticism in Crisis? The Impact of the Canonical Approach on Old Testament Studies* (Cambridge: Cambridge University Press, 1991), 89–93.

irreconcilable with traditional belief."[84] The impasse was intrinsic and inevitable. However, Troeltsch's own approach did not find a viable way out of this impasse. He affirmed a doctrine of *correlation*: events must be understood in relation to their contexts and in terms of antecedent causes. The problem with this is that in advance it outlaws any claim to absolute or final truth in religious matters.[85] It erodes the uniqueness of Christianity by placing it in relation to outside religious and cultural influences, thus eliminating the possibility of calling Christianity true and other religions false. This is exemplified in the history of religions approach to the Old Testament. Likewise Troeltsch's principle of *analogy* eliminates the category of miracle. This principle is the historiographical vindication of Hume. "In tandem with the principle of correlation, Troeltsch's principle of analogy produces what is perhaps the single most decisive result of modern historical method for an older Protestant orthodoxy—namely, the elimination of supernatural intervention as a possible category of historical explanation."[86] Finally, Troeltsch also proposed a principle of criticism: historical results are always corrigible so that our claims about the past are always provisional.

Much twentieth-century theology and biblical studies accepted Troeltsch's way of framing the problem; so a sure ground for faith apart from history had to be found. Hence Martin Kähler distinguished between *Historie* and *Geschichte*; for Herrmann, the inner life of Jesus was the true ground of faith; Bultmann engaged in his hermeneutic of demythologization; and so on. Michalson rightly observes that "mainstream Protestant theology from roughly 1920 to 1960 proceeded on the basis of a kind of double-entry bookkeeping, one column for faith and one column for historiography."[87] Much Protestant thought in the twentieth century thus involves a series of attempts to mediate some truce between the competing demands of these alternative views on history and revelation. Ironically, as Michalson states, Troeltsch's principle of criticism is itself impossible to state in a way that is not self-refuting.[88]

This brings us into the time of the literary turn and then the postmodern turn in biblical interpretation. The literary turn raised the most fundamental questions about much historical criticism; ironically, even as it demonstrated again and again that biblical books and sections were literary wholes, it thereby

---

84. V. A. Harvey, *The Historian and the Believer: The Morality of Historical Knowledge and Christian Belief* (New York: Macmillan, 1966), 5.

85. E. Troeltsch, "Historiography," in *Encyclopedia for Religion and Ethics*, ed. J. Hastings (New York: Charles Scribner's Sons, 1913), 716–23.

86. Michalson, *Lessing's "Ugly Ditch,"* 95.

87. Ibid., 98. See Heinz Zahrnt, Helmut Thielicke, et al.

88. Michalson, *Lessing's "Ugly Ditch,"* 101.

raised the question of reference and historicity in a new way. One might ask, Can carefully constructed literature accurately refer to events? Sternberg and Ricoeur[89] have both pointed out that fiction and history writing share narrative poetics: "There are simply no universals of historical vs. fictive form."[90] In this sense both are forms of literature. Intriguingly, nineteenth-century German historians like von Humboldt and Droysen are well aware of the *art* of history and the role of the imagination. Thus there can be no question that literature *can be* historiography. Criteria other than poetics will determine one's judgment on this issue. Sternberg argues in relation to the Hebrew Bible, "Of course the narrative is historiographic, inevitably so considering its teleology and incredibly so considering its time and environment. Everything points in this direction."[91] As he writes,

> Were the narrative written or read as fiction, then God would turn from the lord of history into a creature of the imagination, with the most disastrous results. The shape of time, the rationale of monotheism, the foundations of conduct, the national sense of identity, the very right to the land of Israel and the hope of deliverance to come: all hang in the generic balance. Hence the Bible's determination to sanctify and compel literal belief in the past. It claims not just the status of history but, as Eric Auerbach rightly maintains, [the status] of *the* history—the one and only truth that, like God himself, brooks no rivals.[92]

Sternberg insightfully links the Bible's view of God and history with that of the intent of the narrators of the Old Testament to refer truthfully to the events they narrate. One may argue that they were poor historians, but this should not detract from their intentions.

Awareness of the inseparable links between the biblical view of God, of history, and of the historicity of its narratives alerts us to the fact that judgments of historicity will have to take into account all three factors. Provan, Long, and Longman bracket their theological commitments in their admirable construction of a *hermeneutics of testimony* for the Old Testament, but my sense is that openness to the biblical testimony at both the theological *and* historical levels will be deeply affected by one's *religiously* directed view of history.

89. P. Ricoeur, *Time and Narrative*, trans. K. McLaughlin and D. Pellauer, 3 vols. (Chicago: University of Chicago Press, 1984–88; reprint, 1990); idem, *Memory, History, Forgetting*, trans. D. Pellauer (Chicago: University of Chicago Press, 2004).
90. M. Sternberg, *The Poetics of Biblical Narrative: Ideological Literature and the Drama of Reading* (Bloomington: Indiana University Press, 1987), 30.
91. Ibid.
92. Ibid., 32.

Two works on philosophy of history that make for a fascinating comparison are Gordon Graham's *The Shape of the Past* (1997) and Genevieve Lloyd's *Providence Lost* (2008). Graham examines the different options available in philosophy of history—progress, decline, collapse, recurrence, providence— and concludes that the only viable options are progress and providence. These are not necessarily contradictory since evaluation of progress depends on the telos of history. Narrative is unavoidable: "to locate my experience in a narrative of past and present gives it meaning in a way that makes the world my home."[93] However, to pursue such a personal narrative inevitably leads to wider and wider dimensions: "In this sense universal history is implicit in it; to seek to understand oneself is, in the end, to seek to understand the human condition and the purposes of human existence." And that brings in the religious question.

Lloyd, like Martha Nussbaum, thinks that belief in providence is largely absent today. According to Nussbaum, "Few of us now believe that we live in a world providentially ordered for the sake of the overall good; few even believe in a teleology of human social life moving toward greater perfection."[94] In contrast to Graham, Nussbaum thus deletes providence *and* progress. Amid the contemporary renaissance of religion, it is intriguing to wonder which world Nussbaum lives in to be able so casually to discard providence; but leaving that aside, where does such an approach leave us? Lloyd refers to Bernard Williams's work *Shame and Necessity*, in which he suggests that ethically we can see important affinities between "our" mentality and that of the Greeks. "We are in an ethical situation more like human beings in antiquity than any Western people have been in the meantime."[95] Lloyd concludes her *Providence Lost* with a quote from Samuel Beckett: "In the silence you don't know, you must go on, I can't go on, I'll go on."[96]

Williams's point is important. In many respects modernity has led us in the West back into a situation similar to that of the Greeks, with similar options in terms of how we view history; whether consciously or not, it is such views of history that shape much contemporary biblical interpretation. In recent decades postmodernism made its presence felt strongly in historiography and also in biblical interpretation. In its reaction to modernity, postmodernism has on the whole not sought a *post*modern return to providence but has instead

---

93. G. Graham, *The Shape of the Past* (Oxford: Oxford University Press, 1997), 218.
94. M. Nussbaum, *The Fragility of Goodness: Luck and Ethics in Greek Tragedy and Philosophy*, 2nd ed. (Cambridge: Cambridge University Press, 2009), xv.
95. B. A. O. Williams, *Shame and Necessity* (Berkeley: University of California Press, 1993), 166.
96. G. Lloyd, *Providence Lost* (Cambridge, MA: Harvard University Press, 2008), 331.

resurrected pre-Christian views of history. Derrida, for example, positively invokes Nietzsche's concept of eternal recurrence. Elsewhere I have discussed the development of postmodernism and its embodiment in biblical studies.[97] Suffice it here to quote Keith Jenkins's revealing conclusion to his *On "What Is History?" From Carr and Elton to Rorty and White*:

> History is arguably a verbal artefact, a narrative prose discourse of which, après White, the content is as much invented as found, and which is constructed by present-minded, ideologically positioned workers.... Operating at various levels of reflexivity, such a discourse, to appear relatively plausible, [is] looking simultaneously towards the once real events and situations of the past and towards the narrative type "mythoi" common—albeit on a dominant-marginal spectrum—in any given social formation. That past, appropriated by historians, is never the past itself, but a past evidenced by its remaining and accessible traces and transformed into historiography through a series of theoretically and methodologically disparate procedures.... Such historiography... [is then] subject to a series of uses which are logically infinite but which, in practice, correspond to the range of power bases that exist at any given juncture and which distribute/circulate the meanings drawn from such histories along a dominant-marginal spectrum.[98]

Postmodernism has resulted in a wild pluralism in historical methods as it has in biblical studies. In its extreme forms it is downright dangerous, as Gertrude Himmelfarb has pointed out particularly in relation to history.[99] Positively, it has alerted us to the perspectives shaping all historical inquiry and the narrative dimension of such work. One would have hoped that, at its best, postmodernism would have facilitated a genuine and open pluralism, but it is deeply rooted in Western liberalism; while ever ready to critique its host, it has been far more cautious about abandoning it. In biblical-historical studies, this has often manifested itself as an extreme secularism, combining some postmodern insights with old-school scientism.

How ought the Christian biblical scholar to respond to the context in which we find ourselves? First, by waking up to the importance of philosophy and theology of history and its formative implications for biblical exegesis. Second, by recognizing that we are once again in a situation not unlike that of

---

97. See, e.g., C. G. Bartholomew, *Reading Ecclesiastes: Old Testament Exegesis and Hermeneutical Theory* (Rome: Pontificio Istituto Biblico, 1998), 173–206.

98. K. Jenkins, *On "What Is History?": From Carr and Elton to Rorty and White* (London: Routledge, 1995), 178–79.

99. G. Himmelfarb, *On Looking into the Abyss: Untimely Thoughts on Culture and Society* (New York: Knopf, 1994).

the church fathers. Third, by courageously retrieving a nuanced providential understanding of history for today,[100] however unpopular this might be, and allowing it to play a formative role in our work on the historicity of the Bible. In this context theology and Christian philosophy of history become vital for biblical interpretation.

Theology of History and Biblical Interpretation

Pannenberg's extensive work on history and theology deserves mention at this point. He repudiated the entire Kantian-Kierkegaardian legacy in modern German Protestantism and argued for a positive correlation between theology and historical enquiry. Pannenberg insisted on grounding faith in historical inquiry. Faith presupposes, inter alia, *faith that* so that faith is dependent for its meaning on adequate historical knowledge of the past to which it refers. Indeed, Pannenberg thinks an argument can be made for the historicity of the resurrection. Pannenberg—mistakenly, in my view—has no room for the "eyes of faith" in his view of history. However, he rightly rejects the bifurcation of event and meaning, maintaining that no event is what it is until the end of history.[101]

Karl Barth asserted that proper theology "begins just at the point where the difficulties disclosed by Strauss . . . are seen and then laughed at."[102] However, as Morgan recognizes, that does not make them go away. Barth rightly states that time[103] "is the form of our existence. To be man is to live in time."[104] In terms strongly reminiscent of Ecclesiastes, Barth acknowledges how time can confront us as a monstrous enigma:[105] "Infinite, also, is the impossibility of escaping its enigma as the enigma of man himself, man who is, and who would like to be in time and have time, who is in point of fact temporal, and whose being in time is of this nature."[106] Time is a "given": it is part of our

---

100. See C. G. Bartholomew and B. Ashford, *The Doctrine of Creation* (Downers Grove, IL: IVP Academic, forthcoming).

101. W. Pannenberg, "Insight and Faith," in *Basic Questions in Theology: Collected Essays*, trans. G. H. Kehm (reprint, Minneapolis: Fortress, 2008), 1:28–45.

102. K. Barth, *Protestant Theology in the Nineteenth Century: Its Background and History*, trans. B. Cozens and J. Bowden, new ed. (London: SCM, 2001), 554.

103. K. Barth, *CD* III:2 §47; titled "Man in His Time," this section is over 200 pages long. Here we cannot discuss it in any detail, yet it is a deeply insightful examination of the theology of time. In Barth's thought, time is a category more or less equivalent to history. See T. W. Ogletree, *Christian Faith and History: A Critical Comparison of Ernst Troeltsch and Karl Barth* (New York: Abingdon, 1965), 158.

104. K. Barth, *CD* III:2, 521.

105. Ibid., 511–17.

106. Ibid., 515. Hence Barth speaks of "creation time," "fallen time," "the time of grace," and "fulfilled time." See ibid., 158.

creamingly condition, and for Barth it becomes a monstrous enigma because of our alienation from God, and thus from ourselves. Time confronts us with the boundaries and limits of human existence. For Barth, we can come to terms with time only when we recognize God as creator:

> What emerges . . . is that man is not God, but a needy creature of God. . . . To say "man" or "time" is first and basically, even if unwillingly and unwittingly, to say "God." For God is for man as He has time for him. It is God who gives him his time. . . . Time as the form of human existence is always in itself and as such a silent but persistent song of praise to God.[107]

The secret of time is, for Barth, "the will and act of God."[108] God is the chief actor in history, and a true view of history can be obtained only in relation to the history of Jesus as narrated in Scripture. The fundamental nature of history is the history of the covenant, so that Barth can speak of the microcosmic character of the history of Israel as the "key to understanding of world history."[109] "For He [Jesus Christ] is the history of God with man and the history of man with God."[110] Thus all history must be interpreted in relation to salvation history. To elucidate this, Barth uses the image of a circle: the covenant is the center, and world history is the circumference.[111] World history is the theater or external context of the history of the covenant.[112]

Barth discusses time as present, past, and future. The loss entailed in "the past" can be profoundly disturbing, and two unhelpful ways of responding to this are by seeking to re-create it in memory[113] or by relegating it to oblivion. Again, for Barth the problem of the past is resolved only in relation to God. Of the past he declares, "Because God was then, its reality and fullness cannot be taken away by the fact that it has gone. What he willed and created cannot disintegrate into nothing. It has merely lost its character as our present,

---

107. Ibid., 525.

108. Ibid., 527. The indispensability of relating time to God as creator is underscored in Barth's emphatic statement, "We understood time and our being in time as real by considering it as the form of human existence willed and created by God. We thus purged the concept of time from all the abstractions by which it is inevitably confused and darkened when the divine will and action are left out of account and time is not understood as His creation" (551).

109. K. Barth, *CD* IV/3.1:64.

110. Ibid., *CD* IV/1:158.

111. Ibid., *CD* III/3:50.

112. Ibid., *CD* III/3:48.

113. K. Barth defines memory in this context as "an attempt to restore to the past the duration and extension which it obviously does not have any longer" (Ogletree, *Christian Faith and History*, 534).

which it once had. But it has not perished as one of the terms of our time."[114] And so it is with the future: "we can count on the fact that the will and act of God are the meaning and ground not only of our being in time generally but also of our being in the future."[115]

Barth makes an important distinction between *Geschichte* and *Historie*. *Geschichte* refers to history understood christologically, whereas *Historie* refers to history as a characteristic of modern historical thinking. The latter has its place but becomes transgressive when it denies or ignores the Christ event.[116] There remains a nature-grace tension in Barth's work between his recognition of *Historie* and his positive interpretation of the Bible as telling the true story of the world. His vision of universal history centered in Christ is correct, in my view, but surely one would expect such a vision to shape the practice of *Historie* as well.

Finally, mention must be made of *von Balthasar's* dramatic theology of history in his multivolume *Theodramatik*. For von Balthasar, God's life as revealed to us is somehow dramatic and thus is particularly well-expressed in the terms drama offers to us. Drama is significant in at least five ways:[117]

1. It reflects the indeterminacy that characterizes human life.
2. It operates through the dynamic staging of particulars so that the unity it imparts is dynamic.
3. It is irreducibly social.
4. Anticipation is central to drama.
5. Drama, as noted above, is uniquely suitable for expressing God's ways to us.

Von Balthasar turns to drama as a means of overcoming the rift between nature and freedom that he discerns as problematic in modernity.[118] In the context of the world understood as theodrama, we become living witnesses to wisdom. He draws on Hegel's categories of epic, lyric, and drama: theologically, epic stands for the objective discussions of systematic theology, and lyric for prayer and personal involvement. For von Balthasar, "We shall not get beyond the alternatives of 'lyrical' and 'epic,' spirituality (prayer and involvement) and

114. Ogletree, ibid., 537.
115. Ibid., 545.
116. On Karl Barth, historical method, and Jesus, see ibid., 192–219.
117. See B. Quash, *Theology and the Drama of History* (Cambridge: Cambridge University Press, 2005), 35–39.
118. Cf. H. Dooyeweerd, *Roots of Western Culture*, The Collected Works of Herman Dooyeweerd B/3 (Lewiston: E. Mellen, 2003), 149–87, who discerns a nature-freedom dialectic as central to the ground motive of modernity.

theology (the objective discussion of facts), so long as we fail to include the dramatic dimension of revelation, in which alone they discover their unity."[119]

The acting subject is the central difference between epic and dramatic poetry, and von Balthasar focuses on the apostolic witness as the dramatic "person" whose voice most approximates a unifying and heightening of epic and lyric ways of speaking. The apostolic witness is not an impartial report but a participatory witness from his whole life. The Gospel writers "do not recount stories in which they are not involved; in fact, they know that their only chance of being objective is by being profoundly involved in the event they are describing."[120] Scripture is inside the drama as well; it mirrors the drama that is manifested by the Spirit, and it can "only be understood in reference to" this drama.[121]

The Drama of Scripture

Von Balthasar's rich work provides a fertile entry into what our discussion thus far means for biblical studies on the ground, as it were. We assume that the reader is convinced that historical studies of the Bible are far from theologically and philosophically neutral; so what does this mean in practice for the history of the patriarchs, of Kings, of Chronicles, of the Gospels, to mention a few of many areas?

What our discussion does, I suggest, is to clarify the ring within which solutions can be sought. Tom Wright, in terms strongly cognizant of von Balthasar, has presented the Bible as a drama in five acts, as we saw in chapter 3. In *The Drama of Scripture*, Mike Goheen and I have proposed six acts: creation, fall, Israel, Jesus, mission, and new creation.[122] As with von Balthasar, this dramatic approach embodies a theology of history. God is the central actor in the drama; it originates from him in creation, and he remains deeply involved in it, with the climax in the Christ event. We ourselves can understand the drama only from *within*, immersed as we are in the fifth act of the drama. As *a* drama, Scripture reveals to us *the* drama we are involved in *and* invites us to

---

119. H. U. von Balthasar, *Theo-Drama: Theological Dramatic Theory*, vol. 2, *Dramatis Personae: Man in God* (San Francisco: Ignatius, 1990), 50.
120. Ibid., 57.
121. Ibid.
122. Greek drama works with five acts. Mike Goheen and I have proposed six acts in *The Drama of Scripture: Finding Our Place in the Biblical Story* (Grand Rapids: Baker Academic, 2004), and I will follow this approach in what follows. See also Max Harris, *Theater and Incarnation* (Grand Rapids: Eerdmans, 2005); T. A. Hart and S. R. Guthrie, eds., *Faithful Performances: Enacting Christian Tradition* (Burlington, VT: Ashgate, 2007).

actively participate in it. In the process of accepting this invitation, we come to understand the dramatic nature of universal history and our place in it.

The Old Testament is mainly concerned with act 3 of the drama of Scripture,[123] but crucially and uniquely God's way with Israel is contextualized in relation to creation, fall, and the destiny of the entire world. God's creation purposes and his way with Israel find their fulfillment in acts 4–6. In this way a clearly *providential* view of history is affirmed, and central to it is God's involvement in actual history. To embrace this drama makes it quite ridiculous to imagine that God does not speak or act in history, and the Christian biblical scholar will bring all this to bear while working on the historicity of the Bible.[124] In terms of the drama, many participants—including biblical scholars!—refuse to embrace act 4 and resist its existence and implications. Clearly acceptance and resistance are antithetical and will result in very different approaches to the Bible and its history.

Acceptance of the drama *will* predispose one positively toward the historicity of the Bible. In philosophical terms, acceptance of the basic truth of the biblical story has been rigorously defended by Alvin Plantinga.[125] But this does not mean that one will or should adopt a fundamentalist approach in which problems are simply denied. Christian motivation should work in the exact opposite direction. The Christian scholar has a vested interest in history and truth, not ill-informed prejudice.

Our interest in history stems from *the way in which God has revealed himself*. He has done so by immersing himself in the life of an ancient Near Eastern nation, Israel, and in the life of a first-century Jew, Jesus. This means, for example, that we will be deeply concerned to learn all we can about the ancient Near East and how the Old Testament fits within that context. This is not to subvert the clarity of Scripture but to recognize that "clarity" is a metaphor, and its shadow side reminds us that much in the Bible is obscure and repeatedly needs to be made clear. Historical study has an important role to play in this area.

This century an immense amount of new knowledge has been gained about the ancient Near East, and this should be taken with the utmost seriousness. G. Ernest Wright's *The Old Testament against Its Environment* remains an important indicator of the direction such work could take, in my opinion; yet it needs to be updated. As noted in chapter 4, Barr and Gilkey are often

---

123. See chap. 3 above.
124. See N. Wolterstorff, *Reason within the Bounds of Religion*, 2nd ed. (Grand Rapids: Eerdmans, 1999).
125. A. Plantinga, "Two (or More) Kinds of Scripture Scholarship," in *Warranted Christian Belief* (New York: Oxford University Press, 2000), 374–421.

credited with bringing about the demise of the BTM, with which G. E. Wright was associated. Their critiques must be taken seriously, but they are far from fatal. Yet sadly the effect of their critiques has been for the rich work of the BTM to literally disappear from view. This needs to change; for those of us who support a "maximalist" view of biblical history, their work contains rich mines to excavate and update.

Thus, G. E. Wright rightly rejects the developmental hypothesis of the Old Testament and its inability to take seriously the story of God's revelation and covenant at Mount Sinai. In an ancient Near Eastern context of highly developed polytheism and myth, Israel's sense of "the LORD" as utterly transcendent is unique and prompts a move away from the mythological worldviews of surrounding nations. From Genesis 2 onward, the drama of life in God's world is related to history.[126] Neither Eden[127] nor the kingdom of God is separated from earth or its history; they are anchored in that history.

Genesis 1–3 is commonly dated as exilic by Old Testament scholars. As Arthur Gibson perceptively notes, "The earlier chapters of Genesis are by now heavily governed by distinguished exegetical policies that police the limiting or limited boundaries of possibility."[128] Von Rad was highly influential in arguing that a doctrine of creation was a late development in Israelite faith, with exodus and God's acting in history as more foundational. However, from what we know of the ancient Near East, creation stories are widespread and ancient. As G. E. Wright observes, "It is inconceivable that Israel did not possess such a doctrine earlier, both from the standpoint of form criticism and from the fact that creation was a basic concern of all people of the day, at least to judge from polytheistic mythology."[129] Albright based his support for such a view on the etymology of YHWH, which he understood as "causes to be."[130] Canonically, creation is foundational, and there certainly is nothing intrinsically problematic with Israel being brought to Yahweh, and then on the basis of his redemptive work in freeing them, coming to understand that this redeemer God is also the creator. However, the ancient Near Eastern background makes this unlikely.

---

126. Genesis 1:1–2:3 is clearly a prologue. The *tôlĕdôt* in 2:4 indicate a connection with history.

127. For a detailed discussion of Eden as a place, see C. G. Bartholomew, *Where Mortals Dwell: A Christian View of Place for Today* (Grand Rapids: Baker Academic, 2011).

128. A. Gibson, *Text and Tablet: Near Eastern Archaeology, the Old Testament and New Possibilities* (Burlington, VT: Ashgate, 2000), 121. However, see the rigorous and sane comments by G. Wenham, *Genesis 1–15*, WBC 1 (Waco: Word, 1987), xlii–xlv.

129. G. E. Wright, *The Old Testament against Its Environment* (London: SCM, 1950), 29–30.

130. W. F. Albright, *From the Stone Age to Christianity: Monotheism and the Historical Process* (Baltimore: Johns Hopkins University Press, 1957), 259–61.

Here we cannot explore the literature in detail.[131] Suffice it to refer to Arthur Gibson's provocative work as an indication of the possibilities if we think outside the box of popular scholarly orthodoxies. Pettinato, the original epigraphist at Ebla, published what he took to be a Sumerian creation hymn, for which Gibson proposes the following translation:

> The lord of heaven and earth
> It existed not,
> Then he created the earth.
> Light had not been formed, then he created it.
> He had not made learning's light.
> Then the Lord manifested the Word:
> The Lord's fullness,
> The Lord's omnipotence,
> The Lord's headship,
> The Lord's own counsel,
> The Lord's divinity,
> The Lord's salvation,
> The Lord's fortune.[132]

Gibson notes a number of parallels with Genesis 1:

- the contrast of a created earth with a prior state of it not existing.
- the creation of light.
- Pettinato's understanding of Genesis 1:3a to refer to "solar light" may parallel the creation of sun and moon.
- the Word as causal agent.

He concludes, "Now with the Sumerian at Ebla, whether or not one posits an underlying Southeast Sumerian literary influence in the Ebla text, the probability of a third-millennium [BC] basis for Genesis 1–2 is increased by the existence of such a tablet in the geographical orbit of the Abrahamic historical setting."[133]

Over the past century the scholarly pendulum has swung from side to side when it comes to the historicity of *the Patriarchal Narratives* (PN). All agree that there are no explicit extrabiblical attestations of the patriarchs, but views have shifted in terms of contextual affirmation of their historicity. The

---

131. For full bibliographies, see Wenham, *Genesis 1–15*.
132. A. Gibson, *Text and Tablet*, 123–24.
133. Ibid., 124.

discovery of the Nuzi tablets and the Mari material was taken by scholars such as Albright, Gordon,[134] and Speiser to provide confirmation of the historical context against which the PN fit. Speiser's articulation of the Nuzi background for Sarah being Abraham's wife/sister was, however, later debunked, and scholars such as Van Seters and Thomas L. Thompson have argued strongly against the historicity of the PN.

So too has *Giovanni Garbini*.[135] He argues that several points in the Abraham narrative provide a fairly precise date: the reference to Ur of the Chaldeans, to Haran, and the choice of the name Terah for the father of Abraham. These details have a precise aim: "to give Abraham a geographical and chronological base which pointed to Mesopotamia and Syria in the time of Nabonidus."[136] Nabonidus (556–539 BC), the last king of the Neo-Babylonian Empire, had his most important sanctuaries at Ur and Haran, and the PN are politically motivated at this point; the Jews in exile in Babylon wanted to create an original link between themselves and Nabonidus. "By having Abraham born in Mesopotamia the Jews acted in precisely the same way as the Romans, who at a certain moment thought it opportune to call themselves descendants of the Trojan hero Aeneas."[137] The relationship instituted between God and Abraham has nothing to do with "covenant"; in the agreements there is a strong antimonarchic tendency as the ideology associated with the king is transferred to the people.

This operation of projecting the narrative of Abraham back on origins was only possible, according to Garbini, if the Jews had a tradition of a founder of their people, namely, Abraham. Thus certain traditions about Abraham must be earlier than the exile, at which time others were created and added to the earlier ones. Regarding the patriarchs, "It is a generally accepted fact that the figure of Isaac is somewhat flimsy"[138] so that there are really only two patriarchs, Abraham and Jacob. The traditions about Abraham were originally completely independent from Jacob, and it was the Israelites of Judah who put Abraham above Jacob and made Jacob his grandson. After the demise of the northern kingdom in 722 and around the time of Hezekiah, a historical process began which was highly innovative:

> The result was that at that time a completely new view of the history of the Jewish people was established, the main features of which could be summed up

---

134. See C. H. Gordon and G. Rendsburg, *The Bible and the Ancient Near East*, 4th ed. (New York: Norton, 1997).
135. I use Garbini as my prime example because he is well known among Semitic scholars.
136. G. Garbini, *History and Ideology in Ancient Israel*, trans. J. Bowden (London: SCM, 1988), 77.
137. Ibid., 80.
138. Ibid.

in three points: the exiles from Judah affirmed their right to represent all Israel, making their ancestor Abraham the direct ancestor of Jacob and the repository of the divine promise; the institution of the monarchy was repudiated and the sacral figure of the king with his direct relationship with the deity was replaced by the people as a whole, who in this way automatically became a sacred people; and the distant origins of the Jewish people were put in southern Mesopotamia.[139]

For Garbini, this is the history that Israel "created at a certain moment of its existence."[140] It is a mythical and legendary past, similar to that which Rome created for itself not much later. The PN are *logoi*, akin to the stories Herodotus wrote about Gigas, Croessus, and Tomiris. What is remarkable, according to Garbini, is that outside the Jewish and Greek world such prose narratives are nonexistent. Garbini argues that the link is not accidental; both emerged in the Axial Age (800–200 BC), and he suggests that the Philistines may have been the conduit of Greek thought among the Israelites. Furthermore, the ancient world knew of written stories only about rulers; only the patriarchs have such *logoi* about them without being kings.

Garbini's reading demonstrates the range of current approaches to the historicity of the PN, ranging from his largely fictional reading akin to those of Van Seters and Thomas L. Thompson, to Dever,[141] to the far more historical approaches of Gordon and Rendsburg,[142] Wenham, Kitchen, and Longman.[143] And similar discussions exist in relation to almost every aspect of the history of the Old Testament and of the New Testament.

Take Moses, for example. It is common practice nowadays to dismiss him as a nonhistorical figure as well as the events at Sinai.[144] John Van Seters, for example, declares, "The quest for the

139. Ibid., 82.
140. Ibid.
141. William G. Dever was a student of G. Ernest Wright, and although he writes in critique of the radical revisionists in his *What Did the Biblical Writers Know and When Did They Know It? What Archaeology Can Tell Us about the Reality of Ancient Israel* (Grand Rapids: Eerdmans, 2001), he, unlike Wright, says of the PN, "After a century of exhaustive investigation, all respectable archaeologists have given up hope of recovering any context that would make Abraham, Isaac, or Jacob credible 'historical figures.' Virtually the last archaeological word was written by me more than 20 years ago for a basic handbook of biblical studies, *Israelite and Judean History*" (98). For a critique of J. Maxwell Miller and John H. Hayes, eds., *A History of Ancient Israel and Judah* (Philadelphia: Westminster, 1986), see Provan et al., *A Biblical History of Israel*, 15–18.
142. In *Bible and the Ancient Near East*, Gordon and Rendsburg continue to argue that a Nuzi and Ugaritic background rightly contextualizes the PN: "the fact remains that no set of known texts offers as many parallels to the patriarchal narratives as do the Nuzu [Nuzi] tablets" (111).
143. With Provan et al., *Biblical History of Israel*, 107–21.
144. For a recent review of the ancient and modern literature on Moses, see D. M. Beegle, "Moses," *ABD* 4:909–18. Cf. also J. K. Hoffmeier, "Moses," *ISBE* 3 (1986): 415–25; idem,

historical Moses is a futile exercise. He now belongs only to legend."[145] By contrast Albright asserted: "It is absurd to deny that Moses was actually the founder of the Israelite commonwealth and the framer of Israel's religious system. This fact is emphasized so unanimously by tradition that it may be regarded as absolutely certain.... If we regard Zoroaster, Buddha, and Confucius as the founders of nomistic religions, we cannot deny this right to Moses."[146]

Knierim alerts us to the reason why Moses is so commonly ignored nowadays. Speaking of the critical reconstruction of the origins of Israel, Knierim insightfully reports, "In this critical reconstruction of Israel's historical beginnings, Moses has played an ever-decreasing role which is the exact opposite of the ever-increasing role asserted for Moses in the tradition-historical process resulting in the Pentateuch."[147] According to Knierim, "Due to the prevalent historical interest, the importance of Moses in the late form of Exodus–Deuteronomy has played no role in modern scholarship."[148]

It should, first, be recognized that this historical interest has been of a very particular sort, as we have mentioned in this chapter. By comparison, James Hoffmeier's work moves in a very different direction. Hoffmeier discloses, "One of the glaring weaknesses of much of the recent literature that has questioned the historicity of the biblical records is that it has lacked serious investigation of Egyptian historical and archaeological materials."[149] He points out that when Egyptologists write about connections between Egypt and the Old Testament, they have on the whole accepted the Bible's claims. In his *Israel in Egypt*, chapter 6, Hoffmeier explores the Egyptian elements in the narratives of Moses's birth, name, and time spent in Pharaoh's court being educated; his time as a refugee; and his "enactment" of the plagues. Hoffmeier reports, "The picture of Moses in Exodus 2 being taken to the court by a princess where he was reared and educated is quite consistent with the emerging information about the *k3p* [nursery (of the palace)] in the New Kingdom, the only period for which there is evidence of foreigners being included in this royal institution."[150] Regarding the Sinai legislation, to which we will come below, Hoffmeier argues, "As will be clear from the following discussion of the development of the Semitic alphabet, there is no reason to deny that the heart of Sinai legislation could have originated in the Late Bronze Age."[151]

As we have discussed above, far too much historical criticism failed to focus on the literary shape of Old Testament texts before plunging into what lies behind them. Hence "it should be asserted that the serious study of the literary form and genre of the extant Pentateuch, and with it the story of the portrait of Moses, is just as necessary as the study of the historical Moses or of the Moses in the pre-Pentateuchal traditions."[152] As Knierim points out, in Exodus–Deuteronomy, Moses is mentioned more often (some 510 times) than Israel (460 times).[153] Indeed, Knierim proposes that we see the Pentateuch as the biography of Moses: "We must

---

Israel in Egypt: The Evidence for the Authenticity of the Exodus Tradition (New York: Oxford University Press, 1997).

145. J. van Seters, *In Search of History: Historiography in the Ancient World and the Origins of Biblical History* (New Haven: Yale University Press, 1983), 23.

146. Albright, *From the Stone Age to Christianity*, 258.

147. R. P. Knierim, *The Task of Old Testament Theology: Substance, Method, and Cases* (Grand Rapids, Eerdmans, 1995), 371.

148. Ibid. With most OT scholars, Knierim assumes that the Pentateuch reached its final form late, after a long process.

149. Hoffmeier, *Israel in Egypt*, x.

150. Ibid., chap. 6, Kindle loc. v.

151. J. K. Hoffmeier, *Ancient Israel in Sinai: The Evidence for the Authenticity of the Wilderness Tradition* (Oxford: Oxford University Press, 2005), 177.

152. Knierim, *Task of Old Testament Theology*, 372.

153. Ibid.; cf. J. A. Motyer, *The Pentateuch and Criticism: Three Lectures by the Rev. J. A. Motyer* (Leicester, UK: Theological Students Fellowship, 1974).

be prepared for the thesis that *the Pentateuch is not the story or history of Israel's beginnings but the story of the life of Moses which is fundamental for the beginnings of Israel's history; that it is the vita, or the biography, of Moses.*"[154]

The question of Moses thus pushes us toward the relationship between the literary shape of the Pentateuch and its historicity. Indeed, Knierim's discussion of Moses occurs as he analyzes the shape of the Pentateuch as a whole.[155] The narrative of Moses holds together Exodus–Deuteronomy so that the Pentateuch is essentially bipartite: before Moses (Genesis) and the time of Moses (Exodus–Deuteronomy). Genesis is the introduction, the prelude to the time of Moses. The link between the two parts is vital since it shows that "the time of Moses must be understood in world-historical perspective as the culmination of the long process of world history in one short period. The Pentateuch is the story, or history, of the time of Moses in the light of universal creation and history, or the history of universal creation and history culminating in the time of Moses."[156] Moses is the link between creation and Israel, a theologically crucial link:

> In Moses' mediation of the revelation of Sinai as well as in his testament, the program is laid down by which Israel is called to be the paradigm for humanity in God's/Yahweh's creation. The decisive person for mediating this revelatory paradigm is Moses. Thus, just as Moses is seen as the single most decisive person for Israel's history and existence, so is he the decisive person for all of humanity's history and existence.[157]

It is fascinating and important to see how this brief discussion of Moses has led us to historical, literary, and theological issues. In my view this is unavoidable and essential in any assessment of the historicity of Moses.[158] What is missing from Knierim's analysis is the fundamental role of *Yahweh*, and his role acutely raises the theological dimension of the Pentateuch. Moses may be central, but not nearly so much as Yahweh, who leads the way at every point and is undoubtedly *the* central character in the Pentateuch. Thus I would not recommend seeing the Pentateuch as the biography of Moses. Exodus–Deuteronomy is better seen as Yahweh forming his people, with Moses as the leader through whom Yahweh works in this process.

The elephant in the room of such discussions is whether we take seriously the possibility of Yahweh, as the creator God, acting in history in this way. If we do, as indeed I do, then it simply will not do to bracket out such theism in the process of developing theories about the Pentateuch. Such a theistic approach far from solves all the difficult issues in the Pentateuch, issues that historical criticism has fingered repeatedly, but it orients one to the Pentateuch in a significantly different way.

What would such a theistically shaped criticism and exegesis look like? That is the million-dollar question, one that I hope to address in future work. Suffice it to state that it will not involve a relapse into an unthinking fundamentalism. Instead it will involve a third way or a variety of third ways of developing theories that account for the data of the Old Testament while taking seriously God's revelation to and in Israel.

Old Testament law is a case in point. A great deal of creative work has been done on the so-called law collections in the Old Testament. David Wright's fascinating *Inventing God's Law* is one of the more recent works, arguing that the Covenant Code (Exod. 19–24) is deliberately modeled

---

154. Knierim, *Task of Old Testament Theology*, 372, with original emphasis. On this issue, cf. the sane comments by G. Wenham, *Exploring the Old Testament: A Guide to the Pentateuch* (Downers Grove, IL: IVP Academic, 2003), 2–4.

155. Knierim, *Task of Old Testament Theology*, 351–79.

156. Ibid., 355.

157. Ibid., 378.

158. On Deuteronomy and the historicity of Moses, see C. G. Bartholomew, "The Composition of Deuteronomy: A Critical Analysis of the Approaches of E. W. Nicholson and A. D. H. Mayes" (MA thesis, Potchefstroom University for Christian Higher Education, 1992), 243–51.

on Hammurabi's (1792–1750 BC) Code,[159] so that it is to be seen as "an academic abstraction rather than a digest of laws practiced by Israelites and Judeans over the course of centuries. Its selective character and the manner in which it reshapes the political and theological landscape of the Laws of Hammurabi, in fact, make it appear to be predominantly an ideological document, a response to Assyrian political and cultural domination."[160] According to David Wright, Mesopotamian influence did not extend to Israel until after the mid-ninth century BC. Wright suggests the Neo-Assyrian period, when Israel and Judah were under Assyrian control, for the origin of the Covenant Code since then "a window of opportunity opens for the use of the Laws of Hammurabi as a source text."[161]

David Wright's is a detailed and controversial view, and we cannot explore it in any detail here. Suffice it here to raise some questions. The French Egyptologist Nicolas Grimal, in his *A History of Ancient Egypt*, notes, "It is considered possible that the Jewish Exodus may have taken place during the reign of Ramesses II."[162] Similarly Ronald J. Williams argued that Egyptian influence could be found within the Old Testament. He asserts, "Due caution must always be observed in assessing the claims of direct influence, but the evidence is overwhelming that Israel drank deeply at the wells of Egypt. In a very real sense the Hebrews were 'a people come out of Egypt' (Num. xxii 5, 11)."[163] In a fascinating work on the time of Ramesses II (1303–1213 BC), most likely the pharaoh under whose reign Moses grew up, Van de Mieroop notes that the Egyptians certainly did not live in isolation. During the centuries around Ramesses's reign, several kingdoms coexisted with Egypt with corresponding widespread interaction.[164] Members of Ramesses's court would have met visitors from the south of Egypt, to the Black Sea in the north of Anatolia, and from the Greek mainland to western Iran, and may have been there themselves. Van de Mieroop describes the "traveling specialists" of the time, among whom were scribes.[165] Some of the scribes at Hattusa in the Hittite heartland, for example, were Babylonians and Assyrians, who perhaps wanted to make a career abroad. "The picture we get is thus quite similar throughout the region: people who knew how to read and write did so in multiple languages. Two literary traditions coexisted, an indigenous and an international one that was heavily influenced by Babylonia."[166]

By the mid-second millennium, Babylonia and Egypt had the oldest and most developed literary traditions. Writing had been invented, probably independently, more than 1,500 years earlier in both places. A way in which texts like the Code of Hammurabi could move around is illustrated by the loot the Elamite Shutruk-Nahhunte brought home after his raid of Babylonia in the mid-twelfth century. His campaign took his troops through cities where stone monuments, some more than a thousand years old, were on display. Shutruk-Nahhunte took these off to his

---

159. See M. E. J. Richardson, *Hammurabi's Laws: Text, Translation and Glossary* (Sheffield: Sheffield Academic Press, 2000); M. Van de Mieroop, *King Hammurabi of Babylon: A Biography* (Oxford: Blackwell, 2005).

160. D. P. Wright, *Inventing God's Law: How the Covenant Code of the Bible Used and Revised the Laws of Hammurabi* (New York: Oxford University Press, 2009), 4.

161. Ibid., 46.

162. Hoffmeier, *Israel in Egypt*, ix, quoting N. Grimal, *A History of Ancient Egypt* (Oxford: Blackwell, 1992), 258.

163. Ibid., quoting R. J. Williams. "'A People Come out of Egypt': An Egyptologist Looks at the Old Testament," *Congress Volume, Edinburgh 1974*, VTSup 28 (Leiden: Brill, 1975), 231–52, esp. 252.

164. M. Van de Mieroop, *The Eastern Mediterranean in the Age of Ramesses II* (Oxford: Blackwell, 2010).

165. Cf. K. Van der Toorn, *Scribal Culture and the Making of the Hebrew Bible* (Cambridge, MA: Harvard University Press, 2007).

166. Van de Mieroop, *Eastern Mediterranean*, chap. 8.

capital city, Susa, and they included some of the famous early Babylonian monuments: the stele of Naram-Sin, king of the twenty-third century, and the Code of Hammurabi.[167]

This alerts us to the fact that if Moses grew up in Egypt and was well educated in Pharaoh's court, as Hoffmeier argues, then it is surely possible that he could have been exposed to Hammurabi's Code. Thus, *if* there is a close relationship between the Covenant Code and Hammurabi's Code, this does *not* mean that the Covenant Code has to be dated long after the time of Moses. Hammurabi's Code also alerts us to the possibility, in the ancient Near East, of a single influential person promulgating a law code. Doubtless there are various sources for this code, but such promulgation raises questions about the assumption in so much Old Testament scholarship that texts like Exodus and the Covenant Code came into existence slowly over a long period of time. This is not to argue that the Covenant Code as we have it is exactly as Moses delivered it to the Israelites from Yahweh, but it is to argue that it could be substantially Mosaic, *and from Yahweh*.

Childs, for example, alerts us to the literary technique in Exodus that brought together an account of an event with the portrayal of ongoing celebration of that event. As he notes, "The canonical effect of this literary device is of profound theological significance. The original events are not robbed of their historical particularity; nevertheless, the means for their actualization for future Israel is offered in the shape of scripture itself."[168] Such an approach allows for textual layers and updating of texts,[169] yet also for original historical events underlying the narratives and laws as we have them. And such events include the speaking of God to Moses. Indeed, from a theistic perspective, a jarring aspect of D. P. Wright's work is the title of his book, *Inventing God's Law*, which carries with it the widespread view in the history of religions school that the Covenant Code is a purely human invention.

How, amid such diversity, are we to evaluate Garbini's type of reading of the PN?[170] Several points are worth making:

1. There is the important point, on which all are agreed, that we have no firm extrabiblical attestation of the PN. Bearing in mind who the patriarchs were—not kings or great ones—and their transience, this is not surprising. Thus everything will depend on how we read the PN and the probability of the patriarchs fitting into ancient Near Eastern contexts that we know of.

167. Ibid., chap. 7.
168. B. S. Childs, *Introduction to the Old Testament as Scripture* (Philadelphia: Fortress, 1979), 176.
169. But see R. Westbrook's fascinating chapter, "What Is the Covenant Code?," in *Theory and Method in Biblical and Cuneiform Law: Revision, Interpolation and Development*, ed. B. M. Levinson, JSOTSup 181 (Sheffield: Sheffield Academic Press, 1994), 15–36, and the responses thereto; Westbrook states, "The most striking feature of the cuneiform legal material, on the other hand, is its static nature" (21). He agrees with H.-J. Kraus and others that in the ancient Near East, "law codes were essentially academic documents, which may accurately have described the law but did not prescribe it" (24). A model for the view of a legal code being carefully edited and updated for changing situations is found in the Digest of Justinian, in the sixth century AD. Hammurabi's Code has been seen as a type of Justinian Digest, but Westbrook denies this and concludes, "The starting point for interpretation must therefore be the presumption that the Covenant Code is a coherent text comprising clear and consistent laws, in the same manner as its cuneiform forbears" (36). Not surprisingly, there is strong disagreement from his respondents.
170. A. R. Millard and D. J. Wiseman, eds., *Essays on the Patriarchal Narratives* (Leicester, UK: Inter-Varsity, 1980), remains a useful source.

2. The place to begin is surely with a close reading of the PN as Hebrew narrative. Yet Garbini shows no evidence of doing this at all. He works with tradition history and refers to de Vaux, Van Seters, Thomas L. Thompson, and several other scholars but manifests no awareness of recent literary readings of the PN that demonstrate their artistry.[171] Isaac does not play a major role in the PN, but he is the long-awaited son, and one wonders what "flimsy" means when the narrator may have all sorts of reasons to focus far more on Jacob/Israel as the immediate father of the nation.[172]

It is through a close reading of the PN that a decision will have to be made as to the *historical intent* of these narratives. Are they largely fictional creations, and should they be categorized as myth and legend? The poetics alone will not resolve this issue, but as we have argued above in agreement with Sternberg and others, the intent *is* historical.

3. Methodologically it is simply inadequate to start with "Chaldeans" as an anachronism and to identify Ur and Haran as important sites in the time of Nabonidus, and then to read the PN in this exilic context. Garbini makes an argument, but *the strength* of the argument needs evaluation; is it certain, highly likely, probable, possible, or unlikely? In my opinion, although this would need to be argued for point by point, it is unlikely and should therefore be discarded.

The discernment of possible anachronisms in the PN is no new issue. The mention of "Chaldeans," of Dan, of the Philistines, and of camels have been repeatedly discussed as possible anachronisms. Garbini dismisses the hypothesis of later updating, but it is unclear why this is so unacceptable. It would seem "natural" for scribes to update texts to ensure they are rightly understood by later generations. Despite that, there is the problem with identifying a clear anachronism, which is far more complex than Garbini's approach suggests. Gordon and Rendsburg plus many others provide, for example, a credible argument for the mention of the Philistines.[173]

Arthur Gibson suggests the Septuagint (LXX) as the text that produced the anachronism of the "Chaldees." Ur was one of the city-states of Sumer, and in translation "Chaldea" renders the Hebrew word *kaśdîm*, whereas the later Akkadian is *kaldu*. The linguistic evidence for a proposed shift from *kasdu* to *kaldu* is not extant, and H. W. F. Saggs notes that the two terms *kaśdîm* and *kaldu* are not synonymous in all contexts. Thus Gibson suggests:

171. See Wenham, *Genesis 1–15*, 256–64, and his bibliography on 256.
172. On Isaac in the patriarchal narratives, see J. Goldingay, "The Patriarchs in Scripture and History," in *Essays on the Patriarchal Narratives*, ed. A. R. Millard and D. J. Wiseman (Leicester, UK: Inter-Varsity, 1980), 16–20.
173. Wenham, *Genesis 1–15*, 118.

> It is possible, as a hypothesis for investigation, to propose that, since *kaldu* is late and the Old Testament Hebrew *kasdim* corresponds to a postulated Old Babylonian form (circa 2000 BC) **kasdu* from which *kasdim* is said to derive, *kasdim* is not anachronistic, but originally contemporary with a circa 2,000 BC use of "Abraham."[174]

It is important to notice that Gibson is proposing this as a hypothesis for further investigation and not asserting it as a fact. When some of the polemic is taken out of the debate,

> instead of prescriptive censorship, one can find that the map of meaning and its geography in ancient history do not have to yield anachronism from the Hebrew Bible in this case.... Decisive solutions to this problem should await further discoveries and results; we should not prejudge scholarly history of the future over this issue. In view of the importance this question has for the Abrahamic era, it is odd that there has been a trend to omit and failure logically to assess these data.[175]

And so we could continue with a discussion of the alleged anachronisms in the PN. They simply will not bear the weight that Garbini's view places on them. However, conversely, we should see that Wenham has pointed out a long list of patriarchal customs that would be anachronistic to a later period.[176]

4. In terms of biblical theology, the PN are integral to the biblical story, and the promises to Abraham frame the biblical story as a whole. The relationships established between God and Abraham are indeed covenants;[177] in their absence someone like Abraham would need to be posited behind Sinai to make sense of the story as a whole. Literary sense does not equate to historicity, but neither are they unconnected.

5. My sense is that rather than deal with the historicity of the Old Testament piecemeal, as is so often the case, a new approach is required akin to that of Tom Wright's project on the origins of the New Testament, *within which* detailed issues should be considered. Historicity will have to be assessed in combination with the literary and theological dimensions of the Old Testament, taken as a whole. Both Wright as a New Testament scholar and C. Stephen Evans[178] as a philosopher have done superb work on the historicity

174. A. Gibson, *Text and Tablet*, 127.
175. Ibid., 128.
176. G. Wenham, *Genesis 16–50*, WBC 2 (Waco: Word, 1994), xx–xxv, xxx–xxxv.
177. See S. W. Hahn, *Kinship by Covenant: A Canonical Approach to the Fulfillment of God's Saving Promises* (New Haven: Yale University Press, 2009).
178. C. S. Evans, *The Historical Christ and the Jesus of Faith: The Incarnational Narrative as History* (Oxford: Oxford University Press, 1996). As with Sternberg's *Poetics of Biblical Narrative*, I do not think that Evans's work has received the attention it deserves. Both of these

of the New Testament and its philosophical foundations. Comparable work remains to be done in Old Testament studies, I think.[179] Yet the challenges are different. In New Testament studies one is dealing with a limited time period in a common culture, whereas with the Old Testament one is dealing with literature that emerged over centuries and in very different cultural contexts. Nevertheless, approaching the Old Testament with a sense of its artistry and kerygma against the backdrop of the ancient Near Eastern context as more and more data surface would enable us to assess *The Old Testament against Its Environment* in an updated version of the sort of work G. Ernest Wright did. As with Tom Wright's multivolume work, we would find, I suspect, the precise genres hard to determine, as literary, historical, and kerygmatic dimensions intermingle richly.

It is worthwhile here to recognize Tom Wright's *critical realist* historical methodology.[180] History writing is the *"meaningful narrative of events and intentions,"*[181] not just at the level of individuals, but also at the level of mindsets, of whole societies, and thus of worldviews. Historians address the "why" question at all possible levels and proceed by the telling of new stories.

All history writing is selective and interpretive; it is an Enlightenment myth to think otherwise. "All history, then, consists of a spiral of knowledge, a long-drawn-out process of interaction between interpreter and source material."[182] With biblical (New Testament) texts, we are, however, dealing with documents that many readers regard as authoritative. Both those who do and do not affirm the authority of Scripture need to take this fact into account. The New Testament (Bible) is theological through and through, but this does not mean that it is unhistorical. A critical-realist perspective takes the interpretive dimension of history writing seriously,[183] but this does not mean there are no facts. In writing the history of the New Testament, all data must be included, letting an overall simplicity emerge. However, for the task of New Testament history, we need new tools: the premodern and modern tools are inadequate.[184]

---

works are extremely important, and yet neither has, e.g., resulted in a collection of detailed essays engaging their arguments. If they are right, the implications are momentous.

179. Provan et al., *Biblical History of Israel*, is an important step in this direction.
180. See N. T. Wright, *NTPG* 81–120.
181. Ibid., 82.
182. Ibid., 86.
183. Ricoeur states: "Representation constitutes a fully legitimate operation that has the privilege of bringing to light the intended reference of historical discourse" (*Memory, History, Forgetting*, 236). He says, "An impoverished concept of event goes along with an impoverished concept of narrative" (239).
184. Provan et al., (*Biblical History of Israel*) rightly declare:
    Indeed, we must face the remarkable fact that for most of the twentieth century, the discipline "history of Israel" proceeded in apparent ignorance of the furious debate

History 373

Wright recognizes the philosophical issues at stake in such a project: "If we are eventually to mount a new theory of knowledge itself, we will also need a new theory of being or existence, that is, a new ontology."[185] Ontologies based on a nature/supernature dualism will not do.[186] Wright courageously declares:

> I find myself driven, both from my study of the New Testament and from a wide variety of other factors which contribute to my being who I am, to tell a story about reality which runs something like this. Reality as we know it is the result of a creator god bringing into being a world that is other than himself, and yet which is full of his glory. As part of the means to this end, the creator brought into being a creature which, by bearing the creator's image, would bring his wise and loving care to bear upon the creation. By a tragic irony, the creature in question has rebelled against this intention. But the creator has solved this problem in principle in an entirely appropriate way, and as a result is now moving the creation towards its originally intended goal. The implementation of this solution now involves the indwelling of this god within his human creatures and ultimately within the whole creation, transforming it into that for which it was made in the beginning.[187]

This story grounds ontology in the being and nature of the creator-redeemer god; it subverts other stories and fits better with reality than the usual post-Enlightenment ones.

History writing works on the basis of hypotheses and verification. A hypothesis is a story explaining a set of phenomena. A good hypothesis must include the data, construct a coherent overall picture, and prove fruitful in related areas. Verification is complex but must proceed by examining the

---

about the nature of history that was raging among historians more generally, so that the nineteenth-century scientific model should still be widely seen at present as the only viable scholarly model that exists and, as such, requires no justification. (52)

185. Ibid., 97.

186. W. Brueggemann ("Response to J. Richard Middleton," *HTR* 87, no. 3 [1994]) rightly states,

The claim that "God acts in history" is not compatible with our Enlightenment notions of control, reason, objectivity, and technique. Indeed, if one begins with the assumptions of modernity, history can only be thought of as a bare story of power, in which the God of the Bible can never make a significant appearance. The claim that "God acts in history," that God's word impinges upon the human process, requires a very different beginning point. (279)

187. N. T. Wright, *NTPG* 97–98; cf. J. Pieper, *Hope and History* (San Francisco: Ignatius, 1994): Wright says, "The Christian expects this present Creation, the reality we see before our eyes, to pass through death and disaster in order to achieve perfection. This is the 'salvation' we hope for. The 'Kingdom of God' will be realized nowhere but in the midst of this historical world" (*NTPG* 88).

evidence on its own terms.[188] Naturally, more than one hypothesis may arise that fits the evidence, especially with the underdetermination resulting from the limited data.

Wright perceptively assesses the field:

> A great many people within the guild of New Testament specialists have written very little history as such. Attention to particular problems, yes; attempts to write the connected history of even part of the first century, no. . . . More characteristic of the discipline as it has been practised . . . are commentaries on particular books, detached studies of smaller-scale problems, and exegetical notes on detailed texts. There is no recent work which does for the early church, or yet for Jesus, what the new edition of Schürer's classic *History of the Jewish People in the Age of Jesus Christ* does for its subject-matter, showing *en route* that despite the fears of New Testament scholars first-century history is alive and well.[189]

In my view, the same can be said of Old Testament studies.

Tom Wright's genius has been in breaking free of the detailed, detached work that so often characterizes biblical studies today and—without for a moment ignoring the detail—in insisting on focusing attention on the bigger picture, which after all is always in play anyway but is so often assumed or ignored. And he rightly recognizes that ontology is crucial and that a decision at this point cannot be avoided, since it *will* affect one's historical epistemology. As Pieper states, "The fundamental question of the philosophy of history is this: Where is the historical process as a whole going? . . . It is plain that no one can meaningfully pose and elucidate this question unless he can refer back to extra-empirical prophetic knowledge."[190]

Arthur Gibson rightly pleads for a new approach to analyzing and evaluating ancient Near Eastern data, but one "which does not proceed with any theological assumptions."[191] Similarly Provan, Long, and Longman rightly and creatively attend to the epistemological issues of testimony in relation to Old Testament historiography, but again seek to bracket out theological concerns. At an apologetic level this is helpful, yet *theological* claims that bear heavily on the view of history of the Old Testament and its historical claims are built into Old Testament testimony. The theological dimension of the Bible, to which we will come in chapter 12, is indispensable, as is a historical sense of the oral-literary nature of Old Testament historical narrative; indeed, a

---

188. See N. T. Wright, *NTPG* 104–9.
189. Pieper, *Hope and History*, 113–14.
190. Ibid., 81.
191. A. Gibson, *Text and Tablet*, 14.

holistic view of biblical history will emerge only as the total picture is taken into account. Wright's work, in my view, models what such an approach might look like, and we urgently need comparable work on the Old Testament. As the quote from Murray Rae at the beginning of this chapter argues, such an approach will need to be rooted in a robust doctrine of creation. Undoubtedly different hypotheses will emerge, but in their relative absence, this would be a welcome phenomenon and allow serious dialogue at the deepest *and* most detailed levels to begin.

11

Literature

To assure maximum presence through history, the Word came in the ripeness of time, when a sense of the oral was still dominant and when at the same time the alphabet could give divine revelation among men a new kind of endurance and stability. The believer finds it providential that divine revelation let down its roots into human culture and consciousness after the alphabet was devised but before print had overgrown major oral structures and before our electronic culture further obscured the basic nature of the word.

Walter Ong[1]

Introduction

In the early church the relationship between literature and Christianity was controversial. Jerome asked, "What communion hath light with darkness? And what concord hath Christ with Belial? How can Horace go with the psalter, Virgil with the gospels, Cicero with the apostle?"[2] In his *Confessions*, Augustine laments his education, which initiated him through dramas like Terence's *Eunuchus* into the stories of the god Jupiter, who punishes the wicked and

---

1. Walter Ong, *The Presence of the Word: Some Prolegomena for Cultural and Religious History* (New Haven: Yale University Press, 1967), 191.
2. Jerome, "Letter XXII: To Eustochium" 29, in NPNF² 6, *St. Jerome: Letters and Select Works*, 35 (http://www.ccel.org/ccel/schaff/npnf206.v.XXII.html).

yet commits adultery himself; which had him reciting the speech of Juno in Virgil's *Aeneid*; and so on. Augustine does, however, explain, "I have nothing against the words themselves. They are like choice and costly glasses, but they contain the wine of error which had already gone to the heads of the teachers who poured it out for us to drink."[3] Similarly Alcuin, whom we encountered in chapter 5, concerned about the monks' fondness for stories about heroes such as Beowulf and Ingeld, asked, "What does Ingeld[4] have to do with Christ?"[5] Understandably, many of the church fathers were concerned about the immorality portrayed in such literature, but they were in danger of confusing the misdirection of literature in this way with the fundamental goodness and gift of literature. As it turns out, Ingeld has a great deal to do with Christ!

The Literary Turn

In chapter 7 we noticed the literary turn in biblical studies from the 1970s onward. On the whole this has been a remarkably creative and fruitful development in biblical studies, yielding an immense body of work. Some examples will suffice to indicate just how revolutionary and productive this turn has been. David Clines's *The Theme of the Pentateuch* remains a very helpful introduction to the literary theme of the Pentateuch *as a whole*. In studies of the *Psalter*, the literary turn has focused attention on the shape of the Psalter as a whole, with Psalms 1 and 2 as the introduction, Psalms 145–150 as the conclusion, and the kingship psalms in Psalms 90–106 as the high point of the book. The fivefold division of the Psalter has been recognized as modeled after the five books of the Pentateuch, as a guide to living the answer to the demands of God's torah/instruction.[6] David Beldman's recent work on the literary shape of Judges and in particular his analysis of *narrative* time in relation to *chronological* time raises major questions about the typical reading of Judges as a spiral down into chaos.[7]

3. Augustine of Hippo, *Confessions* 1.16, trans. R. S. Pine-Coffin (London: Penguin, 1961), 17. His approach to literature is more complex than book 1 of *Confessions* suggests. See esp. his *Christian Instruction* (*DDC*).
4. Ingeld was a legendary warrior in early English and Norse legends.
5. B. Mitchell and F. C. Robinson, eds., *Beowulf: An Edition with Relevant Shorter Texts* (Oxford: Wiley, 1998), 225.
6. See the highly creative works by Gerald Wilson, James Luther Mays, Walter Brueggemann, Eugene Peterson, Clinton McCann, et al. For an introduction to the Psalms at a popular level, see C. G. Bartholomew and A. West, eds., *Praying by the Book: Reading the Psalms* (Carlisle, UK: Paternoster, 2001).
7. D. J. H. Beldman, "The Completion of Judges: Strategies of Ending in Judges 17–21" (PhD diss., University of Bristol, 2013).

Attention has also been given to the book of Proverbs *as a whole*. There remain many parts of Proverbs, especially after chapter 9, where patterns cannot easily be discerned, but an overarching pattern and even patterns amid the aphoristic proverbs are evident.[8] Proverbs begins with its recurring motif of "the fear of the LORD" (1:7) and culminates in an extraordinary picture of wisdom incarnate in its acrostic poem of the valiant woman (31:10–31). Proverbs 1–9 is an introduction setting out the ABC's of wisdom, as it were, with much greater nuance introduced in the proverbial sections that follow.[9] Studies of Ecclesiastes were revolutionized when Michael Fox asserted that we need to focus on Ecclesiastes as literature by attending to the different voices and their interrelationship in the book.[10]

Similarly in New Testament studies, the literary turn has been very fruitful. Rather than starting with detailed comparative studies of the Gospels, the literary turn has catalyzed studies of the Gospels as individual wholes before turning to comparative analysis. We will use the Gospel of Luke as our main example in this chapter. Extensive work has been done on the shape of Luke-Acts as a two-part narrative work by one author. Tom Wright has used narrative as the key to his major project on the New Testament, and Richard Hays has probed the theology of several of Paul's Epistles along narrative lines.

And so we could continue. Because the Bible is literature, its literary dimension *resists* being ignored. Ironically, what was called "literary criticism" by historical critics was an attempt to get behind the text to the sources while effectively bypassing the literary shape of texts. One can dismiss the literary nature of texts, but as a result much historical criticism worked with naive views of the Bible as literature, moving quickly to indications of sources without attending to the literary and synchronic shape of the text *first*. It is always possible that a text is so unintegrated that such a move becomes necessary, but only as a last resort. Alas, for much historical criticism seeking sources became the first goal.

Intriguingly, similar moves can be observed among some church fathers *and* postmodern interpreters. Some church fathers worked, as it were, with the maxim that when one encounters a difficulty in the text, one should resort to

---

8. See, e.g., R. C. Van Leeuwen, *Context and Meaning in Proverbs 25–27*, SBLDS 96 (Atlanta: Scholars Press, 1988); K. M. Heim, *Poetic Imagination in Proverbs: Variant Repetitions and the Nature of Poetry*, Bulletin for Biblical Research Supplements 4 (Winona Lake, IN: Eisenbrauns, 2013).

9. See C. G. Bartholomew and R. P. O'Dowd, *Old Testament Wisdom Literature: A Theological Introduction* (Downers Grove, IL: IVP Academic, 2011), which contains bibliographies for further reading.

10. See C. G. Bartholomew, *Reading Ecclesiastes: Old Testament Exegesis and Hermeneutical Theory* (Rome: Pontificio Istituto Biblico, 1998); idem, *Ecclesiastes* (Grand Rapids: Baker Academic, 2009).

allegory! Many postmoderns are quick to attend to the ideological substructures of texts without first reading them along the grain, an indispensable *first* step. As Sternberg rightly insists, biblical interpretation must work with the synchronic and diachronic dimensions of the text in close dialogue, but the synchronic is primary in the sense that we encounter the books of the Bible as literary texts with literary shapes.[11]

The Received Literary Form

If we work with a communicative hermeneutic for biblical interpretation, which I proposed in my *Reading Ecclesiastes*[12] and which fits integrally with an approach to Scripture aimed at listening for God's address, then in such a context, a literary approach focuses primarily on *the text* and its literary dimension in order to listen to the *message* being communicated. At its most basic level a communicative hermeneutic attends to the text in the context of three terms:

SENDER—MESSAGE—RECEIVER

The contention of this model of exegesis is that the biblical texts in the form that we have them should be the focus of interpretation, since it is through *these* texts that we receive their message.[13] Lategan is thus correct in saying,

> The text represents the solidification of a preceding communication event. It is the deposit of a prior encounter between sender (e.g., Moses or Jesus) and receiver (e.g., Israel or the disciples). In the process of becoming a written text, the message may pass through various stages, . . . *but the text represents also the first stage in the process of reinterpretation. The latter has as its aim a new communication event, this time between text and contemporary receiver.*[14]

A communicative approach directs us to this new communication event as the focus of interpretation, and clearly the text in its present form mediates the message that is at the heart of the new communication event.

---

11. M. Sternberg, *The Poetics of Biblical Narrative: Ideological Literature and the Drama of Reading* (Bloomington: Indiana University Press, 1987).

12. Bartholomew, *Reading Ecclesiastes*, 212–26.

13. In some cases the form of the text is unclear. In this case the different possible "final forms" will need to be explored. Cf. D. J. A. Clines, *The Esther Scroll. The Story of the Story*, JSOTSup 30 (Sheffield: Sheffield Academic, 1984); F. Watson, *Text, Church, and World: Biblical Interpretation in Theological Perspective* (Grand Rapids: Eerdmans, 1994). Watson refers to "the relative stabilization of the text" (16).

14. B. Lategan, "Hermeneutics," *ABD* 3:149–52, esp. 152, with added emphasis.

The expression commonly used to refer to this object of interpretation is "*final form.*" I am hesitant about this nomenclature because it may imply that we have access to the earlier forms of *these* texts but that we choose to make the final form the object of our exegesis. In this case "final form" falsely implies that these *same texts* exist/ed in a number of different forms. In fact, this is never so. We have only the biblical texts that we have, and apart from firm text-critical evidence, any reconstructed earlier "forms" are generally speculative and too often based on poor readings of the "final form." "Final form" also tends to carry with it the synchronic-diachronic tension between historical-critical and canonical readings of the Old Testament. A text may have a very complex prehistory, but in its literary form it is far more than the sum of its component parts, and it is the literary form that must be the focus of interpretation.

Written versus Oral

Does a view of the text as communicative address take sufficient account of the difference between a written and a spoken act of communication? According to Ricoeur, "No interpretation theory is possible that does not come to grips with the problem of writing."[15] In Ricoeur's view, writing differs from an oral speech act in that it fixes the "said" of speaking, alters the connection of the message to the speaker so that the text becomes semantically autonomous, potentially universalizes the message, makes the relation between message and code more complex, and shatters the grounding of reference in the dialogical situation.[16] Nevertheless, in Ricoeur's view the semantic autonomy of the text is still governed by the dialectic of event and meaning.[17]

This is a complex issue, but in my opinion Wolterstorff is correct when he argues that "Ricoeur was right to look for a practice of interpretation located in the space between Romanticism[18] and structuralism.[19] But what occupies that space is not the practice of textual-sense interpretation but the practice of authorial-discourse interpretation—a specific version of this being the practice of reading sacred texts to discern divine discourse."[20] Elsewhere Wolterstorff elaborates on this:

---

15. P. Ricoeur, *Interpretation Theory: Discourse and the Surplus of Meaning* (Fort Worth: Texas Christian University Press, 1976), 25.
16. Ibid., 25–37.
17. Cf. M. J. Valdés, ed., *A Ricoeur Reader: Reflection and Imagination* (Toronto: University of Toronto Press, 1991), 6.
18. With its emphasis on the creativity of *the author*.
19. With its emphasis on the *underlying structures* from which the particular text emerges.
20. N. Wolterstorff, *Divine Discourse: Philosophical Reflections on the Claim That God Speaks* (Cambridge: Cambridge University Press, 1995), 152; see 130–52 for a thorough discussion

We have to liberate ourselves from the grip of the notion that there is nothing between Romanticism and Structuralism. In addition to an author's intentions, and in addition to an author's text, there is what the author did in fact say by authoring his text. Not what he *intended* to say; [but] what he *did* say. . . . So we can set as the goal of our interpretation discerning what an author said.[21]

On this matter New Criticism (NC), as we will see below, is a helpful reaction to Romanticism and positivism by insisting that the focus of literary study should be texts themselves, and that the literary unity of texts is often complex and full of tensions. In biblical studies the literary nature of biblical texts has been repeatedly confirmed through the application of literary methods to them, thereby showing that what readers have often assumed to be contradictions and reduplications are actually literary features of the text.

It must also be borne in mind that in ancient Israel and in the early church, oral reception of the biblical texts played a major role. Indeed, the relationship between orality and literacy is of vital significance for biblical studies. The Jesuit scholar Walter Ong has written a series of important studies on orality and literacy and declares, "Orality-literary theorems challenge biblical study perhaps more than any other field of learning, for, over the centuries, biblical study has generated what is doubtlessly the most massive body of textual commentary in the world."[22] "The orality of the mind-set in the Biblical text, even in its epistolary sections, is overwhelming."[23]

In Ong's terms, neither ancient Israel nor the world of the New Testament were cultures of "primary orality,"[24] in which writing was unknown. By the time of Abraham, the patriarchs, and Moses, writing had already been in existence in the ancient Near East for a long time. Nevertheless such expertise was confined to the elite, and even for those who could read, manuscripts would not have been readily available, so that reception of the Old Testament texts

---

of this aspect of Ricoeur's proposal; and cf. A. C. Thiselton, *New Horizons in Hermeneutics* (Grand Rapids: Zondervan, 1992), 361-68, on Ricoeur's rejection of a dialogue model with respect to texts, and the resulting failure to take "implicature" seriously. Also see Thiselton's theological arguments (68-75) for reading Scripture as communicative address rather than as disembodied texts; he prefers the term "address" to "communication" since in people's minds the latter is often linked with an unproblematic transfer of information.

21. N. Wolterstorff, "The Importance of Hermeneutics for a Christian Worldview," in *Disciplining Hermeneutics: Interpretation in Christian Perspective*, ed. R. Lundin (Grand Rapids: Eerdmans, 1997), 44. For a more detailed discussion of authorial intention, see Bartholomew, *Reading Ecclesiastes*, 215-18.

22. W. J. Ong, *Orality and Literacy: The Technologizing of the Word* (New York: Methuen, 1982), 170.

23. Ibid., 74. Cf. Ong, *Presence of the Word*, 188-89.

24. Ong, *Orality and Literacy*, 6.

would have been primarily oral among the people of God. We have noticed how the codex took hold in the early church, but once again New Testament texts would primarily have been received by early Christians through hearing them read (e.g., Col. 4:16). Ong finds this providential:

> To assure maximum presence through history, the Word came in the ripeness of time, when a sense of the oral was still dominant and when at the same time the alphabet could give divine revelation among men a new kind of endurance and stability. The believer finds it providential that divine revelation let down its roots into human culture and consciousness after the alphabet was devised but before print had overgrown major oral structures and before our electronic culture further obscured the basic nature of the word.[25]

And if, as we have argued, ecclesial reception of the Bible is primary, then Christianity remains deeply committed to oral reception of the Bible.

Ong explains how writing changes orality. Writing locks words into a visual field; orality privileges listening, while writing encourages analysis. The ancient Greeks specialized in the art of rhetoric, which became the most comprehensive academic subject in all of Western culture for some two thousand years. Writing initially thus "did not reduce orality but enhanced it, making it possible to organize the 'principles' or constituents of oratory into a scientific 'art,' a sequentially ordered body of explanation that showed how and why oratory achieved and could be made to achieve its various specific effects."[26] Nevertheless writing introduces a major shift into a primarily oral culture.

Ong's work is peppered with examples of how orality relates to the Bible. In an oral culture words are powerful, and language is a form of action. Ong relates this to the fact that in Hebrew *dābār* can mean both word and event. Adam's naming of the animals in Genesis 2:20 does not just reflect an archaic belief: names do give people power over what they name.[27] To facilitate memory, oral thought is full of rhythmically based expressions as found, for example, in proverbs. Even law is enshrined in formulaic sayings in oral cultures. Sound is central: "the phenomenology of sound enters deeply into human beings' feel for existence, as possessed by the spoken word."[28] Orally based thought is additive rather than subordinate. Ong refers to Genesis 1:1–5 as an example, with its repetitive use of the introductory *wă* (9 times). Contemporary translations, however, provide a flow of narration appropriate to their literate contexts by

---

25. Ong, *Presence of the Word*, 191.
26. Ong, *Orality and Literacy*, 9.
27. But see chap. 2 (above) for Chrétien's reading of this.
28. Ong, *Orality and Literacy*, 72.

translating *wă* in a variety of ways.[29] Repetition is common in oral thought and language since it aids memory. In an oral culture, "narrative originality lodges not in making up new stories but in managing a particular interaction with the audience at this time."[30] Oral cultures tend to use concepts in minimally abstract frames of reference that are closely situated to the human lifeworld. Memorization was generally not verbatim in oral cultures but involved storytellers making the story their own. Oral thought forms help to explain the penchant in the Torah for geographical markers, such as those in Numbers 33:16–49, and in genealogies, which in effect are "commonly narrative."[31]

It is not just writing but the invention of print that transforms literacy in a culture. Print enables hearing-dominance to yield to sight-dominance and enhances a sense of closure: "Before print, writing itself encouraged some sense of noetic closure. By isolating thought on a written surface, . . . writing presents utterance and thought as uninvolved with all else, somehow self-contained, complete."[32] It is print, according to Ong, that gives rise in literary theory to formalism, NC, and intertextuality.

The genre most studied in terms of orality-literacy is *narrative*. Everywhere narrative is a major genre of culture, from primary oral cultures until today.

> In a sense narrative is paramount among all verbal art forms because of the way it underlies so many other art forms, often even the most abstract.[33] Human knowledge comes out of time. Behind even the abstractions of science, there lies narrative of the observations on the basis of which the abstractions have been formulated. . . . Knowledge and discourse come out of human experience, and the elemental way to process human experience verbally is to give an account of it more or less as it really comes into being and exists, embedded in the flow of time. Developing a story line is a way of dealing with this flow.[34]

Oral cultures lack abstract categories, and so they use narrative to store and communicate much of what they know. To facilitate retention of knowledge, oral cultures require poetic structures unfamiliar to us. Ong observes how oral cultures handle plot differently from us, who commonly think along the lines of Freytag's pyramid: an ascending action rising to a climactic point, which brings

---

29. For a discussion of the translation of Gen. 1:1–2:3, see C. G. Bartholomew and B. Ashford, *The Doctrine of Creation* (Downers Grove, IL: IVP Academic, forthcoming).
30. Ong, *Orality and Literacy*, 41.
31. Ibid., 98.
32. Ibid., 129–30.
33. Notice how this relates to my making a *narrative* biblical theology primary in chaps. 3 and 4 (above).
34. Ong, *Orality and Literacy*, 137.

about a reversal of action and is followed by a denouement. In ancient Greek oral narrative, there is a disregard for temporal sequence: the poet starts in the middle of things and casts the hearer into the midst of the action. Oral culture has no experience of a novel-length, climactic, linear plot. Episodic structure and patterning was the only path available, with skill in flashbacks and other techniques. This was the natural way to talk out a lengthy story because it is closer to real life than a Freytag pyramid. Narrative does, however, have to do with temporal sequence, and in all narrative there is some story line. "Oral narrative is not greatly concerned with exact sequence parallelism between the sequence in the narrative and the sequence in extra-narrative referents. Such a parallelism becomes a major objective only when the mind interiorizes literacy."[35] Writing also facilitated the move from flat to round characters, a move that Scholes and Kellogg connect to the interiorizing drive in the Old Testament and its intensification in the New Testament.[36]

It is apparent just how important Ong's work is if we are to avoid anachronistic readings of the Bible. The *sensorium*—Ong's word for the way in which the senses function in a culture—of biblical times is very different from that of our own, and biblical scholarship in particular must be attuned to these differences. Ong reports how even from patristic times and onward, scholars have veered away from considering Jesus the Word as sound toward a knowledge-by-vision approach. Intriguingly, he ponders what an oral-aural theology of the Trinity would look like but recognizes that "such a theology is still so underdeveloped as to be virtually nonexistent."[37] Below we will attend to Luke as a narrative, and it will be apparent how helpful Ong's approach is in avoiding the application of literary analyses that do not fit writing that is still powerfully shaped by orality.

Yet as we notice, Ong does not propose that we revert to practicing the literacy and recovering the mentality of the biblical period. A sense of history is indispensable, but "if God's presence is to be known, it must be found while man is living in a newly arranged constellation of sensory apprehensions."[38]

Literature and History

Several aspects of the complex relationship between literature and history should be recognized.

---

35. Ibid., 144.
36. R. E. Scholes and R. Kellogg, *The Nature of Narrative* (Oxford: Oxford University Press, 1966), 165–77.
37. Ong, *Presence of the Word*, 180.
38. Ibid., 288.

1. As literature, the biblical texts came into existence in particular cultures and at particular times *in* history, and they bear all the marks of such historical and cultural shaping. The books of the Old Testament are ancient Near Eastern texts, and the books of the New Testament are Greek texts and must be read as such. Thus, as Ong's work makes crystal clear, an emic (analysis from within the culture) approach to their literary nature is vital; we have to read the Old Testament as ancient Near Eastern literature, for example, and be wary of anachronistically applying contemporary views of literature to it. Similarly, we need to know about how literature functioned in the Greco-Roman world of the New Testament day and attend to the literary nature of the New Testament books in this light.

An excellent example is that of *the genre of the Gospels*. Traditionally, they were read as biographies of Jesus, a "window" onto Jesus by those who wanted to learn about him. During the nineteenth century, with the emergence of the comprehensive and psychologically oriented biography, several major German scholars declared in the 1920s that the Gospels were not biographies but sui generis. This approach saw the Gospels as popular folk literature, as collections of stories passed down orally, and remarkably this view dominated Gospel studies for some fifty years. The Gospels were now seen more as a window onto the life of the early church.

The emergence of redaction criticism focused attention on the theology of each Gospel and the community it reflected. The Gospels became windows onto particular communities, and then under the influence of social-scientific approaches became mirrors in which the communities were reflected. In some subsequent postmodern readings, the Gospels have become self-reflecting mirrors, in which all we see is a reflection of ourselves!

Intriguingly, the approach to the Gospels as biographies is back on the New Testament agenda, largely through comparing them carefully to biographies *of the time*, which were very different from biographies today. Greco-Roman βίοι (lives) is a flexible genre that does not provide a linear, chronological discussion of the whole of a person's life. Burridge concludes,

> Thus the Gospels are a form of ancient biography, and we must study them with the same biographical concentration upon their subject to see the particular way each author portrays his understanding of Jesus.... The historical, literary, and biographical methods combine to show us that the Gospels are nothing less than Christology in narrative form, the story of Jesus.[39]

---

39. R. A. Burridge, "About People, by People, for People: Gospel Genre and Audiences," in *The Gospels for All Christians: Rethinking the Gospel Audiences*, ed. R. Bauckham (Grand Rapids: Eerdmans, 1997), 123–24.

Of course, comparative work extends beyond genre. The extraordinary example in this respect is Auerbach's *Mimesis*, written while he was exiled from Germany and in Istanbul. "I am a Prussian and of the Jewish faith,"[40] he wrote in 1922. Auerbach's work is rooted in the tradition of Romance philology, Hegel, and Vico. This period marked the emergence of historicism in philosophy of history; in line with this, Auerbach embodies the view that "in order to be able to understand a humanistic text, one must try to do so as if one is the author of that text, living the author's reality, undergoing the kind of life experiences intrinsic to his or her life, and so forth, all by that combination of erudition and sympathy that is the hallmark of philological hermeneutics."[41] *Mimesis* is a riveting work and not least because Auerbach's work is "ideologically unintelligible without the Christian doctrine of Incarnation."[42] He argues that until Christianity, the idea of everyday human life as something to be represented through an appropriate style was unavailable and is a remarkable achievement of the Gospels.

In chapter 1 of *Mimesis*, Auerbach compares Genesis 22, the story of Abraham journeying to sacrifice Isaac, with book 19 of Homer's *Odyssey*. He notices the contrasting brevity in Genesis 22; the only gesture in the narrative is on the third day, when Abraham lifts up his eyes and sees the place from afar: "It is as if, while he traveled on, Abraham had looked neither to the right nor to the left, had suppressed any sign of life in his followers and himself save only their footfalls."[43] By comparison with Homer, the multilayeredness of the characters is notable. Auerbach sees the fuller development of Old Testament characters and relates that to the involvement of the one God with them.[44] The narrative creates an overwhelming sense of suspense, and the words spoken serve to evoke thoughts unexpressed.

From Genesis 22, Auerbach comments in general on the biblical stories. Intriguingly he observes:

> Their religious intent involves an absolute claim to historical truth. The story of Abraham and Isaac is not better established than the story of Odysseus, Penelope, and Eurycleia; both are legendary. But the Biblical narrator, the Elohist, had to believe in the objective truth of the story of Abraham's sacrifice—the

---

40. E. W. Said, "Introduction to the Fiftieth-Anniversary Edition," in *Mimesis: The Representation of Reality in Western Literature*, by E. Auerbach, Princeton Classics (Princeton: Princeton University Press, 1953; pbk., 2003), ix–xxxii, xvii.
41. Ibid., xiii.
42. Ibid., xi.
43. E. Auerbach, *Mimesis* (1953), 9–10.
44. Ibid., 17.

existence of the sacred ordinances of life rested upon the truth of this and similar stories. He had to believe in it passionately; or else (as many rationalistic interpreters believed and perhaps still believe) he had to be a conscious liar, . . . lying in the interest of a claim to absolute authority.[45]

The Elohist aimed not primarily at realism but at *truth*:

> The Bible's claim to truth is not only far more urgent than Homer's, it is tyrannical—it excludes all other claims. The world of the Scripture stories is not satisfied with claiming to be a historically true reality—it insists that it is the only real world, it is destined for autocracy. . . . Far from seeking, like Homer, merely to make us forget our own reality for a few hours, it seeks to overcome our reality: we are to fit our own life into its world, feel ourselves to be elements in its structure of universal history.[46]

Auerbach is adamant that the Old Testament presents *universal history*, beginning with the creation of the world and time and ending with the last days, the fulfilling of the covenant. Over time this metanarrative had to be modified and enlarged, but "this process nearly always also reacts upon the frame."[47] The most striking example of such enlargement took place as a result of Paul's mission to the gentiles, with the Jewish tradition reinterpreted in the light of the Christ event. "As a composition, the Old Testament is incomparably less unified than the Homeric poems, it is more obviously pieced together—but the various components all belong to one concept of universal history and its interpretation."[48]

A fascinating aspect of Auerbach's reading of the Bible is that its literary nature forges a vision in which the sublime (divine) and the everyday are inseparable.[49] In chapter 2 of *Mimesis*, Auerbach examines chapter 37 and part of 38 in Petronius's *Satyricon*, offering description of Trimalchio's wife, *Fortunata*, whose name signifies the ancient view of the instability of fortune, plus part of Tacitus's *Annals*, book 1, and compares these writings with the story of Peter's denial of Jesus in the Gospel of Mark. In contrast with this other ancient literature, Peter "is the image of man in the highest and deepest and most tragic sense,"[50] and the scene of his denial "fits into

---

45. Ibid., 14. This is not to suggest that Auerbach simply sees all OT narratives as historical. There is legendary material present, but "the material of the Old Testament comes closer and closer to history as the narrative proceeds" (19). C. S. Lewis held a similar view.
46. Ibid., 14–15. The reader should note that Lesslie Newbigin makes comparable points.
47. Ibid., 16.
48. Ibid., 17.
49. Cf. ibid., 22–23.
50. Ibid., 41.

no antique genre."⁵¹ Auerbach asks why this narrative arouses in us the most serious sympathy.

> Because it portrays something which neither the poets nor the historians of antiquity ever set out to portray: the birth of a spiritual movement in the depths of the common people, from within the everyday occurrences of contemporary life, which thus assumes an importance it could never have assumed in antique literature. What we witness is the awakening of "a new heart and a new spirit." All this applies not only to Peter's denial but also to every other occurrence which is related in the New Testament.... Peter and the other characters in the New Testament are caught in a universal movement of the depths which at first remains almost entirely below the surface and only very gradually ... emerges into the foreground of history.... What we see here is a world which on the one hand is entirely real, average, identifiable as to place, time and circumstances, but which on the other hand is shaken in its very foundations, is transforming and renewing itself before our eyes. For the New Testament authors who are their contemporaries, these occurrences on the plane of everyday life assume the importance of world-revolutionary events, as later on they will for everyone.⁵²

Mimesis is a tour de force. Auerbach tracks the development of this biblical representation of reality, using his comparative method, through Jerome and Augustine (chap. 3); Gregory of Tours (chap. 5); Bernard of Clairvaux and the Victorines, medieval Christian drama, Francis of Assisi (chap. 7); and its climax in Dante's *Inferno* (chap. 8). Auerbach notes of medieval Christian drama that

> everything in the dramatic play which grew out of the liturgy during the Middle Ages is part of one—and always of the same—context: of one great drama whose beginning is God's creation of the world, whose climax is Christ's Incarnation and Passion, and whose expected conclusion will be Christ's second coming and the Last Judgment.... In principle, this great drama contains everything that occurs in world history. In it all the heights and depths of human conduct and all the heights and depths of stylistic expression find their morally or aesthetically established right to exist; and hence there is no basis for a separation of the sublime from the low and everyday, for they are indissolubly connected in Christ's very life and suffering.⁵³

For Auerbach, this view of reality finds its climax *and* deconstruction in Dante's *Inferno*. Through his near miraculous language, Dante evokes

51. Ibid., 45.
52. Ibid., 43.
53. Ibid., 158.

the sublime, yet with an overwhelming realism and rich evocations of sensory human life, so that "Dante, then, took over earthly historicity into his beyond."[54] Dante's vision is based on a figural view of reality, but both figure and its fulfillment have "the character of actual historical events and phenomena."[55] Dante, with his figural pattern,

> brings to life the whole historical world and, within that, every single human being who crosses his path! To be sure, this is only what was demanded from the first by the Judaeo-Christian interpretation of the phenomenal; that interpretation claims universal validity. But the fullness of life which Dante incorporates into that interpretation is so rich and strong that its manifestations force their way into the listener's soul independently of any interpretation.[56]

For Auerbach, Dante's achievement in such representation is so powerful that "the image of man eclipses the image of God."[57] Dante's work thus marks the emergence of a humanism increasingly devoid of God; in the rest of *Mimesis*, Auerbach tracks the emergence of the historicism of his own day.

Auerbach's work needs to be compulsory reading for every exegete. Sadly, one suspects that it is little known among biblical interpreters. Certainly one will not find it referred to in commentaries on Genesis 22 and Mark 14:66–72.[58] If we are concerned with theological interpretation, this needs to change, and so it is important to reflect on what we can learn from Auerbach.

First, from Auerbach we should learn the value of historical, *comparative study*, but of a particular sort.[59] Biblical studies today is full of comparative work, but it is rare to find comparative work of this sort that allows the Scriptures to speak with freshness and power. A key, I think, is a comparative method with the focus on the world represented by the text; it is such a focus that makes Auerbach's work, that of Frankfort and coauthors' *Intellectual Adventure of Ancient Man*, René Girard's work on myth and the Bible, and Tom Wright's work on the New Testament against the Old Testament and Second Temple background—all to be so fresh and powerful.

54. Ibid., 193.
55. Ibid., 197.
56. Ibid., 201.
57. Ibid., 202.
58. A quick examination of ten major commentaries on each of these books confirms this fact.
59. Cf. C. S. Lewis, *Undeceptions: Essays on Theology and Ethics* (London: Bles, 1971), for his critique of seeing the Gospels as legends: "Now, as a literary historian, I am perfectly convinced that whatever else the Gospels are, they are not legends. . . . Apart from bits of the Platonic dialogues, there are no conversations that I know of in ancient literature like the Fourth Gospel. There is nothing, even in modern literature, until about a hundred years ago when the realistic novel came into existence" (126).

Second, Auerbach's work ought to awaken in us the need for developing a *literary sensibility* that is more important than the detailed literary studies so prominent in biblical scholarship. The latter, as we will see below, are invaluable, but only in the context of a refined literary sensibility. Indeed, the most creative work on the Bible as literature has largely emerged not only from Jews but also from Jews whose primary specialty is not biblical studies but literature. Central examples in this effort are Robert Alter and Meir Sternberg. Training in biblical studies would need to change to facilitate a renewed engagement with the Bible as the God-speaking literature[60] that it is. In a very useful essay, Janine Langan exhorts us to develop educated Christian imaginations.[61] She proposes that such an imagination would be antignostic, typological, iconic, sacramental, and eschatological. Such an imagination would enable us to begin to do justice to the literary, imaginative aspects of biblical texts.

Third, it is clear from Auerbach's work that the literary, the historical, and the theological are finally inseparable. For purposes of analysis, we can and are separating them from one another, but in practice they interpenetrate into a seamless whole.

2. We recognize that attending to the literary nature of biblical books does not prejudge their *historical* reference. This theme has already cropped up in our discussion of Auerbach (above). Ricoeur in particular has attended to the close similarities and differences between nonhistorical and history writing: both forms share the characteristics of literary narrative, as we noted in chapter 10.

3. As careful as we need to be about not imposing alien literary categories on the Bible, there is validity to an etic (analysis from outside a culture) approach. We remain recipients of the biblical message, and over the centuries progress has been made in our understanding of how literature works, what would generally be called *philosophy of literature*.[62] It would be folly to refuse to bring such insights to bear on the Bible.

However, recent and contemporary views of literature are diverse, and postmodernism has shattered any illusion we may have had about an objective science of literature. We are now in a situation where any new development in literary studies is soon applied to the Bible, for better or for worse.[63] For

---

60. This phrase is from the Canadian aesthetician Calvin Seerveld in his *How to Read the Bible to Hear God Speak* (Toronto: Toronto Tuppence Press, 2003).

61. J. Langan, "The Christian Imagination," in *The Christian Imagination: The Practice of Faith in Literature and Writing*, ed. Leland Ryken (Colorado Springs: Shaw, 2002), 63–80.

62. Nowadays the genitive in "of literature" is understood in at least three ways: as referring (1) to how literature works (our use here); (2) to the relationship between philosophy and literature as autonomous disciplines; (3) to philosophy as found in literature.

63. On this issue, esp. see the journal *Semeia*; e.g., "Postcolonialism and Scriptural Reading" (2005).

example, no sooner had *new historicism* emerged in literary studies than a body of new historicist work appeared in biblical studies.

Two lessons emerge from this:

a. We need to know something of the history of literary theory and especially of recent developments and their application in biblical interpretation. We will attend to this below.
b. We cannot avoid critically engaging these developments, not least because they are diverse and contradictory. As Louis Mackey observes, "Given the present near-chaos in criticism, the future of literary theory is unpredictable."[64] In my view there are very rich models on offer, but also some dangerously unhelpful ones. Care is needed, and so is critical Christian insight, which is able to identify the helpful insights in all theories—and distortions—on offer, while positioning such insights in the context of a Christian view of literature. Fortunately there is available a growing body of work on a Christian view of literature from which we can draw, as we will see below.

We must seek to avoid imposing an alien theory of literature on the Bible. What we are looking for is a theory that the facts on the ground will rise up to meet, as it were. Here Sternberg's work is exemplary, focusing *inductively* on the Old Testament to see what poetics are at work in the text. The hermeneutical circle comes into play here again: we need a view of literature in order to attend to the literary aspect of the Bible, but this must be continually refined by the Bible itself.

Literary Theory and the Bible

According to David Lyle Jeffrey, "[C. S.] Lewis's God is Lord also of the literary word, the very Master of metaphor and parable. It is thus to the heart of the faithful reader, not to the skeptic or technophile, that some of the meaning in irreducible mysteries may most likely come."[65]

Literary theory is "a reasoned account of the nature of the literary artifact, its causes, effects, and distinguishing features."[66] In *The Republic*, Plato discusses the formative role of stories in education, but the first major work

---

64. L. H. Mackey, "Literary Theory," in *The Cambridge Dictionary of Philosophy*, ed. R. Audi, 2nd ed. (Cambridge: Cambridge University Press, 1999), 506.
65. D. L. Jeffrey, "Reading Wisely, Reading Well," in *Houses of the Interpreter: Reading Scripture, Reading Culture*, ed. D. L. Jeffrey (Waco: Baylor University Press, 2003).
66. Mackey, "Literary Theory," 505.

in this area is Aristotle's *Poetics*. Ironically, this work had little influence in antiquity, but it was given fresh life in the Renaissance and since then has remained very influential.[67]

Aristotle composed his *Poetics* with the Greek traditions of epic, tragedy, dithyramb (an elaborate choral song with narrative content),[68] comedy, and rhetoric mature before his eyes in Athens. The *Poetics* is literary theory; it is a *technē* (art) of poetry that describes the nature of poetry, discerns its major parts, and sets out its most effective procedures, viewing poetical composition mainly from within rather than from the spectator's viewpoint. A central presupposition, not original to Aristotle, is that poetry is *imitation* of humans in action and designed to give pleasure to an audience. The *Poetics* defines epic poetry, tragedy, and comedy, then examines the six constituent parts of tragedy: plot, character, thought, language, spectacle, and music. Plot is the most important and the final cause (*telos*) of the other parts. For a poem to have maximum effect, the action depicted and the poem itself must be complete and whole.

In chapter 5 we recognized the importance of Augustine's *De doctrina christiana*. This work is directed toward biblical interpretation, but in the process Augustine develops a theory of signification that became the foundation for general literary theory in the Middle Ages.[69] Like Aristotle, Augustine takes the system of signs to be conventional; while this system may appear arbitrary, *the use* of signs is not. Signification is also volitional, involving the will, so that literature is subject to misdirection: it can lead to truth, but it can also lie and distort. Augustine makes his famous distinction between use and enjoyment, situating his semiotics in the full light of the Word made flesh.

The *caveat* to intellectual enterprise, including perhaps any theory of signs, is the basic question of priority and purpose:

> Whatever else appeals to the mind as being loveable should be directed into that channel into which the whole current of love flows. (*DDC* 1.22.21)

For Augustine even a theory of signs is therefore ultimately based on considerations of intention and the ordering of values. That is, he does not believe

---

67. See J. Hutton, introduction to *Aristotle's Poetics*, translated, introduced, and annotated by J. Hutton (New York: Norton, 1982), 1–34.

68. Hutton, *Aristotle's Poetics*, 81.

69. D. L. Jeffrey, *People of the Book: Christian Identity and Literary Culture* (Grand Rapids: Eerdmans, 1996), 89. Valuable recent studies of Augustine's *DDC* include D. W. H. Arnold and P. Bright, eds., *De doctrina christiana: A Classic of Western Culture*, Christianity and Judaism in Antiquity 9 (Notre Dame, IN: University of Notre Dame Press, 1995); E. D. English, *Reading and Wisdom: The "De doctrina Christiana" of Augustine in the Middle Ages*, Notre Dame Conferences in Medieval Studies 6 (Notre Dame, IN: University of Notre Dame Press, 1995).

it possible to elaborate a theory of signs without first taking into account the sphere of the ethical. A self-centered or self-serving (let alone self-referential) use of signs cannot maintain an ordered relationship of means to end.[70]

For Augustine, no fallen individual can be sure of complete understanding; hence the conversation of readers in the body of Christ exercises an important control on interpretation. All truth is God's truth, and Augustine is alert and positive toward the utility of any disciplines that can help to interpret Scripture. "What Augustine advocates is not a syncretism but a discriminating borrowing according to fixed and ordinate principles laid down in Scripture itself."[71] He distinguishes between *useful* reading and *useless* reading: the latter is a product of cupidity, of the soul turned away from God and turned in on itself, its neighbor, or any material thing for the sake of something other than God. Useful reading is a product of charity, "the motion of the soul toward the enjoyment of God for his own sake and the enjoyment of one's self and one's neighbor for the sake of God."[72] Useful reading can be shared; in book 4 of *De doctrina christiana*, Augustine turns to communication of what has been read. The eloquence of rhetoric can be misused, as he knew too well, so he stresses that eloquence is to serve truth and wisdom, not the reverse. Jeffrey eloquently sums up Augustine's theory:

> Above all Augustine's theory is teleological: the distinction and ordering of means and end, enjoyment and use, cupiditous and charitable motivation, eloquence and sapience, letter and spirit, sign and thing, are such as to carry the energies of textual study outward into the whole realm of human inquiry, the *universitas* of humane wisdom, but only to draw their comprehension back again into concrete enactment of the world and will of God as summarized in the Great Commandment.[73]

A paradigm shift in literary theory occurred among the Romantics, of which Coleridge's *Biographia literaria* (1817) is the great symbol. For the Romantics, in reaction to the aridity of Enlightenment rationalism but still within a humanist perspective, poetry and literature are the imaginative *self-expression* of the creative subject.[74] Abrams helpfully explains:

70. Jeffrey, *People of the Book*, 83.
71. Ibid., 87.
72. Augustine, *DDC* 3.10.16.
73. Jeffrey, *People of the Book*, 89.
74. The standard work on the transition from classical theory (imitation) to Romantic expressivism is by M. H. Abrams, *The Mirror and the Lamp: Romantic Theory and the Critical Tradition* (London: Oxford University Press, 1953); idem, *Doing Things with Texts: Essays in Criticism and Critical Theory* (New York: Norton, 1989), 3–30, distinguishes five types of

The mimetic poet is the agent who holds the mirror up to nature; the pragmatic poet is considered mainly in terms of the inherent powers ("nature") and acquired knowledge and skills ("art") he must possess to construct a poetic object intricately adapted, in its parts and as a whole, to its complex aims. In the expressive orientation, the poet moves into the center of the scheme and himself becomes the prime generator of the subject matter, attributes, and values of a poem.[75]

The main historical source for this view is Pseudo-Longinus's *On the Sublime*,[76] which was very influential after it became well known in the last quarter of the seventeenth century. In expressivist theories, the source of a work of literature is no longer the external world but the poet's own self. Literature is above all about self-expression, and intriguingly the most thorough exponent of poetry in this vein was John Keble in his *Lectures on Poetry* (1832–41), who argues that a good poem is the indirect expression of some overpowering emotion. In 1778 J. G. Herder declared: "This *living reading*, this divination into the soul of the author, is the *sole* mode of reading, and the most profound means of self-development."[77]

Positivism emerged in the late nineteenth and early twentieth centuries. Philosophical positivism, especially with its concern to extend scientific method to all areas of life, played an important role in developing these traits, but the complexities and diversities of these developments in literary studies must not be overlooked.[78] In the latter nineteenth century it was common for literature to be studied in relation to "the genesis of the art-work in terms of 'influences' and 'sources'; to search for similar or analogous motifs and themes in earlier literature; to probe the origins of the political, cultural and social background of the period or the biographical background of the author—all in order to give a causal explanation of how the work came into being."[79] Scientific causality was used to explain literary phenomena in relation to economic, social, and political conditions; for example, Brunetière (1849–1906) and Symonds (1840–93) argued

---

critical theories of literature: mimetic, pragmatic, expressive, objective, and recent developments. His section (11–17) on expressive theories is a good summary of Romanticism's influence on literary theory.

75. Abrams, *Doing Things with Texts*, 11.
76. It is spuriously attributed to Longinus.
77. Abrams, *Doing Things with Texts*, 15. Quoting J. G. Herder, *Vom Erkennen und Empfinden der menschlichen Seele* (Riga: Hartknoch, 1778), 56–57.
78. Note, e.g., R. Wellek's references to the interrelationship between historicism and positivism, and to how different views of the natural sciences' methods affect literary criticism: *Concepts of Criticism* (New Haven: Yale University Press, 1963), 257–58.
79. Meir Weiss, *The Bible from Within: The Method of Totality Interpretation* (Jerusalem: Magnes, 1984), 2.

for an understanding of the evolution of genres, based on the analogy of biological sciences. "Positivism" in literary studies is summed up in an exaggerated form in Taine's introduction to his 1863 history of English literature. In his view a literary text is an expression of the psychology of an individual, which in turn is an expression of the writer's milieu and race, captured in the French phrase *"la race, le milieu, et le moment."* Literary scholarship must therefore take as its object the causal explanation of texts in relation to these three factors. By so doing it will become a form of scientific history comparable in status and method to the natural sciences. In an exaggerated way, Taine expressed assumptions that guided European and American scholarship in the late nineteenth and early twentieth centuries. Jefferson and Robey sum these up as follows:

> In its pure form positivistic scholarship studied literature almost exclusively in relation to its factual causes or genesis: the author's life, his recorded intentions in writing, his immediate social and cultural environment, his sources.... It was not interested in the features of the literary text itself except from a philological and historical viewpoint.... It disregarded questions concerning the value or the distinctive properties of literature, since these could not be dealt with in a factual and historical manner. Or more exactly, while it took for granted that literary texts possessed a special value, in practice it treated them as if they were indistinguishable from other sorts of historical document.[80]

In his essay "The Revolt against Positivism in Recent Literary Scholarship," Wellek outlines the reaction to positivism in literary studies across Europe in the early twentieth century.[81] It was widespread and part of a broader philosophical reaction against positivism. Philosophically, there was a shift from positivism to a wide variety of idealisms, as exemplified in the work of Bergson in France, Croce in Italy,[82] and Alexander and Whitehead in England. Whereas in positivism the natural science paradigm was imposed on other disciplines, in philosophy of history this imposition was now questioned and rejected. Several philosophers now offered a defense of the methods of the historical sciences, which they sharply distinguished from the natural sciences. In literary studies too it was stressed that literary scholarship is a system of knowledge with its own aims and methods. This called for a methodologically precise criticism that deals with the *distinctive properties* of literature. Wellek

---

80. A. Jefferson and D. Robey, eds., *Modern Literary Theory: A Comparative Introduction* (London: Batsford, 1986), 9.
81. Wellek, *Concepts of Criticism*.
82. See C. G. Seerveld, *Benedetto Croce's Earlier Aesthetic Theories and Literary Criticism: A Critical Philosophical Look at the Development during the Rationalistic Years* (Kampen, Netherlands: J. H. Kok, 1958).

explores the diverse ways in which this common reaction manifested itself across Europe, ranging from Croce in Italy; to Richards, Eliot, Empson, and Lewis in England; and to Russian formalism. New Criticism's (NC) roots lie in the English reaction of Richards and Eliot. We will therefore briefly explore aspects of Richards's and Eliot's approaches before making some comments about NC as a manifestation of this reaction.

For Richards, the key to establishing the autonomy of the literary field lies in emphasizing the reader's response. He stresses the need for a theory of communication and valuation in literary studies. Toward this end he distinguishes between referential and emotive functions of language. The value of literature lies in its use of the emotive function of language, in its effect on the reader. In its effect good literature is disconcerting and thereby carries the reconciliation of conflicting values to an exceptionally high level. "They renovate and enhance our reactions to life by disrupting established habits of response, and creating in us a state of equilibrium of a kind that other sorts of experience can rarely achieve."[83] Richards's influence in literary theory is seen above all in the close reading of texts. This approach was developed by his pupil William Empson, who in his *Seven Types of Ambiguity*, according to Wellek, did "more than anybody else to inaugurate the subtle and sometimes even over[ly] ingenious analyses of poetic diction and its implications which are flourishing today both in England and in the United States."[84]

If NC derives its emphasis on close reading from Richards, it derives its antiaffectivity and stress on the objective reality of the poem from Eliot. In his celebrated essay "Tradition and Individual Talent," published in 1919, Eliot attacks the approach to poetry that seeks its significance in the marks of individual talent setting it off from its immediate predecessors.[85] He stresses that a literary work positions itself within the literary tradition, within which it must be understood, and that this context depersonalizes it and objectifies it. Thus "the poet has, not a 'personality' to express, but a particular medium, which is only a medium and not a personality, in which impressions and expressions combine in peculiar and unexpected ways."[86] Poetry thus becomes not an expression of emotion and personality but an escape from both of these.[87]

83. D. Robey, "Anglo-American New Criticism," in *Modern Literary Theory: A Comparative Introduction*, ed. A. Jefferson, D. Robey, and D. Forgacs, 2nd ed. (London: Batsford, 1986), 73–91, esp. 76.
84. Wellek, *Concepts of Criticism*, 266.
85. T. S. Eliot, "Tradition and the Individual Talent" (1919) and "The Function of Criticism" (1923), in *20th Century Literary Criticism*, ed. D. Lodge (London: Longman, 1972), 69–84, esp. 71.
86. Ibid., 75.
87. On the influence of Eliot on NC, see R. Selden and P. Widdowson, *A Reader's Guide to Contemporary Literary Theory*, 3rd ed. (Lexington: University Press of Kentucky, 1993), 11–12.

The New Critics shared Richards's and Eliot's reaction to positivism. The New Critics also shared with Richards a stress on the need for a theory of literature and his emphasis on close reading of texts. However, in common with Eliot, the New Critics rejected Richards's focus on the reader and the emotive effect of the text as the way into a properly theoretical approach to literary studies.

New Criticism focuses on the distinctive properties of literature and attempts to deal with these theoretically. Complexity and coherence constitute the key considerations in the analysis of literary texts. A literary work is a system of tensions, which may operate without ultimate solution; indeed, the presence of these tensions is the sign of a truly valuable work of art. Mature works resist easy satisfactions. However, the various elements are integrated into a whole.

The New Critical understanding of literature, and especially poetry, as a distinct type of writing needs to be taken seriously because, unlike that of many postmodern literary theorists, NC's methodology is restricted to literary texts. Thus on the whole notion of intentionality, for example, Wimsatt and Beardsley draw a clear distinction between poetry and practical messages: "In this respect poetry differs from practical messages, which are successful if and only if we correctly infer the intention. They are more abstract than poetry."[88]

New Criticism shifts the focus of literary study to the literary text itself:

> The natural and sensible starting-point for work in literary scholarship is the interpretation and analysis of the works of literature themselves. After all, only the works themselves justify all our interest in the life of an author, in his social environment and the whole process of literature. But, curiously enough, literary history has been so preoccupied with the setting of a work of literature that its attempts at an analysis of the works themselves have been light in comparison with the enormous efforts expended on the study of the environment.[89]

Criticism should focus on the poem/literary work itself, not the reader/author. The objective features of the medium thus become the focus of study; criticism is the study of the form and structure of a text. "Only one who will explain without looking to the right or left, above all without inquiring what is before and what is after, only he will fulfil his obligations to the creation, and only he will refrain from undermining the sovereignty of literary study."[90]

---

88. W. K. Wimsatt and M. C. Beardsley, "The Intentional Fallacy," in Lodge, *20th Century Criticism*, 335; cf. M. Weiss, *Bible from Within*, 21–24.

89. R. Wellek and A. Warren, *Theory of Literature*, 3rd ed. (London: Penguin, 1963), 139.

90. M. Weiss, *Bible from Within*, 6; quoting E. Staiger, *Die Kunst der Interpretation* (Zurich: Atlantis, 1957).

Two of the best-known products of NC theory are Wimsatt's and Beardsley's "The Intentional Fallacy" and "The Affective Fallacy."[91] These two essays are central to NC's attempt to construct a theoretical base that is an alternative to positivism. They acknowledge that "the words of a poem ... come out of a head, not out of a hat"; yet they reject design or intention as a standard by which to judge a poem; the intentional fallacy is a Romantic error.[92] We do not have access to a poet's intention,[93] and furthermore, a literary work is an object in the public domain and not the private creation of an individual. The author's experiences and so forth are only of historical interest and do not determine the meaning or effect of his creation. What counts is what is embodied in the text, and that is wholly accessible to anyone with a knowledge of the language and culture to which the text belongs. In this way the significance of authorial intention for literary interpretation is severely curtailed. This is not an ahistorical approach but one that severely restricts the role of history in literary study, "relegating questions about 'how the poem came to be' to a different, and by implication, inferior, branch of enquiry."[94] The "affective fallacy" refers to the type of approach that Richards represents, judging literature by its effect. This too is rejected.

The reduction of literature to a paraphrase is just that, a reduction, and it can never be equivalent to the work itself. Hence comes Brooks's essay "The Heresy of Paraphrase."[95] The structural properties that draw literature into a unity are of a dramatic and not a logical nature; the form/content distinction, as often applied to literature as though the poetic form is only the vehicle for the message, is invalid. This understanding of the integrity of the literary work affects the New Critics' view of the relationship of the artwork to its historical context of origin. Source criticism is, for example, severely curtailed. "That ancient text which gave the push to the artist was at the most some raw material in the hands of the creator but in no sense the

---

91. Wimsatt and Beardsley, "Intentional Fallacy," 334–45; idem, "The Affective Fallacy," in Lodge, *20th Century Criticism*, 345–58.

92. Wimsatt and Beardsley, "Intentional Fallacy," 334, 336.

93. M. Weiss (*Bible from Within*, 13–17) points out that since the time of Socrates, the importance of intention for interpretation has been disputed. From time to time poets themselves have admitted that they did not fully understand their intentions in producing a poem. In the nineteenth century it was suggested that the creative activity of the poet flowed from the unconscious like a prophet who does not know what he is prophesying. Weiss also suggests that intentionality is intellectually focused, whereas poetry touches on areas neglected by intellect and memory.

94. Robey, "Anglo-American New Criticism," 82.

95. In C. Brooks, *The Well Wrought Urn: Studies in the Structure of Poetry* (New York: Reynal & Hitchcock, 1947), 192–214.

source of his creation. This new creation ... springs completely from the poet's mind and soul. Therefore Knight asserts that the expression 'source' is only a misleading metaphor."[96] New Criticism stresses that the literary work, even if entirely constructed from other texts, is in its present form an integral whole and must be understood as such. The literary creation is much more than the sum of its sources.

New Critics do seek objectivity in their interpretation of literary works. "The true interpretation is the outcome of that fortunate occasion when the interpreter does not subjugate the creation but is subjugated by it."[97] The method best suited to such interpretation is close reading; close, attentive reading of the literary text is regarded as the best key for unlocking its secrets. Ong explains, "The New Critics have assimilated the verbal art work to the visual object-world of texts rather than to the oral-aural event-world. They have insisted that the poem or other literary work be regarded as an object, a 'verbal icon.'"[98]

The reaction to positivism within literary studies has a parallel in biblical studies. Meir Weiss's *The Bible from Within*, published in Hebrew in 1962, presents a New Critical approach to biblical literature as the key to resolving the distorting influence of what he calls "historicism" on biblical studies.[99] Another early advocate of NC as the method for biblical study was Alonso-Schökel,[100] who used NC in studies on prophetic poetry and poetic imagery. In many ways the influence of NC remains, but as it was superseded in literary theory, so too it has been superseded in biblical studies.

Meir Weiss's work is particularly interesting since the Hebrew version of his *The Bible from Within* was published in 1962 and the revised, enlarged, and fully updated English edition in 1984. He had twenty-two years in which to reassess his commitment to NC, but has not shifted his position. Weiss coined the expression "Total Interpretation" to describe his method of interpreting

---

96. M. Weiss, *Bible from Within*, 24.
97. Ibid., 19.
98. Ong, *Orality and Literacy*, 157. For Ong on NC, structuralism, and speech-act theory, and the difference taking account of orality-literacy makes to these approaches, see ibid., 157–68.
99. What Meir Weiss calls "historicism" is equivalent to what Wellek calls positivism. Historicism, even more than positivism, is a notoriously slippery word. For a useful discussion of the diverse ways in which it has been used, see M. Mandelbaum, "Historicism," in *The Encyclopedia of Philosophy*, ed. P. Edwards (New York: Macmillan, 1967), 4:22–25. The general definition that Mandelbaum proposes fits with Meir Weiss's use: "Historicism is the belief that an adequate understanding of the nature of anything and an adequate assessment of its value are to be gained by considering it in terms of the place it occupied and the role it played within a process of development" (4:24).
100. See L. Alonso-Schökel, *A Manual of Hebrew Poetics*, Subsidia biblica 11 (Rome: Editrice Pontificio Istituto Biblico, 1988), 205–6, for a list of his works.

the poetic parts of the Bible.[101] This method is "total" because it seeks to grasp the literary creation in its totality, using an explanation based on all the formal elements working together to create the literary work. Weiss welcomes the reaction to historicism that NC represents since this allowed the literary work itself to become the focus of literary study. Weiss is well aware that nowadays New Criticism tends to be regarded as out of date. However, he defends it against structuralism and continues to argue that "Total Interpretation" is the best method for reading biblical poetry. New Criticism does have a lot in common with structuralism, but it is focused on the individual text, while structuralism tends to be concerned with underlying and general structures.[102] Criticisms of NC are often either a result of the abuse of the method or stem from a lack of understanding. Indeed, Meir Weiss's *The Bible from Within* is an excellent example of just how sophisticated NC methodology can be.

Weiss regards form criticism as wedded to historicist presuppositions and rejects it as an external approach, utilizing an outmoded notion of form.[103] A good scientific method must be appropriate to its object, and Weiss regards the internal method of "Total Interpretation" as the most appropriate way to interpret biblical poetry.

Weiss's carefully nuanced understanding of the relationship between historical context and poetic interpretation is worth examining. In observing that NC is opposed to historicism, he distinguishes between two shades of opposition, as we saw above. As an opponent of historical background as the sole method, Weiss is concerned to restore the methodological imbalance resulting from historicism[104] but has no desire to deny the legitimate role of historical concerns in literary studies. Yet this role is restricted. Biographical and philological data can confirm one's interpretation but cannot replace it. The limitations and problems of historical criticism have to be faced, however good its intentions:

> This [historical-critical] method seems now to have come to the point where its deficiencies are becoming more obvious than its merit. The keys which have been cut and shaped with such care certainly opened a door; but the door only

---

101. M. Weiss, *Bible from Within*, 27.

102. To support this statement, Meir Weiss quotes the structuralist Elmar Holenstein: "We cannot understand and elucidate something until its appropriate place in its polymorphous and polyvalent universal code has been found, until it is clear which partial system of this general code is to be actualized for its constitution and comprehension" (ibid., 8).

103. Cf. ibid., 47–64, for a thorough critique of Gunkel's form-critical approach in relation to Ps. 23:1.

104. Quoting Cleanth Brooks in *Well Wrought Urn*, M. Weiss states: "The danger now, it seems to me, is not that we will forget the differences between poems of different historical periods, but that we may forget those qualities which they have in common, . . . those qualities that make them *poems*" (*Bible from Within*, 9).

seems to lead into another room with a door which is locked, and the lock on that door the keys do not fit. And the room we have got into is plainly not the heart of the building, but only another antechamber.[105]

Indeed, historical criticism as practiced is not truly historical because of its unbalanced idea of the relationship between literature and history. New Criticism seeks to redress this balance and in so doing argues for a different understanding of literary texts in history; it opposes their reduction to historical documents and recognizes their resistance to historical reconstruction. Weiss argues that literature will only yield what it has to give if it is approached as literature.

The strength of Meir Weiss's work is that he is at pains to show how his "Total Interpretation" bears fruit in actual exegesis. This, in his view, is the ultimate test of a method: "It can only be tested and proved in practice. If the results it produces appear to be *eis*egesis instead of *ex*egesis, then a thorough philological-critical examination of the text should point up the inadequacy and illuminate the source of the error."[106] The major part of Weiss's work is devoted to showing the difference that his method makes in exegesis.

New Criticism was "followed" by structuralism in literary criticism.[107] It is not easy to generalize about *structuralism*, but we can sum up its approach to literary texts in three ways. First, structuralism looks at a text as a manifestation of a deep, underlying structure. This has led to the well-known distinction between surface and deep structure. Because of structuralism's fascination with deep structure, some have concluded that it is not interested in the final form of the text and therefore in interpretation.[108] Certainly the focus of structuralism is deep, underlying structure, but it would be wrong to conclude, therefore, that it has no concern with interpretation. Polzin's work on Job, for example, and N. T. Wright's work on the Gospels are fine examples of how concern with deep structure may illumine the surface structure and overall interpretation of the message of the text.

Second, structuralism constructs a hypothetical-deductive model, not an inductive one.[109] Third, structuralism is conscious of the reader of the text.

---

105. H. Gardner, *The Business of Criticism* (Oxford: Clarendon, 1959), 152.
106. Ibid., 73.
107. See F. Lentricchia, *After the New Criticism* (Chicago: University of Chicago Press, 1980).
108. D. Greenwood (*Structuralism and the Biblical Text*, Religion and Reason 32 [New York: Mouton, 1985], 8–9) notes that structuralists are not primarily concerned with the meaning of a text. J. Barton (*Reading the Old Testament: Method in Biblical Study*, 2nd ed. [London: Darton, Longman & Todd, 1996], 121) stresses that structuralists are more concerned with analysis than exegesis. They are not so much concerned with providing new interpretations as explaining how an interpretation comes to be appropriate.
109. Greenwood, *Structuralism and the Biblical Text*, 112–13; R. M. Polzin, *Biblical Structuralism: Method and Subjectivity in the Study of Ancient Texts* (Philadelphia: Fortress, 1977), 19.

"Structural analysis as sign can be viewed in its dual role as the *meaning* (= content) of an object but [also] the *expression* of a subject. It is the crucial awareness and self-consciousness of the latter role of analysis that most often signals the study of an object as truly structural."[110]

The literature related to the development and application of structuralism is vast and multidisciplinary.[111] Terence Hawkes traces the origins of structuralism back to Vico in the eighteenth century,[112] but the major impetus for linguistic structuralism came from the French linguist Saussure. The English translation of Saussure's *Cours* only appeared in 1959, and it was mainly in the 1960s that it experienced the height of its influence, being taken up and developed in a variety of disciplines. In Prague a functional type of structuralism developed, focusing on the functions that language fulfils in society as a distinct structure. Key figures were Troubetskoy and Roman Jakobson (1896–1982). Jakobson focused on *the poetic function* of language and sought to give an account of this within the context of linguistics.[113]

Poeticalness is an aspect of all uses of language; poetry appears when "poeticalness" is raised to a higher degree than other competing functions. Hence, when dealing with poetic function, linguistics cannot limit itself to the field of poetry.[114] We therefore need a poetics of poetry and prose that attends to metonymy and metaphor at all levels, and this is what Jakobson seeks to provide. To this end he draws attention to six constituent factors that make up any speech event. All communication entails a *message* initiated by an *addresser* and directed toward an *addressee*. The message requires a *contact* between the two (e.g., oral, visual, electronic), must be formulated in terms of a *code* (speech, writing, numbers), and must refer to a *context* understood by both addresser and addressee. This can be diagrammatically represented as follows.

We need to notice that the message cannot be the sole carrier of meaning in this act; rather, meaning resides in the total act of communication.

---

110. Polzin, *Biblical Structuralism*, 38, with original emphasis.
111. See, e.g., the bibliography in T. Hawkes, *Structuralism and Semiotics* (London: Routledge, 1977).
112. Ibid.
113. For a useful summary of Jakobson's view, see ibid., 76–87.
114. Ibid., 377.

All meaning is context-sensitive and thus is not a stable entity that passes untrammeled from sender to receiver. The six constitutive elements are never in perfect balance. One is always dominant so that, for example, if the act is directed toward the context, then the referential function of the act dominates; if toward the addresser, the emotive dominates; if toward the addresser, the conative dominates; and so on. The above scheme of the six factors in communication can be rewritten in terms of their six functions:

	referential	
	message	
emotive	poetic[a]	conative
	phatic[b]	
	metalingual[c]	

a. R. Jakobson, "Closing Statement: Linguistics and Poetics," in *Style in Language*, ed. T. A. Sebeok (Cambridge, MA: Technology Press of Massachusetts Institute of Technology, 1960), 350–77. Jakobson states, "The set (*Einstellung*) toward the MESSAGE as such, focus on the message for its own sake, is the POETIC function of language" (356).
b. Messages serving to establish, prolong, or discontinue communication. Jakobson, "Closing Statement," 355.
c. Speech focused on the code.

Jakobson's work was most strongly directed toward poetic texts. In terms of structuralist analysis of prose, Vladimir Propp (1895–1970) was most probably the linking figure between the Russian formalists, of which group Jakobson was a member, and structuralists, especially French ones.[115] Propp's work was refashioned and developed by Algirdas Julien Greimas (1917–92).

Greimas's primary concern is semantics. He focuses on narrative structure in particular and describes it in terms of a Saussurean linguistic model of an underlying *langue* generating a *parole*. Stories spring from a common grammar so that, although stories differ considerably at a *surface level*, at a *structural level* they derive from a common grammar. At a surface level the structure of the enunciation spectacle is manifested through the actants who embody it, and these actants operate at a functional/phonemic level rather than in terms of content. An actant may be embodied in a single character or reside in the function of more than one character. "The content of the actions changes all the time, the actors vary, but the enunciation-spectacle remains always the same, for its permanence is guaranteed by the fixed distribution of the roles."[116]

Like Propp, Greimas argues for a grammar of narrative in which a finite number of elements, organized in a finite number of ways, generate stories. Greimas reorganizes Propp's seven spheres of action into the following three relationships, which he calls *actants*: subject versus object, sender versus receiver, helper versus opponent. If these three relationships form a type of

115. Cf. Hawkes, *Structuralism and Semiotics*, 87.
116. Algirdas Julien Greimas, quoted in ibid., 89.

phonemic analysis, then a syntactic analysis is required at the surface level, which will show how these elements can be joined to form a narrative in a number of *sequences*. Greimas's work on narrative constitutes a refinement of Propp's, with the same basic aim: to establish the plot models and to explore their combinatory potential.

The application of structuralism to biblical studies began in the early 1960s with the work of Leach, who used methods deeply influenced by Claude Lévi-Strauss (1908–2009) and attempted a structural analysis of the creation stories in Genesis.[117] By September 1969 close to two hundred biblical scholars, including Roland Barthes, gathered at Chantilly to discuss the relationship between structuralism and biblical interpretation. In 1970 Güttgemanns founded the journal *Linguistica Biblica* to promote structuralist approaches to the Bible.

Structuralist interpretation of the Old Testament has produced a sizable body of literature, although the latter is concentrated on Old Testament narrative texts. Greenwood maintains that the methodologies of Lévi-Strauss, Barthes, Greimas, and Güttgemanns are the most established structural procedures for biblical interpretation.[118] In my *Reading Ecclesiastes* I discuss Polzin's structuralist work on Job, so the reader is referred to that discussion.[119]

Intriguingly, Tom Wright makes substantial use of Greimas's approach in his *The New Testament and the People of God* in order to access the narrative structure of the New Testament stories, albeit within the context of more recent work on narrative.[120] Wright explains that a typical, basic story—he uses the example of "Little Red Riding Hood"—can be divided into an initial sequence, a topical sequence, and a final sequence. Most stories are more complex than this one; the twists and turns of a plot are mostly subdivisions of the topic sequence. Wright argues that such analysis of Gospel narratives "can and often does enable us to sort out, for example, where the main emphases of a narrative lie . . . and how the diverse parts relate to the whole. . . . In an (academic) world that has largely forgotten what stories are, and are for, it is a necessary task if we are to recapture important dimensions of the text."[121]

Tom Wright applies this structuralist analysis to Mark 12:1–12, the parable of the wicked tenants.[122] He discerns the following five sequences in the parable:

---

117. Cf. Greenwood, *Structuralism and the Biblical Text*, 16–22.
118. Ibid., 11. See Polzin, *Biblical Structuralism*, as well for useful bibliographies relating to the application of structuralism in Old Testament studies.
119. Bartholomew, *Reading Ecclesiastes*, 128–31. Cf. R. M. Polzin, "The Framework of the Book of Job," *Int* 28, no. 2 (1974): 182–200; Polzin, *Biblical Structuralism*.
120. N. T. Wright, *NTPG* 69–80.
121. Ibid., 73.
122. Greenwood (*Structuralism and the Biblical Text*, 63–69) uses Greimas's approach for a structural analysis of the parable of the good Samaritan in Luke 10:30–35.

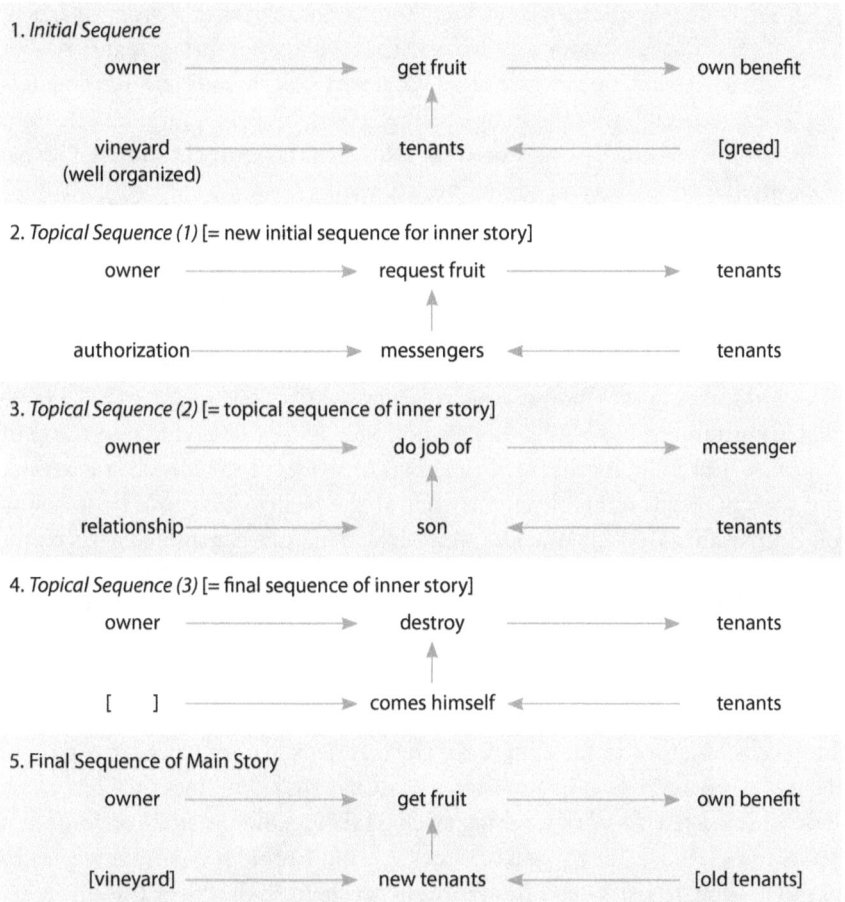

As Tom Wright notes, such analysis highlights the following issues:

a. The owner's intentions. Clearly the vineyard is there for a purpose, and within the historical setting the vineyard is Israel. Israel was created not for its own benefit but for the purposes of its covenant God.
b. The role of the son is less prominent than a strong christological reading might suggest. There is no suggestion that the death of the son might be the turning point of the story.
c. In sequences 2 and 4 the tenants appear in different positions. The characters who were designed to be in a different role end up as the opponents!
d. Within the story itself the new tenants cannot be identified.
e. The blank under "owner" in sequence 4 is pregnant with implications and will turn out to be military action taken by Rome.

f. Of wider significance is the fact that the parable tells the story of Israel: "it sets out the Jewish worldview in the regular appropriate manner—but gives it a startling new twist."[123] What is at stake in the New Testament is different tellings of the story of Israel's God, his people, and his creation.
g. Characteristically this story, like stories in the Gospels and the Gospel itself, articulates tragedy within comedy.

Wright makes use of similar structural analysis to articulate the Jewish worldview[124] and the stories told by Matthew and Luke. Appropriately, Wright's reading is not restricted to structural analysis but positions Luke-Acts in its historical context. For example, he spots striking similarities between Josephus's *Jewish War* and Luke-Acts.[125] Wright is also alert to the Old Testament and Hellenistic background to Luke-Acts. Luke's prologue is very different from those of Matthew and John; it evokes the openings of works of the Hellenistic period, but then proceeds to an obscure corner of the Hellenistic world by focusing on Zechariah and Elizabeth. The allusion here in Luke is not to Genesis but to 1 Samuel and the formation of Israel's monarchy. The story of Elizabeth and Zechariah clearly alludes to the story of Hannah and Elkanah (1 Sam. 1:1–2:1). The message is one of judgment and salvation, with John the Baptist playing Samuel to Jesus's David. "Luke has told the story of Jesus in such a way as to legitimate him as the true Davidic king."[126] As much by its outline as shape, Luke tells his story as the climax to which Israel's history has been building. Tom Wright argues that in a masterly way Luke thus combines the Hellenistic βίος with the Jewish story reaching its climax: "He told the story of Jesus *as* a Jewish story, indeed as *the* Jewish story. . . . But he told it in such a way as to say to his non-Jewish Greco-Roman audience: here, in the life of this one man, is the Jewish message of salvation that you pagans need."[127] Thus Luke's story is only meaningful as part of public world history, as well as being theology.

In terms of Greimas's categories, Luke presents his Gospel as the topical sequence of a larger drama, and the book of Acts as initiating the final sequence. This can be depicted as follows, first with the initial sequence:

123. N. T. Wright, *NTPG* 76.
124. Ibid., 221–23.
125. Ibid., 373–78.
126. Ibid., 382.
127. Ibid., 381.

Thus, in Acts the author Luke can show how the final sequence achieves what the initial sequence was unable to do:

Tom Wright's work is an excellent example of the appropriate combination of the emic and the etic. Historical context and comparative work is indispensable, but so too is the utilization of insights from contemporary literary theory, in his case Greimas's structuralism.

Derrida's lecture on structuralism in 1961 in the United States is regarded as initiating poststructuralism! Within literary theory, continental thought spawned a bewildering variety of competing theories: Russian formalism, structuralism, deconstruction, new historicism, ideological critique, queer reading, and so forth[128]—all of which have found their way into biblical studies. None of these should be ignored. Positively, postmodernism has alerted us to the presuppositions of modernism—one's worldview *does* influence one's view of literature—but negatively, postmodernism has exalted the reader over the author and the text, and we are in a situation where just about anything can be done with the Bible apart from close readings along the grain. In my view postmodernism is now in demise, but it is astonishing how many exegetes have leapt aboard this wagon uncritically. Sertillanges's advice on this matter is highly relevant:

> People talk of keeping *au courant*, and no doubt an intellectual cannot ignore the human race, nor be indifferent to what is written in his special field; but take care lest the current should carry away with it all your capacity for work, and, instead of bearing you onwards, prevent you from making any headway against it. It is only by rowing oneself that one goes forward; no current can take you to the point you aim at reaching. Go your own way and do not drift into the wake of everybody else.[129]

---

128. The best summary is Frank Lentricchia's *After the New Criticism*.
129. A. G. Sertillanges, *The Intellectual Life: Its Spirit, Conditions, Methods* (Washington, DC: Catholic University of America Press, 1998), 148.

I recall a formative conversation with Meir Sternberg when I visited him in Tel Aviv. He encouraged me to do positive, constructive work of the sort he has done in *The Poetics of Hebrew Narrative*, rather than trying to follow all the current fashions. George Steiner perceptively observes that for most of history, *a covenant between word and world* was assumed so that being and texts are sayable. Steiner rightly notes that in the philosophy of language, the shattering of this covenant in the twentieth and twenty-first centuries is one of the most significant developments in our view of language. This shattering has generated a secondary city of critical theory, which occludes engagement with the major texts of history. In the wake of such a shattering, deconstruction becomes inevitable; hence Derrida confronts us with the choice of either nihilism or "In the beginning was the Word."[130] No matter how unfashionable, it is the latter approach that we must choose and work within. Such a choice also means that we should continue to take the best from NC and structuralism and other such "modernist" theories. Indeed, as the postmodern fog subsides, it is to such theories that we will need to look for constructive ways forward.

Hence our telling of the story of literary theory must include the major contributions of Christian scholars, whose work we can build on today as we seek to retrieve that covenant between word and world; at best, their theories can orient us amid the bewildering diversity of approaches today. We have already flagged the importance of Augustine in this area, but attention needs to be given as well to the significant contributions of Christians in recent years. T. S. Eliot's, C. S. Lewis's, and Northrop Frye's work remains fertile for today; then we also have a growing body of more contemporary work by scholars such as Ruth Etchells, Walter Ong,[131] Michael Edwards, Robert Coles, Leland Ryken, David Jasper, René Girard,[132] Stephen Prickett, Wendell Berry,[133] David Lyle Jeffrey, Peter Leithart, Calvin Seerveld, Roger Lundin, Valentine Cunningham, and others.

The works of such authors contain a rich resource for thinking about the Bible as literature. A few examples will suffice. Jeffrey writes that the reader of literature requires intellectual toughness *and* imaginative sympathy. Leithart claims that reading must be an act of humility: "homage to the *auctoritatis* of an *auctor*."[134] As Leithart says, such humility includes

---

130. G. Steiner, *Real Presences* (London: Faber & Faber, 1989).

131. Ong, *Orality and Literacy*; plus many other publications.

132. See esp. R. Girard, *Deceit, Desire, and the Novel: Self and Other in Literary Structure* (Baltimore: Johns Hopkins University Press, 1965).

133. W. Berry, *Standing by Words* (Berkeley: Counterpoint, 1983); idem, *The Poetry of William Carlos Williams of Rutherford* (Berkeley: Counterpoint, 2011); idem, *Imagination in Place* (Berkeley: Counterpoint, 2010).

134. P. J. Leithart, "Authors, Authority and the Humble Reader," in *The Christian Imagination: The Practice of Faith in Literature and Writing*, ed. L. Ryken (Colorado Springs: Shaw, 2002), 210.

following the contours of plot, imagery, and character by which a work of fiction progresses. It means paying attention to what the author thinks is important, and noticing how he signals that it is important. It means paying attention to the metaphors, analogies, and symbols that the author is using to explain the significance of his story.... We may not want the emphasis placed where the author has placed it.... There will be time for such criticism, but unless we first receive what the author has given us, our criticisms will be confused at least.[135]

Similarly Lewis (and also Steiner) stresses the need for readers to be as receptive as possible to what they are reading. Lewis rightly states, "Especially poisonous is that kind of teaching which encourages [us] to approach every literary work with suspicion."[136] "No man who values originality will ever be original."[137] Jeffrey refers to Steiner's distinction between critic and reader: "The reader is servant to the text, [...] called to a clerisy of service."[138]

Lewis insists that it is not enough to make sense of a text: we want to find the sense the author intended. In the light of legitimate postmodern critique, I would nuance this, as explained above, in terms of what the author *actually said*. We do not have direct access to authorial intention, but since a work is the product of an author or authors, we *do* read texts to find out what particular authors have to say. Postmodernism's ideology of the death of the author is not only dangerous;[139] it also manifests a hubris beyond belief. The author is killed off and the reader exalted as the source of meaning. Rather than *post*modernity, this is *late modernity* with a vengeance, in which *we* become the source of all meaning.

Scholars such as Lewis, Eliot, and Jeffrey also attend to the divine authorship of Scripture, a topic that the best secular literary critics tend to avoid.[140] Intriguingly, Lewis was not a great fan of the KJV; as literature it is great, but Scripture was written in the ordinary language of the day, and we need translations that enable us to hear it as such today. Both Lewis and Eliot were wary of exclusively literary approaches to the Bible. Eliot says:

> I could fulminate against the men of letters who have gone into ecstasies over "the Bible as literature," the "Bible as the noblest monument of English prose."

---

135. Ibid., 211–12.
136. C. S. Lewis, *An Experiment in Criticism* (Cambridge: Cambridge University Press, 1961; reprint, 1996), 93.
137. C. S. Lewis, *The Weight of Glory* (Grand Rapids: Eerdmans, 1949), 41.
138. G. Steiner, *George Steiner: A Reader* (New York: Oxford University Press, 1984), 95.
139. See S. Burke, *The Death and Return of the Author: Criticism and Subjectivity* (Edinburgh: Edinburgh University Press, 1992), and note in particular the De Mann affair (1–7).
140. See D. L. Jeffrey, "Reading the Bible with C. S. Lewis," in *Houses of the Interpreter: Reading Scripture, Reading Culture* (Waco: Baylor University Press, 2003), 181–93.

Those who talk of the Bible as a "monument of English prose" are merely admiring it as a monument over the grave of Christianity. . . . The Bible has had a *literary* influence upon English literature not because it has been considered as literature, but because it has been considered as the report of the Word of God. And the fact that men of letters now discuss it as "literature" probably indicates the end of its literary influence.[141]

Clearly a Christian approach to literature at its best reorients us to a constructive approach to the literary dimensions of the Bible, and such reorientation will enable us to draw from the best, moderate, yet highly creative contemporary work, such as Wayne Booth's *The Rhetoric of Fiction*, and Ricoeur's extraordinary reinvigoration of literature as mimesis (representation) in dialogue with Aristotle and Augustine in particular.[142] And yes, this will look like a move back to modernism from the perspective of postmodernism, but so be it. We are after *truth*, not fashion.

The *Sender-Message* Relationship: The Question of Authorial Intent

For biblical interpretation, we have discussed (above) the importance of retaining an emphasis on the author and what the author has said. In reaction to positivism, NC often went too far in denying the need to take the historical aspect seriously in interpretation. In criticism, the legacy of this focus on the literary, at the expense of the historical, is the tension that many biblical scholars feel today between synchronic and diachronic readings of biblical texts. The weakness of Frei's and Lindbeck's narrative hermeneutic, for example, is its failure to do justice to the referential/historical aspect of biblical texts.[143] The model of biblical hermeneutics that I am proposing insists on privileging the biblical texts as we have them for the focus of interpretation; yet this model refuses to drive a wedge between the synchronic and diachronic aspects of biblical texts. The text as the instantiation of a communication event comes into existence at a certain historical point: in all its synchronicity, it is embedded in history, and it is crucial that this historical aspect of the text be taken seriously in interpretation.

The assumption of a tension between synchronic and diachronic readings of texts is common in biblical studies today. Jon Levenson is a good example

---

141. T. S. Eliot, *Selected Prose*, ed. J. Hayward (London: Penguin, 1953), 32–33; Jeffrey, *Houses of the Interpreter*, 276.
142. See our discussion of Ricoeur in chap. 3 above.
143. As argued by F. Watson, *Text, Church, and World*, 19–29; and K. J. Vanhoozer, *Biblical Narrative in the Philosophy of Paul Ricoeur: A Study in Hermeneutics and Philosophy* (Cambridge: Cambridge University Press, 1990).

of such a view.[144] He exposes the radical tension between a historical-critical reading as opposed to a literary reading of the Old Testament. In the preface he expresses his "own intuition . . . that the two seemingly opposite directions in which these essays move are each indispensable avenues to the larger and more encompassing truth. The dignity both of traditional interpretation and of modern criticism depends on a careful separation of the two and a reengagement on new terms."[145] How these two antithetical approaches might lead to this larger truth is never explained; indeed, Levenson has driven a wedge between the historical and the traditional contexts, and what Thiselton asks of Morgan should be asked of Jon Levenson at this point: "Rather than aim for a shift of emphasis between two paradigms, might not a more constructive task be the welding together of a more comprehensive hermeneutical model which seeks to draw on the strength of each approach while avoiding its distinctive weaknesses?"[146] Sternberg too points in a similar direction in his strong denial that a literary interpretation can avoid historical questions.

However, "welding together" will not be enough if the underlying assumptions of Levenson are not also exposed. Levenson exposes the Enlightenment underpinnings of the historical method but still tends to affirm its neutral validity.[147] In my opinion this retaining of an area of study as neutral is a legacy of "positivism," which itself needs to be undermined.

A communication model of textuality alerts us to the need to explore the questions of authorship and readership and their respective worlds, doing so in a way that refuses to set the diachronic and the synchronic at odds with each other. With most Old Testament texts, we have no external information in these respects; hence we are inevitably pushed back to the text itself for information. The critical question is *how* to take the historical aspect seriously in biblical exegesis. Francis Watson (intratextual realism), Wright (critical realism), Vanhoozer (speech-act theory), and Thiselton (pastoral hermeneutic) all argue, albeit in different ways, for a "final-form" approach that still takes the historical aspect of biblical texts seriously.

Within Old Testament poetics, Sternberg has made what I regard as the most helpful proposals about reconstructing the relationship between source criticism and literary readings of the text.[148] Sternberg regards NC as an

---

144. J. D. Levenson, *The Hebrew Bible, the Old Testament, and Historical Criticism: Jews and Christians in Biblical Studies* (Louisville: Westminster John Knox, 1993).
145. Ibid., xiv-xv.
146. A. C. Thiselton, "On Models and Methods: A Conversation with Robert Morgan," in *The Bible in Three Dimensions: Essays in Celebration of Forty Years of Biblical Studies in the University of Sheffield*, ed. D. J. A. Clines et al., JSOTSup 87 (Sheffield: JSOT Press, 1990), 341.
147. Levenson, *Hebrew Bible*, 106-26.
148. Sternberg, *Poetics of Biblical Narrative*, 7-23.

unbalanced reaction to the excesses of historical scholarship in that it sought to bracket out historical questions in textual interpretation. This is just impossible, according to Sternberg; even to understand biblical Hebrew requires historical study, and "as with linguistic code, so with artistic code."[149] "But is the language any more or less of a historical datum to be reconstructed than the artistic conventions, the reality-model, the value system?"[150] The text has no meaning outside a historical context: "The appropriate coordinates are historical, and the main trouble with the historical approaches to the Bible is their antihistorical performance."[151]

This antihistorical tendency is clearly seen, according to Sternberg, in the faulty application of source criticism that has been so dominant in Old Testament studies. "Rarely has there been such a futile expense of spirit in a noble cause; rarely have such grandiose theories of origination been built and revised and pitted against one another on the evidential equivalent of the head of a pin; rarely have so many worked so long and so hard with so little to show for their trouble."[152] This is not to deride the question of genesis: "the only point at issue between them is where and how the appeal to the genetic option serves a purpose."[153]

Sternberg maintains that, broadly speaking, approaches to the Bible are of two sorts: source- and discourse-oriented inquiries.[154] These approaches are distinguished by the object of inquiry. Source criticism is dealt with by the theologian, historian, linguist, and geneticist. It focuses on the biblical world (usually part of it) as it really was. The historian, for example, tries to determine what happened in Israelite history. The geneticist focuses on the processes that shaped the biblical text, the passage from oral to written transmission, and so forth. Discourse analysis focuses on the text itself as a pattern of meaning and effect; by pursuing this line of questioning, one tries to make sense of the discourse in terms of communication. Discourse-oriented analysis seeks to understand the text as a

> pattern of meaning and effect. What does this piece of language ... signify in context? What are the rules governing the transaction between storyteller or poet and reader? Are the operative rules, for instance, those of prose or verse, parable or chronicle, omniscience or realistic limitation, historical or fictional

149. Ibid., 12.
150. Ibid., 10.
151. Ibid., 11.
152. Ibid., 13.
153. Ibid., 14.
154. Ibid., 14–15.

writing? . . . To pursue this line of questioning is to make sense of the discourse in terms of communication, always goal-directed on the speaker's part and always requiring interpretive activity on the addressee's.[155]

Sternberg strongly argues for a community of labor; the better we understand the context, the better we will understand the text, and vice versa. Source analysis is particularly dependent on understanding the text because apart from the biblical texts, we know very little of the context. Thus "the movement from text to reality cannot but pass through interpretation. If the Bible is a work of literature, therefore, nobody can evade the consequences. As reader, for example, the historian must take into account that every item of reality given in the text may have been stylized by conventions and for purposes alien to historical science."[156]

Discourse and source analysis do not even enjoy temporal priority over each other. "Both the interpreter and the historian must perforce combine the two viewpoints throughout, incessantly moving between given discourse and source in an endeavor to work out the best fit, until they reach some firm conclusion."[157] What varies is the object of study. Where the object is to make sense of the discourse, conjecture about the source operates as an aid to interpretation and discovery of its artful rules. Discourse and genetic analysis become rivals only when they cross their boundaries and, for example, when the source critic imposes one's own reconstruction of the sources and process of composition on the text's structure.

In biblical interpretation, we maintain that the primary object of study is the text as discourse; hence source analysis will always be secondary to interpretation of the text. Form, source, redaction, and tradition criticism all have their place in the study of the sender-message relationship,[158] but understanding the text as a whole must remain the goal toward which interpretative energies are directed. Clearly the type of model for understanding genetic criticism that Sternberg has proposed has radical implications for traditional genetic criticism as historical critics have practiced it. Historical critics have tended to focus on the genetic pole of the genetic-discourse dialectic, often with disastrous consequences for discourse analysis. While maintaining the validity of the genetic aspect of biblical interpretation, it is vital that the dialectic between source and discourse analysis be recognized.

155. Ibid., 15.
156. Ibid., 16.
157. Ibid., 19.
158. Although they need to be reconfigured in this light. On form criticism and NT studies, see N. T. Wright, *NTPG* 418–35.

Literary Genre

Genre is inseparable from the communicative nature of texts, as some of the metaphors used by scholars to describe genre indicate. Wellek and Warren refer to genre as an "institution." "One can work through, express oneself through, existing institutions, create new ones, or get on, so far as possible, without sharing in polities or rituals; one can also join, but then reshape, institutions. Theory of genres is a principle of order. ... Any critical and evaluative—as distinct from historical—study involves, in some form, the appeal to such structures."[159]

Other metaphors used of genre are contracts, codes, games, deep and surface structure, and patterns of expression.[160] These metaphors point to the character of genres as general, publicly known means of expressing a type of message. Ricoeur helpfully points out that

> genres are generative devices to produce discourse as. ... Before being classificatory devices used by literary critics to orient themselves in the profusion of literary works, therefore being artifacts of criticism, they are to discourse what generative grammar is to the grammaticality of individual sentences. ... The function of these generative devices is to produce new entities of language longer than the sentence, organic wholes irreducible to a mere addition of sentences. ... Language is submitted to the rules of a kind of craftsmanship, which allows us to speak of production and works of art, and, by extension, of works of discourse. Poems, narratives, and essays are such works of discourse. The generative devices, which we call literary genres, are the technical rules presiding over their production.[161]

Consequently, at the macrolevel one of the major constraints of the way we read texts is the textual type or genre of the text. Morgan argues that "texts, like dead men and women, have no rights, no aims, no interests. They can be used in whatever way readers or interpreters choose. ... In all cases it is the interests or aims of the interpreter that are decisive, not the claims of the text as such. Any suggestion that the text has rights is a deception concealing someone else's interests."[162]

A communicative model, however, refuses to make the aims of the interpreter decisive in this way but insists that the primary responsibility of the

---

159. Wellek and Warren, *Theory of Literature*, 226.
160. T. Longman, *Fictional Akkadian Autobiography: A Generic and Comparative* (Winona Lake, IN: Eisenbrauns, 1991), 8–9.
161. Ricoeur, *Interpretation Theory*, 32–33.
162. R. Morgan with J. Barton, *Biblical Interpretation* (Oxford: Oxford University Press, 1988), 7. Morgan's view is more nuanced than this lone quote may suggest; see ibid., chap. 1.

interpreter is to read the text along the grain, as it were, in order to discern the message of the text.[163] Texts in this view do have rights, aims, and interests, and these need to be taken seriously if the text is to be read and criticized *objectively*. Texts are an expression of *interpersonal* communication: just as we cannot do as we like with people, so there are ethics of reading. A communicative model reminds us of the need to respect the otherness of the text and to allow *its* voice to be heard.

This stress on reading biblical texts objectively should not be seen as a reassertion of historical criticism in its classic modern mode. A distinction should, I suggest, be made between *thick* and *thin* notions of objectivity. The thin[164] rationalist understanding of objectivity, which reduces the truth of biblical texts to rational propositions, and the thin historical-critical approach, which generally fails to recognize the literary and kerygmatic nature of biblical texts because of its overwhelming interest in history—both should be rejected as distorting the biblical texts.[165] However, it would be quite wrong to relinquish *any* notion of objectivity or realism, as some postmoderns do. The point is that a reductionistic Enlightenment understanding of objectivity should be rejected because it fails to take into account a variety of factors that influence the acquisition of knowledge,[166] and it yields a narrow view of biblical textuality. A thicker notion of method *and* of biblical textuality is required, since interpretation involves both of these elements. But this means broadening the quest for objectivity rather than abandoning it entirely, as some postmodern thinkers are prone to do.

A thicker notion of biblical texts is required, which takes into account their historical, literary, *and* ideological/theological aspects.[167] Such a notion

---

163. However important it may be to read texts against the grain, before this can be done, they first must be read along the grain.

164. I am using "thin" here as a metaphor for "reductionistic."

165. Note that both fundamentalist hermeneutics (propositionalism) and liberal hermeneutics have been deeply influenced by modernity, albeit in quite different directions.

166. Feminist epistemology, e.g., has alerted us to the role of gender and subjectivity in the knowing process. S. G. Harding (ed., *Feminism and Methodology: Social Science Issues* [Milton Keynes, UK: Open University Press, 1987]) helpfully points out, "The beliefs and behaviors of the researcher . . . must be open to critical scrutiny no less than what is traditionally defined as relevant evidence. Introducing this 'subjective' element into the analysis in fact increases the objectivity of the research and decreases the 'objectivism' which hides this kind of evidence from the public" (9). R. A. Clouser (*The Myth of Religious Neutrality: An Essay on the Hidden Role of Religious Belief in Theories* [Notre Dame, IN: University of Notre Dame Press, 1991]) argues for taking religious presuppositions seriously in accounts of theory. In my opinion, a thick objectivity, or what one might call a critical realism, needs to take all these factors into account.

167. In NT studies, N. T. Wright, *NTPG*, has tried to develop such a thick notion of biblical texts; in OT studies, Sternberg, *Poetics of Biblical Narrative*, has argued along similar lines.

of textuality needs to be matched by a thicker notion of readers, which takes into account religion, gender, culture, historical period, and so on. In our history-dominated context, careful consideration of the genre of texts can be particularly helpful in resisting imposition of thin methodologies on texts since it forces one to take the different aspects of the biblical texts seriously.[168]

In *discourse analysis* some highly creative work is being done on textual types, particularly as these relate to narrative biblical texts.[169] Textual type/genre shapes the entire work, so to produce correct interpretation it is crucial for the interpreter to detect the type and to be aware of the rules for that genre. Genre determination will be a joint historical-literary venture. We saw (above) how an anachronistic application of "contemporary" biography to the Gospels misdirected Gospels studies for some fifty years. Genre analysis needs to be a careful combination of etic and emic approaches. Take the classification of Proverbs, Job, and Ecclesiastes as *wisdom books*. This is a modern and thus etic construct, which is very useful. However, awareness of its etic nature will make us far more sensitive to the fluid interrelationship between Old Testament genres than are too many Old Testament scholars, as well as sensitive to the fact that books like Job and Ecclesiastes combine narrative and wisdom genres. We also need to be aware that genre is not a wooden concept, cast in concrete, especially when dealing with books that embody the freshness of God's revelation. For example, the Gospels are usefully classified as βίοι, but as we noted in relation to Auerbach's work, they exceed this genre in important ways. The concept of genre thus needs to be flexible, refusing to squeeze texts into preconceived patterns and recognizing the individual structure of a text.[170] Genre remains, however, a crucial factor in objective interpretation. When we read a biblical text, we need to do the hard work of determining its genre through a combination of historical study and reading of the text. Many of the books on hermeneutics contain excellent and extensive work in this area, and I will not repeat that work here.

168. As we saw in chap. 5 above.
169. The literature is immense. See, e.g., D. A. Dawson, *Text-Linguistics and Biblical Hebrew* (Sheffield: Sheffield Academic, 1994); S. E. Runge, *Lexham Discourse Greek New Testament Bundle*, 6 vols. (Bellingham, WA: Lexham, 2008–11); S. E. Runge and J. R. Westbury, *Lexham Discourse Hebrew Bible Bundle*, 6 vols. (Bellingham, WA: Lexham, 2012).
170. Benedetto Croce's denial of the existence of genre is an extreme position, but it is understandable as a reaction against the "genre tranché" of classicism (Wellek and Warren, *Theory of Literature*, 233–34). This overreaction correctly recognizes the individuality of each text and the importance of an inductive, historical approach to the question of genre.

Text Structure

A communication model of interpretation alerts us to the particularity of each text; genre is something a text shares with other texts, but structure is more specific to a text. All texts have some structure. The idea of a text or work carries with it notions of developing unity and coherence. Where these break down completely, the reader concludes that one is not dealing with a work or unified text. Bradbury rightly argues that

> all critical theories have some notion of structure: the developing unity of a work.... I here assume what I think must be assumed for criticism effectively to exist: that every work is a distinct and verbally-created universe and must have a self-created logic or sequence for which the author is responsible. The work will have its own expectations and probabilities which constitute the unity of that universe.[171]

Coherence of relationships, actions, rhetorical devices, and attitudes are part of this unity, as Bradbury points out. Structural analysis seeks to lay bare the way in which these different elements contribute to the developing coherence of *a particular text*.

Internal (derived from the text itself) and external (derived from outside the text) means exist for gaining access to the coherence of a work. For biblical interpretation, the surface structure of the text is most important; insofar as the connection between deep and surface structures can be articulated, structuralism has much to offer. Discourse analysis of the way textual type shapes syntax[172] is another example of how external means can be helpful in discerning textual structure. And analyses of the poetics of narrative structure have been found to illuminate the coherence of biblical texts in all sorts of insightful ways.

If we can think of deep structure as analysis of genre, then what we are after is the way in which a genre, or deep structure, has come to the *particular* shape of the text we are examining. In the latter respect the internal means of deriving structure are particularly important; these means involve study of the individual texts' rhetorical techniques, such as inclusions, repetitions, chiasm, and so on. Clearly these cannot be separated either from the content of the text or from "external" and historical studies of such techniques. Structural analysis will inevitably involve a dialectic between generalized notions

---

171. M. Bradbury, "Structure," in *A Dictionary of Modern Critical Terms*, ed. R. Fowler (London: Routledge & Kegan Paul, 1987), 235.
 172. See references in note 169 above.

of deep structure, genre, discourse type, and rhetoric, plus the shape of the individual text.[173]

Intertextuality

Here I am using "intertextuality" not in the polemical sense of *intertextuality* as opposed to *intersubjectivity*,[174] but in the sense of preunderstanding and inner-biblical exegesis.[175] A communication model of biblical hermeneutics will involve exploring the world of the text, the world of the sender, and their interrelationship. In terms of genetic criticism, the Old Testament forms an indispensable part of the historical context of any Old Testament text. However, the Old Testament also comes to us as part of Hebrew and Christian Scripture, and this aspect of the text cannot be ignored, as Childs has repeatedly pointed out.[176] An approach to the Old Testament as Christian Scripture would expect a general understanding of the whole to be a helpful prejudice, or preunderstanding, in approaching the part. In this sense biblical theology and Christian doctrine should form part of the prejudice with which the reader comes to the text. However, particular care must be taken that this prejudice is not simply read into the biblical text (eisegesis) but that it allows the text to speak on its own terms. Inner-biblical exegesis can be of help in this project of examining how a text uses parts of other biblical texts.[177]

The Message of the Text: The Implied Author

A communication model of hermeneutic alerts us to discernment of the message as the goal of biblical interpretation.[178] In literary texts, including the Old Testament, the message is not always immediately obvious. This remains true even if we agree with Sternberg that the biblical authors adopted

---

173. Sternberg (*Poetics of Biblical Narrative*) states,
   In most of the theoretical work that I have done, on narrative and other subjects, the Bible has proved a corrective to widely held doctrines about literary structure and analysis, often a pointer to the formation of alternatives. In my biblical work, conversely, seldom have I found a narrative or strategy proceeding along the theoretically expected grooves or, after the event, failing to illuminate a host of other corpora and traditions. (56–57)

174. See Thiselton, *New Horizons in Hermeneutics*, 41.

175. This is M. A. Fishbane's expression, in *Biblical Interpretation in Ancient Israel* (Oxford: Oxford University Press, 2004); see esp. 2–19.

176. See also Wolterstorff, *Divine Discourse*, 204–8.

177. See Thiselton, *New Horizons in Hermeneutics*, 39–42, for some helpful comments on Fishbane's inner-biblical exegetical method.

178. See Wolterstorff, *Divine Discourse*, 183–222, for a discussion of the relationship between interpreting the mediating human discourse and interpreting for the mediated divine discourse.

a foolproof method of composition.[179] The movement from the truth to the whole truth of a biblical text is always via the literary contours of a biblical text. Here Ricoeur's notion of the world opened up in front of the text is most helpful. Another helpful way of getting at this overall message of the text is the notion of the implied author.

The notion of the implied author is developed by Booth.[180] The implied author refers to where the author wants the reader to stand in the world of values. "In short, the author's judgement is always present, always evident to anyone who knows how to look for it."[181] "As he writes, he creates not simply an ideal, impersonal 'man in general' but an implied version of 'himself' that is different from the implied authors we meet in other men's works."[182] Other terms for the implied author are the *official scribe* and the author's *second self*.[183] The implied author is not to be confused with the narrator or the "I" of a work; these more commonly refer to the speaker in the work "who is after all only one of the elements created by the implied author and who may be separated from him by large ironies. 'Narrator' is usually taken to mean the 'I' of a work, but the 'I' is seldom if ever identical with the implied image of the artist."[184]

> Our sense of the implied author includes not only the extractable meanings but also the moral and emotional content of each bit of action and suffering of all the characters. It includes, in short, the intuitive apprehension of a completed artistic whole; the chief value to which *this* implied author is committed, regardless of what party his creator belongs to in real life, is that which is expressed by the total form.[185]

In his work on biblical narrative, Sternberg finds Booth's notion of the implied author irrelevant because in biblical narrative the implied author

---

179. See Sternberg, *Poetics of Biblical Narrative*, 230–35. In conversation with Sternberg, it became clear to me that he uses *foolproof composition* to refer to the basic contours of the narrative rather than specifically to the message of the text. The latter may be located more at the indeterminate margins of the text, and it is always arrived at via the poetics of the narrative.
180. W. C. Booth, *The Rhetoric of Fiction*, 2nd ed. (London: Penguin, 1983).
181. Ibid., 20.
182. Ibid., 70.
183. Ibid., 71.
184. Ibid., 73. As Booth points out, "In any reading experience there is an implied dialogue among author, narrator, the other characters, and the reader. Each of the four can range, in relation to each of the others, from identification to complete opposition" (155).
185. Ibid., 73–74, with original emphasis.

and narrator merge into each other. For Sternberg, what is important is that "the distance between the historical writer and the implied author/narrator is so marked, indeed unbridgeable, that they not only can but must be distinguished."[186] Either way, to think in terms of an implied author or an implied author-narrator is helpful in focusing biblical interpretation on the message of the text. As Sternberg points out, this is inevitable:

> The author/narrator exists only as a construct, which the reader infers and fills out to make sense of the work as an ordered design of meaning and effect.... Where our interpretations differ, so do our reconstructions of his image—ways, means, and all. But reconstruct him according to our lights we must, all of us, not excluding the most dedicated geneticist. For a moment's thought will reveal that the very fragmentation of a biblical tale into sources, documents, etc. presupposes a unity distinctive of some teller, and the triumphant pointing to some version as *the* original form announces his disentanglement from the overall process of transmission.[187]

The Reader/s and the Text

The reader is the recipient of the message embodied in the text, according to a communication model of hermeneutic. The notion of the implied reader fits well with this approach. Each biblical text is historically embedded, and the way to the message is via the first horizon. As with the sender of the message, the initial readership has to be reconstructed mainly via the text. Although the implied author and the implied reader are always constructs of the reader, this approach maximizes the constraints of the text in interpretation. Fundamental to the process of biblical interpretation is the attempt to hear the message of the text in this way.

Current methods of interpretation have often undermined this approach to biblical interpretation. Clines has gone so far as to suggest that this approach to interpretation may be unethical, because it may require a reader to position oneself against the reader's deepest beliefs.[188] Clines has a point in that Booth is, I think, wrong in suggesting that the most successful reading is always that in which the created selves find complete agreement. Ethically, certain texts are most successfully read when reader and implied author/implied reader are opposed. The point is, though, that before one can disagree with a text, one must read it, and to do so along the grain. Feminist and materialist critiques,

---

186. Sternberg, *Poetics of Biblical Narrative*, 74–75.
187. Ibid., 75, with original emphasis.
188. D. J. A. Clines, "Possibilities and Priorities of Biblical Interpretation in an International Perspective," *Biblical Interpretation* 1, no. 1 (1993): 86–87.

to mention only two, can *follow* such a reading but should not—indeed cannot—precede it.[189]

Defending the importance of the first horizon in biblical interpretation does not mean ignoring the second horizon. In any textual interpretation the two will be in constant dynamic interaction. As the history of biblical interpretation demonstrates, what is brought to a text influences the way it is read. Subjective and communal factors play a significant role in all interpretation, and critical consciousness of these is vital in biblical interpretation. Biblical interpretation is about the fusion of two horizons, that of the biblical text and that of the reader. Interpretation takes place at the fusion of these horizons, and the biblical interpreter needs to be sensitive to the elements in both horizons and how these affect interpretation.

For example, Western individualism and privatized religion have regularly been read into biblical texts, whereas in fact they are concepts deeply alien to biblical religion.[190] I have suggested that there is a certain reader "baggage" that aids the objective reading of biblical texts, baggage such as a commitment to these texts as Christian Scripture. However, in order to bring hidden baggage to light, interpretations within one community ought to be in dialogue with interpretations of the same text within other communities. Thus dialogue of Christian interpreters with Enlightenment historical-critical readings or other religious readings can be very helpful.

A Christian model of biblical interpretation should ultimately never be

---

189. For a useful survey of the variety of approaches to the reader in literary theory, see S. R. Suleiman, "Introduction: Varieties of Audience-Oriented Criticism," in *The Reader in the Text: Essays on Audience and Interpretation*, ed. S. R. Suleiman and I. Crosman (Princeton: Princeton University Press, 1980), 3–45. Suleiman distinguishes between positive and negative hermeneutics. The former upholds the pervasive notion of the unity and wholeness of the text, plus the existence and possibility of discovering meaning, the very things that negative hermeneutics deny. This denial of the unity of the text is connected with fragmented views of the self, i.e., with anthropology. As Suleiman perceptively comments,

> That there exists a strong correlation between theories of the self and theories of the text has not escaped the more perspicacious of today's literary critics; nor has the correlation between both theories of self and of text and larger philosophical issues. Indeed, I think it is the recognition of these correlations and of their consequences that accounts for the passionately polemical tone in the debate between "positive" and "negative" theorists of interpretation. (ibid., 42)

A positive hermeneutic and the sort of view of the reader for which I argue follow from a Christian hermeneutical model.

190. On the issue of the modern distinction between secular and religious and its relationship to wisdom literature see R. E. Murphy, "Wisdom—Theses and Hypotheses," in *Israelite Wisdom: Theological and Literary Essays in Honor of Samuel Terrien*, ed. J. G. Gammie et al. (Missoula, MT: Scholars Press, 1978), 35–42, esp. 40. Murphy rightly points out that this modern conceptual disjunction is not applicable to OT thought. On community and primarily oral cultures, see Ong, *Orality and Literacy*, 73–74.

individual. Scripture can be approached as Scripture only in community, and this implies a system of checks and balances by the community within which one works. This does not mean, however, that academic biblical interpretation should all ideally be done within the institutional church. In my view, academic biblical interpretation fits within the university as long as the biblical scholar is genuinely free to allow one's own religious presuppositions to shape the exegesis.

Listening to Luke Tell the Story of Jesus

I am aware of no equivalent for the Gospel of Luke that is similar to Jean Vanier's lectio divina reading of the Gospel of John.[191] Suffice it here to remind the reader that such a reading is indispensable preparation and conclusion to our examination of Luke as literature.

The history of the interpretation of Luke is vast. Sean Kealy has left us all in his debt with his two-volume survey of work on Luke through the centuries.[192] Of primary importance for the interpretation of Luke is the question of genre: it is a *narrative*. Luke himself categorizes his work as "an orderly account" or "narrative" (διήγησις). "Luke has in mind the use of history to preach, to set forth a persuasive proclamation of God's work in Jesus and the early church, and *the medium of that proclamation is the narrative account whose 'order' is crucial for our understanding of that interpretation.*"[193] This may seem obvious, but it is an area where recent scholarship has made real progress. Henry Cadbury was one of the first to attend to the coherent plot-like structure in Luke-Acts.[194] Since then W. C. Robinson,[195] Charles Talbert,[196]

---

191. But see T. Clayton, *Exploring Advent with Luke: Four Questions for Spiritual Growth* (Notre Dame, IN: Ave Maria Press, 2012).

192. S. P. Kealy, *The Interpretation of the Gospel of Luke*, vol. 1, *From Apostolic Times through the Nineteenth Century*; vol. 2, *In the Twentieth Century* (Lewiston, NY: E. Mellen, 2005–7). For a very useful overview of recent scholarship, see A. C. Thiselton, "The Hermeneutical Dynamics of 'Reading Luke' as Interpretation, Reflection, Formation," in *Reading Luke: Interpretation, Reflection, and Formation*, ed. C. G. Bartholomew, J. B Green, and A. C. Thiselton, SAHS 6 (Carlisle, UK: Paternoster; Grand Rapids: Zondervan, 2006), 3–54. I will footnote references only where essential.

193. J. B. Green, *The Gospel of Luke* (Grand Rapids: Eerdmans, 1997), 38, with added emphasis.

194. H. J. Cadbury, *The Making of Luke-Acts*, 2nd ed. (London: SPCK, 1958).

195. W. C. Robinson, *Der Weg des Herrn: Studien zur Geschichte und Eschatologie im Lukas-Evangelium* (Hamburg-Bergstedt: Reich, 1964).

196. C. H. Talbert, *Literary Patterns, Theological Themes, and the Genre of Luke-Acts* (Cambridge, MA: SBL, 1974); idem, *Reading Luke: A Literary and Theological Commentary* (New York: Crossroad, 1982).

Robert Tannehill,[197] Luke Timothy Johnson,[198] David Moessner,[199] Joel Green, and a host of others have made major contributions in this area.

That Luke has the genre of narrative immediately alerts us to the following elements as significant for its interpretation: temporality, plot, sequencing, beginnings and ends, and narrative frames.[200] Typical of the Gospel writers, Luke does not insert his voice at regular intervals to make sure we understand the significance of what is being narrated. It is *by* attending to Luke as narrative that we hear its message.[201] We need, however, to be alert to avoid applying anachronistic understandings of narrative to Luke, as Ong's work reminds us.

The identification of Luke as narrative prevents us from pitting history, theology,[202] and formation against one another. *As* narrative, Luke represents for us a world in which the main actors are God, Jesus, and the Spirit sent by Jesus in Acts. The validity of this representation depends for its truth on the events recorded having happened in time and space,[203] but it is *through* narrative that the events recorded are interpreted and a world opened up in front of the text, a world that the reader is invited to explore and inhabit. Attending to Luke as narrative is fundamental to the explication of all three of these dimensions of Luke: its theology, its historicity, and its role in spiritual formation. In cultures in which orality played a large part, narrative *was the means* by which knowledge was communicated.

Very detailed literary analyses of Luke are available, yet they do not always agree in how to analyze the literary structure. This is especially true of the Lukan Travel Narrative (9:51–19:48).[204] What is often lacking in such analyses is an assessment of the degree of probability of particular readings.[205]

---

197. R. C. Tannehill, *The Narrative Unity of Luke-Acts: A Literary Interpretation*, 2 vols. (Philadelphia: Fortress, 1986–90).

198. L. T. Johnson, *The Gospel of Luke* (Collegeville, MN: Liturgical Press, 1991).

199. D. P. Moessner, *Lord of the Banquet: The Literary and Theological Significance of the Lukan Travel Narrative* (Minneapolis: Fortress, 1989).

200. See B. Richardson, ed., *Narrative Dynamics: Essays on Time, Plot, Closure, and Frames* (Columbus: Ohio State University Press, 2002).

201. But cf. S. Sheeley, *Narrative Asides in Luke-Acts* (London: Bloomsbury, 2015).

202. See I. H. Marshall, *Luke: Historian and Theologian*, 3rd ed. (Downers Grove, IL: InterVarsity, 1998).

203. This is not to suggest that the historicity of the Gospels is a simple matter, but I assert that the effectiveness of the Gospels as speech acts depends on historicity and also that historical comparisons between the Gospels should follow after narrative analysis of each Gospel, not earlier.

204. See, e.g., K. E. Bailey, *Poet and Peasant: A Literary-Cultural Approach to the Parables in Luke* (Grand Rapids: Eerdmans, 1976), 79–85; Moessner, *Lord of the Banquet*; Talbert, *Reading Luke*, 111–13; idem, *Literary Patterns*, 51–56.

205. See G. J. Wenham, "Method in Pentateuchal Source Criticism," *VT* 40, no. 1 (1991): 84–109; C. G. Bartholomew, "The Composition of Deuteronomy: A Critical Analysis of the

Especially bearing in mind the oral reception of Luke's Gospel, some of the analyses proposed are less than convincing, not least in the light of Ong's work. In what follows we will concentrate on the narrative shape of Luke *as a whole* while taking note of detailed work where appropriate.

1. *Luke 1:1–4, The Prologue.* Here Luke identifies the genre of his work, positions it among other such narratives, alerts us to the historical base of his narrative in eyewitness testimony, and tells of his decision to write a similar narrative,[206] on the basis of his own careful investigation, for Theophilus, so that he may "know the truth" concerning the things in which he has been instructed. Moessner suggests that Luke distinguishes his narrative from others, writing one that will lead Theophilus to "certain clarity."[207] However, it is unlikely that this is what Luke has in mind in the prologue, implying as it would that similar accounts also based on eyewitness testimony do not lead to such clarity; the difference rather seems to be the intended audience: "most excellent[208] Theophilus" and the circle of his friends that such a dedication would open up. Alas, we know very little about Theophilus, but the clearly Hellenistic style of the prologue[209] and the public status of Theophilus clue us in to the gentile character of Luke's Gospel. As is often mentioned, there is something of an *apologetic* character to this Gospel; Luke wants to show that the story of Jesus is the answer to the Greco-Roman world as well as the Jewish one. Hence the Hellenistic style—unique among the Gospels—of the prologue and Luke's particular telling of the story for the audience he has in view.

In a narrative the beginning and ending are important. Thus it appears necessary to decide whether Luke ends in Acts 28 or Luke 24. Green states, "The narrative unity of Luke-Acts has important implications for our reading of Luke's work. Most significantly, it requires that our understanding of the

---

Approaches of E. W. Nicholson and A. D. H. Mayes" (MA thesis, Potchefstroom University for Christian Higher Education, 1992), 252–54, on the development of a more nuanced assessment of probability. On the limits of some detailed approaches to Luke, see Green, *Gospel of Luke*, 399.

206. As Ong's work (e.g., *Orality and Literacy*, discussed above) reminds us, Luke, in his significantly oral context, would want tell the same story in his own way for his audience, not tell a different story.

207. D. P. Moessner, "'Listening Posts' along the Way: 'Synchronisms' as Metaleptic Prompts to the 'Continuity of the Narrative' in Polybius's *Histories* and Luke's Gospel-Acts; A Tribute to David E. Aune," in *The New Testament and Early Christian Literature in Greco-Roman Context: Studies in Honor of David E. Aune*, ed. J. Fotopoulos, NovTSup 122 (Leiden: Brill, 2006), 129–50, 131–32.

208. "Most excellent" was normally reserved for Roman political officials but may be an honorary title; either way, Theophilus is a person of significant status.

209. On this, see Henry Cadbury, Loveday Alexander.

need(s) and audience he addressed account *for all the evidence*, both the Gospel and Acts."[210] This is undoubtedly true, although canonically Luke has been separated off from Acts as one of four Gospels, and as noted in our chapter (8) on canon, the "fourfold Gospel" collection arose very early. In my view we need to read Luke both as a coherent whole and as part 1 of a two-part work. The endings of Luke *and* of Acts are significant for Luke. The action of Luke begins in the temple, and it ends there, with the disciples continually meeting there, blessing God. Indeed, Jerusalem is central to the Gospel. The prologue alerts us to the significance of the gospel for the Roman world; thus it is noteworthy that Acts ends with Paul proclaiming the kingdom of God in Rome and teaching freely about the Lord Jesus Christ.

Luke's Gospel begins with the prologue, but the action begins in 1:5. Green observes that "Luke's prologue (1:1–4) is external to the narrative per se"[211] and that the transition to the action is abrupt. However, as both Tom Wright and Green say, this abrupt transition from the world of Hellenistic history writing to the world of small-town Jewish folk is significant: "The intersection of these two worlds is of critical importance for Luke, who will show through his orderly account how the unfolding events in this world of ancient Galilee and Judea are of universal significance."[212] In Greek the style of language also changes from the balanced, complex prologue to a more plodding style filled with Semitisms. "Imaginatively, then, the reader begins in the biblical world of Temple and torah, and instinctively feels, 'this is part of *our* story.'"[213]

2. *Luke 1:5–2:52, God at Work: The Births of John and Jesus.* The geographical and historical indicators in 1:5 and 3:1 demarcate this section, as does the summarizing conclusion in 2:52. So too does the content, dealing as it does with the births of John and Jesus. This section contains numerous markers: chronological, geographical, geopolitical, topographical, all designed to provide dramatic narrative movement and a concrete representation of the events in time and space, as well as a sense of God decisively at work in the midst of the events.

The central human figures introduced in this section are John and Jesus. Unlike Mark and John, Luke has chosen to tell us at length about the events surrounding their births, believing rightly that these events provide major clues to the mission of Jesus. Most of the extensive material in this section is unique to Luke, and thus L. T. Johnson writes, "These chapters are, therefore, like Acts, of particular importance in showing the reader how Luke intended

---

210. Green, *Gospel of Luke*, 10, with original emphasis.
211. Ibid., 47.
212. Ibid.
213. L. T. Johnson, *Gospel of Luke*, 35.

his story to be understood."[214] Indeed, all the seeds of the forthcoming narrative development are planted in this section. As Ong says of oral narrative, we are thrown into the midst of the action straightaway. There are extensive parallels drawn between John and Jesus,[215] although more text is devoted to the birth of Jesus, and he is clearly highlighted as *the one*.[216] Both births are described as "gospel" ("good news," 1:19; 2:10),[217] thus linking John closely to Jesus from the outset.

In addition to the parallelism between John and Jesus, the motif of "promise—fulfillment—praise response" recurs in the cases of Zechariah, Mary, and Simeon so that their three "songs" connect this section integrally. The roles played by Zechariah, Mary, and Simeon serve to position the two births in the broader context of Israel's story. In the spirit and power of Elijah, John will prepare a people for the Lord (1:17). Gabriel announces to Mary that her son will be "the Son of the Most High," who will be given "the throne . . . of David" (2:32). The three songs all integrate the births unequivocally into Israel's story and indicate that God, who is the major actor in this section, is now acting to fulfill his purposes in history. This is more than confirmed by the Old Testament intertextuality in this section in relation to Genesis 11–21; Daniel 7–10; Genesis 27–43; and so forth—to the extent that Green describes this section as an echo chamber of Old Testament texts. Sanders observes, "What is remarkable about Luke's knowledge of his scripture was that apparently it came from his assiduous reading of it, or portions of it."[218]

Undoubtedly this would connect with the messianism of the day: it is intriguing to compare the three songs in this respect. Zechariah's song contains a strong emphasis on God delivering Israel from its enemies, whereas Simeon's song is more alert to the equivocal response Jesus would evoke in Israel.[219] J. M. Ford evocatively argues that Luke deliberately heightens messianic expectations in this section, those of the Zealots in particular, so that they can be contrasted with Jesus's approach in the rest of the Gospel. From the start the question of how Israel's story is truly to be fulfilled is raised, heightening expectation as to how the narrative will unfold.

This section thus anticipates the forthcoming development of the narrative in many ways. In this material unique to Luke, the reader, as is often

214. Ibid, 34.
215. Green, *Gospel of Luke*, 50.
216. In light of Acts 13:24–25; 18:25; 19:1–4, Green, *Gospel of Luke*, 51, finds this significant.
217. In both cases a verbal form is used.
218. J. A. Sanders, "Isaiah in Luke," *Int* 36 (1992): 144–55, esp. 146.
219. See D. Bosch, *Transforming Mission: Paradigm Shifts in Theology of Mission* (Maryknoll, NY: Orbis Books, 2003), 108–13.

the case in narrative (cf. Job), is made privy to much information that later characters will not be aware of. In this way the reader is invited, like Mary, to ponder and reflect on the epochal events as they unfold. In Luke 1:66 we read that all who heard about the circumstances of John's birth "pondered them" (καὶ ἔθεντο πάντες οἱ ἀκούσαντες ἐν τῇ καρδίᾳ αὐτῶν); in Luke 2:19 (cf. 2:51) we read that Mary "treasured all these words and pondered them in her heart" (ἡ δὲ Μαριὰμ πάντα συνετήρει τὰ ῥήματα ταῦτα συμβάλλουσα ἐν τῇ καρδίᾳ αὐτῆς). Such pondering is at the heart of lectio divina; at these points the Gospel invites its readers similarly to reflect on, chew over, and live into these epochal events.

3. *Luke 3:1–4:13, From Personal to Public: The Emergence of Jesus.* In this section we leap forward to the time when John and Jesus are adults and to the start of their public ministries. Sections 2, 3, and 4 of Luke are like three beginnings, all connected back into previous ones. In section 2 we have the births of John and Jesus, clearly flagged as the start of God's climactic act in history. Here in section 3 we have the transition of Jesus from personal life to public figure, another beginning. And section 4 reports the beginning of his public ministry.

Once again God is the main actor: in Luke 3:2, John's public ministry is initiated in true prophetic fashion by the word of God coming to him, while his identity as "son of Zechariah" connects this beginning back into section 2. This section clearly sets out the diverse identities of John and Jesus. John is the Isaianic messenger preparing the way of the Lord, while Jesus is the coming one, more powerful than John. Jesus's baptism is highly significant, with God himself speaking and affirming him as "my Son," even as Jesus identifies himself with sinners in the waters of baptism, thereby flagging, for the perceptive reader, that his Sonship will turn out radically different from what might have been expected. "Thus we are reminded that, though the narrative spotlight turns first on John then on Jesus, this is not their story. God is the primary actor around whose purpose the narrative develops."[220]

4. *Luke 4:14–9:50, The Start and Practice of Jesus's Public Ministry.* There is no straightforward narrative structure in this section, consisting as it does of complex, interactive cycles. Jesus's ministry consists of both proclamation and miracles, and responses to him vary. For those who receive him, there is significant instruction about discipleship. Narrative summaries are found in 4:14–15, 44; 5:15; 7:17; 8:1–3; these are necessitated by the episodic character of this section. As Ong notes, such an episodic style is typical of oral narrative.

220. Green, *Gospel of Luke*, 160.

As with beginnings in general, the start of Jesus's public ministry in 4:16–21 is pregnant with meaning in terms of the ongoing development of the story. It prefaces Jesus's entire ministry and is a condensed version of the gospel story as a whole; its programmatic function has been compared to the Sermon on the Mount in Matthew's Gospel. Clearly Jesus is claiming to be the Messiah, the Servant of Isaiah 61, who is anointed by the Spirit and sent to bring liberty. Intriguingly, Jesus halts his reading from Isaiah before "the day of vengeance of our God," and it was probably this that enraged his audience, who held to a messianism that would crush Israel's enemies.

Jesus's reading and halting where he did goes to the heart of what Israel's story is all about and how the gentiles fit in it. Jesus is radically different from what has been expected. As the Anointed One, he will announce a Jubilee for the Jews *and* their opponents! The liberty he brings is creation-wide and not in service of a narrow Jewish nationalism. As Nissen notices, by this means Jesus challenged the congregation's "ethics of election."[221] J. M. Ford sees Jesus's strategy as in deliberate opposition to the expectations evoked in the birth narratives.[222] Jesus's "Nazareth Manifesto" generated severe conflict (4:20–30), a theme that becomes stronger and stronger in Luke. Here we see the cause of opposition: what is the true nature of the climax of Israel's story? As Bosch declares, "The Nazareth pericope thus sets the stage for Jesus' entire ministry."[223]

5. *Luke 9:51–19:48, Jesus's Journey to Jerusalem.* Luke's Gospel is exceptional in the long travel narrative that dominates the middle of his book, clearly marked with notes along the way. The historicity of the journey is debated; Bailey, for example, argues, "Obviously there is no 'traveling' done at all and the title 'Travel Narrative' is a misnomer. . . . We prefer to call it the 'Jerusalem Document.'"[224] However, there is no reason why literary artifice and historicity ought to conflict at this point. Either way the journey is highly metaphorical: it is Jesus's unavoidable journey through which he must pass before being "taken up," and it is full of instruction for disciples also on "the way."

"The repetition of Jerusalem on the outside and at the center gives it a prominence that is unmistakeable."[225] The precise ending of the narrative is unclear since "for him to be taken up" in 9:51 is fulfilled only in 24:51. However,

---

221. J. Nissen, *Poverty and Mission: New Testament Perspectives*, IIMO Research Pamphlet 10 (Leiden: Inter-university Institute for Missiological and Ecumenical Research, 1984), 75. See also J. Jeremias, *Jesus' Promise to the Nations* (London: SCM, 1958), 41–46.

222. J. M. Ford, *My Enemy Is My Guest: Jesus and Violence in Luke* (Maryknoll, NY: Orbis Books, 1984), 36.

223. Bosch, *Transforming Mission*, 111.

224. Bailey, *Poet and Peasant*, 82.

225. Ibid., 83.

Jesus's triumphal entry into Jerusalem and his cleansing of the temple appear to mark the conclusion of his journey to Jerusalem. Luke unequivocally alerts the reader to the centrality of Jerusalem and that it was by no mistake that Jesus arrived there around the time of the Passover. The events that will follow are thus marked as no accident: they are central to the ministry of Jesus and the fulfillment of Israel's story.

Indeed, a central theme in this section is the opposition to Jesus and the stress of recognizing that the Son of Man must suffer and die (cf. 9:22, 44). For the reader, this section explains how Israel's rejection of Jesus came about: the Samaritans reject him because he is going to Jerusalem (9:51–55); some accuse him of being possessed (11:14–23); his critique of scribes and Pharisees heightened the opposition (11:37–54); in 12:49–53 he explains that he will cause deep division; in 13:31–35 he is told that Herod wants to kill him, but he insists that "it is impossible for a prophet to be killed outside of Jerusalem"; he enters Jerusalem triumphantly, but his cleansing of the temple calls forth dangerous opposition as the chief priests, scribes, and leaders look for a way to kill him.

Essentially, Jesus's teaching and practices are what evoke opposition. The story of Zacchaeus is instructive on this issue (19:1–10). His acceptance of Zacchaeus's hospitality evokes criticism, but Jesus insists that "the Son of Man came to seek out and save the lost" (19:10).

6. *Luke 20:1–21:38, Jesus Reclaims the Temple*. This section is demarcated by an inclusio about Jesus's *continual* teaching in the temple in 20:1 and 21:37–38. If the reader wonders why it was so important for Jesus to head to Jerusalem, then the answer is found here, in his "Father's house" (cf. 2:46–47, 49). "The reasoning of this narrative segment proceeds on the basis of this common understanding of the essential prominence of the temple as sacred space that establishes the order of the world and provides the axial point around which social life is aligned."[226] The chief priests and scribes rightly recognize that the question of *authority* is at the heart of the matter (20:2). The temple is the microcosm of the macrocosm of creation, and if salvation—the central theme of Luke—is to come, then it must come here, where God dwells amid his people.

It is in this context that we find the parable of the wicked tenants, which we discussed above in relation to Tom Wright's structuralist analysis of it, albeit the Markan version. It is not hard to see how this goes to the heart of the matter and how incendiary such teaching is in this scene, as also Jesus's prophecy of the destruction of the temple.

---

226. Green, *Gospel of Luke*, 697.

7. *Luke 22:1–23:56, Jesus Is Crucified.* In close connection to previous chapters, the theme of conflict comes to a climax in this section. The time is highly significant; the Feast of Unleavened Bread and the Passover enact the drama of Israel's identity, the very question that is evoking such opposition to Jesus and that is at the heart of his ministry. In section 6 (above) the people provided a protective barrier between Jesus and his opponents, but this buffer is porous; as the opposition increases, so do the holes in his buffer. The institution of the Lord's Supper at the time of the Passover is symbolically loaded,[227] as is Jesus's insistence that his crucifixion is not accidental but "as it has been determined" (22:22; cf. Acts 2:23). The Jewish opposition to Jesus as depicted by Luke, although not uniform (23:50–56), is tragic and not anti-Semitic. A "war of interpretation" is under way in which Jesus's identity is grasped by unlikely people but opposed by most of the leaders.

8. *Luke 24:1–53, Jesus Enthroned.* Luke 24 vividly tells the story of the resurrection, Jesus's appearances to his disciples, his commissioning them as witnesses—a major theme in Acts, and of his ascension. Gabriel told Mary that Jesus would occupy the throne of David; at the outset of the travel narrative, we learned that Jesus would be "taken up"; here in the climax of Luke's Gospel, these predictions are fulfilled in his enthronement as Lord over the universe. At the same time Luke 24 and Acts 1 provide the transition from the story of Jesus to that of the witnesses.

A powerful story indeed! Green sums up the theme of Luke's narrative as follows:

> Throughout, the Lukan narrative focuses attention on a pervasive, coordinating theme: salvation. Salvation is neither ethereal nor merely future, but embraces life in the present, restoring the integrity of human life, revitalizing human communities, setting the cosmos in order, and commissioning the community of God's people to put God's grace into practice among themselves and toward ever-widening circles of others. The Third Evangelist knows nothing of such dichotomies as those sometimes drawn between social and spiritual or individual and communal. Salvation embraces the totality of embodied life, including its social, economic, and political concerns. For Luke, the God of Israel is the Great Benefactor whose redemptive purpose is manifest in the career of Jesus, whose message is that this benefaction enables and inspires new ways for living in the world.[228]

---

227. Cf. our discussion in chap. 6 above, esp. in the footnotes.
228. Green, *Gospel of Luke*, 24–25.

12

Theology

> Moreover, it has been my purpose in this labor to prepare and instruct candidates in sacred theology for the reading of the divine Word, in order that they may be able both to have easy access to it and to advance in it without stumbling.
>
> John Calvin[1]

Introduction

A formative moment in my early studies in systematic theology was my encounter with the work of the Reformed theologian John Murray. Murray would inevitably begin his theological work with detailed exegesis of biblical texts before moving from there to doctrinal exposition. It is many years since I read Murray, but that rich sense of a deep, integral relationship between Scripture and doctrine lingers.

A second formative encounter in this respect was with Karl Barth's *Church Dogmatics*. An effect of Cornelius Van Til's critique of Barth in the evangelical circles in which I was trained was to disparage Barth *theologically* without reading him. Years later I discovered the extraordinary exegetical and theological riches in Barth's *Church Dogmatics*. Barth is a model of what has become so

---

1. J. Calvin, "John Calvin to the Reader," in *Institutes of the Christian Religion*, ed. J. T. McNeill, trans. F. L. Battles. LCC 20–21 (Philadelphia: Westminster, 1960), 1:4.

rare nowadays; as his theological framework takes hold, he does more—much more!—exegesis. An extraordinary percentage of the *Dogmatics* consists of theological exegesis. Up to the present his exegesis remains largely ignored by biblical scholars: it is rare to find Barth referenced in works of biblical exegesis.

Calvin wrote his *Institutes* in order to deepen the reading of the Bible by Christians, as noted above.[2] Too often nowadays the move is the reverse: from Scripture to theology, with no return to Scripture; or we find a practice of theology largely divorced from Scripture. Neither is acceptable. Scripture is the primary norm and resource for theology, and we need a truly *biblical* theology. Thus we need theology that openly emerges from deep and wide-ranging exegesis, informed by the tradition and the best contemporary practice in biblical studies. At the same time biblical exegesis needs to be theologically informed so that theology deepens our exegesis. Whether we agree with Barth's theology and his exegesis or not, his is *the* major model for the Scripture-doctrine relationship,[3] and it is one that needs to be received and developed anew today.

What Is Doctrine/Theology, and Why Does It Matter for Biblical Interpretation?

Defining Doctrine

We begin with some prominent examples of the definition of doctrine. *Karl Barth* says of dogmatics that it

> is a science. . . . By science we understand an attempt at comprehension and exposition, at investigation and instruction, which is related to a definite object and sphere of activity. . . . The subject of this science is the Church. It is the place, the community, charged with the object and the activity with which dogmatics is concerned—namely, the proclamation of the Gospel. . . . In the science of dogmatics the Church draws up its reckoning in accordance with the state of its knowledge at different times.[4]

Kevin Vanhoozer defines doctrine as follows: "Doctrine has to do with what faith seeking understanding gets when its search is successful. To be precise:

---

2. For similar comments, see A. E. McGrath, *Studies in Doctrine* (Grand Rapids: Zondervan, 1997), 248–49; McGrath declares, "A systematic presentation of the main themes of Christian doctrine is an excellent guide to Scripture. It provides a sort of route map by which the various scriptural landmarks may be located and identified, and related to each other" (249).

3. Yet there are important areas in which I personally disagree with Karl Barth. Bonhoeffer is another example of a major theologian in whose work exegesis plays a formative role.

4. K. Barth, *Dogmatics in Outline* (London: SCM, 2001), 9–10.

Christian doctrine is the reward that faith finds at the end of its search for the meaning of the apostolic testimony to what God was doing in the event of Jesus Christ."[5]

Rowan Williams identifies three dimensions of theology: as celebration or doxology, as communication and meaning, and as criticism to discern true from false witness.[6] David Ford asserts that "theology deals with questions of meaning, truth, beauty, and practice."[7] *Dalferth* asserts of theology, "Its fundamental reflective task is thus twofold: it must explicate the orientational knowledge derived from revelation in a system of doctrines, and elucidate the whole of reality in the light of it."[8]

Tom Wright approaches the question of theology through the concept of worldview.[9] Theology focuses on certain aspects of the questions and answers a worldview provides; theologians need to go about this while fully conscious of the interrelationship between questions and stories, and praxis and symbol. Wright helpfully quotes Petersen's comment that "we can speak of a symbolic universe as a primary (pre-reflective) form of knowledge and theology as a secondary (reflective) form that is dependent on it."[10] For Wright, theology both tells stories about humans and the world *and also* explores questions in the light of this storytelling activity: "'theology' highlights what we might call the god-dimension of a worldview."[11] Wright's critical-realist model identifies various levels of "theology," and he rightly declares,

> The overall point here is that a good deal of what is called "Christian theology" consists of discussions and debates at the level of basic belief or consequent belief, not necessarily at the level of the Christian worldview itself. If theological study is to be fully aware of its own nature, however, it must include study of the whole range, from worldviews to every level of belief.[12]

N. T. Wright has evocatively described doctrines as portable narratives.[13] They enable us to "bundle up" the biblical narratives related to a theme such as

---

5. K. J. Vanhoozer, *The Drama of Doctrine: A Canonical-Linguistic Approach to Christian Theology* (Louisville: Westminster John Knox, 2005), 4, with original emphasis.
6. R. Williams, *On Christian Theology* (Oxford: Blackwell, 2000), xiii.
7. D. F. Ford, *Theology: A Very Short Introduction* (Oxford: Oxford University Press, 2000), 17.
8. I. U. Dalferth, *Theology and Philosophy* (Oxford: Blackwell, 1988), ix–x.
9. N. T. Wright, *NTPG* 121–44.
10. N. R. Petersen, *Rediscovering Paul: Philemon and the Sociology of Paul's Narrative World* (Philadelphia: Fortress, 1985), 30; cf. 57–60.
11. N. T. Wright, *NTPG* 130.
12. Ibid., 134.
13. N. T. Wright, "Reading Paul, Thinking Scripture," in *Scripture's Doctrine and Theology's Bible*, ed. M. Bockmuehl and A. J. Torrance (Grand Rapids: Baker Academic, 2008), 59–71.

the cross under the label of "atonement," for example, without having to continually refer to the entirety of the matter.

Alister McGrath asserts that doctrine serves four major purposes:[14]

1. to tell the truth about the way things are,
2. to respond to the self-revelation of God,
3. to address, interpret, and transform human experience,
4. to provide Christians with a sense of purpose and identity.

And so we could continue, but this at least gives us a taste of several influential definitions. What are we to make of these? A problem that emerges from a comparison of these definitions is that there is a tendency to define theology and doctrine so comprehensively that some definitions fail to get at the distinctive element of doctrine/theology. Philosophy is, for example, often defined etymologically as "the love of wisdom," but this fails to articulate the distinctive focus of philosophy and thus is an unhelpful definition. David Ford's, Vanhoozer's, and McGrath's definitions seem to me to be vulnerable to a similar danger. How can theology be distinctive in dealing with "questions of meaning, truth, beauty, and practice"? Would it not be true to say that every discipline deals with, or should deal with, such issues? Similarly, McGrath's four purposes of doctrine could be applied to every discipline. Psychology, for example, when conducted in the spirit of faith seeking understanding, should clearly fulfill purposes 1, 3, and 4. Regarding purpose 2, it has been rightly said that all of life is a response to God, so that psychology is as much a response to God's self-revelation, albeit his general revelation, as is theology. And is it true that only "doctrine has to do with what faith seeking understanding gets when its search is successful"? When the Christian sociologist or biologist embarks on research in the spirit of *faith seeking understanding*, is what they get "doctrine"? Surely not, unless we define doctrine so widely that it ceases to be meaningful.

Vanhoozer's qualification of this sentence by relating theology to the apostolic testimony seems to me closer to the mark. God's revelation extends way beyond Scripture to the whole creation (cf. Ps. 19), but Scripture is his written revelation of his way with Israel and in Jesus and the church. Historically, the focus of theologians has rightly been God's revelation *in Scripture*, whereas other disciplines focus on his revelation in the many-splendored diversity of creation. Thus a distinctive of doctrine and theology is its focus on God's revelation *in Scripture*. As Pannenberg states, "The evangelical understanding

---

14. McGrath, *Studies in Doctrine*, 237.

of dogma and dogmatics is characterized by its *intimate relationship to Scripture*. The confrontation of church dogmas with revelation has the concrete form of their being *bound to Scripture*."[15]

Karl Barth, Abraham Kuyper, Bavinck,[16] and many others are right, in my opinion, to see theology as a *science* since it is about systematic, logically qualified knowledge. McGrath takes the relationship of Scripture to doctrine and compares it to the relationship of wild flowers and plants in nature, which are collected and arranged in species and studied in botanical gardens. He asserts, "Doctrine represents the human attempt to order the ideas of Scripture, arranging them in a logical manner in order that their mutual relation can be better understood."[17] While "ideas" needs careful definition, I think McGrath is correct about the systematic, logical nature of doctrine/theology. However, it is important to distinguish different levels of "theology," ranging from

- biblical creeds such as the Shema,
- to the rules of faith we find among the church fathers,
- creeds such as the Apostles' Creed,
- the more developed Nicene and Athanasian Creeds,
- denominational confessions,
- and systematic theology or dogmatics per se.

Scientific analysis inevitably involves *abstraction* since the focus of analysis is abstracted from its context and studied by itself. Abstraction is most in play at the level of systematic theology and far less involved in the biblical creeds and the rules of faith. The stronger the degree of abstraction, the more strongly the philosophical element enters into play, so that the relationship between theology and philosophy becomes increasingly important. Doctrine attempts to state systematically that which is universally true; as Pannenberg explains, "The inevitability of using philosophical terminology in dogmatics is another implication of the universality of dogmatic statements."[18]

---

15. W. Pannenberg, "What Is a Dogmatic Statement?," in *Basic Questions in Theology: Collected Essays* (reprint, Minneapolis: Fortress, 2008), 1:182–211, esp. 184, with added emphasis.

16. H. Bavinck, *Reformed Dogmatics: Prolegomena*, ed. J. Bolt., trans. J. Vriend, 4 vols. (Grand Rapids: Baker Academic, 2003–8), 25–58.

17. McGrath, *Studies in Doctrine*, 249.

18. Pannenberg, "What Is a Dogmatic Statement?"; he states, "While philosophy asks about the whole of reality on the basis of everyday experience of reality, dogmatics asks this question only in such a way that it proceeds from the Christ-event and pursues its universal significance for reality. Thus, dogmatics understands the unity of reality only in the light of the Christ-event" (201).

In the context of systematic theology or dogmatics, doctrine involves *analysis* in the attempt to set out systematically (in logical order) the central elements of a particular doctrine in their right relationship for today, be it the doctrine of God, of humankind, sin, Jesus, the Spirit, or the church. Such analysis always abstracts the particular doctrine from its contexts in the biblical narrative; hence, an important test of the formulation of a doctrine will be whether it deepens reading of the Scriptures in the light of its doctrinal formulation. I find Tom Wright's analysis illuminating, yet it seems to me important to distinguish worldview and storytelling *from* doctrinal analysis. Doctrinal analysis has a systematic or propositional dimension that is lacking in worldview and storytelling. Beliefs surely are embedded in and enacted by the biblical narrative,[19] but doctrines are more than "portable narratives." Doctrines abstract the cognitive, *belief* element from the biblical story and seek to systematize that knowledge.

"Propositional" and "logical" need not imply dry and boring! There is a tendency to try to renew doctrine by giving it a dramatic, narrative flavor, but it is surely Scripture, rather than doctrine, that has these characteristics, which need to be recovered. Doctrine should attend to the network of relations amid doctrines even as it abstracts from the biblical grand story, and *in this sense* it would share in the narrative character of Scripture. Furthermore, propositional language certainly does not exclude *metaphor*, as philosophy of science has reminded us in recent years. Indeed, an element that makes Barth's and Bonhoeffer's theologies so attractive is their evocative use of metaphor. Nevertheless it is a mistake to translate the drama of Scripture into the drama of doctrine without carefully attending to the important differences in the two uses of "drama" in these phrases.[20]

The Importance of Doctrine

The relationship between Scripture and doctrine/theology is akin, in my view, to the relationship between *lived experience and theory*. Lived experience is primary, and theory always develops from lived experience. Indeed, the test of theory is whether it deepens lived experience. As we live in modernity, there can be no doubting the power of theory: again and again it has demonstrated

---

19. For an excellent example, see R. Sokolowski, *The God of Faith and Reason: Foundations of Christian Theology* (Washington, DC: Catholic University of America Press, 1995), 122–23; he notes the fundamental importance of the distinction between God and the world, and not least for biblical interpretation, but then asks, Does Scripture provide us with this distinction? He argues that it is enacted in the biblical narratives and has to be lived before it can be stated.

20. On this issue, see my comments in chap. 3 above.

its power to alter our lives. Alas, this has not always been for the good; theory has often taken on a life of its own and become the royal road to truth, yet without being tested by its relationship to lived experience.[21] The danger of such an approach is built into the genius of theory. Theory *abstracts* a part of reality from its embeddedness in lived experience and focuses intensively and logically on this part of reality. However, unless there is a return to and testing by lived experience, such theory easily leads to reductionism and a distortion of life.

Similarly with doctrine, or systematic theology: in terms of God's revelation of himself, Scripture is primary, with its character of a sprawling, capacious narrative that came into existence over hundreds of years, as the deposit of God's way with Israel, culminating in the Christ event. Doctrine abstracts landmarks of belief from the story of Scripture and seeks to articulate the nature of that belief systematically for today.

Clearly the articulation of the central beliefs of Scripture will be of great value in reading it aright. If doctrine can be compared to the belief-skeleton of Scripture, then having a sense of that belief-structure will assist the exegete, just as a thorough knowledge of the skeletal system of the body will assist the health practitioner. Like the human body, Scripture is complex, diverse, and constituted by many parts. Assuming the unity of the Bible, an assumption fundamental to both biblical interpretation and dogmatics, healthy doctrine will richly enhance the work of the exegete both in terms of what to look for in Scripture and in terms of sensitivity to the *otherness* of Scripture where it calls doctrinal formulations into question. Take the doctrine of creation, for example, which we will examine in more detail below. A healthy *doctrine of creation* would never have remained silent when history was privileged over nature in so much twentieth-century Old Testament interpretation, and when, as in von Rad's work, creation was made subsidiary to redemption. A well-articulated doctrine of creation would have compelled Christian exegetes to revisit this issue and to find alternative, more biblical articulations of Old Testament theology without succumbing to the misdirected creation-order theology that was so destructive in Nazi Germany and in apartheid South Africa.[22] As we will see below, a biblical view of creation order is *the* basis for cultural critique, and its use to reinforce the worst ideologies is a tragic perversion of Scripture.

---

21. On this theme, see C. G. Bartholomew, *Where Mortals Dwell: A Christian View of Place for Today* (Grand Rapids: Baker Academic, 2011).

22. Cf. G. J. Spykman, *Reformational Theology: A New Paradigm for Doing Dogmatics* (Grand Rapids: Eerdmans, 1992), 176–77. See R. P. Knierim, *The Task of Old Testament Theology: Substance, Method, and Cases* (Grand Rapids: Eerdmans, 1995), a valuable work as a good example of a corrective.

Scripture contains a great deal of doctrinal material, not least in Paul's explication of the gospel in Romans. However, it is neither a systematic theology nor a doctrinal textbook. Instead, God has given us narrative, song, poetry, law, prophecy, Gospels, epistles, and so forth, in which beliefs are embedded. Early on the church rightly and naturally recognized the need to provide coherent answers to questions about *what* Christians believe; hence, doctrine came to be essential in the *communication of the faith* both within the church and also outside the church in *apologetics* as Christians gave a reason for the hope within them. Central to trinitarian monotheism is the belief that truth is one and unified; thus coherent, logical articulations of the unity of truth in Christ flow naturally from the Scriptures. Doctrinal formulation also became essential as the church faced threats from groups such as Marcion, the gnostics, and Arians. Historically, the formulation of doctrine thus served multiple purposes; it is not something achieved once and for all, but instead it is a communal task for each new generation as it faces new challenges. Christians have done this since the inception of the church, and so such work will always be done in the context of *the tradition* of the church,[23] not least because doctrine *develops*. The development of doctrine is a matter of controversy between Roman Catholics and Protestants, but there can be no doubt that doctrine is developed over time.[24] The doctrine of the Trinity is *implicit* on virtually every page of the New Testament, but it only became *explicit* as the early church wrestled with the identity of Jesus; once the doctrine of the Trinity became explicit, its theological and biblical fertility became apparent, as we see, for example, in Colin Gunton's trinitarian theology of creation.[25]

The recent histories of both theology and biblical studies have made us far more aware of the complexities involved in formulating doctrine; as Thiselton rightly recognizes, we need a *hermeneutics of doctrine*.[26] As with Christian scholarship, which we will explore in the next chapter, there is *an ecology* of doctrine, and nowadays it is simply unacceptable to remain ignorant of the complexity of elements involved in formulating doctrine, elements such as

---

23. See A. C. Thiselton's constructive emphasis on reception history in his *The Hermeneutics of Doctrine* (Grand Rapids: Eerdmans, 2007). Historical theology is an indispensable element in the ecology of doctrine.

24. See John Henry Newman's influential (1845) book *An Essay on the Development of Christian Doctrine*, 6th ed. (Notre Dame, IN: University of Notre Dame Press, 1989); A. E. McGrath, *The Genesis of Doctrine: A Study in the Foundations of Doctrinal Criticism* (Cambridge, MA: Blackwell, 1990); etc.

25. See C. E. Gunton, *The Triune Creator: A Historical and Systematic Study*, Edinburgh Studies in Constructive Theology (Grand Rapids: Eerdmans, 1998).

26. See Thiselton, *Hermeneutics of Doctrine*.

exegesis, tradition, concept formation, philosophy, and so forth. Take the *doctrine of faith*, for example. Once we use faith as a unified *concept*, we are using it in a way different from the multiple occurrences of "faith" in the two Testaments. We need to be conscious of this difference in use. A comparable example would be *covenantal theology*. In both Testaments, "covenant," like "faith," is used with a variety of nuances and in multiple contexts by different authors. Thus proof-texting is dangerous without an awareness of the diverse uses of these words in diverse contexts, as well as the process of abstraction involved once we use "covenant" or "faith" as a dogmatic concept. And it should be impossible to develop a doctrine of faith or covenant without an awareness of the variety of ways in which the church has articulated these doctrines down through the ages.

Doctrine and Biblical Theology

From the foregoing, it is clear that the task of doctrinal formulation is challenging and complex. Doctrine aims at universal truth "from the standpoint of the distinctiveness of the history of Jesus as the eschatological event,"[27] which is no easy task! Doctrine and systematic theology will, therefore, have a vested interest in grasping Scripture as God's Word in its totality. *Tota Scriptura* will be of enormous importance in the ecology of doctrine; the *discrimen*, the distinct and decisive criterion by which theologians seek to take hold of Scripture in this way, has been addressed by David Kelsey in his important *The Uses of Scripture in Recent Theology*. Kelsey argues that the *discrimen* will have to come from outside Scripture, but in my view this runs the danger of making Scripture subject to an alien framework.

In this way biblical theology as the technical discipline that seeks to articulate the inner unity of Scripture according to its own categories comes into its own. Biblical theology allows the inner unity of Scripture to emerge from within, in biblical rather than systematic categories. An effect of historical criticism and postmodernism has been to keep biblical scholars focused on small parts of the canon; few, very few, have had the nerve to work away on comprehensive biblical theologies. Ironically, this is one of the great needs of our day, not least if we wish to renew the Scripture-doctrine relationship.

The neglect of biblical theology is evident in biblical studies *and* in theology.[28] A notable exception to this is Gordon Spykman in his rich *Reformational*

---

27. Pannenberg, "What Is a Dogmatic Statement?," 200.
28. Neither Vanhoozer, *Drama of Doctrine*, nor Thiselton, *Hermeneutics of Doctrine*, has a single reference to biblical theology in the indexes of their books.

Theology: A New Paradigm for Doing Dogmatics. Spykman respects the distinct identities of biblical theology and systematics yet comments:

> At the same time, there is an underlying unity between work in biblical and systematic theology. Differentiation of tasks may not be allowed to negate the basic religious unity which binds them together. They stand in coexisting and proexisting relationships to each other within the larger arena of theological scholarship. This project in dogmatics aims to draw heavily on this relationship of mutual interdependence.[29]

Spykman lists the insights of recent biblical studies that he finds particularly helpful[30] and states:

> In all these valuable insights, . . . we can discern a golden thread weaving its way through the total fabric of biblical revelation, lending it a coherent perspective on life. Perhaps for Reformed dogmatics it can be captured most succinctly in the pervasive biblical teaching on covenant and kingdom. Covenant and kingdom are like two sides of a single coin. Accordingly, we may say that in creation God covenanted his kingdom into existence. After the fall, God renewed the covenant with a view toward the coming of his kingdom. The ultimate goal is the restoration of all creation in the renewed earth. Thus, the original covenant stands forever as the abiding foundation and norm for life in God's world. . . . In this sense covenant and kingdom are two ways of viewing the one all-embracing reality of God's way with his world. Covenant is kingdom looking back to its original and abiding charter given with the creation. Kingdom is covenant looking forward programmatically toward its promised goal of perfect renewal.[31]

The result is a rich and important one-volume systematics structured according to: the good creation, sin and evil, the way of salvation, and the consummation. What sort of biblical work, we should ask, would best fund this sort of project? Detailed work on small parts of the canon remain indispensable, but it is the larger picture of biblical-theological work that is invaluable, work such as Clines's *The Theme of the Pentateuch*, Dumbrell's *Covenant and Creation*,[32] John Stek's superb work on creation in his "What

---

29. Spykman, *Reformational Theology*, 9–10.
30. Ibid., 10–11.
31. Ibid., 11–12.
32. W. J. Dumbrell has written several important works on biblical theology, such as *The Faith of Israel: A Theological Survey of the Old Testament* (Grand Rapids: Baker Academic, 2002) and *The End of the Beginning: Revelation 21–22 and the Old Testament* (Eugene, OR: Wipf & Stock, 2001).

Says the Scripture?,"[33] Childs's *BTONT*, Scobie's *The Ways of Our God*, Tom Wright's *Jesus and the Victory of God*, Herman Ridderbos's *Paul*, Chris Wright's works on biblical ethics, Richard Bauckham's many works, Leon Kass's *The Beginning of Wisdom*, and so forth.

The relationship between such theology and biblical interpretation is wonderfully reciprocal. The more systematic theology is informed by biblical theology, the richer and more biblical it will become, and the more it will inform biblical interpretation in fresh and fertile ways.

Within theological interpretation it is inevitable that there will be a dialogical relationship between the theological framework and interpretation. However, it should be recognized that not all theological frameworks are equal. Luther's law-gospel and two-kingdoms approach seems to me far less helpful than Bonhoeffer's brand of Lutheranism, which resolutely resists the two-spheres approach and thus emerges with healthier doctrines of creation, society, and eschatology.[34] O'Donovan's framework of resurrection as the reaffirmation of creation proves wonderfully fertile in his *Resurrection and Moral Order*. Indeed, O'Donovan is a rare example of a theologian, like Karl Barth, who does more exegesis as his theological framework takes hold.[35]

Scripture, Kerygma, and Doctrine

Theological interpretation remains a fluid enterprise. From some proponents, one gathers the impression that it involves reading the Bible for theology or doctrine. In my opinion this is a mistake or at least reductionistic. What has often been lacking in commentaries and exegesis is not so much reading the Bible for doctrine but making the telos (ultimate end/purpose) listening for God's address.[36] In the light of the hermeneutic of listening outlined in chapter 2 (above), exegetical and commentary work, however rigorous, is incomplete if it is not directed toward listening for God's Word. Biblical interpretation should move *from* listening and *toward* listening. Indeed, the aim of hard

---

33. In H. J. Van Til et al., *Portraits of Creation: Biblical and Scientific Perspectives on the World's Formation* (Grand Rapids: Eerdmans, 1990), 203–65. On the relationship between John Henry Stek's work and William Dumbrell's work, see C. G. Bartholomew, "Covenant and Creation: Covenant Overload or Covenantal Deconstruction?," *Calvin Theological Journal* 30, no. 1 (April 1995): 11–33.

34. See D. Bonhoeffer, *Ethics* (New York: Macmillan, 1955).

35. See also O. O'Donovan, *The Desire of the Nations: Rediscovering the Roots of Political Theology* (Cambridge: Cambridge University Press, 1996).

36. For an attempt to redirect OT studies in this direction, see C. G. Bartholomew and D. J. H. Beldman, eds., *Hearing the Old Testament: Listening for God's Address* (Grand Rapids: Eerdmans, 2012).

exegetical work is to deepen the process of listening and to enable us to hear more clearly and with greater power the address of God.

Under the influence of historical criticism, the focus—across the spectrum—tended to be on the world *behind the text*, or what we might call the referential dimension of the text. As noticed in our chapter on history, this is certainly legitimate but only insofar as it is in service of the world opened up *in front of the text*, which the reader is invited to indwell.

Recent years have seen a welcome emphasis on *rhetorical readings* of biblical texts, which at their best go a long way toward filling out the telos of the hermeneutic in this direction. The earliest rhetorical handbook that we know of is The Instruction of Ptahhotep, composed in Egypt sometime before 2000 BC.[37] Among the ancient Greeks, Aristotle (384–322 BC) produced the first systematic study of the subject in his work *Rhetoric*. Aristotle defines rhetoric as "an ability, in each [particular] case, to see the available means of persuasion."[38] For Aristotle, rhetoric is partly a method and partly a practical art derived from ethics and politics. For Socrates and Plato,[39] rhetoric was controversial because of its misuse by the Sophists. The main difference between Aristotle and Isocrates (436–338 BC), the most influential teacher of rhetoric in Aristotle's day, was the emphasis Aristotle put on truth, knowledge of a subject, and logical argument. It has become commonplace in the history of rhetoric to identify two traditions: the Isocratean, which emphasizes the literary aspect of rhetoric, and the Aristotelian, which emphasizes the logical aspect. Aristotle identifies three modes of persuasion: *ēthos*, the projection of the speaker's character as trustworthy; *pathos*, the consideration of the emotions of the audience; and *logos*, inductive or deductive argument.[40]

There is a long history of rhetoric since Aristotle. Rhetoric flourished during the Middle Ages and Renaissance but was made subordinate to science and philosophy in the Enlightenment and post-Enlightenment period. The twentieth century witnessed a revival of interest in rhetoric through the work of such luminaries as I. A. Richards (1893–1979), Ernesto Grassi (1902–91), the parents of the new rhetoric[41] Chaïm Perelman (1912–84) and Lucie Olbrechts-Tyteca (1899–1987), Richard Weaver, Stephen Toulmin, Kenneth Burke, Jürgen

---

37. G. A. Kennedy, introduction to *On Rhetoric: A Theory of Civic Discourse*, by Aristotle, trans. G. A. Kennedy, 2nd ed. (Oxford: Oxford University Press, 2007), 1–25, esp. 7, states that some of what we find in this Egyptian text (The Instruction of Ptahhotep) resembles OT precepts such as those in Ps. 16 (yet the verses Kennedy quotes are not from Ps. 16).

38. Aristotle, *Rhetoric* 1.2.1; cf. 1.1.14.

39. See Plato, *Phaedrus*, esp. 277b5–c6.

40. Aristotle, *On Rhetoric* 1356a.

41. The new rhetoric emphasizes rationality, logic, and argumentation more than what was perceived as a reductionistic emphasis on style.

Habermas,[42] and others. The works of these theorists contain rich pickings for biblical studies; suffice it for our purposes to see how rhetorical criticism emphasizes persuasion and aims "to explore the function of a text within a communicative act and the means by which this function is fulfilled."[43]

The focus of rhetorical criticism on the communicative trajectory of the text as a whole is fertile for biblical interpretation. It reminds us, for example, that narrative historical texts were not written for the players in the events described but for a later generation/s. Especially in Old Testament texts, it is often hard to be sure of the audience, but one can be sure that books like 1 and 2 Kings, for example, were not written for those living during the reigns of the monarchs described. The rhetorical trajectory is aimed at a later generation, be that exilic or postexilic, and it is *this* rhetorical trajectory that needs to be the focus of attention if we are to discern the message or kerygma of the text.

The communicative act of a narrative, prophetic, wisdom, or Gospel text is rich and multidimensional; hence it is helpful to connect the rhetorical trajectory with Paul Ricoeur's notion of *the world opened up in front of the text*. This is not to deny the text's initial rhetorical horizon but to see contemporary readers connecting with that initial horizon and the *Wirkungsgeschichte* (reception history/theory) of the text.

For the purposes of this chapter, what is crucial is that the world/s opened up in front of the biblical text/s is always more than "mere" belief or doctrine. Belief is an important element of this world/s and may be more to the fore in some texts than others, but the persuasive world that biblical texts seek to open up in front of their readers is inevitably richer than abstract doctrine. Beliefs can and should be abstracted from the worlds opened up, but this should not be *the* focus of theological interpretation. Priority must be given to the communicative act of the biblical texts individually and as a whole. Kerygma, not doctrine, should be the primary focus.

Doctrine and Philosophy

In chapter 9 we discussed the relationship between philosophy and biblical interpretation. Underlying the relationship between philosophy and biblical interpretation *and also* the relationship between theology and philosophy is

---

42. J. Rogerson, *A Theology of the Old Testament: Cultural Memory, Communication, and Being Human* (Minneapolis: Fortress, 2010), has sought to utilize Jürgen Habermas's work in OT studies.

43. T. Renz, *The Rhetorical Function of the Book of Ezekiel* (Leiden: Brill, 1999), 1.

the deeper question of the relationship between faith and reason. That this is the central issue in relation to theology and philosophy is recognized by Dalferth in his *Theology and Philosophy*, probably the most rigorous discussion of this issue. At the heart of his book is part 2, in which he develops a sevenfold typology of the faith-reason relationship:

a. the two-books model (Augustine)
b. the nature-grace model (Thomas Aquinas)
c. the law-gospel model (Luther)
d. the reason-revelation model (Enlightenment)
e. the difference-in-unity model (Schleiermacher)
f. the unity-in-difference model (K. Barth)

In a book on biblical hermeneutics, we cannot work through these models in detail: hence the reader is referred to Dalferth's work. One may even wonder why we should deal with this issue in relation to biblical studies. The reason is that theology invariably affects biblical interpretation: we have argued that it should! So if philosophy skews one's theology, then it *will* impact exegesis. Indeed, a theme of this book is that far too often profound philosophical shaping of biblical interpretation has gone undetected because of the mistaken belief that "pure" biblical criticism is untainted by philosophy.

Dalferth argues that none of the above models provides a final solution to the problem that in fact "allows of no definitive solution."[44] "All we can (and must) do, therefore, is to secure harmony between the perspectives of Faith and Reason by designing rational means of translating between them."[45] The problem with this approach is that it affirms the autonomy of philosophy, and thereby it ends up conceding the epistemic grounds in all disciplines except, perhaps, theology. Buckley alerts us to the danger of such a concession in his *At the Origins of Modern Atheism*. A bifurcation between theology and philosophy in Dalferth's way means that philosophy can and will work in any tradition apart from the Christian one. The best one can do, then, is to bend philosophy toward theology while aware that it is rooted in a perspective on the world different from Christian theology's perspective.

In my view the two-books approach is worth revisiting.[46] Dalferth rightly observes that in Augustine's thought the two are not understood as independent in a nature-grace type way. Rather, Scripture is the key to the book of nature and is granted epistemic priority. "For the Christian this fundamental

---

44. Dalferth, *Theology and Philosophy*, ix.
45. Ibid. Dalferth's work is detailed, nuanced, and well worth reading on this topic.
46. For helpful comments, see Spykman, *Reformational Theology*, 170–72.

frame of frames is the *creation*: he does not know of the world apart from knowing it as creation."⁴⁷

Dalferth argues that this model broke down when the focus shifted from the common authorship of the two books to their different languages so that, ironically, the two-books model achieved the opposite of what it set out to do. He refers to Galileo's view that the book of nature is written in mathematics, and hence Scripture is obviously of little help in deciphering it. However, there is more going on here than the two-books model becoming unraveled. Galileo's reductionist approach to nature is part of the emerging Enlightenment tradition, with its scientism, facilitated far more by the nature-grace model than the Augustinian tradition.

Indeed, in recent decades the Augustinian tradition in philosophy has experienced a major revival, particularly in the Reformed epistemology of Nicholas Wolterstorff and Alvin Plantinga.⁴⁸ Wolterstorff's position in *Reason within the Bounds of Religion* is a nuanced, robust defense of what Dalferth calls Augustine's two-books approach. As Wolterstorff declares, "The Christian scholar ought to allow the belief-content of his authentic Christian commitment to function as control within his devising and weighing of theories."⁴⁹ Wolterstorff, Alvin Plantinga, and a host of others have been exemplary in showing what this might mean for philosophy.

Theology therefore needs to draw on the current renaissance of Christian philosophy. Doctrine inevitably brings philosophy with it as it seeks to define itself systematically. It has always been so. Early trinitarian doctrine drew on Greek concepts of substance and essence; anthropology has inevitably drawn on philosophical understanding of the human person.⁵⁰ Christian philosophy can help theology in ensuring that the conceptual framework is consistent with Scripture.

The perceptive reader will have picked up a possible contradiction above. Theology needs Christian philosophy, but is it not theology that helps define the belief-content of authentic Christian commitment? In the following chapter we will explore the role of Scripture in the ecology of Christian scholarship,

---

47. Dalferth, *Theology and Philosophy*, 68.
48. For an introduction and references, see C. G. Bartholomew and M. W. Goheen, *Christian Philosophy: A Systematic and Narrative Introduction* (Grand Rapids: Baker Academic, 2013). For Alvin Plantinga's locating himself in the Augustinian tradition, see his "Augustinian Christian Philosophy," in *The Augustinian Tradition*, ed. G. B. Matthews (Berkeley: University of California Press, 1998), 1–26.
49. N. Wolterstorff, *Reason within the Bounds of Religion*, 2nd ed. (Grand Rapids: Eerdmans, 1999), 76.
50. See J. W. Cooper, *Body, Soul, and Life Everlasting: Biblical Anthropology and the Monism-Dualism Debate* (Grand Rapids: Eerdmans, 1989).

but here, in brief, the answer is Yes! Here there is a circular, what we will call symbiotic, relationship that is unavoidable. Scripture is authoritative for all of life, and insofar as a doctrine adequately articulates the witness of Scripture, it aims at universal truth from the perspective of God's written revelation. Take anthropology, for example. Scripture nowhere provides a detailed, logical anthropology, but it does *orient* us authoritatively toward what it means to be human; hence Christians, including Christian scholars, must take seriously its witness in this area. A certain view of what it means to be human will indeed be part of the belief-content of authentic Christian commitment. At the same time, the more the theologian tries to articulate a Scriptural anthropology for today, the more philosophy will play a part. The two need to work in close relation with each other.

The Doctrine of Creation

The biblical drama begins with creation and ends with the new creation. Here in the final section of this chapter, we will explore some of the multiple ways in which doctrine and biblical interpretation can and should inform each other through an examination of the doctrine of creation.

1. *The eclipse of creation.* In much twentieth-century theology and biblical studies, we witnessed an eclipse of the doctrine of creation. Evangelical theology regularly placed, and still places, so much emphasis on the second article of the Apostles' Creed that the first article became marginalized, and the second and third articles were truncated as a result. "This is a faulty and shortsighted approach. For the full biblical import of our sinful predicament, of the call to conversion and sanctification, and of our future hope comes to its own only against the backdrop of a solidly based commitment to the work of God in creation."[51]

Similarly, Zahrnt evaluates Karl Barth's mature theology:

> The whole creation—nature, the world, man and history—is now forced into the christological pattern and so deprived of its own meaning and status. Everything takes place from Christ and for Christ. . . . No one will object to the way Barth draws together the beginning and the end of the whole historical process in Jesus Christ. But the question is whether in Barth it is still a matter of an historical *process*: does he present anything in history as still *happening*?[52]

---

51. Spykman, *Reformational Theology*, 176.
52. H. Zahrnt, *The Question of God: Protestant Theology in the Twentieth Century* (London: Collins, 1969), 113.

Ironically, an eclipse of creation is also present in much liberation theology. Gutiérrez, for example, asserts in relation to the exodus that "the God of Exodus is the God of history and of political liberation more than he is the God of nature";[53] thereby Gutiérrez sets up a false dichotomy between history and "nature." In theology and biblical studies, the perversion of creation order by Germans to support the Third Reich and by many South African Christians to support apartheid led to a reaction among theologians and biblical scholars,[54] which downplayed the doctrine of creation, as though it were somehow inherently vulnerable to such abuse.

However, this is a far more wide-ranging problem than specific theologies; it extends to modernity and the church's response to it. Colin Gunton says of his *The One, the Three and the Many*, an acute analysis of the culture of modernity, that "what began as a study of culture became both that and a study of the doctrine of creation.... The created world provides the framework within which human activity takes place."[55] Modernity privatized religion and secularized the public dimensions of culture so that for much of modernity the church has been caught on its back foot in reaction to the overwhelming juggernaut of scientific modernity. An understandable but fatal temptation has been to go along with the privatization of religion by keeping the focus on the second- and third-article elements of faith while downplaying the first-article confession of belief in God as creator. I say "fatal" because this not only distorts belief in Jesus and the Spirit but also removes from the church an essential dimension in its faith for responding comprehensively to modernity, both critically and affirmatively.

At the outset of the twenty-first century, modernity is clearly in crisis as it lurches from one disaster to another. Within the West the name of that crisis has often been postmodernism, in many ways an acute critic of modernity but dismally lacking in constructive grounds for moving forward. Several scholars have recognized similarities between postmodernism and gnosticism; one way in which the parallel is clear is in the lack of a robust theology of creation. As we move beyond postmodernism in the West and confront the challenges of globalization, few things are more important

---

53. G. Gutiérrez, *A Theology of Liberation: History, Politics, and Salvation* (Maryknoll, NY: Orbis Books, 1973), 157.

54. See esp. G. von Rad, "The Theological Problem of the Old Testament Doctrine of Creation," in *The Problem of the Hexateuch and Other Essays* (New York: McGraw-Hill, 1966), 131–43. Both A. LaCocque and P. Ricoeur discuss von Rad's view in their *Thinking Biblically: Exegetical and Hermeneutical Studies*, trans. D. Pellauer (Chicago: University of Chicago Press, 1998), 3–67.

55. C. E. Gunton, *The One, the Three, and the Many: God, Creation, and the Culture of Modernity* (Cambridge: Cambridge University Press, 1993), xiii.

than the recovery of a doctrine of creation. Its eclipse cannot be allowed to continue.

2. *The doctrine of creation.* The Christian doctrine of creation has a long history. Irenaeus and Tertullian were the first to articulate a doctrine of creation in response to the gnostic and Marcionite disparagement of creation, affirming the one God as creator and the creation as good. In his engagement with neoplatonism, Augustine repeatedly returned to Genesis in his struggle to take account of creation.[56] Augustine insists on *creatio ex nihilo*. Everything outside God is produced by him. Ex nihilo embraces two phases: the creation of formless matter and the formation of that matter. In contrast to Thomas Aquinas, Augustine explains the production of creatures on the basis of their *participation* in the divine ideas. Aquinas, however, attributes creation to God's efficient causality. God's creation is, for Augustine, a manifestation of his overflowing goodness. God is transcendent, separate from his creation, perfectly free before creation, and not dependent on his creation afterward. Time is part of creation, but God inhabits eternity.

The effect of Platonism and, in a different way, Aristotelianism, on theology was to subvert a biblical doctrine of creation. The gravitational pull of Platonism is always upward, away from the material creation. The effect of Aristotelianism, especially the atheist sort that gathered momentum in the Renaissance, was to insist on reason as adequate to understand nature, thereby reducing the realm of grace and revelation. A major contribution of the Reformers was their recovery of a robust doctrine of creation, whereby all of earthly life could be seen as part of the theater of God's glory.[57] In his *Sources of the Self*, Charles Taylor evocatively titles the chapter in which he deals with this recovery of the ordinary: "God Loveth Adverbs."

The secularism of the Enlightenment put theology on the defensive, with many seeking mistakenly to correlate doctrine with Enlightenment belief.[58] Fertile doctrines of creation can nevertheless be found in the thought of Søren Kierkegaard, Anglican sacramentalism, the Dutch Calvinism of Kuyper and Bavinck, and on into the works of Paul Tillich, Karl Barth, Emil Brunner, Pannenberg, Helmut Thielicke, Thomas Torrance, Hendrikus Berkhof, Moltmann, Gunton, McGrath, and others.[59] In developing a contemporary

---

56. Augustine of Hippo, *On Genesis*, trans. E. Hill (Hyde Park, NY: New City, 2002); also C. J. O'Toole, *The Philosophy of Creation in the Writings of St. Augustine* (Washington, DC: Catholic University of America Press, 1944).

57. Calvin's phrase, and one also much loved by Karl Barth.

58. See Bartholomew, *Where Mortals Dwell*, 219–21.

59. See ibid., 222–32. On Moltmann and Pannenberg, see Thiselton, *Hermeneutics of Doctrine*, 214–22.

doctrine of creation, Christians have a rich tradition of reflection on which to draw.

Colin Gunton argues that the doctrine of creation includes six components:[60]

1. the agency of the whole Trinity
2. *creatio ex nihilo*
3. creation as an expression of God's love
4. God's interactive relationship with the world and humankind
5. divine preservation
6. continuity with history and the work of redemption

The Whole Trinity and Creation

For biblical interpretation, creation is of prime importance. A theology may not begin with it, but the drama of Scripture does; as the first act in the drama, it is utterly fundamental to all that follows. To go wrong here is potentially to skew one's understanding of the whole of Scripture.

The trinitarian nature of God comes into view first in the New Testament, yet does so in the light of *tota Scriptura*. Gunton is right to insist that a Christian doctrine of creation involves the agency of the whole Trinity. Trinitarian doctrine sees the members of the Trinity as primarily responsible for different acts in the drama of Scripture; the Father in creation, the Son in redemption, and the Spirit in mission, but perichoresis insists that in all their acts, all three are integrally involved. "Father, Son, and Holy Spirit are involved jointly in every act along the biblical story line of creation, redemption (including sanctification), and consummation."[61] This is an important insight because it relates to the one problem that Ricoeur says "has dominated the exegesis and theology of the Old Testament: what degree of independence is to be accorded the doctrine of creation in relation to the fundamental soteriological affirmation that is assumed to run through both testaments of the Bible. . . . Within Christian communities, then, the stakes of this discussion are high."[62]

A trinitarian doctrine of creation means that we should expect creation, redemption, and mission to cohere so that redemption and mission will not be at odds with the Father's purpose in creation but integrally related to it. The biblical evidence for this integrality is found across Scripture, yet it is

---

60. C. E. Gunton, "The Doctrine of Creation," in *The Cambridge Companion to Christian Doctrine*, ed. C. E. Gunton (Cambridge: Cambridge University Press, 1977), 141–44.
61. Spykman, *Reformational Theology*, 140.
62. P. Ricoeur, in Lacocque and Ricoeur, *Thinking Biblically*, 31.

the very thing that has so often been eclipsed in recent centuries. Take God's redemption of Israel, for example. Von Rad, writing on the biblical story of creation, rightly states:

> What is strange, however, is that this book, Israel's great etiology, does not begin as one might expect it would with Abraham . . . but rather with the creation of the world. That, of course, encompasses an enormous claim: to speak properly about Israel, to understand Israel correctly, one must begin with the creation of the world; for Israel has its place in God's plans for the world. . . . One misunderstands Israel, her faith and her worship, unless one sees it all from the vantage point of the creation of the world. Only from that perspective are the things that this book says about Israel placed in proper proportion.[63]

Von Rad is quite correct, and this is an insight with major implications for biblical interpretation. Even as Genesis 2:4–4:26 moves the focus from the whole of creation to Eden and the first couple in their relationality, the unusual use of "Yahweh Elohim" for God is a powerful reminder that the God who walks in Eden, giving it a sanctuary-like quality, *is* the creator God.

In Genesis 12:1–3 the word "bless" or some form of it is used five times in relation to the original intention of God to bless his creation, and in opposition to the fivefold use of "curse" to express God's judgment in Genesis 1–11.[64] The point is that God's election of Abraham and thus of Israel is aimed at a recovery of God's purposes for his creation, bringing the blessing of all nations. Karl Barth's view of covenant as the internal basis of creation is a poignant insight, and it is surely right to see the foundational covenantal text in the Bible as Genesis 1. As a priestly royalty and a holy *nation* (Exod. 19:3–6), Israel is intended to be a picture for the nations, a sign of what life lived under the creator-redeemer God looks like. History flows out of the timed creation, and Israel's law understandably bears many resemblances to ancient Near Eastern law while also manifesting important differences. The integrity of creation and redemption reminds us that Israel's law is not an alien imposition on God's order for creation but an actualization of this order at this time and place. As Patrick Miller reminds us, the Decalogue establishes the ethos of the good neighborhood.[65]

Recent studies of Israel's cultus have rightly recognized the creational resonances in the priestly law and narratives. The cultus is a microcosm of the macrocosm of creation. Old Testament prophecy is comprehensive in the

---

63. G. von Rad, *God at Work in Israel* (Nashville: Abingdon, 1980), 98–99.
64. See Claus Westermann, William Dumbrell, et al.
65. P. D. Miller, *The Way of the Lord: Essays in Old Testament Theology* (Grand Rapids: Eerdmans, 2007).

covenant-based charges the prophets bring against Israel; hence *all of life* is in view. Wisdom too is based in a theology of creation. Blocher suggests that Genesis 1 was written by a wise man. Others have suggested that it has the character of a liturgical hymn, whereas von Rad stresses its nature as compact, priestly doctrine: "Everything that is said here is to be accepted exactly as it is written; nothing is to be interpreted symbolically or metaphorically."[66] What Genesis 1 certainly shares with wisdom is a doctrine of creation order.[67] The creation is shaped according to God's repeated "Let there be," an evocative way of alerting the reader to the fact that "The LORD by wisdom founded the earth; by understanding he established the heavens" (Prov. 3:19).

Truly God's redemptive way with Israel cannot be understood aright apart from creation. But neither can his way with Jesus of Nazareth. It is remarkable how much New Testament scholarship fails to recognize the creation-wide dimensions of Christ's redemption. To take a central example, for much of the twentieth century a false dichotomy was made between the kingdom of God as *reign* versus *realm*. According to the Synoptic Gospels, the kingdom of God/heaven was the central theme of Jesus's teaching, and so there is a great deal at stake in how it is interpreted. Eventually we came to accept that there was a "now" and "not-yet" dimension to this preaching of the kingdom, but the view persisted that kingdom was about reign and not realm. Often this was tied to the view that the New Testament spiritualizes the earthy Old Testament materiality of land, people, temple, and so forth. An articulate doctrine of creation would never have allowed such views to remain for so long. As I have argued in *Where Mortals Dwell*, kingdom evokes both reign *and* realm; the realm in view is nothing less than the entire creation. The Gospels are full of creation motifs, and the Matthean Great Commission in Matthew 28:16-20 is encompassed in a declaration of Christ's sovereign authority over heaven and earth, even as the command is given to disciple "*all nations*." Paul's Letters—especially Romans, 1 Corinthians, Ephesians, Colossians—are full of profound Christology that unequivocally connects creation to God's redemption in Christ.

Ola Tjørhom articulates the theological implications of our discussion poignantly:

> The Father is the creator, the Son is the ultimate liberator of creation, and the Holy Spirit conveys life to all created beings. Surely, a misplaced confusion of creation and redemption must be avoided.[68]

---

66. Von Rad, *God at Work in Israel*, 99.
67. For an excellent discussion of this issue, see Spykman, *Reformational Theology*, 171-91.
68. O. Tjørhom, *Embodied Faith: Reflections on a Materialist Spirituality* (Grand Rapids: Eerdmans, 2009), 33.

Actually, without creation there is nothing to save—creation is the "stuff" of salvation.[69]

When the first Christians—being a tiny and insignificant minority in society—were able to maintain the immense cosmic scope of the drama of salvation in Christ, it becomes odd when we today are so bent on retracting into cramped, personalized, or private positions.[70]

Recovery of the doctrine of creation and the agency of the whole Trinity in it will alone enable us to recover and maintain the *immense* scope of the cosmic drama of salvation in Christ.

Creatio ex nihilo

John 1:3, as with other verses in the New Testament, clearly teaches *creatio ex nihilo*: "All things came into being through him, and without him not one thing came into being."[71] As theologians and Christian philosophers have long recognized, there is much at stake in this doctrine, since it safeguards the sovereignty and transcendence of God and prevents any aspect or part of creation from being equated with the divine. However, when it comes to Genesis 1:1-2, a seminal text in this regard, there is widespread disagreement as to whether it affirms *creatio ex nihilo*.[72] In his wonderfully stimulating commentary on Genesis, Leon Kass says of verse 2

> The origin of the primordial chaos is absolutely unclear; there is no explicit assertion of its creation out of nothing. The ultimate beginnings—and even the status quo ante, before God's creative acts—are shrouded in mystery. And well they should be, for neither of the two options—"came from nothing" and "it was there always"—can we humans picture to ourselves.[73]

The translation of verse 1 is also contested.[74] The NRSV translates verses 1-2 as "In the beginning when God created the heavens and the earth, the earth

---

69. Ibid., 36.
70. Ibid., 37.
71. Cf. Heb. 11:3; and in the intertestamental period, 2 Macc. 7:28.
72. P. Ricoeur (in LaCocque and Ricoeur, *Thinking Biblically*) argues that the idea of *creatio ex nihilo* emerged only in Hellenism.
73. L. R. Kass, *The Beginning of Wisdom: Reading Genesis* (Chicago: University of Chicago Press, 2003), 28–29.
74. For a discussion of the four main alternatives, see G. J. Wenham, *Genesis 1–15*, WBC 1 (Waco: Word, 1987), 11–13. The debate continues; see, e.g., R. Holmstedt, "The Restrictive Syntax of Genesis i 1," *VT* 58, no. 1 (2008): 56–67; J. C. M. Van Winden, "In the Beginning: Some Observations on the Patristic Interpretation of Genesis 1:1," *Vigiliae Christianae* 17,

was a formless void." This translation treats verse 1 as a temporal clause, subordinate to the main clause in verse 2. Clearly this translation leaves open the possibility that the chaos of verse 2 preexisted God's creation of the heavens and the earth. By comparison the NIV presents the traditional translation: "In the beginning God created the heavens and the earth." Verses 2–3 then describe subsequent acts in God's creative work.

It is unlikely that the tortuous syntactic debates will finally resolve this issue.[75] What may illumine it, however, is consideration of the orality underlying Genesis 1. Ong argues that Genesis 1:1–5 is a typical example of *additive oral style*—rather than subordinative—in which the opening statement is followed by nine introductory "ands." Thus the 1610 Douay version of the Bible, produced in a culture with a significant oral residue, translates verse 1 as an independent sentence and each of the following *wă* uses simply as "and." Our modern versions

> provide a flow of narration with the analytic, reasoned subordination that characterizes writing, ... and that appears more natural in twentieth-century texts.... The Douay is closer in that it renders *we* or *wa* always by the same word, but it strikes the present-day sensibility as remote, archaic, and even quaint. Peoples in oral cultures or cultures with high oral residue, including the culture that produced the Bible, do not savor this sort of expression as so archaic or quaint. It feels natural and normal to them somewhat as the New American version feels natural and normal to us.[76]

If Ong is right, this would seem to support the traditional translation of 1:1. Two of the four possibilities Wenham explores treat 1:1 as a *subordinate* clause, contrary to the additive structure discerned by Ong. Apart from the traditional reading, the other alternative is to read 1:1 as a heading or title for what follows. However, this is unlikely for, as Gunkel noted, verse 2 would then imply that the earth preexisted what verse 1 tells us the chapter is all about, namely, the creation of heaven and *earth*.[77] As I have argued elsewhere, what is possible is that verse 1 serves as a heading *and* as the first act in creation.[78]

Attempts have been made to support *creatio ex nihilo* in Genesis from the use of the verb *bārā'*. God is indeed always the subject of this verb, but it

---

no. 2 (1963): 105–21; G. Anderson, "The Interpretation of Genesis 1:1 in the Targums," *CBQ* 52, no. 1 (1990): 21–29.

75. See C. G. Bartholomew, "Genesis 1:2 and the Doctrine of Creation," forthcoming.

76. W. J. Ong, *Orality and Literacy: The Technologizing of the Word* (New York: Methuen, 1982), 37–38.

77. See Wenham, *Genesis 1–15*, 13.

78. Bartholomew, "Genesis 1:2."

is not exclusively used of creation ex nihilo. It does, however, "preserve the same idea, namely 'God's effortless, totally free and unbound creating, his sovereignty.'"[79] Stek surveys the rich variety of Old Testament language use of God's creative activity and concludes:

> It must also be noted that whereas the Christian doctrine of creation has tended to focus almost exclusively on the origin of the creation in the beginning, that limitation does not apply to Old Testament creation language. In the speech of the Old Testament authors, whatever exists now and whatever will come into existence in the creaturely realm has been or will have been "created" by God. He is not only the Creator of the original state of affairs but also of all present and future realities.[80]

That Genesis 1 speaks of an absolute beginning, and creation ex nihilo is confirmed by the theology of Genesis 1 as a whole. Eichrodt rightly points out that the author's monotheism, the difference between his cosmogony and that of the current myths, his emphasis on creation by divine fiat, his choice of the word *bārā'*—all incline toward a depiction of creation in which, in more abstract language, anything short of ex nihilo would fail to do justice.[81]

Creation and Providence

This theme relates to points 4–6 in Gunton's list of the key elements in a doctrine of creation: point 4, God's interactive relationship with the world and humankind; point 5, divine preservation; point 6, continuity with history and the work of redemption.

Historically, theologians have made a sharp distinction between creation and providence;[82] while this has clear *logical* merit, it may be an area where Scripture would reshape theology. Abraham Kuyper is unusual in his somewhat different approach. By appropriating the term *creatio continuata*, he endeavored to safeguard the distinction between origination and the continuation of the creation, yet while holding fast to the total dependence of the created on the creator:[83]

---

79. Ibid., 14. Cf. J. H. Stek, "What Says the Scripture?," in *Portraits of Creation*, ed. Van Til et al., 207–13, esp. 212–13.
80. Stek, "What Says the Scripture?," 211.
81. W. Eichrodt, *Theology of the Old Testament*, trans. J. A. Baker, 2 vols. (Philadelphia: Westminster, 1961–67), 2:101–6.
82. Examples are Herman Bavinck, Gerrit C. Berkouwer, Emil Brunner, Otto Weber, et al. Bavinck held that God's resting signifies the separation between creation and providence.
83. A. Kuyper, *Dictaten dogmatiek* (Kampen, Netherlands: J. H. Kok, 1910).

> We must definitely insist that providence is a *creatio continuata*, to be understood in the sense that from the hour of original creation until now, God, the Lord, has done the same thing as in the moment of creation: he has given all things power of existence through his power.[84]
>
> In the Bible the language of creation is not just used of origination but also of the ongoing sustaining and development of the creation by God.[85]

Furthermore, as Stek rightly observes, the repeated "Let there be" of Genesis 1, the creation decrees, not only originate but also maintain the creation in existence. Stek says:

> Since God's creating word called into being not merely an aggregate of entities but components designed to function within the economy of an integrated realm, the preserving and governing power of the creation word cannot be isolated from the functioning economy of the creatures, from their "concurrence." The creation's economy continues to be governed by the Creator's decrees—his *creation* decrees. ... There is indeed not continuous creating (no *creatio continuata* in its classic sense); there is rather the continuing effectiveness of the Creator's "Let there be . . ."[86]

According to Stek, the narrative mode of Genesis 1 transcends the problem of the relationship between creation and providence that has exercised theologians for so long. God's repeated "Let there be" is effective to originate and to govern and maintain the economy of creation.

This seems right to me. History and providence issue forth from creation, and it is helpful to see providence anchored deeply into creation in this way. It is also a reminder of the potential for the rich biblical material on creation to refashion dogmatics.

Creation Order

As we noticed above, the doctrine of creation order has not been without its detractors. However, it is biblical and fundamentally important, provided it is rightly understood. In its first article the Apostles' Creed affirms, "We believe in God the Father Almighty, creator of *heaven and earth*." The distinction between heaven and earth, the *separation* of heaven and earth, is the most fundamental aspect of God's ordering of his creation. Creation order provides

---

84. Quoted by G. C. Berkouwer, *The Providence of God* (Grand Rapids: Eerdmans, 1952), 62.
85. Stek, "What Says the Scripture?," 246.
86. Ibid., 248.

the basis for existence and flourishing. Contrary to many of its detractors, it is not static; but creation order means that even for history and change there are God-given norms.[87] Humans have freedom and response-ability, but it is freedom within creational limits. As Berkouwer declares in an article on divine revelation, the whole of human life is a response to God, in one way or another.

We have referred (above) to the *separation* of heaven and earth. Separation (*hibdîl*) is a significant word in Genesis 1,[88] and several scholars have noted its importance for a theology of creation. Kass asserts, "We could say that *the* fundamental principle through which the world is created is separation. Creation is the bringing of order out of chaos largely through acts of separation, division, distinction."[89] Kass illustrates his *creation by division* as indicated in figure 12.1.

Thus Kass argues that Genesis provides us with "an intelligible account of a cosmic order based on noetic or intelligible principles, not mythic or sensuous ones. . . . When we grasp the intelligible order, the text that bespeaks and reveals that order gains our trust."[90] In Genesis 1, God creates primarily by speech,[91] the divine fiat, and Kass argues that this fits creation by division because speech implies the making and recognizing of divisions. "A formed world is necessarily a world of distinction, a world whose ordered divisions can be made articulate in intelligible speech."[92]

In my view, Kass is right that Genesis 1, with its view of creation order, sees the world as having a discernible shape: it presents a version of *realism*. A question is what type of realism it presents. Kass argues that once the intelligible principles of being "are presented to the mind's eye, by means of carefully wrought speech, any human can appreciate them."[93] There is certainly truth to this, but I think LaCocque is closer to the mark in his resistance to calling the creation a *cosmos* because this is easily understood as a harmony based on reason, "whereas the harmony of the world according to Genesis is by decree, by

---

87. P. Ricoeur (in LaCocque and Ricoeur, *Thinking Biblically*, 54–62) expresses several cautions about creation order: we need to think of it as contingent; we need to think of it as an event; we need to discern a vulnerability intrinsic to order. Ricoeur (in ibid., 57) is certainly right to state that the idea of order takes on a more dynamic sense when we move from the cosmic to the human level of right and justice.

88. See Gen. 1:4, 6, 7, 14, 18. The idea is implicit in "of every [after its] kind," occurring ten times.

89. Kass, *Beginning of Wisdom*, 32.

90. Ibid., 33.

91. See J. D. Levenson's *Creation and the Persistence of Evil: The Jewish Drama of Divine Omnipotence* (San Francisco: Harper & Row, 1988), important work on the different metaphors for creation in the OT.

92. Kass, *Beginning of Wisdom*, 35.

93. Ibid., 33.

Figure 12.1
Creation by Division

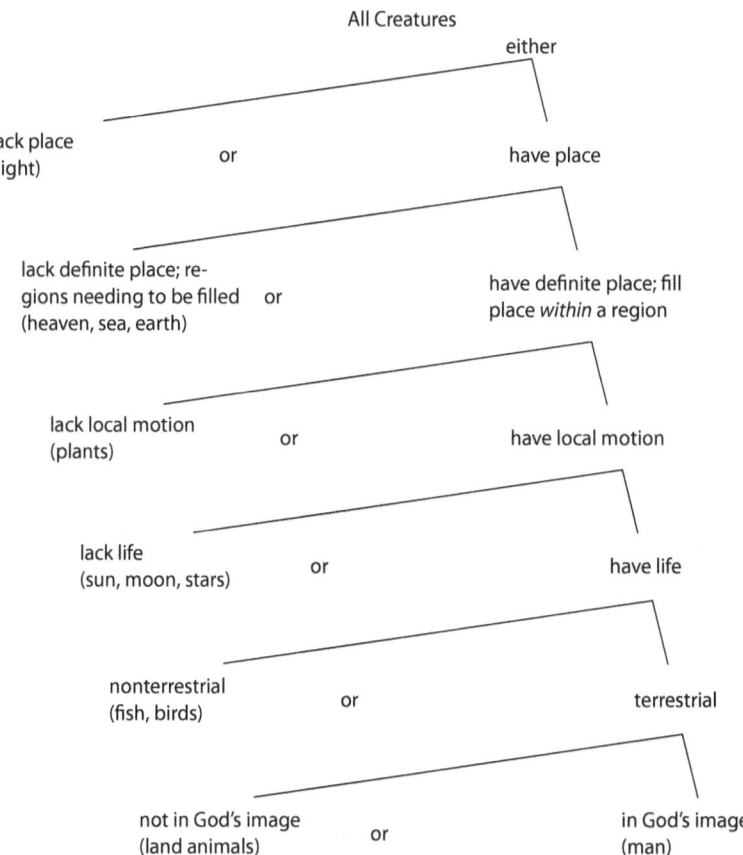

Law, and an equation is established between harmony and obedience."[94] Thus true knowledge of the creation is dependent on responding correctly to God. LaCocque evocatively reads the repeated *ṭôb* in Genesis 1 as expressing "the vocational capacity of the creature to fulfill the expectation of its Creator."[95] "God is good and declares his creature also good (*ṭôb*). The creature's goodness is its capability to respond to the Creator's goodness. Psalm 94:7–9 shows incisively that the essence of being human is to be in communication with others, to be turned *ad extra*. This is the human responsibility."[96]

---

94. LaCocque and Ricoeur, *Thinking Biblically*, 6.
95. Ibid., 6.
96. Ibid., 10.

This leaves us, rightly, with a more *critical* realism than that presented by Kass. O'Donovan has, in my view, provided us with the richest articulation of a biblical epistemology in his *Resurrection and Moral Order*. With Brunner, he agrees that the creation has a discernible shape and order; but with Karl Barth, he agrees that we can only know this order aright *in Christ*.

It remains to be recognized that creation order is a great blessing. Spykman expresses this eloquently:

> This network of structures and functions, governed by creational law, manifests his loving care for all creatures. Every creature, each in its own unique way, is subject to this constant yet dynamic ecosystem of creational laws. Compliance with it is not an odious burden. For it was not imposed by some alien force. The creation order is evidence of the caring hand of the Creator reaching out to secure the well-being of his creatures, of a Father extending a universe full of blessings to his children. Willing obedience to this life-enveloping, love-impelling, shalom-enhancing framework of law and order brings with it freedom, righteousness, and joy. It enables us to become all we are meant to be.[97]

Christ and Creation

Weber rightly states that "every section of dogmatics includes, in its own way and from its own point of view, the whole of dogmatics within itself."[98] This is certainly the case when we attend to Jesus and creation. Perichoresis would lead us to expect that Jesus has much to do with creation, but the abundance of New Testament material is rarely resourced for a doctrine of creation.[99] The more the foundational reality of creation for the biblical drama is understood, the more we will see its role in every major doctrine. History emanates from creation, and as Bonhoeffer declares, "History lives between promise and fulfillment. It carries the promise within itself, to become full of God, the womb of the birth of God."[100] Creation is thus deeply intertwined with history and eschatology, and nowhere is this clearer than in a consideration of Jesus and creation. The Gospels are chock-full of creation motifs, and the Letters of the New Testament contain a rich theology of the cosmic

---

97. Spykman, *Reformational Theology*, 178.
98. O. Weber, *Foundations of Dogmatics* (Grand Rapids: Eerdmans, 1981), 1:349.
99. Useful works that do attend to this issue are J.-F. Bonnefoy, *Christ and the Cosmos*, trans. and ed. M. D. Meilach (Paterson, NJ: St. Anthony Guild, 1965); C. E. Gunton, *Christ and Creation* (1992; reprint, Eugene, OR: Wipf & Stock, 2005); A. König, *The Eclipse of Christ in Eschatology: Toward a Christ-Centered Approach* (Grand Rapids: Eerdmans, 1989).
100. D. Bonhoeffer, *Christ the Center*, trans. E. Bethge (New York: Harper & Row, 1966), 61-62.

Christ, especially Romans 8, Ephesians, Colossians, and Revelation.[101] As König admits, "There is no consensus on the relationship between God and creation. Because eschatology speaks of the goal of creation, we will need to investigate this relationship between Creator and creation more fully."[102] "Through the centuries, this cosmic significance of Jesus's ministry and lordship has frequently been misrepresented in the Church's preaching."[103] Such misrepresentation has been exceedingly damaging, and the New Testament understanding of the relationship between Jesus and creation needs to be recovered.

We have already referred (above) to the great theme of the kingdom of God/heaven and its comprehensive range. Unlike the Gospels, Paul does not often use the language of the "kingdom of God." Generally Paul uses a different vocabulary in his postresurrection context. Intriguingly, we do find *kingdom language* twice in Colossians: 1:13; 4:11. In 1:13 Christians are those who have been "rescued . . . from the power of darkness and transferred into *the kingdom of his beloved Son*." In 4:11 Paul speaks of his "co-workers for the kingdom of God."

"*The kingdom of his beloved Son*" is a rich expression. It alludes to Jesus's baptism and his transfiguration (cf. Luke 3:22; 9:28–36). At his baptism a voice came from heaven saying, "You are my Son, the Beloved; with you I am well pleased." On the mountain when Jesus was transfigured and Moses (representing *the Law*) and Elijah (representing *the Prophets*) were talking to him about his coming "departure [*exodos*]," a cloud overshadowed them, reminiscent of Mount Sinai. From the cloud came a voice, saying, "This is my Son, my Chosen; listen to him!"

There is so much to unpack from this expression. Suffice it to see that the allusion to Jesus's baptism reminds us that this is an unusual kingdom. It is the kingdom of the Son, who came not as a conquering monarch in all his majesty, but as the one who, though rich, for our sake became poor, that we through his poverty might become rich (cf. 2 Cor. 8:9). In Karl Barth's words, this is the kingdom of the God who went into the far country in order that we might return from it and come home.[104]

The allusion to the transfiguration reminds us that this is the Son of the kingdom of *GOD*. The veil is lifted, and the disciples "saw his glory" (Luke 9:32). Moses and Elijah are present because he fulfills the Old Testament, sometimes referred to as the Law and the Prophets. His coming passion is

---

101. The genre of Revelation is certainly more than that of a letter.
102. König, *Eclipse of Christ in Eschatology*, 50.
103. Ibid., 112.
104. K. Barth, *CD* IV/2, 20–21.

described with the word *exodos* because he will accomplish, not the release of slaves from Egypt, but the exodus of *the entire creation* from its bondage to sin and evil.

Paul's christocentric creation theology comes to the fore particularly in Colossians, through the "hymn" in 1:15–20. Scholars divide the hymn in different ways; Murray Harris suggests that we divide it into two parts:[105]

verses 15–17: the supremacy of Christ in creation
verses 18–20: the supremacy of Christ in redemption

This is useful, but the text also resists such a useful division because creation and redemption are utterly interwoven in this hymn. The vital point to notice is that the Christ who is the head of the church is also the creator, and his work of redemption is aimed at nothing less than the recovery of his purposes *for the whole creation*!

Christ is *"the image of the invisible God"*: "image" here speaks of Jesus as the exact visible representation of the invisible God. Dunn argues that Paul here utilizes the imagery of divine Wisdom to explicate the Christ event, thereby affirming the immanence of God in Jesus while safeguarding God's utter transcendence.[106] Note the irony: Jesus is the exact *image* of the *invisible* God. In relation to verse 14, which speaks of *redemption*, verse 15 affirms the deity of Christ: "It is Christ in his revelatory and redemptive significance who is the subject of praise here. . . . And the praise is that his redemptive work . . . is entirely continuous with and of a piece with God's work in creation. It is the same God who comes to expression in creation and definitively in Christ."[107] This is confirmed by the expression "the firstborn of all creation." "Firstborn" does not evoke the idea of Christ as created,[108] but as supreme in rank as well as prior in time. It declares his absolute preexistence and his sovereignty over all creation.

In verse 16 the preposition "ἐν" can be translated as "by" or "in." In terms of what "in him" might mean, Murray Harris suggests that creation occurred "within the person of" Christ; in him resided the energy that produced all creation; the Father acted with the Son in creation.[109] Note the conclusion of

---

105. Murray J. Harris, *Colossians and Philemon* (Grand Rapids: Eerdmans, 1991), 42.
106. J. D. G. Dunn, *The Epistles to the Colossians and to Philemon: A Commentary on the Greek Text*, NIGTC (Grand Rapids: Eerdmans, 1996), 87–89.
107. Ibid., 89.
108. See J. B. Lightfoot, *St. Paul's Epistles to the Colossians and to Philemon: A Revised Text with Introductions, Notes and Dissertations* (Grand Rapids: Zondervan, 1959), 148–50.
109. Murray J. Harris, *Colossians and Philemon*, 40.

verse 16: "all things have been created through him and for him." Lightfoot explains the phrase "for him": "The Eternal Word is the goal of the Universe, as He was the starting point. It must end in unity, as it proceeded from unity; and *the centre* of this unity is Christ."[110] König perceptively notes, "It is precisely because Christ is the goal of creation that it is not possible to contemplate his significance without considering 'things' (i.e., created realities)."[111]

The way in which Christ is depicted in relation to creation in this hymn is quite remarkable. Creation comes into existence by and in him, and the goal of creation is . . . him! "The fact that Christ himself is the last and the end means that God's creation goal is both revealed in him and attained by him."[112] Verse 17 declares that "in him all things hold together." In the Old Testament, creation involves not just bringing into being but also sustaining in being, and here Christ is depicted as "the principle of cohesion in the universe. He impresses upon creation that unity and solidarity which makes it a cosmos instead of a chaos. Thus (to take one instance) the action of gravitation, which keeps in their places things fixed and regulates the motions of things moving, is an expression of His mind."[113]

Paul continues in verse 18: "He is the beginning [ἀρχή], the firstborn from the dead, so that he might come to have first place *in everything*." "Beginning" connects back into creation yet looks forward to the new creation that Christ ushers in by his resurrection. "Firstborn from the dead" parallels "firstborn of all creation," so that resurrection is connected with creation. Christ's resurrection unequivocally marks the breaking in of the new age into the creation, and in time to come, his resurrection will drag the whole creation with it into the new heavens and new earth. Karl Barth says: "The raising of [Jesus] is to the men of the New Testament the guarantee of their own future resurrection and that of all men, in whose resurrection they have the basis of a life in this world which is assured of a future resurrection, which hastens towards it, which anticipates in hope their own future life out of death."[114]

God's plan of redemption is to reconcile to himself all things in Christ; to restore *shalom* to every aspect of his creation as he always intended it. "Reconciliation is more than a reaction to faithlessness; it is the pursuit of God's original act, through which he intends to realize his goal, the covenant."[115] Thereby Christ will come to have first place in everything!

110. Ibid., 155, with added emphasis.
111. König, *Eclipse of Christ in Eschatology*, 42.
112. Ibid., vii.
113. Lightfoot, *St. Paul's Epistles*, 156.
114. K. Barth, *CD* IV/1:299.
115. König, *Eclipse of Christ in Eschatology*, 57; cf. K. Barth, *CD* IV/1:34–39.

A theologian who has excavated the rich New Testament language about Jesus and creation is the South African Adrio König in his *The Eclipse of Christ in Eschatology*.[116] In a section titled "Jesus the Goal of Creation," König rightly explains: "Christ is not merely the beginning of creation in a temporal sense, but that as pilot and ruler he accompanies creation—or rather takes it along with him. He is not the deist's "beginning" who left creation to its own devices; he is rather the helmsman of creation, which is why everything can be brought together in him (Eph. 1:10)."[117] In dialogue with Karl Barth, König affirms a view of creation as grace; we may, he suggests, distinguish between creation grace and redemption grace.[118] He identifies covenant as the goal of creation and affirms Schoonenberg's statement "Salvation consists in the covenant between God and man, and the God-man is the covenant in person."[119]

In a marvelous exploration, König unpacks eschatology under the headings of "Christ Realizes the Goal for Us," "Christ Realizes the Goal in Us," and "Christ Realizes the Goal with Us." König's work gives us a taste of how fruitful genuinely creative cooperation between biblical scholars and theologians can be. As Ricoeur declares, much is at stake in how we conceive of the relationship between creation and redemption. Enormous biblical and theological riches remain to be excavated for our day in relation to the doctrine of creation.

---

116. See also A. König, *New and Greater Things: Re-Evaluating the Biblical Message on Creation* (Pretoria: University of South Africa, 1988).
117. König, *Eclipse of Christ in Eschatology*, 24.
118. Ibid., 54; cf. K. Barth, CD IV/1:8–9.
119. Quoted in König, *Eclipse of Christ in Eschatology*, 58.

13

Scripture and the University

The Ecology of Christian Scholarship

What have I to do for this panting, palpitating century? More than ever before thought is waiting for men, and men for thought. The world is in danger for lack of life-giving maxims. We are in a train rushing ahead at top speed, no signals visible. The planet is going it knows not where, its law has failed: who will give it back its sun?

A. G. Sertillanges[1]

At a time of unparalleled elimination of taboos, is God to be the last taboo? No, the question of God is too important and too explosive to be left solely to theologians. . . . Unless we are completely mistaken, the time is coming when people will begin to be aware not only of the socio-political but also the closely connected ethical-religious dimension of each department.

Hans Küng[2]

The point then is not that we must now cling to faith in ascetic nakedness. Instead we must pass beyond the all-too-modern fideism of neo-orthodoxy

---

1. A. G. Sertillanges, *The Intellectual Life: Its Spirit, Conditions, Methods* (Washington, DC: Catholic University of America Press, 1998), 14–15.
2. H. Küng, "God: The Last Taboo?," in *Theology and the University: Essays in Honor of John B Cobb, Jr.*, ed. D. R. Griffin and J. C. Hough Jr. (Albany: State University of New York Press, 1991), 62.

toward a radical orthodoxy that refuses the duality of reason over against faith.

John Milbank[3]

How does such a perspective impact upon the task of theology today? Primarily, it absolutely forbids us to baptize the secular desert as the realm of pure reason, pure nature, natural law, or natural rights, and so forth. . . . So the answer cannot be responsibility before a uniform liberal court.

John Milbank[4]

While Paul's demand to take every thought captive to Christ is incumbent on all Christians, the ecclesially based university provides a distinct context within which Christians can be introduced to the habits, practices, and dispositions that will enable them to think Christianly across the entire spectrum of knowledge. There is no aspect of knowing that Christians can rule out of bounds.

Stephen Fowl[5]

It's time to recognize that what has been lost is the Judeo-Christian cosmic theater, with its penetrating vision of a future, its broader grasp of the limits of human knowledge, its deeper sense of time, and its larger universe that includes unknown as well as unknowable meanings of our existence as a human species.

David Rosenberg[6]

But there is a storm breaking upon the university again, and this time from north, south, east, and west.

Jaroslav Pelikan[7]

Introduction

I am not aware of any other book on biblical hermeneutics that includes a chapter on Christian scholarship. However, if Scripture is God's word *for all*

---

3. J. Milbank, "The Last of the Last: Theology in the Church," in *Conflicting Allegiances: The Church-Based University in a Liberal Democratic Society*, ed. M. L. Budde and J. Wright (Grand Rapids: Brazos, 2004), 244.
4. Ibid., 245.
5. S. Fowl, "The Role of Scripture in an Ecclesially Based University," in Budde and J. Wright, *Conflicting Allegiances,* 172.
6. D. Rosenberg, *The Educated Man: A Dual Biography of Moses and Jesus* (Berkeley: Counterpoint, 2010).
7. J. Pelikan, *The Idea of a University: A Reexamination* (New Haven: Yale University Press, 1992), 11.

of life, then one would expect Scripture to be taken seriously in every discipline. In the above quote from Sertillanges's classic and extraordinary work *La vie intellectuelle*,[8] he poses the question, "Who will give it [our world] back its sun?" Hamann rightly says, "All the colors of this most beautiful world grow pale once you extinguish its light, the firstborn of creation."[9] Jesus is the light, the sun of our world; and Scripture is that field in which we find hid the pearl of great price. Therefore in our intellectual work, if we desire to contribute to giving the world back its sun, then the role of Scripture in scholarship should be high on our agendas. Biblical scholars, I suggest, have a particular responsibility to produce work that is aimed at enabling scholars in other disciplines to engage Scripture in their disciplines.

In chapter 15 (below) on preaching, we honor the comprehensive scope of Christ's lordship. Christ's lordship is not for a moment alien to the rich, textured, visceral nature of earthy, material life; his redemption is aimed precisely at the creation that *he* brought into existence. Bonhoeffer thus rightly asserts:

> The lordship of Christ is not the rule of a foreign power; it is the lordship of the Creator, Reconciler and Redeemer, the lordship of Him through whom and for whom all created beings exist, of Him in whom indeed all created beings alone find their origin, their goal and their essence. Jesus Christ imposes no alien law upon creation. . . . The commandment of Jesus Christ, the living Lord, sets creation free for the fulfillment of the law which is its own, that is to say, the law which is inherent in it by virtue of its having its origin, its goal and its essence in Jesus Christ. . . . Jesus Christ's claim to lordship, which is proclaimed by the Church, means at the same time the emancipation of family, culture and government for the realization of their own essential character which has its foundation in Christ.[10]

Rather than faith in Christ being an escape from the creation,[11] it is the very thing that enables humans and the creation to become fully themselves; it is *liberation* for the whole creation. A major critique of Christianity has been that it detracts from and subverts the glory of ordinary, everyday life in all its richness;[12] while this has sadly been true of certain types of

---

8. It would serve us well to have all our students and scholars read this extraordinary work.
9. J. G. Hamann, *Writings on Philosophy and Language*, trans. and ed. K. Haynes (Cambridge: Cambridge University Press, 2007), 78. On Hamann see C. G. Bartholomew and M. W. Goheen, *Christian Philosophy: A Systematic and Narrative Introduction* (Grand Rapids: Baker Academic, 2013), 147–50.
10. D. Bonhoeffer, *Ethics* (New York: Macmillan, 1955), 264.
11. Bonhoeffer acutely declares, "Any attempt to escape from the world must sooner or later be paid for with a sinful surrender to the world" (ibid., 66).
12. For a good critique of such views, see B. Ingraffia, *Postmodern Theory and Biblical Theology: Vanquishing God's Shadow* (Cambridge: Cambridge University Press, 1995).

Christianity, it is not true of biblical Christianity, as so wonderfully expressed by Bonhoeffer.

Bonhoeffer's insights are premised on the belief that God has spoken finally and definitively *in Christ*, the redeemer and creator. Yet many today, not least in the West and among biblical scholars, reject this belief. And it is a belief that cannot be proved: "*The reality of the church is a reality of revelation, a reality that essentially must be* either believed or denied. Thus an adequate criterion for judging the claim of the church to be God's church-community can be found only by stepping inside, by bowing in faith to its claim."[13] Thus the challenge to Christian scholars is that their faith lays comprehensive claim to all of reality in a *pluralistic* world, in which a diversity of belief systems operate. How then should we live and practice our scholarship in such a context?

First, we need to become aware that the admirable freedom of religion in the West has severe limits. Modernity is characterized by the privatization of religion and seeks to keep religion out of the public square, including education and scholarship, in which "neutral, objective reason" is supposed to dominate. Far too much contemporary Christianity has succumbed to this privatization and concentrated on building churches that embody this dualism. The history of the twentieth century and postmodernism have alerted us to the fact that "neutral, objective reason" is far from neutral but is itself invariably traditioned. What we urgently need in the West is a different, *just* model of pluralism,[14] which acknowledges the diverse worldviews in our cultures and creates the space for them to come to fruition in all areas of life and not just in the private domain.

Second, Christians need to resist modern privatization of faith. On the one hand we need to be seriously committed to protecting the *freedom of all* to give expression to their beliefs; yet on the other hand we need to take equally seriously the comprehensive scope of Christ's redemption, and this not least in our scholarship. Scholarship is not neutral, and the insights of faith make a profound difference to all disciplines, including biblical interpretation. In different ways Alvin Plantinga, Nicholas Wolterstorff, Mark Noll, and George Marsden have drawn attention to this, but we have a long way to go in actually incarnating this vision in practice. Especially in North America, with

---

13. D. Bonhoeffer, *Sanctorum communio: A Theological Study of the Sociology of the Church*, trans. R. Krauss and N. Lukens, ed. C. J. Green (Minneapolis: Fortress, 1998), 127, with original emphasis.

14. Excellent work has been done in this area. See, e.g., J. W. Skillen and R. M. McCarthy, eds., *Political Order and the Plural Structure of Society*, Emory University Studies in Law and Religion (Atlanta: Scholars Press, 1991); R. J. Mouw and S. Griffioen, *Pluralisms and Horizons: An Essay in Christian Public Philosophy* (Grand Rapids: Eerdmans, 1993).

its plethora of Christian colleges and universities, significant progress has been made, and in some disciplines—such as philosophy—the contribution has been outstanding. The renaissance of Christian philosophy needs to be complemented by a similar renaissance in all the other disciplines. A rising tide should lift all boats, and certainly this *should* be true of biblical studies. Alas, too often material from other disciplines is imported uncritically, so that biblical studies become a hodgepodge of diverse views, with no *integrality*, the very thing that Plantinga has rightly encouraged us to aim for in our scholarship.[15] As biblical studies draws on the rich insights of sociology, anthropology, linguistics, literary theory, and so forth, it needs to be able to attend to major Christian work in these areas so that it does indeed plunder the Egyptians rather than invite the Trojan horse into its camp.

Philosophers have already made a major contribution to biblical interpretation, but one suspects that it has not yet been recognized or fully appropriated by biblical scholars. Eleonore Stump,[16] Alvin Plantinga,[17] Leon Kass,[18] and C. Stephen Evans[19] are all major philosophers who have attended to biblical interpretation. But sadly, none of their work has prompted serious engagement by biblical scholars.[20] If we do not wake up to the importance of these issues, it may come to be said of biblical studies what Betz says of Hamann and his reception: "Some of the most potent and influential thinkers of a generation go unnoticed."[21] Particularly in an age in which so many books are published, we need a holy discernment so that we do not miss the really important work when it appears.

Third, genuinely Christian scholarship is not just for the church but *for the world*. A casualty of postmodernism and the wild pluralism in the academy is *truth*, and yet this is precisely the goal of Christian scholarship.[22] Bonhoeffer

---

15. See A. Plantinga, "Advice to Christian Philosophers," *Faith and Philosophy* 1, no. 3 (1984): 253–71.

16. E. Stump, *Wandering in Darkness: Narrative and the Problem of Suffering* (Oxford: Oxford University Press, 2010).

17. See A. Plantinga's discussion of biblical interpretation as a possible defeater of Christian faith in his *Warranted Christian Belief* (New York: Oxford University Press, 2000).

18. L. Kass, *The Beginning of Wisdom: Reading Genesis* (Chicago: University of Chicago Press, 2003).

19. C. S. Evans, *The Historical Christ and the Jesus of Faith: The Incarnational Narrative as History* (Oxford: Oxford University Press, 1996).

20. For a dialogue with Alvin Plantinga by C. G. Bartholomew and Robert Gordon, see C. G. Bartholomew et al., eds., *"Behind" the Text: History and Biblical Interpretation* (Grand Rapids: Zondervan, 2003).

21. J. R. Betz, "Reading 'Sibylline Leaves': J. G. Hamann in the History of Ideas," *Journal of the History of Ideas* 70, no. 1 (2009): 93–118, esp. 118.

22. I have found Sertillanges, *The Intellectual Life*, to be a helpful antidote to the jaded lostness of postmodern pluralism in the academy.

rightly argues that the church has its own space, but that this space does not exist on its own account. The space of the church

> is from the outset something which reaches out far beyond itself.... It is the place where testimony is given to the foundation of all reality in Jesus Christ. The space of the Church is not there to deprive the world of a piece of its territory, but precisely in order to prove to the world that it is still the world, the world which is loved by God and reconciled with Him.... The only way in which the Church can defend her own territory is by fighting not for it but for the salvation of the world.[23]

Christian scholarship must insist on doing its work "in Christ" and should not make the mistake of yielding the epistemic foundations and then trying to reach Christian conclusions from alien starting points.[24] Certainly Christian scholarship should serve the church, but in its quest for truth it should always aim to contribute to the commons of our cultures, to keep proving to the world that it is the world!

Christian scholarship is often hard to talk about because it is so often misunderstood, and sometimes there are few outstanding examples to point to. When I worked in the United Kingdom, the very notion of a Christian university seemed implausible because there was no significant example that one could point to. Several aspects of Christian scholarship thus need to be highlighted.

1. *It is Christian scholarship.* In the Christian tradition we are heirs to a rich tradition of scholarship. There is our foundational document, the Scriptures, whose legacy echoes in myriad cultural ways down to the present. One thinks of Augustine's *Confessions* and his *The City of God*, which has never been out of print since it was published. One thinks of Thomas Aquinas with his *Summas*; of Hamann, contemporary and critic of Kant, whose contribution is now being recognized;[25] of Søren Kierkegaard, with his remarkably creative corpus of writings produced in such a short life; of the world-renowned work of philosopher Alvin Plantinga, whose free-will argument in relation to the problem of evil has been described by a non-Christian philosopher as a thing of beauty. Theology and philosophy are heirs to a tradition jam-packed

---

23. Bonhoeffer, *Ethics*, 68.

24. See M. J. Buckley, *At the Origins of Modern Atheism* (New Haven: Yale University Press, 1987). Cf. J. Milbank, "The Last of the Last: Theology in the Church"; idem, "Knowledge: The Theological Critique of Philosophy in Haman and Jacobi," in *Radical Orthodoxy*, ed. J. Milbank, C. Pickstock, and Graham Ward (New York: Routledge, 1999), 21–37.

25. For an excellent introduction to Hamann, see J. R. Betz, *After Enlightenment: The Postsecular Vision of J. G. Hamann* (Oxford: Blackwell, 2012).

with a feast of outstanding contributions. And this is to say nothing of the major contributions of Christians to the variety of other disciplines in the academy today. For example, ornithologist T. Birkhead, in his *The Wisdom of Birds: An Illustrated History of Ornithology*, argues that the most influential ornithologist of all time was John Ray, a devout Christian.[26]

This rich tradition, it should be recognized, has been remarkably influential. In his *Justice*, Wolterstorff argues that it was Augustine's scriptural scholarship that broke the back of the *eudaemonia* tradition in Western thought, thereby creating the space for the emergence of human rights.[27] When we are thinking about Christian scholarship, we are not therefore thinking about scholarship done only for the Christian community, although that clearly has its place, but of scholarship that genuinely contributes to the commons.

We should therefore not underestimate what is at stake in Christian scholarship making its own contribution to the commons. In his highly creative three-volume work, *Sacred Order / Social Order*, the Jewish sociologist Philip Rieff titles volume 1 *My Life amidst the Deathworks*. He argues that the work of culture is always to translate sacred order into social order and that the health of societies depends on a "vertical in authority," which he playfully abbreviates to "via": "Our own motions in sacred order are locatable once each of us has restored to himself the notion of sacred order. The basic restorative is to understand the purity and inviolate nature of the vertical in authority. Those arbitrary meanings warranted not by any man, but by the one God, are necessary if we are to find some safety in any world."[28]

Rieff argues that we are entering into a "third culture," which abandons the *via* with devastating consequences. "Happiness means that sense of being blessed in our lives, and the pursuit of the good life in its modest forms comes from obeying the commanding truths inseparable from creation."[29] However, "the self-dispossession of the world of commanding truths is the project of modern culture."[30] These commanding truths are

> Nots. As my grandfather well knew, before permission there must be prohibition. This is true in first world taboos and second world commanding truths. The

---

26. See C. G. Bartholomew, *Where Mortals Dwell: A Christian View of Place for Today* (Grand Rapids: Baker Academic, 2011), 21.

27. N. Wolterstorff, *Justice: Rights and Wrongs* (Princeton: Princeton University Press, 2008), 180–206.

28. P. Rieff, *My Life among the Deathworks: Illustrations of the Aesthetics of Authority*, ed. K. S. Piver, vol. 3 of *Sacred Order / Social Order* (Charlottesville: University of Virginia Press, 2006), 13.

29. Ibid., 176.

30. Ibid., 184.

unprecedented character of the abolitionist movements is that they are against taboos and commanding truths. . . . The word, not nature, is primordial, and the word was with God and the word was God.[31]

Rieff's work requires detailed engagement, but the basic insight is right: the health of the world and our cultures depends on their relationship to God. Similarly, there is John Carroll's profound diagnosis of Western culture today[32] and in particular of the crisis of the university. Carroll is clear that the university "requires a unifying vision,"[33] and he declares:

> The humanist university has run down. The Christian university founded in medieval form, is too culturally alien to the contemporary West to be revived. Likewise the church, the one institution that could replace the university as the master teacher of eternal truths, is in a state of hopeless disrepair. Yet the university is here to stay, for a bureaucratically organised society will, of its nature, maintain an educational hierarchy with the universities at the pinnacle.[34]

Carroll is sure that the "first problem is one of faith. The entire story of the failure of upper-middle-class nerve in modernity is one of the loss of a place to stand."[35] Indeed, "the search for meaning is predicated on some kind of knowing of the mystery of things beyond."[36] But Carroll despairs of the church being up to the challenge.

Rieff may be too negative about contemporary culture, and one may need to complement his work with that of Charles Taylor, for example, in looking for the redemptive moments in modern culture.[37] In my view, Carroll is too negative about the potential of Christianity to provide a unifying vision for the university and culture today. Either way, the sustained engagement with our culture—at the highest and most practical levels, by particular religious traditions, and not least by Christianity—is of great importance at this time. *Christian scholarship matters.*

---

31. Ibid., 190–91.
32. J. Carroll, *Humanism: The Wreck of Western Culture* (London: Fontana, 1993).
33. Ibid., 154.
34. Ibid., 155.
35. Ibid.
36. Ibid., 159.
37. C. Taylor, *The Malaise of Modernity* (Toronto: House of Anansi, 2003); idem, *Sources of the Self: The Making of the Modern Identity* (Cambridge: Cambridge University Press, 1989); idem, *A Secular Age* (Cambridge, MA: Belknap, 2007); idem, *Modern Social Imaginaries* (Durham, NC: Duke University Press, 2004). Another example of a more positive approach is B. K. Ward, *Redeeming the Enlightenment: Christianity and the Liberal Virtues* (Grand Rapids: Eerdmans, 2010).

2. *Christian scholarship does not claim to have an exclusive hold on the truth.* God alone possesses the truth; while we do argue, as does Newbigin, that Christ is *the* clue to the whole creation, this clue has to be pursued. In many, many subjects, non-Christians are brighter and more insightful than most Christians. With Augustine, Christian scholarship recognizes that all truth is God's truth and remains open to learning from any and all. What cannot be conceded, however, is the starting point in Christ, or as Proverbs (9:10) puts it, "The fear of the LORD is the beginning of wisdom."[38] As the space is created in the context of a generous pluralism and as Christian scholarship flourishes, across the academic spectrum more dialogue needs to be opened up with dialogue partners wherever they are open to such dialogue.

3. *Scripture should play a foundational role in Christian scholarship.* This follows logically from our exploration of the scope of Scripture in our discussion of preaching and interpretation. Scripture is that field in which we find hidden the pearl of great price, and when that pearl is found, it needs to adorn all our work. Augustine similarly uses an economic metaphor for the teaching of Christ, calling it "the Lord's money to be distributed."[39] The Christ found in Scripture is the creator and redeemer, and from this perspective it would be madness, indeed rebellion, not to take the witness of Scripture seriously in all our attempts to understand the world, which is rightly Christ's. Scripture is to be lavishly distributed in our scholarship as a means by which we spread the fragrance of Christ's presence (2 Cor. 2:14–16) in his world and contribute to the health of our world for all its citizens. This means that Christian scholars will need to be grounded in ecclesial reception of Scripture and lectio divina *and also* be aware of the best biblical scholarship. Intriguingly, in the medieval era the Psalter embodied this sort of dual role: "the Psalter served not only as the daily text in the recitation of the monastic hours and in the liturgy but, because of that central position, also became both the educational primer and the most studied text of the Middle Ages."[40]

Biblical studies clearly has a crucial role to play in making the Lord's money available to other scholars. This is, however, easier said than done, and there are not a multitude of great examples to cite. Below we will refer to some

---

38. See G. von Rad's insightful comments in this respect in his *Wisdom in Israel* (Nashville: Abingdon, 1972).

39. Augustine, *Instructing Beginners in Faith* [*Catechizing the Uninstructed*] 1.2, translated, introduced, and annotated by R. Canning, ed. B. Ramsey (Hyde Park, NY: New City, 2006), 55.

40. G. H. Brown, "The Psalms as the Foundation of Anglo-Saxon Learning," in *The Place of the Psalms in the Intellectual Culture of the Middle Ages*, ed. N. van Deusen (Albany: State University of New York Press, 1999), 3. Cf. M. P. Kuczynski, "The Psalms and Social Action in Late Medieval England," in *The Place of the Psalms in the Intellectual Culture of the Middle Ages*, ed. N. van Deusen (Albany: State University of New York Press, 1999), 191–214.

models of good practice. For now it is important to identify two dangers that need to be avoided. First, there is the danger of mistaking Scripture for a scientific textbook that provides all the answers we need in different disciplines. Such an approach often parades as a high view of Scripture, but it actually diminishes Scripture by expecting it to answer questions it never intended to answer. There certainly *are* areas of life that Scripture addresses directly and that should be taken seriously in the relevant disciplines. Examples are Scripture's clear teaching in relation to family life and sexuality. Yet in many areas of modern life, Scripture has nothing directly to say, and it is a dangerous mistake to try to force it in this direction. An example I often use with my students is the development of a theory of rape counseling. Clearly this is an important enterprise; if done well, it can help bring healing to victims of rape. Nevertheless, nowhere is such a theory to be found in Scripture. Does Scripture then have nothing to contribute to such a theory?

This brings us to our second danger, that of restricting the scope of Scripture to personal and church life. If the first danger is that of *biblicism*, the danger here is that of *dualism*.[41] Scripture *is* authoritative for all of life, but *how*? That is the crucial question. In my view, Scripture orients us toward the world in a particular way, and we need to take this orientation as authoritative. Take anthropology, our view of the human person, as an example. Scripture certainly does not provide us with a *philosophical* anthropology; instead, it orients us toward a particular understanding of what it means to be human, and that orientation needs to be taken seriously, even in developing a theory of rape counseling. Any theory of counseling will *eo ipso* assume a certain anthropology, and a Christian theory of rape counseling should be informed by a scriptural anthropology. Certainly there is far more to the ecology of such a theory than Scripture. For example, it needs to be informed by empirical research into the effect of rape on victims, but our point here is that Scripture, appropriately understood, should function authoritatively within that ecology.

---

41. See Milbank, "The Last of the Last," who traces this dualism between "theology" and reason back to Cajetan's reception of Thomas Aquinas. He sees the thirteenth century as the major time of transition: "What has been outgrown is not a natural childhood, but a noninnocent childhood of error which need never have happened—which is not at all to say that we should have remained forever in the culture of the twelfth and thirteenth centuries. No, it is an unknown future that we have missed and must seek to rejoin" (243). To tell his story, Milbank draws on M. de Certeau, *The Mystic Fable* (Chicago: University of Chicago Press, 1992); O. Boulnois, *Être et représentation: Une généalogie de la métaphysique moderne à l'époque de Duns Scot, XIIIe–XIVe siècle* (Paris: Presses Universitaires de France, 1999); Jean-Luc Marion; Jean-Yves Lacoste; and others. Cf. Küng, "God: The Last Taboo?," 51–56. I am more optimistic about the Reformed and Calvinist tradition than is Milbank.

All of this raises the issue of the shape of such an ecology, and it is to such a model that we will turn below. Before we do that, we call attention to the important work of the British theologian David Ford. In his *Christian Wisdom: Desiring God and Learning in Love*, Ford does indeed attend to the relationship between faith, wisdom, and the university, particularly in relationship to the University of Cambridge. David Ford's work is always stimulating, biblically engaged, and evocative, and *Christian Wisdom* is no exception. In my view, however, he is overly hopeful that, amid the religious and disciplinary diversity of a university like Cambridge, serious dialogue can and will lead to wisdom. Theology has become multifaith at Cambridge, and it is hard to imagine any of the major disciplines there taking Scripture and a Christian perspective seriously in their academic work. Chapels abound, and so does stunning Christian architecture, but one suspects that nowadays the major work of Cambridge proceeds without serious attention to the Christian tradition.

In recent years David Ford has been involved in and written on an emerging practice called *scriptural reasoning*.[42] In his response to Habermas, Nicholas Adams appeals to this practice as a possible way forward for the public involvement of theology.[43] Scriptural reasoning is a contemporary form of interfaith dialogue, and without doubt it is valuable in the global context today, where we are witnessing a major resurgence of religion. One does wonder, however, whether the elephant in the room is not the lack of identifying secular humanism—Habermas, for example—also as a dialogue partner, with its own religious commitments.[44] Either way, scriptural reasoning is a very different entity from what I have in mind in this chapter. In my view, it is only as different traditions are allowed the space to come to fruition that creative dialogue can really take place. John Carroll speaks of the need for a new Reformation, and I suggest that we need to think along such lines as we contemplate a renewal of Christian scholarship in our day. Bill Readings rightly explains how the idea of excellence in education has been hijacked by the consumer university, with the result that it has been nearly voided of

---

42. D. F. Ford and C. C. Pecknold, *The Promise of Scriptural Reasoning* (Oxford: Blackwell, 2006); D. F. Ford, "An Interfaith Wisdom: Scriptural Reasoning between Jews, Christians and Muslims," *Modern Theology* 22, no. 3 (2006): 345–66; P. Ochs and N. Levene, *Textual Reasonings: Jewish Philosophy and Text Study at the End of the Twentieth Century* (Grand Rapids: Eerdmans, 2002). See the website for The Society of Scriptural Reasoning at http:/www.scripturalreasoning.org.uk/scriptural_reasoning_covenant.pdf. The Society's Community Ethic and Scriptural Reasoning Covenant make clear what the Society is about.

43. N. Adams, *Habermas and Theology* (Cambridge: Cambridge University Press, 2006), 234–55.

44. Newbigin perceptively noted that the West is the great missionary challenge today. See his *Foolishness to the Greeks: The Gospel and Western Culture* (Grand Rapids: Eerdmans, 1986).

content apart from high placing in university rankings. John Henry Newman argues that "excellence needs a centre," and, we confess, that center is Christ. Our challenge today is the production of scholarship that genuinely stems from that center which is Christ and as a result enhances Christ's reputation in his world and enables the commons of our cultures to flourish *for all*. Such scholarship will therefore need to be biblical.

Toward an Ecology of Christian Scholarship

Redeemer University College, at which I teach, has a fine document among its foundational commitments, The Cross and Our Calling,[45] which needs to be more widely known than it is. The Cross and Our Calling articulates, inter alia, a vision for Christian scholarship that moves from Scripture to worldview to philosophy to particular disciplines. I have no major critique of this approach apart from rethinking the role of theology, but propose that this linear representation of Christian scholarship is better conceived of as an *ecology* of scholarship, with a delicate balance of ingredients, feedbacks, and interactive dimensions that an ecology more accurately evokes.

Scripture and the Ingredients of the Ecology of Christian Scholarship

I propose that we think of the ecology of Christian scholarship as a *tree of knowledge* (see fig. 13.1).

This diagram shows that all scholarship is ultimately rooted in faith. Academic study is never religiously neutral, as is increasingly recognized.[46] With faith comes the conviction that Scripture is God's trustworthy word: as Hamann perceptively states, it interprets *ourselves to ourselves* and provides us with an orientation toward the world as God's good but fallen creation, which is being redeemed. In terms of chapter 3 (above), Scripture tells us the true story of the world and calls us to indwell that story and become an active participant in God's purposes for his creation. The biblical story can be articulated as a worldview, and the discipline of biblical theology plays an important role in deepening our understanding of the unity of Scripture.

---

45. Available at http://www2.redeemer.ca/about/The-Cross-and-our-Calling.pdf.
46. See R. A. Clouser (*The Myth of Religious Neutrality: An Essay on the Hidden Role of Religious Belief in Theories* [Notre Dame, IN: University of Notre Dame Press, 1991]), who argues that all theorists have religious beliefs, which are defined as beliefs in that entity on which everything else depends, but that entity depends on nothing else.

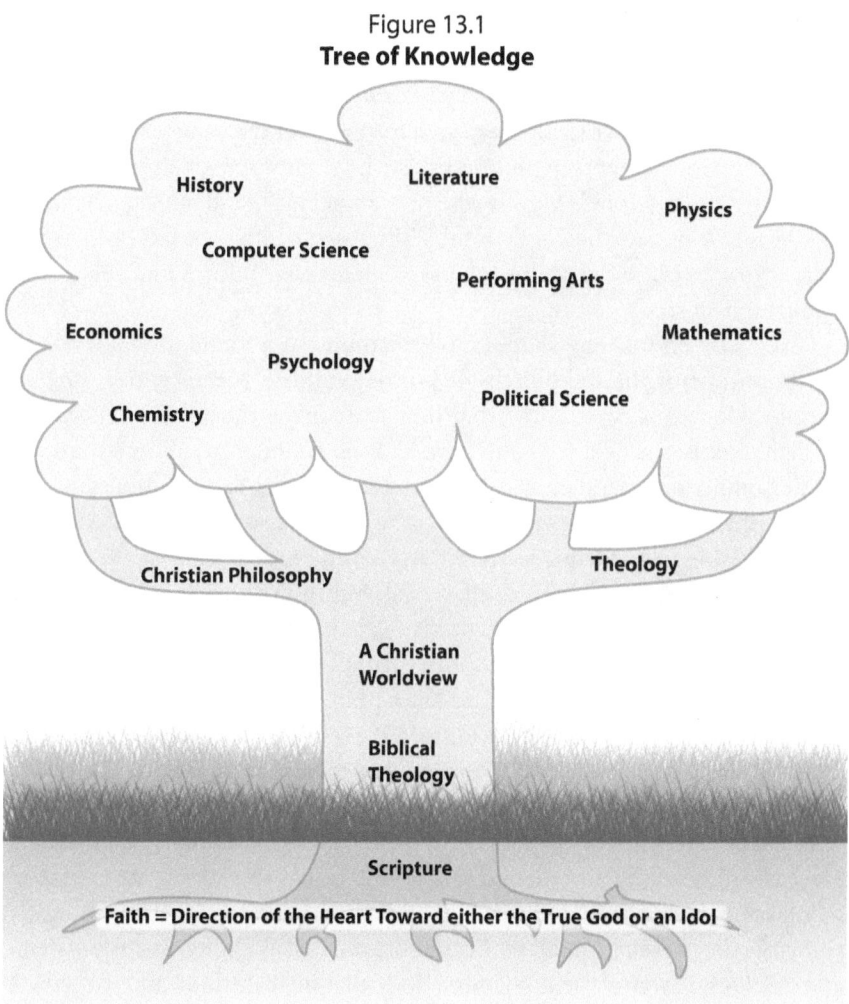

Figure 13.1
Tree of Knowledge

As explained in chapter 3, the biblical story is comprehensive and encompasses all of life, *including biblical studies*. Ecclesial reception of Scripture, in contrast to academic biblical study, is primary (chap. 2), and thus we need to reflect carefully on the role of biblical studies as an *academic* discipline in our ecology. Hence it is helpful to think from the top down rather than from the bottom up!

Charles Taylor makes the point that the deeper and deeper you go into any discipline, including biblical studies, you eventually ask the really foundational questions, and that is *philosophy*. Take epistemology, for example. My working definition is "how to go about knowing something so that you can trust the results of the knowing process." A moment's reflection will reveal that in every course we take or teach, every article/book we write, an epistemology will eo ipso be involved. It cannot fail to be. The problem is that epistemologies are generally at work *unconsciously* and thus powerfully shape a discipline uncritically and undetected. And the same can be said of the other major elements in philosophy, such as ontology (one's view of reality), anthropology (one's view of the human person), and ethics. In chapter 10 (above) we noticed how unhelpful Wellhausen's influence has been in this area, trying to erase the philosophical elements that inform and shape academic biblical study.

Given that philosophy shapes biblical studies at a foundational level, we encounter one of the shibboleths of our day, namely, *the autonomy of philosophy*. Hence the two quotes from John Milbank at the outset of this chapter. Milbank is one of a few who have had the courage to call into question the autonomy of reason and philosophy. Roy Clouser rightly argues that all philosophy ultimately depends on religious beliefs, so that religion or faith is unavoidable in academic work.[47] Even among proponents of theological interpretation, this remains controversial, but in my view it is unavoidable if we are to practice integrally Christian scholarship in biblical studies and to allow Scripture its rightful authority for all of life. Hence arises the importance of the renaissance of Christian philosophy in our day. We do not need to reinvent the wheel: instead, we have a corpus of Christian work to draw on, both in the analytical-philosophical tradition[48] and in the European continental tradition.[49]

A particular distinctive of the tree of knowledge (see fig. 13.1) is that it identifies philosophy and theology as foundational disciplines for Christian scholarship. Here theology should be understood in terms of the *theological encyclopedia*, which includes biblical studies as well as church history, systematic theology, practical theology, missiology, theological ethics, and so forth. A model has its limits, and it is possible that theology should also be positioned as a discipline in the foliage of the tree! Certainly, in such an ecology there will be loops and feedback mechanisms in play all over the place. However, I do think that *dogmatics* and *biblical studies* are foundational disciplines. Historically, what theologians have done is to reflect on God's revelation *in*

---

47. Ibid.
48. William P. Alston, Alvin Plantinga, Nicholas Wolterstorff, C. Stephen Evans, et al.
49. The most exciting development in philosophy today is the so-called theological turn in phenomenology represented by philosophers such as Jean-Luc Marion, Jean-Louis Chrétien, Jean-Yves Lacoste, Michel Henry, Emmanuel Falque, et al. In my opinion it is the continental tradition that holds the most riches for engagement with biblical studies. Cf. Bartholomew and Goheen, *Christian Philosophy*.

Scripture and seek systematically to articulate the central doctrines of the faith for their day. Clearly this kind of work is of foundational importance, and if done well, will be of immeasurable help in any discipline trying to do Christian scholarship. Gordon Spykman, in his *Reformational Theology*, makes the point, for example, that a theology of the human person orients us biblically in terms of the human person, and that any work on anthropology will need to be normed by such an orientation. This will need further theoretical development to become a systematic view of the human person, whether in theology or philosophy. So too with biblical studies. If we are looking for a type of Christian scholarship deeply engaged with the biblical text, as I suggest we should, then thorough biblical work that reads the text for all of life will be indispensable.

The relationship between systematic theology and philosophy is controversial.[50] As is evident from the tree of knowledge (see fig. 13.1), in my view both should work out of a Christian worldview. The relationship between worldview and philosophy-theology is likewise controversial.[51] Mike Goheen and I define a worldview as follows: "*Worldview is an articulation of the basic beliefs embedded in a shared grand story which are rooted in a faith commitment and which give shape and direction to the whole of our individual and corporate lives.*"[52] A worldview is not yet tightly theoretical, but it is more systematic than an articulation of the biblical grand story. A worldview attempts to articulate the major elements of the biblical story and their coherence such that it can shape a Christian mind. In our *Christian Philosophy*, Goheen and I argue that a worldview can yield—be developed into—a philosophy and a theology.

But how then do philosophy and theology relate to each other?[53] I propose that we conceive of their relationship symbiotically or, to use a theological term, perichoretically. Christian philosophy will need to be conscious of the doctrines of the faith as it develops; the more theology becomes systematic, the more it will need foundational insights from Christian philosophy. Such a symbiotic or perichoretic relationship is far less common than it needs to be, and it may be that we need to turn back to someone like Augustine in our quest for such a model. In Augustine we find no sharp distinction between

---

50. See, e.g., I. U. Dalferth, *Theology and Philosophy* (Oxford: Blackwell, 1988), which explores seven different models; C. G. Bartholomew, "Uncharted Waters: Philosophy, Theology, and the Crisis in Biblical Interpretation," in *Renewing Biblical Interpretation*, ed. C. G. Bartholomew, C. Greene, and K. Möller (Grand Rapids: Zondervan, 2000).

51. For Albert M. Wolter's typology of the four main views of the relationship, see Bartholomew and Goheen, *Christian Philosophy*, 17–20.

52. C. G. Bartholomew and M. W. Goheen, *Living at the Crossroads: An Introduction to Christian Worldview* (Grand Rapids: Baker Academic, 2008).

53. Cf. chap. 12 above.

theology and philosophy; the two are deeply intertwined in the service of Christian scholarship.

As theology and philosophy develop, they become more and more theoretical, in the sense of becoming systematic, logical, and conceptually tight. The importance of this move should not be underestimated. All theoretical work in every discipline requires *concepts* with which to do analysis. As Oliver O'Donovan points out, *sola narratione* will not do when it comes to—in his case—political theology.[54] A conceptual framework is required, and then the question becomes whether this is normed by Scripture or embraced apart from Scripture, an issue that David Kelsey has explored in detail.[55] With O'Donovan, I argue that the *discrimen* for taking hold of Scripture as a whole should emerge from *within* Scripture and that concepts need to be normed by Scripture, albeit mediated through a worldview and philosophy/theology. At this level of concepts and frameworks for theoretical work, a healthy philosophy and theology pays dividends.

From the above discussion, it will be obvious that the ecology of (Christian) scholarship is complex! Many of the best scholars practice Christian scholarship intuitively. Nevertheless, there is much to be gained from becoming conscious of the key elements in such an ecology if we are serious about Christian scholarship. Far more work needs to be done in this area; meanwhile I welcome criticism of and development of my tree of knowledge. What must *not* be missed is that in all scholarship there is *always already* an ecology in operation; hence we need help in becoming aware of the ecologies at work in our own and other scholarship.

Clearly in my proposed model, Scripture is of fundamental importance. At the base of the tree it functions ecclesially as the Word of the living God, which shows us who we are and orients us to the world as God's good creation. This role is *never* abandoned and needs to be carried with us along the journey of scholarship. The Christian biblical scholar needs to be as at home in receiving the preached word and in lectio divina as in the most rigorous linguistic analysis of a word in a text.

In terms of our tree, a worldview mediates the norming relationship between Scripture and philosophy-theology. It is thus of great consequence that we are clear how a Christian worldview is grounded in Scripture and emerges out of Scripture, a theme that Goheen and I have addressed in *The Drama of Scripture* and *Living at the Crossroads*. In my experience, even among

---

54. O. O'Donovan, *The Desire of the Nations: Rediscovering the Roots of Political Theology* (Cambridge: Cambridge University Press, 1996).

55. D. Kelsey, *The Uses of Scripture in Recent Theology* (Philadelphia: Fortress, 1975).

scholars who are well acquainted with a Christian worldview, there is often a significant lack of awareness as to how a worldview is grounded in Scripture. The danger of this will be obvious; such a worldview can take on a life of its own and be absolutized or, ironically, easily discarded.

In his superb book *The Spirit of Early Christian Thought*, Robert Wilken aims to "show how a Christian intellectual tradition came into being, how Christians thought about the things they believed."[56] The early church, according to Wilken, achieved the "Christianization of Hellenism." How did it achieve this transformation? In multiple ways, but Wilken reports:

> What has impressed me most is the omnipresence of the Bible in early Christian writings. Early Christian thought is biblical, and one of the lasting accomplishments of the patristic period was to forge a way of thinking, scriptural in language and inspiration, that gave to the church and to Western civilization a unified and coherent interpretation of the Bible as a whole.[57]

When the early Christians read the Bible, they were overwhelmed. "It came upon them like a torrent leaping down the side of a mountain."[58] The Bible both formed a community and gave that community a language. According to Wilken, it is in the writings of Clement of Alexandria that the Bible first emerges as the foundation for a Christian culture. On average there are seven or eight citations of Scripture on every page of his works. "When he cites the Scriptures there is a sense of discovery, that something extraordinary is to be learned in its pages, that it is not one book among many. For Clement the Bible was a source of revelation and instruction, 'our wisdom,' as he called it in one place."[59]

It is sadly rare nowadays to find Christian scholarship that is even comparably biblically engaged. In theology two figures stand out to me: Karl Barth's *Church Dogmatics* is remarkable in that as his conceptual framework takes hold, he does more and not less exegesis. Oliver O'Donovan's *The Desire of the Nations* is similar in this respect. In philosophy two comparable figures are Hamann and Kierkegaard, both of whose writings *require* a biblical index. How then do we pursue the tree of knowledge without letting go of Scripture?

Calvin can help us here. He wrote his *Institutes* to help Christians read the Bible better! Alas, nowadays we tend to envisage the move from Scripture to

---

56. R. L. Wilken, *The Spirit of Early Christian Thought: Seeking the Face of God* (New Haven: Yale University Press, 2003), xiv.
57. Ibid., xvii.
58. Ibid., 53.
59. Ibid., 57.

worldview and theology or philosophy, but not the other way around. It has long seemed to me that a healthy philosophy, theology, and worldview will lead to deeper engagement with Scripture and not to its far too common neglect.

But how are we to reengage Scripture in our scholarship? Intriguingly, on this issue Wilken refers to Irenaeus's approach to Scripture as a single story.[60] This, I argue, provides an important clue to *a* major way of ensuring that Scripture remains fully engaged in our scholarship. In this way we return to where we began in chapter 3 (above), perhaps now to understand our starting point more fully. We need a way to grasp Scripture in its totality and allow it to grasp us in an ongoing fashion in our scholarly work. As Newbigin alerts us, we need to *indwell* the story of the Bible so that it increasingly becomes our default mode—our home away from home—amid our life and scholarship. Thus an indispensable element in Christian scholarship must be a renewed sense of *tota Scriptura*. Scripture is God's Word in its totality, and it is as such that we need to bring it into engagement with our scholarship. This is no easy task in our day, when biblical scholarship has contributed to an endless fragmenting of the Bible into thousands of irreconcilable pieces. Fortunately scholars like Tom Wright and some others have insisted on continuing to attend to *the big-picture* aspects of biblical studies. Such approaches are invaluable for the Christian scholar.

The significance of a genuine recovery of the biblical story in contemporary language should not be underestimated. In his work *The Existential Jesus*, John Carroll asserts, "The waning of Christianity as practiced in the West is easy to explain. The Christian churches have comprehensively failed in their one central task—to retell their foundation story in a way that might speak to the times."[61]

Construed in this way, the biblical story provides a hermeneutic for understanding our world and our times. The Christian church is in the fifth act (see chap. 3 above), and we are called to use all the insights from the others to live fully for Christ today, including via our scholarship and teaching. As scholars and teachers, we are called to witness to Christ *in our teaching and scholarship*. Scripture needs to become that story in which we are deeply at home so that we can begin to discern the crossroads at which the biblical story and our cultural/disciplinary story intersect. This crossroads,[62] as Newbigin pointed out, is the place of mission, the place of a painful tension. Christian scholarship will feel this tension as it seeks to be faithful to Christ, to recognize

---

60. Cf. Fowl, "Scripture in an Ecclesially Based University," 172–74.
61. J. Carroll, *The Existential Jesus* (Berkeley: Counterpoint, 2007), 7.
62. See Goheen and Bartholomew, *Living at the Crossroads*.

the positive elements in contemporary scholarship, and to stand antithetically against other elements. Inter alia, this will mean a deep acquaintance with *the story of our discipline* within which we labor. Years ago I learned from the Canadian aesthetician Calvin Seerveld that if things are unhealthy in the present state of your discipline, you need to go back in its history to find healthy nodes and then transfuse these into the present. This is impossible without an ability to tell the story of one's discipline.

A major challenge for Christian scholarship is thus to become intimately acquainted with the biblical story[63] *and* the story of one's discipline, then to consciously live at the intersection of both. As I have discovered in Old Testament studies and in philosophy, the way in which the story of a discipline is told is far from neutral.[64] Only in this way will the challenges of the discipline become conscious, and then we can begin to orient ourselves toward our discipline to embrace its riches and to work to reorient its distortions.

Christian Scholarship and Cultural Analysis

The early church shaped a distinctive intellectual culture in *its* context. We need to do it in *ours*. But what exactly is our context? Is it postmodernity, late modernity, ultramodernity, globalization, or what? John Stott helpfully emphasizes the need for us to learn to listen with both ears, what he called "double listening," one ear attuned to Scripture, the other to our culture. In order to live effectively at the crossroads, Christian cultural analysis is essential. When Tom Wright wrote his monumental *The New Testament and the People of God*, he wisely added a question to Brian Walsh and J. Richard Middleton's diagnostic questions for a worldview: "What time is it in our culture?"[65] George Weigel poignantly remembers that John Paul II scouted out the future in order to discern how to lead the church in its mission to the world.

This missional question is vital if we are to practice missional scholarship. We will need some sense of where we are in Western culture at this time and

---

63. Fowl ("Scripture in an Ecclesially Based University") notes the challenge this presents to Bible and theology faculty, let alone those in other disciplines, because of the lack of integration in theological training. He rightly declares, "Faculty are going to need to learn how to teach against the grain of their theological training" (174). An excellent practice would be for every faculty member to take a turn in teaching the biblical story as a core part of the curriculum.

64. See, e.g., Bartholomew and Goheen, *Christian Philosophy*; Bartholomew, "Uncharted Waters."

65. See B. J. Walsh and J. R. Middleton, *The Transforming Vision: Shaping a Christian World View* (Downers Grove, IL: InterVarsity, 1984), 35.

place, as well as a sense of where biblical studies is at this time and place. The two are integrally related. This is a fascinating but challenging time in the history of the world, and we need the insights of scholars like Philip Jenkins and others to begin to orient us in relation to the challenges of our day. John Stott suggests that we discern our vocation by asking two questions: "What are our gifts?" "What are the needs of the day?" Then we need to stretch our gifts to relate to the needs of the day.

Such cultural analysis will also alert us to the urgent need for *interdisciplinary* engagement.[66] A legacy of the German philosophy of the university is separate and separated disciplines, but the great need of our day is for connectivity. Cultural analysis will require input from all disciplines, and all disciplines will need one another if we are to genuinely produce significant Christian scholarship today.

Back to That Ecology Again

I have hinted (above) at the advantages of an ecological model of Christian scholarship versus a linear one. This is vital for a number of reasons.

1. It alerts us to the fact that the Christian biblical scholar does not need to become a philosopher or theologian in order to do Christian scholarship. You are *already* doing scholarship, and an ecology is *already* at work in your scholarship. The vital point is to become aware of the different elements in that ecology and to work hard to strengthen the weak areas.

2. To do this we will undoubtedly need one another, that is, Christian scholarly community and genuine interdisciplinarity. Fowl rightly declares: "Especially in ecclesially based universities, we cannot think and reflect on the curriculum apart from its maintenance and execution by a concrete community of scholars. What and how we teach shapes and is shaped by the sorts of people we are, the friendships we form, and the departments and institutions we inhabit."[67]

The reader should notice the need for feedback loops and connecting lines in the tree diagram (above). Indeed, in a Christian scholarly community, one envisages a situation in which we are shuttling back and forth from classes and offices, drinking endless *leisurely* cups of coffee (and other drinks?!) together, as we wrestle with the shape of Christian scholarship in particular

---

66. Or what Eric Johnson and I prefer to call "transdisciplinary scholarship." In our view the agenda of "integration" has largely failed at Christian institutions: we need a new paradigm for Christian scholarship.

67. Fowl, "Scripture in an Ecclesially Based University," 175.

areas. In political theory, imagine a discussion on the civil rights of gays in North American culture today. Would this not be enriched by

- a historical perspective?
- insights from biblical scholars?
- insights from psychologists?
- insights from theologians?
- insights from sociologists? And so forth.

3. Critical questions can emerge from any part of the ecology and not just from the bottom up. Indeed, I suspect that the most interesting discussions will ensue from the bottom-down questions. Imagine a biblical scholar struggling with the experience of Job and whether the book of Job makes sense as a unity (most Old Testament scholars think it does not). Would not such a discussion be immeasurably enriched by psychological insight? And enriched by the history of art and dramatic and literary representation of Job? In almost any discussion, our foreign-language teachers could be of immense help in bringing the riches of other-language intellectual cultures to bear on our discussions.

This chapter has presented a plea for taking Scripture with the utmost seriousness in scholarship, but my hunch is that if this were to take place, it would also *transform biblical interpretation*. For much of modern biblical interpretation, the discipline has been turned incestuously in on itself until doctorates are done on smaller and smaller fragments of the Bible. A repositioning of biblical studies within Christian scholarship would compel biblical scholars to engage with a raft of questions they often never consider. Just how fertile this can prove is evident in Ellen Davis's excellent *Scripture, Culture, and Agriculture*,[68] in which she opens up a dialogue between the new agrarianism—Wendell Berry in particular—and the Old Testament. Suddenly books like Leviticus—yes, Leviticus!—come alive and contemporary in ways we had not imagined. Issues of food production and consumption are suddenly "on the table," and the agribusiness of the day is under the critical spotlight of Scripture.

4. An ecology is organic, and one becomes familiar with it by practice and by immersion in outstanding examples of good practice. There is value in attempting to map the ecology as I have done; yet each discipline will have its own delightful eccentricities, and invariably a healthy ecology in one's

---

68. E. F. Davis, *Scripture, Culture, and Agriculture: An Agrarian Reading of the Bible* (Cambridge: Cambridge University Press, 2009).

discipline will emerge from actually doing scholarship and teaching. It would, for example, be helpful to identify outstanding examples of scholarship in one's area—Christian and non-Christian—and then take a close look at them to discern the ecologies at work. What are the ingredients that contributed to such good work? Are some elements missing that would improve the work? What role does Scripture play in the particular ecology of a discipline, and what difference does it make? And so on.

Conclusion: *It's Personal!*

Amid a time of nauseating mediocrity, the call to Christian scholarship is great and humbling. Who are we to contribute to the great challenges of our day? Personally, I take great comfort from Lewis Mumford's tome on the history of the city in the West.[69] He reports that even as the Roman Empire was collapsing inwardly and in a terrible state of decay, the answer was waiting in the wings. It was available in microcosm in the monasteries. Medieval society was the macrocosm of which the monasteries were the microcosm. Let us not despise the day of small things but be faithful in the opportunities available to us, continually aspiring to excellence in genuinely Christian scholarship that seeks to contribute to the flourishing of all. Such excellence will not be possible without a recovery of Scripture as foundational to Christian scholarship.

In the Christian tradition, unlike the Greek one, truth is a person first of all and not propositions alone. Amid the malaise of pluralism and postmodernism, we should make the goal of our scholarship to *tell the truth*. In order to do this, we also need to live *in the truth*, ever more deeply into Christ:

> Study itself is a divine office, an indirect divine office; it seeks out and honors the traces of the Creator, or His images, according as it investigates nature or humanity; but it must make way at the right moment for direct intercourse with Him. If we forget to do this, not only do we neglect a great duty, but the image of God in creation comes between us and Him, and His traces only serve to lead us far from Him to whom they bear witness.[70]

---

69. L. Mumford, *The City in History: Its Origins, Its Transformation, and Its Prospects* (New York: MJF Books, 1998).
70. Sertillanges, *The Intellectual Life*, 28–29.

Part 5

The Goal of Biblical Interpretation

14

The "Epistle" to the Hebrews

But We Do See Jesus

> We cannot venture into the Bible as tourists; we must become inhabitants of the land. . . . To become part of this world we must enter it, immerse ourselves in it in order to be absorbed by it.
>
> M. Magrassi[1]

Hebrews

In this penultimate chapter, we will focus on one book of the Bible, Hebrews, and seek to bring the long journey we have been on to a penultimate conclusion in a close examination of it. In keeping with the hermeneutic we have outlined, our aim will be to listen for God's address through Hebrews. The reader might rightly wonder, why *Hebrews*? For one reason, it is not too long! Indeed, the author describes it as "brief" (13:22) in his epistolary conclusion. However, this is clearly not sufficient motivation.

In much ecclesial and scholarly life, Hebrews is marginal; yet as I have worked on it and come to appreciate its extraordinary riches, it has struck me

---

1. M. Magrassi, *Praying the Bible: An Introduction to Lectio Divina*, trans. E. Hagman (Collegeville, MN: Liturgical Press, 1998), 68.

that it is comparable to Romans in the New Testament. Romans is a letter, but as Paul unpacks "the gospel of God" (1:1), it grows far beyond the normal limits of a letter, exploring the expanding largesse of the gospel. Scholars continue to debate whether Hebrews is a letter, as we will see below, but whether a rewritten sermon or a letter, it expands far beyond these genres as the author unpacks the fact that in these last days, God "has spoken to us by a Son" (1:2). In very different and yet complementary ways, both these New Testament books unpack the Christ event *in depth*; thus they are worthy of close attention. Hebrews is utterly christological and is exemplary for biblical theology. Indeed, Guthrie insightfully characterizes Hebrews:

> Its astute scholar has crafted what might be called the "Queen" when it comes to the use of the OT in the NT. No NT book, with perhaps the exception of Revelation, presents a discourse so permeated, so crafted, both at the macro- and microlevels, by various uses to which the older covenant texts are put, and his appropriation of the text is radically different from the book's apocalyptic cousin.[2]

Furthermore, Hebrews is designed to be heard as a "word of exhortation" (13:22). "For more than any other NT book, Hebrews, from beginning to end, *preaches* the OT. . . . His Christology vies for a christocentric life."[3] As I have deepened my knowledge of Hebrews, it has struck me that this is a book we would do well to recover to a greater extent in the church today. If "we would see Jesus" (cf. 2:9; John 12:21 KJV), then this is an indispensable part of the canon.

Lectio Divina

Interpretation, we have argued, should emerge out of and return to ecclesial reception of Hebrews. The genre of Hebrews is that of a "word of exhortation" (13:22), a reminder that Hebrews is not presented to us simply for analysis, but first of all for *listening*. As Lane states, "Hebrews was crafted to communicate its point as much aurally as logically."[4] In 2:9 the author tells us that "we do see Jesus," and it fits entirely with Hebrews to find a mode of listening to and studying it that enables us to surface again and again in the presence of Jesus, so that after all our listening and work, we too are able to say, "*But* we do *see Jesus.*"

---

2. G. H. Guthrie, "Hebrews," in *Commentary on the New Testament Use of the Old Testament*, ed. G. K. Beale and D. A. Carson (Grand Rapids: Baker Academic, 2007), 919.
3. Ibid., 923, with original emphasis.
4. W. L. Lane, *Hebrews 1–8*, WBC 47A (Dallas: Word Books, 1991), lxxv.

Lectio is a practice, and it is hard to enact it in a chapter like this. Nevertheless, I encourage the reader to intersperse the reading of this chapter and the study of Hebrews with the practice of lectio on sections of Hebrews. We will start with an outline of a suggested practice[5] and then punctuate the chapter with reminders to return to lectio with suggested passages.

1. *Entering into the silence.* Take five minutes to slow down and become centered in Jesus. Let the thoughts and stresses of the day go, and . . . be still. Choose a prayer word—if you don't have one, I suggest "Jesus"—and repeat it as you breathe in and out, opening yourself to God.
2. *The presence of God.* Hebrews is all about the presence of God and how our great high priest, Jesus, has opened the way for us into God's presence. To be present is to arrive as we are and open up to the other. At this instant, as we pause in our reading of this chapter, God is present and waiting for us. He arrives before us, desiring to connect with us even more than our most intimate friend. We take a moment to greet our living God, who comes to us in Jesus.
3. *Freedom.* "In these days God taught me as a schoolteacher teaches a pupil" (Ignatius of Loyola). We remind ourselves that there are things God has to teach us yet, and we ask for the grace to hear them and to be changed by them.
4. *Consciousness.* How am I really feeling? We acknowledge how we really are. Jesus, we remind ourselves, became fully human and was tempted as we are. He is able to "sympathize with our weaknesses" (4:15). It is the real me that the Lord loves.
5. *The Word.* We take time to read Hebrews 1:1–4 slowly, a few times, allowing ourselves to dwell on anything that strikes us.
6. *Conversation.* What feelings rise up in me as I pray and reflect on Hebrews 1:1–4? I imagine Jesus himself sitting in a chair opposite me, and I open my heart to him and share with him my thoughts, feelings, reflections.
7. *Conclusion.* Now may the God of peace, who through the blood of the eternal covenant brought back from the dead our Lord Jesus, that great shepherd of the sheep, equip you with everything good for doing his will, and may he work in us what is pleasing to him, through Jesus Christ, to whom be glory for ever and ever.
Amen. (Heb. 13:20–21 NIV)

---

5. Here I follow the wonderfully creative work of the Irish Jesuits in their website and book, *Sacred Space.* www.sacredspace.ie/.

Canonicity and Authorship

In our use of lectio, we have approached Hebrews as canonical, but it is one of a few New Testament books whose canonicity was contested in the early church. *First Clement*, written from Rome to the church in Corinth in the late first century or early second century AD, manifests clear knowledge and use of Hebrews.[6] As a pastoral letter, *1 Clement* is deliberative in style, sent to Corinth because of the disruptions the church there was experiencing. In terms of reception history, the author of *1 Clement* has rightly understood the hortatory horizon of Hebrews and appropriately draws on it to address the church at Corinth: "This is the way, dear friends, in which we have found our salvation, namely Jesus Christ, the High Priest of our offerings, the Guardian and Helper of our weakness."[7] Hebrews is likewise known and used by Justin, Irenaeus, and Hippolytus, all of whom recognized that it was not written by Paul.[8]

Amid the persecution the early church experienced, an issue they struggled with was how to handle those who lapsed from their faith. Thus Tertullian appeals to Hebrews, which he thinks was written by Barnabas, to argue *against* a second, postbaptismal repentance.[9] This issue plus questions about its authorship led to Roman Christians excluding Hebrews from the Pauline Letters canon in the late second and early third centuries. The Muratorian Canon, for example, makes no mention of Hebrews.[10]

In the East, Hebrews was accepted as authoritative by the end of the second century. Western fathers who spent time in the East were influenced by such views, and late in the fourth century agreement was reached between East and West that Hebrews was a fourteenth letter of Paul. Jerome's and Augustine's influence was decisive on this question.[11]

---

6. G. L. Cockerill, "Heb 1:1–14, *1 Clem.* 36.1–6, and the High Priest Title," *Journal of Biblical Literature* 97 (1978): 437–40; P. Ellingworth, "Hebrews and *1 Clement*: Literary Dependence or Common Tradition?," *Biblische Zeitschrift* 23 (1979): 262–69.

7. *1 Clement* 36, in M. W. Holmes, ed., *The Apostolic Fathers: Greek Texts and English Translations*, updated ed. (Grand Rapids: Baker Books, 1999).

8. W. L. Lane, *Hebrews 1–8*, clii.

9. Tertullian, *Modesty* 20.3. Calvin opposed the medieval view that Heb. 6:4–6 denies second baptism. See K. Hagen, *Hebrews Commenting from Erasmus to Bèze, 1516–1598* (Tübingen: Mohr, 1981), 64. For a discussion of interpretive proposals for Heb. 6 through the centuries, see P. E. Hughes, *A Commentary on the Epistle to the Hebrews* (Grand Rapids: Eerdmans, 1977), 212–22.

10. The date of the Muratorian Canon is contested. See chap. 8 (above), on "Canon."

11. After its acceptance as canonical, Erasmus was probably the first to express doubts about Pauline authorship. See K. Hagen, *A Theology of Testament in the Young Luther: The Lectures on Hebrews* (Leiden: Brill, 1974), 23–24; see 24–30 for Luther's views. Calvin denied Pauline authorship of Hebrews. On the history of reception of Hebrews, see Hagen, *Hebrews*

We do not know who wrote Hebrews. However, the connection with eyewitness testimony, a central criterion for canonicity (see chap. 8), is strongly affirmed in the first warning passage, namely, 2:1–4. The author declares that "so great a salvation" was first declared by Jesus and then "attested to us by those who heard him," with God adding his testimony "by gifts of the Holy Spirit." As Koester states, "The concern in Heb. 2:3–4 is to connect the message the listeners received with Jesus himself."[12] The phrase διὰ τοῦ κυρίου has a parallel expression in 1:2, ἐν υἱῷ. As διά and ἐν indicate, "through the Lord" should not be conceived of as merely verbal but denotes a rich view of the church as rooted in *the life and ministry of Jesus*. "Basic to the designation of Jesus as Lord (κύριος), however, is the writer's conception of the unity of word and deed in Jesus's ministry. Jesus's word is not simply information about salvation.... He embodied the word of God and accomplished it."[13]

The question in 2:3a is rhetorical: "How can we escape if we neglect so great a salvation?" The implication is clear: such is the enormity of the Christ event that there will be no escape if it is neglected. Then 12:25 speaks of the possibility of *refusing* the one who is speaking. Clearly what is at stake in Hebrews is far more than the reception of information. This emphasis connects with the discussion of Application A in chapter 15 (below) on preaching and the Bible.[14] Hebrews will not let the reader off the hook and calls for a deeply *involved* reading. Certainly, from the author's perspective, one will read the letter differently depending on one's view of Jesus.

The link between the church of Hebrews and the Christ event is established through "at first," "attested to us by those who heard him," and "God added his testimony" (2:3–4). Here we have the kernel of a doctrine of *tradition* in which Christ and apostolic testimony are held in the closest relationship with the recognition that the apostolic testimony is authenticated for the listeners by the Spirit. Lane explains, "The present participle (rendered 'while God endorsed')

Commenting; B. Demarest, *A History of Interpretation of Hebrews 7, 1–10 from the Reformation to the Present* (Tübingen: Mohr, 1976); E. Grässer, *Aufbruch und Verheissung: Gesammelte Aufsätze zum Hebräerbrief* (Berlin: de Gruyter, 1992), 1–99. Martin Luther and Johannes Bugenhagen see Christ as the end of the whole law. For Calvin and most other exegetes of the Reformation era, Christ marks the ends of parts of the OT law, but there is significant continuity so that law and gospel are not in opposition.

12. C. R. Koester, *Hebrews: A New Translation with Introduction and Commentary*, AB 36 (New York: Doubleday, 2001), 211.

13. W. L. Lane, *Hebrews 1–8*, 39. According to H. W. Attridge, *The Epistle to the Hebrews: A Commentary on the Epistle to the Hebrews*, Hermeneia (Philadelphia: Fortress, 1989), "The reference to the Lord does not indicate when the inauguration of his salvific message was to have taken place" (66), but that seems to be beside the point since the whole "Christ event" is in view.

14. J. Y. Jang, "Communicative Preaching: A Homiletical Study in the Light of Hebrews" (PhD diss., North-West University, Potchefstroom, South Africa, 2007).

implies that the corroborative evidence was not confined to the initial act of preaching, but continued to be displayed within the life of the community."[15] It is from this sort of biblical data that Thomas Aquinas and Calvin rightly develop their doctrine of the internal testimony of the Spirit in relationship to Scripture as the Word of God. Indeed, any notion of canonicity needs to hold together the Christ event, the apostolic and eyewitness testimony, and the witness of the Spirit. The vital role of the Spirit in a biblical hermeneutic flows from this, as does the ecclesial context of the reception of the Word as primary. As we say in our chapter (15) on preaching, it is as the Word is preached in the ecclesia that the Spirit loves to apply the Word to the hearts of the hearers and open their lives to the "so great a salvation" made available in Jesus. In his powerful evocation of Mount Zion and the "assembly of the firstborn" in 12:18–25, the author exhorts his readers not to refuse the one who *is speaking*. In 13:7 he encourages his audience, "Remember your leaders, those who *spoke the word of God to you*." Clearly, for the author, the God who "*has* spoken" (1:2) definitively and finally in the Son *continues to speak the same* Word in the ecclesia, as the apostolic testimony is taught and preached. Koester rightly comments, "The author of Hebrews gives a human speech that calls listeners to give attention to divine speech."[16] I would extend this by stating that the author *expects* his audience to hear the divine address through his words.

As we admitted above, we do not know who wrote Hebrews, but the author deliberately establishes the link between himself[17] and the eyewitnesses of Jesus. This is confirmed by the intriguing reference to "our brother Timothy" in 13:23. This Timothy is most likely Paul's coworker and coauthor of several of Paul's Letters and recipient of two of Paul's Letters.[18] If this is correct, then it places the author of Hebrews firmly within Paul's circle so that it is not surprising that Apollos, Barnabas, and Luke have been proposed as possible authors of Hebrews. Indeed, recently there have been renewed attempts to argue that Luke wrote Hebrews.[19] We cannot solve this issue, but it is clear that the author of Hebrews was in intimate contact with the leaders of the early church, so we should presuppose his familiarity with Paul's teaching and the apostolic tradition about Jesus. Hebrews was most likely written around the same time as the Gospels were being published. Lane suggests that Hebrews be dated

---

15. W. L. Lane, *Hebrews 1–8*, 39.
16. Koester, *Hebrews*, 79.
17. The use of the masculine participle in 11:32 ("to tell") confirms that the author was male.
18. Cf. Attridge, *Epistle to the Hebrews*, 409, who agrees with this but argues that Timothy is the "fictional recipient of two letters on church order."
19. D. L. Allen, *Lukan Authorship of Hebrews*, NAC Studies of the Bible & Theology (Nashville: Broadman & Holman, 2010). Cf. R. A. Thiele, "A Reexamination of the Authorship of the Epistle to the Hebrews" (PhD diss., University of Wisconsin–Milwaukee, 2008).

between the aftermath of the great fire in Rome in AD 64 and Nero's suicide in AD 68.[20] We should not assume that the author of Hebrews had access to the written Gospels, but we *should* assume that he was well acquainted with the apostolic tradition that would be or was being written up in the Gospels.[21]

In terms of the recipients of Hebrews, "the cumulative weight of the evidence points to men and women who participate in a small house fellowship, loosely related to other house churches in an urban setting,[22] whose theological vocabulary and conceptions were informed by the rich legacy of Hellenistic Judaism."[23] Proposals for the social location of the congregation range from Jerusalem in the East to Spain in the West; a common view is that they were located in or near Rome, if one is right to read οἱ ἀπὸ τῆς Ἰταλίας (13:24) as in Acts 18:2 to mean "from outside Italy," outside the Italian peninsula.[24] Isaacs raises some penetrating critiques of the Roman view,[25] whether of Rome as the place of origin or destination, and proposes that "a specific historical situation gave rise to the theology we find in Hebrews. Christians of Jewish origin, whether in Judaea or the Diaspora, especially those with a priestly frame of mind, would have mourned the loss of Jerusalem. It is this which is the most likely scenario of our Epistle."[26] Simply put, it is hard to be certain about the provenance or destination of Hebrews.

Genre and Literary Structure

An enormous amount of work has been done since the 1950s on the literary structure of Hebrews, a quest inseparably related to its genre.[27] A background

---

20. Koester (*Hebrews*, 50–54) suggests a date of AD 60–90; and Attridge (*Epistle to the Hebrews*, 6–9) proposes AD 60–100. M. E. Isaacs (*Sacred Space: An Approach to the Theology of the Epistle to the Hebrews*, JSNTSup 73 [Sheffield: Sheffield Academic Press, 1992], 43–44) says that Hebrews may well be written after AD 70.

21. J. L. Terveen, "Jesus in Hebrews: An Exegetical Analysis of the References to Jesus' Earthly Life in the Epistle to the Hebrews" (PhD diss., University of Edinburgh, 1986).

22. The emphasis on the "city" in Hebrews plus the social references in 13:1–6 indicate an urban setting.

23. W. L. Lane, *Hebrews 1–8*, lv.

24. We cannot be sure of this. Cf. P. Ellingworth and E. A. Nida, *Hebrews: A Translator's Handbook on the Letter to the Hebrews* (New York: United Bible Societies, 1983).

25. Isaacs, *Sacred Space*, 35–37. However, cf. E. B. Aitken, "Portraying the Temple in Stone and Text: The Arch of Titus and the Epistle to the Hebrews," in *Hebrews: Contemporary Methods, New Insights*, ed. G. Gelardini, BIS 75 (Leiden: Brill, 2005), 131–48, who argues that Hebrews was composed *in Rome*, shortly after the death of Titus in AD 81.

26. Isaacs, *Sacred Space*, 67.

27. For surveys, see W. L. Lane, *Hebrews 1–8*, lxxxiv–lxxxix; G. H. Guthrie, *The Structure of Hebrews: A Text-Linguistic Analysis*, NovTSup 73 (Leiden: Brill, 1994), 3–41; D. J. MacLeod, "The Literary Structure of the Book of Hebrews," *BSac* 146 (April–June 1989): 185–97.

has been sought in ancient rhetoric with the appropriate recognition that Hebrews embodies both *deliberative* (advising on a course of action in the future) and *epideictic* (reinforcing the present values of the readers) rhetoric.[28] This is helpful but does not take us very far in discerning the genre and structure of Hebrews.

For centuries Hebrews was regarded as a letter, and indeed its conclusion in 13:22–25 has such elements.[29] However, it lacks the typical shape and introductory elements of a letter; hence, during the past two hundred years the view that Hebrews is a sermon with an epistolary ending has become common.[30] The genres of a speech and a letter are not antithetical, but Koester argues that in formal terms the distinction is worth maintaining and that the ancients distinguished between a speech and a letter.[31] Koester does not find the classification of Hebrews as a homily very helpful because we know so little about the shape of Jewish and Christian preaching in the first century.[32]

---

28. For an overview of attempts to apply rhetorical categories to the structure of Hebrews, see D. F. Watson, "Rhetorical Criticism of Hebrews and the Catholic Epistles Since 1978," *Currents in Research: Biblical Studies* 5 (1997): 182–83; C. C. Black II, "The Rhetorical Form of the Hellenistic Jewish and Early Christian Sermon: A Response to Lawrence Wills," *HTR* 81 (1988): 1–18.

29. The following continue to see Hebrews as a letter: P. Ellingworth, *The Epistle to the Hebrews: A Commentary on the Greek Text*, NIGTC (Grand Rapids: Eerdmans, 1993), 59–62; H. Feld, *Der Hebräerbrief*, Erträge der Forschung 28 (Darmstadt: Buchgesellschaft, 1985), 23; S. Kistemaker, *Exposition of the Epistle to the Hebrews* (Grand Rapids: Baker, 1984), 3–4; B. Lindars, *The Theology of the Letter to the Hebrews* (Cambridge: Cambridge University Press, 1991), 6; J. Dunnill, *Covenant and Sacrifice in the Letter to the Hebrews*, SNTSMS 75 (Cambridge: Cambridge University Press, 1992), 72.

30. First proposed by J. Berger, "Der Brief an der Hebräer, eine Homilie," in *Göttinger theologische Bibliothek* 3 (1797): 449–59; since then, this view has been adopted by many scholars, including W. L. Lane, *Hebrews 1–8*, lxix–lxxv; H. W. Attridge, "Paraenesis in a Homily (λόγος παρακλήσεως): The Possible Location of, and the Socialization in, the 'Epistle to the Hebrews,'" *Semeia* 50 (1990): 211–26; and G. L. Cockerill, *The Epistle to the Hebrews*, NICNT (Grand Rapids: Eerdmans, 2012), 11–16. G. Gelardini, "Hebrews, an Ancient Synagogue Homily for *Tisha be-Av*: Its Function, Its Basis, Its Theological Interpretation," in *Hebrews: Contemporary Methods, New Insights*, ed. G. Gelardini, BIS 75 (Leiden: Brill, 2005), argues that Hebrews is an ancient synagogue homily.

31. Koester, *Hebrews*, 81, follows R. D. Anderson, *Ancient Rhetorical Theory and Paul* (Kampen, Netherlands: Kok Pharos, 1996), 93–109. H.-F. Weiss, *Der Brief an der Hebräer*, KEK 13 (Göttingen: Vandenhoeck & Ruprecht, 1991), 40, argues that "word of exhortation" (τοῦ λόγου τῆς παρακλήσεως) in Heb. 13:22 is a technical synagogue term for the sermon following the readings from the Torah and Prophets; cf. Acts 13:15 for the only other use of this phrase in the NT.

32. Koester, *Hebrews*, 81. On Hellenistic Jewish sermons, see F. Siegert, *Drei hellenistisch-jüdische Predigten*, WUNT 61 (Tübingen: Mohr Siebeck, 1992), 1–29; L. Wills, "The Form of the Sermon in Hellenistic Judaism and Early Christianity," *HTR* 77 (1984): 277–99. On rabbinic

To a large extent, therefore, the genre and structure of Hebrews has finally to be determined inductively. In the epistolary conclusion Hebrews 13:22 reads, "I exhort[33] you, therefore, brothers, to give patient attention to[34] my word of exhortation [παρακλήσεως]."[35] The noun παράκλησις is used several times in the New Testament for preaching (Rom. 12:8; 1 Thess. 2:3; 1 Tim. 4:13). Paul encourages Timothy, for example, to "give attention to the public reading of scripture, to exhortation [παρακλήσει], to teaching" (1 Tim. 4:13). Thus the oral, hortatory, pastoral nature[36] of Hebrews is a constituent element of its genre; it is *a form of preaching*. The hortatory nature of Hebrews comes to the fore particularly in the so-called warning passages scattered throughout Hebrews (e.g., 2:1–4; 2:12–15; 6:1–4; 10:26–29; etc).

Even those of us used to long sermons will, nevertheless, be surprised to hear the author describe his work as one "written to you briefly" (13:22)![37] It would appear to be far too long to be a written sermon; instead it should, I suggest, be considered a developed form of preaching made possible by crafting it in written form as a document to be read to and consulted by the church/es to which it is sent. If "briefly" is not ironic, and I doubt that it is, and if the Gospels are also a form of παράκλησις, then perhaps the author is thinking of the literature like the Gospels, in comparison with which it is indeed brief. As with so much of the Bible, Hebrews has a literary[38] and oral nature; both characteristics need to be taken into account in its interpretation. The book is crafted in this way for the particular situation of the Hebrews and thus also has an epistolary dimension.

Since the second half of the twentieth century, a great deal of work has been done on the literary structure, with no sign of an emerging consensus.

---

preaching, see W. R. Stegner, "The Ancient Jewish Synagogue Homily;" in *Greco-Roman Literature and the New Testament: Selected Forms and Genres*, ed. D. E. Aune (Atlanta: Scholars Press, 1988), 51–69; H. Thyen, *Der Stil der jüdisch-hellenistischen Homilie*, FRLANT 47 (Göttingen: Vandenhoeck & Ruprecht, 1955).

33. Translated as "exhort" to foreground the paronomasia in the verse.

34. Attridge, *Epistle to the Hebrews*, 408, translates this verb as "to put up with" and thus as a coy, somewhat ironic appeal.

35. My translation.

36. Cf. O. Kuss, "Der Verfasser des Hebräerbriefes als Seelsorger," *TTZ* 67 (1958): 1–12, 65–80; see also F. V. Filson, *"Yesterday": A Study of Hebrews in the Light of Chapter 13*, Studies in Biblical Theology 2/4 (London: SCM, 1967).

37. Cf. Koester, *Hebrews*, 580. Attridge (*Epistle to the Hebrews*, 408) suggests that "briefly" may be ironic but that the irony may be conventional. The same expression is used in 1 Pet. 5:12, but 1 Peter is much shorter than Hebrews.

38. For Attridge's development of A. Vanhoye's analysis of the structure (see next note) as well as insightful comments on the highly literary nature of Hebrews, see his *Epistle to the Hebrews*, 13–21.

Father Albert Vanhoye has repeatedly returned to the issue of the structure of Hebrews.[39] He argues that apart from the frame introduction (1:1–4) and conclusion (13:20–25), it consists of five parts:

1. The situation of Christ (1:5–2:18)
   2. High priest worthy of faith and merciful (3:1–5:10)
      3. Unique value of the priesthood and of the sacrifice of Christ (5:11–10:39)
   4. Faith and endurance (11:1–12:13)
5. The straight paths (12:14–13:19)

Vanhoye arranges these five parts concentrically around the theme of the priesthood of Christ, which he takes to be the heart of Hebrews (8:1), and suggests that parts 1 and 5 deal with eschatology, 2 and 4 with ecclesiology, with 3 as the central section discussing sacrifice.

Vanhoye's analysis of the structure has been contested, but many continue to follow it, albeit in modified form.[40] More recently a number of discourse analyses of Hebrews have appeared.[41] The variety of proposals for the structure of Hebrews and the lack of consensus should alert us to the problem with searching for a tight *logical* structure. As I found in my work on Ecclesiastes, books like this *are integrated* but resist the sort of logical structure scholars find irresistible. Thus Lane reports, "Although an impression of careful composition according to a well-ordered plan is conveyed on every page of Hebrews, there has been no common agreement concerning the literary structure of the document."[42] Hebrews has a literary, organic structure as befits its sermonic, oral/literary nature, and it resists neat, logical analysis. However, as we will see, attention to literary markers is important as we journey with the author along his word of exhortation. As is typical of oral/literary material, the prologue in 1:1–4 puts all the major themes on the table, as it were, and in the remainder of the book these are worked out around exposition of Old Testament texts.

---

39. See A. Vanhoye, *Structure and Message of the Epistle to the Hebrews*, Subsidia biblica 12 (Rome: Editrice Pontificio Istituto Biblica, 1989). His analysis is far more detailed than presented here.

40. See, e.g., W. L. Lane, *Hebrews 1–8*, lxxxiv–xcviii.

41. Guthrie, *Structure of Hebrews*; C. L. Westfall, *A Discourse Analysis of the Letter to the Hebrews: The Relationship between Form and Meaning*, LNTS 297 (London: T&T Clark, 2005).

42. W. L. Lane, *Hebrews 1–8*, 1. Guthrie states, "The problems caused by the complex structure of Hebrews are not easily answered; they may never be answered with a consensus of New Testament scholarship" (*Structure of Hebrews*, 146).

Prologue, 1:1–4

The distinct rhetorical and literary nature of Hebrews is immediately evident in the prologue, a long, carefully crafted "period."[43] "The writer has cultivated the instincts of an orator, which are now brought into the service of preaching."[44] The prologue begins in verse 1 by affirming the Old Testament as God's Word. "By the prophets" is a parallel expression to "by a son," suggesting that the dative ἐν τοῖς προφήταις is instrumental, but it is also possible that this phrase refers to the Old Testament Scriptures themselves (cf. Luke 24:25; John 6:45).[45] The alternatives are not exclusive; either way, as Westcott perceptively states, "The O.T. does not simply contain prophecies, but . . . it is one vast prophecy, in the record of national fortunes, in the ordinances of a national Law, in the expression of a national hope. Israel in its history, in its ritual, in its ideal, is a unique enigma among the peoples of the world, of which the Christ is the complete solution."[46] In 1:1, προφήταις also fits well with the author's emphasis on God speaking and rightly evokes the view of the whole of the Old Testament as God's Word.[47]

Excursus A: Hebrews and the Old Testament

Hebrews is awash with the Old Testament,[48] and its use of the Old Testament is central to its structure.[49] So prevalent is the Old Testament in Hebrews that it is unclear just how many quotations and allusions there are! Longenecker identifies 38 quotations; Caird, 29; Spicq, 36; and Michel, 32.[50] Some 19 or 20 of the passages quoted are not cited elsewhere in the New Testament. Hebrews draws most heavily on the Pentateuch and the Psalms, "the fundamental Law and the Book of common devotion," as Westcott describes them.[51] Lane says in his exposition of Hebrews 3:7–19, for example, "It would appear that the writer had the Book of Numbers opened before him when he composed this section of the sermon."[52] The Psalter is,

---

43. It is a single sentence.
44. W. L. Lane, *Hebrews 1–8*, 6.
45. So BDAG 891.
46. B. F. Westcott, *The Epistle to the Hebrews: The Greek Texts with Notes and Essays* (London: Macmillan, 1892), 493.
47. It also fits with the repeated use of the Greek letter π in 1:1. Cf. Heb. 4:12–13 for the author's view of the word of God.
48. There is a great deal of recent and older literature to explore in this respect. See, e.g., J. Swetnam, *Jesus and Isaac: A Study of the Epistle to the Hebrews in the Light of the Aqedah*, Analecta biblica 94 (Rome: Biblical Institute Press, 1981); on 189 he notes that Gen. 22 is treated more explicitly and extensively than anywhere else in the NT.
49. P. Ellingworth, "The Old Testament in Hebrews: Exegesis, Method and Hermeneutics" (PhD diss., University of Aberdeen, 1977). See the very useful article by G. H. Guthrie, "Hebrews' Use of the Old Testament: Recent Trends in Research," *Currents in Biblical Research* 1, no. 2 (2003): 271–94.
50. W. L. Lane, *Hebrews 1–8*, cxvi.
51. Westcott, *Epistle to the Hebrews*, 475.
52. W. L. Lane, *Hebrews 1–8*, 90.

however, the primary source for his Christology, especially Psalms 110:1, 4.[53] Throughout his work he makes use of the Septuagint (LXX), but it is impossible to be precise about exactly which version of the LXX.[54]

Already in the eighteenth century, Bengel drew attention to the role of the Old Testament in Hebrews, especially Psalms 2; 8; 110.[55] He noticed that the introduction of a quote from the Old Testament provided a platform for the ensuing discussion. In a formative article George Caird proposed that the argument of Hebrews is arranged around four Old Testament texts: Psalms 110:1-4; 8:4-6; 95:7-11; and Jeremiah 31:31-34 (rather than Ps. 40). In each section after the first, the main quote is placed at the beginning. These texts make the case for the ineffectiveness of the Old Testament institutions, and other scriptural references are ancillary to these four. A weakness in Caird's creative theory is how to account for the paraenesis in 10:19-13:21 as integral to the structure. J. Walters developed Caird's approach by arguing that the author of Hebrews arranged his argument in a series of six scriptural explications, each framed with exhortation. In addition to Caird's four, he added Habakkuk 2:3-4[56] and Proverbs 3:11-12.[57]

Caird's work has been illuminating in terms of the hermeneutic of the author of Hebrews. Rather than his exegesis being Alexandrian and fanciful, it was "one of the earliest and most successful attempts to define the relationship between the Old and the New Testaments, and ... a large part of the value of the book is to be found in the method of exegesis which was formerly dismissed with contempt."[58] Thus if we are looking for a biblical warrant for biblical theology, we find a strong one in Hebrews. The author is alert to the diversity in the Old Testament ("in many and various ways," 1:1) but clearly sees the *same* God at work there as the one who has now spoken in a Son: Jesus. Although he does not use the word, clearly he embraces a theology of *fulfillment*.[59] As we will see below, the author's theology of fulfillment is one of continuity and discontinuity: "At the heart of his exegetical endeavors is the quite straightforward query: What do the Scriptures mean when viewed from a Christocentric perspective? ... What he seems to be doing is basing himself upon an accepted exegetical tradition within the Church and straightforwardly explicating relationships within that tradition and implications for his addressees in light of their circumstances."[60]

Psalm 110 is utterly central to Hebrews and might strike us as a strange psalm on which to base so much of Hebrews' Christology. However, as C. H. Dodd rightly says of Psalm 110:1, "This

---

53. Hebrews quotes the Psalms more often than does any other NT book. The next closest is Romans. See the diagram in G. J. Steyn, *A Quest for the Assumed LXX Vorlage of the Explicit Quotations in Hebrews* (Göttingen: Vandenhoeck & Ruprecht, 2011), 12.

54. W. L. Lane, *Hebrews 1-8*, cxviii. Cf. R. Gheorghita, *The Role of the Septuagint in Hebrews: An Investigation of Its Influence with Special Consideration to the Use of Hab 2:3-4 in Heb 10:37-38*, WUNT 2/160 (Tübingen: Mohr Siebeck, 2003); Steyn, *Quest for the Assumed LXX Vorlage*.

55. J. A. Bengel, *Gnomon Novi Testamenti* (Tübingen: Schramm, 1742), 2.2.333-505; ET, C. T. Lewis and M. R. Vincent, *John Albert Bengel's Gnomon of the New Testament*, 2 vols. (Philadelphia: Perkinpine & Higgins, 1860), reprint of 3rd ed. as *New Testament Word Studies* (Grand Rapids: Kregel, 1971).

56. On the use of Hab. 2:3-4 LXX in Heb. 10:37-38, see Gheorghita, *Septuagint in Hebrews*, 147-224.

57. J. Walters, "The Rhetorical Arrangement of Hebrews," *Asbury Theological Journal* 51, no. 2 (1996): 59-70. See W. L. Lane, *Hebrews 1-8*, cxiv-cxv.

58. G. B. Caird, "The Exegetical Method of the Epistle to the Hebrews," *Canadian Journal of Theology* 5 (1959): 44-51. Cf. Guthrie, "Hebrews' Use," 920.

59. See R. N. Longenecker, *Biblical Exegesis in the Apostolic Period*, 2nd ed. (Grand Rapids: Eerdmans, 1999), 175.

60. Ibid., 185.

particular verse was one of the most fundamental texts of the kerygma."[61] It was interpreted messianically by Jesus himself in Mark 12:36 and is cited by Peter at Pentecost in Acts 2:34. Thus, as Longenecker notes, "Once the κύριος of Ps. 110:1 became ascribed to Jesus (evidently under his own instigation), it would have been inevitable as Christological thought developed for other passages where deity is addressed to be also so ascribed particularly in such a passage as Ps. 45:6[-7]."[62]

The author of Hebrews does not simply impose christological readings on Old Testament texts in a distorted way. His reading of Psalm 8 in Hebrews 2:5-9, for example, clearly understands the psalm as referring to humankind and their dominion over the creation. Indeed, his christological reading of the Old Testament is *typological* rather than allegorical. As Alexander Nairne puts it, "Philo deals with allegories, the Epistle with symbols."[63] Typology looks for links between persons, events, and things within the historical context of salvation and under the assumption that the same God is at work in the whole story. As Daniélou asserts, "We must make a rigorous distinction between such a typology—which is historical symbolism—and the kind of allegorism practiced by Philo and adopted by certain Fathers of the Church. For the latter is really a reappearance of a cosmic symbolism without an historical basis."[64] Hebrews' use of the Old Testament thus supports a typological biblical theology rather than allegorical interpretation.[65]

Hebrews sees continuity and discontinuity between the Old Testament and the Christ event. The same God is speaking, but Hebrews 1:2-4 emphasizes the superiority and newness of what God has done in *a Son*. "Last days" is a technical term for the breaking in of the eschaton and alerts us to the fact that Hebrews espouses *the same eschatology* found throughout the New Testament.[66] Tom Wright points out that entering the world of Hebrews after studying Paul is like listening to Monteverdi after Bach! "We are clearly in the same world, but the texture is different, the allusions are different, the whole flavour is changed."[67] N. T. Wright draws attention to the parallel between the climax of Sirach 44:1-50:21 and Hebrews. This section in Sirach climaxes with the ministry of the high priest Simon in the temple. The list of heroes in Hebrews 11 aims at making the same point but with a christological twist. Instead of the present high priest in the temple being the telos of Israel's history, it is Jesus, the true high priest: "Hebrews 12.1-3

---

61. C. H. Dodd, *According to the Scriptures: The Sub-Structure of New Testament Theology* (London: Nisbet, 1952), 35.

62. Longenecker, *Biblical Exegesis*, 178-79.

63. A. Nairne, *The Epistle of Priesthood: Studies in the Epistle to the Hebrews* (Edinburgh: T&T Clark, 1913), 37.

64. J. Daniélou, "The New Testament and the Theology of History," in *Studia evangelica I*, ed. Kurt Aland et al. (Berlin: Akademie-Verlag, 1959), 25-34, esp. 30.

65. Discussion about the precise nature of the author's exegetical method continues. Cf. S. E. Docherty, *The Use of the Old Testament in Hebrews: A Case Study in Early Jewish Bible Interpretation*, WUNT 2/260 (Tübingen: Mohr Siebeck, 2009).

66. Cf. C. K. Barrett, "The Eschatology of the Epistle to the Hebrews," in *The Background of the New Testament and Its Eschatology: Studies in Honour of Charles Harold Dodd*, ed. W. D. Davies and D. Daube (Cambridge: Cambridge University Press, 1956).

67. N. T. Wright, *NTPG* 409.

stands to 11.4–40 as Sirach 50.1–21 does to 44.1–49.16."[68] As Wright thus explains:

> Underneath the poetic sequence of Hebrews, then, lies a clear implicit narrative sequence. The story of the world, and of Israel, has led up to a point, namely, the establishment of the true worship of the true god. . . . Hebrews focuses on the Temple cult rather than on more general theological or practical issues, but the underlying story corresponds to what we found in the synoptics and Paul. Jesus has brought Israel's story to its paradoxical climax.[69]

In Hebrews 1:2–4 the author draws on Old Testament allusions, the wisdom tradition, and cultic terminology to unpack the Christ event. "A Son, whom he appointed heir of all things," is an allusion to Psalm 2:7–8. Jesus is thus the true Davidic king, but his inheritance is *the whole of creation*, just as he, like Wisdom, is the agent of creation. Dunn evocatively speaks of "Jesus as the man Wisdom became."[70] The aorist form of the verb "created" speaks of the Son's activity in history *past*. "The worlds" (τοὺς αἰῶνας) may refer to periods of time, be primarily spatial, or indicate the visible and invisible aspects of creation.[71] Bateman suggests "universe" as an all-inclusive description.[72] Hebrews 1:3ab, which some think comes from an early hymn, establishes the deity of the Son, who radiates God's glory. Not only was the Son the agent of creation, but he also sustains or bears (φέρων) all things along by his word. Φέρων implies rulership, sustaining, and directing toward a goal, all of which are true of the Son.[73]

A notable aspect of the prologue is how the roles of the Son as *creator and redeemer* are interwoven (cf. Col. 1:15–20). Truly the word that God has spoken in the Son is a speech *act*. Hebrews 1:3c marks a transition from the Son as Davidic king and creator to the Son as priest, *the* major theme of Hebrews. Only twice does καθαρισμός (purification) occur in the New Testament in relation to Christ's atoning death (here and 2 Pet. 1:9), but it occurs frequently in the LXX and the New Testament for cultic purification. In Leviticus 16,

---

68. Ibid., 410.
69. Ibid.
70. J. D. G. Dunn, *Christology in the Making: A New New Testament Inquiry into the Origins of the Doctrine of the Incarnation*, 2nd ed. (Grand Rapids: Eerdmans, 1989), 212.
71. H. W. Bateman IV, *Early Jewish Hermeneutics and Hebrews 1:5–13: The Impact of Early Jewish Exegesis on the Interpretation of a Significant New Testament Passage* (New York: Peter Lang, 1997), 210.
72. Ibid., 210–11.
73. See our discussion of the doctrine of creation in chap. 12 above. Also see C. G. Bartholomew and B. Ashford, *The Doctrine of Creation* (Downers Grove, IL: IVP Academic, forthcoming).

which deals with the Day of Atonement, the verb is found three times in verses 19 and 30 (cf. Exod. 29:36–37, with the noun and the verb [twice]; 30:10, with the noun). The cultic metaphor the author has appropriated is that of *pollution* to refer to anything that prevents God's presence among his people. "For sins" qualifies this metaphor of cleansing from pollution, and the aorist "had made" evokes the finality and once-for-all nature of Christ's priestly work. In 1:4 "the name" is probably "Son," evoking Jesus's royalty. "Superior" is a common word in Hebrews and relates to the author's purpose to draw unequivocally to the attention of his hearers the complete superiority of Jesus. "Angels" provides the link into the following section.

The dense, theologically pregnant single sentence of the prologue is programmatic for the entire work. Here in a kernel are all the themes that the author will unpack, as Paul does after his similarly programmatic introduction in Romans 1:1–6. What Paul and the author to the Hebrews want us to grasp is the sheer enormity of the gospel; having introduced it, they unpack it, and it becomes bigger and bigger. Such introductory passages and the expositions that follow often remind me of Blackwell's Bookstore on Broad Street in Oxford. It looks small from the outside, but once you enter, it opens out into room after room and goes from one level to another, turning out to be huge. Such is the largesse of the gospel that it can be unpacked in different but complementary ways, as a comparison of Romans with Hebrews reveals. Perhaps now we can begin to understand why the author of Hebrews describes his word of exhortation as "brief." There is so much more to say!

Lectio Divina

Good biblical interpretation should deepen our reception of Hebrews as God's Word addressed to us. Return to the lectio exercise at the outset of the chapter, work through it again, and see whether this turns out to be the case!

The Superiority of Jesus

"Angels" occurs repeatedly in 1:4–2:18, and not again after 2:18. There has been much discussion as to why, at the outset of his work, the author focuses on angels. In the Old Testament and Second Temple Judaism, angels were ascribed a role in revelation and redemption and are here most likely the counterparts to *the prophets* in 1:1.[74] Just as Jesus is superior to

---

74. W. L. Lane, *Hebrews 1–8*, 17.

the prophets, so too is he superior to the angels. In line with the aim of Hebrews "superior" (κρείττων) occurs thirteen times in Hebrews, nineteen times in the entire New Testament.

Indeed a unifying theme in Hebrews is the superiority of Jesus over the prophets, the angels, Moses, Joshua, the Aaronic high priests, the Levitical priests, Abraham, the tabernacle ministry, the old covenant, and so forth. Amid the author's development of this recurring motif, many other details enter into the picture; indeed, the more one works on Hebrews, the richer it becomes. Christology is utterly central to Hebrews, and two titles dominate the book: Son and high priest. Since Jesus's priesthood in particular is at the heart of Hebrews, we will focus on it, and then examine the paraenetic section that concludes the book. Lane identifies five major sections in Hebrews, including section 2, "The High Priestly Character of the Son," 3:1–5:10; and 3, "The High Priestly Office of the Son," 5:11–10:39; these two sections cover Jesus's priesthood and will be our focus.

Jesus's Priesthood

Hebrews 2:17 alerts the reader to the major themes of what follows, Jesus as "a *merciful and faithful* high priest,"[75] which is dealt with in reverse order: 3:1–4:14 focuses on the faithfulness of Jesus and our need to remain faithful; 4:15–5:10 focuses on Jesus as a merciful high priest. Lane observes that whereas in the Old Testament the priesthood is directed primarily toward service *for God*, the author emphasizes the solidarity of Jesus as high priest with his people. Similarly Helmut Thielicke asserts that whereas the prophetic office is on the side of God, "in contrast the priestly office expresses the fact that Christ is on the side of man, that in solidarity with him he lets himself come under the pressure of history, its guilt, its oppression (*thlipsis*), and its finitude. Here then, being true man, he is man's representative and in this capacity stands over against God."[76]

We do not commonly think of Moses along priestly lines,[77] and so the comparison with Moses in 3:1–6 may strike us initially as strange. However, not only can the veneration of Moses in Judaism hardly be exaggerated but he is also called a priest once in the Old Testament (Ps. 99:6), and his Levitical

---

75. Heb. 2:17 contains the first reference to Jesus as high priest.
76. H. Thielicke, *The Evangelical Faith: The Doctrine of God and of Christ* (Edinburgh: T&T Clark, 1974), 2:366.
77. In Hellenistic Judaism, a likely background to Hebrews, Moses was venerated as a high priest, as attested by Philo, *Life of Moses*, I.149.

background (Exod. 2:1–10), his unique access to the presence of God, and his building of and service at the altar (Exod. 24:4–8)—all relate him to priestly functions.[78]

The author emphasizes Moses's faithfulness "in all God's house as a servant" (Heb. 3:4). In comparing Moses to Jesus, he could have drawn attention to Moses's rebellion (Num. 20:10–12) but chooses to emphasize Moses's *faithfulness*, as he does with the list of heroes of the faith in Hebrews 11. The point of comparison is between Moses's faithfulness as *a servant* versus Jesus as *a son*,[79] as well as the extent of the house over which they were faithful. As in the prologue, creation and redemption are held closely together; "God's house," while clearly referring to the people of God, has strong creational overtones (cf. 3:4), just as the tabernacle and temple do in the Old Testament.[80] As a Son, Jesus is the Davidic king who rules over all things,[81] and we know from 1:2 that Jesus is the agent of creation and thus also "the builder of all things" (3:4). Similarly with the kingdom of God/heaven in the Gospels, redemption and thus a people are clearly in view, but so too is *all of creation*. The description of the addresses as "*holy* partners" (3:1) draws them into association with Jesus's priestly ministry.

The implications of Jesus's faithfulness are developed in 3:7–4:16, using an extract from Psalm 95 as the basis, the second major Old Testament text the author makes use of. If Jesus is worthy of more "glory" than Moses, then the readers are bound to imitate Jesus's—and Moses's—faithfulness. From Psalm 95 the author uses the wilderness generation as a type of his addressees and exhorts them to respond "today," an expression now charged eschatologically, here with belief rather than unbelief. In Hebrews 3:1 he refers to "our confession" and in 4:14 urges them to "hold fast to our confession." As an aside, the author's typological use of Moses is *historically* grounded. His entire case would collapse if Moses were not a historical figure and if the narratives about him in the Old Testament were not true.[82]

---

78. Cf. W. L. Lane, *Hebrews 1–8*, 74.

79. Only in Heb. 3:1 is Jesus described as an "apostle" in the NT. For different views of this see W. L. Lane, *Hebrews 1–8*, 75–76.

80. See G. J. Wenham, "Sanctuary Symbolism," *Proceedings of the 9th World Congress of Jewish Studies* 9 (1986): 19–25; G. K. Beale, *The Temple and the Church's Mission: A Biblical Theology of the Dwelling Place of God*, New Studies in Biblical Theology (Downers Grove, IL: InterVarsity, 2004); C. G. Bartholomew, *Where Mortals Dwell: A Christian View of Place for Today* (Grand Rapids: Baker Academic, 2011).

81. Likely "faithful" in Heb. 3:2 alludes to similar use of *pistis* (or a verbal cognate) in the LXX: 1 Chron. 17:14; 1 Sam. 2:35; Num. 12:7. See W. L. Lane, *Hebrews 1–8*, 76–77.

82. Cf. our discussion of the historicity of Moses in chap. 10 above.

In 4:1–8 the author develops from Psalm 95 his theology of *rest*, linking Psalm 95, Joshua, and Genesis 1 together,[83] so that rest becomes the eschatological goal of history. "The theology of rest developed in 4:1–11 takes account of the pattern of archetype (God's primal rest, v. 4), type (the settlement of the land under Joshua, v. 8), and antitype (the Sabbath celebration of the consummation, v. 9)."[84] Once again, redemption and creation are closely tied together.

Montefiore explains, "This 'rest,' like everything else God has made, was created when the universe came into being. . . . That which was created at the beginning is reserved for the end."[85] That the writer's theology of rest does not deny the doctrine of a new creation is also apparent from Psalm 95, which celebrates God as our creator (cf. vv. 4–7). Thus Hurst is unhelpful in commenting, "The 'rest' of God in Acts 7:49 is, fittingly, something entirely independent of any earthly fixture or particularity, an idea perhaps closer to the general argument of Hebrews than anything else in the Christian tradition."[86] On the contrary, Acts 7:49 quotes Isaiah 66:1, which is all about the connection between heaven and earth: Isaiah 66 culminates in verse 22 with the creation of the new heavens and the new earth! In Isaiah 66:1, the question "What could serve as my resting place?" is not a denial of God's presence in the temple or his presence in creation; rather, as Childs rightly states,

> The issue within the Old Testament, and especially in chapter 66, is not whether God is too exalted even to tolerate an earthly dwelling place, but is the motivation of those desiring to construct a temple. Those arrogant people who feel God is thereby beholden to them are flatly rejected. God asserts his complete sovereignty over all creation and all its works. Then v. 2b reaffirms the theme of chapter 65 that the transcendent and creative God is fully accessible to the one who is humble, contrite and respectful of God's word.[87]

The reference to Jesus as "a great high priest" in 4:14 is not an afterthought but the conclusion to this section. "Our confession" in 3:1 and 4:14 is an inclusio; central to this confession is Jesus as high priest. Jesus as high priest has done his priestly work *in the heavens*, an emphasis that will be developed

---

83. As in Exod. 20, rest and Sabbath are held together: cf. Heb. 4:9, "*sabbath* rest."

84. W. L. Lane, *Hebrews 1–8*, 104.

85. H. Montefiore, *A Commentary on the Epistle to the Hebrews* (New York: Harper & Row, 1964), 83–84.

86. L. D. Hurst, *The Epistle to the Hebrews: Its Background of Thought* (Cambridge: Cambridge University Press, 1990), 102.

87. B. S. Childs, *Isaiah*, Old Testament Library (Louisville: Westminster John Knox, 2001), 540.

in Hebrews 9. The emphasis in 4:15–5:10 is on Jesus as the *merciful* high priest, with the central Old Testament text being Psalm 110:4. As our high priest, Jesus is able to feel our weakness and actively help us in every way (cf. συμπαθῆσαι in 4:15).[88] The emphasis on Jesus's sympathy and gentleness (cf. 5:2) is extraordinary and has no clear parallel in sources from contemporary Judaism.[89] As Thielicke declares, "Nowhere is his [Jesus's] function as both the fulfillment and the crisis of humanity so pregnantly portrayed as in Hebrews."[90]

Hebrews 4:15 says that "in every respect" Jesus was tempted as we are, yet he remained "without sin." According to Thielicke, "For Hebrews, . . . being tempted as we are is the true mark of Christ's humanity. Christ entered the sphere between God and Satan. He faced the possible failure of his mission and the fall of the Messiah."[91] The obvious reference is to Jesus's temptation in the wilderness before the start of his public ministry, where all three of those temptations involve the possibility of avoiding the cross: "all three temptations focus on the attractive possibility of usurping divine power without serving, suffering, loving or obeying."[92] Thielicke observes how theologians struggle to relate Jesus's real susceptibility to temptation to his deity.[93] There is mystery here, but Hebrews is adamant with its "in every respect." On this subject, Thielicke stresses Christ's choice to come "under the burden that we bear constitutionally as the burden of human existence"[94] and that Christ overcame the susceptibility to temptation through prayer, just as in 4:16 we are encouraged to do.[95] "Without sin" points to his success in this area and to what Thielicke calls the elusive aspect of Christ's being tempted: "In the very depths in which he is so close to us that we are delivered from our sufferings in virtue of his pain and anguish, he is also distant from us in uncompromising majesty and remoteness. . . . The humanity of Christ escapes us at the very point where it seems closest to us."[96]

The juxtaposed quotes from Psalms 2:7 and 110:4 emphasize the two aspects of Jesus's person central to Hebrews: he is both the Son and the priest. "According to the order of Melchizedek" enables the author to develop his theology of Jesus as superior to both Aaron (cf. 5:4) and Abraham (Heb. 7). Psalm 110 is the most-quoted psalm in the New Testament. Its messianic

---

88. W. L. Lane, *Hebrews 1–8*, 114.
89. Ibid., 116.
90. Thielicke, *Evangelical Faith*, 2:371.
91. Ibid., 376.
92. Ibid.
93. See the discussion in Thielicke, *Evangelical Faith*, 2:376–82.
94. Ibid., 381.
95. On the cultic terminology in Heb. 4:16, see W. L. Lane, *Hebrews 1–8*, 115.
96. Thielicke, *Evangelical Faith*, 2:371–72.

application comes from Jesus himself (Matt. 22:41–46) during his dialogue with the Pharisees about the nature of the Messiah (as noted above).

Psalm 110 is a bit like Melchizedek; Goldingay says of this psalm, "We will never know its origin."[97] Scholars debate the messianic nature of the psalm: Derek Kidner, for example, claims that it is messianic,[98] whereas Goldingay argues that it is only in the light of Jesus's coming that the Spirit inspires interpreters to find a significance in this text that was not there before.[99] This is a complex issue, but Bateman seems to me helpful in his description of the psalm as "typological-prophetic."[100] One assumes that the psalm meant something to its original hearers that may well not have had overt messianic overtones "originally"; but in the light of the Psalter as a whole, it does seem that Jesus's interpretation and that of Hebrews fits well with it. As Goldingay explains, Psalm 110 is the twin to Psalm 2, with its emphasis on the anointed king. Psalms 93; 95–99 form the editorial and thus theological center of the Psalter and emphasize Yahweh's kingship while diminishing the emphasis on the Davidic king. The Psalter as a whole reached its final form when Israel was without a king, and in that context psalms like 2 and 110 would easily be viewed as connected with God's future purposes for Israel. Thus I find Goldingay's statement too strong in declaring, "The text's theological implications then do not lie in its application to Jesus; that is to ignore its meaning."[101] As Clinton McCann has demonstrated in his outstanding work on the Psalter, when the psalms are read holistically and when Jesus is seen as fulfilling the Old Testament as a whole, then the move from the psalms to Jesus becomes natural and not forced. According to Mays, "Hebrews is right on target in its use of verse 4 when it differentiates the priesthood of Aaron from that of Jesus because the priesthood of Jesus is a messianic, a royal priesthood, the Priesthood of the Son (Heb 1:3; 5:6; 7:17, 21). . . . The New Testament uses the psalm as language to speak about the true identity and role of Jesus in the coming kingdom of God."[102]

The intriguing thing about Psalm 110 is that the Davidic king ("my lord" in 110:1) is affirmed as both king *and priest*, and "priest forever according to the order of Melchizedek" (110:4). Israelite kings were not priests and got into serious trouble when they tried to adopt the priestly role, as

---

97. J. Goldingay, *Psalms*, vol. 3, *Psalms 90–150* (Grand Rapids: Baker Academic, 2008), 292. Cf. J. Kurianal, *Jesus Our High Priest: Ps 110,4 as the Substructure of Heb 5,1–7, 28*, European University Studies Series 23: Theology 693 (Frankfurt: Peter Lang, 2000).
98. D. Kidner, *Psalms*, 2 vols. (Downers Grove, IL: InterVarsity, 1973–75), 2:391–92.
99. Ibid., 299.
100. H. W. Bateman, "Psalm 110:1 and the New Testament," *BSac* 149 (1992): 453.
101. Goldingay, *Psalms*, 3:299.
102. J. L. Mays, *Psalms*, Interpretation (Louisville: John Knox, 1994), 354.

is well known in Saul's case (1 Sam 13:1–15). We read of Melchizedek in Genesis 14:17–24. He is the first priest mentioned in the Bible, a priest of El-Elyon, one of the names by which God was worshiped by the patriarchs. He manifests his priesthood in *blessing* Abraham, a key word in Genesis, and the verb occurs three times in 14:19–20. It is related to God's promise that through Abraham he will bless the nations, except that here *Abraham himself* is being blessed by Melchizedek. In response to this priestly blessing, Abraham gives Melchizedek a tithe of "everything." As Wenham notes, "Here Abram (cf. Jacob [in Gen.] 28:22), father of the nation, sets an example for all his descendents to follow (cf. later legislation on tithing: Num. 18; Lev. 27:30–33)."[103]

We know almost nothing about Melchizedek, a point exploited by the author of Hebrews (7:3), but in the light of Jesus's application of Psalm 110 to himself, the theology the author develops from this text is understandable.[104] Not surprisingly, however, the author describes his teaching about Jesus as a priest according to the order of Melchizedek as "hard to explain" (5:11). In chapter 7 the author draws on the details of Genesis 14 as well as Psalm 110:4 to establish the superiority of Jesus over Abraham (7:1–9) as well as over the Levitical priesthood (7:11–28). A central plank in his argument is his assumption that Psalm 110 was written after the establishment of the Levitical priesthood. Jesus's priesthood is contrasted with the Levitical priesthood along several lines: Jesus is not of the tribe of Levi, but his priesthood is established "through the power of an indestructible life" (7:16); his priesthood is established with an oath (7:20); his priesthood is effective, whereas the Levitical priesthood was weak and ineffectual (7:18–19); his priesthood is permanent (7:23–24); his priesthood is holy and perfect (7:26–28).

---

103. G. J. Wenham, *Genesis 1–15*, WBC 1 (Waco: Word, 1987), 317.

104. There is much discussion about the background to Hebrews's view of Melchizedek. See, e.g., W. L. Lane, *Hebrews 1–8*, 160–63; Attridge, *Epistle to the Hebrews*, 192–95; E. F. Mason, *"You Are a Priest Forever": Second Temple Jewish Messianism and the Priestly Christology of the Epistle to the Hebrews* (Leiden: Brill, 2008), who concludes, "Two elements contributing to Hebrews' presentation of Jesus as priest—the notion of a heavenly priesthood and an angelic understanding of Melchizedek—are best paralleled in ideas found in the Dead Sea Scrolls" (203). By comparison, see B. A. Demarest, "Hebrews 7:3: A *Crux Interpretum* Historically Considered," *Evangelical Quarterly* 49 (1997): 141–62; idem, *A History of Interpretation of Hebrews 7, 1–10*. Lane sides with Demarest's literal reading and observes that Heb. 7:3 is a "polished example of condensed reference. . . . The silence of the Genesis narrative . . . was significant because of the contrast it posed with the Levitical priesthood, where recorded line of descent was required for accession to the priestly office" (*Hebrews 1–8*, 165). Both Koester (*Hebrews*, 348) and Attridge (*Epistle to the Hebrews*, 190) state that 7:3 is an argument developed from silence, an interpretive device shared with rabbinic exegesis and Philo.

Already in 7:22 the author relates Jesus's priesthood to the introduction of a "better covenant." This is now expanded in chapters 8–10 with an excerpt from Jeremiah 31 as the central Old Testament text.[105] The new-covenant material from Jeremiah is prefaced (Heb. 8:1–7) and followed by discussion of the cultic aspects of Jesus's priesthood, an emphasis that is not surprising from this author. In 8:6 Jesus's "more excellent ministry" results in him being the mediator of "a better covenant." Cultus was, after all, a fundamental part of the Sinai covenant, as the lengthy chapters on the building of the tabernacle in Exodus 25–40 bear eloquent witness. We have noticed (above) that the author's main Old Testament sources are the Pentateuch and the Psalter, and thus it is not surprising that he focuses on the mobile tabernacle rather than the temple.

Hebrews 8:2 flows directly from 8:1. The author uses "the terminology of the heavenly sanctuary and the true tabernacle as spatial expressions for the session at God's right hand, as the collocation of the two ideas in 8:1–2 shows"[106] (cf. 1:3c). Cody has demonstrated that the idea of a heavenly sanctuary corresponding to the earthly sanctuary was common in Judaism, and he argues that this theme in Hebrews reflects direct dependence on the Old Testament (Exod. 25:9, 40; 26:30; 27:8; Num. 8:4) and has more in common with rabbinic and Jewish apocalyptic literature than with Philo.[107] Therefore, Nomoto rightly, in my view, argues that the earthly-heavenly contrast is *not* an expression of Platonic metaphysics but is the author's means of expressing the typological relationship (see "symbol," παραβολή, in 9:9)[108] between the old and new covenants, between the Old Testament cultus and the new situation achieved by Jesus as high priest.[109]

In 9:1–10 the author stresses the severe limitations of access to God under the old covenant. The high priest had to make atonement once a year, every year, whereas Jesus has made atonement "once for all" (9:12), thus "obtaining eternal redemption" (cf. 9:25–26). "The superiority of Christ's cultic action derives from the uniqueness of the sanctuary that he entered and from the uniqueness of the sacrifice that he presented."[110] In 9:11–28 the theme of

---

105. For the literary structure of these chapters, see W. L. Lane, *Hebrews 1–8*, 202–4; idem, *Hebrews 9–13*, 217–18, 233–35, 257–59.

106. W. L. Lane, *Hebrews 1–8*, 206.

107. A. Cody, *Heavenly Sanctuary and Liturgy in the Epistle to the Hebrews: The Achievement of Salvation in the Epistle's Perspectives* (St. Meinrad, IN: St. Meinrad Archabbey, 1960), 9–46; cf. A. J. McNicol, "The Relationship of the Image of the Highest Angel to the High Priest Concept in Hebrews" (PhD diss., Vanderbilt University, 1974), 54–113.

108. Koester states, "Hebrews uses the term for typological connections between the old and new covenants" (*Hebrews*, 398).

109. S. Nomoto, "Herkunft und Struktur der hohenpriestervorstellung im Hebräerbrief," *NovT* 10 (1968): 10–25.

110. W. L. Lane, *Hebrews 9–13*, 237.

Christ himself *as the sacrifice* comes to the fore. In 9:12 he enters the heavenly holy of holies "with his own blood." The atonement is here cultically viewed as achieved by "the blood of Christ, who through the eternal Spirit offered himself without blemish to God" (9:14).

As is well known in the New Testament and in the history of theology, a variety of metaphors have been used to describe Christ's atoning work. Thielicke identifies three major metaphors for the atonement *within* Christ's priestly office: political and military, penal, and cultic.[111] For our purposes the cultic metaphor is most relevant, with its two foci in Hebrews of priest and victim. As Thielicke states, "This metaphor is particularly significant because it enables us to locate the death of Jesus within the process of salvation history,"[112] as we have seen in relation to the old and new covenants. Oliver O'Donovan rightly associates Hebrews with an apophatic hermeneutic of the Old Testament since it stresses fulfillment and the obsolescence of the old,[113] but this point should not be overplayed. In an intriguing comment in 4:2, the author says of the wilderness generation that "the good news came [εὐηγγελισμένοι] to us *just as to them*." This is a remarkable affirmation of continuity (cf. 1:1–4) between old and new covenants.

An important element discussed by Thielicke is that Christ's sacrifice has an expiatory function. He rightly claims that this only makes sense against a view of God as personal.[114] The issue at stake is "fellowship with the majesty of God,"[115] and atonement is all grace, with God taking the initiative to provide a sacrifice: "The OT concept of sacrifice is thus inverted.... Man does not bring God an offering; God brings man an offering, he brings himself. To forgive means entering the breach and taking up the burden of loss. Golgotha means pain in God."[116]

In relation to the Passover and the Last Supper, Thielicke notices that what is too often overlooked in our eucharistic theology is that the meal calls us to break camp and march on. It involves going forth as sheep in the midst of wolves. Similarly in 10:19–39, the author exhorts the Hebrews to persevere in their faith; they are to "hold fast to the confession of our hope" (10:23; cf. 3:1 and 4:14).

The enormity of what Christ has achieved is wonderfully articulated in 10:19–22. Christ has opened the way for us into the very holy of holies, into

---

111. Thielicke, *Evangelical Faith*, 2:392–406.
112. Ibid., 392.
113. O. O'Donovan, "The Loss of a Sense of Place," *Irish Theological Quarterly* 55 (1989): 39–58.
114. Thielicke, *Evangelical Faith*, 2:394.
115. Ibid.
116. Ibid., 397.

the very presence of God. Such a great salvation calls forth faithfulness and holiness, taking the gathering of the local ecclesia seriously (10:25), and enduring suffering (10:32–36). The atonement that Christ has achieved remains articulated in the typical eschatological framework by the author. In 9:28 he affirms that Christ, "having been offered," will appear a second time, and in 10:37 the readers are reassured that he "will come and will not delay."

At several points we have compared Hebrews to Romans, but nowhere is this comparison so poignant as in the different use the two books make of Habakkuk 2:4 (cf. Heb. 10:38 with Rom. 1:17 and Gal. 3:11).[117] If we want to know how the author understands "faith" in Habakkuk 2:4, we only have to look at the exposition of faith that follows in Hebrews 11. As Lane observes, the author has inverted the clauses in 2:4 and added an adversative καί, "to buttress the paraenetic call to boldness and endurance in vv 35–36, corresponding to the original function of the passage in Habakkuk."[118]

Paul seems to read Habakkuk 2:4 as "It is the one who is righteous by faith that will live,"[119] a clause that might be regarded as *the* text of Romans (as in 1:17). Bruce declares, "There is no fundamental difference in this respect between Paul and the author of Hebrews; but our author, reproducing this clause together with part of its context, emphasizes the forward-looking character of saving faith, and in fact includes in 'faith' not only what Paul means by the word but also what Paul more often expresses by the companion word 'hope.'"[120]

Habakkuk 2:4 provides the lead-in to the author's exposition of faith in Hebrews 11. As he sees it, faith is the only adequate response to the enormity of the Christ event. His call to faith evokes Paul's call to offer our "bodies as a living sacrifice" in Romans 12:1, after he has expounded the gospel for eleven chapters. We will return to the challenge of faith below. After a further pause for lectio, we are now in a position, via an excursus, to explore the contested issue of creation and eschatology in Hebrews.

Lectio Divina

1. *Entering into the silence*. Take five minutes to slow down and become centered in Jesus. Let the thoughts and stresses of the day—and of

---

117. Cf. Dodd, *According to the Scriptures*, 49–51; F. F. Bruce, *The Epistle to the Hebrews*, 2nd ed. (Grand Rapids: Eerdmans, 1990), 274–75; Gheorghita, *Septuagint in Hebrews*, 147–224.
118. W. L. Lane, *Hebrews 9–13*, 305.
119. Bruce, *Epistle to the Hebrews*, 274.
120. Ibid., 274–75.

reading this chapter!—go, and be still. Choose a prayer word and repeat it as you breathe in and out, opening yourself to God.
2. *The presence of God.* Hebrews is all about the presence of God and how our great high priest, Jesus, has opened the way for us into God's presence. Reflect for a moment on the fact that "we have confidence to enter the sanctuary by the blood of Jesus" (Heb. 10:19). At this instant, as we pause in our reading of this chapter, God is present and waiting for us. He arrives before us, desiring to connect with us even more than does our most intimate friend. We take a moment to greet our living God, who comes to us in Jesus.
3. *Freedom.* "In these days God taught me as a schoolteacher teaches a pupil" (Ignatius of Loyola). We remind ourselves that there are things God has to teach us yet, and we ask for the grace to hear them and to be changed by them.
4. *Consciousness.* How am I really feeling? We acknowledge how we really are. Jesus, we remind ourselves, became fully human and was tempted as we are. He is able to "sympathize with our weaknesses" (4:15). It is the real me that the Lord loves.
5. *The Word.* We take time to read Hebrews 7:26–28 slowly, a few times, allowing ourselves to dwell on anything that strikes us.
6. *Conversation.* What feelings rise up in me as I pray and reflect on Hebrews 7:26–28? I imagine Jesus himself, our great high priest, sitting in a chair opposite me, and I open my heart to him and share with him my thoughts, feelings, reflections.
7. *Conclusion.* Glory be to the Father, and to the Son, and to the Holy Spirit. As it was in the beginning, is now, and ever shall be, world without end.
Amen.

Excursus B: Creation and Eschatology in Hebrews

Hurst reports that "the Epistle to the Hebrews continues to be a storm-center of debate in NT study,"[121] and this is certainly the case for creation and eschatology in Hebrews. If there is one New Testament book that might appear to be a fire wall against the idea of a new *creation*, then Hebrews is that book. In his major commentary on Hebrews, Spicq finds the background in Philo and Platonism; clearly, if such is the case, then this will incline one to read "the heavenly Jerusalem" (12:22) as entirely in the realm above. Similarly, Käsemann finds the background to Hebrews in pre-Christian gnosticism, with its motif of "the heavenly pilgrimage of the self from the enslaving world of matter to the heavenly realm of the spirit."[122] Hebrews provides a paradigm

---

121. Hurst, *Epistle to the Hebrews*, 2.
122. W. L. Lane, *Hebrews 1–8*, cix. See E. Käsemann, *The Wandering People of God: An Investigation of the Letter to the Hebrews* (Minneapolis: Augsburg, 1984).

example for William D. Davies—and many others—of what he sees as the New Testament tendency to transfer Christian hope from the earthly Jerusalem, the heart of *the land* in Judaism, to the heavenly Jerusalem. Davies refers to Hebrews 12:18–24, where the earthly Mount Zion is a symbol of the city of God. He argues, "It is because God has his seat there that Zion is the city with foundations. But God's habitat is not on earth: he is in heaven, and Zion, therefore, must be a heavenly reality.... Christians ... have no permanent home on earth but are seekers for a city to come ... a city that cannot be touched, eternal in the heavens."[123]

Perhaps no one articulates the implications of such an approach as clearly as does Josipovici when he comments on how the author of Hebrews uses Jeremiah 31:

> The law may be inscribed in the hearts of men, but here [in Jer. 31] a real Jerusalem and real fields and farms are being referred to. It is not simply that the author of Hebrews has given the passage a meaning which the original did not have, but that by so doing he has *obscured the meaning it did have*. The concreteness of God's dealings with Israel, his concern not with an abstract entity but with animals and trees and buildings, has completely vanished from Hebrews. It is not that an old meaning has been subsumed into a new one but that a new meaning has blotted out the old.[124]

However, much in our interpretation of Hebrews and especially of its eschatology depends on the worldview background against which one reads it. Already in 1950, Schmidt recognized the significance of whether one reads "the heavenly city" against a Platonic or apocalyptic background.[125] More recently, a Platonic and gnostic background has been subjected to major critique. Hurst's work on this issue is particularly significant; he argues that while Philo and the author of Hebrews share a common conceptual background in the Old Greek version of the Old Testament, Philo developed these concepts Platonically while the author of Hebrews did so *eschatologically*. From this perspective the background to Hebrews is to be located in Jewish apocalyptic and early Christian tradition.

That the primary background to Hebrews is to be found in *Jewish* apocalyptic is vitally important for its interpretation since, as N. T. Wright has shown, "*there is virtually no evidence that Jews were expecting the end of the space-time universe.*"[126] Such a view would flatly contradict Israel's creational monotheism. "As good creational monotheists, mainline Jews were not hoping to escape from

---

123. W. D. Davies, *The Gospel and the Land: Early Christianity and Jewish Territorial Doctrine* (Berkeley: University of California Press, 1974), 162.

124. G. Josipovici, *The Book of God: A Response to the Bible* (New Haven: Yale University Press, 1988), 266–67, with original emphasis. He asserts, "If the author of Hebrews does see Jesus in terms of the OT past, his sense of that past is remarkably thin" (ibid., 270). Similarly he says that even the Gospels with their emphasis on the kingdom of God not being of this world mark

> a fundamental shift in the way we are to conceive of human nature and culture. And there are good reasons for this. From the start Christianity was a religion not of people but of individuals, not of a locality but of all places and times. It was natural therefore that despite its attempt to retain much of the vocabulary of the Hebrew culture from which it sprang, it would be forced to drain that vocabulary of its original meaning. (ibid., 274)

From our examination of the Gospels, it is clear that here Josipovici sets up a series of false dichotomies. Isaacs (*Sacred Space*) examines the theology of Hebrews through the grid of sacred space. Her final discussion about the nature of "heaven" as our destiny is equivocal, caught between heaven as God's place and the typical biblical eschatology of a new creation.

125. K. L. Schmidt, "Jerusalem als Urbild und Abbild," in *Eranos-Jahrbuch*, vol. 18, *Aus der Welt der Urbilder: Sonderband for C. G. Jung* (Zurich: Rhein Verlag, 1950), 207–48; W. D. Davies, *Gospel and the Land*, 163.

126. N. T. Wright, *NTPG* 333.

the present universe into some Platonic realm of eternal bliss enjoyed by disembodied souls after the end of the space-time universe."[127] Important as the background is, the text of Hebrews itself must be determinative, and it is to this we now (re)turn.

As we have seen, Hebrews manifests a strong doctrine of creation as well as a sense of the age to come breaking in on the present, consistent with what we find in the rest of the New Testament. As Lane rightly explains, "Apocalyptic eschatology provided him [the author] the categories with which to interpret the entire history of God's redemptive action."[128] In 1:1–4 as elsewhere in Hebrews, the Son is described in the language of divine Wisdom. In 1:2 the Son is "heir of all things, through whom he [God] also created the worlds." In 1:3 the Son "sustains all things by his powerful word."

> The new clause ascribes to the Son the providential government of all created existence, which is the function of God himself. As the pre-creational Wisdom of God, the Son not only embodies God's glory but also reveals this to the universe as he sustains all things and bears them to their appointed end by his omnipotent word. The ascription of cosmic dimensions to the work of the Son was prompted by the total estimate which the writer had formed of his transcendent dignity.[129]

In 1:10–12 the traditional belief in God as creator is affirmed; the heavens and the earth are described as God's creation—they will "perish" and "wear out," but like clothing they will "be changed." In 2:10 God is described as the one "for whom and through whom all things exist."

Hebrews 11:3 is particularly interesting in relation to creation. In a reflection on Genesis 1, the author argues that creation is understood by *faith*; πίστει is placed at the start of the sentence for emphasis. In line with Genesis 1,[130] the author holds to a doctrine of creation order: κατηρτίσθαι is used in the LXX to mean "to establish," "to order," "to create," and it is translated by Lane as "was ordered by the word of God."[131] As we wrote (above) in our comments on 1:2, τοὺς αἰῶνας is best translated as "universe." The second half of 11:3 is important for our purposes since it appears to teach *creatio ex nihilo*, although this has been challenged by several commentators. The word order is unusual, and the negative μή can either qualify φαινομένων to read "not from anything visible," or qualify the entire infinitive clause to read "was not brought into being from anything observable."[132] Lane favors the latter translation, but I do not think there is a great deal at stake in this issue. The more important issue is whether the author rules out creation from preexistent matter. Several writers detect Platonic influence here,[133] but for Philo and Plato the world was created out of a visible mass, precisely the point the author here negates. As Lane says, "It may, in fact, have been the writer's intention to correct a widespread tendency in Hellenistic Judaism to read Gen. 1 in the light of Plato's doctrine of creation in the *Timaeus* (e.g., Wis 11:17: God's 'all-powerful hand created the world out of formless matter')."[134] My conclusion is that Hebrews

---

127. Ibid., 286.
128. W. L. Lane, *Hebrews 1–8*, 10.
129. Ibid., 14.
130. Bruce (*Epistle to the Hebrews*, 279–80) notes that Genesis is probably uppermost in the author's mind since he is about to refer to seven examples of faith from that book.
131. W. L. Lane, *Hebrews 9–13*, 325.
132. See ibid., 326–27.
133. S. G. Sowers, *The Hermeneutics of Philo and Hebrews: A Comparison of the Interpretation of the Old Testament in Philo Judaeus and the Epistle to the Hebrews* (Richmond: John Knox, 1965), 134–35; R. A. Stewart, "Creation and Matter in the Epistle to the Hebrews," *New Testament Studies* 12 (1965–66): 284–93; J. A. Thompson, *The Beginnings of Christian Philosophy: The Epistle to the Hebrews* (Washington, DC: Catholic Biblical Association of America, 1982), 75.
134. W. L. Lane, *Hebrews 9–13*, 332.

11:3 does indeed teach *creatio ex nihilo*.[135] Either way the clear emphasis is that our ordered universe has its origin in God and his word.

It is in Hebrews 8–9 that the new covenant comes into clear view. However, as Dunnill rightly notices, covenant imagery and allusions are found throughout the book.[136] The author uses Jeremiah 31:31–34[137] as his Old Testament basis for asserting that Christ has inaugurated the new covenant, which is superior to the old. The new covenant enables believers to receive the "promised eternal inheritance" (9:15). The discussion of Christ's heavenly redemptive ministry reaches its climax in 9:15. As elsewhere in the New Testament, "eternal" (αἰώνιος) does not mean "heavenly" but "of the age to come": it is an eschatological term for the renewed creation.

The author of Hebrews does, however, have a major and very important emphasis on heaven as the place of God, and in chapters 8–9 the earthly tabernacle is contrasted with the heavenly holy place, as we have seen. The crucial question is whether this expresses a *duality* or a Platonic-type *dualism*. The duality of heaven and earth is found throughout Scripture, and clearly in this duality, heaven as God's abode has primacy. However, throughout the New Testament this duality is connected with an eschatology moving toward a new heaven and a new earth. It would be surprising and jarring if the author is indeed arguing for a Platonic type of dualism since this would undercut his doctrine of creation and salvation history. A closer examination of the key texts is required.

In Hebrews 1:10–12 the author quotes from Psalm 102:26–27 in order to demonstrate that the Son is superior to the creation. Through quoting a version of the Septuagint, the author is able to take these verses as addressed by the Father to the Son.[138] For our purposes the key question is the eschatology in view in Hebrews 1:11–12. Of the earth and the heavens, it is said that they will

- perish
- wear out like clothing
- be rolled up like clothing
- be changed like clothing

Lane, E. Adams, J. A. Thompson, and others insist that the author here teaches the dissolution of the cosmos, its perishibility. In Adams's words:

> The statements of vv. 11a–12b express, as much as they do in their original psalmic context, the destructibility of the natural world. Heaven and earth had a beginning, they will grow old and they will eventually be dissolved. The cosmic order is viewed as "naturally" perishable: it deteriorates with age. It was not created to be everlasting, but with the propensity to decay. When the time comes, the creator himself . . . will dissolve the works of his hands; he will actively "roll them up."[139]

Similarly J. A. Thompson argues:

> By using this psalm as an exaltation text, the author has introduced the spatial framework into the argument. His argument is reminiscent of the Platonic view in which the "becoming"

---

135. Cf. Bruce (*Epistle to the Hebrews*, 278–80) who affirms *creatio ex nihilo* here; Attridge (*Epistle to the Hebrews*, 315–16) is more cautious and suggests that the unseen realities from which the visible is created are the constituents of the heavenly realm; Koester (*Hebrews*, 474) argues that what cannot be seen is the word of God.

136. See Dunnill, *Covenant and Sacrifice*, 149–87.

137. Heb. 8:8–12 is in substantial agreement with the LXX manuscript A (Codex Alexandrinus).

138. W. L. Lane, *Hebrews 1–8*, 30.

139. E. Adams, *The Stars Will Fall from Heaven: Cosmic Catastrophe in the New Testament and Its World* (London: T&T Clark, 2007), 184–85.

(*genesis*) in this creation is distinguished from the eternal world of "forms."... It is probable, therefore, that the author has read Ps. 102:26-28 [25-27 ET] with Platonic assumptions in order to interpret the exaltation and to demonstrate the precise way in which Christ is "better" than angels.[140]

There can be no question that the sovereignty of the Son over the creation is clearly asserted through this quote. Indeed, in Hebrews 1:13-14 this is precisely the point that is drawn from the previous verses: the Son's enemies will be made "a footstool" for his feet, whereas the angels are merely "spirits in . . . [God's] service." However, it is indeed questionable whether these verses teach, as E. Adams and J. A. Thompson argue, the destruction of the cosmos. For 1:11, Westcott comments on ἀπολοῦνται (they will perish): "The idea, as it is afterwards developed (xii. 26ff.), is of change, transfiguration, and not of annihilation."[141]

Clearly what is said about the earth and the heavens is highly metaphorical, and everything will depend on right interpretations of the metaphors. Verses 11b and 12a elaborate on what it means for the earth and the heavens to "perish," using the imagery of clothing. The verb ἀπολοῦνται by itself does not make this clear; it can mean "to die" or, as in Luke (5:37), "to be broken." Like clothing they will wear out, like a cloak they will be rolled up, and like clothing they will be changed. Nothing in this imagery of clothing, it should be recognized, suggests annihilation. If E. Adams is correct in seeing the image of rolling up (v. 12a) as evoking Isaiah 34:4, according to which "the heavens shall be rolled up like a scroll" (NKJV), then it is likely that what we have here, as in Isaiah, is the apocalyptic language of judgment; and as in Isaiah, this should not be taken literally but as the use of cosmic catastrophic language to evoke the notion of judgment. Indeed, this is the very theme picked up in Hebrews 1:13, with its evocation of Isaiah 66:1 and Psalm 2:12, verses that refer not to the annihilation of creation but to the changing of creation: the eradication of evil and revolt against the Son.

And Hebrews 1:12 does speak of transformation: "they will be changed." We are not told just what this change will constitute, but the imagery is reminiscent of 1 Corinthians 15:50-54, which also uses the imagery of clothing, of "putting on." In 1 Corinthians 15:53 what must be put on is "imperishability" and "immortality," but it is precisely "this perishable body" and "this mortal body" that must put these on so that death will have finally been conquered (cf. 15:54-57). As in Hebrews 1:13, this change is related to the overcoming of sin and its power, and precisely *not* to the annihilation of the cosmos. The problem in view is not that of a mutable creation but of a creation cursed with death as a result of sin. Thus the contrast being drawn in Hebrews 1:10-14 is not between the imperishable Son and the perishable creation, but between the perfect Son and a creation in dire need of redemption and transformation! The Son remains (v. 11) in the sense, as verse 12 puts it, that he is "the same" and his years never end.

So far so good. The writer's eschatology is basically the same as that of Jesus and Paul. Indeed, the idea of the Son as "heir of all things" (1:2) and the one through whom God created the world is paralleled in many places in Paul's Letters.[142] Particularly interesting is the use that Paul and Hebrews make of Psalm 8.[143] In Hebrews 2, Psalm 8 is used in relation to "the coming world" (2:5). Psalm 8 intertextually evokes Genesis 1:26-28 and is read this way by the author of Hebrews: the doctrine of royal stewardship is stated unequivocally in 2:8, but it admits that we do not yet see all things subject to human beings. However, Jesus has already achieved this role since he is

---

140. J. A. Thompson, *Beginnings of Christian Philosophy*, 137-38.

141. Westcott, *Epistle to the Hebrews*, 28. Similarly, Montefiore comments, "The Psalmist looks forward to a new heaven and a new earth. . . . It will be as though God were to give them a new suit of clothes" (*Epistle to the Hebrews*, 48).

142. On Hebrews and Pauline theology, see Hurst, *Epistle to the Hebrews*, 107-24; on 124 he suggests that the description of Hebrews as "deutero-Pauline" might be appropriate.

143. See ibid., 110-13.

now crowned with glory and honor. Jesus has achieved the state for which Adam was created, to be "crowned with *glory*" (cf. 2:9 with 2:7). Jesus is enthroned as the representative of humanity, and his crowning anticipates ours![144] The context of Psalm 8 is crucial in understanding the author's use of "glory." "Glory" refers to the dignity of being royal stewards over the creation; although humans do not yet have everything in subjection to themselves (2:8), Jesus is already crowned with "glory" (2:9). Verse 10 therefore, when it speaks of the creator God as "bringing many children to glory," is not talking about "taking them to heaven" but about leading them to the fulfillment of their human destiny as royal stewards of the new creation. The representative and corporate nature of Jesus's redemptive work is clearly stated in 2:10–13. Jesus became incarnate because he came to help "the descendents of Abraham" (2:16), and the problem he came to help them with was not their embodiment but the problem of death (2:14–15).

Paul alludes to or quotes Psalm 8 in 1 Corinthians 15:27; Romans 8:20; Philippians 2:10; and 3:21. It is particularly Paul's discussion in 1 Corinthians 15 that invites comparison with Hebrews. Hebrews makes much of Psalm 110, and in 1 Corinthians 15 Paul links Psalm 110:1 with Psalm 8:6 in the midst of his "second Adam" discourse, thereby "indicating that he is developing Ps. 8 not in terms of the unique dignities of an individual but in terms of one who represents and leads humankind to its appointed destiny."[145] The central point of 1 Corinthians 15:24–28 is "the predestined role of humankind as the mirror reflection, in the new creation, of God's universal rule."[146]

Hebrews 2:9, coming in the exposition immediately following the quote from Ps. 8, is worth revisiting in relation to the author's statement that "so that by the grace of God he might taste death for everyone" (ὅπως χάριτι θεοῦ ὑπὲρ παντὸς γεύσηται θανάτου). Πάντα occurs twice in verse 8, where it clearly refers to *every created thing*. Most scholars translate παντός in verse 9 as "everyone," but παντός could be masculine (everyone) or neuter (everything). In the context of the two preceding uses of the same word (in 2:8, in the plural form, πάντα), it seems to me that the most natural translation is "everything," so that Christ's priestly work is aimed at the redemption of the whole creation.

In Hebrews 11:8–16 Abraham is held up as a paradigm of faith for the Hebrews in that "he looked forward to the city that has foundations, whose architect and builder is God" (11:10). Hebrews 11:14 speaks of "a homeland," and verse 16 of "a better country, that is, a heavenly one." Verse 16 also states that God "has prepared a city for them." As we noticed above, the urban imagery would speak powerfully to the Hebrews, threatened as they were by the power of Rome, a city that repeatedly showed itself not to be built by God! In 12:22 the author speaks of "Mount Zion" and "the city of the living God, the heavenly Jerusalem." The image of a city fits well with New Testament eschatology because there is never an indication that God plans to lead his creation back to Eden, but rather forward to its destiny. But what of the adjective "heavenly"? Does it indicate that our destiny is not a new heavens and a new earth but "heaven"? The answer is, I think, No, not necessarily. In John 18:36 Jesus says to Pilate that his "kingdom is not from this world. If my kingdom were from this world, my followers would be fighting to keep me from being handed over to the Jews." As with Hebrews, the fact that Jesus's kingdom is from heaven does not for a moment mean it is of no earthly significance. In fact, the opposite is true: because the origin of his rule is from heaven, its political and earthly significance is cosmic! Heavenly, I suggest, qualifies "city" and "Jerusalem" not in the sense of going to heaven, but in the sense of a city and a place that is dominated by God, the one who dwells in heaven.

In Hebrews 12:25–29, "the main eschatological passage of the epistle,"[147] the author alerts the readers to the fact that God will shake the earth and the heaven. The NRSV translates verse 27: "This phrase, 'Yet once more,' indicates the removal of what is shaken—that is, created things—so that

---

144. See ibid., 110–11.
145. Ibid., 111.
146. Ibid., 112.
147. E. Adams, *Stars Will Fall from Heaven*, 185.

what cannot be shaken may remain." This translation appears to indicate the removal of "created things," the whole creation. Most recently, E. Adams has argued strongly for this interpretation. He notices that 12:26 is referring to the promise in Haggai 2:6, although the author omits Haggai's "and the sea and the dry land," in order to keep the focus on earth and heaven. The time when God's "voice shook the earth" (v. 26) is a reference to Sinai, but now God is about to shake the entire cosmos. Adams rightly points out that μετάθεσιν can mean "change" or "alteration," but in Hebrews and here probably means "removal."[148] What is removed are the shakable things, and according to Adams, these are defined as πεποιημένων (created things).

> The author of Hebrews thus envisions in this passage a cosmic catastrophe that results in the dissolution of the cosmos. By declaring that heaven and earth, as created things, are destined for "removal," is he indicating that they are to be annihilated, that is, reduced to nothing? This seems unlikely since such a thought probably lay beyond his horizon. Most likely, he means that they will be reduced to their pre-created, *material* condition.[149]

In a footnote Adams invokes Hebrews 11:3, which he takes to indicate that the world was formed out of invisible matter. Yet 11:3 is a very weak foundation for this view, as we have seen. But what of the phrase ὡς πεποιημένων (12:27)? Lane rightly notes that this expression stands in apposition to τῶν σαλευομένων (what is shaken) and translates it "as of these things having been made." An important clue as to how to interpret this verse lies in the metaphor of "shaking." The author gets this metaphor from Haggai, where it clearly refers to judgment. In 12:27-28 the shaking refers to the final eschatological judgment of God. The crucial question thus becomes how this judgment relates to the "removal" of verse 27. E. Adams's reading makes no sense of this passage since in verse 28 the readers, "we," who are very much part of the creation, are already receiving a kingdom that cannot be shaken! In biblical terms, creation is hardly thinkable apart from humans, and the dissolution of the creation would imply the dissolution of the readers of Hebrews, but verse 28 clearly denies this. Thus Caird is right, in my view, that the difference between the shakable and the unshakable lies, contra Adams, not in their status as created, but in their relationship to God in terms of judgment.[150] Verse 27, in other words, does *not* teach the dissolution of the creation but its purification. The picture is similar to that in 1 Corinthians 3:10-15, in which "the Day will disclose" how one has built on the foundation of Jesus Christ. Fire will destroy that which is wood, hay, and stubble. Intriguingly, Hebrews 12:29 declares that "our God is a consuming fire." In 12:25-29 it is thus God's final judgment that is in view, a judgment that will remove all that can be shaken, all that is ripe for judgment; that which is righteous will remain, and the Hebrews are encouraged to persevere because they "are receiving a kingdom that cannot be shaken" (12:28).[151]

Positively, Hebrews does envision a new temple. In 12:22-23 the readers are reminded that they have already come to Mount Zion, a new-temple image. This is juxtaposed with the images of "the city of the living God," "the heavenly Jerusalem," and "the assembly of the firstborn." The description of Christians as "the firstborn" is related to the description of Christ in 1:6 as "the firstborn." Lane argues that 1:6 refers not to Jesus's incarnation but to his ascension. If this is right, then firstborn would be associated with the resurrection of the dead, a major element in Jewish new-creation eschatology. Certainly the language of heavenly place must be read within the eschatological framework of Hebrews so that, as in other parts of the New Testament, the

---

148. Cf. W. L. Lane, *Hebrews 9-13*, 482.

149. E. Adams, *Stars Will Fall from Heaven*, 190-91, with original emphasis.

150. G. B. Caird, "The Christological Basis of Christian Hope," in *The Christian Hope*, by G. B. Caird et al. (London: SPCK, 1970), 21-24, esp. 23.

151. E. Adams (*Stars Will Fall from Heaven*, 194-99) ends up with a mass of contradictions by reading Heb. 12:25-29 in the way he does. Despite his view of 12:27, he nevertheless is compelled to acknowledge tantalizing indications that the author does indeed anticipate a new creation.

vision of a new temple does not mean going to heaven but refers to a creation in which God dwells, precisely the picture we find in Revelation 21. As C. K. Barrett points out, "The heavenly tabernacle in Hebrews is not the product of Platonic idealism, but the eschatological temple of apocalyptic Judaism, the temple which is in heaven primarily in order that it be manifested on earth."[152]

Josipovici is thus quite wrong to argue that the author's reading of Jeremiah 31 obliterates the material dimensions of the Old Testament. In Hebrews 6:7–8 the author uses an illustration that points in quite the opposite direction. Ground that drinks up the rain and produces a crop useful for those for whom it is cultivated "receives a blessing from God." Here in one verse we have ground, rain, agriculture, consumption of the fruits of the earth—all equated, as in Genesis, with God's *blessing*. Hebrews does not obliterate the material spirituality of the Old Testament but moves the focus from the land to *the whole creation*.[153]

A Faith-Full Response

The major Old Testament texts in Hebrews 10–12 are Habakkuk 2:4 and Proverbs 3:11–12, from which the two major themes of (1) faith and (2) endurance and discipline (*paideia*) emerge. In chapters 11–12 the hortatory dimension of Hebrews builds to a crescendo as the author reaches for evocative images, such as the "cloud of witnesses" (12:1), to spur his addresses on to faith, hope, and endurance. In this final section we will concentrate on faith as the appropriate response to Jesus as Son and high priest.

Hebrews 11:1 declares, Ἔστιν δὲ πίστις ἐλπιζομένων ὑπόστασις, πραγμάτων ἔλεγχος οὐ βλεπομένων. Here ὑπόστασις has been much discussed;[154] central to it are the connotations of objectivity and certainty.[155] Hence Lane translates verse 1 as follows: "*Now faith celebrates the objective reality [of the blessings] for which we hope, the demonstration of events as yet unseen.*"[156] Faith is trust,[157] but a trust that has a *certainty* about it. Belief in creation (11:3), for example, cannot be proved, but by faith it is understood (νοοῦμεν). *Hope* (the verb ἐλπιζομένων is used in v. 1) is an assurance about the eschatology, the history of salvation as we find it in the Bible. In 11:4–40 the author assembles a vast cloud of witnesses, who serve as examples of lives lived in the light of such faith. We may wonder why some of them are included, such as

---

152. C. K. Barrett, "Eschatology of the Epistle to the Hebrews," 389.

153. Hebrews' universal vision should be carefully distinguished from the soteriological universalism that is popular nowadays. With its creation-wide scope, Hebrews articulates a very strong doctrine of judgment.

154. For a survey of views, see E. Grässer, *Der Glaube im Hebräerbrief* (Marburg: Elwert, 1965), 46–47.

155. W. L. Lane, *Hebrews 9–13*, 325–26.

156. Ibid., 325, with original emphasis.

157. K. Barth says, "Perhaps the strongest New Testament account of this New Testament faith which is not only bound up with hope but ultimately identical with it, is the eleventh chapter of the Epistle to the Hebrews" (*CD* IV/1:331).

the judges mentioned in 11:32, but as we saw with the author's treatment of Moses, he chooses to focus on their positive achievements while well aware of their "weaknesses" (4:15).[158]

As with the cloud of witnesses, we are called to stake our lives on the objective reality of creation and redemption. The author deliberately follows chapter 11 with 12:1-3; as we noticed above, N. T. Wright draws attention to the parallel between the climax of Sirach 44:1–50:21 and Hebrews. This section in Sirach climaxes with the ministry of the high priest Simon in the temple. The list of heroes in Hebrews 11 aims to make the same point, but with a christological twist. Instead of the present high priest in the temple being the telos of Israel's history, it is Jesus, the true high priest: "Hebrews 12.1–3 stands to 11.4–40 as Sirach 50.1–21 does to 44.1–49.16."[159] In the light of this telos of the true story of the world, *we*[160] are called to run the race of life with perseverance, keeping our eyes on "Jesus, the pioneer and perfecter of our faith." We have—already—come to the city of the living God, to the assembly of the firstborn, and we are to live in the light of this reality. We are to be a people of faith and hope. Thus Karl Barth applies Hebrews 11:

> Waiting quietly for the Lord, hope restrains faith, preventing it from rushing forward in too great a hurry. It confirms it so that it does not waver in its trust in God's promises or begin to doubt. It revives it so that it does not grow weary. It keeps it fixed on its final goal so that it does not give up half-way or when it is in captivity. It continually renews and re-establishes it, thus seeing to it that it continually rises up in more vital forms and perseveres to the end.[161]

Like all good sermons, Hebrews recontextualizes the life and worldview of its readers and hearers within the true story of the world centered in Jesus. Hebrews 13:2 has a fascinating reference to "entertaining angels unawares" (cf. KJV). This verse inspired the title of Peter Berger's classic *A Rumour of Angels: Modern Society and the Rediscovery of the Supernatural*.[162] Berger has

---

158. P. M. Eisenbaum, "Heroes and History in Hebrews 11," in *Early Interpretation of the Scriptures of Israel: Investigations and Proposals*, ed. C. A. Evans and J. A. Sanders, JSNTSup 148 (Sheffield: Sheffield Academic, 1997), 380–96; idem, *The Jewish Heroes of Christian History: Hebrews 11 in Literary Context*, SBLDS 156 (Atlanta: Scholars Press, 1997). Eisenbaum explores the criteria for the heroes included in Heb. 11 and concludes that the author deliberately chose figures marginalized in Israel. Thus they are good examples for Christians struggling with marginalization.

159. N. T. Wright, *NTPG* 410.

160. Note the plural verbs in Heb. 12:1–3.

161. K. Barth, *CD* IV/1:332.

162. P. L. Berger, *A Rumour of Angels: Modern Society and the Rediscovery of the Supernatural* (London: Allen Lane, 1970), 95.

consistently alerted us to the fact that we do not have to adopt the secular plausibility structures of our day: we have a choice. As Backhaus therefore declares, in a rich chapter on the ethics of Hebrews, "The way, therefore, is open to set out to explore those rumors of angels and to follow them to their source."[163]

Faith-Full Biblical Interpretation

It is simply impossible to take the message of Hebrews seriously and then to argue that faith has nothing to do with biblical interpretation, that we ought to keep faith and exegesis hermetically sealed in separate compartments. In the light of Hebrews, the whole of our lives is to be lived in faith, and that will certainly include our practice of interpretation. Theological interpretation will be faith-*full* and seek to work on the basis of the objective certainties of creation and redemption. It will be characterized, as we have argued in this book, by *faith seeking understanding*, thus precisely not by unbelief seeking understanding, and not by doubt seeking understanding.

Such an approach inevitably privileges the ecclesial context as the primary context for the reception of Scripture via listening. We have seen this to be true of Hebrews, whose goal is to facilitate attentive listening to "the one who is speaking" (12:25).[164] Where then does academic interpretation fit in this context? As I hope this chapter has demonstrated, privileging the ecclesial context does not for a moment subvert utmost rigor in academic interpretation. Academic interpretation is a *holy* calling (cf. Heb. 3:1), a priestly calling that works from faith and toward faith and in the process provides an indispensable contribution in deepening our reception of Hebrews as part of God's Word. We have seen how close attention to the Greek in which it was written, taking Hebrews seriously as a literary/oral composition, paying close attention to its use of the Old Testament, engaging with its theology in relation to that of the rest of the canon, and so forth, are of vital importance in reading and listening to Hebrews. The clear goal of all this work, however, has been to enable us to hear God's address today.

Above we have already given some indication of what Hebrews might mean for the contemporary biblical scholar. In terms of Application B in chapter 15 (below), how might Hebrews address us today? This will vary depending on our cultural context. For the many, many believers suffering persecution for

---

163. K. Backhaus, "How to Entertain Angels: Ethics in the Epistle to the Hebrews," in *Hebrews: Contemporary Methods, New Insights*, ed. G. Gelardini (Leiden: Brill, 2005), 149–75.

164. See J. I. Griffiths, *Hebrews and Divine Speech*, LNTS (London: Bloomsbury T&T Clark, 2015).

their faith today, Hebrews will speak directly and powerfully. For those of us in the comfortable consumer West, the message may be harder to hear amid a Christianity-lite that is often dualistic and privatized. Take the United States, for example, aptly characterized by Peter Berger as a nation of Indians (i.e., very religious) ruled by a Swedish elite (i.e., very secular).[165] A privatized faith fits easily in such a context since it never challenges the cultural direction provided by the secular elite. In biblical studies, for example, which many enter as a result of coming to a living faith in Jesus, the temptation is to have one foot in the ecclesia and the other in the secular academy, without ever exploring the connection between faith in Jesus and the practice of biblical interpretation. The "drift" away from Jesus[166] inevitably sets in, and we end up part of that desperate situation in too much Western theology in which "Christian doctrine is bowdlerized by its own theologians and deep literal conviction is not conspicuous by its presence."[167] Hebrews addresses this situation incisively in its awareness of the "power of unbelief" (cf. 3:12, 19). Unbelief has a power all of its own and directs biblical interpretation along distinctive lines as formatively as does faith. Clearly this is a far cry from Hebrews 11:1 (cf. 10:22). At times as biblical scholars, we will certainly find ourselves crying, "I believe! Help my unbelief," itself a cry of faith, but we are called to work out of faith and toward faith.

As I worked on Hebrews, I was struck with just how rich and extraordinary a work it is, leading us again and again to see Jesus. Like the rest of the Bible, Hebrews serves up a feast and invites us to nourish ourselves at its table again and again, even if in our cultural and academic context it is a table in the wilderness. It is time, *today* (Heb. 3:7–19), for exegetes to contribute all their gifts and energy to serving up bread and not stones.

Closing Lectio Divina

1. *Entering into the silence.* Take five minutes to slow down and become centered in Jesus. Let your mind slow down, and become centered in your heart, the core of your being. Repeat your prayer word slowly as you breathe in and out, opening yourself to God.
2. *The presence of God.* In Jesus you have already arrived at the city of the living God, the assembly of the firstborn. As you reflect on this reality,

---

165. P. Berger, G. Davie, and E. Folks, *Religious America, Secular Europe? A Theme and Variations* (Burlington, VT: Ashgate, 2008), 12.
166. Scholars nowadays see Hebrews as less about a lapse back into Judaism as a drift away from faith in Christ and the associated Christian practices.
167. E. Gellner, *Postmodernism, Reason and Religion* (London: Routledge, 1992), 5.

anticipate entering the sanctuary to meet with God. God is present, waiting for us. He arrives before us, desiring to connect with us even more than our most intimate friend. We take a moment to greet our living God, who comes to us in Jesus.

3. *Freedom.* "In these days God taught me as a schoolteacher teaches a pupil" (Ignatius of Loyola). We remind ourselves that there are things God has to teach us yet, and we ask for the grace to hear them and to be changed by them.
4. *Consciousness.* How am I really feeling? We acknowledge how we really are. Jesus, we remind ourselves, became fully human and was tempted as we are. He is able to "sympathize with our weaknesses" (4:15). It is the real me that the Lord loves.
5. *The Word.* We take time to read Hebrews 12:1–4 slowly, a few times, allowing ourselves to dwell on anything that strikes us.
6. *Conversation.* What feelings rise up in me as I pray and reflect on Hebrews 12:1–4? I imagine Jesus, my great high priest, sitting in a chair opposite me, and I open my heart to him and share with him my thoughts, feelings, reflections.
7. *Conclusion.* Glory be to the Father, and to the Son, and to the Holy Spirit. As it was in the beginning, is now, and ever shall be, world without end.
Amen.

15

Preaching the Bible for All It's Worth

The Resurrection of the Sermon and the Incarnation of the Christ

The Word of God comes home to us, as no word of man as such can come home to us, and as even death does not come home to us, because it is the Word of our Creator, the Word of him who bounds our existence and the end of our existence, from whose side it is affirmed and denied, because through this Word everything has its being and is preserved, and without it would not exist. To Him we belong who here makes Himself heard. Whatever He may say, it will at least also be said within this relation of the Creator to His creature.

Karl Barth[1]

Modernist thought hears man answer without any one having called him. It hears him talk to himself.

Karl Barth[2]

Of the living God, on the other hand, we read that *his word runs very swiftly* (Ps. 147:15). It goes forth from Jerusalem still, the place of God's self-disclosure on earth, and the gate by which it issues is that of Holy Scripture, the testimony of the apostles and prophets who saw with their eyes and touched with their

---

1. K. Barth, *The Doctrine of the Word of God* (CD I/1), 161.
2. Ibid., 68.

hands God come among us in Jerusalem. And the Word still circles the earth and returns to where it came from, bringing God back the praise he covets, the true tale of what he has done.

Oliver O'Donovan[3]

This means that we shall never look upon the prophets and apostles as merely objects for the study and assessment of later readers; they will always be living, acting, speaking subjects on their own account. The fact that they have spoken once does not mean that they have now ceased to speak. On the contrary, they take up and deliver the Word afresh in every age and to every people, at every cultural level and to every individual.

Karl Barth[4]

If the Holy Spirit is speaking in those who are handed over to the persecutors on Christ's account, why not also in those who are handing Christ over to the learners?

Augustine of Hippo[5]

It's a futile preacher outwardly of God's word, who isn't also inwardly a listener.

Augustine of Hippo[6]

Introduction

In churches in which preaching is taken seriously, we expect ministers to draw on the commentaries and other works of biblical scholars. But would we regard exposure to—and perhaps even the practice of—preaching as an indispensable part of the formation of a biblical scholar?[7] Doubtless in most

---

3. O. O'Donovan, *The Word in Small Boats: Sermons from Oxford* (Grand Rapids: Eerdmans, 2010), 3, with original emphasis.
4. K. Barth, *CD* III.3:49.
5. Augustine of Hippo, *DDC* 4.32.
6. Augustine, *Essential Sermons*, trans. E. Hill (Hyde Park, NY: New City, 2007), 235.
7. H. Thielicke (*The Trouble with the Church: A Call for Renewal*, trans. J. W. Doberstein [New York: Harper & Row, 1965]) comments, "In these days when my Hamburg faculty of theology is completing its first decade, I remember with gratitude that here every member of the faculty also preaches. We have sworn to raise this banner in order to help bridge this chasm in our little corner" (29). On Thielicke and preaching, see H. O. Old, *The Reading and Preaching of the Scriptures in the Worship of the Christian Church*, 7 vols. (Grand Rapids: Eerdmans, 1998–2010), 1:836–55.

departments of biblical studies nowadays, the very idea would go down like a lead balloon! Ellen Davis rightly reports, "Indeed, it is now widely regarded as axiomatic that one should not do exegesis in the pulpit. Conversely 'homiletical treatments' of Scripture are dismissed by biblical scholars as inherently lacking in substance."[8]

As suggested in this volume, however, if we privilege *listening and the ecclesial context* as the primary modes for reception of the Word, then not only should biblical studies inform preaching, but preaching also should form a fertile soil from which biblical studies emerges. I have sought to reconfigure biblical interpretation within an arc traced *from* listening and *toward* listening, with biblical interpretation nested in between these two poles. Within these poles preaching plays a fundamental role.

The Primacy of Preaching

Few theologians and exegetes have emphasized the primacy of preaching as much as Karl Barth[9] and Bonhoeffer.[10] The day before Bonhoeffer was martyred, he preached. In his work *Ethics*, Bonhoeffer argues that in the church the commandment of God confronts us in two ways: it is addressed to the individual in confession and to the assembly in preaching.[11] He argues that these two possibilities alert us to the shortcomings of the Protestant and Catholic churches respectively. The Protestant church is in danger of losing the concrete, individual application of the confessional, whereas the Catholic church is in danger of losing the proclamation to the assembly. Personally I have found in my experience as a pastor that the interchange between pulpit and counseling room/spiritual direction is rich and most productive when one feeds off the other.

In terms of practical theology, it is important to notice that for Bonhoeffer *both* of these activities are forms of divine proclamation. Cornick similarly points out that for the Reformers, and Zwingli in particular, preaching *was* pastoral care:

---

8. E. F. Davis, *Wondrous Depth: Preaching the Old Testament* (Louisville: Westminster John Knox, 2005), xii. See in this respect Wallace M. Alston Jr.'s useful chapter, "The Recovery of Theological Preaching," in *The Power to Comprehend with All the Saints*, ed. W. M. Alston Jr. and C. A. Jarvis (Grand Rapids: Eerdmans, 2009), 221–36.

9. On Karl Barth and preaching, see Old, *Reading and Preaching*, who comments, "As with Dietrich Bonhoeffer and a number of others, Barth may be better known as a theologian to the outside world, but in his own heart he was above all a preacher" (6:773–86).

10. On Bonhoeffer and preaching see ibid., 801–25.

11. D. Bonhoeffer, *Ethics* (New York: Macmillan, 1955), 258–59.

> Preaching was not a rarified academic activity, although in [Zwingli's] eyes it demanded the very best of scholarship. Applying the Word of God to the life of God's people, indeed of God's world, was at its heart a pastoral activity, just as it was for the Old Testament prophets in whose work he delights. It was all of a piece—public, prophetic, private, consoling, broken into the multiplicity of the minister's work, baptizing, administering the sacraments, visiting the sick, caring for the poor from the Church's resources, but above all teaching.[12]

Bonhoeffer, in the light of this comprehensive understanding of proclamation, asserts:

> The mandate which is given to the Church is the mandate of proclamation. God desires a place at which His Word is repeatedly spoken, expounded, interpreted and disseminated until the end of the world. The word which came from heaven in Jesus Christ desires to return again in the form of human speech. The mandate of the Church is the word of God. God Himself desires to be present in this word. God Himself desires to speak His word in the Church.[13]

Like Karl Barth, Bonhoeffer holds the proclaimed word close to that of *the* Word: "the proclaimed word ... is the Christ himself walking through his congregation as the Word."[14] "The proclaimed word is the Christ bearing human nature. This word is no new incarnation, but the Incarnate One who bears the sins of the world. Through the Holy Spirit this word becomes the actualization of his acceptance and sustenance."[15] The Word creates community and by its nature is directed toward the congregation: "It seeks community, it needs community, because it is already laden with humanity."[16]

Barth, however, rightly states that not all language about God in the church is proclamation. Proclamation is

> human language in and through which God Himself speaks, like a king through the mouth of his herald, which moreover is meant to be heard and apprehended as language in and through which God Himself speaks, and so heard and apprehended in faith as the divine decision upon life and death, as the divine judgment and the divine acquittal, the eternal law and the eternal gospel both together.[17]

---

12. D. Cornick, "The Reformation Crisis in Pastoral Care," in *A History of Pastoral Care*, ed. G. R. Evans (London: Cassell, 2002), 236.

13. Bonhoeffer, *Ethics*, 259.

14. D. Bonhoeffer, "Lectures on Preaching," in *Bonhoeffer: Worldly Preaching*, trans. and ed. Clyde E. Fant (Nashville: Nelson, 1975), 126.

15. Ibid., 127.

16. Ibid.

17. K. Barth, *Doctrine of the Word of God*, 57.

God's Word cannot be confined to preaching. Barth claims that God may speak to us through communism, a concerto, a flowering plant, or a dead dog! He may address us through an atheist or a pagan and "in that way give us to understand that the boundary between Church and the profane still and repeatedly takes a course quite different from that which we hitherto thought we saw."[18] Where God genuinely so speaks, we should listen to him, but this is *not* what we are called to proclaim.[19] The church has the commission to preach *Scripture*: "The fact of the canon tells us simply that the church has regarded the Scriptures as the place where we can expect to hear the voice of God."[20] And Scripture is designed to be *preached*: "Preaching is such proclamation; i.e., the attempt, essayed by one called thereto in the Church, to express in his own words in the form of an exposition of a portion of the Biblical testimony to revelation, and to make comprehensible to men of his day, the promise of God's revelation, reconciliation and calling, as they are to be expected here and now."[21]

Barth discerns a threefold form of the one Word of God: the Word of God preached; the written Word of God, Scripture; and the Word of God revealed, Jesus Christ himself. "In this threefold form and not otherwise, . . . it is given us, and in this form we must endeavour to understand it conceptually."[22] There is certainly room for reflection on just how closely Barth and Bonhoeffer hold preaching in relation to the Word,[23] and on the different forms proclamation takes in the church, as well as the vital role of other forms of language in the church, such as liturgy. What *is* insightful about their views is the high view of preaching as facilitating God's address, as an event that enables and produces personal encounter with the living God.

Barth's and Bonhoeffer's high view of preaching as proclamation of the Word evokes the ministry of the Old Testament prophets. Yet there are

18. Ibid., 61.
19. Cf. Wallace M. Alston, "Recovery of Theological Preaching," 229–30.
20. K. Barth, *Homiletics*, trans. G. W. Bromiley and D. E. Daniels (Louisville: Westminster John Knox, 1991), 78.
21. K. Barth, *Doctrine of the Word of God*, 61.
22. Ibid., 135–36.
23. For an evangelical evaluation, see G. W. Bromiley, "The Authority of Scripture in Karl Barth," in *Hermeneutics: Authority and Canon*, ed. D. A. Carson and J. D. Woodbridge (Downers Grove, IL: InterVarsity, 1986), 271–94. The Second Helvetic Confession (written by H. Bullinger, 1562; rev., 1564, https://www.ccel.org/creeds/helvetic.htm), chap. 1, states: "Wherefore when this Word of God is now preached in the church by preachers lawfully called, we believe that the very Word of God is proclaimed, and received by the faithful." W. Brueggemann (*The Practice of Prophetic Imagination: Preaching an Emancipatory Word* [Minneapolis: Fortress, 2012], 2) suggests that we think of the preacher as a scribe rather than a prophet, as "a 'scribe' who handles old texts and permits them to be seen with contemporary force and authority." See also A. Kuyper, *Our Worship* (Grand Rapids: Eerdmans, 2009), 162–63.

important differences between preaching and Old Testament prophecy, not least the mode of direct inspiration, but the similarities are instructive. They remind us, for example, that much of the Old Testament consists of preaching, as does much of the New Testament. This in itself should alert us to the fundamental connection between preaching and biblical interpretation, as discussed above. The canon simply will not allow us to relegate preaching to the role of a second-class citizen in relation to academic biblical interpretation. The analogy with prophecy also reminds us that God rules over his people through his Word, and that in our fifth act of the drama of Scripture, Christ rules over his church through his Word.

There is thus a great deal at stake in the relationship between biblical hermeneutics and preaching. To explore this relationship, we will need to take note of the major homiletical models in practice today, examine the history of homiletics, and focus on the crucial issue of application. As we will see, it is in and around application that the relationship between biblical interpretation and preaching emerges most clearly into focus.

The History of Homiletics[24]

Especially in the wake of the emergence of hermeneutics as a philosophical discipline, diverse schools of homiletics can be identified: contemporary traditional homiletics, new homiletics, postliberal homiletics, and postmodern homiletics.[25] *Contemporary traditional* homiletics conceives of the relationship between Scripture and the congregation in terms of the historical-cultural gap between today's hearers and the original recipients of the biblical texts. With the *right method*, the preacher abstracts timeless truths from the Bible and applies these truths to the congregation. *New homiletics* focuses on the event of understanding and aims, not at applying propositional truth, but at the evocation of a Word-event experienced by the congregation.[26] *Postliberal homiletics* makes narrative central and seeks to allow the Word to absorb the world via its narrative shape. *Postmodern homiletics* seeks to open up a conversation between Scripture and congregation that generates meaning/s.

---

24. On the history of preaching see Y. Brilioth, *A Brief History of Preaching* (Philadelphia: Fortress, 1965); P. S. Wilson, *A Concise History of Preaching* (Nashville: Abingdon, 1992); Old, *Reading and Preaching*.

25. For much of this discussion, I am indebted to the very useful work by A. Spears, "The Theological Hermeneutics of Homiletical Application and Ecclesiastes 7:23–29" (PhD diss., University of Liverpool, 2006).

26. For a recent example, see P. S. Wilson, *Setting Words on Fire: Putting God at the Center of the Sermon* (Nashville: Abingdon, 2008), esp. chap. 3.

In many ways, these types of homiletics are clearly not antithetical. There *is* a historical gap between the Bible and contemporary hearers, and the preacher needs to be aware of it. *Contemporary traditional* homiletics also alerts us to the instructional element in preaching: there *is* truth to be conveyed. As articulated by Barth in particular, preaching is also an event that facilitates an encounter with the living God. In our exploration of biblical theology, we argued for a narrative approach that itself functions as a hermeneutic and interprets our place in God's story; thus there are important insights in the postliberal approach. And there is much to learn from postmodern approaches about congregational involvement in the sermon.

Nevertheless, there are important differences among these approaches. Some of these are at the *surface level* and fairly obvious. Contemporary traditional homiletics easily becomes a type of instruction that makes it difficult to take the event aspect of preaching seriously. The most obvious difference is between strongly postmodern homiletics and the other three, since such postmodern approaches tend to place the hearer on the same level as the biblical text or even, in practice, above it, and they may overemphasize the creative input of the congregation and the preacher. More important differences lurk beneath the surface at the hermeneutical level, differences related to issues of language, epistemology, textuality, and history, as Spears has so ably pointed out.[27] Differences at this deeper level are often antithetical and move back into alternative worldviews. Language and textuality have been central to postmodernism, and McClure's postmodern view of textuality in his *Other-Wise Preaching*,[28] for example, cannot be reconciled with narrative approaches such as that of Mathewson in his *The Art of Preaching Old Testament Narrative*.

Spears examines the hermeneutical substrata of homiletics in relation to the "most vexing problem facing homiletics today," namely, *application*.[29] As his research shows, one's view of preaching, and of application in particular, is deeply rooted in hermeneutical issues, issues that far too often control preaching unconsciously, at the subterranean level. A way to get at this deeper level is to explore the history of homiletics. Clearly, in a single chapter we cannot do this in any detail, and so, following Spears, we will focus on aspects of the history of the oldest and most influential approach today, that of contemporary traditional homiletics.

---

27. Spears, "Theological Hermeneutics."
28. J. S. McClure, *Other-Wise Preaching: A Postmodern Ethic for Homiletics* (St. Louis: Chalice, 2001), 13–26.
29. Spears, "Theological Hermeneutics," 3.

The History of Contemporary Traditional Homiletics (CTH)

The major exponent of this tradition today is Haddon W. Robinson (1930–). Robinson's textbook *Biblical Preaching* has sold over 200,000 copies and is used in over 160 colleges and seminaries.[30] Robinson emphasizes the role of the thesis in preaching: "To ignore the principle that a central, unifying idea must be at the heart of an effective sermon is to push aside what experts in both communication theory and preaching have to tell us."[31] This unifying idea is a proposition; for Robinson it consists of a subject and a complement.[32] Duane Litfin, a student of Robinson, says, "If we are to handle the text of Scripture with integrity, Haddon Robinson has taught us, we must listen to it at the level of its ideas."[33] Similarly James Daane asserts, "Every properly selected text expresses a truth which can be stated in propositional form."[34] Thus Spears rightly states, "This dual focus, on propositional sermons and Scripture as propositional, is a defining characteristic of CTH that radically shapes the approach to application."[35] It is important to recognize that CTH is a strong version of propositionalism. Clearly Scripture contains propositions and is chock-full of instruction and teaching, but CTH follows the sort of view of Scripture expressed by Carl Henry as "a propositional revelation of the unchanging truth of God."[36] The effect of this approach to homiletics is that *method* becomes central to exegesis, hence comes the popularity in many evangelical circles of Ed Hirsch's distinction between meaning and significance in interpretation.[37] From this perspective, application follows the methodological analysis of meaning in relating the propositional truth abstracted from Scripture and delivered to the congregation.

There are multiple problems with CTH. First, it distorts the nature of Scripture by reducing it to propositions.[38] Clearly there is a propositional dimension

---

30. Ibid., 19.

31. Haddon W. Robinson, *Biblical Preaching: The Development and Delivery of Expository Messages* (Grand Rapids: Baker, 2001), 37.

32. Ibid., 41.

33. D. Litfin, "New Testament Challenges to Big Idea Preaching," in *The Big Idea of Biblical Preaching: Connecting the Bible to People*, ed. K. Willhite and S. Gibson (Grand Rapids: Baker Academic, 1998), 53–66, esp. 56.

34. J. Daane, *Preaching with Confidence: A Theological Essay on the Power of the Pulpit* (Grand Rapids: Eerdmans, 1980), 132.

35. Spears, "Theological Hermeneutics," 21–22.

36. C. F. H. Henry, *God, Revelation, and Authority* (Waco: Word Books, 1979; reprint, Wheaton: Crossway, 1999), 3:457. See Spears, "Theological Hermeneutics," 22–23.

37. See E. D. Hirsch, *Validity in Interpretation* (New Haven: Yale University Press, 1967); idem, *The Aims of Interpretation* (Chicago: University of Chicago Press, 1976); Spears, "Theological Hermeneutics," 36–37.

38. Note the debate in this respect between Charles Hodge and Horace Bushnell. See A. C. Thiselton, "Biblical Interpretation," in *The Modern Theologians: An Introduction to Christian*

to Scripture, and this is more pronounced in some texts than others. But the glory of Scripture is that God has given us a library of books containing an immense diversity of literature, ranging from narrative to prophecy, law, wisdom, gospels, letters, and the sort of apocalyptic-prophetic material we find in Revelation. Speech-act theory is helpful in alerting us to the many different intentions of biblical texts. Their illocutionary force often cannot be reduced to telling the truth in a propositional form. Instruction in the sense of conveying truth is one illocutionary force that needs to be seen in the context of many other such forces, such as warning, opening a dialogue, encouraging, rendering a world, inviting, and so forth. The rich diversity of these illocutionary forces needs to be fully in play in order for us to hear Scripture address us with power.

The desire of CTH to preserve the *objectivity* of the biblical text is admirable; Scripture does have a determinate shape and resists being treated like a wax nose. This shape is, however, literary rather than logical, and what is needed instead is a *thick* notion of objectivity that does justice to the literary, kerygmatic, and historical dimensions of the biblical text.

A distinction should thus, as suggested in chapter 11 (above), be made between *thick* and *thin* notions of objectivity. However, it would be quite wrong to relinquish *any* notion of objectivity or realism, as some postmoderns do. The point is that a reductionistic Enlightenment understanding of objectivity should be rejected because it fails to take into account a variety of factors that influence the acquisition of knowledge, and it yields a narrow view of biblical textuality. A thicker notion of method *and* of biblical textuality is required, since interpretation involves both of these elements. But this means broadening rather than abandoning the quest for objectivity entirely, as some postmodern thinkers are prone to do. In our history-dominated context, careful consideration of the genre of texts can be particularly helpful in resisting imposition of thin methodologies on them; such care forces one to take the different aspects of the biblical texts seriously. Drawing on Eco's notion of open and closed texts, Spears observes the tendency of CTH to read all biblical texts as closed, whereas in fact they range from being more open to being more closed, and interpretation will vary accordingly. What must be clear is that open texts are not open to any and every interpretation, but may allow a range of readings within clear bounds.

In order to understand what is at stake in CTH, an examination of its roots is crucial. Spears identifies the following as central historical ingredients in CTH:[39]

Theology in the Twentieth Century, ed. D. Ford with R. Mears, 2nd ed. (Oxford: Blackwell, 1997), 287–304, esp. 300; Spears, "Theological Hermeneutics," 16–17.

39. Spears, "Theological Hermeneutics," 10–18.

1. *The rhetoric of Pierre de la Ramée (Petrus Ramus, 1515–72/75).* The effect of Ramus's reconfiguration of rhetoric was to turn the sermon into an act of logic, into "logical discourse rather than oral persuasions."[40]

2. *Protestant preaching.* Ramus's approach deeply influenced Puritan preaching, with its emphasis on plain thinking.[41] William Perkins's *The Art of Prophesying* was the seminal work in this area. Spears describes his homiletics as "Ramist rhetoric baptized into homiletics."[42] In France a similar shift can be observed in Jean Claude's *Traité de la composition d'un sermon* (1688), one of the most prized Protestant books on homiletics. In 1796 Charles Simeon translated Claude's work into English and appended it to his *Horae homileticae.*

The shift embodied in Perkins's and Claude's approaches is more than cosmetic: "It is part of a fundamental epistemological shift in Western culture, a change in the way that truth itself is understood, or at least how we grasp truth."[43] The epistemological shift is that of the early Enlightenment philosophers and in particular Descartes, with his emphasis on clear ideas as utterly central to truth.

3. *Richard Whately (1787–1863).* In his *Elements of Rhetoric*, Whately, the Anglican archbishop of Dublin, affirmed Aristotle's view of rhetoric as the art of persuasion, but unlike Aristotle and like Ramus, Whately separated logic from rhetoric. Logic discovers truth by investigation whereas rhetoric is about the presentation of that truth in a persuasive manner.

4. *Charles Hodge (1797–1878).* The emergence of Cartesian rationalism and the scientific revolution required a response from theology. The Princeton school, of which Hodge was a leading figure, accepted the epistemological changes of the Enlightenment and sought to secure biblical truth on this basis. Thus Hodge notoriously argued, "The Bible is to the theologian what nature is to the man of science. It is his store-house of facts; and his method of ascertaining what the Bible teaches, is the same as that which the natural philosopher adopts to ascertain what nature teaches."[44] As Buckley has cogently argued in his *At the Origins of Modern Atheism*, this acceptance of the epistemic foundations of the Enlightenment was a fatal step, one that more insightful theologians such as Abraham Kuyper in the Netherlands refused to take.[45]

---

40. O. C. Edwards Jr., *A History of Preaching* (Nashville: Abingdon, 2004), 363.

41. See J. C. Adams, "Ramist Conceptions of Testimony, Judicial Analogies, and the Puritan Conversion Narrative," *Rhetorica* 9 (1991): 251–68.

42. Spears, "Theological Hermeneutics," 12.

43. E. F. Davis, *Imagination Shaped: Old Testament Preaching in the Anglican Tradition* (Valley Forge, PA: Trinity Press International, 1995), 3.

44. C. Hodge, *Systematic Theology* (Peabody, MA: Hendrickson, 1999), 1:27.

45. See Kuyper, *Our Worship*, esp. 159–206. Kuyper notes that the minister will see that preaching involves instruction, but that this is only one aspect of his task as an ambassador. "As

5. John Broadus (1827–95). It is in Broadus's *On the Preparation and Delivery of Sermons* that we see the closest connections with CTH. The sermon "must have a subject . . . the focal idea . . . one main point."[46] The subject or idea must be combined with a predicate so that it can be expressed as a proposition.[47] "The discourse is the proposition unfolded, and the proposition is the discourse condensed."[48]

This history is illuminating in that it reveals unequivocally that CTH is modern in its understanding of truth, reason, and textuality—yet largely unhelpfully so, as we have argued above. The emphasis on propositional truth, the distinction between investigating the proposition and applying it, the centrality of an idea, and many other aspects of CTH—these stem directly from the impact of the Enlightenment on rhetoric and homiletics. The result is a form of preaching that too often addresses the head but fails to penetrate to the heart. Martyn Lloyd-Jones shares that the sort of preaching he wishes to hear is preaching that ushers us into the presence of God. Preaching reduced to propositions will not be conducive to what Lloyd-Jones rightly applauds.

Homiletics and Application

> I have aimed at being practical. . . . In any case, as appears in many of these lectures, I thoroughly dislike any theoretical or abstract treatment of this subject.
>
> Martyn Lloyd-Jones, *Preaching and Preachers*[49]

Lloyd-Jones sees little value in the sort of theoretical discussion we will engage in here. This, I suggest, is a mistake. Provided it is organically linked into practice, theory has a major contribution to make, as we will see in our discussion of application. In his hermeneutical ecology of application, Spears distinguishes three types, based on their view of the relationship between application and understanding: distinct (Hirsch), involved (Gadamer), and determinate (Derrida). In order to get at the depth issues involved in these three types, Spears begins with Eco's distinction between closed and open

---

such he has something to proclaim, to command, and to bind on the hearts of the congregation on behalf of his Sender. In that position *proclaiming* or thematic preaching answers the purpose much better than *analytic* preaching" (192–93, with original emphasis).

46. Old, *Reading and Preaching*, 6:37–38.

47. J. A. Broadus, *On the Preparation and Delivery of Sermons*, 4th ed., rev. V. L. Stanfield (New York: HarperOne, 1979), 45–47.

48. Ibid.

49. M. Lloyd-Jones, *Preaching and Preachers* (Grand Rapids: Zondervan, 1972), 4. On Lloyd-Jones and preaching, see Old, *Reading and Preaching*, 6:935–52.

texts.⁵⁰ Closed texts "obsessively aim at arousing a precise response on the part of more or less empirical readers."⁵¹ The distinct approach treats all texts as closed, and hence understanding is clearly distinct from application.⁵²

Open texts are written with the active role of the reader—the model reader—in mind, who is encouraged to explore and choose between a plurality of interpretations. Texts differ in terms of their requirements of the reader's participation, so readers must read in a way that fits with "the type of cooperation requested of the reader" by the text.⁵³ Such openness does not equate to wild pluralism, in which meaning is entirely a construct of the reader: "To say that a text has potentially no end does not mean that every act of interpretation can have a happy end."⁵⁴ Eco's open-text model fits well with the involved approach to application. Meaning emerges through the active engagement of the reader, particularly in relation to literary texts such as we have in the Bible.

The determinate approach grants all the power to the reader so that texts have as many meanings as they have readers. Derrida's view of interpretation is complex, involving his doctrine of two ways: that of reading according to the guardrail of authorial intention, and that of setting texts in play. However, as much as his followers might protest, it is the latter approach that he privileges especially in his reading of other philosophers. Knowledge is reduced to language, and language can never be saturated with meaning to the extent that there is no slippage, with the result that texts become radically indeterminate. Ironically, this is a determinate strategy in that the desires and will of the reader end up controlling the interpretation. Spears perceptively recognizes that "Derrida's private, antihistorical, asocial, essentially anarchic experience of reading and Hirsch's approach are actually the flip side of the same coin. Both ignore the position of the reader in history."⁵⁵

At this point it is helpful to identify two meanings of application, what we can call Application A and Application B. Spears is concerned to show that in literary texts like the Bible, the reader/s is/are always actively and concretely involved in the construction of meaning, so in this sense application is *always already* in play. We call this Application A. This does *not* mean that the

---

50. U. Eco, *The Limits of Interpretation* (Bloomington: Indiana University Press, 1990), 44–63.
51. Ibid., 45. A. C. Thiselton, *New Horizons in Hermeneutics* (Grand Rapids: Zondervan, 1992), 20, suggests that Philemon primarily functions in this way.
52. See Spears, "Theological Hermeneutics," 49–51.
53. U. Eco, *The Role of the Reader: Explorations in the Semiotics of Texts* (Bloomington: Indiana University Press, 1979), 33.
54. U. Eco, *Interpretation and Overinterpretation* (Cambridge: Cambridge University Press, 1992), 23–24.
55. Spears, "Theological Hermeneutics," 67.

intricate movement from Scripture to congregation is erased. We will call this Application B. What Spears is rightly critiquing is a "scientific" understanding of Application A, which ignores the element of application already at work.

Especially with the sort of open texts we find in the Bible, the concrete involvement of the reader is indispensable in their interpretation. Spears makes this case *philosophically* so that Application A would be present in all open texts. When it comes to Scripture this is even more the case. As the Word of God, there is no neutral place from which to read "objectively." We are *eo ipso* involved in Heidegger's hermeneutical circle, and the key question is not how we escape from it—we cannot!—but whether it is inevitably vicious. Heidegger himself poses the question of the right way in which to enter the circle. In my view, the right way is "in Christ," with all that this rich expression entails. Spears demonstrates that the three different types of application are rooted in *particular* views of language (ideality), history, and epistemology.[56] A question inevitably arises: What view of language, history, and epistemology should the Christian interpreter of the Bible adopt? As we argued in our chapters (9–10) on philosophy, hermeneutics, and history, faith bears formatively on these issues, and Christian exegetes have a responsibility to ensure that their views on these issues line up with their view of Scripture as God's Word.

In terms of Application A, Spears, following Wittgenstein and Thiselton, argues that application is a polymorphous concept. It varies from text to text: "With a polymorphic view, one approaches every text in such a way as to allow the nature of application as that particular text shapes it to inform the nature of homiletical application for that particular text."[57] In this quote, Spears connects Application A with that of B, a connection that bears unpacking. Ecclesiastes, for example, is an open text, calling for intense reader engagement as one follows the tracking back and forth of Qohelet on his quest for meaning in life. Application A is clearly in play, but once one has come to an understanding of Ecclesiastes, how does one or should one preach it?

Spears explores this issue in relation to Ecclesiastes 7:23–29. The challenge is that while one must structure Application B in light of Application A, one cannot simply reproduce the poetics of the text in the sermon. Ecclesiastes is a written text; a sermon is oral. Ecclesiastes was written for an Israelite audience, probably in the postexilic period; the sermon is preached to a particular congregation at a particular time in a particular context. How does one preach a biblical text for all it's worth so as to allow its full force to address a contemporary congregation?

---

56. Ibid., 55–100.
57. Ibid., 102.

Doubtless there is more than one answer to this question! The answer lies, I think, in the two different but related *rhetorical trajectories*. Careful, engaged study of the text will uncover the original rhetorical trajectory, at least to some extent. With Ecclesiastes, for example, we know that it was written for Israelites and not for New Testament Christians! Application B will involve bringing the full force of this trajectory into relationship with the rhetorical context of the congregation one is preaching to. The analogy between preaching and Old Testament prophecy is helpful here, in my view. Old Testament prophecy is always *contextual* and involves primarily forthtelling rather than foretelling. The prophets never proclaim God's Word in a vacuum but in the concrete *matrix* within which Israel finds itself. The preacher must do the same, and to do this, the preacher will need to develop a finely tuned understanding of the cultural matrix within which one is preaching.

The context of the contemporary congregation can be thought of as ever-diminishing circles. Let us take Ecclesiastes as our focus once again. At the broadest level the congregation, like Qohelet, are humans living in God's good creation, so there is a great deal they share in common. At a closer level they are, however, in a different act in the drama of Scripture, act 5, which issues from the Christ event. Preaching Ecclesiastes in act 5 must take account of the way in which the drama of Scripture has developed. Here biblical theology is an indispensable aid as the preacher reads Ecclesiastes within the context of the biblical metanarrative as a whole.

Cultural analysis is vital in order to gain a sense of the competing metanarratives of the culture within which the congregation lives. The church lives at the intersection of two stories, that of the Bible and that of the culture. Mission, in our case preaching, takes place at the intersection of those two stories, a place Newbigin describes as one of painful tension. Brueggemann explains, "Prophetic proclamation is the staging and performance of a contest between two narrative accounts of the world and an effort to show that the YHWH account of reality is more adequate and finally more reliable than the dominant narrative account that is cast among us as though it were true and beyond critique."[58]

Just as we need a biblical hermeneutics, so we need a hermeneutics of modern culture. John Stott evocatively notes that evangelicals launch their sermonic missiles from the Bible, but one has no idea where they are aimed. Liberals launch their missiles into the contemporary context but one has no idea where they have come from![59] Scripture is what must be preached,

---

58. Brueggemann, *Practice of Prophetic Imagination*, 3.
59. For a comparable comment on German versus American preachers, see Thielicke, *Trouble with the Church*, 30.

but *contextually*, and the only way to do this is to develop a growing understanding of the dynamics of contemporary culture, the matrix in which one's congregation swims every day.[60] Thielicke says of Schleiermacher that although we may not agree with him in every area,

> there is not a single theologian since the Reformation who can hold a candle to him for depth, systematizing power, and continuing influence. Why? Because he did not simply go on spinning old threads and threshing the empty straw, but rather found his questions in a living dialogue with his time, and out of this polarity there came to him ideas which in many different variations are still our own problems.[61]

And so one could continue until one arrives at the dynamics of the particular, local congregation to which one is preaching. If we hope for the sermon to be Christ walking amid his people and addressing *them*, then preachers will need to know their congregations well; they too will need to walk among their people and be in dialogue with them. Spiritual direction, which is pastoral care of the individual, needs to be revived and recovered as a pastoral practice so that preachers are also pastors and are intimately acquainted with the journeys of their parishioners.[62]

It is at the intersection of these two trajectories that the sermon will take shape. The form of the sermon can and will vary—there is room for immense creativity at this point—but in my experience the pastor, while exploring this intersection, begins to see how Scripture addresses the congregation, and the logic of the sermon will flow from this dynamic. Perhaps the virtue that needs to be invoked at this point is that of *wisdom*, of fittingness.

Proverbs has much to say about language, speaking, and listening,[63] topics that are central to preaching. "To make an apt answer is a joy to anyone, and a word in season, how good it is!" (Prov. 15:23). Proverbs itself enunciates a hermeneutics of what is fitting, and not least in 26:1–12. Verse 1 introduces a theme central to this section and to wisdom: what is *fitting*.[64] Snow is fitting

---

60. See C. G. Bartholomew and M. W. Goheen, *Living at the Crossroads: An Introduction to Christian Worldview* (Grand Rapids: Baker Academic, 2008). Brueggemann (*Practice of Prophetic Imagination*, 2–4) observes how preachers neglect cultural analysis and characterizes our age as one of "military consumerism" (3).

61. Thielicke, *Trouble with the Church*, 28.

62. See E. H. Peterson, *Working the Angles: The Shape of Pastoral Integrity* (Grand Rapids: Eerdmans, 1987).

63. See C. G. Bartholomew, *Reading Proverbs with Integrity* (Cambridge: Grove Books, 2001). Augustine, *DDC*, chap. 4, has much useful advice about language and preaching.

64. See N. Wolterstorff's use of this theme in his *Art in Action: Toward a Christian Aesthetic* (Grand Rapids: Eerdmans, 1980).

in winter and rain in summer; "honor is not fitting for a fool." Verses 4–5 are fascinating in terms of this hermeneutic of fittingness. The two verses provide contradictory advice: "Do not answer fools according to their folly" and "Answer fools according to their folly"! What are we to make of this contradictory juxtaposition? The answer is that wisdom involves working out what is fitting in a particular situation, a task that the preacher is constantly involved in while repeatedly negotiating the journey from Scripture to congregation. Thus there is no easy formula for working out what fits in a particular situation. Method has its place in preaching, and preaching should certainly draw on the best academic work, but wisdom—and preaching—is far more an art than a technique, and it has to be learned through practice. Augustine delightfully describes preachers as "sons and ministers of this wisdom."[65]

Application and the Preacher: The Fecundity of the Incurable Wound

If we need any persuasion that application is inherent in the reception and interpretation of Scripture, then the Old Testament prophets provide us with what we need. Their whole lives were bound up with being prophets, and often at great cost. One need only reflect on the ministries of Hosea, Amos, Habakkuk, and Jeremiah to sense the cost involved.

The entanglement of life with proclamation is perhaps nowhere clearer than in the "Confessions" of Jeremiah (Jer. 11:18–23; 12:1–6; 15:10–21; 17:14–18; 18:18–23; 20:7–18). Jeremiah was called to prophesy during the last forty years of the kingdom of Judah, before it went into exile. Anyone who preaches and pastors will know that life on the *inside* is very different from what a congregation may perceive. Uniquely in his confessions, Jeremiah provides us with an insight into the internal struggle that being called to proclaim the Word of God may involve.[66] From his call in 1:4–19, it is clear that God will need to form and fortify him in order for him to execute his ministry.

The *involvement* of Jeremiah with the word he is called to preach is evoked in Yahweh touching his mouth and putting his words in his mouth (1:9). In one of the confessions, Jeremiah (15:16) declares:

---

65. Augustine, *DDC* 4.7. In book 4 Augustine turns from understanding the truth of Scripture to communicating it. It is remarkable how often he uses the language of wisdom in this final book of *DCC*.

66. On Jeremiah and the preaching ministry, esp. see J. Skinner, *Prophecy and Religion: Studies in the Life of Jeremiah* (Cambridge: Cambridge University Press, 1922), 201–30; R. Davidson, *Courage to Doubt: Exploring an Old Testament Theme* (London: SCM, 1983), 121–39; E. H. Peterson, *Run with the Horses: The Quest for Life at Its Best* (Downers Grove, IL: InterVarsity, 1983).

> Your words were found, and I ate them,
>   and your words became to me a joy
>   and the delight of my heart;
> for I am called by your name,
>   O LORD, God of hosts.

This verse evokes the deepest internalization of the word from God. As Peterson says, "Jeremiah was constitutionally unable to say something just because he was told it was true; he *lived* the truth and then he spoke it."[67] The phrase "for I am called by your name" reads literally, "Your name was upon me," and evokes the language used in Deuteronomy (e.g. 12:5, 11) to refer to the place where Yahweh will choose to put his name and habitation.[68] It thus speaks of Yahweh's ownership as he inhabits the prophet. Jeremiah has to "become" Jerusalem in order to prophesy to Jerusalem! He needs to be on the *inside* of God's purposes *with* God in order to receive and proclaim God's word to his people. He has to live the Word, and as he testifies in 15:10, he has done so, unlike his contemporaries: "I have not lent, nor have I borrowed." As Brueggemann explains, "He has not practiced the social exploitation of which he accuses others."[69]

Clearly Jeremiah engaged in no distant, "objective" reading or hearing of God's words. Application, to refer back to our previous discussion, is inherent in his reception of the Word at every point. He must be owned by God, obedient to God, confident in God, and at God's disposal in order to be his prophet. So far, so good. What the confessions do, however, is open up to us the struggles that attend such a ministry.

In 15:18 Jeremiah speaks of his "wound" as "incurable." One is reminded of Henri Nouwen's book *The Wounded Healer*. Being a prophet involved Jeremiah in the deepest wounding. From the confessions we can discern several aspects of this:

1. We know from the book as a whole that Jeremiah's ministry was met with opposition, hatred, and persecution. His ministry was primarily one of proclaiming judgment, a huge burden to carry during forty years:

> For whenever I speak, I must cry out,
>   I must shout, "Violence and destruction!"

---

67. Peterson, *Run with the Horses*, 102, with original emphasis.
68. J. A. Thompson, *The Book of Jeremiah* (Grand Rapids: Eerdmans, 1980), 396.
69. W. Brueggemann, *A Commentary on Jeremiah: Exile and Homecoming* (Grand Rapids: Eerdmans, 1998), 144.

> For the word of the LORD has become for me
> a reproach and derision all day long. (Jer. 20:8)

2. We know that Jeremiah's ministry was very *lonely*, and not only because of the opposition. As part of a symbolic witness to his hearers, he was not to marry and have a family (16:1–4), and even his own family members turned against him (12:6). Hence Peter Berger challenges the theologian amid our secular culture:

> Unless our theologian has the inner fortitude of a desert saint, he has only one effective remedy against the threat of cognitive collapse in the face of these pressures. He must huddle together with like-minded fellow deviants—and huddle very closely. Only in a counter community of considerable strength does cognitive deviance have a chance to maintain itself. This counter community provides continuing therapy against the creeping doubt as to whether after all one may not be wrong and the majority right.[70]

Jeremiah was called to a very difficult ministry *without* such a countercommunity.

3. Jeremiah appeared to be a failed and thus a false prophet. Over his long ministry, he must have appeared to many of his hearers as the classic example of a false prophet (cf. Deut. 18:22). Israel was not short of prophets willing to proclaim far more acceptable messages than that of Jeremiah (cf. Jer. 28). Not surprisingly, in one of his confessions Jeremiah raises this very issue of apparent failure: "See how they say to me, 'Where is the word of the LORD? Let it come!'" (Jer. 17:15).

4. Imprecation and emotional turmoil. In 17:16, Jeremiah says to God, "I have not run away from being a shepherd in your service, nor have I desired the fatal day." This, however, was a hard position to sustain, and in other sections of the confessions, an imprecatory element is understandably strongly to the fore (cf. 18:20–23). Indeed, parts of the confessions are reminiscent of Lamentations, Habakkuk, the psalms of lament and imprecation, and of Job and Ecclesiastes. Jeremiah 20:7–18 moves from anguish in verses 7–10, to hope in verses 11–13, and then to complete despair in verses 14–18, providing an insight into the emotional roller-coaster that Jeremiah experienced amid his ministry. Nevertheless he cannot fail to speak; the word within him is "like a burning fire" that cannot be restrained (20:9).

Jeremiah's experience is perhaps not common among preachers; few of us are called to such a lifelong ministry of judgment and severe opposition.

---

70. P. L. Berger, *A Rumour of Angels: Modern Society and the Rediscovery of the Supernatural* (London: Allen Lane, 1970), 32.

And yet the parallels are real: preachers know the emotional cost of bringing God's Word to God's people week in and week out, knowing that we are not called to say what the listeners want to hear but what they need to hear. And any preaching that positions the narratives of our day against that of the biblical story, highlighting the contextual points of antithesis, will call forth opposition.[71] South Africa, where I grew up, is an obvious example. More than 70 percent of the population claimed to be Christian, but there were few contexts in which a searching call for repentance from racism would not evoke strong and sometimes violent opposition. And now in the new South Africa, there are new idols that similarly resist searching exposure.

Clearly the preacher is one who is deeply involved with God's Word, but how does one sustain such a ministry over a lifetime? Jeremiah's confessions provide important clues. First, his confessions are prayers:

> Apart from a few brief sections which are in the form of words from the Lord to Jeremiah (11.21–23; 12.5–6; 15.19–21), all the material in the confessions is in the form of prayers. This is not a man thinking his own thoughts as in some Shakespearean soliloquy; this is a man pouring out his whole self to God; his despondency, his doubts, his disillusionment, his curses, his unanswered questions, his hurt cries for healing and vindication.[72]

It is through his cultivation of a deep prayer life that Jeremiah endures, is restored and restored again, and maintains his witness against impossible odds. As Peterson states, "It is not enough to remember; we must *hear* it again. Prayer is the act in which we hear it again."[73]

Nowadays it is rare to find prayer as a topic in books on biblical hermeneutics.[74] Jeremiah reminds us just how mistaken this is. To grasp and be grasped by God's Word, prayer is indispensable. Hence our starting this book with listening to, and open reception of, the Word.

Second, his wounds become the means for his formation. In 1:18 God says to Jeremiah that he has made him "an iron pillar, and a bronze wall." In 15:19–21 God responds to Jeremiah's pointed lament (cf. 15:18c) by saying that if he turns back, repents, God will make him a "fortified wall of bronze."

---

71. See Thielicke, *Trouble with the Church*, 37: a remarkable example of contextualization in Nazi Germany.
72. Davidson, *Courage to Doubt*, 138–39.
73. Peterson, *Run with the Horses*, 106, with original emphasis.
74. See C. G. Bartholomew and R. Holt, "Prayer in/and the Drama of Redemption in Luke: Prayer and Exegetical Performance," in *Reading Luke: Interpretation, Reflection, and Formation*, ed. C. G. Bartholomew, J. B Green, and A. C. Thiselton, SAHS 6 (Grand Rapids: Zondervan, 2006), 350–75.

He has to become, as it were, what God has already made him. Such is the fiery furnace of formation out of which Jeremiah emerges stronger and again equipped for his calling.

Without his wound we would never have received such a rich book as we have in Jeremiah. And so it is with the preacher *and* the biblical scholar. In the academy it would be regarded as scandalous nowadays to draw attention to the inner life of the exegete and its importance for biblical interpretation.[75] Nevertheless, depth is acquired through spiritual formation, which inevitably, according to the best authorities in the Christian tradition, involves dark nights of the soul. These wounds ironically become the very points of growth and formation. Rich theological interpretation will not emerge simply from the recovery of a method of exegesis: it will require formation not only of minds, important as that is, but also of hearts, just as with Jeremiah.[76]

We all know of Thomas Aquinas as a great theologian, philosopher, and exegete. What is less commonly known nowadays is the complete immersion of Thomas's work in prayer:

> Rainald, his confessor, knew, for certain, that the Saint gained everything by prayer. On one occasion, during class, the conversation fell on the great Angelical [Thomas]. Rainald burst into tears, and exclaimed, "Brothers, my master forbade me, during his life, to tell the wonderful things he did:—one thing I know of him, that it was not human talent, but *prayer*, that was the secret of his great success. He never discussed, read, wrote, or dictated, without begging with tears for illumination."[77]

Preaching the Bible for *All* It's Worth

> How greatly the socioethical potential and sociological relevance of the message of Jesus Christ has been neglected through the centuries!
>
> Hans Küng[78]

---

75. Point 6 of Robert of Sorbon's advice to students as to how to profit from study is "to pray—for this is, in point of fact, one of the best means of learning." Quoted via R. Vaughan, *The Life and Labours of Saint Thomas of Aquin*, ed. J. Vaughan, 2nd ed. (New York: Catholic Publication Society, 1890), 148.

76. The best book that I know of on the intellectual life is A. G. Sertillanges, *The Intellectual Life: Its Spirit, Conditions, Methods* (Washington, DC: Catholic University of America Press, 1998); see esp. chap. 2, "Virtues of a Catholic Intellectual."

77. Vaughan, *Saint Thomas of Aquin*, 195–96.

78. H. Küng, "God: The Last Taboo?," in *Theology and the University: Essays in Honor of John B Cobb, Jr.*, ed. D. R. Griffin and J. C. Hough Jr. (Albany: State University of New York Press, 1991), 54.

There is a suffering humanity whose way of the cross has as many stations as that of the Lord when he suffered among us in Palestine.

Leonardo Boff[79]

As we noted in chapter 4, Brevard Childs identified *a* reason for the demise of the Biblical Theology Movement (BTM) in its failure to address the wider issues of culture. This is not a failure unique to the BTM. It is rare, even amid the renaissance of theological interpretation, to find deep explorations of how the Word addresses all of life today. Take Ecclesiastes, for example. Qohelet is relentless in exploring every aspect of life in his quest for meaning: pleasure, sex, justice, oppression, grand projects, politics, justice and oppression, music, work, and so forth. Yet in his exploration he fails to find an answer in any of these areas. However, his quest does come to resolution finally in remembering his *creator* (12:1). What is rarely noticed by commentators is that if he finds resolution to life "under the sun," then *retrospectively* all the areas he examines are indeed *full of meaning*. As Gordon Spykman eloquently puts it, "Nothing matters but the kingdom, but because of the kingdom everything matters."[80] In this light Ecclesiastes provides fertile theological resources for explorations of all the areas Qohelet attends to.

Yet Ecclesiastes is far from alone in this. Leon Kass's superb commentary on Genesis, *The Beginning of Wisdom*, is unique in exploring, via a "wisdom seeking" hermeneutic,[81] the many, many ways in which Genesis connects with all of life. Take Babel and Pentecost, for example, standing like two great mountains at either ends of the Bible. Clearly both events have to do with *language*, but once again this is a point rarely picked up by modern commentators.[82] While I have reservations on some aspects of liberation theology, authors like Gutiérrez and Boff have alerted us unequivocally to the importance

---

79. L. Boff, *Passion of Christ, Passion of the World: The Facts, Their Interpretation, and Their Meaning Yesterday and Today*, trans. R. R. Barr, 2nd ed. (Maryknoll, NY: Orbis Books, 2001), ix.

80. G. J. Spykman, *Reformational Theology: A New Paradigm for Doing Dogmatics* (Grand Rapids: Eerdmans, 1992), 478.

81. L. Kass (*The Beginning of Wisdom: Reading Genesis* [Chicago: University of Chicago Press, 2003], 1) describes his hermeneutic as "philosophic," meaning "wisdom-seeking" and "wisdom-loving."

82. Jacques Ellul is a scholar whose works attend to Scripture and the contemporary scene. See his *The Presence of the Kingdom* (New York: Seabury, 1967); *Hope in Time of Abandonment* (New York: Seabury, 1973); *The New Demons* (New York: Seabury, 1975); *The Judgment of Jonah* (Grand Rapids: Eerdmans, 1971); *The Subversion of Christianity* (Grand Rapids: Eerdmans, 1986). Two vital books by Ellul for understanding our age are *The Technological Society* (New York: Knopf, 1964); *Propaganda: The Formation of Men's Attitudes* (New York: Knopf, 1965). Jean-Luc Porquet, in his *Jacques Ellul: L'homme qui avait presque tout prévu* (Paris: Cherche Midi, 2003), explores the multitude of ways in which Ellul's predictions about the future have come true.

of reading Scripture in relation to the poor and oppressed of the world. In his *The Desire of the Nations*, O'Donovan distinguishes between "our" questions in the North compared with the liberation questions in the South. Amid globalization, however, their questions are, or should be, our questions too.

Scripture is God's Word for *all* of created life, and it is astonishing that exegetes can work on a daily basis with biblical texts without seeing the connections with life as a whole. Sometimes one gets the impression that God has provided us with a church view rather than a *world*view. The great themes of covenant and kingdom are utterly comprehensive and relate to the reign of God over his entire creation. How is it possible, one wonders, to preach and research the Old Testament and Jesus without sounding this comprehensive note again and again? Bonhoeffer evocatively asserts:

> On the basis of Holy Scripture, the office of preaching proclaims Christ as the Lord and Saviour of the world. . . . This means that no created thing can be conceived and essentially understood without reference to Christ, the Mediator of creation. . . . It is vain to seek to know God's will for created things without reference to Christ. . . . A life in genuine worldliness is possible only through the proclamation of Christ crucified; true worldly living is not possible or real in contradiction to the proclamation or side by side with it, that is to say, in any kind of autonomy of the secular sphere: it is possible and real only "in, with and under" the proclamation of Christ.[83]

In the light of this comprehensive vision and claim, what needs to be teased out carefully is the relationship between the church and the world. Again, Bonhoeffer is very helpful with his model of "Christonomy": "The word of God, proclaimed by virtue of a divine mandate, dominates and rules the entire world; the 'community' which comes into being around this word does not dominate the world, but it stands entirely in service of the fulfillment of the divine mandate."[84] *Jesus* not only designates the individual human but embraces the whole of humanity. The congregation of God is the new humanity in Jesus. This means that people there accept the gospel and "allow that to happen to themselves which properly, as an act of God, should happen to all."[85]

The law of the Christian community must, however, be distinguished from the law of the worldly order. Neither must be imposed on the other. At the heart of the mission of the church is *proclamation*: "In the very limitation of her [the church's] spiritual and material domain she gives expression to the

---

83. Bonhoeffer, *Ethics*, 261-63.
84. Ibid., 265.
85. Ibid.

unlimited scope of the message of Christ."[86] According to Bonhoeffer, the church exists for the sake of the world. Through its willingness to be such an instrument, "the congregation has become the goal and center of all God's dealings with the world.... The Christian congregation stands at the point at which the whole world ought to be standing; to this extent it serves as deputy for the world and exists for the sake of the world."[87]

The dynamic inner connection between preaching and the mission of the church in the world needs close attention. The preacher is *not* called to be an expert in all the many areas in which members of his congregation function as full-time servants of Christ. Christians in health care, business, law, homemaking, education, and so forth, have a God-given responsibility to work out *together* for *themselves* what the lordship of Christ means in their areas of vocation. Preaching will inevitably and rightly be limited in how particular it can become in relation to policy making, aesthetics, scholarship, and so on. What preaching *must* do is repeatedly sound the kingdom note so that all Christians, all of whom are, as Peterson puts it, "in holy orders," hear the call to submit all of their lives to the reign of the king. And naturally this includes biblical scholars!

In the quote with which we began this chapter, Karl Barth confessed, "To Him we belong who here makes Himself heard." Having heard and encountered the living God, academic biblical interpretation cannot proceed as though this has not happened. Instead, it will be placed in service of this God. Ecclesial reception of the Word *is* primary, and all the hard exegetical work of scholars, and preachers, will emerge from encounter with God through his Word and be placed in service of it.

---

86. Ibid., 266. On p. 267 he declares that Catholics are in danger of seeing the church as an end in itself, while Protestants are in danger of neglecting the church as an entity, with a consequent liturgical poverty and weak ecclesiastical organizations.
87. Ibid., 266.

Bibliography

Abegg, M., Jr., P. Flint, and E. Ulrich, trans. *The Dead Sea Scrolls Bible: The Oldest Known Bible Translated for the First Time into English*. San Francisco: HarperSanFrancisco, 1999.

Abraham, W. J. *Canon and Criterion in Christian Theology: From the Fathers to Feminism*. Oxford: Oxford University Press, 2002.

Abrams, M. H. *Doing Things with Texts: Essays in Criticism and Critical Theory*. New York: Norton, 1989.

———. *The Mirror and the Lamp: Romantic Theory and the Critical Tradition*. London: Oxford University Press, 1953.

Achtemeier, E. "The Canon as the Voice of the Living God." In *Reclaiming the Bible for the Church*, edited by C. Braaten and R. Jenson, 119–30. Grand Rapids: Eerdmans, 1995.

Adams, A. K. M., ed. *Handbook of Postmodern Biblical Interpretation*. St. Louis: Chalice, 2000.

Adams, E. *The Stars Will Fall from Heaven: Cosmic Catastrophe in the New Testament and Its World*. London: T&T Clark, 2007.

Adams, J. C. "Ramist Concepts of Testimony, Judicial Analogies, and the Puritan Conversion Narrative." *Rhetorica* 9 (1991): 251–68.

Adams, N. *Habermas and Theology*. Cambridge: Cambridge University Press, 2006.

Addinall, P. *Philosophy and Biblical Interpretation: A Study in Nineteenth-Century Conflict*. Cambridge: Cambridge University Press, 1991.

Agamben, G. *The Time That Remains: A Commentary on the Letter to the Romans*. Translated by P. Dailey. Stanford, CA: Stanford University Press, 2005.

Aitken, E. B. "Portraying the Temple in Stone and Text: The Arch of Titus and the Epistle to the Hebrews." In Gelardini, *Hebrews: Contemporary Methods, New Insights*, 131–48.

Albrektson, B. *History and the Gods: An Essay on the Idea of Historical Events as Divine Manifestations in the Ancient Near East and in Israel*. Lund: Gleerup, 1967. Reprint, Winona Lake, IN: Eisenbrauns, 2011.

Albright, W. F. *From the Stone Age to Christianity: Monotheism and the Historical Process*. Baltimore: Johns Hopkins University Press, 1957.

Alexander, P. S. "Retelling the Old Testament." In *It Is Written: Scripture Citing Scripture*, edited by D. A. Carson and H. G. M. Williamson, 99–121. Cambridge: Cambridge University Press, 1988.

Alexander, T. D., and B. S. Rosner, eds. *New Dictionary of Biblical Theology: Exploring the Unity and Diversity of Scripture*. Downers Grove, IL: InterVarsity, 2000.

Allen, D. L. *Lukan Authorship of Hebrews*. NAC Studies of the Bible & Theology. Nashville: B&H Academic, 2010.

Alonso-Schökel, L. *Apuntes de hermenéutica*. 2nd ed. Colección Estructuras y Procesos. Madrid: Editorial Trotta, 1997.

———. *A Manual of Hebrew Poetics*. Subsidia biblica 11. Rome: Editrice Pontificio Istituto Biblico, 1988.

Alston, Wallace M., Jr. "The Recovery of Theological Preaching." In *The Power to Comprehend with All the Saints*, edited by W. M. Alston Jr. and C. A. Jarvis, 221–36. Grand Rapids: Eerdmans, 2009.

Alston, William P. "Divine and Human Action." In *Divine and Human Action: Essays in the Metaphysics of Theism*, edited by T. V. Morris, 257–80. Ithaca, NY: Cornell University Press, 1988.

———. "How to Think about Divine Action: Twenty-Five Years of Travail for Biblical Language." In *Divine Action: Studies Inspired by the Philosophical Theology of Austin Farrer*, edited by B. Hebblethwaite and E. Henderson, 51–70. Edinburgh: T&T Clark, 1990.

Alter, R. *The Art of Biblical Narrative*. New York: Basic Books, 1981. Rev., updated ed., 2011.

Alter, R., and F. Kermode. *The Literary Guide to the Bible*. Cambridge, MA: Harvard University Press, 1999.

Andersen, F. I., and D. N. Freedman. *Amos: A New Translation with Introduction and Commentary*. AB 24A. New York: Doubleday, 1989.

Anderson, B. W. "Politics and the Transcendent: Voegelin's Philosophical and Theological Exposition of the Old Testament in the Context of the Ancient Near East." In *Eric Voegelin's Search for Order in History*, edited by S. A. McKnight, 62–100. Lanham, MD: University Press of America, 1987.

Anderson, G. "The Interpretation of Genesis 1:1 in the Targums." *CBQ* 52, no. 1 (1990): 21–29.

Anderson, R. D. *Ancient Rhetorical Theory and Paul*. Kampen, Netherlands: Kok Pharos, 1996.

Angeles, P. A. *Dictionary of Philosophy*. New York: Harper & Row, 1981.

Aristotle. *On Rhetoric: A Theory of Civic Discourse*. 2nd ed. Translated by G. A. Kennedy. Oxford: Oxford University Press, 2007.

Arnold, D. W. H., and P. Bright, eds. *De doctrina christiana: A Classic of Western Culture*. Christianity and Judaism in Antiquity 9. Notre Dame, IN: University of Notre Dame Press, 1995.

Attridge, H. W. *The Epistle to the Hebrews: A Commentary on the Epistle to the Hebrews*. Hermeneia. Philadelphia: Fortress, 1989.

———. "Paraenesis in a Homily (λόγος παρακλήσεως): The Possible Location of, and Socialization in, the Epistle to the Hebrews." *Semeia* 50 (1990): 211–26.

Auerbach, E. *Mimesis: The Representation of Reality in Western Literature*. Princeton Classics. Princeton: Princeton University Press, 1953. Pbk., 2003.

Augustine of Hippo. *City of God*. Middlesex, UK: Penguin, 1972.

———. *Confessions*. Translated by R. S. Pine-Coffin. London: Penguin, 1961.

———. *Essential Sermons*. Translated by E. Hill. Hyde Park, NY: New City, 2007.

———. *Instructing Beginners in Faith*. Translated, introduced, and annotated by R. Canning. Edited by B. Ramsey. Hyde Park, NY: New City, 2006.

———. *On Christian Teaching*. Translated by R. P. H. Green. Oxford: Oxford University Press, 1997.

———. *On Genesis*. Translated by E. Hill. Hyde Park, NY: New City, 2002.

———. *On the Morals of the Catholic Church*. http://www.newadvent.org/fathers/.

———. *The Retractions*. FC 60. Washington, DC: Catholic University of America Press, 1968.

———. *Sermons on Selected Lessons of the New Testament*. http://www.newadvent.org/fathers.

———. *Sermons on the Old Testament, 20–50*. In *The Works of Saint Augustine: A*

Translation for the 21st Century, translated and annotated by E. Hill, part 3, vol. 2. Hyde Park, NY: New City, 1990.

Auneau, J. *Écrits didactiques: Le livre de Tobie; Les Psaumes et les autres Écrits*. Petite bibliothèque des sciences bibliques Ancien Testament 5. Tournai: Desclée, 1990.

Bachelard, G. *The Poetics of Space*. Boston: Beacon, 1964, 1994.

Backhaus, K. "How to Entertain Angels: Ethics in the Epistle to the Hebrews." In Gelardini, *Hebrews: Contemporary Methods, New Insights*, 149–75.

Baildam, J. D. *Paradisal Love: Johann Gottfried Herder and the Song of Songs*. JSOTSup 298. Sheffield: Sheffield Academic, 1999.

Bailey, K. E. *Jacob and the Prodigal: How Jesus Retold Israel's Story*. Downers Grove, IL: IVP Academic, 2003.

———. *Poet and Peasant: A Literary-Cultural Approach to the Parables in Luke*. Grand Rapids: Eerdmans, 1976.

Balthasar, H. U. von. *The Glory of the Lord: A Theological Aesthetics*. 7 vols. San Francisco: Ignatius, 1983–91; 2nd ed., 2009.

———. *Prayer*. San Francisco: Ignatius, 1986.

———. *Theo-Drama: Theological Dramatic Theory*. Vol. 2, *Dramatis Personae: Man in God*. San Francisco: Ignatius, 1990.

———. *Theologik*. Vol. 2, *Wahrheit Gottes*. Einsiedeln: Johannes-Verlag, 1985.

———. *Theologik*. Vol. 3, *Der Geist der Wahrheit*. Einsiedeln: Johannes-Verlag, 1987.

Barr, J. *The Bible in the Modern World: The Croall Lectures Given in New College, Edinburgh in November 1970*. London: SCM, 1973.

———. *Biblical Words for Time*. 2nd ed. London: SCM, 1969.

———. *The Concept of Biblical Theology: An Old Testament Perspective*. Minneapolis: Fortress, 1999.

———. *History and Ideology in the Old Testament: Biblical Studies at the End of a Millennium*. Oxford: Oxford University Press, 2005.

———. *Holy Scripture: Canon, Authority, Criticism*. Oxford: Clarendon, 1983.

———. *Old and New in Interpretation: A Study of the Two Testaments*. 2nd ed. London: SCM, 1982.

———. *The Semantics of Biblical Language*. London: SCM, 1982. Reprint, Eugene, OR: Wipf & Stock, 2004.

———. "The Theological Case against Biblical Theology." In *Canon, Theology and Old Testament*, edited by G. M. Tucker, D. L. Petersen, and R. R. Wilson, 3–19. Minneapolis: Fortress, 1988.

———. "Trends and Prospects in Biblical Theology." *JTS* 24 (1974): 265–82.

Barrett, C. K. "The Allegory of Abraham, Sarah, and Hagar in the Argument of Galatians." In *Rechtfertigung: Festschrift für Ernst Käsemann zum 70. Geburtstag*, edited by J. Friedrich, W. Pöhlmann, and P. Stuhlmacher, 1–16. Tübingen: Mohr, 1976.

———. "The Eschatology of the Epistle to the Hebrews." In *The Background of the New Testament and Its Eschatology: Studies in Honour of Charles Harold Dodd*, edited by W. D. Davies and D. Daube, 363–93. Cambridge: Cambridge University Press, 1956.

———. *The Second Epistle to the Corinthians*. London: Continuum, 1973.

———. *Westcott as Commentator*. Cambridge: Cambridge University Press, 1959.

Barrett, L. C., and J. Stewart. *Kierkegaard and the Bible*. Tome 1, *The Old Testament*. Tome 2, *The New Testament*. Farnham: Ashgate, 2010.

Barry, J. *The Resurrected Servant in Isaiah*. Colorado Springs: Biblica, 2010.

Barth, K. *Church Dogmatics*. Edited by G. W. Bromiley and T. F. Torrance. Translated by G. W. Bromiley et al. First pbk. ed. 4 vols. in 14. Edinburgh: T&T Clark, 2004.

———. *The Doctrine of the Word of God*. Vol. I/1 of *Church Dogmatics*.

———. *Dogmatics in Outline*. London: SCM, 2001.

———. *The Epistle to the Romans*. Translated by E. C. Hoskyns from the 6th German ed. London: Oxford University Press, 1933.

———. *Homiletics*. Translated by G. W. Bromiley and D. E. Daniels. Louisville: Westminster John Knox, 1991.

———. *Protestant Theology in the Nineteenth Century: Its Background and History*. Translated by B. Cozens and J. Bowden. New ed. London: SCM, 2001.

———. *The Theology of John Calvin*. Translated by G. W. Bromiley. Grand Rapids: Eerdmans, 1995.

Barth, M. "The Old Testament in Hebrews: An Essay in Biblical Hermeneutics." In *Current Issues in New Testament Interpretation: Essays in Honor of Otto A. Piper*, edited by W. Klassen and G. F. Snyder, 53–78. London: SCM, 1962.

Barthélemy, D. *Studies in the Text of the Old Testament: An Introduction to the Hebrew Old Testament Text Project*. Translated by S. Lind. Textual Criticism and the Translator 3. Winona Lake, IN: Eisenbrauns, 2012.

Barthes, R. "The Death of an Author." In *Modern Criticism and Theory: A Reader*, edited by D. Lodge, 167–71. London: Longman, 1988.

Bartholomew, C. G. "Before Babel and after Pentecost: Language, Literature, and Biblical Interpretation." In *After Pentecost: Language and Biblical Interpretation*, edited by C. G. Bartholomew, C. Greene, and K. Möller, 131–70. Scripture and Hermeneutics 2. Grand Rapids: Zondervan, 2001.

———. "The Composition of Deuteronomy: A Critical Analysis of the Approaches of E. W. Nicholson and A. D. H. Mayes." MA thesis, Potchefstroom University for Christian Higher Education, 1992.

———. "Covenant and Creation: Covenant Overload or Covenantal Deconstruction?" *Calvin Theological Journal* 30, no. 1 (April 1995): 11–33.

———. *Ecclesiastes*. BCOTWP. Grand Rapids: Baker Academic, 2009.

———. "Genesis 1:2 and the Doctrine of Creation." Forthcoming.

———. "Hearing the Old Testament Wisdom Literature: The Wit of Many and the Wisdom of One." In Bartholomew and Beldman, *Hearing the Old Testament*, 302–31.

———. "Hermeneutics." In *Dictionary of the Old Testament: Historical Books*, edited by B. T. Arnold and H. G. M. Williamson, 392–407. Downers Grove, IL: IVP Academic, 2005.

———. "The Intertextuality of Ecclesiastes and the New Testament." In *Reading Ecclesiastes Intertextually*, edited by K. Dell and W. Kynes, chap. 19. London: T&T Clark, 2014.

———. Introduction to *A Royal Priesthood? The Use of the Bible Ethically and Politically*, edited by C. G. Bartholomew et al., 1–45. Grand Rapids: Zondervan, 2002.

———. Introduction to Bartholomew et al., *"Behind" the Text*, 1–16.

———. *Reading Ecclesiastes: Old Testament Exegesis and Hermeneutical Theory*. Rome: Pontificio Istituto Biblico, 1998.

———. *Reading Proverbs with Integrity*. Cambridge: Grove Books, 2001.

———. "Uncharted Waters: Philosophy, Theology, and the Crisis in Biblical Interpretation." In *Renewing Biblical Interpretation*, edited by C. G. Bartholomew, C. Greene, and K. Möller, 1–39. SAHS 1. Grand Rapids: Zondervan, 2000.

———. "Warranted Biblical Interpretation: Alvin Plantinga's 'Two or More Kinds of Scripture Scholarship.'" In Bartholomew et al., *"Behind" the Text*, 58–78.

———. *When You Want to Yell at God: The Book of Job*. Bellingham, WA: Lexham, 2014.

———. *Where Mortals Dwell: A Christian View of Place for Today*. Grand Rapids: Baker Academic, 2011.

Bartholomew, C. G., and B. Ashford. *The Doctrine of Creation*. Downers Grove, IL: IVP Academic, forthcoming.

Bartholomew, C. G., and D. J. H. Beldman, eds. *Hearing the Old Testament: Listening for God's Address*. Grand Rapid: Eerdmans, 2012.

Bartholomew, C. G., and M. W. Goheen. *Christian Philosophy: A Systematic and Narrative Introduction*. Grand Rapids: Baker Academic, 2013.

———. *The Drama of Scripture: Finding Our Place in the Biblical Story*. Grand Rapids: Baker Academic, 2004.

———. *Living at the Crossroads: An Introduction to Christian Worldview*. Grand Rapids: Baker Academic, 2008.

———. "Story and Biblical Theology." In Bartholomew, Healy, Möller, and Parry, *Out of Egypt*, 172–84.

Bartholomew, C. G., and R. Holt. "Prayer in/ and the Drama of Redemption in Luke: Prayer and Exegetical Performance." In *Reading Luke: Interpretation, Reflection, and Formation*, edited by C. G. Bartholomew, J. B. Green, and A. C. Thiselton, 350–75. SAHS 6. Grand Rapids: Zondervan, 2006.

Bartholomew, C. G., and T. Moritz. *Christ and Consumerism: Critical Reflections on the Spirit of Our Age*. Carlisle, UK: Paternoster, 2000.

Bartholomew, C. G., and R. P. O'Dowd. *Old Testament Wisdom Literature: A Theological Introduction*. Downers Grove, IL: IVP Academic, 2011.

Bartholomew, C. G., and H. Thomas. *Manifesto for Theological Interpretation*. Grand Rapids: Baker Academic, forthcoming.

———. *The Minor Prophets: A Theological Introduction*. Downers Grove, IL: IVP Academic, forthcoming.

Bartholomew, C. G., and A. West, eds. *Praying by the Book: Reading the Psalms*. Carlisle, UK: Paternoster, 2001.

Bartholomew, C. G., M. Healy, K. Möller, and R. Parry, eds. *Out of Egypt: Biblical Theology and Biblical Interpretation*. SAHS 5. Grand Rapids: Zondervan, 2004.

Bartholomew, C. G., et al., eds. *"Behind" the Text: History and Biblical Interpretation*. SAHS 4. Grand Rapids: Zondervan, 2003.

Bartholomew, C. G., et al., eds. *Canon and Biblical Interpretation*. SAHS 7. Grand Rapids: Zondervan, 2006.

Barton, J. *The Future of Old Testament Study*. Oxford: Clarendon, 1993.

———. *Holy Writings, Sacred Text: The Canon in Early Christianity*. Louisville: Westminster John Knox, 1997.

———. *Reading the Old Testament: Method in Biblical Study*. 2nd ed. London: Darton, Longman & Todd, 1996.

Bateman, H. W., IV. *Early Jewish Hermeneutics and Hebrews 1:5–13: The Impact of Early Jewish Exegesis on the Interpretation of a Significant New Testament Passage*. New York: Peter Lang, 1997.

———. "Psalm 110:1 and the New Testament." *BSac* 149 (1992): 438–53.

Bauckham, R. *Bible and Mission: Christian Witness in a Postmodern World*. Grand Rapids: Baker Academic, 2003.

———, ed. *The Gospels for All Christians: Rethinking the Gospel Audiences*. Grand Rapids: Eerdmans, 1997.

———. *Jesus and the Eyewitnesses: The Gospels as Eyewitness Testimony*. Grand Rapids: Eerdmans, 2006.

———. *Jude, 2 Peter*. WBC 50. Waco: Word Books, 1983.

———. "Tobit as a Parable for the Exiles of Northern Israel." In *The Jewish World around the New Testament: Collected Essays I*, 433–59. WUNT 233. Tübingen: Mohr Siebeck, 2008.

Bavinck, H. *The Doctrine of God*. Translated by W. Hendriksen. Edinburgh: Banner of Truth, 1978.

———. *Reformed Dogmatics*. Edited by J. Bolt. Translated by J. Vriend. 4 vols. Grand Rapids: Baker Academic, 2003–8.

Beale, G. K. *A New Testament Biblical Theology: The Unfolding of the Old Testament in the New*. Grand Rapids: Baker Academic, 2011.

———. *The Temple and the Church's Mission: A Biblical Theology of the Dwelling Place of God*. New Studies in Biblical Theology. Downers Grove, IL: InterVarsity, 2004.

Bebbington, D. *Patterns in History: A Christian Perspective on Historical Thought*. Leicester, UK: Inter-Varsity, 1979. Reprint, Leicester, UK: Apollos, 1990.

Beckwith, R. T. *The Old Testament Canon of the New Testament Church and Its Background in Early Judaism*. Grand Rapids: Eerdmans, 1986.

Bede, the Venerable. *A Biblical Miscellany.* Translated by W. T. Foley and A. G. Holder. Translated Texts for Historians. Liverpool: Liverpool University Press, 1999.

———. *Commentary on Revelation.* Translated by F. Wallis. Translated Texts for Historians. Liverpool: Liverpool University Press, 2013.

———. *On Ezra and Nehemiah.* Translated by S. DeGregorio. Translated Texts for Historians. Liverpool: Liverpool University Press, 2006.

———. *On Genesis.* Translated by C. Kendall. Translated Texts for Historians. Liverpool: Liverpool University Press, 2008.

———. *On the Tabernacle.* Translated by A. G. Holder. Translated Texts for Historians. Liverpool: Liverpool University Press, 1994.

———. *On the Temple.* Translated by S. Connolly. Translated Texts for Historians. Liverpool: Liverpool University Press, 1996.

Bedouelle, G. *La réforme du catholicisme, 1480–1620.* Paris: Cerf, 1989.

Beiser, F. C. *The Fate of Reason: German Philosophy from Kant to Fichte.* Cambridge, MA: Harvard University Press, 1993.

———. *The German Historicist Tradition.* Oxford: Oxford University Press, 2011.

———. *Hegel.* London: Routledge, 2005.

———. *The Romantic Imperative: The Concept of Early German Romanticism.* Cambridge, MA: Harvard University Press, 2003.

Beisser, F. *"Claritas scripturae" bei Martin Luther.* Forschungen zur Kirchen- und Dogmengeschichte 18. Göttingen: Vandenhoeck & Ruprecht, 1966.

Beldman, D. J. H. "The Completion of Judges: Strategies of Ending in Judges 17–21." PhD diss., University of Bristol, 2013.

Bellah, R. N., et al. *Habits of the Heart: Individualism and Commitment in American Life.* Updated edition. Berkeley: University of California Press, 2008.

Ben-Eliyahu, E., Y. Cohn, F. Millar, and P. S. Alexander, eds. *Handbook of Jewish Literature from Late Antiquity, 135–700 CE.* Oxford: Oxford University Press, 2012.

Bengel, J. A. *Gnomon Novi Testamenti.* Tübingen: Schramm, 1742.

Berger, J. "Der Brief an der Hebräer, eine Homilie." *Göttinger theologische Bibliothek* 3 (1797): 449–59.

Berger, P. L. *A Rumour of Angels: Modern Society and the Rediscovery of the Supernatural.* London: Allen Lane, 1970.

Berger, P., G. Davie, and E. Folks. *Religious America, Secular Europe? A Theme and Variations.* Burlington, VT: Ashgate, 2008.

Berkouwer, G. C. "General and Special Divine Revelation." In *Revelation in the Bible: Contemporary Evangelical Thought*, ed. C. F. H. Henry, 13–24. Grand Rapids: Baker, 1959.

———. *The Providence of God.* Grand Rapids: Eerdmans, 1952.

———. *The Triumph of Grace in the Theology of Karl Barth.* Grand Rapids: Eerdmans, 1956.

Berliner, A., ed. *Rashi: The Commentary of Solomon B. Isaac on the Torah* [Hebrew]. 2nd ed. Frankfurt: Kauffmann, 1905.

Bernstein, M. J. "'Rewritten Bible': A Generic Category Which Has Outlived Its Usefulness?" *Textus* 22 (2005): 169–96.

Bernstein, R. J., ed. *Habermas and Modernity.* Cambridge: Polity, 1985.

Berry, W. *Imagination in Place.* Berkeley: Counterpoint, 2010.

———. *The Poetry of William Carlos Williams of Rutherford.* Berkeley: Counterpoint, 2011.

———. *Standing by Words.* Berkeley: Counterpoint, 1983.

Bertens, J. W. *The Idea of the Postmodern: A History.* London: Routledge, 1995.

Betz, J. R. *After Enlightenment: The Postsecular Vision of J. G. Hamann.* Oxford: Blackwell, 2009.

———. "Enlightenment Revisited: Hamann as the First and Best Critic of Kant's Philosophy." *Modern Theology* 20 (2004): 291–301.

———. "Reading 'Sibylline Leaves': J. G. Hamann in the History of Ideas." *Journal of the History of Ideas* 70, no. 1 (2009): 93–118.

Bireley, R. *The Refashioning of Catholicism, 1450–1700*. London: Macmillan, 1999.

Black, C. C., II. "The Rhetorical Form of the Hellenistic Jewish and Early Christian Sermon: A Response to Lawrence Wills." *HTR* 81 (1988): 1–18.

Bleicher, J. *Contemporary Hermeneutics: Hermeneutics as Method, Philosophy, and Critique*. London: Routledge & Kegan Paul, 1980.

Blocher, Henri. *In the Beginning: The Opening Chapters of Genesis*. Downers Grove, IL: InterVarsity, 1984.

Block, D. I. *How I Love Your Torah, O Lord! Studies in Deuteronomy*. Eugene, OR: Cascade Books, 2011.

Blowers, P. M. "The *Regula Fidei* and the Narrative Character of Early Christian Faith." *Pro Ecclesia* 6, no. 2 (1997): 199–228.

———. "The World in the Mirror of Holy Scripture: Maximus the Confessor's Short Hermeneutical Treatise in *Ambiguum ad Joannem* 37." In *In Dominico Eloquio—In Lordly Eloquence: Essays on Patristic Exegesis in Honor of Robert Louis Wilken*, edited by P. M. Blowers, A. R. Christman, D. G. Hunter, and R. D. Young, 408–26. Grand Rapids: Eerdmans, 2002.

Boff, L. *Passion of Christ, Passion of the World: The Facts, Their Interpretation, and Their Meaning Yesterday and Today*. Translated by R. R. Barr. 2nd ed. Maryknoll, NY: Orbis Books, 2001.

Böhm, T. "Allegory and History." In Kannengiesser, *HPE* 1:213–26.

Bonaventure. *St. Bonaventure's Commentary on the Gospel of Luke*. With introduction, translation, and notes by R. J. Karris. 3 vols. Works of St. Bonaventure 8.1–3. St. Bonaventure, NY: Franciscan Institute Publications, 2001–4.

Bonhoeffer, D. *Christ the Center*. Translated by E. Bethge. New York: Harper & Row, 1966.

———. *Ethics*. New York: Macmillan, 1955.

———. "Lectures on Preaching." In *Bonhoeffer: Worldly Preaching*, edited and translated by C. E. Fant, 123–80. Nashville: Nelson, 1975.

———. *Life Together; Prayerbook of the Bible*. Dietrich Bonhoeffer Works 5. Minneapolis: Fortress, 1996.

———. *Sanctorum communio: A Theological Study of the Sociology of the Church*. Translated by R. Krauss and N. Lukens. Edited by C. J. Green. Minneapolis: Fortress, 1998.

Bonnefoy, J.-F. *Christ and the Cosmos*. Translated and edited by M. D. Meilach. Paterson, NJ: St. Anthony Guild, 1965.

Booth, W. *The Rhetoric of Fiction*. 2nd ed. London: Penguin, 1983.

Borgen, P. "Philo of Alexandria as Exegete." In Hauser and Watson, *History of Biblical Interpretation*, 1:114–43.

Bornkamm, H. *Luther and the Old Testament*. Translated by E. W. Gritsch and R. C. Gritsch. Philadelphia: Fortress, 1969.

Bosch, D. J. *Transforming Mission: Paradigm Shifts in Theology of Mission*. Maryknoll, NY: Orbis Books, 2003.

Botha, M. E. *Metaphor and Its Moorings: Studies in the Gounding of Metaphorical Meaning*. Bern: Peter Lang, 2007.

———. "Understanding Our Age: Philosophy at a Turning Point of the 'Turns'?—The Endless Search for the Elusive Universal." *TCW* 30, no. 2 (1994): 16–31.

Boulnois, O. *Être et représentation: Une généalogie de la métaphysique moderne à l'époque de Duns Scot, XIIIe–XIVe siècle*. Paris: Presses Universitaires de France, 1999.

Boyarin, D. "Origen as Theorist of Allegory: Alexandrian Contexts." In Copeland and Struck, *Cambridge Companion to Allegory*, 39–56.

Braaten, C. E., and R. W. Jenson, eds. *The Last Things: Biblical and Theological Perspectives on Eschatology*. Grand Rapids: Eerdmans, 2002.

Bradbury, M. "Structure." In *A Dictionary of Modern Critical Terms*, edited by R. Fowler, 235. London: Routledge & Kegan Paul, 1987.

Brassier, R. *Nihil Unbound: Enlightenment and Extinction*. Basingstoke, UK: Palgrave Macmillan, 2007.

Breck, J. *Scripture in Tradition: The Bible and Its Interpretation in the Orthodox Church.* Crestwood, NY: St. Vladimir's Seminary Press, 2001.

Brett, M. G. *Biblical Criticism in Crisis? The Impact of the Canonical Approach on Old Testament Studies.* Cambridge: Cambridge University Press, 1991.

Brettler, M. Z. *The Creation of History in Ancient Israel.* London: Routledge, 1995.

Bright, J. *The Authority of the Old Testament.* Nashville: Abingdon, 1967.

Bright, P., ed. *Augustine and the Bible.* Notre Dame, IN: University of Notre Dame Press, 1999.

Brilioth, Y. *A Brief History of Preaching.* Philadelphia, Fortress, 1965.

Brinkmann, H. *Mittelalterliche Hermeneutik.* Tübingen: Niemeyer, 1980.

Broadus, J. A. *On the Preparation and Delivery of Sermons.* 4th ed. Revised by V. L. Stanfield. New York: HarperOne, 1979.

Brody, R. "The Geonim of Babylonia as Biblical Exegetes." In Saebø, *HB/OT* 1.2 (2000): 74–88.

Bromiley, G. W. "The Authority of Scripture in Karl Barth." In *Hermeneutics: Authority and Canon*, edited by D. A. Carson and D. Woodbridge, 271–94. Downers Grove, IL: InterVarsity, 1986.

Brooke, G. J. *Reading the Dead Sea Scrolls: Essays in Method.* Atlanta: SBL, 2013.

———. "Rewritten Bible." In Schiffman and VanderKam, *Encyclopedia of the Dead Sea Scrolls*, 2:777–81.

Brooks, C. *The Well Wrought Urn: Studies in the Structure of Poetry.* New York: Reynal & Hitchcock, 1947.

Brown, G. H. "The Psalms as the Foundation of Anglo-Saxon Learning." In *The Place of the Psalms in the Intellectual Culture of the Middle Ages*, edited by N. van Deusen, 1–24. Albany: State University of New York Press, 1999.

Brownlee, W. H. "Biblical Interpretation among the Sectaries of the Dead Sea Scrolls." *Biblical Archaeologist* 14 (1951): 60–62.

Bruce, F. F. *The Books and the Parchments: Some Chapters on the Transmission of the Bible.* 2nd ed. London: Pickering & Inglis, 1963.

———. *The Canon of Scripture.* Downers Grove, IL: InterVarsity, 1988.

———. *The Epistle to the Galatians: A Commentary on the Greek Text.* NIGTC. Exeter, UK: Paternoster, 1982.

———. *The Epistle to the Hebrews.* 2nd ed. Grand Rapids: Eerdmans, 1990.

Brueggemann, W. *A Commentary on Jeremiah: Exile and Homecoming.* Grand Rapids: Eerdmans, 1998.

———. *The Practice of Prophetic Imagination: Preaching an Emancipatory Word.* Minneapolis: Fortress, 2012.

———. "Response to J. Richard Middleton." *HTR* 87, no. 3 (1994): 279–89.

———. *Theology of the Old Testament: Testimony, Dispute, Advocacy.* Minneapolis: Fortress, 2005.

Buber, M. *I and Thou.* Translated by W. Kaufmann. Edinburgh: T&T Clark, 1970.

Buckley, M. J. *At the Origins of Modern Atheism.* New Haven: Yale University Press, 1987.

Bullinger, H. *The Second Helvetic Confession.* 1562; rev., 1564. https://www.ccel.org/creeds/helvetic.htm.

Burke, S. *The Death and Return of the Author: Criticism and Subjectivity.* Edinburgh: Edinburgh University Press, 1992.

Burnett, F. S. "Historiography." In A. K. M. Adams, *Postmodern Biblical Interpretation*, 106–12.

Burridge, R. A. "About People, by People, for People: Gospel Genre and Audiences." In Bauckham, *Gospels for All Christians*, 113–46.

Burrows, M. S., and P. Rorem, eds. *Biblical Hermeneutics in Historical Perspective: Studies in Honor of Karlfried Froehlich on His Sixtieth Birthday.* Grand Rapids: Eerdmans, 1991.

Burtness, J. H. *Shaping the Future: The Ethics of Dietrich Bonhoeffer.* Philadelphia: Fortress, 1985.

Buss, M. J. "The Meaning of History." In *Theology as History*, edited by J. M. Robinson and J. B. Cobb, 135–54. New York: Harper Books, 1967.

Byrskog, S. S. *Story as History—History as Story: The Gospel Tradition in the Context of Ancient Oral History*. Tübingen: Mohr Siebeck, 2000.

Cadbury, H. J. *The Making of Luke-Acts*. 2nd ed. London: SPCK, 1958.

Caird, G. B. "The Christological Basis of Christian Hope." In *The Christian Hope*, by G. B. Caird et al., 21–24. London: SPCK, 1970.

———. "The Exegetical Method of the Epistle to the Hebrews." *Canadian Journal of Theology* 5 (1959): 44–51.

Caird, G. B., and L. D. Hurst. *New Testament Theology*. Oxford: Clarendon, 1995.

Calvin, John. *Institutes of the Christian Religion*. Edited by J. T. McNeill. Translated by F. L. Battles. 2 vols. LCC 20–21. Philadelphia: Westminster, 1960.

Cancik, H. *Grundzüge der hethitischen und alttestamentlichen Geschichtsschreibung*. Wiesbaden: Harrassowitz, 1976.

Caputo, J. D. *Philosophy and Theology*. Nashville: Abingdon, 2006.

———. *Radical Hermeneutics: Repetition, Deconstruction, and the Hermeneutic Project*. Bloomington: Indiana University Press, 1987.

Caputo, N. *Nahmanides in Medieval Catalonia: History, Community, and Messianism*. Notre Dame, IN: University of Notre Dame Press, 2008.

Carasik, M., ed. *The Commentators' Bible: The JPS Miqra'ot Gedolot: Exodus*. Philadelphia: Jewish Publication Society, 2005.

Carr, D. M. "Canonization in the Context of Community: An Outline of the Formation of the Tanakh and the Christian Bible." In *A Gift of God in Due Season: Essays on Scripture and Community in Honor of James A. Sanders*, edited by R. D. Weis and D. M. Carr, 22–64. JSOTSup 225. Sheffield: Sheffield Academic, 1996.

Carroll, J. *The Existential Jesus*. Berkeley: Counterpoint, 2007.

———. *Humanism: The Wreck of Western Culture*. London: Fontana, 1993.

Carroll, R. P. "Toward a Grammar of Creation: On Steiner the Theologian." In *Reading George Steiner*, edited by N. A. Scott and R. A. Sharp, 262–74. London: Johns Hopkins University Press, 1994.

Chadwick, H. "Tyconius and Augustine." In *Heresy and Orthodoxy in the Early Church*, edited by H. Chadwick, 49–55. Aldershot, UK: Ashgate, 1991.

Chapman, S. B. *The Law and the Prophets: A Study in Old Testament Canon Formation*. Tübingen: Mohr Siebeck, 2000.

Chazelle, C., and B. V. N. Edwards, eds. *The Study of the Bible in the Carolingian Era*. Medieval Church Studies 3. Turnhout: Brepols, 2003.

Childs, B. S. *Biblical Theology in Crisis*. Philadelphia: Westminster, 1970.

———. *Biblical Theology of the Old and New Testaments: Theological Reflection on the Christian Bible*. Minneapolis: Fortress, 1992.

———. *The Book of Exodus: A Critical, Theological Commentary*. Philadelphia: Westminster, 1974.

———. "The Canon in Recent Biblical Studies: Reflections on an Era." In Bartholomew et al., *Canon and Biblical Interpretation*, 33–57.

———. "Critiques of Recent Intertextual Canonical Interpretation." *ZAW* (2003): 173–84.

———. "Interpretation in Faith. The Theological Responsibility of an Old Testament Commentary." *Int* 18 (1964): 432–49.

———. *Introduction to the Old Testament as Scripture*. Philadelphia: Fortress, 1979.

———. *Isaiah*. Old Testament Library. Louisville: Westminster John Knox, 2001.

———. *Myth and Reality in the Old Testament*. 2nd ed. Eugene, OR: Wipf & Stock, 2009.

———. "The Nature of the Christian Bible: One Book, Two Testaments." In *The Rule of Faith: Scripture, Canon, and Creed in a Critical Age*, edited by E. Radner and G. Sumner, 115–26. Harrisburg, PA: Morehouse, 1998.

———. *Old Testament Theology in a Canonical Context*. Minneapolis: Fortress, 1990.

———. "On Reclaiming the Bible for Christian Theology." In *Reclaiming the Bible for the Church*, edited by C. E. Braaten and R. W. Jenson, 1–19. Edinburgh: T&T Clark, 1995.

———. *The Struggle to Understand Isaiah as Christian Scripture*. Grand Rapids: Eerdmans, 2004.

Chilton, B., and J. Neusner. *The Intellectual Foundations of Christian and Jewish Discourse: The Philosophy of Religious Argument*. New York: Routledge, 1997.

Chrétien, J.-L. *The Ark of Speech*. Translated by A. Brown. New York: Routledge, 2004.

———. *The Call and the Response*. Translated by A. A. Davenport. Bronx, NY: Fordham University Press, 2004.

———. *Hand to Hand: Listening to the Work of Art*. Translated by S. E. Lewis. Bronx, NY: Fordham University Press, 2003.

———. *Sous le regard de la Bible*. Paris: Bayard, 2008. ET, *Under the Gaze of the Bible*. Translated by J. M. Dunaway. Bronx, NY: Fordham University Press, 2015.

Chrysostom, John. *Commentary on the Psalms*. Translated by R. C. Hill. 2 vols. Brookline, MA: Holy Cross Orthodox Press, 1998.

Church, C. L. "Westcott, B. F., and F. J. A. Hort." In McKim, *Historical Handbook*, 389–93.

Churgin, P. *Targum Jonathan to the Prophets*. New York: Ktav, 1983.

Clark, S. H. *Paul Ricoeur*. London: Routledge, 1990.

Clayton, A. L. "The Orthodox Recovery of a Heretical Proof-Text: Athanasius of Alexandria's Interpretation of Proverbs 8:22–30 in Conflict with the Arians." PhD diss., Southern Methodist University, 1988.

Clayton, T. *Exploring Advent with Luke: Four Questions for Spiritual Growth*. Notre Dame, IN: Ave Maria Press, 2012.

Clement of Alexandria. *Stromata*. In ANF 2. http://www.earlychristianwritings.com.

———. *Who Is the Rich Man That Shall Be Saved?* In ANF 2. http://www.earlychristianwritings.com.

Clements, R. E. *A Century of Old Testament Study*. Rev. ed. Guildford, UK: Lutterworth, 1983.

Clines, D. J. A. *The Esther Scroll: The Story of the Story*. JSOTSup 30. Sheffield: Sheffield Academic, 1984.

———. "Possibilities and Priorities of Biblical Interpretation in an International Perspective." *Biblical Interpretation* 1, no. 1 (1993): 67–87.

———. "The Ten Commandments: Reading from Left to Right." In *Words Remembered, Texts Renewed: Essays in Honour of John F. A. Sawyer*, edited by J. Davies, G. Harvey, and W. Watson, 97–112. Sheffield: Sheffield Academic Press, 1995.

Clouser, R. A. *The Myth of Religious Neutrality: An Essay on the Hidden Role of Religious Belief in Theories*. Notre Dame, IN: University of Notre Dame Press, 1991.

Clowney, E. P. *Preaching and Biblical Theology*. Phillipsburg, NJ: P&R, 1979.

Cochrane, C. N. *Christianity and Classical Culture: A Study of Thought and Action from Augustus to Augustine*. Oxford: Oxford University Press, 1957.

———. *Thucydides and the Science of History*. London: Oxford University Press, 1929.

Cockerill, G. L. *The Epistle to the Hebrews*. NICNT. Grand Rapids: Eerdmans, 2012.

———. "Heb. 1:1–14, *1 Clem.* 36.1–6, and the High Priest Title." *Journal of Biblical Literature* 97 (1978): 437–40.

Cody, A. *Heavenly Sanctuary and Liturgy in the Epistle to the Hebrews: The Achievement of Salvation in the Epistle's Perspectives*. St. Meinrad, IN: St. Meinrad Archabbey, 1960.

Cohen, J. J. *Major Philosophers of Jewish Prayer in the Twentieth Century*. Bronx, NY: Fordham University Press, 2000.

Cohen, M. "The Qimhi Family." In Saebø, *HB/OT* 1.2 (2000): 388–415.

Cohen, S. J. D. *From the Maccabees to the Mishnah*. 2nd ed. Louisville: Westminster John Knox, 2006.

Colet, J. *An Exposition of St. Paul's Epistle to the Romans*. London: Bell & Daldy, 1873.

Collingwood, R. G. *The Idea of History*. Oxford: Oxford University Press, 1946.

Collins, J. J. *The Dead Sea Scrolls: A Biography*. Princeton: Princeton University Press, 2012.

Collins, J. J., and D. C. Harlow, eds. *Early Judaism: A Comprehensive Overview*. Grand Rapids: Eerdmans, 2012.

Congregation for Institutes of Consecrated Life and Societies of Apostolic Life. *Starting Afresh from Christ: A Renewed Commitment to Consecrated Life in the Third Millennium*. Sherbrooke, Quebec: Médiaspaul, 2002.

Cook, J., ed. *Septuagint and Reception: Essays Prepared for the Association for the Study of the Septuagint in South Africa*. VTSup 127. Leiden: Brill, 2009.

Cooper, J. W. *Body, Soul, and Life Everlasting: Biblical Anthropology and the Monism-Dualism Debate*. Grand Rapids: Eerdmans, 1989.

Copeland, R., and P. T. Struck, eds. *The Cambridge Companion to Allegory*. Cambridge: Cambridge University Press, 2010.

Cornick, D. "The Reformation Crisis in Pastoral Care." In *A History of Pastoral Care*, edited by G. R. Evans, 223–51. London: Cassell, 2002.

Corpus Christianorum: Series graeca. Turnhout: Brepols, 1977–.

Crawford, S. W. *Rewriting Scripture in Second Temple Times*. Grand Rapids: Eerdmans, 2008.

Cullmann, O. *Christ and Time: The Primitive Christian Conception of Time and History*. 3rd, rev. ed. London: SCM, 1967.

———. *Salvation in History*. Translated by S. G. Sowers. New York: Harper & Row, 1967.

Cyprian. *On the Lord's Prayer*. In *Tertullian, Cyprian, and Origen, On the Lord's Prayer*. Popular Patristics 29. Crestwood, NY: St. Vladimir's Seminary Press, 2004.

Daane, J. *Preaching with Confidence: A Theological Essay on the Power of the Pulpit*. Grand Rapids: Eerdmans, 1980.

Dalferth, I. U. *Theology and Philosophy*. Oxford: Blackwell, 1988.

Dan, J. *Gershom Scholem and the Mystical Dimension of Jewish History*. Translated by N. Abercrombie. New York: New York University Press, 1987.

Daniélou, J. *From Shadows to Reality: Studies in the Biblical Typology of the Fathers*. Westminster, MD: Newman, 1960.

———. *The Lord of History: Reflections on the Inner Meaning of History*. Cleveland: World, 1968.

———. "The New Testament and the Theology of History." In *Studia evangelica I*, edited by K. Aland et al., 25–34. Berlin: Akademie-Verlag, 1959.

Daube, D. *The New Testament and Rabbinic Judaism*. Peabody, MA: Hendrickson, 1995.

Davidson, R. *The Courage to Doubt: Exploring an Old Testament Theme*. London: SCM, 1983.

Davies, P. R. "Ethics and the Old Testament." In *The Bible in Ethics*, edited by J. W. Rogerson et al., 164–73. JSOTSup 207. Sheffield: Sheffield Academic, 1995.

Davies, W. D. *The Gospel and the Land: Early Christianity and Jewish Territorial Doctrine*. Berkeley: University of California Press, 1974.

Davis, E. F. *Imagination Shaped: Old Testament Preaching in the Anglican Tradition*. Valley Forge, PA: Trinity Press International, 1995.

———. *Scripture, Culture, and Agriculture: An Agrarian Reading of the Bible*. Cambridge: Cambridge University Press, 2009.

———. *Wondrous Depth: Preaching the Old Testament*. Louisville: Westminster John Knox, 2005.

Davis, S. T., ed. *Encountering Evil: Live Options in Theodicy*. New ed. Edinburgh: T&T Clark, 2001.

Dawson, D. A. *Allegorical Readers and Cultural Revision in Ancient Alexandria*.

Berkeley: University of California Press, 1992.

———. *Text-Linguistics and Biblical Hebrew*. JSOTSup 177. Sheffield: Sheffield Academic, 1994.

Dearman, J. A. *The Book of Hosea*. Grand Rapids: Eerdmans, 2010.

de Certeau, M. *The Mystic Fable*. Chicago: University of Chicago Press, 1992.

DeGregorio, S., trans. Introduction to *Bede: On Ezra and Nehemiah*, xiii–xliv. Liverpool: Liverpool University Press, 2006.

Delegue, Y. *Les machines du sens: Fragments d'une sémiologie médiévale*. Paris: Archives du Commentaire, 1987.

de Man, P. Introduction to *Toward an Aesthetic of Reception*, by H. R. Jauss, translated by T. Bahti, vii–xxv. Minneapolis: University of Minnesota Press, 1982.

Demarest, B. A. *A History of Interpretation of Hebrews 7, 1–10 from the Reformation to the Present*. Beiträge zur Geschichte der biblischen Exegese. Tübingen: Mohr, 1976.

Dempster, S. G. "Torah, Torah, Torah: The Emergence of the Tripartite Canon." In *Exploring the Origins of the Bible: Canon Formation in Historical, Literary, and Theological Perspective*, edited by C. Evans and E. Tov, 87–128. Grand Rapids: Baker Academic, 2008.

Descartes, R. *Discourse on the Method of Rightly Conducting the Reason, and Seeking the Truth in the Sciences*. https://ebooks.adelaide.edu.au/d/descartes/rene/d44dm/part1.html.

de Vaux, R. *Ancient Israel: Its Life and Institutions*. New York: McGraw-Hill, 1961. Reprint, Grand Rapids: Eerdmans, 1997.

Dever, W. G. *What Did the Biblical Writers Know, and When Did They Know It? What Archaeology Can Tell Us about the Reality of Ancient Israel*. Grand Rapids: Eerdmans, 2001.

Dewald, C., and J. Marincola, eds. *The Cambridge Companion to Herodotus*. Cambridge: Cambridge University Press, 2013.

Dickson, G. G. *Johann Georg Hamann's Relational Metacriticism*. Berlin: de Gruyter, 1995.

Docherty, S. E. *The Use of the Old Testament in Hebrews: A Case Study in Early Jewish Bible Interpretation*. WUNT 2/260. Tübingen: Mohr Siebeck, 2009.

Dodd, C. H. *According to the Scriptures: The Sub-Structure of New Testament Theology*. London: Nisbet, 1952.

Dohmen, C. "Probleme und Chancen biblischer Theologie aus alttestamentlicher Sicht." In Dohmen and Söding, *Eine Bibel—zwei Testamente*, 15–35.

Dohmen, C., and M. Oeming. *Biblischer Kanon, warum und wozu? Eine Kanontheologie*. Quaestiones disputatae 137. Freiburg: Herder, 1992.

Dohmen, C., and T. Söding, eds. *Eine Bibel—zwei Testamente: Positionen biblischer Theologie*. Paderborn: Schöningh, 1995.

Dohmen, C., and G. Stemberger. *Hermeneutik der Jüdischen Bibel und des Alten Testaments*. Stuttgart: Kohlhammer, 1996.

Donovan, M. A. *One Right Reading? A Guide to Irenaeus*. Collegeville, MN: Liturgical Press, 1997.

Dooyeweerd, H. *Roots of Western Culture*. The Collected Works of Herman Dooyeweerd B/3. Lewiston, NY: E. Mellen, 2003.

Duke, P. *Irony in the Fourth Gospel*. Atlanta: John Knox, 1985.

Dumbrell, W. J. *Covenant and Creation: A Theology of Old Testament Covenants*. Nashville: Nelson, 1984.

———. *The End of the Beginning: Revelation 21–22 and the Old Testament*. Reprint, Eugene, OR: Wipf & Stock, 2001.

———. *The Faith of Israel: A Theological Survey of the Old Testament*. Grand Rapids: Baker Academic, 2002.

Dungan, D. L. "The New Testament Canon in Recent Study." *Int* 29 (1975): 339–51.

Dunn, J. D. G. *Christianity in the Making*. Vol. 1, *Jesus Remembered*. Grand Rapids: Eerdmans, 2003.

———. *Christology in the Making: A New New Testament Inquiry into the Origins* of the Doctrine of the Incarnation. 2nd ed. Grand Rapids: Eerdmans, 2003.

———. The Epistles to the Colossians and to Philemon: A Commentary on the Greek Text. NIGTC. Grand Rapids: Eerdmans, 1996.

Dunnill, J. Covenant and Sacrifice in the Letter to the Hebrews. SNTSMS 75. Cambridge: Cambridge University Press, 1992.

Düringer, H. Universale Vernunft und partikularer Glaube: Eine theologische Auswertung des Werkes von Jürgen Habermas. Leuven: Peeters, 1999.

Ebeling, G. "Hermeneutik." In Religion in Geschichte und Gegenwart: Handwörterbuch für Theologie und Religionswissenschaft, edited by H. D. Betz et al., 3:243–62. 4th ed. Tübingen: Mohr Siebeck, 2008.

———. Wort Gottes und Tradition: Studien zu einer Hermeneutik der Konfessionen. Göttingen: Vandenhoek & Ruprecht, 1964.

Eco, U. Interpretation and Overinterpretation. Cambridge: Cambridge University Press, 1992.

———. The Limits of Interpretation. Bloomington: Indiana University Press, 1990.

———. The Role of the Reader: Explorations in the Semiotics of Texts. Bloomington: Indiana University Press, 1979.

———. Semiotics and the Philosophy of Language. Bloomington: Indiana University Press, 1984.

———. A Theory of Semiotics. Bloomington: Indiana University Press, 1976.

Edgar, A. "Kant's Two Interpretations of Genesis." Literature and Theology 6, no. 3 (1992): 280–90.

Edwards, O. C., Jr. A History of Preaching. Nashville: Abingdon, 2004.

Edwards, T. M. Exegesis in the Targum of Psalms: The Old, the New, and the Rewritten. Piscataway, NJ: Gorgias, 2007.

Eichrodt, W. Theology of the Old Testament. Translated by J. A. Baker. 2 vols. Philadelphia: Westminster, 1961–67.

Eisen, R. The Book of Job in Medieval Jewish Philosophy. New York: Oxford University Press, 2004.

———. Gersonides on Providence, Covenant, and the Chosen People: A Study in Medieval Philosophy and Biblical Commentary. Albany: State University of New York Press, 1995.

Eisenbaum, P. M. "Heroes and History in Hebrews 11." In Early Interpretation of the Scriptures of Israel: Investigations and Proposals, edited by C. A. Evans and J. A. Sanders, 380–96. JSNTSup 148. Sheffield: Sheffield Academic, 1997.

———. The Jewish Heroes of Christian History: Hebrews 11 in Literary Context. SBLDS 156. Atlanta: Scholars Press, 1997.

Eliezer of Beaugency. Commentaries on Ezekiel and the Twelve Minor Prophets by Eliezer of Beaugency [Hebrew]. Edited by S. Poznanski. Warsaw: Mikize Nirdamm, 1913.

———. Commentary on the Latter Prophets by R. Eliezer of Beaugency: Isaiah [Hebrew]. Edited by J. W. Nutt. London: Baer, 1879.

Eliot, T. S. Selected Prose. Edited by J. Hayward. London: Penguin, 1953.

———. "Tradition and the Individual Talent" (1919) and "The Function of Criticism" (1923). In 20th Century Literary Criticism, edited by D. Lodge, 69–84. New York: Longman, 1972.

Ellingsen, M. The Integrity of Biblical Narrative: Story in Theology and Proclamation. Minneapolis: Fortress, 1990.

Ellingworth, P. The Epistle to the Hebrews: A Commentary on the Greek Text. NIGTC. Grand Rapids: Eerdmans, 1993.

———. "Hebrews and 1 Clement: Literary Dependence or Common Tradition?" Biblische Zeitschrift 23 (1979): 262–69.

———. "The Old Testament in Hebrews: Exegesis, Method, and Hermeneutics." PhD diss., University of Aberdeen, 1997.

Ellingworth, P., and E. A. Nida. Hebrews: A Translator's Handbook on the Letter to the Hebrews. New York: United Bible Societies, 1983.

Ellis, E. E. History and Interpretation in New Testament Perspective. Leiden: Brill, 2001.

———. "The New Testament's Use of the Old Testament." In *Biblical Hermeneutics: A Comprehensive Introduction to Interpreting Scripture*, edited by B. Corley et al., 72–89. Nashville: B&H, 2002.

———. *The Old Testament in Early Christianity: Canon and Interpretation in the Light of Modern Research*. Tübingen: Mohr, 1991.

Ellul, J. *Hope in Time of Abandonment*. New York: Seabury, 1973.

———. *The Judgment of Jonah*. Grand Rapids: Eerdmans, 1971.

———. *The New Demons*. New York: Seabury, 1975.

———. *The Presence of the Kingdom*. New York: Seabury, 1967.

———. *Propaganda: The Formation of Men's Attitudes*. New York: Knopf, 1965.

———. *The Subversion of Christianity*. Grand Rapids: Eerdmans, 1986.

———. *The Technological Society*. New York: Knopf, 1964.

Elman, Y. "Moses ben Nahman/Nahmanides (Ramban)." In Saebø, *HB/OT* 1.2 (2000): 416–32.

English, E. D. *Reading and Wisdom: The "De doctrina christiana" of Augustine in the Middle Ages*. Notre Dame Conferences in Medieval Studies 6. Notre Dame, IN: University of Notre Dame Press, 1995.

Ernest, J. D. *The Bible in Athanasius of Alexandria*. The Bible in Ancient Christianity 2. Leiden: Brill, 2004.

Evans, C. S. *The Historical Christ and the Jesus of Faith: The Incarnational Narrative as History*. Oxford: Oxford University Press, 1996.

———. *Kierkegaard: An Introduction*. Cambridge: Cambridge University Press, 2009.

———. *Subjectivity and Religious Belief: An Historical, Critical Study*. Washington, DC: University Press of America, 1982.

Fackre, G. "Narrative Theology from an Evangelical Perspective." In *Faith and Narrative*, edited by K. E. Yandell, 188–201. Oxford: Oxford University Press, 2001.

Fahey, M. A. *Cyprian and the Bible: A Study in Third-Century Exegesis*. Beiträge zur Geschichte der biblischen Hermeneutik 9. Tübingen: Mohr, 1971.

Farge, J. K. *Orthodoxy and Reform in Early Reformation France: The Faculty of Theology of Paris, 1500–1543*. Leiden: Brill, 1985.

Farrow, D. *Ascension and Ecclesia: On the Significance of the Doctrine of the Ascension for Ecclesiology and Christian Cosmology*. Grand Rapids: Eerdmans, 1999.

Feld, H. *Der Hebräerbrief*. Erträge der Forschung 28. Darmstadt: Buchgesellschaft, 1985.

Feldmeier, R., and H. Spieckermann. *God of the Living: A Biblical Theology*. Waco: Baylor University Press, 2011. ET of *Der Gott der Lebendigen: Eine biblische Gotteslehre*. Tübingen: Mohr Siebeck, 2011.

Filson, F. V. *"Yesterday": A Study of Hebrews in the Light of Chapter 13*. Studies in Biblical Theology 2/4. London: SCM, 1967.

Fishbane, M. A. *Biblical Interpretation in Ancient Israel*. Oxford: Oxford University Press, 2004.

———, ed. *The Midrashic Imagination: Jewish Exegesis, Thought, and History*. Albany: State University of New York Press, 1993.

Fiumara, G. C. *The Other Side of Language: A Philosophy of Listening*. London: Routledge, 1995.

Flusser, D. *Judaism of the Second Temple Period*. Translated by A. Yadin. Vol. 1. Grand Rapids: Eerdmans, 2007.

Fodor, J. *Christian Hermeneutics: Paul Ricoeur and the Refiguring of Theology*. Oxford: Oxford University Press, 1995.

Ford, D. F. "An Interfaith Wisdom: Scriptural Reasoning between Jews, Christians and Muslims." *Modern Theology* 22, no. 3 (2006): 345–66.

———. *Theology: A Very Short Introduction*. Oxford: Oxford University Press, 2000.

Ford, D. F., and C. C. Pecknold. *The Promise of Scriptural Reasoning*. Oxford: Blackwell, 2006.

Ford, J. M. *My Enemy Is My Guest: Jesus and Violence in Luke*. Maryknoll, NY: Orbis Books, 1984.

Foss, S. K., K. A. Foss, and R. Trapp, eds. *Contemporary Perspectives on Rhetoric*. 3rd ed. Prospect Heights, IL: Waveland, 2002.

Foster, E., and D. Lateiner, eds. *Thucydides and Herodotus*. Oxford: Oxford University Press, 2012.

Foucault, M. "What Is an Author?" In *The Foucault Reader*, edited by P. Rabinow, 101–20. New York: Pantheon, 1984.

Fowl, S. "The Role of Scripture in an Ecclesially Based University." In *Conflicting Allegiances: The Church-Based University in a Liberal Democratic Society*, edited by M. L. Budde and J. Wright, 171–82. Grand Rapids: Brazos, 2004.

Frank, D. "Karaite Exegesis." In Saebø, *HB/OT* 1.2 (2000): 110–28.

———. *Search Scripture Well: Karaite Exegesis and the Origins of the Jewish Bible Commentary in the Islamic East*. Leiden: Brill, 2004.

Frankfort, H., H. A. Frankfort, J. A. Wilson, T. Jacobsen, and W. A. Irwin. *The Intellectual Adventure of Ancient Man: An Essay on Speculative Thought in the Ancient Near East*. Chicago: University of Chicago Press, 1946.

Freedman, D. N., ed. *Anchor Bible Dictionary*. 6 vols. New York: Doubleday, 1992.

———. Preface to *Pomegranates and Golden Bells: Studies in Biblical, Jewish, and Near Eastern Ritual, Law, and Literature in Honor of Jacob Milgrom*, edited by D. P. Wright et al., ix–xi. Winona Lake, IN: Eisenbrauns, 1995.

Frei, H. W. *The Eclipse of Biblical Narrative: A Study in Eighteenth and Nineteenth Century Hermeneutics*. New Haven: Yale University Press, 1974.

Frendo, A. *Pre-Exilic Israel, the Hebrew Bible, and Archaeology*. London: T&T Clark, 2011.

Freund, E. *The Return of the Reader: Reader-Response Criticism*. London: Methuen, 1987.

Friedlander, M., ed. *Essays on the Writings of Abraham Ibn Ezra*. London: Society of Hebrew Literature / Trübner, 1877. Reprint, 1964.

Froehlich, K. "Church History and the Bible." In Burrows and Rorem, *Biblical Hermeneutics in Historical Perspective*, 1–15.

———. "Postscript." In Burrows and Rorem, *Biblical Hermeneutics in Historical Perspective*, 339–49.

Gabler, J. P. "An Oration on the Proper Distinction between Biblical and Dogmatic Theology and the Specific Objectives of Each." In *Old Testament Theology: Flowering and Future*, edited by B. C. Ollenburger, 1:497–506. Winona Lake, IN: Eisenbrauns, 2004.

Gadamer, H.-G. *Truth and Method*. New York: Seabury, 1975.

Gamble, H. Y. *The New Testament Canon: Its Making and Meaning*. Philadelphia: Fortress, 1985.

Garbini, G. *History and Ideology in Ancient Israel*. Translated by J. Bowden. London: SCM, 1988.

Gardner, Helen. *The Business of Criticism*. Oxford: Clarendon, 1959.

Garfinkel, S. "Clearing *Peshat* and *Derash*." In Saebø, *HB/OT* 1.2 (2000): 129–34.

Gehring, H.-U. *Schriftprinzip und Rezeptionsästhetik: Rezeption in Martin Luther's Predigt und bei Hans Robert Jauss*. Neukirchen-Vluyn: Neukirchener Verlag, 1999.

Gelardini, G., ed. "Hebrews, an Ancient Synagogue Homily for *Tisha be-Av*: Its Function, Its Basis, Its Theological Interpretation." In Gelardini, *Hebrews: Contemporary Methods, New Insights*, 107–27.

———. *Hebrews: Contemporary Methods, New Insights*. BIS 75. Leiden: Brill, 2005.

Gelles, B. J. *Peshat and Derash in the Exegesis of Rashi*. Leiden: Brill, 1981.

Gellner, E. *Postmodernism, Reason and Religion*. London: Routledge, 1992.

Genette, G. *Narrative Discourse: An Essay in Method*. Translated by J. E. Lewin. Ithaca, NY: Cornell University Press, 1983.

Gentry, P. J., and S. J. Wellum. *Kingdom through Covenant: A Biblical-Theological Understanding of the Covenants*. Wheaton: Crossway, 2012.

Gerkin, C. V. *Widening the Horizons: Pastoral Responses to a Fragmented Society*. Philadelphia: Westminster, 1986.

Gerstenberger, E. S. *Theologies in the Old Testament*. Translated by J. Bowden. London: T&T Clark, 2002.

Gheorghita, R. *The Role of the Septuagint in Hebrews: An Investigation of Its Influence with Special Consideration to the Use of Hab 2:3–4 in Heb 10:37–38*. WUNT 2/160. Tübingen: Mohr Siebeck, 2003.

Gibson, A. *Text and Tablet: Near Eastern Archaeology, the Old Testament and New Possibilities*. Burlington, VT: Ashgate, 2000.

Gibson, M. "Lanfranc's Commentary on the Pauline Epistles." *JTS* 22 (1971): 86–112.

Gilbert, P. "The Catholic Counterpart to the Protestant Orthodoxy." In Saebø, *HB/OT* 2 (2008): 758–73.

Gilkey, L. "Cosmology, Ontology, and the Travail of Biblical Language." *JR* (1961): 194–205.

Girard, R. *Deceit, Desire, and the Novel: Self and Other in Literary Structure*. Translated by Y. Freccero. Baltimore: Johns Hopkins University Press, 1965.

Glatzer, N. N., ed. *The Schocken Passover Haggadah*. New York: Schocken, 1953.

Goheen, M. W. *A Light to the Nations: The Missional Church and the Biblical Story*. Grand Rapids: Baker Academic, 2011.

Goldingay, J. *Old Testament Theology*. 3 vols. Downers Grove, IL: IVP Academic, 2003–9.

———. "The Patriarchs in Scripture and History." In Millard and Wiseman, *Essays on the Patriarchal Narratives*, 11–42.

———. *Psalms*. Vol. 3, *Psalms 90–150*. Grand Rapids: Baker Academic, 2008.

———. *Theological Diversity and the Authority of the Old Testament*. Grand Rapids: Eerdmans, 1987.

Goldstein, L. J. *Historical Knowing*. Austin: University of Texas Press, 1976.

Goldsworthy, G. L. *Preaching the Whole Bible as Christian Scripture: The Application of Biblical Theology to Expository Preaching*. Downers Grove, IL: InterVarsity, 2000.

Goodman, L. E., ed. *The Book of Theodicy: Translation and Commentary on the Book of Job, by Saadiah ben Joseph al-Fayyūmī*. Yale Judaica 25. New Haven: Yale University Press, 1988.

———. *Love Thy Neighbor as Thyself*. Oxford: Oxford University Press, 2008.

Goppelt, L. *Typos: The Typological Interpretation of the Old Testament in the New*. Translated by D. H. Madvig. Grand Rapids: Eerdmans, 1982.

Gorday, P. *Principles of Patristic Exegesis: Romans 9–11 in Origen, John Chrysostom, and Augustine*. New York: E. Mellen, 1983.

Gordis, R. *Koheleth the Man and His World: A Study of Ecclesiastes*. New York: Schocken Books, 1968.

Gordon, C. H., and G. R. Rendsburg. *The Bible and the Ancient Near East*. 4th ed. New York: Norton, 1997.

Graf-Stuhlhofer, F. *Der Gebrauch der Bibel von Jesus bis Euseb: Eine statistische Untersuchung zur Kanonsgeschichte*. Wuppertal: Brockhaus, 1988.

Graham, G. *The Shape of the Past*. Oxford: Oxford University Press, 1997.

Grant, G. *Technology and Justice*. Toronto: Anansi, 1986.

Grant, R. M., with D. Tracy. *A Short History of the Interpretation of the Bible*. 2nd ed. Reprint, Eugene, OR: Wipf & Stock, 2001.

Grässer, E. *Aufbruch und Verheissung: Gesammelte Aufsätze zum Hebräerbrief*. Berlin: de Gruyter, 1992.

———. *Der Glaube im Hebräerbrief*. Marburg: Elwert, 1965.

Green, J. B. *The Gospel of Luke*. NICNT. Grand Rapids: Eerdmans, 1997.

Green, J. B., and M. C. McKeever. *Luke-Acts and New Testament Historiography*. Grand Rapids: Baker, 1994.

Greene, T. M. "The Historical Context and Religious Significance of Kant's Religion."

In Kant, *Religion within the Limits of Reason Alone*, ix–cxxxiv.

Greene-McCreight, K. *Ad Litteram: How Augustine, Calvin, and Barth Read the "Plain Sense."* New York: Peter Lang, 1999.

Greenslade, S. L., ed. *Early Latin Theology: Selections from Tertullian, Cyprian, Ambrose, and Jerome.* LCC 5. Philadelphia: Westminster, 1956.

Greenspoon, L. "Hebrew into Greek: Interpretation in, by, and of the Septuagint." In Hauser and Watson, *History of Biblical Interpretation*, 1:80–113.

———. "It's All Greek to Me: The Septuagint in Modern English Translations of the Hebrew Bible." In *7th Congress of the International Organization for Septuagintal and Cognate Studies*, edited by C. Cox, 1–21. SCS 31. Atlanta: Scholars Press, 1991.

———. "The Use and Abuse of the Term 'LXX' and Related Terminology in Recent Scholarship." *BIOSCS* 20 (1987): 21–29.

Greenwood, D. *Structuralism and the Biblical Text*. Religion and Reason 32. New York: Mouton, 1985.

Greidanus, S. *The Modern Preacher and the Ancient Text: Interpreting and Preaching Biblical Literature*. Grand Rapids: Eerdmans, 1988.

———. *Sola scriptura: Problems and Principles in Preaching Historical Texts*. Toronto: Wedge, 1970.

Grillmeier, A. *Christ in the Christian Tradition*. Vol. 1, *From the Apostolic Age to Chalcedon (451)*. Translated by J. Bowden. 2nd ed. London: Mowbrays, 1975.

Grondin, J. *Hans-Georg Gadamer: A Biography*. New Haven: Yale University Press, 2003.

———. *Introduction to Philosophical Hermeneutics*. New Haven: Yale University Press, 1995.

———. *Sources of Hermeneutics*. Albany: State University of New York Press, 1995.

Grossman, A. *Rashi*. Portland, OR: Littman Library of Jewish Civilization, 2012.

———. "The School of Literal Jewish Exegesis in Northern France." In Saebø, *HB/OT* 1.2 (2000): 321–71.

Gruber, M. I. *Rashi's Commentary on the Psalms*. Philadelphia: Jewish Publication Society, 2008.

Gruenler, R. G. *Meaning and Understanding: The Philosophical Framework for Biblical Interpretation*. Foundations of Contemporary Interpretation 2. Grand Rapids: Zondervan, 1991.

Grunhaus, N. *The Challenge of Received Tradition: Dilemmas of Interpretation in Radak's Biblical Commentaries*. Oxford: Oxford University Press, 2012.

Gundry, R. H., et al., eds. *To Tell the Mystery: Essays on New Testament Eschatology in Honor of Robert H. Gundry*. Sheffield: Sheffield Academic, 1994.

Gunkel, H. *Creation and Chaos in the Primeval Era and the Eschaton: A Religio-historical Study of Genesis 1 and Revelation 12*. Grand Rapids: Eerdmans, 2006.

Gunn, D. M. "New Directions in the Study of Biblical Hebrew Narrative." *JSOT* 39 (1987): 65–75.

Gunneweg, A. H. J. *Biblische Theologie des Alten Testaments: Eine Religionsgeschichte Israels in biblisch-theologischer Sicht*. Stuttgart: Kohlhammer, 1993.

Gunton, C. E. *Christ and Creation*. [1992.] Reprint, Eugene, OR: Wipf & Stock, 2005.

———. "The Doctrine of Creation." In *The Cambridge Companion to Christian Doctrine*, edited by C. E. Gunton, 141–57. Cambridge: Cambridge University Press, 1977.

———. *The One, the Three, and the Many: God, Creation, and the Culture of Modernity*. Cambridge: Cambridge University Press, 1993.

———. *The Triune Creator: A Historical and Systematic Study*. Edinburgh Studies in Constructive Theology. Grand Rapids: Eerdmans, 1998.

Guthrie, G. H. "Hebrews." In *Commentary on the New Testament Use of the Old Testament*, edited by G. K. Beale and D. A. Carson, 919–95. Grand Rapids: Baker Academic, 2007.

———. "Hebrews' Use of the Old Testament: Recent Trends in Research." *Currents in Biblical Research* 1, no. 2 (2003): 271–94.

———. *The Structure of Hebrews: A Text-Linguistic Analysis.* NovTSup 73. Leiden: Brill, 1994.

Gutiérrez, G. *A Theology of Liberation: History, Politics, and Salvation.* Maryknoll, NY: Orbis Books, 1973.

Habermas, J. *Erläuterung zur Diskursethik.* Frankfurt: Suhrkamp, 1991.

———. *On the Logic of the Social Sciences.* Cambridge: Polity, 1994.

———. *The Philosophical Discourse of Modernity: Twelve Lectures.* Cambridge: Polity, 1987.

———. *Religion and Rationality: Essays on Reason, God, and Modernity.* Cambridge: Polity, 2002.

Habermas, J., and J. Ratzinger. *The Dialectics of Secularization: On Reason and Religion.* San Francisco: Ignatius, 2006.

Hafemann, S. J. "Baur, F[erdinand] C[hristian] (1792–1860)." In McKim, *Historical Handbook*, 285–89.

———, ed. *Biblical Theology: Retrospect and Prospect.* Downers Grove, IL: InterVarsity, 2002.

Hagen, K. *Hebrews Commenting from Erasmus to Bèze, 1516–1598.* Tübingen: Mohr, 1981.

———. *A Theology of Testament in the Young Luther: The Lectures on Hebrews.* Leiden: Brill, 1974.

Hagman, E. "To the Reader." In Magrassi, *Praying the Bible*, vii–ix.

Hahn, H. F. *The Old Testament in Modern Research.* Philadelphia: Fortress, 1966.

Hahn, S. W. *The Kingdom of God as Liturgical Empire: A Theological Commentary on 1–2 Chronicles.* Grand Rapids: Baker Academic, 2012.

———. *Kinship by Covenant: A Canonical Approach to the Fulfillment of God's Saving Promises.* New Haven: Yale University Press, 2009.

Hahn, S. W., and B. Wiker. *Politicizing the Bible: The Roots of Historical Criticism and the Secularization of Scripture 1300–1700.* New York: Herder and Herder, 2013.

Hailperin, H. *Rashi and the Christian Scholars.* Pittsburgh: University of Pittsburgh Press, 1963.

Hamann, J. G. "Biblische Betrachtungen eines Christen." In *Londoner Schriften*, edited by O. Bayer and B. Weissenborn, 65–104. Munich: C. H. Beck, 1993.

———. *Sämtliche Werke.* Edited by J. Nadler. Vol. 2. Vienna: Herder, 1950.

———. *Writings on Philosophy and Language.* Translated and edited by K. Haynes. Cambridge: Cambridge University Press, 2007.

Harbison, H. E. *The Christian Scholar in the Age of the Reformation.* Grand Rapids: Eerdmans, 1983.

Harding, S. G., ed. *Feminism and Methodology: Social Science Issues.* Milton Keynes, UK: Open University Press, 1987.

Harrington, A. *Hermeneutic Dialogue and Social Science: A Critique of Gadamer and Habermas.* New York: Routledge, 2001.

Harris, H. *The Tübingen School: A Historical and Theological Investigation of the School of F. C. Baur.* Grand Rapids: Baker, 1990.

Harris, Max. *Theater and Incarnation.* Grand Rapids: Eerdmans, 2005.

Harris, Murray J. *Colossians and Philemon.* Grand Rapids: Eerdmans, 1991.

Harris, Robert A. "The Literary Hermeneutic of Rabbi Eliezer of Beaugency." PhD diss., Jewish Theological Seminary, 1997.

———. "Medieval Jewish Biblical Exegesis." In Hauser and Watson, *History of Biblical Interpretation*, 2:141–71.

Harris, Roy. *Reading Saussure: A Critical Commentary on the "Cours de linguistique générale."* London: Duckworth, 1987.

———. *Saussure and His Interpreters.* Edinburgh: Edinburgh University Press, 2003.

Harrisville, Roy A., and M. C. Mattes. "Translators' Epilogue." In *A Contemporary in Dissent: Johann Georg Hamann as a Radical Enlightener*, edited by O. Bayer, 209–23. Grand Rapids: Eerdmans, 2011.

Harrisville, Roy A., and W. Sundberg. *The Bible in Modern Culture: Theology and Historical-Critical Method from Spinoza to Käsemann*. Grand Rapids: Eerdmans, 1995.

Hart, T. A., and S. R. Guthrie, eds. *Faithful Performances: Enacting Christian Tradition*. Burlington, VT: Ashgate, 2007.

Harvey, V. A. *The Historian and the Believer: The Morality of Historical Knowledge and Christian Belief*. New York: Macmillan, 1966.

Hasel, G. *Old Testament Theology: Basic Issues in the Current Debate*. 4th ed. Grand Rapids: Eerdmans, 1991.

Hauerwas, S. *The Peaceable Kingdom: A Primer in Christian Ethics*. Notre Dame, IN: University of Notre Dame Press, 1983.

Hauerwas, S., and L. G. Jones. *Why Narrative? Readings in Narrative Theology*. Grand Rapids: Eerdmans, 1989.

Hauret, C. "Comment lire la Bible?" *La Table Ronde*, no. 107 (November 1956): 141.

Hauser, A. J., and D. F. Watson, eds. *A History of Biblical Interpretation*. Vol. 1, *The Ancient Period*. Vol. 2, *The Medieval through the Reformation Periods*. Grand Rapids: Eerdmans, 2003–9.

Hawkes, T. *Structuralism and Semiotics*. London: Routledge, 1977.

Hays, R. B. *Echoes of Scripture in the Letters of Paul*. New Haven: Yale University Press, 1989.

———. *The Faith of Jesus Christ: An Investigation of the Narrative Substructure of Galatians 3:1–4:11*. Chico, CA: Scholars Press, 1983.

Hazony, Y. *The Philosophy of Hebrew Scripture*. Cambridge: Cambridge University Press, 2012.

Hebblethwaite, B. "Recent British Theology." In *One God in Trinity: An Analysis of the Primary Dogma of Christianity*, ed. P. Toon and J. D. Spiceland, 158–71. London: Samuel Bagster, 1980.

Heidegger, M. *Being and Time*. Oxford: Blackwell, 1962.

———. *Letter on Humanism* (1949). wagner.edu/psychology/files/2013/01/Heidegger-Letter-On-Humanism-Translation-GROTH.pdf.

Heim, K. M. *Poetic Imagination in Proverbs: Variant Repetitions and the Nature of Poetry*. Bulletin for Biblical Research Supplements 4. Winona Lake, IN: Eisenbrauns, 2013.

Held, J. S. "Rembrandt and the Spoken Word." In *Rembrandt Studies*, 164–83. Princeton: Princeton University Press, 1991.

Helvetic Confession, The Second. https://www.ccel.org/creeds/helvetic.htm.

Henry, C. F. H. *God, Revelation, and Authority*. Vol. 3. Waco: Word Books, 1979. Reprint, Wheaton: Crossway, 1999.

Henry, M. "Eric Voegelin on the Incarnate Christ." *Modern Age* 50, no. 4 (2008): 332–44.

———. *I Am the Truth: Toward a Philosophy of Christianity*. Translated by S. Emanuel. Stanford, CA: Stanford University Press, 2003.

———. *Words of Christ*. Translated by C. M. Gschwandtner. Interventions. Grand Rapids: Eerdmans, 2012.

Henze, M., ed. *A Companion to Biblical Interpretation in Early Judaism*. Grand Rapids: Eerdmans, 2012.

Herder, J. G. "Nachricht von einem neuen Erläuterer der H. Dreieinigkeit." In *Sämtliche Werke*, edited by B. Suphan, C. Redlich, and R. Stein, 1:28–42. Berlin: Weidmann, 1877.

———. *Vom Erkennen und Empfinden der menschlichen Seele*. Riga: Hartknoch, 1778.

Herodotus. *The Histories*. Edited by J. M. Marincola. Translated by A. de Selincourt. Rev. ed. New York: Penguin, 2003.

Herrera, R. A. *Reasons for Our Rhymes: An Inquiry into the Philosophy of History*. Grand Rapids: Eerdmans, 2001.

Hesse, M. B. "The Cognitive Claims of Metaphor." *Journal of Speculative Philosophy* 2 (1988): 1–16.

———. "How to Be Postmodern without Being a Feminist." *The Monist* 77/4 (1994): 445–61.

Hill, R. C. Introduction to *Diodore of Tarsus: Commentary on Psalms 1–51*, xi–xxxvii. Atlanta: SBL, 2005.

———. *Reading the Old Testament in Antioch*. Bible in Ancient Christianity 5. Leiden: Brill, 2005.

———. "Zechariah in Alexandria and Antioch." *Augustinianum* 48, no. 2 (2008): 323–43.

Himmelfarb, G. *On Looking into the Abyss: Untimely Thoughts on Culture and Society*. New York: Knopf, 1994.

Hirsch, E. D. *The Aims of Interpretation*. Chicago: University of Chicago Press, 1976.

———. *Validity in Interpretation*. New Haven: Yale University Press, 1967.

Hodge, C. *Systematic Theology*. 3 vols. Peabody, MA: Hendrickson, 1999.

Hoffmeier, J. K. *Ancient Israel in Sinai: The Evidence for the Authenticity of the Wilderness Tradition*. New York: Oxford University Press, 2005.

———. *Israel in Egypt: The Evidence for the Authenticity of the Exodus Tradition*. New York: Oxford University Press, 1997.

———. "Moses." *ISBE* 3 (1986): 415–25.

Holder, R. W. *John Calvin and the Grounding of Interpretation: Calvin's First Commentaries*. Leiden: Brill, 2005.

Holmes, M. W., ed. *The Apostolic Fathers: Greek Texts and English Translations*. Updated ed. Grand Rapids: Baker Books, 1999.

———. *The Apostolic Fathers in English*. 3rd ed. Grand Rapids: Baker Academic, 2006.

Holmstedt, R. "The Restrictive Syntax of Genesis i 1." *VT* 58, no. 1 (2008): 56–67.

Holub, R. C. *Reception Theory: A Critical Introduction; New Accents*. London: Routledge, 1984.

———. "Reception Theory: School of Constance." In *The Cambridge History of Literary Criticism*, vol. 8, *From Formalism to Poststructuralism*, edited by R. Selden, 319–46. Cambridge: Cambridge University Press, 1995.

Honorius III, Pope. *Regula Bullata*, for Francis of Assisi and the Friars Minor. November 29, 1223. http://www.liturgies.net/saints/francis/writings.html#RegulaBullata.

Horton, M. S. *Covenant and Eschatology: The Divine Drama*. Louisville: Westminster John Knox, 2002.

House, P. R. *Old Testament Theology*. Downers Grove, IL: IVP Academic, 1998.

How, A. *The Habermas-Gadamer Debate and the Nature of the Social: Back to Bedrock*. Aldershot, UK: Avebury, 1995.

Howard, T. A. *Religion and the Rise of Historicism: W. M. L. de Wette, Jacob Burckhardt, and the Theological Origins of Nineteenth-Century Historical Consciousness*. Cambridge: Cambridge University Press, 2000.

Hübner, H. *Biblische Theologie des Neuen Testaments*. Vol. 2. Göttingen: Vandenhoeck & Ruprecht, 1993.

Hughes, P. E. *A Commentary on the Epistle to the Hebrews*. Grand Rapids: Eerdmans, 1977.

Humboldt, W. von. "On the Task of the Historian." In Mueller-Vollmer, *Hermeneutics Reader*, 105–18.

Hurst, L. D. *The Epistle to the Hebrews: Its Background of Thought*. Cambridge: Cambridge University Press, 1990.

Hutton, J. Introduction to *Aristotle's Poetics*, translated, introduced, and annotated by J. Hutton, 1–34. New York: Norton, 1982.

Ibn Ezra, A. *Abraham Ibn Ezra's Commentary on the First Book of the Psalms*. Translated by H. N. Strickman. Brighton, MA: Academic Studies, 2009.

———. *Abraham Ibn Ezra's Commentary on the Second Book of Psalms*. Translated by H. N. Strickman. Brighton, MA: Academic Studies, 2009.

———. *The Commentary of Ibn Ezra on Isaiah*. Edited and translated by M. Friedlander. 4 vols. London: Society of Hebrew Literature / Trübner, 1873–77.

———. *The Commentary of Rabbi Abraham Ibn Ezra on Hosea*. Edited and translated by A. Lipshitz. New York: Sepher-Hermon, 1988.

Ingraffia, B. D. *Postmodern Theory and Biblical Theology: Vanquishing God's Shadow*.

Cambridge: Cambridge University Press, 1995.
Irenaeus of Lyons. *On the Apostolic Preaching*. Translated by J. Behr. Popular Patristics 17. Crestwood, NY: St. Vladimir's Seminary Press, 1997.
Irwin, W. "Against Intertextuality." *Philosophy and Literature* 28, no. 2 (October 2004): 227–42.
Isaacs, M. E. *Sacred Space: An Approach to the Theology of the Epistle to the Hebrews*. JSNTSup 73. Sheffield: Sheffield Academic Press, 1992.
Jacobi, F. H. *The Main Philosophical Writings and the Novel "Allwill."* Translated by G. di Giovanni. McGill-Queen's Studies in the History of Ideas. Montreal: McGill-Queen's University Press, 1994.
Jakobson, R. "Closing Statement: Linguistics and Poetics." In *Style in Language*, edited by T. A. Sebeok, 350–77. Cambridge, MA: Technology Press of Massachusetts Institute of Technology, 1960.
Jang, J. Y. "Communicative Preaching: A Homiletical Study in the Light of Hebrews." PhD diss., North-West University, Potchefstroom, South Africa, 2007.
Japhet, S. *The Commentary of Rabbi Samuel Ben Meier (Rashbam) on the Book of Job* [Hebrew]. Jerusalem: Magnes, 2000.
———. *I and II Chronicles: A Commentary*. Old Testament Library. London: SCM, 1993.
———. "Rashbam's Commentary on Job—The History of Its Discovery [Hebrew]." *Tarbiz* 66 (1996): 5–39.
Japhet, S., and R. B. Salters, eds. *The Commentary of R. Samuel Ben Meir, Rashbam, on Qoheleth*. Jerusalem: Magnes; Leiden: Brill, 1985.
Jauss, H. R. *Question and Answer: Forms of Dialogic Understanding*. Minneapolis: University of Minnesota Press, 1989.
———. *Toward an Aesthetic of Reception*. Translated by T. Bahti. Minneapolis: University of Minnesota Press, 1982.
———. *Wege des Verstehens*. Munich: Wilhelm Fink, 1994.

Jeanrond, W. G. *Text and Interpretation as Categories of Theological Thinking*. Dublin: Gill & Macmillan, 1988.
———. *Theological Hermeneutics: Development and Significance*. London: SCM, 1994.
Jedin, H. *A History of the Council of Trent*. Translated by E. Graf. London: Nelson, 1949.
Jefferson, A., and D. Robey, eds. *Modern Literary Theory: A Comparative Introduction*. London: Batsford, 1986.
Jeffrey, D. L. *Houses of the Interpreter: Reading Scripture, Reading Culture*. Waco: Baylor University Press, 2003.
———. *Luke*. Brazos Theological Commentary on the Bible. Grand Rapids: Brazos, 2012.
———. *People of the Book: Christian Identity and Literary Culture*. Grand Rapids: Eerdmans, 1996.
———. "Reading the Bible with C. S. Lewis." In Jeffrey, *Houses of the Interpreter*, 181–93.
Jenkins, K. *On "What Is History?": From Carr and Elton to Rorty and White*. London: Routledge, 1995.
Jeremias, J. *Abba: Studien zur neutestamentlichen Theologie und Zeitgeschichte*. Göttingen: Vandenhoeck & Ruprecht, 1966.
———. *The Eucharistic Words of Jesus*. Translated by N. Perrin. Philadelphia: Fortress, 1966.
———. *Jesus' Promise to the Nations*. London: SCM, 1958.
———. *New Testament Theology*. Translated by J. Bowden. London: SCM, 1971.
Jerome. "Letter XXII: To Eustochium." In NPNF[2] 6, *St. Jerome: Letters and Select Works*. http://www.ccel.org/ccel/schaff/npnf206.v.XXII.html.
———. *St. Jerome: Commentary on Galatians*. Translated by A. Cain, FC. Washington, DC: Catholic University of America Press, 2010.
Jobes, K. H., and M. Silva. *Invitation to the Septuagint*. Grand Rapids: Baker Academic, 2000.

Johnson, L. T. *The Gospel of Luke*. Collegeville, MN: Liturgical Press, 1991.

Johnson, P. *The Renaissance: A Short History*. London: Phoenix, 2000.

Jonker, L. C. *Exclusivity and Variety: Perspectives on Multidimensional Exegesis*. Contributions to Biblical Exegesis and Theology 19. Kampen, Netherlands: Kok Pharos, 1997.

Josipovici, G. *The Book of God: A Response to the Bible*. New Haven: Yale University Press, 1988.

Kaiser, W. *The Promise-Plan of God: A Biblical Theology of the Old and New Testaments*. Grand Rapids: Zondervan, 2008.

Kalimi, I. *An Ancient Israelite Historian: Studies in the Chronicler, His Time, Place and Writing*. Studia semitica neerlandica 46. Assen: Van Gorcum, 2006.

———, ed. *Jewish Bible Theology: Perspectives and Case Studies*. Winona Lake, IN: Eisenbrauns, 2012.

———. *The Retelling of Chronicles in Jewish Tradition and Literature: A Historical Journey*. Winona Lake, IN: Eisenbrauns, 2009.

Kalin, E. "How Did the Canon Come to Us? A Response to the Leiman Hypothesis." *Concordia Theological Monthly* 4 (1997): 47–52.

Kalman, J. "Medieval Jewish Biblical Commentaries and the State of *Parshanut* Studies." *Religion Compass* 2, no. 5 (2008): 820–34.

———. "With Friends Like These: Turning Points in the Jewish Exegesis of the Biblical Book of Job." PhD diss., McGill University, 2005.

Kannengiesser, C., ed. *Handbook of Patristic Exegesis*. 2 vols. The Bible in Ancient Christianity. Leiden: Brill, 2004. 2 vols. in 1, 2006.

Kant, I. *Der Streit der Fakultäten*. Hamburg: Felix Meiner, 2005.

———. *Religion within the Limits of Reason Alone*. Translated by T. M. Greene and H. H. Hudson. New York: Harper & Row, 1960.

Karris, R. J. "Bonaventure and Talbert on Luke 8:26–39: Christology, Discipleship, and Evangelization." *Perspectives in Religious Studies* 28, no. 1 (2001): 57–66.

———. Introduction to *Works of St. Bonaventure*, vol. 8.1, *St. Bonaventure's Commentary on the Gospel of Luke, Chapters 1–8*. St. Bonaventure, NY: Franciscan Institute Publications, 2001.

———. "Luke 8:26–39: Jesus, the Pigs, and Human Transformation." *New Theological Review* 4, no. 3 (1991): 39–51.

———. *Prayer and the New Testament*. Companions to the New Testament. New York: Crossroad, 2000.

Käsemann, E. *The Wandering People of God: An Investigation of the Letter to the Hebrews*. Minneapolis: Augsburg, 1984.

Kass, L. R. *The Beginning of Wisdom: Reading Genesis*. Chicago: University of Chicago Press, 2003.

Kealy, S. *The Interpretation of the Gospel of Luke from Apostolic Times through the Twentieth Century*. 2 vols. Lewiston, NY: E. Mellen, 2005–7.

Kelsey, D. *The Uses of Scripture in Recent Theology*. Philadelphia: Fortress, 1975.

Kereszty, R. A. *Wedding Feast of the Lamb: Eucharistic Theology from a Historical, Biblical, and Systematic Perspective*. Chicago: Hillenbrand Books, 2004.

Kermode, F. "Deciphering the Big Book." Review of *The Birth of the Messiah*, by Raymond E. Brown. *New York Review of Books* 25, no. 11 (June 29, 1978): 39–42.

Kessler, J. *Old Testament Theology: Divine Call and Human Response*. Waco: Baylor University Press, 2013.

Kidner, D. *Psalms*. 2 vols. Downers Grove, IL: IVP Academic, 1973–75.

Kierkegaard, S. *Concluding Unscientific Postscript*. Edited by A. Hanney. Cambridge Texts in the History of Philosophy. Cambridge: Cambridge University Press, Kindle edition, 2009.

———. *Either/Or*. 2 vols. Edited and translated by H. V. Hong and E. H. Hong. Princeton: Princeton University Press, 1987.

———. *Fear and Trembling: Repetition*. Translated by H. V. Hong and E. H. Hong. Princeton: Princeton University Press, 1983.

———. *Kierkegaard's Journals and Papers*. Vol. 6. Translated and edited by H. V. Hong and E. H. Hong. Bloomington: Indiana University Press, 2009.

———. *The Point of View for My Work as an Author: A Report to History and Related Writings*. Translated by W. Lowrie and B. Nelson. New York: Harper & Row, 1962.

———. *Purity of Heart Is to Will One Thing*. New York: Harper & Row, 1938, 1948.

———. *Spiritual Writings: Gift, Creation, Love; Selections from the Upbuilding Discourses*. Translated by G. Pattison. New York: Harper Perennial, 2010.

Kimball, C. A. *Jesus' Exposition of the Old Testament in Luke's Gospel*. JSOT 94. Sheffield: JSOT Press, 1994.

Kirwin, C. "Augustine's Philosophy of Language." In *Cambridge Companion to Augustine*, edited by E. Stump and N. Kretzmann, 186–204. Cambridge: Cambridge University Press, 2001.

Kistemaker, S. *Exposition of the Epistle to the Hebrews*. Grand Rapids: Baker, 1984.

Kitchen, K. A. *On the Reliability of the Old Testament*. Grand Rapids: Eerdmans, 2003.

———. *Pharaoh Triumphant: The Life and Times of Ramesses II King of Egypt*. Warminster, UK: Aris & Phillips, 1982.

———. *The Third Intermediate Period in Egypt, 1100–650 BC*. 2nd ed. Warminster, UK: Aris & Phillips, 1986.

Kiuchi, N. *The Purification Offering in the Priestly Literature: Its Meaning and Function*. Sheffield: Sheffield Academic, 1987.

Klein-Braslavy, S. "The Philosophical Exegesis." In Saebø, *HB/OT* 1.2 (2000): 302–20.

Klink, E. W., III, and D. R. Lockett. *Understanding Biblical Theology: A Comparison of Theory and Practice*. Grand Rapids: Zondervan, 2012.

Knierim, R. P. *The Task of Old Testament Theology: Substance, Method, and Cases*. Grand Rapids: Eerdmans, 1995.

Koester, C. R. *Hebrews: A New Translation with Introduction and Commentary*. AB 36. New York: Doubleday, 2001.

Kolb, R. "Flacius Illyricus, Matthias." In McKim, *Historical Handbook*, 190–95.

König, A. *The Eclipse of Christ in Eschatology: Toward a Christ-Centered Approach*. Grand Rapids: Eerdmans, 1989.

———. *New and Greater Things: Re-Evaluating the Biblical Message on Creation*. Pretoria: University of South Africa, 1988.

Kraemer, H. *The Christian Message in a Non-Christian World*. London: Edinburgh House, 1938.

Krentz, E. *The Historical-Critical Method*. London: SPCK, 1975.

Kristeller, P. O., and M. Mooney. *Renaissance Thought and Its Sources*. New York: Columbia University Press, 1979.

Kristeller, P. O., and J. H. Randall Jr. Introduction to *The Renaissance Philosophy of Man*, edited by E. Cassirer, P. O. Kristeller, and J. H. Randall Jr., 1–20. Chicago: University of Chicago Press, 1948.

Kristeva, J. *Desire in Language: A Semiotic Approach to Literature and Art*. New York: Columbia University Press, 1980.

———. *Revolution in Poetic Language*. Translated by M. Waller. New York: Columbia University Press, 1984.

Kuczynski, M. P. "The Psalms and Social Action in Late Medieval England." In *The Place of the Psalms in the Intellectual Culture of the Middle Ages*, edited by N. van Deusen, 191–214. Albany: State University of New York Press, 1999.

Kugel, J. L. "The Beginnings of Biblical Interpretation." In Henze, *Companion to Biblical Interpretation*, 3–23.

———. *The Bible as It Was*. Cambridge, MA: Belknap, 1997.

Kuhrt, A. *The Ancient Near East, c. 3000–330 BC*. London: Routledge, 1995.

Küng, H. "God: The Last Taboo?" In *Theology and the University: Essays in Honor of John B. Cobb, Jr.*, edited by D. R. Griffin and J. C. Hough Jr., 51–66. Albany: State University of New York Press, 1991.

Kurianal, J. *Jesus Our High Priest: Ps. 110,4 as the Substructure of Heb 5,1–7, 28.* European University Studies 23: Theology 693. Frankfurt: Peter Lang, 2000.

Kuss, O. "Der Verfasser des Habräerbriefes als Seelsorger." *TTZ* 67 (1958): 1–12, 65–80.

Kuyper, A. *Dictaten dogmatiek.* Kampen, Netherlands: J. H. Kok, 1910.

———. *Our Worship.* Grand Rapids: Eerdmans, 2009.

LaCocque, A., and P. Ricoeur. *Thinking Biblically: Exegetical and Hermeneutical Studies.* Translated by D. Pellauer. Chicago: University of Chicago Press, 1998.

Lacoste, J.-Y. *Experience and the Absolute: Disputed Questions on the Humanity of Man.* Perspectives in Continental Philosophy. Bronx, NY: Fordham University Press, 2004.

Lakoff, G., and M. Johnson. *Metaphors We Live By.* Chicago: University of Chicago Press, 1980.

———. *Philosophy in the Flesh: The Embodied Mind and Its Challenge to Western Thought.* New York: Basic Books, 1999.

Lampe, G. W. H., ed. *The Cambridge History of the Bible.* Vol. 2, *The West from the Fathers to the Reformation.* Cambridge: Cambridge University Press, 1983.

Lancaster, I. *Deconstructing the Bible: Abraham ibn Ezra's Introduction to the Torah.* Routledge Jewish Studies. New York: Routledge, 2003.

Lane, A. N. S. *John Calvin: Student of the Church Fathers.* Grand Rapids: Baker, 1999.

Lane, W. L. *Hebrews 1–8.* WBC 47A. Dallas: Word Books, 1991.

———. *Hebrews 9–13.* WBC 47B. Dallas: Word Books, 1991.

Langan, J. "The Christian Imagination." In *The Christian Imagination: The Practice of Faith in Literature and Writing*, edited by L. Ryken, 63–80. 2nd ed. Colorado Springs: Shaw, 2002.

Lash, N. *Believing Three Ways in One God: A Reading of the Apostles' Creed.* Notre Dame, IN: University of Notre Dame Press, 1993.

———. "Performing the Scriptures." In *Theology on the Way to Emmaus*, edited by N. Lash, 37–46. London: SCM, 1986.

———. "When Did Theologians Lose Interest in Theology?" In *Theology and Dialogue: Essays in Conversation with George Lindbeck*, edited by B. D. Marshall, 131–47. Notre Dame, IN: University of Notre Dame Press, 1990.

Lategan, B. "Hermeneutics." *ABD* 3:149–52.

Law, T. *When God Spoke Greek.* Oxford: Oxford University Press, 2013.

Lawee, E. "Isaac Abarbanel: From Medieval to Renaissance Jewish Biblical Scholarship." In Saebø, *HB/OT* 2 (2008): 190–214.

Leclercq, J. *The Love of Learning and the Desire for God: A Study of Monastic Culture.* Bronx, NY: Fordham University Press, 1961.

Legaspi, M. C. *The Death of Scripture and the Rise of Biblical Studies.* Oxford: Oxford University Press, 2010.

Legrand, L. "Christ the Fellow Traveller: The Emmaus Story in Luke 24:13–35." *ITS* 19 (1984): 33–34.

Leiman, S. Z. *The Canonization of the Hebrew Scripture: The Talmudic and Midrashic Evidence.* Hamden, CT: Archon, 1976.

Leithart, P. J. "Authors, Authority, and the Humble Reader." In *The Christian Imagination: The Practice of Faith in Literature and Writing*, edited by L. Ryken, 209–24. Colorado Springs: Shaw, 2002.

Lentricchia, F. *After the New Criticism.* Chicago: University of Chicago Press, 1980.

Lerch D., and L. Vischer. "Die Auslegungsgeschichte als notwendige theologische Aufgabe." *Studia patristica* 1 (1957): 414–19.

Lessing, G. E. *Philosophical and Theological Writings.* Cambridge Texts in the History of Philosophy. Cambridge: Cambridge University Press, 2005.

Levenson, J. D. *Creation and the Persistence of Evil: The Jewish Drama of Divine Omnipotence.* San Francisco: Harper & Row, 1988.

———. *The Hebrew Bible, the Old Testament, and Historical Criticism: Jews and*

Christians in Biblical Studies. Louisville: Westminster John Knox, 1993.

Lévi-Strauss, C. *Structural Anthropology.* New York: Basic Books, 1963.

Levy, S. *The Bible as Theatre.* Portland, OR: Sussex Academic, 2000.

Lewis, C. S. *An Experiment in Criticism.* Cambridge: Cambridge University Press, 1961. Reprint, 1996.

———. *Undeceptions: Essays on Theology and Ethics.* London: Bles, 1971.

———. *The Weight of Glory.* Grand Rapids: Eerdmans, 1949.

Lichtheim, M. *Ancient Egyptian Literature: A Book of Readings.* Vol. 1, *The Old and Middle Kingdoms.* Berkeley: University of California Press, 1973.

———. *Ancient Egyptian Literature: A Book of Readings.* Vol. 2, *The New Kingdom.* Berkeley: University of California Press, 1976.

Lightfoot, J. B. *St. Paul's Epistles to the Colossians and to Philemon: A Revised Text with Introductions, Notes and Dissertations.* Grand Rapids: Zondervan, 1959.

Lillback, P. A. "The Binding of God: Calvin's Role in the Development of Covenant Theology." PhD diss., Westminster Theological Seminary, 1985.

Lim, T. H. *The Formation of the Jewish Canon.* New Haven: Yale University Press, 2013.

Lincoln, A. *Truth on Trial: The Lawsuit Motif in the Fourth Gospel.* Peabody, MA: Hendrickson, 2000.

Lindars, B. *The Theology of the Letter to the Hebrews.* Cambridge: Cambridge University Press, 1991.

Linn, D., S. F. Linn, and M. Linn. *Sleeping with Bread: Holding What Gives You Life.* Mahwah, NJ: Paulist Press, 1995.

Litfin, D. "New Testament Challenges to Big Idea Preaching." In *The Big Idea of Biblical Preaching: Connecting the Bible to People,* edited by K. Willhite and S. Gibson, 53–66. Grand Rapids: Baker Academic, 1998.

Lloyd, G. *Providence Lost.* Cambridge, MA: Harvard University Press, 2008.

Lloyd-Jones, M. *Preaching and Preachers.* Grand Rapids: Zondervan, 1972.

Loewe, R. "Jewish Exegesis." In *A Dictionary of Biblical Interpretation,* edited by R. J. Coggins and J. C. Houlden, 346–54. London: SCM, 1990.

Lohfink, N. *Der niemals gekündigte Bund: Exegetische Gedanken zum christlich-jüdischen Gespräch.* Freiburg: Herder, 1989.

Longenecker, R. N. *Biblical Exegesis in the Apostolic Period.* 2nd ed. Grand Rapids: Eerdmans, 1999.

———. *Galatians.* WBC 41. Dallas: Word, 1990.

Longman, T. *Fictional Akkadian Autobiography: A Generic and Comparative.* Winona Lake, IN: Eisenbrauns, 1991.

Loughlin, G. *Telling God's Story: Bible, Church, and Narrative Theology.* Cambridge: Cambridge University Press, 1996.

Lubac, Henri de. *Catholicism: A Study of the Corporate Destiny of Mankind.* Translated by L. C. Sheppard. New York: Sheed & Ward, 1958.

———. *Exégèse médiévale: Les quatre sens de l'Écriture.* Part 2.1–2. Paris: Aubier, 1961–64.

———. *Medieval Exegesis: The Four Senses of Scripture.* Vol. 1. Grand Rapids: Eerdmans, 2000.

———. *Scripture in the Tradition.* Translated by L. O'Neill. New York: Crossroad, 2000.

Lundin, R., ed. *Disciplining Hermeneutics: Interpretation in Christian Perspective.* Grand Rapids: Eerdmans, 1997.

Luraghi, N., ed. *The Historian's Craft in the Age of Herodotus.* New York: Oxford University Press, 2001.

Luther, M. D. *Martin Luthers Werke: Kritische Gesamtausgabe* [Weimarer Ausgabe]. Edited by J. K. F. Knaake, G. Kawerau, et al. 127 vols. Weimar: Böhlau, 1883–.

Lyon, D. *Postmodernity.* Concepts in the Social Sciences. Buckingham, UK: Open University Press, 1994.

Lyotard, J.-F. *The Postmodern Condition: A Report on Knowledge.* Translated by G.

Bennington and B. Massumi. Minneapolis: University of Minnesota Press, 1984.

MacIntyre, A. C. *After Virtue: A Study in Moral Theory*. 2nd ed. Notre Dame, IN: University of Notre Dame Press, 1984.

———. *Whose Justice? Which Rationality?* Notre Dame, IN: University of Notre Dame Press, 1988.

Mackey, L. H. "Literary Theory." In *The Cambridge Dictionary of Philosophy*, edited by R. Audi, 505–6. 2nd ed. Cambridge: Cambridge University Press, 1999.

MacLeod, D. J. "The Literary Structure of the Book of Hebrews." *BSac* 146 (April–June 1989): 185–97.

Madison, G. B. *The Hermeneutics of Postmodernity: Figures and Themes*. Studies in Phenomenology and Existential Philosophy. Bloomington: Indiana University Press, 1988.

Magness, J. *The Archaeology of Qumran and the Dead Sea Scrolls*. Grand Rapids: Eerdmans, 2002.

Magrassi, M. *Praying the Bible: An Introduction to Lectio Divina*. Translated by E. Hagman. Collegeville, MN: Liturgical Press, 1998.

Maimonides, M. *Guide of the Perplexed*. Translated by S. Pines. Chicago: University of Chicago Press, 2010.

Mandelbaum, M. "Historicism." In *The Encyclopedia of Philosophy*, edited by P. Edwards, 4:22–25. New York: Macmillan, 1967.

———. *History, Man, and Reason. A Study in Nineteenth-Century Thought*. Baltimore: Johns Hopkins University Press, 1971.

Manguel, A. *A History of Reading*. New York: Penguin, 2008.

Marcel, G. *The Mystery of Being*. Vol. 2, *Faith and Reality*. South Bend, IN: St. Augustine's Press, 2001.

Marcos, N. F. *The Septuagint in Context: Introduction to the Greek Versions of the Bible*. Translated by W. G. E. Watson. Leiden: Brill, 2000.

Marenbon, J. *From the Circle of Alcuin to the School of Auxerre: Logic, Theology, and Philosophy in the Early Middle Ages*. Cambridge: Cambridge University Press, 1981.

Marsden, G. *C. S. Lewis's "Mere Christianity": A Biography*. Princeton: Princeton University Press, 2011.

Marshall, B. D. *Trinity and Truth*. Cambridge: Cambridge University Press, 2000.

Marshall, I. H. *Last Supper and Lord's Supper*. Carlisle, UK: Paternoster, 1980.

———. *Luke: Historian and Theologian*. 3rd ed. Downers Grove, IL: InterVarsity, 1998.

———. *New Testament Theology: Many Witnesses, One Gospel*. Downers Grove, IL: InterVarsity, 2004.

Martens, E. A. *God's Design: A Focus on Old Testament Theology*. 3rd ed. N. Richland Hills, TX: Bibal, 1998.

Martin, G. D. *Multiple Originals: New Approaches to Hebrew Bible Textual Criticism*. Atlanta: SBL, 2010.

Mason, E. F. *"You Are a Priest Forever": Second Temple Jewish Messianism and the Priestly Christology of the Epistle to the Hebrews*. Leiden: Brill, 2008.

Maurer, W. *Der junge Melanchthon zwischen Humanismus und Reformation*. Göttingen: Vandenhoeck & Ruprecht, 1996.

Maximus the Confessor. *On the Cosmic Mystery of Jesus Christ*. Popular Patristics 25. Crestwood, NY: St. Vladimir's Seminary Press, 2003.

Mayeski, M. A. "Early Medieval Exegesis: Gregory I to the Twelfth Century." In Hauser and Watson, *A History of Biblical Interpretation*, 2:86–112.

Mays, J. L. *Psalms*. Interpretation. Louisville: John Knox, 1994.

McCann, J. C., Jr. *A Theological Introduction to the Book of Psalms: The Psalms as Torah*. Nashville: Abingdon, 1993.

McCarthy, T. "Rationality and Relativism: Habermas' 'Overcoming' of Hermeneutics." In *Habermas: Critical Debates*, edited by J. B. Thompson and D. Held, 57–78. London: Macmillan, 1982.

McClendon, J. W., Jr. *Biography as Theology: How Life Stories Can Remake Today's Theology*. Philadelphia: Fortress, 1983. Reprint, Eugene, OR: Wipf & Stock, 2002.

McClure, J. S. *Other-Wise Preaching: A Postmodern Ethic for Homiletics*. St. Louis: Chalice, 2001.

McComiskey, L. E. "Hosea." In *The Minor Prophets: An Exegetical and Expository Commentary*, edited by L. E. McComiskey, 1–238. Grand Rapids: Baker, 1992.

McDonald, L. M. *The Biblical Canon: Its Origin, Transmission, and Authority*. 3rd ed. Peabody, MA: Hendrickson, 2007.

———. *The Formation of the Christian Biblical Canon*. Rev., exp. ed. Peabody, MA: Hendrickson, 1996.

McDonald, L. M., and J. A. Sanders, eds. *The Canon Debate*. Peabody, MA: Hendrickson, 2002.

McGrath, A. E. *The Genesis of Doctrine: A Study in the Foundations of Doctrinal Criticism*. Cambridge, MA: Blackwell, 1990.

———. *Studies in Doctrine*. Grand Rapids: Zondervan, 1997.

McIntyre, J. *The Christian Doctrine of History*. London: Oliver & Boyd, 1957.

———. "Historical Criticism in a 'History-Centered Value System.'" In *Language, Theology, and the Bible: Essays in Honour of James Barr*, edited by S. E. Balentine and J. Barton, 370–84. Oxford: Clarendon, 1994.

McKim, D. K., ed. *Calvin and the Bible*. Cambridge: Cambridge University Press, 2006.

———, ed. *Historical Handbook of Major Biblical Interpreters*. Downers Grove, IL: InterVarsity, 1998.

McKnight, S. *Jesus and His Death: Historiography, the Historical Jesus, and Atonement Theory*. Waco: Baylor University Press, 2005.

McLay, R. T. *The Use of the Septuagint in New Testament Research*. Grand Rapids: Eerdmans, 2003.

McLeod, F. G. *The Roles of Christ's Humanity in Salvation: Insights from Theodore of Mopsuestia*. Washington, DC: Catholic University of America Press, 2005.

———. *Theodore of Mopsuestia*. London: Routledge, 2009.

McNamara, M. *Targum and Testament: Aramaic Paraphrases of the Hebrew Bible*. 2nd ed. Grand Rapids: Eerdmans, 2010.

McNicol, A. J. "The Relationship of the Image of the Highest Angel to the High Priest Concept in Hebrews." PhD diss., Vanderbilt University, 1974.

Meek, J. A. *The Gentile Mission in Old Testament Citations in Acts: Text, Hermeneutic, and Purpose*. LNTS 385. London: T&T Clark, 2008.

Meier, J. P. *A Marginal Jew: Rethinking the Historical Jesus*. Vol. 3. New York: Doubleday, 2001.

Merkley, P. *The Greek and Hebrew Origins of Our Idea of History*. Toronto Studies in Theology 32. Lewiston, NY: Edwin Mellon, 1987.

Michalson, G. E., Jr. *The Historical Dimensions of a Rational Faith: The Role of History in Kant's Religious Thought*. Washington, DC: University Press of America, 1977.

———. *Kant and the Problem of God*. Oxford: Blackwell, 1999.

———. *Lessing's "Ugly Ditch": A Study of Theology and History*. University Park: Pennsylvania State University Press, 1985.

Migne, J.-P., ed. *Patrologia graeca*. 162 vols. Paris: Imprimerie Catholique. 1857–66. Index, 1912.

Milbank, J. "Knowledge: The Theological Critique of Philosophy in Haman and Jacobi." In *Radical Orthodoxy*, edited by J. Milbank, C. Pickstock, and G. Ward, 21–37. New York: Routledge, 1999.

———. "The Last of the Last: Theology in the Church." In *Conflicting Allegiances: The Church-Based University in a Liberal Democratic Society*, edited by M. L. Budde and J. Wright, 239–54. Grand Rapids: Brazos, 2004.

———. *The Word Made Strange: Theology, Language, Culture*. Oxford: Blackwell, 1999.

Milgrom, J. *Leviticus 1–16: A New Translation with Introduction and Commentary*. AB 3. New York: Doubleday, 1991.

Millard, A. R. *Reading and Writing in the Time of Jesus*. Sheffield: Sheffield Academic, 2000.

Millard, A. R., and D. J. Wiseman, eds. *Essays on the Patriarchal Narratives*. Leicester, UK: Inter-Varsity, 1980.

Millard, A. R., J. Hoffmeier, and D. W. Baker, eds. *Faith, Tradition, and History: Old Testament Historiography in Its Near Eastern Context*. Winona Lake, IN: Eisenbrauns, 1994.

Miller, J. M., and J. H. Hayes, eds. *A History of Ancient Israel and Judah*. Philadelphia: Westminster, 1986.

Miller, P. D. *The Way of the Lord: Essays in Old Testament Theology*. Grand Rapids: Eerdmans, 2007.

Mitchell, B., and F. C. Robinson, eds. *Beowulf: An Edition with Relevant Shorter Texts*. Oxford: Wiley, 1998.

Mittleman, A. *Hope in a Democratic Age: Philosophy, Religion, and Political Theory*. New York: Oxford University Press, 2009.

———. "The Job of Judaism and the Job of Kant." *HTR* 102, no. 1 (2009): 25–50.

Moberly, R. W. L. *Old Testament Theology: Reading the Hebrew Bible as Christian Scripture*. Grand Rapids: Baker Academic, 2013.

Moessner, D. P. "'Listening Posts' Along the Way: 'Synchronisms' as Metaleptic Prompts to the 'Continuity of the Narrative' in Polybius' *Histories* and Luke's Gospel-Acts; A Tribute to David E. Aune." In *The New Testament and Early Christian Literature in Greco-Roman Context: Studies in Honor of David E. Aune*, edited by J. Fotopoulos, 129–50. NovTSup 122. Leiden: Brill, 2006.

———. *Lord of the Banquet: The Literary and Theological Significance of the Lukan Travel Narrative*. Minneapolis: Fortress, 1989.

Molnar, P. D. *Incarnation and Resurrection: Toward a Contemporary Understanding*. Grand Rapids: Eerdmans, 2007.

Moltmann, J. *God in Creation. An Ecological Doctrine of Creation*. Translated by M. Kohl. London: SCM, 1985.

Montefiore, H. *A Commentary on the Epistle to the Hebrews*. New York: Harper & Row, 1964.

Monti, D. "Bonaventure's Use of 'The Divine Word' in Academic Theology." In *That Others May Know and Love: Essays in Honor of Zachary Hayes, OFM, Franciscan, Educator, Scholar*, edited by M. F. Cusato and F. E. Coughlin, 65–88. New York: Franciscan Institute, 1997.

Moore, G. F. *Judaism in the First Centuries of the Christian Era: The Age of the Tannaim*. 3 vols. Cambridge, MA: Harvard University Press, 1927–30.

Morgan, R., with J. Barton. *Biblical Interpretation*. Oxford: Oxford University Press, 1988.

Moscati, S. *The Face of the Ancient Orient: A Panorama of Near Eastern Civilizations in Pre-Classical Times*. Chicago: Quadrangle, 1960.

Most, G. W. "Hellenistic Allegory and Early Imperial Rhetoric." In Copeland and Struck, *Cambridge Companion to Allegory*, 26–38.

Motyer, J. A. *The Pentateuch and Criticism: Three Lectures by the Rev. J. A. Motyer*. Leicester, UK: Theological Students Fellowship, 1974.

Mouw, R. J., and S. Griffioen. *Pluralisms and Horizons: An Essay in Christian Public Philosophy*. Grand Rapids: Eerdmans, 1993.

Moyise, S. *Jesus and Scripture*. London: SPCK, 2010.

Mudge, L. S. "Paul Ricoeur on Biblical Interpretation." In Ricoeur, *Essays on Biblical Interpretation*, 9–15.

Mueller-Vollmer, K., ed. *Herder Today: Contributions from the International Herder Conference, Nov. 5–8, 1987, Stanford, California*. Berlin: de Gruyter, 1990.

———, ed. *The Hermeneutics Reader: Texts of the German Tradition from the Enlightenment to the Present*. New York: Continuum, 1988.

Mulchahey, M. *"First the Bow Is Bent in Study": Dominican Education before 1350*. Toronto: Pontifical Institute of Medieval Studies, 1998.

Muller, R. A. "Biblical Interpretation in the Era of the Reformation: The View from the Middle Ages." In *Biblical Interpretation in the Era of the Reformation: Essays Presented to David C. Steinmetz in Honor of His Sixtieth Birthday*, edited by R. A. Muller and J. L. Thompson, 3–22. Grand Rapids: Eerdmans, 1996.

———. "Biblical Interpretation in the 16th and 17th Centuries." In McKim, *Historical Handbook*, 123–52.

———. *Post-Reformation Reformed Dogmatics: The Rise and Development of Reformed Orthodoxy, ca. 1520 to ca. 1725.* Vol. 2. 2nd ed. Grand Rapids: Baker Academic, 2003.

Müller-Sievers, H. "'Gott als Schriftsteller': Herder and the Hermeneutic Tradition." In Mueller-Vollmer, *Herder Today*, 319–30.

Mumford, L. *The City in History: Its Origins, Its Transformation, and Its Prospects.* New York: MJF Books, 1998.

Munslow, A. *Deconstructing History.* London: Routledge, 1997.

Murphy, R. E. "Wisdom—Theses and Hypotheses." In *Israelite Wisdom: Theological and Literary Essays in Honor of Samuel Terrien*, edited by J. G. Gammie, W. A. Brueggemann, W. L. Humphreys, J. M. Ward, et al., 35–42. Missoula, MT: Scholars Press, 1978.

Nägele, S. *Laubhütte Davids und Wolkensohn: Eine auslegungsgeschichtliche Studie zu Amos 9,11 in der jüdischen und christlichen Exegese.* AGJU 24. Leiden: Brill, 1995.

Nairne, A. *The Epistle of Priesthood: Studies in the Epistle to the Hebrews.* Edinburgh: T&T Clark, 1913.

Neill, S. *The Interpretation of the New Testament, 1861–1961.* Oxford: Oxford University Press, 1964.

Neill, S., and N. T. Wright. *The Interpretation of the New Testament, 1861–1986.* 2nd ed. Oxford: Oxford University Press, 1988.

Nelson, E. *The Hebrew Republic: Jewish Sources and the Transformation of European Political Thought.* Cambridge, MA: Harvard University Press, 2010.

Neuhaus, R. Foreword to *Requiem: A Lament in Three Movements*, by T. C. Oden, 9–12. Nashville: Abingdon, 1995.

Neusner, J. *Glory of God Is Intelligence: Four Lectures on the Role of Intellect in Judaism.* Salt Lake City: Religious Studies Center, Brigham Young University, 1978.

———. *Introduction to Rabbinic Literature.* Anchor Bible Reference Library. New York: Doubleday, 1999.

———. *Judaism in the Beginning of Christianity.* Philadelphia: Fortress, 1984.

———. *Midrash in Context: Exegesis in Formative Judaism.* Philadelphia: Fortress, 1983.

———. *A Midrash Reader.* Minneapolis: Fortress, 1990.

———. *The Mishnah: An Introduction.* Northvale, NJ: Jason Aronson, 1989. Reprint, Lanham, MD: Rowman & Littlefield, 2004.

Newbigin, L. "Christ and Cultures." *SJT* 31 (1978): 1–22.

———. *Foolishness to the Greeks: The Gospel and Western Culture.* Grand Rapids: Eerdmans, 1986.

———. *The Good Shepherd: Meditations on Christian Ministry in Today's World.* Oxford: Mowbray, 1977.

———. *The Gospel in a Pluralist Society.* Grand Rapids: Eerdmans, 1989.

———. *The Light Has Come: An Exposition of the Fourth Gospel.* Grand Rapids: Eerdmans, 1982.

———. "Missions." In *Concise Encyclopedia of Preaching*, edited by W. H. Willimon and R. Lischer, 335–36. Louisville: Westminster John Knox, 1995.

———. *The Open Secret: An Introduction to the Theology of Mission.* Rev. ed. Grand Rapids: Eerdmans, 1995.

———. *The Other Side of 1984: Questions for the Churches.* Geneva: World Council of Churches, 1983.

———. *Proper Confidence: Faith, Doubt, and Certainty in Christian Discipleship.* Grand Rapids: Eerdmans, 1995.

———. "Response to 'Word of God?,'" by John Coventry, SJ. *The Gospel and Our Culture Newsletter* 8 (1991): 2.

———. "The Role of the Bible in Our Church." Unpublished remarks given at a meeting of the United Reformed Forward Policy Group, April 17–18, 1985.

———. *The Sending of the Church—Three Bible Studies*. Edinburgh: Church of Scotland Board of World Mission and Unity, 1984.

———. *Truth and Authority in Modernity*. Valley Forge, PA: Trinity Press International, 1996.

———. *Unfinished Agenda: An Autobiography*. Rev., exp. ed. Edinburgh: St. Andrew Press, 1993.

———. *A Walk through the Bible*. Louisville: Westminster John Knox, 1999.

———. *A Word in Season: Perspectives on Christian World Missions*. Grand Rapids: Eerdmans, 1994.

Newman, C. C., ed. *Jesus and the Restoration of Israel: A Critical Assessment of N. T. Wright's "Jesus and the Victory of God."* Downers Grove, IL: InterVarsity, 1999.

Newman, J. H. *An Essay on the Development of Christian Doctrine*, 6th ed. Notre Dame, IN: University of Notre Dame Press, 1989.

Nicholson, E. W. *Interpreting the Old Testament: A Century of the Oriel Professorship*. Oxford: Clarendon, 1981.

———. *The Pentateuch in the Twentieth Century: The Legacy of Julius Wellhausen*. Oxford: Oxford University Press, 1998.

Nickelsburg, G. W. E. *Jewish Literature between the Bible and the Mishnah*. Minneapolis: Augsburg, 2009.

Nissen, J. *Poverty and Mission: New Testament Perspectives*. IIMO Research Pamphlet 10. Leiden: Inter-university Institute for Missiological and Ecumenical Research, 1984.

Nobile, M. *Teologia dell'Antico Testamento*. Logos: Corso di studi biblici 8.1. Leumann [Torino]: Elle Di Ci, 1998.

Noll, M. A., and J. Turner. *The Future of Christian Learning: An Evangelical and Catholic Dialogue*. Edited by T. A. Howard. Grand Rapids: Brazos, 2008.

Nolland, J. *Luke 18:35–24:53*. WBC 35C. Dallas: Word, 1993.

Nomoto, S. "Herkunft und Struktur der Hohenpriestervorstellung im Hebräerbrief." *NovT* 10 (1968): 10–25.

Norris, C. *The Contest of Faculties: Philosophy and Theory after Deconstruction*. London: Methuen, 1985.

———. "Criticism." In *Encyclopedia of Literature and Criticism*, edited by M. Coyle et al., 27–65. London: Routledge, 1990.

———. *Spinoza and the Origins of Modern Critical Theory*. The Bucknell Lectures in Literary Theory. Oxford: Blackwell, 1991.

———. *Truth and the Ethics of Criticism*. Manchester, UK: Manchester University Press, 1994.

———. *What's Wrong with Postmodernism?* London: Harvest Wheatsheaf, 1990.

Norris, R. A., Jr. "Augustine and the Close of the Ancient Period." In Hauser and Watson, *History of Biblical Interpretation*, 1:380–408.

Nussbaum, M. C. *The Fragility of Goodness: Luck and Ethics in Greek Tragedy and Philosophy*. 2nd ed. Cambridge: Cambridge University Press, 2009.

Oakes, K. *Karl Barth on Theology and Philosophy*. New York: Oxford University Press, 2012.

Obbink, D. "Early Greek Allegory." In Copeland and Struck, *Cambridge Companion to Allegory*, 15–25.

Ochs, P., and N. Levene. *Textual Reasonings: Jewish Philosophy and Text Study at the End of the Twentieth Century*. Grand Rapids: Eerdmans, 2002.

Ocker, C. *Biblical Poetics before Humanism and Reformation*. Cambridge: Cambridge University Press, 2002.

———. "Scholastic Interpretation of the Bible." In Hauser and Watson, *History of Biblical Interpretation*, 2:254–79.

O'Donovan, O. *The Desire of the Nations: Rediscovering the Roots of Political Theology*. Cambridge: Cambridge University Press, 1996.

———. "The Loss of a Sense of Place." *Irish Theological Quarterly* 55 (1989): 39–58.

———. *Resurrection and Moral Order: An Outline for Evangelical Ethics*. Grand Rapids: Eerdmans, 1986.

———. *The Word in Small Boats: Sermons from Oxford*. Grand Rapids: Eerdmans, 2010.

Ogletree, T. W. *Christian Faith and History: A Critical Comparison of Ernst Troeltsch and Karl Barth*. New York: Abingdon, 1965.

Old, H. O. *The Reading and Preaching of the Scriptures in the Worship of the Christian Church*. 7 vols. Grand Rapids: Eerdmans, 1998.

Olivier, J.-M. *Diodori Tarsensis Commentarii in Psalmos*. Vol. 1, *Commentarii in Psalmos I–L*. CCSG 6. Turnhout: Brepols, 1980.

O'Malley, J. W. *Catholicism in Early Modern History: A Guide to Research*. Reformation Guides to Research 2. St. Louis, MO: Center for Reformation Studies, 1988.

———. *The First Jesuits*. Cambridge, MA: Harvard University Press, 1995.

———. *Trent and All That: Renaming Catholicism in the Early Modern Era*. Cambridge, MA: Harvard University Press, 2000.

———. *Trent: What Happened at the Council*. Cambridge, MA: Harvard University Press, 2013.

O'Neill, O. "Vindicating Reason." In *The Cambridge Companion to Kant*, edited by P. Guyer, 280–308. Cambridge: Cambridge University Press, 1992.

Ong, W. J. *Orality and Literacy: The Technologizing of the Word*. New York: Methuen, 1982.

———. *The Presence of the Word: Some Prolegomena for Cultural and Religious History*. New Haven: Yale University Press, 1967.

———. "The Word in Chains." In *In the Human Grain: Further Explorations in Contemporary Culture*, edited by W. J. Ong, 52–59. New York: MacMillan, 1967.

Origen. *First Principles*. (*De principiis*. In *ANF* 4.) http://www.newadvent.org/fathers/.

———. *Homilies on Numbers*. Translated by T. P. Scheck. Ancient Christian Texts. Downers Grove, IL: IVP Academic, 2009.

Orlinsky, H. M. *The So-Called "Servant of the Lord" and "Suffering Servant" in Second Isaiah*. VTSup 14. Leiden: Brill, 1977.

Orr, M. *Intertextuality: Debates and Contexts*. Cambridge: Polity, 2003.

Östborn, G. *Cult and Canon: A Study in the Canonization of the Old Testament*. Uppsala Universitets Årsskrift 10. Uppsala: Almqvist & Wiksell, 1950.

O'Toole, C. J. *The Philosophy of Creation in the Writings of St. Augustine*. Washington, DC: Catholic University of America Press, 1944.

Palmer, R. E. *Hermeneutics: Interpretation Theory in Schleiermacher, Dilthey, Heidegger, and Gadamer*. Evanston, IL: Northwestern University Press, 1988.

Pannenberg, W. "Insight and Faith." In *Basic Questions in Theology: Collected Essays*, translated by G. H. Kehm, 1:28–45. Philadelphia: Fortress, 1970. Reprint, Minneapolis: Fortress, 2008.

———. "Response to Discussion." In *Theology as History*, edited by J. M. Robinson and J. B. Cobb, translated by W. A. Beardslee et al., 221–76. New York: Harper, 1967.

———. *Revelation as History*. New York: Macmillan, 1969.

———. "What Is a Dogmatic Statement?" In *Basic Questions in Theology: Collected Essays*, 1:182–211. Philadelphia: Fortress, 1970. Reprint, Minneapolis: Fortress, 2008.

Parker, T. H. L. *Calvin's New Testament Commentaries*. 2nd ed. Edinburgh: T&T Clark, 1993.

———. *Calvin's Old Testament Commentaries*. Edinburgh: T&T Clark, 1993.

Parry, R. A., and H. A. Thomas, eds. *Great Is Thy Faithfulness? Reading Lamentations as Sacred Scripture*. Eugene, OR: Pickwick, 2011.

Patrick, D. *The Rendering of God in the Old Testament*. Philadelphia: Fortress, 1981.

Pelikan, J. *The Idea of a University: A Reexamination.* New Haven: Yale University Press, 1992.

Perdue, L. G. *Wisdom and Creation: The Theology of Wisdom Literature.* Nashville: Abingdon, 1994.

Perlitt, L. *Vatke und Wellhausen.* BZAW 94. Berlin: Töpelmann, 1965.

Petersen, N. R. *Rediscovering Paul: Philemon and the Sociology of Paul's Narrative World.* Philadelphia: Fortress, 1985.

Peterson, E. H. *Run with the Horses: The Quest for Life at Its Best.* Downers Grove, IL: InterVarsity, 1983.

———. *Working the Angles: The Shape of Pastoral Integrity.* Grand Rapids: Eerdmans, 1987.

Petrie, H. G., and Oshlag, R. S. "Metaphor and Learning." In *Metaphor and Thought*, edited by A. Ortony, 579–609. 2nd ed. Cambridge: Cambridge University Press, 1993.

Pfister, M. *The Theory and Analysis of Drama.* Translated by J. Halliday. Cambridge: Cambridge University Press, 1988.

Phillips, A. *Ancient Israel's Criminal Law: A New Approach to the Decalogue.* Oxford: Blackwell, 1970.

Pieper, J. *Hope and History.* San Francisco: Ignatius, 1994.

———. *Scholasticism: Personalities and Problems of Medieval Philosophy.* South Bend, IN: St. Augustine's Press, 2001.

Pitkin, B. "John Calvin and the Interpretation of the Bible." In Hauser and Watson, *History of Biblical Interpretation*, 2:341–71.

Pitre, B. *Jesus and the Jewish Roots of the Eucharist: Unlocking the Secrets of the Last Supper.* New York: Doubleday, 2011.

Plantinga, A. "Advice to Christian Philosophers." *Faith and Philosophy* 1, no. 3 (1984): 253–71.

———. "Augustinian Christian Philosophy." In *The Augustinian Tradition*, edited by G. B. Matthews, 1–26. Berkeley: University of California Press, 1998.

———. "Christian Philosophy at the End of the 20th Century." In *Christian Philosophy at the Close of the Twentieth Century: Assessment and Perspective*, edited by S. Griffioen and B. M. Balk, 30–37. Kampen, Netherlands: Kok, 1995.

———. "Two (or More) Kinds of Scripture Scholarship." In Plantinga, *Warranted Christian Belief*, 374–421.

———. *Warranted Christian Belief.* New York: Oxford University Press, 2000.

Plantinga, T. "Dilthey's Philosophy of the History of Philosophy." In *Hearing and Doing: Philosophical Essays Dedicated to H. Evan Runner*, edited by J. Kraay and A. Tol, 199–214. Toronto: Wedge, 1979.

———. *Historical Understanding in the Thought of Wilhelm Dilthey.* Toronto: University of Toronto Press, 1980.

Plato. *The Republic.* 2nd ed. Translated by D. Lee. New York: Penguin, 1974.

Polk, T. *The Biblical Kierkegaard: Reading by the Rule of Faith.* Macon, GA: Mercer University Press, 1997.

Polliack, M., ed. *Karaite Judaism: A Guide to Its History and Literary Sources.* Handbook of Oriental Studies: Section 1, The Near and Middle East 73. Leiden: Brill, 2003.

Polzin, R. M. *Biblical Structuralism: Method and Subjectivity in the Study of Ancient Texts.* Philadelphia: Fortress, 1977.

———. "The Framework of the Book of Job." *Int* 28, no. 2 (1974): 182–200.

Pons, J. *Stealing a Gift: Kierkegaard's Pseudonyms and the Bible.* Bronx, NY: Fordham University Press, 2004.

Popovic, M., ed. *Authoritative Scriptures in Ancient Judaism.* Leiden: Brill, 2010.

Porquet, J.-L. *Jacques Ellul: L'homme qui avait presque tout prévu.* Paris: Cherche Midi, 2003.

Prestige, G-L. *Fathers and Heretics: Six Studies in Dogmatic Faith with Prologue and Epilogue; Being the Bampton Lectures for 1940.* London: SPCK, 1977.

Preus, J. S. "A Hidden Opponent in Spinoza's *Tractatus*." *HTR* 88, no. 3 (1995): 361–88.

Preuss, H. D. *Old Testament Theology.* Translated by L. G. Perdue. 2 vols. Louisville: Westminster John Knox, 1995–96.

Provan, I. W., P. Long, and T. Longman III. *A Biblical History of Israel*. Louisville: Westminster John Knox, 2003.

Puckett, D. L. *John Calvin's Exegesis of the Old Testament*. Louisville: Westminster John Knox, 1995.

Quash, B. *Theology and the Drama of History*. Cambridge: Cambridge University Press, 2005.

Rad, G. von. *God at Work in Israel*. Nashville: Abingdon, 1980.

———. "The Theological Problem of the Old Testament Doctrine of Creation." In *The Problem of the Hexateuch and Other Essays*, 131–43. New York: McGraw-Hill, 1966.

———. *Wisdom in Israel*. Nashville: Abingdon, 1972.

Radcliffe, T. *Sing a New Song: The Christian Vocation*. Springfield, IL: Templegate, 1999.

Rae, M. "Creation and Promise: Towards a Theology of History." In Bartholomew et al., *"Behind" the Text*, 263–95.

Raeder, S. "The Exegetical and Hermeneutical Work of Martin Luther." In Saebø, *HB/OT* 2 (2008): 363–406.

Rajak, T. *Translation and Survival: The Greek Bible of the Ancient Jewish Diaspora*. Oxford: Oxford University Press, 2011.

Randolph, F. *Know Him in the Breaking of the Bread: A Guide to the Mass*. San Francisco: Ignatius, 1994.

Ranke, L. von. *The Theory and Practice of History*. Edited and introduced by G. G. Iggers. London: Routledge, 2011.

Reardon, B. M. G. *Religion in the Age of Romanticism*. Cambridge: Cambridge University Press, 1985.

Redford, D. B. *Pharaonic King-Lists, Annals, and Day-Books: A Contribution to the Study of the Egyptian Sense of History*. Mississauga, ON: Benben, 1986.

Redmond, M. "The Hamann-Hume Connection." *Religious Studies* 23 (1987): 95–107.

Reist, T. *Saint Bonaventure as a Biblical Commentator: A Translation and Analysis of His Commentary on Luke XVIII, 34–XIX,* 42. Lanham, MD: University Press of America, 1985.

Rendtorff, R. *Canon and Theology: Overtures to an Old Testament Theology*. Translated and edited by M. Kohl. Philadelphia: Fortress, 1993.

———. *Theologie des Alten Testaments: Ein Kanonischer Entwurf*. 2 vols. Neukirchen-Vluyn: Neukirchener, 1999–2001.

Renz, T. *The Rhetorical Function of the Book of Ezekiel*. Leiden: Brill, 1999.

Reventlow, H. G. *The Authority of the Bible and the Rise of the Modern World*. London: SCM, 1984.

———. *History of Biblical Interpretation*. 4 vols. Leiden: Brill, 2010.

———. *Problems of Biblical Theology in the Twentieth Century*. London: SCM, 1986.

———. *Problems of Old Testament Theology in the Twentieth Century*. Philadelphia: Fortress, 1985.

Rhodes, A. B. *The Mighty Acts of God*. Richmond: CLC Press, 1964.

Richardson, A. "The Rise of Modern Biblical Scholarship and Recent Discussion of the Authority of the Bible." In *The Cambridge History of the Bible*, vol. 3, *The West from the Reformation to the Present Day*, edited by S. L. Greenslade, 294–338. Cambridge: Cambridge University Press, 1975.

Richardson, B., ed. *Narrative Dynamics: Essays on Time, Plot, Closure, and Frames*. Columbus: Ohio State University Press, 2002.

Richardson, M. E. J. *Hammurabi's Laws: Text, Translation and Glossary*. Sheffield: Sheffield Academic Press, 2000.

Ricoeur, P. "Biblical Time." In *Figuring the Sacred: Religion, Narrative, and Imagination*, 167–80. Minneapolis: Fortress, 1995.

———. "The Critique of Religion." In *The Philosophy of Paul Ricoeur: An Anthology of His Work*, edited by C. E. Reagan and D. Stewart, 212–22. Boston: Beacon, 1978.

———. *Essays on Biblical Interpretation*. Edited and introduced by L. S. Mudge. Philadelphia: Fortress, 1980.

———. "Ethics and Culture: Habermas and Gadamer in Dialogue." *Philosophy Today* 17 (1973): 153–65.

———. *Hermeneutics and the Human Sciences*. Translated and edited by J. B. Thompson. Cambridge: Cambridge University Press, 1981.

———. *Interpretation Theory: Discourse and the Surplus of Meaning*. Fort Worth: Texas Christian University Press, 1976.

———. *Memory, History, Forgetting*. Translated by D. Pellauer. Chicago: University of Chicago Press, 2004.

———. Preface to *Hermeneutic Phenomenology: The Philosophy of Paul Ricoeur*, by D. Ihde. Evanston, IL: Northwestern University Press, 1971.

———. *The Rule of Metaphor: Multi-Disciplinary Studies of the Creation of Meaning in Language*. Toronto: University of Toronto Press, 1977.

———. *The Symbolism of Evil*. Boston: Beacon, 1969.

———. *Time and Narrative*. Translated by K. McLaughlin and D. Pellauer. 3 vols. Chicago: University of Chicago Press, 1984–88; reprint, 1990.

Ridderbos, H. N. *The Coming of the Kingdom*. Translated by H. de Jongste. Phillipsburg, NJ: P&R, 1962.

———. *The Gospel of John: A Theological Commentary*. Grand Rapids: Eerdmans, 1997.

———. *Paul: An Outline of His Theology*. Translated by J. R. de Witt. Grand Rapids: Eerdmans, 1975.

———. *Redemptive History and the New Testament Scriptures*. Translated by H. de Jongste. Revised by R. B. Gaffin. 2nd, rev. ed. Phillipsburg, NJ: P&R, 1988.

———. *When the Time Had Fully Come: Studies in New Testament Theology*. Grand Rapids: Eerdmans, 1957. Reprint, Jordan Station, ON: Paideia, 1982.

Rieff, P. *My Life among the Deathworks: Illustrations of the Aesthetics of Authority*. Edited by K. S. Piver. Vol. 3 of *Sacred Order / Social Order*. Charlottesville: University of Virginia Press, 2006.

Roberts, J. T. *Herodotus: A Very Short Introduction*. Oxford: Oxford University Press, 2011.

Robey, D. "Anglo-American New Criticism." In *Modern Literary Theory: A Comparative Introduction*, by A. Jefferson, D. Robey, and D. Forgacs, 73–91. 2nd ed. London: Batsford, 1986.

Robinson, H. W. *Biblical Preaching: The Development and Delivery of Expository Messages*. 2nd ed. Grand Rapids: Baker Academic, 2001.

Robinson, W. C. *Der Weg des Herrn: Studien zur Geschichte und Eschatologie im Lukas-Evangelium*. Hamburg-Bergstedt: Reich, 1964.

Rogerson, J. *Old Testament Criticism in the Nineteenth Century: England and Germany*. London: SPCK, 1984.

———. "Philosophy and the Rise of Biblical Criticism: England and Germany." In *England and Germany: Studies in Theological Diplomacy*, edited by W. Sykes, 63–79. Frankfurt: Peter Lang, 1982.

———. *A Theology of the Old Testament: Cultural Memory, Communication, and Being Human*. Minneapolis: Fortress, 2010.

———. *Theory and Practice in Old Testament Ethics*. JSOTSup 405. London: T&T Clark, 2004.

———. *W. M. L. de Wette, Founder of Modern Biblical Criticism: An Intellectual Biography*. JSOTSup 126. Sheffield: Sheffield Academic, 1992.

Rorty, R. "Postmodernist Bourgeois Liberalism." *Journal of Philosophy* 80, no. 10 (1983): 583–89.

Rosenberg, D. *The Educated Man: A Dual Biography of Moses and Jesus*. Berkeley: Counterpoint, 2010.

Roth, N., ed. *Medieval Jewish Civilization: An Encyclopedia*. Routledge Encyclopedias of the Middle Ages 7. New York: Routledge, 2007.

Rothen, B. *Die Klarheit der Schrift*. Vol. 1, *Martin Luther: Die wiederentdeckten Grundlagen*. Göttingen: Vandenhoeck & Ruprecht, 1990.

Routledge, R. *Old Testament Theology: A Thematic Approach*. Downers Grove, IL: IVP Academic, 2008.

Rummel, E. "The Renaissance Humanists." In Hauser and Watson, *History of Biblical Interpretation*, 2:280–98.

———. "The Textual and Hermeneutic Work of Desiderius Erasmus of Rotterdam." In Saebø, *HB/OT* 2 (2008): 215–30.

Runge, S. E. *Lexham Discourse Greek New Testament Bundle*. 6 vols. Logos Bible Software. Bellingham, WA: Lexham, 2008–11.

Runge, S. E., and J. R. Westbury. *Lexham Discourse Hebrew Bible Bundle*. 6 vols. Logos Bible Software. Bellingham, WA: Lexham, 2012.

Rush, O. *The Reception of Doctrine: An Appropriation of Hans Robert Jauss' Reception Aesthetics and Literary Hermeneutics*. Tesi Gregoriana, Serie Teologia 19. Rome: Pontifical Gregorian University, 1997.

Ryle, H. E. *The Canon of the Old Testament: An Essay on the Gradual Growth and Formation of the Hebrew Canon of Scripture*. 2nd ed. London: Macmillan, 1925.

Saebø, M. ed. *Hebrew Bible / Old Testament: The History of Its Interpretation*. Vol. 1.2, *The Middle Ages*. Vol. 2, *From the Renaissance to the Enlightenment*. Göttingen: Vandenhoeck & Ruprecht, 2000–2008.

Sáenz-Badillos, A. "Early Hebraists in Spain: Menaḥem ben Saruq and Dunash ben Labraṭ." In Saebø, *HB/OT* 1/2 (2000): 96–109.

Said, E. "Introduction to the Fiftieth-Anniversary Edition." In Auerbach, *Mimesis*, ix–xxxii.

Sailhamer, J. H. *Introduction to Old Testament Theology: A Canonical Approach*. Grand Rapids: Zondervan, 1995.

Sanders, J. A. "Adaptable for Life: The Nature and Function of Canon." In *Magnalia Dei, the Mighty Acts of God: Essays on the Bible and Archaeology in Memory of G. Ernest Wright*, edited by F. M. Cross et al., 531–60. New York: Doubleday, 1976.

———. *Canon and Community: A Guide to Canonical Criticism*. Guides to Biblical Study. Philadelphia: Fortress, 1984.

———. "Isaiah in Luke." *Int* 36 (1992): 144–55.

———. *Torah and Canon*. Philadelphia: Fortress, 1972.

Saperstein, M. *Jewish Preaching, 1200–1800: An Anthology*. New Haven: Yale University Press: 1989.

Sasso, S. E. *God's Echo: Exploring Scripture with Midrash*. Brewster, MA: Paraclete, 2007.

Saussure, F. de. *Cours de linguistique générale*. Paris: Payot & Rivage, 1995.

Scheffler, I. *Beyond the Letter: A Philosophical Inquiry into Ambiguity, Vagueness, and Metaphor in Language*. London: Routledge, 1979.

Schenker, S., ed. *The Earliest Text of the Hebrew Bible: The Relationship between the Masoretic Text and the Hebrew Base of the Septuagint Revisited*. Septuagint and Cognate Studies. Leiden: Brill, 2003.

Schiffman, L. H., and J. C. VanderKam, eds. *Encyclopedia of the Dead Sea Scrolls*. 2 vols. Oxford: Oxford University Press, 2000.

Schleiermacher, F. *Hermeneutics and Criticism: And Other Writings*. Translated and edited by A. Bowie. Cambridge: Cambridge University Press, 1998.

———. *The Hermeneutics Reader: Texts of the German Tradition from the Enlightenment to the Present*. Edited by K. Mueller-Vollmer. New York: Continuum, 1988.

Schmidt, K. L. "Jerusalem als Urbild und Abbild." In *Eranos-Jahrbuch*, vol. 18, *Aus der Welt der Urbilder: Sonderband für C. G. Jung zum 75. Geburtstag*, 207–48. Zurich: Rhein Verlag, 1950.

Schneider, J. R. *Philip Melanchthon's Rhetorical Construal of Biblical Authority: Oratio Sacra*. Test and Studies in Religion 51. Lewiston, NY: E. Mellen, 1990.

Schnelle, U., and M. E. Boring. *Theology of the New Testament*. Grand Rapids: Baker Academic, 2009.

Scholder, K. *The Birth of Modern Critical Theology: Origins and Problems of Biblical Criticism in the Seventeenth Century*. London: SCM, 1990.

Scholes, R. E., and R. Kellogg. *The Nature of Narrative.* Oxford: Oxford University Press, 1966.

Schreiner, S. "Calvin as an Interpreter of Job." In McKim, *Calvin and the Bible,* 53–84.

Schreiner, T. R. *The King in His Beauty: A Biblical Theology of Old and New Testaments.* Grand Rapids: Baker Academic, 2013.

———. *New Testament Theology: Magnifying God in Christ.* Grand Rapids: Baker Academic, 2008.

Schwanke, J. *Creatio ex nihilo: Luthers Lehre von der Schöpfung aus dem Nichts in der grossen Genesisvorlesung (1535–1545).* Berlin: de Gruyter, 2004.

Scobie, C. H. H. *The Ways of Our God: An Approach to Biblical Theology.* Grand Rapids: Eerdmans, 2003.

Scott, N. A. "Steiner on Interpretation." In *Reading George Steiner,* edited by N. A. Scott and R. A. Sharp, 1–13. London: Johns Hopkins University Press, 1994.

Scroggs, R. *The Last Adam: A Study in Pauline Anthropology.* Philadelphia: Fortress, 1966.

Scruton, R. *Kant.* Oxford: Oxford University Press, 1982.

Seerveld, C. *Benedetto Croce's Earlier Aesthetic Theories and Literary Criticism: A Critical Philosophical Look at the Development during the Rationalistic Years.* Kampen, Netherlands: J. H. Kok, 1958.

———. "Footprints in the Snow." *Philosophia Reformata* 56 (1991): 1–34.

———. *How to Read the Bible to Hear God Speak.* Toronto: Toronto Tuppence Press, 2003.

———. "Overlooked Herder, and the Performative Nature of שיר השירים as Biblical Wisdom Literature." *Southeastern Theological Review* 4/2 (2013): 197–222.

———. *Rainbows for the Fallen World: Aesthetic Life and Artistic Task.* Toronto: Tuppence, 2005.

———. Review of *Truth and Method,* by H.-G. Gadamer. *Criticism* 36, no. 4 (1978): 487–90.

Segal, M. *The Book of Jubilees: Rewritten Bible, Redaction, Ideology and Theology.* JSJSup 117. Leiden: Brill, 2007.

Segalla, G. *Teologia biblica del Nuovo Testamento: Tra memoria escatologica di Gesù e promessa del futuro regno di Dio.* Logos: Corso di studi biblici 8.2. Leumann [Turin]: Elle Di Ci, 2006.

Seitz, C. R. "The Canonical Approach and Theological Interpretation." In Bartholomew et al., *Canon and Biblical Interpretation,* 58–110.

———. "Christological Interpretation of Texts and Trinitarian Claims to Truth." *SJT* 52 (1999): 209–26.

———. *Figured Out: Typology and Providence in Christian Scripture.* Louisville: Westminster John Knox, 2001.

———. *Word without End: The Old Testament as Abiding Theological Witness.* Grand Rapids: Eerdmans, 1998.

Selden, R., and P. Widdowson. *A Reader's Guide to Contemporary Literary Theory.* 3rd ed. Lexington: University Press of Kentucky, 1993.

Sertillanges, A. G. *The Intellectual Life: Its Spirit, Conditions, Methods.* Washington, DC: Catholic University of America Press, 1998.

Sheeley, S. *Narrative Asides in Luke-Acts.* London: Bloomsbury, 2015.

Shinan, A., and Y. Zakovitch. *From Gods to God: How the Bible Debunked, Suppressed, or Changed Ancient Myths and Legends.* Translated by V. Zakovitch. Lincoln: University of Nebraska Press, 2012.

Sieben, H. J. "Studien zur Psalterbenutzung des Athanasius von Alexandrien im Rahmen seiner Schriftauffassung und Schriftlesung." ThD diss., Institut Catholique zu Paris, 1968.

Siegert, F. *Drei hellenistisch-jüdische Predigten.* WUNT 61. Tübingen: Mohr Siebeck, 1992.

Silva, M. "The New Testament Use of the Old Testament: Text Form and Authority." In *Scripture and Truth,* edited by D. A. Carson and J. D. Woodbridge, 147–65. Leicester, UK: Inter-Varsity, 1983.

Silver, D. J. *The Story of Scripture: From Oral Tradition to the Written Word*. New York: Basic Books, 1990.

Silverman, H. J., ed. *Gadamer and Hermeneutics*. London: Routledge, 1991.

Simon, R. *A Critical History of the New Testament*. London: Taylor, 1689.

———. *A Critical History of the Old Testament*. London: Davis, 1678.

Simon, U. *Four Approaches to the Book of Psalms: From Saadiah Gaon to Abraham Ibn Ezra*. Albany: State University of New York Press, 1991.

———. "Jewish Exegesis in Spain and Provence and in the East in the Twelfth and Thirteenth Centuries: Abraham Ibn Ezra." In Saebø, ed., *HB/OT* 1.2 (2000): 377–87.

Simonetti, M. "Theodore of Mopsuestia (ca. 350–428)." In Kannengiesser, *HPE* 799–839.

Skarsaune, O. "From the Reform Councils to the Counter-Reformation: The Council as Interpreter of Scripture." In Saebø, *HB/OT* 2 (2008): 319–28.

Skillen, J. W., and R. M. McCarthy, eds. *Political Order and the Plural Structure of Society*. Emory University Studies in Law and Religion. Atlanta: Scholars Press, 1991.

Skinner, J. *Prophecy and Religion: Studies in the Life of Jeremiah*. Cambridge: Cambridge University Press, 1922.

Smalley, B. *Medieval Exegesis of Wisdom Literature: Essays by Beryl Smalley*. Edited by R. E. Murphy. Atlanta: Scholars Press, 1986.

———. *The Study of the Bible in the Middle Ages*. Oxford: Blackwell, 1983.

Smit, M. C. *Toward a Christian Conception of History*. Edited by H. D. Morton and H. Van Dyke. Lanham, MD: University Press of America, 2002.

Smolar, L., and M. Aberbach. *Studies in Targum Jonathan to the Prophets*. [Bound with] P. Churgin. *Targum Jonathan to the Prophets*. New York: Ktav, 1983.

Sokolowski, R. *The God of Faith and Reason: Foundations of Christian Theology*. Washington, DC: Catholic University of America Press, 1995.

Sommer, B. D. *The Bodies of God and the World of Ancient Israel*. Cambridge: Cambridge University Press, 2009.

———. *A Prophet Reads Scripture: Allusion in Isaiah 40–66*. Stanford, CA: Stanford University Press, 1998.

Soskice, J. M. *Metaphor and Religious Language*. Oxford: Oxford University Press, 1985.

Sowers, S. G. *The Hermeneutics of Philo and Hebrews: A Comparison of the Interpretation of the Old Testament in Philo Judaeus and the Epistle to the Hebrews*. Richmond: John Knox, 1965.

Spears, A. "The Theological Hermeneutics of Homiletical Application and Ecclesiastes 7:23–29." PhD diss., University of Liverpool, 2006.

Sperling, S. D., ed. *Students of the Covenant: A History of Jewish Biblical Scholarship in North America*. Atlanta: Scholars Press, 1992.

Spinoza, B., de. *The Chief Works of Benedict de Spinoza*. Translated from Latin and introduced by R. H. M. Elwes. Vol. 1, *Introduction; Tractatus Theologico-politicus; Tractatus Politicus*. Rev. ed. London: George Bell & Sons, 1887.

———. *A Theologico-political Treatise and a Political Treatise*. Mineola, NY: Dover, 2004.

Spykman, G. J. *Reformational Theology: A New Paradigm for Doing Dogmatics*. Grand Rapids: Eerdmans, 1992.

Stegemann, H. *The Library of Qumran: On the Essenes, Qumran, John the Baptist, and Jesus*. Grand Rapids: Eerdmans, 1998.

Stegner, W. R. "The Ancient Jewish Synagogue Homily." In *Greco-Roman Literature and the New Testament: Selected Forms and Genres*, edited by D. E. Aune, 51–69. Atlanta: Scholars Press, 1988.

Steiner, G. *After Babel: Aspects of Language and Translation*. 3rd ed. Oxford: Oxford University Press, 1998.

———. *George Steiner: A Reader*. New York: Oxford University Press, 1984.

———. *Grammars of Creation*. London: Faber & Faber, 2001.

———. *Real Presences: Is There Anything in What We Say?* London: Faber & Faber, 1989.

———. "A Responsion." In *Reading George Steiner*, edited by N. A. Scott and R. A. Sharp, 275–85. London: Johns Hopkins University Press, 1994.

———. Review of *The Literary Guide to the Bible*, by R. Alter and F. Kermode. *The New Yorker*, January 11, 1988, 94–98.

Steinmetz, D. C. *Calvin in Context*. 2nd ed. Oxford: Oxford University Press, 2010.

———. "John Calvin as Interpreter of the Bible." In McKim, *Calvin and the Bible*, 282–91.

Stek, J. "What Says the Scripture?" In Van Til et al., *Portraits of Creation*, 203–65.

Stemberger, G. "Elements of Biblical Interpretation in Medieval Jewish-Christian Disputation." In Saebø, *HB/OT* 1.2 (2000): 578–90.

Stephens, W-P. *The Theology of Huldrych Zwingli*. Oxford: Clarendon, 1988.

Sternberg, M. *The Poetics of Biblical Narrative: Ideological Literature and the Drama of Reading*. Bloomington: Indiana University Press, 1987.

Stewart, R. A. "Creation and Matter in the Epistle to the Hebrews." *New Testament Studies* 12 (1965–66): 284–93.

Steyn, G. J. *A Quest for the Assumed LXX Vorlage of the Explicit Quotations in Hebrews*. Göttingen: Vandenhoeck & Ruprecht, 2011.

Stiver, D. R. *The Philosophy of Religious Language: Sign, Symbol and Story*. Oxford: Blackwell, 1996.

Storkey, A. *A Christian Social Perspective*. Downers Grove, IL: InterVarsity, 1979.

Stott, J. *The Contemporary Christian*. Downers Grove, IL: InterVarsity, 1992.

Strauss, L. *The Early Writings (1921–1932)*. Translated and edited by M. Zank. Albany: State University of New York Press, 2002.

———. *Jewish Philosophy and the Crisis of Modernity: Essays and Lectures in Modern Jewish Thought*. Albany: State University of New York Press, 1997.

———. "On the Interpretation of Genesis (1957)." In Strauss, *Jewish Philosophy*, 359–76.

Strazicich, J. *Joel's Use of Scripture and the Scripture's Use of Joel: Appropriation and Resignification in Second Temple Judaism and Early Christianity*. BIS 82. Leiden: Brill, 2007.

Stroup, G. W. *The Promise of Narrative Theology: Recovering the Gospel in the Church*. Atlanta: John Knox, 1981.

Struck, P. T. "Allegory and Ascent in Neoplatonism." In Copeland and Struck, *Cambridge Companion to Allegory*, 57–70.

Stuhlmacher, P. *Biblische Theologie des Neuen Testaments*. Göttingen: Vandenhoeck & Ruprecht, 1999.

———. *Historical Criticism and Theological Interpretation of Scripture: Toward a Hermeneutics of Consent*. Translated by R. A. Harrisville. Philadelphia: Fortress, 1977.

Stump, E. "Biblical Commentary and Philosophy." In *Cambridge Companion to Aquinas*, edited by N. Kretzmann and E. Stump, 252–68. Cambridge: Cambridge University Press, 1993.

———. *Wandering in Darkness: Narrative and the Problem of Suffering*. Oxford: Oxford University Press, 2010.

Suleiman, S. R. "Introduction: Varieties of Audience-Oriented Criticism." In Suleiman and Crosman, *Reader in the Text*, 3–45.

Suleiman, S. R., and I. Crosman, eds. *The Reader in the Text: Essays on Audience and Interpretation*. Princeton: Princeton University Press, 1980.

Sweeney, M. A. *Tanak: A Theological and Critical Introduction to the Jewish Bible*. Minneapolis: Fortress, 2012.

Swetnam, J. *Jesus and Isaac: A Study of the Epistle to the Hebrews in the Light of the Aqedah*. Analecta biblica 94. Rome: Biblical Institute Press, 1981.

Tadmor, H., and M. Weinfeld, eds. *History, Historiography and Interpretation: Studies*

in Biblical and Cuneiform Literatures. Jerusalem: Magnes, 1984.
Talbert, C. H. *Literary Patterns, Theological Themes, and the Genre of Luke-Acts*. Cambridge, MA: SBL, 1974.
———. *Reading Luke: A Literary and Theological Commentary*. New York: Crossroad, 1982.
Tallis, R. *Not Saussure: A Critique of Post-Saussurean Literary Theory*. 2nd ed. Basingstoke, UK: Macmillan, 1995.
Talmage, F., ed. *The Commentaries on Proverbs of the Kimhi Family* [Hebrew]. Jerusalem: Magnes, 1990.
———. *David Kimhi: The Man and His Commentaries*. Cambridge, MA: Harvard University Press, 1975.
Tannehill, R. C. *The Narrative Unity of Luke-Acts: A Literary Interpretation*. 2 vols. Philadelphia: Fortress, 1986–90.
Tarnas, Richard. *The Passion of the Western Mind: Understanding the Ideas That Have Shaped Our World View*. New York: Harmony Books, 1991.
Tauler, J. *Sermons*. Translated by É. Hugueny et al. Paris: Cerf, 1991.
Taylor, C. *The Malaise of Modernity*. Toronto: House of Anansi, 2003.
———. *Modern Social Imaginaries*. Durham, NC: Duke University Press, 2004.
———. *A Secular Age*. Cambridge, MA: Belknap, 2007.
———. *Sources of the Self: The Making of the Modern Identity*. Cambridge: Cambridge University Press, 1989.
———. "Theories of Meaning." In *Human Agency and Language: Philosophical Papers*, 248–92. Cambridge: Cambridge University Press, 1985.
Taylor, J. E. *The Essenes, the Scrolls, and the Dead Sea*. Oxford: Oxford University Press, 2012.
Taylor, M. C. *Erring: A Postmodern A/theology*. 8th ed. Chicago: University of Chicago Press, 2010.
Teigas, D., J. Habermas, and H.-G. Gadamer. *Knowledge and Hermeneutic Understanding: The Habermas-Gadamer Debate and the Nature of the Social*. Lewisburg, PA: Bucknell University Press, 1995.
Terveen, J. L. "Jesus in Hebrews: An Exegetical Analysis of the References to Jesus' Earthly Life in the Epistle to the Hebrews." PhD diss., University of Edinburgh, 1986.
Theodore of Mopsuestia. *Commentary on the Twelve Prophets*. Translated by R. C. Hill. Washington, DC: Catholic University of America Press, 2004.
Theodoret of Cyrus. *Commentary on the Psalms*. Vol. 1, *1–72*. Vol. 2, *73–150*. Translated by R. C. Hill. FC. Washington, DC: Catholic University of America Press, 2000–2001.
Thiele, R. "A Reexamination of the Authorship of the Epistle to the Hebrews." PhD diss., University of Wisconsin-Milwaukee, 2008.
Thielicke, H. *The Evangelical Faith*. 3 vols. Edinburgh: T&T Clark, 1974.
———. *The Trouble with the Church: A Call for Renewal*. Translated by J. W. Doberstein. New York: Harper & Row, 1965.
Thielman, F. *Theology of the New Testament: A Canonical and Synthetic Approach*. Grand Rapids: Zondervan, 2005.
Thiselton, A. C. "Biblical Interpretation." In *The Modern Theologians: An Introduction to Christian Theology in the Twentieth Century*, edited by D. Ford with R. Mears, 287–304. 2nd ed. Oxford: Blackwell, 1997.
———. "Communicative Action and Promise in Interdisciplinary, Biblical, and Theological Hermeneutics." In *The Promise of Hermeneutics*, by R. Lundin, C. Walhout, and A. C. Thiselton, 133–239. Grand Rapids: Eerdmans, 1999.
———. *The First Epistle to the Corinthians: A Commentary on the Greek Text*. NIGTC. Grand Rapids: Eerdmans, 2000.
———. "Further Implications and the Paradigmatic Status of Promise as Communicative Action." In *The Promise of Hermeneutics*, by R. Lundin, C. Walhout, and A. C. Thiselton, 209–40. Grand Rapids: Eerdmans, 2001.
———. "The Hermeneutical Dynamics of 'Reading Luke' as Interpretation, Reflection, Formation." In *Reading Luke:*

Interpretation, Reflection, and Formation, edited by C. G. Bartholomew, J. B Green, and A. C. Thiselton, 3–54. SAHS 6. Carlisle, UK: Paternoster; Grand Rapids: Zondervan, 2006.

———. *The Hermeneutics of Doctrine*. Grand Rapids: Eerdmans, 2007.

———. Introduction to Bartholomew et al., *Canon and Biblical Interpretation*, 1–30.

———. *New Horizons in Hermeneutics*. Grand Rapids: Zondervan, 1992.

———. "On Models and Methods: A Conversation with Robert Morgan." In *The Bible in Three Dimensions: Essays in Celebration of Forty Years of Biblical Studies in the University of Sheffield*, edited by D. J. A. Clines, S. E. Fowl, and S. E. Porter, 337–56. JSOTSup 87. Sheffield: JSOT Press, 1990.

———. *Thiselton on Hermeneutics: Collected Works and New Essays*. Grand Rapids: Eerdmans, 2006.

———. *The Two Horizons: New Testament Hermeneutics and Philosophical Description with Special Reference to Heidegger, Bultmann, Gadamer, and Wittgenstein*. Grand Rapids: Eerdmans, 1980.

Thomas Aquinas. *Commentary on Saint Paul's Epistle to the Galatians*. Translated by F. R. Larcher. Albany, NY: Magi Books, 1966.

———. *Commentary on the Book of Job*. http://dhspriory.org/thomas/SSJob.htm#0.

———. *Commentary on the Gospel of Saint John*. Translated by F. Larcher and J. A. Weisheipl. 3 vols. Washington, DC: Catholic University of America Press. Kindle edition, 2010.

Thomas, D. *Proclaiming the Incomprehensible God: Calvin's Teaching on Job*. Fearn, UK: Mentor, 2004.

Thompson, J. A. *The Beginnings of Christian Philosophy: The Epistle to the Hebrews*. Washington, DC: Catholic Biblical Association of America, 1982.

———. *The Book of Jeremiah*. Grand Rapids: Eerdmans, 1980.

Thompson, M. D. "Biblical Interpretation in the Work of Martin Luther." In Hauser and Watson, *History of Biblical Interpretation*, 2:299–318.

Thompson, T. L. *The Historicity of the Patriarchal Narratives: The Quest for the Historical Abraham*. Berlin: de Gruyter, 1974.

Thulstrup, N. "Commentator's Introduction." In *Philosophical Fragments*, by S. Kierkegaard, xlv–xcvii. Princeton: Princeton University Press, 1962.

Thyen, H. *Der Stil der jüdisch-hellenistischen Homilie*, FRLANT 47. Göttingen: Vandenhoeck & Ruprecht, 1955.

Tjørhom, O. *Embodied Faith: Reflections on a Materialist Spirituality*. Grand Rapids: Eerdmans, 2009.

Torrance, T. F. *The Hermeneutics of John Calvin*. Edinburgh: Scottish Academic, 1988.

———. *Space, Time, and Resurrection*. Grand Rapids: Eerdmans, 1976.

Torrell, J.-P. *Aquinas's "Summa": Background, Structure, and Reception*. Washington, DC: Catholic University of America Press, 2005.

Toulmin, S. *Cosmopolis: The Hidden Agenda of Modernity*. New York: Free Press, 1990. Reprint, Chicago: University of Chicago Press, 1992.

Tov, E. "Post-Modern Textual Criticism?" In *Greek Scripture and the Rabbis*, edited by T. M. Law and A. Salvesen, 1–18. Leuven: Peeters, 2012.

———. "Rewritten Bible Composition and Biblical Manuscripts, with Special Attention to the Samaritan Pentateuch." *Dead Sea Discoveries* 5 (1998): 334–54.

———. *The Text-Critical Use of the Septuagint in Biblical Research*. Jerusalem: Simor, 1981.

———. *Textual Criticism of the Hebrew Bible*. Minneapolis: Fortress, 1992.

Trigg, J. W. *Biblical Interpretation*. Wilmington, DE: M. Glazier, 1988.

Troeltsch, E. "Historiography." In *Encyclopedia for Religion and Ethics*, edited by J. Hastings, 716–23. New York: Charles Scribner's Sons, 1913.

Turner, D. "Allegory in Christian Late Antiquity." In Copeland and Struck, *Cambridge Companion to Allegory*, 71–82.

Ulrich, E. "The Notion and Definition of Canon." In McDonald and Sanders, *The Canon Debate*, 21–35.

Valdés, M. J., ed. *A Ricoeur Reader: Reflection and Imagination*. Toronto: University of Toronto Press, 1991.

Van de Beek, A. *Een lichtkring om het kruis: Scheppingsleer in christologisch perspectief*. Zoetermeer: Meinema, 2014.

Van de Mieroop, M. *The Eastern Mediterranean in the Age of Ramesses II*. Oxford: Blackwell, 2010.

———. *King Hammurabi of Babylon: A Biography*. Oxford: Blackwell, 2005.

Vanderburg, W. H. *The Growth of Minds and Cultures: A Unified Theory of the Structure of Human Experience*. Toronto: University of Toronto Press, 1985.

———. *The Labyrinth of Technology*. Toronto: University of Toronto Press, 2000.

———. *Our War on Ourselves: Rethinking Science, Technology, and Economic Growth*. Toronto: University of Toronto Press, 2011.

———. *Perspectives on Our Age: Jacques Ellul Speaks on His Life and Work*. New York: Seabury, 1981.

Vander Goot, H. "The Modern Settlement: Religion and Culture in the Early Schleiermacher." In *Hearing and Doing: Philosophical Essays Dedicated to H. Evan Runner*, edited by J. Kraay and A. Tol, 173–97. Toronto: Wedge, 1979.

VanderKam, J. C. *The Dead Sea Scrolls and the Bible*. Grand Rapids: Eerdmans, 2012.

Van der Toorn, K. *Scribal Culture and the Making of the Hebrew Bible*. Cambridge, MA: Harvard University Press, 2007.

van der Watt, J. G., ed. *Eschatology of the New Testament and Some Related Documents*. WUNT 2/315. Tübingen: Mohr Siebeck, 2011.

Van Dyke, H. *Groen van Prinsterer's Lectures on Unbelief and Revolution*. Jordan Station, ON: Wedge, 1989.

Vanhoozer, K. J. *Biblical Narrative in the Philosophy of Paul Ricoeur: A Study in Hermeneutics and Theology*. Cambridge: Cambridge University Press, 1990.

———. *The Drama of Doctrine: A Canonical-Linguistic Approach to Christian Theology*. Louisville: Westminster John Knox, 2005.

———. *Is There a Meaning in This Text? The Bible, the Reader, and the Morality of Literary Knowledge*. Grand Rapids: Zondervan, 1998.

———. "The Spirit of Understanding: Special Revelation and General Hermeneutics." In Lundin, *Disciplining Hermeneutics*, 131–65.

Vanhoye, A. *Structure and Message of the Epistle to the Hebrews*. Subsidia biblica 12. Rome: Editrice Pontificio Istituto Biblica, 1989.

Vanier, J. *Drawn into the Mystery of Jesus through the Gospel of John*. Ottawa: Novalis, 2004.

Van Leeuwen, R. C. *Context and Meaning in Proverbs 25–27*. SBLDS 96. Atlanta: Scholars Press, 1988.

van Ruiten, J. "Biblical Interpretation in the Book of Jubilees: The Case of the Early Abram (Jub. 11:14–12:15)." In Henze, *Companion to Biblical Interpretation*, 121–56.

———. *Primaeval History Interpreted: The Rewriting of Genesis 1–11 in the Book of Jubilees*. JSJSup 66. Leiden: Brill, 2000.

Van Seters, J. *In Search of History: Historiography in the Ancient World and the Origins of Biblical History*. New Haven: Yale University Press, 1983.

Van Til, C. *Karl Barth and Evangelicalism*. Philadelphia: P&R, 1964.

Van Til, H. J., R. E. Snow, J. H. Stek, and D. A. Young. *Portraits of Creation: Biblical and Scientific Perspectives on the World's Formation*. Grand Rapids: Eerdmans, 1990.

Van Winden, J. C. M. "In the Beginning: Some Observations on the Patristic Interpretation of Genesis 1:1." *Vigiliae Christianae* 17, no. 2 (1963): 105–21.

Varlamov, I. "Die Heilige Schrift in der Theologie des Heiligen Athanasius des Grossen." PhD diss., Leningrad, 1960.

Vaughan, R. *The Life and Labours of Saint Thomas of Aquin*. Edited by J. Vaughan. 2nd ed. New York: Catholic Publication Society, 1890.

Veltri, G. *Libraries, Translations and Canonic Texts: The Septuagint, Aquila and Ben Sira in the Jewish and Christian Traditions.* JSJSup 109. Leiden: Brill, 2006.

Vermès, G. *The Religion of Jesus the Jew.* Fortress: Minneapolis, 1993.

———. *Scripture and Tradition in Judaism.* Studia Post-Biblica 4. Leiden: Brill, 1961.

Vischer, L., and D. Lerch. "Die Auslegungsgeschichte als notwendige theologische Aufgabe." *Studia Patristica* 1 (1957): 414–19.

Voegelin, E. *Order and History.* Vol. 1, *Israel and Revolution.* The Collected Works of Eric Voegelin 14. Columbia: University of Missouri Press, 2001.

Vriezen, T. C. *An Outline of Old Testament Theology.* Oxford: Blackwell, 1958.

Walfish, B. D. *Esther in Medieval Garb: Jewish Interpretation of the Book of Esther in the Middle Ages.* Albany: State University of New York Press, 1993.

Walker, A. *Telling the Story: Gospel, Mission and Culture.* London: SPCK, 1996.

Wallace, M. I. Introduction to *Figuring the Sacred: Religion, Narrative, and Imagination*, by P. Ricoeur, 1–34. Minneapolis: Fortress, 1995.

Walsh, B., and J. R. Middleton. *The Transforming Vision: Shaping a Christian World View.* Downers Grove, IL: InterVarsity, 1984.

Walsh, K., and D. Wood, eds. *The Bible in the Medieval World: Essays in Memory of Beryl Smalley.* Studies in Church History, Subsidia 4. Oxford: Blackwell, 1985.

Walters, J. "The Rhetorical Arrangement of Hebrews." *Asbury Theological Journal* 51, no. 2 (1996): 59–70.

Waltke, B. K. "The Textual Criticism of the Old Testament." In *Biblical Criticism: Historical, Literary, and Textual*, edited by R. K. Harrison, B. K. Waltke, D. Guthrie, and G. D. Fee, 47–78. Grand Rapids: Zondervan, 1978.

Waltke, B. K., and M. P. O'Connor. *An Introduction to Biblical Hebrew Syntax.* Winona Lake, IN: Eisenbrauns, 1990.

Waltke, B. K., and C. Yu. *An Old Testament Theology: An Exegetical, Canonical, and Thematic Approach.* Grand Rapids: Zondervan, 2007.

Walzer, M. *Exodus and Revolution.* New York: Basic Books, 1985.

———. *In God's Shadow: Politics in the Hebrew Bible.* New Haven: Yale University Press, 2012.

Ward, B. K. *Redeeming the Enlightenment: Christianity and the Liberal Virtues.* Grand Rapids: Eerdmans, 2010.

Ward, George. "Heidegger in Steiner." In *Reading George Steiner*, edited by N. A. Scott and R. A. Sharp, 180–204. London: Johns Hopkins University Press, 1994.

Ward, Graham. *Barth, Derrida, and the Language of Theology.* Cambridge: Cambridge University Press, 1995.

Warnke, G. *Gadamer: Hermeneutics, Tradition, and Reason.* Stanford, CA: Stanford University Press, 1987.

Watson, D. F. "Rhetorical Criticism of Hebrews and the Catholic Epistles since 1978." *Currents in Research: Biblical Studies* 5 (1997): 175–207.

Watson, F. *Gospel Writing: A Canonical Perspective.* Grand Rapids: Eerdmans, 2013.

———. "The Old Testament as Christian Scripture: A Response to Professor Seitz." *SJT* 52 (1999): 227–32.

———. *Text and Truth: Redefining Biblical Theology.* Grand Rapids: Eerdmans, 1997.

———. *Text, Church, and World: Biblical Interpretation in Theological Perspective.* Grand Rapids: Eerdmans, 1994.

Weber, O. *Foundations of Dogmatics.* 2 vols. Grand Rapids: Eerdmans, 1981–83.

Webster, J. B. *Word and Church: Essays in Church Dogmatics.* New York: T&T Clark, 2001.

Weinandy, T. G., D. A. Keating, and J. P. Yocum, eds. *Aquinas on Scripture: An Introduction to His Biblical Commentaries.* London: T&T Clark, 2005.

Weinfeld, M. "God the Creator in Genesis 1 and in the Prophecy of Second Isaiah." *Tarbiz* 37 (1968): 105–32.

Weiss, H.-F. *Der Brief an der Hebräer*. KEK 13. Göttingen: Vandenhoeck & Ruprecht, 1991.

Weiss, M. *The Bible from Within: The Method of Totality Interpretation*. Jerusalem: Magnes, 1984.

Weitzman, S. *Solomon: The Lure of Wisdom*. New Haven: Yale University Press, 2011.

Wellek, R. *Concepts of Criticism*. New Haven: Yale University Press, 1963.

Wellek, R., and A. Warren. *Theory of Literature*. 3rd ed. London: Penguin, 1963.

Wellhausen, J. *Prolegomena to the History of Israel*. Cambridge Library Collection. Cambridge: Cambridge University Press, 2013.

Wendel, F. *Calvin: Origins and Development of His Religious Thought*. Grand Rapids: Baker Books, 2002.

Wengert, T. J. "Biblical Interpretation in the Works of Philip Melanchthon." In Hauser and Watson, *History of Biblical Interpretation*, 2:319–40.

———. "Philip Melanchthon's 1522 Annotations on Romans and the Lutheran Origins of Rhetoric Criticism." In *Philip Melanchthon, Speaker of the Reformation: Wittenberg's Other Reformer*. Burlington, VT: Ashgate Variorum, 2010. Reprinted from *Biblical Interpretation in the Era of the Reformation: Essays Presented to David Steinmetz in Honor of His Sixtieth Birthday*, edited by R. A. Muller and J. L. Thompson, 118–40. Grand Rapids: Eerdmans, 1996.

Wengert, T. J., and M. P. Graham, eds. *Philip Melanchthon (1497–1560) and the Commentary*. Sheffield: Sheffield Academic, 1997.

Wenham, G. J. "The Date of Deuteronomy: Linch-Pin of Old Testament Criticism, Part One." *Themelios* 10, no. 3 (April 1985): 15–20.

———. *Exploring the Old Testament: A Guide to the Pentateuch*. Downers Grove, IL: IVP Academic, 2003.

———. *Genesis 1–15*. WBC 1. Waco: Word, 1987.

———. *Genesis 16–50*. WBC 2. Waco: Word, 1994.

———. "Method in Pentateuchal Source Criticism." *VT* 40, no. 1 (1991): 84–109.

———. "Sanctuary Symbolism in the Garden of Eden Story." *Proceedings of the 9th World Congress of Jewish Studies* 9 (1986): 19–25.

Westbrook, R. "What Is the Covenant Code?" In *Theory and Method in Biblical and Cuneiform Law: Revision, Interpolation and Development*, edited by B. M. Levinson, 15–36. JSOTSup 181. Sheffield: Sheffield Academic Press, 1994.

Westcott, B. F. *The Epistle to the Hebrews: The Greek Texts with Notes and Essays*. London: Macmillan, 1892.

Westermann, C. *Genesis 1–11: A Commentary*. Minneapolis: Augsburg, 1984.

Westfall, C. L. *A Discourse Analysis of the Letter to the Hebrews: The Relationship between Form and Meaning*. LNTS 297. London: T&T Clark, 2005.

Westphal, M. "Christian Philosophers and the Copernican Revolution." In *Christian Perspectives on Religious Knowledge*, edited by C. S. Evans and M. Westphal, 161–79. Grand Rapids: Eerdmans, 1993.

Whitelam, K. *The Invention of Ancient Israel: The Silencing of Palestinian History*. London: Routledge, 1996.

Whybray, R. H. *Thanksgiving for a Liberated Prophet: An Interpretation of Isaiah Chapter 53*. JSOTSup 4. Sheffield: University of Sheffield Press, 1978.

Wicks, J. "Catholic Old Testament Interpretation in the Reformation and Early Confessional Eras." In Saebø, *HB/OT* 2 (2008): 617–68.

Wiesel, E. *Rashi*. Jewish Encounters. New York: Schocken, 2012.

Wilken, R. L. *The Spirit of Early Christian Thought: Seeking the Face of God*. New Haven: Yale University Press, 2003.

Wilkinson, R. H. *Egyptology Today*. Cambridge: Cambridge University Press, 2008.

Williams, B. A. O. *Shame and Necessity*. Berkeley: University of California Press, 1993.

Williams, R. *On Christian Theology*. Oxford: Blackwell, 2000.

Williams, R. J. "'A People Come out of Egypt': An Egyptologist Looks at the Old Testament." *Congress Volume, Edinburgh 1974*. VTSup 28. Leiden: Brill, 1975.

Wills, L. "The Form of the Sermon in Hellenistic Judaism and Early Christianity." *HTR* 77 (1984): 277–99.

Wilson, P. S. *A Concise History of Preaching*. Nashville: Abingdon, 1992.

———. *Setting Words on Fire: Putting God at the Center of the Sermon*. Nashville: Abingdon, 2008.

Wimsatt, W. K., and M. C. Beardsley. "The Affective Fallacy." In *20th Century Criticism*, edited by D. Lodge, 345–58. London: Longman, 1972.

———. "The Intentional Fallacy." In *20th Century Criticism*, edited by D. Lodge, 334–45. London: Longman, 1972.

Windelband, W. *A History of Philosophy*. London: Macmillan, 1901.

Wisse, M. *Scripture between Identity and Creativity: A Hermeneutical Theory Building upon Four Interpretations of Job*. Ars Disputandi: Supplement Series 1. Utrecht: Ars Disputandi, 2003.

Wold, D. J. "The Karet Penalty in P: Rationale and Cases." *SBL Seminar Papers*, 1979, 1–45.

Wolters, A. *Creation Regained: Biblical Basics for a Reformational Worldview*. Grand Rapids: Eerdmans, 1985.

Wolterstorff, N. *Art in Action: Toward a Christian Aesthetic*. Grand Rapids: Eerdmans, 1980.

———. *Divine Discourse: Philosophical Reflections on the Claim That God Speaks*. Cambridge: Cambridge University Press, 1995.

———. "The Importance of Hermeneutics for a Christian Worldview." In Lundin, *Disciplining Hermeneutics*, 25–47.

———. *Justice: Rights and Wrongs*. Princeton: Princeton University Press, 2008.

———. *Reason within the Bounds of Religion*. 2nd ed. Grand Rapids: Eerdmans, 1999.

Wood, A. W. "Rational Theology, Moral Faith, and Religion." In *The Cambridge Companion to Kant*, edited by P. Guyer, 404–16. Cambridge: Cambridge University Press, 1992.

Wood, C. M. *The Formation of Christian Understanding: Theological Hermeneutics*. Eugene, OR: Wipf & Stock, 2000.

Worton, M., and J. Still, eds. *Intertextuality: Theories and Practices*. Manchester, UK: Manchester University Press, 1990.

Wright, D. P. *Inventing God's Law: How the Covenant Code of the Bible Used and Revised the Laws of Hammurabi*. New York: Oxford University Press, 2009.

Wright, G. E. *The Book of Isaiah*. Richmond: John Knox, 1964.

———. *God Who Acts: Biblical Theology as Recital*. London: SCM, 1952.

———. *The Old Testament against Its Environment*. London: SCM, 1950.

Wright, N. T. *Jesus and the Victory of God*. Christian Origins and the Question of God 2. London: SPCK, 1996.

———. *The New Testament and the People of God*. Christian Origins and the Question of God 1. Minneapolis: Fortress, 1992.

———. "Reading Paul, Thinking Scripture." In *Scripture's Doctrine and Theology's Bible*, edited by M. Bockmuehl and A. J. Torrance, 59–74. Grand Rapids: Baker Academic, 2008.

———. *The Resurrection of the Son of God*. Christian Origins and the Question of God 3. London: SPCK, 2003.

Wyschogrod, E. "The Mind of a Critical Moralist: Steiner as Jew." In *Reading George Steiner*, edited by N. A. Scott and R. A. Sharp, 151–79. London: Johns Hopkins University Press, 1994.

Young, F. M. *Biblical Exegesis and the Formation of Christian Culture*. Peabody, MA: Hendrickson, 2002.

Young, F. M., and A. Teal. *From Nicaea to Chalcedon: A Guide to the Literature and Its Background*. Grand Rapids: Baker Academic, 2010.

Zachman, R. C. *Image and Word in the Theology of John Calvin*. Notre Dame, IN: University of Notre Dame Press, 2009.

———. *John Calvin as Teacher, Pastor, and Theologian: The Shape of His Writings and Thought*. Grand Rapids: Baker Academic, 2006.

Zaharopoulos, D. Z. *Theodore of Mopsuestia on the Bible*. New York: Paulist Press, 1989.

Zahrnt, H. *The Question of God: Protestant Theology in the Twentieth Century*. London: Collins, 1969.

Zenger, E. *Einleitung in das Alte Testament*. 3rd ed. Stuttgart: Kohlhammer, 1998.

Zwingli, H. "Of the Clarity and Certainty of the Word of God." In *Zwingli and Bullinger*, edited by G. W. Bromiley, 49–58. London: SCM, 1953.

Subject Index

Abraham, 364–65, 386
Absolute, 214
abstraction, systematic theology as, 435, 437
academic exegesis, 12
academic interpretation
   autonomy of, 43–44
   exalted and humbled by trinitarian hermeneutic, 9
actants, 403
Adam, 204
adaptability, as criterion for canon, 259–60, 268
addresser and addressee, 402
Ad fontes, 195, 196
aesthetic life (Kierkegaard), 302
aesthetics of reception, 115–17
affective fallacy, 398
after-Word, 27
age to come, 62
aggression, 29n77
agrarianism, 483
Alexander the Great, 162, 173
Alexandria, 163
Alexandrian school, 129, 130–31, 133–34, 145, 498
allegorical interpretation, 98, 99, 142
   of Augustine, 139–41, 144, 147
   of Gregory I, 150
   Luther on, 198
   in patristic exegesis, 126, 127–38, 192, 284–85, 338, 378–79
   of Philo, 182–83
American Academy of Religion, 5
Amoraim, 160, 176

analogia Scriptura, 235
analogical language, 93, 94n39
analogical sense of Scripture, 139
analogy (Troeltsch), 353
analogy of faith, 203
analysis, 18
   and listening, 22–24
ancient Near East, 361–62
ancient Near Eastern literature, 385
angels, 501–2
anthropology, 446, 472, 476
Antiochene school, 127, 129, 135–38, 145
Antiochus Epiphanes, 162–63, 173, 174
antiquity, as criterion for canon, 270–71, 273
antirealism, 291
antithetic typology, 129
apartheid South Africa, 253, 437, 447, 541
Apocrypha, 161, 275–76
apologetics, 438
Apostles' Creed, 446, 455
apostolicity, as criterion for canon, 252, 254, 260, 270–71, 273, 277
apostolic testimony, 434
application, 66, 529, 533–42
Arians, 438
Aristotelianism, 190, 192, 194–95, 197, 448
ascent, and interpretation, 139–40
atheism, 217, 448
atonement, 500–501, 508–10
attentiveness, 20, 36
auditory metaphor, 24n50
Augustinian hermeneutic, 326–29
Auslegungsgeschichte, 120

Subject Index

author, death of, 409
authorial intention, 204, 240, 307, 313, 398, 409
autonomy, 110, 217–18, 286, 290, 296, 305, 308, 319
  of academic interpretation, 43–44
  of philosophy, 326
  of scholarship, 45

Babel, 327, 543
Bel and the Dragon, 174
belief, 443
Bible. *See also* Scripture
  in Biblical Theology movement, 96–97
  historicity of, 336, 361
  as literature, 99, 240, 408
  as one true story, 73, 81
  postmodern readings of, 337
  as progressive revelation, 70
  as testimony, 316
  unity of, 86–87, 91
  used to legitimate oppressions, 252, 253
  as Word of God, 231, 233–34
biblical hermeneutics, 283, 329
biblical interpretation
  in community, 422
  and faith, 520–21
  and history, 338–57
  and philosophy of language, 329–34
  and theology, 234
biblical scholarship. *See* modern biblical criticism
biblical studies
  divide with theology, 11, 18
  and preaching, 525
  secularization of, 45
biblical theology, 9, 59, 82–84, 85, 250, 474
  canonical paradigm for, 92
  and doctrine, 439–41
  as historical discipline, 352
  history of, 86–90
  and story, 74–82
  and unity of Scripture, 52
Biblical Theology Movement, 75, 90–97, 102, 229, 332, 343, 362, 543
biblicism, 472
biographies, Gospels as, 385
blessing, 450, 518
British evangelical scholarship, 228–29
"broken myth," 125

California school (narrative theology), 67
Cambridge University, 473

canon, 103, 140, 251–53
  and biblical theology, 92
  and Christology, 257–63
  as closed, 252–53, 277
  and community, 255–56, 273
canonical approach (Childs), 97, 245
canonical biblical theology, 99–102
canonical hermeneutic, 236–37
capitalism, 71n102, 312
Carolingian schools, 151
Cartesianism, 217, 308, 309, 314, 315, 345, 532
catholicity, as criterion for canon, 275, 277
Catholics, 36
causality, 93
Chaldeans, 370
chance, 341
Charlemagne, 151
Chicago school (narrative theology), 67
Christendom, 300
Christian dialetic, 61
Christian philosophy, 192, 235, 445, 467
  and Scripture, 304–5
Christian scholarship, 445, 463–84
Christological hermeneutic, 5–6, 9–10
Christology
  and canon, 257–63
  of Hebrews, 498, 502
"Christonomy," 544
Christum treibet, 199
Chronicles, 172
church, space of, 468
church and world, 544–45
church calendar, 59n45
church fathers, 86, 196
  allegory of, 338, 378–79
Cistercian school, 152–53
classical foundationalism, 57, 59, 303–4, 319
classical historiography, 339–40
cloud of witnesses, 518
Code of Justinian, 285
codex, 57
commanding truths, 469–70
communication, 402–3, 410–15, 420
communion with God, 12–13
community, 545
  and biblical interpretation, 422
  and canon, 255–56, 273
  and story, 66
comparative study, 389
contemplation, 42
contemporary traditional hermeneutics, 528–31
contemptus mundi, 135, 201

context, 413
controlling story, 77n126
correlation (Troeltsch), 353
Council of Nicaea, 135
Council of Trent, 205–6
Counter-Reformation, 205–6
courtesy, 29–31
covenant, 84, 101, 105, 109, 258, 358, 387, 439, 440, 462, 544
Covenant Code, 367–69
covenant theology, 87n11
covenant typology, 129n83
created order, 105–6
creatio continuata, 454–55
creatio ex nihilo, 124, 448, 452–54, 513–14
creation, 33n94, 83, 100, 104, 108, 326, 387, 544
   Barth on, 230
   doctrine of, 437, 446–49
   and eschatology, 511–18
   and Jesus Christ, 458–62
   liberation for, 465
   and providence, 454–55
   and redemption, 83, 108, 450–51, 503–4
   and Trinity, 449–52
creation grace, 462
creation order, 455–58
creation typology, 129n83
"creative idealism" of postmodernism, 348
critical realism, 372, 411, 433
criticism, as debt of love, 31n83
cultural analysis, 481–82, 536–37
cultural linguistic method, 98
cyclic time, 105

darkness, 5
Dasein, 310
Day of Atonement, 501
day of the Lord, 62
Dead Sea Scrolls, 161, 168–70, 254
deconstruction, 27–28, 29, 314, 326, 407
deep and surface structure, 401, 403, 414, 417
defamiliarization, 118
deism, 211, 462
deliberative rhetoric, 494
democracy, 319
demythologization, 353
desire for God, 44
"developmentalism" in Old Testament studies, 14
dictionaries, 122–23, 283n7
discourse analysis, 412–13, 416, 417
discourse ethics, 321

disenchantment, with the world, 4–5
dissimilarity, criterion of, 159
divine command, 291, 321
divine drama, 77
doctrine
   and biblical theology, 439–41
   definition of, 432–36
   development of, 438
   importance of, 436–39
   and philosophy, 443–46
documentary hypothesis, 52, 220, 245
dogma, of Enlightenment, 73
dogmatics, 88, 98, 435–36, 476
double listening, 15, 481
drama, and narrative, 78–80
"drama of reading," 241
dualism, 472, 514, 521
dual Torah, 167n45

eating metaphor, 42
Ebla, 362
ecclesial interpretation, 46
ecclesial reception of the Bible, 9, 12, 113, 250, 382, 475
Ecclesiastes, 135, 141, 155, 201, 416, 536, 543
Ecclesiasticus, 268
ecology, of Christian scholarship, 445, 474–81, 482–84
edification, 323
egalitarianism, 319
Eighteen Benedictions, 167
eisegesis, 401, 418
emic analysis, 385, 407
Emmaus road, 54–56
emotive function of language, 396
empiricism, 290
Enlightenment, 24–25, 72–73, 197, 209, 211–12, 245, 249, 282, 284, 286, 292, 293, 294, 299–300, 314, 444–45, 448, 532–33
   as a story, 78, 80
   prejudice against prejudice, 310–11
   reductionistic understanding of objectivity, 415
Enlightenment rationalism, 289, 325, 393
epideictic rhetoric, 494
epistemology, 60, 216, 223, 247, 323, 475–76, 535
Epistle of Jeremiah, 175
equivocal language, 94n39
eschatology, 61–63, 104, 203, 338, 462
   and creation, 511–18
   of Dead Sea Scrolls, 168

of Hebrews, 499
Essenes, 167, 168–70, 171, 182
ethics, and language, 328
ēthos (rhetoric), 442
etic analysis, 407, 416
Eucharist, 35–36
eucharistic theology, 509
evangelicalism, 228
evidentialism, 179, 303
evolutionism, 219–20, 224, 352
exegesis, 401, 418
  of Barth, 232
  of Calvin, 232
  and philosophy, 222
  and spiritual formation, 46
existential gap (Lessing), 346
existentialism, 300
exitus, 154
exodus, 343
explanation, and interpretation, 315
expressive self, 293
expressivist theories, 394–95
eyewitness testimony, 250, 271–75, 336, 424, 491, 492

faith, 518
  and biblical interpretation, 520–21
  and history, 337, 357
  Kierkegaard on, 350
  and reason, 289, 444
  and theology, 234
faithfulness, 503
faith seeking understanding, 107, 297, 326, 432, 434, 520
false prophet, 540
family, as domestic church, 38–39
fear of the Lord, 378, 471
feminism, 284
fideism, 290, 463
figurative interpretation, 139, 140
final form of text, 380, 411
firstborn of all creation, 460–61
First Clement, 490
formalism, 383
form criticism, 11, 226, 400, 413
foundationalism. *See* classical foundationalism
fourfold Gospel collection, 425
fourfold interpretation, 146, 150, 153. *See also* quadriga
freedom, 30
  with language, 26
freedom of religion, 466

fundamentalism, 91, 320, 361, 415n165
fusion of horizons, 66, 311, 421

general hermeneutics, 285–86, 329
genetic analysis, 412–13
genre, 116, 395, 414–16
  of Gospels, 385
Geonim, 160, 183–84, 187
German historicism, 212
Geschichte, 353, 359
globalization, 319, 447, 544
glory, 516
Glossa ordinaria, 151–52
gnosticism, 62, 98, 325, 438, 448
God
  acting in history, 367
  as creator, 358
  presence of, 25–26
  as primary author of Scriptures, 52
  revelation of himself, 361
  speaks through Christ, 114
Gospels
  genre of, 385
  historicity of, 423n203
  as legends, 389n59
grace, 462
"grammars of creation," 32
grammatical interpretation, 204, 285, 307–8
Great Commission, 451
great-ideas approach, to biblical theology, 98
Greek language, 140
Greek philosophy, 131, 284
Greek texts, 385

habits of the heart, 38
halakah, 184
Hammurabi's code, 368–69
heaven and earth, 453, 455–56
heavenly Jerusalem, 511–12, 516–17
Hebrew language, 140
Hebrews, 487–522
  as a sermon, 493–96
  canonicity and authorship of, 490–93
  and Old Testament, 497–500
  prologue to, 497–501
Hegelianism, 212, 221, 223
Heilsgeschichte, 75n118
Hellenism, 133, 162, 163
Hellenistic Judaism, 163, 254
hermeneutical circle, 307, 309, 391, 535
hermeneutic of suspicion, 314
hermeneutics, 282–84

of doctrine, 438–39
Flacius on, 203
historicity of, 309
as way of coping, 324
hermeneutics of testimony, 354
Hinduism, 73
historical criticism, 52–53, 75, 87, 89, 90, 91, 102, 106, 110, 117, 205, 208–28, 237, 246, 249, 346, 378, 400, 415
   Barth on, 233
   and canon, 257, 264, 266
   conservative responses to, 228–29
   vs. literary reading, 411
historical objectivism, 115
historical order, 105–6
historical revolution, 90, 206, 209
historical sense of Scripture, 139
historical theology, 438n23
historicism, 14, 212, 224, 226, 324, 386
   in biblical studies, 399–401
Historie, 353, 359
historiography, 210, 226–27, 239, 299, 339–41, 351–56
history, 105, 535
   Barth on, 357–59
   and biblical interpretation, 338–57
   as cyclical, 341, 344
   Descartes on, 345–46
   embeddedness in, 329
   and faith, 337, 357
   hypotheses and verification in, 373–74
   Kant on, 347–48
   Kierkegaard on, 349–50
   Lessing on, 346–47
   and literature, 384–91
   and nature, 447
   Pannenberg on, 357
   Ranke on, 351–52
   and theology, 211
history-of-religions approach, 90–91, 110, 257, 352–53
Holocaust, 274
Holy Spirit
   and canon, 253, 278
   internal testimony, 492
   and Scripture, 199
home, as place of listening to the Word, 38–39
homiletics, history of, 528–29
horizon of expectation, 116–18, 119
hospitality, 28–29
humanism, 194–97, 206–8, 293
human rights, 319

humility, 22–23
   in reading, 408–9

idealism, of Kant, 291–92
ideal-speech situation, 318
ideological critique, 407
ideology, 317, 329
illegitimate totality transfer, 95
imagination, 354
imitation of Christ, 61
implied author, 418–20
implied reader, 420
improvisation, 77
inaugurated eschatology, 105
incarnation, 343
incorporation, 29n77
individualism, 39, 302, 421
inner-biblical exegesis, 124, 418
inner reading, 42
Instruction of Ptahhotep, 442
intellectual wonder, 20
intentional fallacy, 398
interdisciplinary engagement, 482
interpretation
   and application, 311, 318
   as an art, 306
   and ascent, 139–40
   demystification in, 315n158
   historicity of, 311
   as semantic event, 314
intertextuality, 116, 121–26, 242, 383, 418
intratextual realism, 411
irony, 140
Islam, and birth of biblical commentary, 187
Isocrates, 442
Israel
   cultus of, 264–65, 268, 450–51, 508
   and history, 343–44

Jamnia, 266
Jeremiah, "confessions" of, 538–42
Jesuits, 206
Jesus Christ
   as center of Scripture, 54, 59–60, 84
   and creation, 458–62, 473
   image of invisible God, 460
   as light of the world, 5
   lordship of, 465
   priesthood of, 502–10
Jewish biblical theology, 61n54, 98
Jewish exegesis, 181–83
Jewish interpretation, 158–60

Subject Index 597

Jewish messianism, 169–70
Jewish philosophers, 192
Job, 138, 148–50, 156–57, 188, 190, 191n177, 192n179, 304, 416, 463
Jonah, 119, 142–44
Jubilees, 173
Judaism, 162–63
Judas Maccabaeus, 163

Kantianism, 211, 216–17, 320
Karaites, 186
kerygma, 34–35
kingdom of God, 62, 84, 105, 108–9, 440, 459, 503, 544
  anchored in history, 362, 373n187
  as reign and realm, 105, 451
knowledge
  as dialectical, 311
  as traditioned, 323, 326, 337
knowledge of God, 107
Konstanz school (literary studies), 114

language, 26, 93, 534, 535, 537
  absolutization of, 326, 328
  and creation, 28
  as hospitality, 28–29
  and interpretation, 307
  philosophy of, 122, 326–28, 282–84, 329–34
language-in-action, 311
langue, 115n11, 121, 403
late modernity, 249, 284, 312, 409, 481
law, third function of, 201n42
law-grace distinction, 201, 441
lectio divina, 12, 39–44, 46, 47, 206, 422, 427, 488–89, 501, 510–11, 521–22
  and liturgy, 42–43
lectio sacra, 39, 40, 146, 152
Letter of Aristeas, 163
letter-spirit distinction, 198
Leviticus, 329–34, 483
liberal theology, 96
  Barth's effect on, 230
liberation theology, 447, 543–44
linear time, 105
linguistics, 283
listening, 15–16, 17–24, 31, 39, 47, 382, 441–42, 488, 525, 537
  and analysis, 22–24
  to God's address in Scripture, 379
  and social transformation, 37
literacy, 383
literal interpretation

  in Jewish biblical interpretation, 188
  in patristic exegesis, 127
  in Reformation, 198–200
literalism, 127
literary application, 119
literary approaches to the Bible, 30–31, 110, 239
  vs. historical-critical reading, 411
literary criticism, 226, 378
literary sensibility, 390
literary theory, 391–410
literary turn, 237–41, 244, 247, 264, 313, 353, 377–79
literature
  and history, 384–91
  philosophy of, 390
liturgical reason, 47
liturgy, 18, 33, 42–43, 46–47
lived experience, 68, 436–37
logocentrism, 319
logography, 339
logos, 19–20, 340–41
logos (rhetoric), 442
Lord's Supper, 179–80
lucid brevity, of Calvin, 202
Luke, 422–30
Lutheranism, 441

Maccabees, 173
Marcionism, 91, 448
Masoretic Text, 164–66, 169
meaning
  as context-sensitive, 403
  and significance, 530
means of grace, 35
mediating theology, 217
medieval biblical interpretation, 145–53
medieval Jewish interpretation, 183–91
meditation, 41–42
Melchizedek, 505–7
memory, 358n113, 382–83
metaphor, 314, 315, 329, 331–34, 436
metaphysical gap (Lessing), 346
method, Enlightenment on, 25
Middle Platonism, 130
middoth, 181–82
midrashic exegesis, 181–83, 185, 187n150, 188–89, 191, 192
midrashim, 177–79, 180, 254
mimesis, 64–66, 410
miracle, 353
Mishnah, 160, 176–77, 180

missiology
  and biblical interpretation, 83
  and narrative, 71–73
mission, and Christian scholarship, 480
missional, Kierkegaard as, 300
misunderstanding, 306
modern biblical criticism, 59, 206–8, 213, 220–22, 227, 337, 465
  faith assumptions of, 73n110
  as reductionistic, 80
modern hermeneutical theory, 284–86
modernism, 407–8
modernist dogmatics, 24–25
modernist/fundamentalist debate, 90
modernity, 207, 209, 215, 220, 225, 415n165, 447, 466
  and Christianity, 319–20
  and historiography, 355–56
  and privatization of religion, 37
  as unfinished project, 319
modern philosophy, 206
modern science, 200n39, 206, 295–96
modern theology, radicalization of, 96
modern Western worldview, 80–81
monasteries, 195–96, 484
monastic theology, 44
monotheism, 6
Moses, 366–69, 502–3
Mount Zion, 516–17
mysticism, 41n130
myth, 80n145, 315, 362, 365
mythology, 214

Nabonidus, 364, 370
narrative, 240–41, 383–84
  and drama, 78–80
  as functional discourse, 239
  and missiology, 71–73
  in philosophy and theology, 63–68
  in practical theology, 68–70
  Ricoeur on, 315
  Wright on, 378
narrative biblical theology, 59, 63, 82
narratology, 239–40
narrator, 419–20
naturalism, 195, 295
natural law, 137
nature-freedom dialectic, 359n118
nature-grace dichotomy, 44–45, 197, 359
nature/supernature dualism, 373
Nazi Germany, 437, 447
neo-Calvinism, 8

neo-orthodoxy, 90
Neoplatonism, 135, 141–42, 144, 147, 149, 154, 194, 338, 448
new covenant, 259, 508
new creation, 70, 104, 105, 137–38, 360, 446, 461, 511, 516
New Criticism, 237–38, 313–14, 381, 383, 396–401, 408, 410, 412
new historicism, 391, 407
new homiletics, 528
New Testament
  authority of, 261
  canon of, 269–75
  citations of the Old Testament, 100
  as "free narrative invention," 336
  historicity of, 371–72
  witness of, 100, 102, 108, 109
New Testament theology, 88–89
Nicene Creed, 113
Noachian covenant, 105
nomism, 34n100
"now" and "not yet," 451

obedient attention, 12
objective reading of biblical texts, 415
objectivism, 117
objectivity, thick and thin versions of, 415–16
Old Greek, 164–67, 275
Old Testament
  canon of, 263–69, 277
  citations in the New Testament, 100
  historicity of, 336, 371–72, 374–75
  as mythology, 214
  preaching in, 528, 536
  witness of, 9–10, 100, 102, 108, 109
Old Testament theology, 88–89
ontology, 60, 93, 216, 374, 476
  of Gadamer, 311
opposition, hatred, and persecution, in ministry, 539–40
oppression, 253
orality, 125, 381–84, 453
oral narrative, 426, 428
ordinary, 201, 448

pan-biblical theology, 85n2
pantheism, 212
parole, 115n11, 121–22, 403
parousia, 62
Passover, 179–81, 509
pastoral care, preaching as, 525
pastoral hermeneutics, 411

Subject Index

pathos (rhetoric), 442
patriarchal narratives, historicity of, 363–71
patristic exegesis, 58, 126–45
patristic period, 86–87
Paul
  allegory in, 128–29
  creation theology of, 460–61
Pax Romana, 163
Pelagianism, 34n100
Pentecost, 327, 543
perichoresis, 10, 449
personality, 341
personal narrative, 67
persuasion, 442
peshat exegesis, 160, 181, 186–87, 188–89, 191
pesher, 182
phenomenology, 314–15n157, 476n49
philology, 226, 285
philosophical hermeneutics, 283
philosophy, 434, 475–76
  autonomy of, 326, 476
  Barth on, 207, 235, 282
  and biblical criticism, 221–23, 348
  de Wette on, 216–17
  and doctrine, 443–46
  narrative in, 63–68
  Spinoza on, 288–89
phonemic analysis, 404
Pietism, 211, 228, 289
Pilate, 6
plain sense of Scripture, 198, 246
Platonism, 62, 132, 141, 143, 338, 448, 511, 512–13
plot, 65–66
pluralism, 466–67, 471
  of postmodernism, 312, 356, 484
poetics, 239–41, 257, 354
poetry, 392, 396–97, 402
politeness theory, 329
political theology, 478
polyglot Bibles, 202
polytheism, 362
positivism, 115, 223, 224, 352, 394, 399, 411
post-Enlightenment, 7, 110, 373, 442
postliberal homiletics, 528–29
postliberal theology, 245
postmodern hermeneutics, 528–29
postmodernism, 5, 6–7, 52–53, 94, 223, 228, 242–45, 407–9, 447
  and Barth, 236
  and biblical studies, 122
  and canon, 257

  "creative idealism" of, 348
  and death of the author, 409
  Habermas on, 319
  and Hamann, 297
  and historiography, 355–56
  in Kierkegaard, 300–301
  on language, 115n11, 122, 283–84
  pluralism of, 467, 484
  and the reader, 118
  and textuality, 529
  Wright on, 238
postmodern turn, 242–45, 247, 312–14, 353
post-Saussurean linguistics, 27, 121, 403
poststructuralism, 118n22, 314, 407
practical theology, narrative in, 68–70
pragmatism, 321, 323–24
prayer, 37–38, 42, 43, 541–42
preacher, life of, 43
preaching, 34–35, 39, 495, 523–45
  and narrative, 70
precritical and critical, 207
prejudice, 114, 310–11
preunderstanding, 418
priesthood, 264–65
primary and secondary causes, 340
Princeton Theological Seminary, 228
printing press, 195, 209, 383
privatization of religion, 37, 447, 466
proclamation, 18n5, 34–36, 39, 526–27, 544
progress, 207, 212, 291, 355
progressive revelation, 106
promise and fulfillment, 103–6
proof-texting, 439
prophecy, as forthtelling, 536
prophets, 343, 451, 501
propositional revelation, 304, 415, 436, 530–31, 533
Protestant Orthodoxy, 202–5
Protestants, on preaching, 39
Proverbs, 378, 382, 416, 537–38
providence, 156–57, 190, 291, 299, 341, 355–57, 361
  and creation, 454–55
pseudepigrapha, 161
pseudonymity, 275
psychoanalysis, 27, 318
psychological aspect of interpretation, 307–8
psychology, 434

quadriga, 142, 146, 198n18
quaestio, 44
queer reading, 407
Qumran, 168, 182

racism, 253
radical orthodoxy, 464
rationalism, 34n100, 289–90, 293, 298
  of Gabler, 87–88
rationalist-humanist story, 71
rationality, 326
reader
  exalted in postmodernism, 407
  overempowerment of, 118
  role of, 534
  in structuralism, 401–2
reading, 41
  drama of, 241
  postmodernism on, 257
real absence, 27
real presence, 27, 32–33
reason
  in Enlightenment, 209
  Gadamer on, 310
  Hamann on, 295–96
  Herder on, 299, 300
  in Judaism, 178–79
  Kant on, 290
  Kierkegaard on, 303
  as neutral and objective, 466
  Schleiermacher on, 306
  Spinoza on, 287–89
recapitulation, 74, 140, 141n147
reception history, 114, 117–20
receptivity, 12, 22–24
reciprocity, 29n77
reconciliation, 102, 461
redaction criticism, 226, 385, 413
redemption
  and creation, 83, 108, 450–51, 503–4
  grace, 462
redemptive historical approach, 74–75, 98, 99
reditus, 154
redundancy, 331, 334
referential function of language, 396
Reformation, 197–202
Reformed epistemology, 445
relativism, 284, 329
relevance theory, 329
religion
  Schleiermacher on, 305
  vs. theology, 88
religious consciousness, Schleiermacher on, 93, 307–8
religious hermeneutic, 245
Renaissance, 186, 194–97, 209–10, 284, 392, 448

repetition, 383
respectful listening, 24
responsible reading, 30–31
rest, 504
resurrection
  in Isaiah, 169–70
  as reaffirmation of creation, 441
retellings, of the Hebrew Bible, 171–72
revelation
  and canon, 267
  Ricoeur on, 316
rhetoric, 140, 442–43, 494
rhetorical criticism, 238, 443
Rishonim, 160, 183, 184–85
Romanticism, 286, 292–93, 300, 305–6, 307, 380–81, 393, 398
Rule of Faith, 57–59, 140, 270
Russian formalism, 403, 407

Sachkritik, 226
Sadducees, 167–68, 170
sapientia, 340
scholasticism, 153–57, 194
science, as coping rather than progressive, 323
scientific revolution, 209–10, 532
scientism, 110, 318, 356, 445
scribe, preacher as, 527n23
scriptural reasoning, 473
Scripture. *See also* Bible
  authority of, 8, 91, 200
  and Christian scholarship, 471–74
  clarity of, 34, 199, 361
  designed to be preached, 527
  discontinuities between Testaments, 89
  and doctrine, 434–35
  drama of, 360–61
  fragmented by modern biblical scholarship, 59
  as kerygmatic, 34–35
  narrative shape of, 63
  as pair of spectacles, 201
  as revelation, 316
  scope of, 472
  as single story, 480
  tells true story of the world, 474
  telos of, 139
  transforms biblical interpretation, 483
  unity of, 52–61, 474
Scripture and Hermeneutics Seminar (Cambridge), 237, 245
secondary conceptualization, 309
Second Helvetic Confession, 527n23

Subject Index

Second Isaiah, 124–25
Second Temple literature, 159, 160–75
secular humanism, 197
secularism, 356, 448
secularization, 26, 45, 320, 322, 447
self-consciousness, 296
semantics, 95, 403
semiotics, 121–22
sensorium, 384
Septuagint, 103, 108, 140, 162, 163–67, 254, 275–76, 370, 498
shalom, 461
Shammai, 167
Shema, 24–25, 38, 42, 45, 125, 167, 435
signs, 139, 392–93
silence, 20–21
Sirach, 172–73
Society of Biblical Literature, 5
sociocritical approaches, 284, 317–23
sociological perspectives, in biblical theology, 98
sociopragmatic hermeneutics, 323–25
Socrates, 442
sola narratione, 478
Soncino Bible, 196
Song of Songs, 299
source criticism, 211–12, 240, 378, 411–13
speech-act theory, 329, 411, 531
spiritual formation, 542
spirituality, 44
spiritual sense, 128n78, 134, 198
Stoics, 127–28, 284n12
story, 125–26
 and biblical theology, 74–82
 N. T. Wright on, 81–82
storytelling, and doctrine, 433, 436
structural analysis, 417
structuralism, 313, 329, 380–81, 400, 401–8
Sturm und Drang, 294
subjectivism, 115–16
subjectivity
 Kierkegaard on, 300–301
 Schleiermacher on, 307
suffering, 4
Susanna, 174
symbol, 314
syntactic analysis, 404
synthetic typology, 129
systematic theology, 435–36

Talmuds, 160, 177, 181
Tannaim, 160, 176, 179

Targums, 161, 177, 254
technique, 23
technology, 23
temple
 desecration of in 167 BC, 162–63
 destruction in AD 70, 160, 167
 as symbol in first-century Judaism, 167
temporal gap (Lessing), 346
temporality, 65–66
text, 379–80, 415
 open and closed, 531, 533–34
 as discourse, 413
 historicity of, 240
 meaning of, 307
 as mediating communication, 314
 New Criticism on, 397–99
 priority of, 31
text structure, 417–18
textual criticism, 276–77
textuality, 314
thematic biblical theology, 98, 103–6
theodicy, 192n179
theological encyclopedia, 476
theological hermeneutic, 245
theological interpretation, 14, 18, 32, 43, 207, 244–50, 441, 443
 and hermeneutics, 282–84
theological reconstruction, 119
theology, 433
 as a science, 435
 and exegesis, 200–201
 narrative in, 63–68
 originates in listening, 18n5
theology of history, 357–60
theology of place, 142
theory, reductiveness of, 26
thick objectivity, 188n22, 531
time, 262
 Barth on, 357–58
 biblical view of, 342
 Cullmann on, 95
Tobit, 174
Tosefta, 177, 180
"Total Interpretation," 399–401
tota Scriptura, 9, 59, 234, 439, 449, 480
tradition, 9, 114, 285, 322, 323–24, 438
tradition criticism, 413
traditum, 124
transcendental turn, in Schleiermacher, 306
transdisciplinary scholarship, 482n66
transfiguration, 459–60
translation, 127

tree of knowledge (diagram), 474–75
trinitarian hermeneutic, 6–11, 12, 14, 247
Trinity, 6, 7, 8, 10–11, 84
   and creation, 449–52
trust, 29n77
truth, 5–7, 71, 327, 387, 410, 473, 484
   as one and unified, 438
   in postmodernism, 324, 467
   as subjectivity, 300
two ages, 61–62
two-books approach (Augustine), 444–45
two-kingdoms approach, 201, 441
type and reality, 339
typology, 9, 98, 99, 145, 499
   of Maximus, 143
   of patristics, 126, 129, 140

unbelief, 521
understanding, 317
universal history, 71–72, 387
universal pragmatics, 318
universities, 196, 470
univocal language, 93, 94
use and enjoyment (Augustine), 392–93

Verstehen, 318
"vertical in authority," 469
Victorines, 152, 388
visual metaphor, 24
vocation, 201
Vulgate, 195

Western church, syncretism in, 72
Wirkungsgeschichte, 323, 443
wisdom, 44, 142, 149, 451, 473, 537–38
wisdom literature, 154, 416
Wisdom of Solomon, 173
word and sacrament, 35
Word and world, 36–37
Word of God, threefold form of, 527
"worldhood," 309
world opened up in front of the text, 443
worldview, 77–78, 474, 477–78
   and doctrine, 433, 436
   stories, 78, 80
writing, 382–83

Yale school, 67, 235, 245

Scripture Index

Old Testament

Genesis
1   101, 105, 118, 230, 363, 451, 453, 454, 456, 457, 513
1–2   363
1–3   204, 362
1–11   450
1–Exod. 12   173
1:1–2   452
1:1–2:3   362n126, 383n29
1:1–2:4a   124
1:1–5   130n89, 382, 453
1:2   124, 125, 452, 453
1:2–3   298, 453
1:3a   363
1:4   456n88
1:6   456n88
1:7   456n88
1:14   456n88
1:18   456n88
1:24–25   235
1:26   124
1:26f   124n58
1:26–28   515
2   118, 230
2–4   188
2:2–3   124
2:4   362n126
2:4–4:26   450
2:8–9   141
2:20   382
2:24   147
3   24n50
3:7   56
4:8   164, 269
11–21   426
12:1–3   166, 450
14   507
14:17–24   507
14:19–20   507
18:22–33   321
22   132, 304, 386, 389, 497n48
22:3–4   130n89, 132
28:22   507
47:31   165n33

Exodus
1:19   177
2   366
2:1–10   503
13:9   189
19–24   367
19:3–6   450
20   185, 504n83
24:4–8   503
24:12–30:31   150
25–40   508
25:9   508
25:40   508
26:30   508
27:8   508
29:36–37   501
30:10   501

Leviticus
4:27–28   330
5:2–4   330
5:5   330
5:17   330, 331
5:23a   330
6:1–7   332
6:4 (ET)   330
8–10   264
10:10–11   264
16   500
16:19   501
16:30   501
18:6–23   333
18:25   333
18:29   333
18:30   333
25:1   333
27:30–33   507

Numbers
5:6b–7   330
8:4   508
12:7   503n81
18   507
20:10–12   503
22:5   368
22:11   368
25:6–12   173
33:16–49   383

Deuteronomy
6:3–4   24
6:4   33
6:4–5   37n112
6:4–9   24, 37
6:6   37, 37n112
12:5   539
12:11   539
18:22   540
25:4   129, 130n87
33:10   264

1 Samuel
1:1–2:1   406
2:35   503n81
13:1–15   507
24:5   331n226
25:31   331n226
28   135

2 Samuel
7:13   166
7:16   166
24:10   331n226

603

1 Kings
5:1–8:51 150

1 Chronicles
17:14 503n81

2 Chronicles
24:20–22 269

Job
1:2 150
3 149
7:15 148, 149
12:11 17
28 149
28:12–15 148
38:2 156

Psalms
1 127, 137, 377
1:1b 127
1:3 127
1:4 127
2 137, 377, 506
2:7 505
2:7–8 500
2:12 515
8 515, 516
8:4–6 498
8:6 516
16 442n37
16:7 331n226
19 137, 434
19:7 137
40 498
42 332
45:6 499
90–99 377
93 506
94:7–9 457
95 503, 504
95–99 506
95:7–11 498
99:6 502
102:26–27 514
102:26–28 515
110 498, 505, 506, 507, 516
110:1 498, 499, 506, 516
110:1–4 498
110:4 498, 505, 506, 507
113–14 180
115–18 180
119 24n50
119:6 24n50
119:15 24n50
119:18 24n50
119:37 24n50
119:82 24n50
119:105 24n50
119:123 24n50
119:148 24n50
145–150 377
147:15 523

Proverbs
1–9 378
1:7 378
3:11–12 498, 518
3:19 149, 451
7:1–6 125
8:22–31 149
9:10 46, 471
15:23 537
26:1–12 537
26:4–5 538
31 144
31:10 144
31:10–31 378
31:13 144
31:22 144
31:24 144

Ecclesiastes
1 341n30
1:1–2 189
1:2–3 141
1:2–11 189

1:14 26n59
1:17 26n59
4:17 18
7:23–29 535
12:1 543

Isaiah
1–39 169
40–55 169
40:12–31 124
40:18 124
40:18f 124n58
40:18–20 124
40:25 124
40:28 124
43:20–21 235
45–46 174
45:7 124, 125
45:18 124
45:23 164
46:5 124
52–53 170
52:13–53:12 169, 170n65
53:11 170
55 15
55:1 144
55:2–3 15
56–66 169
66:1 504, 515
66:2b 504
66:22 504

Jeremiah
1:4–19 538
1:18 541
10:2–15 175
11:18–23 538
11:21–23 541
12:1–6 538
12:5–6 541
12:6 540
15:10 539
15:10–21 538
15:16 538–39

15:18 539
15:18c 541
15:19–21 541
16:1–4 540
17:14–18 538
17:15 540
17:16 540
18:18–23 538
18:20–23 540
20:7–10 540
20:7–18 538, 540
20:8 539–40
20:9 540
20:11–13 540
20:14–18 540
28 540
31 508, 512, 518
31:31–34 498, 514

Ezekiel
34 235

Daniel
7–10 426

Hosea
2:18 235
6:7 204, 204n54

Amos
9:11 166
9:11–12 165–66
9:12 166, 167

Jonah
3:8 235
4:11 143, 230, 235

Habakkuk
2:3–4 498, 498n56
2:4 510, 518
2:20 42

Haggai
2:6 517

New Testament

Matthew
19:21 133
22:41–46 506
26:29 181
26:36–46 181
27:31–36 181
27:48 181
28:16–20 451

Mark
1:13 235
1:16–18 273
12:1–12 404
12:36 499
14:25 180, 181
14:66–72 389
15:36 181
16:7 273

Luke
1–2 55, 56, 272n86
1:1 56
1:1–4 424, 425
1:2 272
1:5 425
1:5–2:52 425
1:17 426
1:19 426
1:66 427
2:10 426
2:19 427
2:32 426
2:46–47 429
2:49 429
2:51 427
2:52 425
3:1 425
3:1–4:13 427
3:2 427
3:6 164
3:22 459
4 426n219
4:14–15 428
4:14–9:50 427
4:16–21 428
4:20–30 428
5:15 428
5:37 515
7:17 428

8:1–3 428
8:22–25 155
9:22 429
9:28–36 459
9:32 459
9:44 429
9:51 429
9:51–55 429
9:51–19:48 423, 428
10:30–35 404n122
10:38–42 18
11:14–23 429
11:37–54 429
11:50–51 269
12:49–53 429
13:31–35 429
19:1–10 429
19:10 429
20:1 429
20:1–21:38 429
20:2 429
21:37–38 429
22:1–23:56 430
22:15 181
22:16 180, 181
22:18 181
22:22 430
23:50–56 430
24 55, 56, 424, 430
24:1–12 55
24:1–53 430
24:13–35 55
24:15 55
24:18 55
24:24 55
24:25 55, 497
24:25–27 55
24:27 55, 55n24, 56
24:31 55, 56
24:32 55, 56
24:35 56
24:36–49 55
24:44 55n24
24:45–48 56
24:48 55
24:50–53 55
24:51 429

John
1 130
1:3 452
1:14 338
1:35–42 273
1:38 273
1:39 273
1:40–42 273
3:16 35
3:31–36 6
5:30 7
6:45 497
6:52–53 159
12:21 488
14:6 6
15:26–27 272
16:13–14 7
18:28–19:16a 6
18:36 516
18:37 6
19:23–30 181
19:30 181
20:30 205
21:20 273
21:22 273
21:24–25 273

Acts
1 430
1:21–26 272
2:23 430
2:34 499
2:42 262
2:46 56
3:15 15, 36
7:49 504
8:26–40 55
10:36–42 272
13:15 494n31
13:24–25 426n216
15 166
15:16 166
15:16–18 165–66
15:17 166
16:10–17 275
18:2 493
18:25 426n216
19:1–4 426n216
20:5–15 275

21:1–18 275
27:1–28 275
28 424

Romans
1:1 488
1:1–6 501
1:17 510
2:17 130
5:12–14 210
7:14 129
8:20 516
9–11 35
12:1 510
12:8 495

1 Corinthians
1:23 169
3:10–15 517
9:8–9 129, 130n87
10:11 147
11:26 36
15:24–28 516
15:27 516
15:50–54 515
15:53 515
15:54–57 515

2 Corinthians
2:14–16 471
3 129
3:4–6 129
3:6 129
8:9 459
10:4–5 236

Galatians
3:11 510
4:21–31 128
4:24 128
5:11 169

Ephesians
1 74
1:10 462
5:32 147

Philippians
2:6–11 108

2:10 164, 516
3:12 107
3:21 516

Colossians
1:13 459
1:14 460
1:15 460
1:15–17 460
1:15–20 36, 460, 500
1:16 460–61
1:17 461
1:18 461
1:18–20 460
4:11 459
4:16 382

1 Thessalonians
2:3 495

1 Timothy
4:13 495
6:13 6

2 Timothy
3:16 136
3:16–17 278

Hebrews
1:1 497, 497n47, 498, 501
1:1–4 258, 489, 496, 497, 509, 513
1:2 3, 488, 491, 492, 503, 513, 515
1:2–4 499, 500
1:3 500, 506, 513
1:3c 508
1:4 501
1:4–2:18 501
1:5–2:18 496
1:6 517
1:10–12 513, 514
1:11 515
1:11–12 514
1:12 515
1:12a 515
1:13 515
1:13–14 515
2 515

2:1–4 491, 495
2:3–4 491
2:3a 491
2:5 515
2:5–9 499
2:7 516
2:8 516
2:9 488, 516
2:10 513, 516
2:10–13 516
2:12–15 495
2:14–15 516
2:16 516
2:17 502, 502n75
2:18 501
3:1 503, 503n79, 504, 509, 520
3:1–6 502
3:1–4:14 502
3:1–5:10 496, 502
3:2 503n81
3:4 503
3:7–19 497, 521
3:7–4:16 503
3:12 521
3:19 521
4:1–8 504
4:1–11 504
4:2 509
4:4 504
4:4–7 504
4:8 504
4:9 504, 504n83
4:12–13 497n47
4:14 503, 504, 509
4:15 489, 505, 511, 519
4:15–5:10 502, 505
4:16 505, 505n95
5:2 505
5:4 505
5:6 506
5:11 507
5:11–10:39 496, 502
6:1–4 495
6:4–6 490n9
6:7–8 518
7 505
7:1–9 507
7:3 507, 507n104
7:11–28 507

7:16 507
7:17 506
7:18–19 507
7:20 507
7:21 506
7:22 508
7:23–24 507
7:26–28 507, 511
8–9 514
8–10 508
8:1 496
8:1–2 508
8:1–7 508
8:2 508
8:6 508
8:8–12 514n137
9 505
9:1–10 508
9:9 508
9:11–28 508
9:12 508, 509
9:14 509
9:15 514
9:25–26 508
9:28 510
10–12 518
10:19 511
10:19–13:21 498
10:19–22 509
10:22 521
10:23 509
10:25 510
10:26–29 495
10:29–39 509
10:32–36 510
10:37 510
10:37–38 498n56
10:38 510
11 499, 503, 510, 519, 519n158
11–12 113, 518
11:1 518, 521
11:1–12:13 496
11:3 452n71, 513, 514, 517
11:4–40 500, 518, 519
11:8–16 516
11:10 516
11:14 516
11:16 516

11:21 165n33
11:32 492n17, 519
11:35–36 510
12:1 518
12:1–3 500, 519
12:1–4 522
12:14–13:19 496
12:18–24 512
12:18–25 492
12:22 114, 511, 516
12:22–23 517
12:23 114
12:25 113, 491, 520
12:25–29 516, 517, 517n151
12:26 515, 517
12:27 516, 517, 517n151
12:27–28 517
12:28 517
12:29 517
13:1–6 493n22
13:2 519
13:7 492
13:20–21 489
13:20–25 496
13:22 487, 488, 494n31, 495
13:22–25 494
13:23 492
13:24 493

James
1:17 301

1 Peter
5:12 495n37

2 Peter
1:9 500

1 John
1:1–3 3, 260

Jude
9 276

Revelation
21 518
21:3 100

Apocrypha

Epistle of Jeremiah
23   175

1 Maccabees
1:10   173
2:23–26   173

2 Maccabees
7:28   452n71

Sirach
24:10   173
44–50   172
44:1–14   172
44:1–49:16   500, 519
44:1–50:21   499, 519
44:2   172
44:12   172
46:11–12   172n76
50   173
50:1–21   172, 500, 519

Tobit
14:4   174
14:15   174

Wisdom of Solomon
11:17   513

Dead Sea Scrolls

4Q252   162

Apostolic Fathers

1 Clement
36   490n7
42.1–2   269n68

Ancient Classical and Christian Writers

Aristotle
On Rhetoric
1.1.14   442n38
1.2.1   442n38
1356a   442n30

Augustine
City of God
12.14   341n30
Instructing Beginners in Faith
1.2   471n39
Retractions
1.1–2   341n26

Clement of Alexandria
Stromata
1.2   131n90
1.9   258n30
3.11   258n30
4.21   258n30
5   131
5.6   131
5.11   132
5.13   258n30
7.18   132n91
20.1   131n90

Gregory the Great
Magna moralia
1.3   148n175

Maximus
Ambigua
37   143n153

Philo
Life of Moses
I.149   502n77

Plato
Phaedrus
277b5–c6   442n39

Tacitus
Annals
1   387

Tertullian
Against Marcion
4.1   258n30
Against Praxeas
15   258n30
Modesty
20.3   490n9
Prescription against Heretics
6   270n70

Author Index

Abarbanel, I., 185–86
Abegg, M., Jr., 182n121
Aberbach, M., 177, 177n94
Abraham, W. J., 252n4
Abraham ibn Ezra, 184–85, 186n142, 190–91, 191nn73–74, 204n54
Abrams, M. H., 393–94, 393–94n74, 394n75, 394n77
Achtemeier, E., 14, 14n41
Adams, A. K. M., 242n231
Adams, E., 514–15, 514n139, 516n147, 517, 517n149, 517n151
Adams, J. C., 532n41
Adams, N., 317n170, 318n172, 319n176, 320, 320n182, 320n185, 320nn187–88, 322, 322nn194–96, 322nn198–99, 329, 473, 473n43
Aelred of Rievaulx, 152
Agamben, G., 27n65
Akiba, Rabbi, 182
Albo, 191
Albrekston, B., 344, 344n43
Albright, W. F., 362, 362n130, 364, 366, 366n146
Alcuin of Northumberland, 151, 377
Alexander, P. S., 162, 162n14
Alexander, T. D., 97n54
Allen, D. L., 492n19
Alonso-Schöckel, L., 399, 399n100
Alston, Wallace M., Jr., 525n8, 527n19
Alston, William P., 94n40
Alter, R., 99, 237–38, 237n206, 238n210, 241, 390

Ambrose, 155, 196, 341
Andersen, F. I., 166nn41–42
Anderson, B. W., 344, 344nn44–45
Anderson, G., 453n74
Anderson, R. D., 494n31
Andrew of St. Victor, 152
Angeles, P. A., 61n57
Anselm, 107
Apel, K.-O., 323n201
Arama, M., 191
Aristeas, 130
Aristobulus, 130
Aristotle, 78, 78n136, 141n147, 151, 154, 201, 392, 410, 442, 442n38, 442n40, 532
Arnobius, 196
Arnold, D. W. H., 392n69
Ashford, B., 52n8, 357n100, 383n29, 500n73
Astruc, J., 211
Athanasius, 12, 13, 58, 146, 340
Attridge, H. W., 491n13, 492n18, 494n30, 495n34, 495nn37–38, 507n104
Auerbach, E., 67n84, 354, 386–90, 386n43–44, 387nn45–50, 388nn51–53, 389nn54–57
Augustine, 9, 15–16, 19, 19n8, 21n26, 43, 43n140, 66, 74n114, 131, 138–42, 139nn134–37, 140nn138–44, 141n147, 142nn149–50, 144–47, 144nn158–59, 146n169, 147nn170–71, 154, 196, 248, 275–76, 340–41, 341n26, 341n30, 349, 376–77, 377n3, 388, 392–93, 393n72, 408, 410, 444, 448, 448n56, 468, 471, 471n39, 477, 490, 524, 524nn5–6, 537n63, 538n65
Auneau, J., 174, 174n86

Bachelard, G., 38n115
Backhaus, K., 520, 520n163
Badrinath, C., 72
Baildam, J. D., 299, 299nn88–89, 299nn91–92
Bailey, K. E., 159n4, 423n204, 428, 428nn224–25
Bakhtin, M., 10
Balthasar, H. U. von, 6n8, 42n136, 78n129, 359–60, 360nn119–21
Barr, J., 8, 8nn19–20, 10, 10n23, 75–76, 75n120, 85n2, 86, 86n3, 90, 91, 92, 92n31, 94–97, 94nn41–42, 95nn43–46, 96nn50–52, 122, 122n51, 223, 223n139, 267, 267n59, 283, 283n8, 332, 332n229, 344, 361
Barrett, C. K., 129, 129n82, 130n86, 229, 229n169, 499n66, 518, 518n152
Barrett, L. C., 304n108
Barry, J., 170, 170nn63–64
Barth, K., 5, 5n5, 7–8, 7n15, 9, 18n5, 24, 25n51, 25n53, 34–35, 34n99, 35n101, 45, 90, 91, 113, 113n1, 192, 202, 207, 224, 230–37, 230n172, 231nn175–81, 232nn182–89, 233nn190–91, 234n192, 234n194, 234n196, 235nn197–99, 236n200, 236n202, 236nn204–5, 245, 249, 282, 357–59, 357nn103–6, 358nn107–13, 359n116, 431, 432–33, 435, 436, 441, 444, 446, 448, 450, 458, 459, 459n104, 461, 461n115, 462, 462n118, 465n9, 479, 518n157, 519, 519n161, 523, 523nn1–2, 524, 524n4, 525, 525n9, 526–27, 526n17, 527n18, 527nn20–22, 529, 545
Barth, M., 114n2
Barthélemy, D., 169n57
Barthes, R., 121, 122, 313, 313n151, 404
Bartholomew, C. G., xn4, 4n2, 11n27, 18n6, 41n132, 52n8, 57n35, 59n46, 63n64, 76n121, 77n124, 79–80, 82n154, 83n157, 105n109, 116n18, 119n27, 125n59, 126n67, 157n210, 179n105, 207n67, 237n207, 248n245, 267n58, 327n212, 356n97, 357n100, 360, 360n122, 362n127, 367n158, 377n6, 378nn9–10, 379n12, 383n29, 404n119, 423n205, 437n21, 441n33, 441n36, 445n48, 448nn58–59, 453n75, 453n78, 454n79, 467n20, 469n26, 476n49, 477, 477nn50–52, 478, 480n62, 481n64, 500n73, 503n80, 537n60, 537n63, 541n74
Barton, J., 31n85, 238n208, 245, 245n237, 262n42, 270, 401n108, 414n162
Basil, 196

Bateman, H. W., 500, 500nn71–72, 506, 506n100
Battles, F. L., 202
Bauckham, R., 71n102, 174–75, 174n85, 175n87, 229, 249–50, 260n37, 270, 272–74, 272n81, 272nn83–86, 273nn87–94, 274n95, 274nn97–98, 276n107, 336, 441
Baudrillard, J., 313
Bauer, B., 256
Bauer, G. L., 88
Baumgarten, J., 298
Baur, F. C., 208, 219–20, 229
Bavinck, H., 12nn30–31, 15, 15n44, 34, 34n100, 36–37, 37nn107–9, 435, 435n16, 448, 454n82
Beale, G. K., 89n18, 503n80
Beardsley, M. C., 397, 397n88, 398, 398nn91–92
Bebbington, D., 94n37, 142n151, 212, 212nn94–95, 212n99, 344
Beckett, S., 355
Beckwith, R., 253, 263, 269nn65–66, 277, 277n109
Bede, 150, 151, 155
Bedouelle, G., 205n57
Beegle, D. M., 365n144
Beiser, F. C., 199n30, 212n95, 217, 217nn112–13, 289n36, 293n57, 294n62, 295, 295n68, 296nn69–70, 297nn76–78, 298, 298nn81–85, 299n86, 299n93, 300n94, 348, 348n64, 348n66, 351n78
Beldman, D., 377, 377n7, 441n36
Bellah, R. N., 38nn116–17
Benedict, 145
Ben-Eliyahu, E., 175n88, 176n90, 177n96
Bengel, J. A., 498, 498n55
Benjamin, W., 351
Berengar of Tours, 152
Berger, J., 494n30
Berger, P., 94n38, 304n109, 519–20, 519n162, 521, 521n165, 540, 540n70
Berkhof, Hendrikus, 448
Berkouwer, G. C., 230–31, 231n174, 454n82, 455n84, 456
Berliner, A., 188n159
Bernard of Clairvaux, 44, 152, 388
Bernstein, M. J., 162n14
Bernstein, R. J., 319n177
Berossus, 342
Berry, W., 408, 408n133, 483
Bertens, J. W., 319n178, 324, 324n203
Betz, J. R., 217n113, 295, 295nn64–65, 295n67, 296, 296n71, 467n21, 468n25

Bireley, R., 205n57
Birkhead, T., 469
Black, C. C., II., 494n28
Bleicher, J., 308n131, 350n71
Blocher, H., 451
Block, D. I., 24nn48–49
Blowers, P., 58–59, 59nn43–44, 143n153
Bodin, J., 210
Boethius, 145
Boff, L., 4, 4n4, 543, 543n79
Böhm, T., 126n68
Boling, R. G., 97n55
Bonaventure, 53, 53n13, 153, 154–55
Bonhoeffer, D., 9, 17–18, 17n2, 18n3, 33n93, 37, 327n213, 436, 441, 441n34, 458, 458n100, 465–66, 465nn10–11, 466n13, 467–68, 468n23, 525, 525nn10–11, 526–27, 526nn13–16, 544–45, 544nn83–85, 545nn86–87
Bonnefoy, J.-F., 458n99
Booth, W. C., 410, 419, 419nn180–85, 420
Borgen, P., 182n123
Boring, M. E., 89n18
Bosch, D. J., 426n219, 428, 428n223
Botha, M. E., 247, 247n243, 333n233
Boulnois, O., 472n41
Bourgoing, R. P. F., 21n28
Boyarin, D., 134n104
Bradbury, M., 417, 417n171
Brassier, R., 4, 4n3
Braudel, F., 351
Bray, G., 87n12
Breck, J., 40n122
Brent, 352n83
Brett, M. G., 352
Bright, J., 91n26
Bright, P., 392n69
Brilioth, Y., 528n24
Broadus, J., 533, 533nn47–48
Brody, R., 183n128, 184, 184n130
Bromiley, G. W., 527n23
Brooke, G. J., 162, 162n14, 168n50
Brooks, C., 398, 398n95, 400n104
Brown, G. H., 471n40
Brownlee, W. H., 182, 182n122
Bruce, F. F., 51, 51nn1–2, 58, 58n42, 129, 129nn80–81, 163nn18–22, 164n25, 166, 166n43, 229, 258n31, 259nn33–35, 266, 266n56, 268, 268n62, 268n65, 274, 275n100, 510, 510n117, 510nn119–20, 513n130, 514n135

Brueggemann, W., 89n18, 245, 373n186, 377n6, 527n23, 536, 536n58, 537n60, 539n69
Bruner, F. D., 249
Brunetière, F., 394
Brunner, E., 51, 90, 448, 454n82, 458
Buber, M., 98, 158–59, 159n2
Buckley, M. J., 45, 217n118, 444, 468n24, 532
Bullinger, H., 87n11
Bultmann, R., 94, 353
Burke, K., 442
Burke, S., 313, 313n152, 409n139
Burnett, F. S., 244n234
Burridge, R. A., 385, 385n39
Burtness, J. H., 327n213
Bushnell, H., 530n38
Buss, M. J., 71–72n103
Byrskog, S. S., 274, 274n96

Cadbury, H., 422, 422n194
Caird, G., 73n110, 89n18, 497, 498, 498n58, 517n150
Cajetan, T., 472n41
Calmer, A., 206
Calvin, J., 9, 74, 86, 87n11, 157, 193, 193n2, 197–202, 199n33–34, 200n41, 201n46, 202n47, 231–33, 248, 431, 431n1, 432n4, 479–80, 490–91n11, 492
Campenhausen, H. von, 256
Cappel, L., 205
Caputo, J. D., 31n84, 218, 218n120, 309n134
Caputo, N., 185n137
Carasik, M., 186n142
Carr, D. M., 255n11
Carr, E. H., 351
Carroll, J., 82, 82n156, 83n157, 209n80, 470, 470nn32–36, 473, 480, 480n61
Carroll, R., 32, 32n89
Carson, D., 229
Carterius, 135
Celan, P., 28
Chadwick, H., 140n145
Chapman, S. B., 268, 268n64
Childs, B., 10nn24–25, 46, 51, 51n3, 52, 52n4, 57, 57n36, 61n55, 75–76, 76n121, 87n8, 87n11, 88n16, 89n18, 90n20–21, 90n23, 91, 91n24, 92nn29–30, 96–97, 98–102, 98n57, 98n59, 99n71–73, 100nn74–76, 101nn77–82, 102nn83–88, 105, 106, 120n36, 125, 125n62, 169n60, 234, 234n195, 236–37, 245, 249, 250, 254–55, 254n9, 255nn12–13, 256–57, 256n14, 257n22, 257n24, 260, 260n38, 369, 369n168, 441, 504, 504n87, 543

Chilton, B., 178–79, 178n103
Chladenius, J. M., 286
Chrétien, J.-L., 15–16, 16n46, 19, 19n13, 21, 21nn27–31, 21nn33–35, 22, 22n36, 22nn38–39, 22nn41–42, 28–29, 28nn69–73, 29n74, 32, 32n90, 37–38, 38n111, 42n138, 47n159, 52–53, 52n9, 53nn10–11, 476n49
Chrysostom, John, 135, 196
Church, C. L., 229, 229n167
Cicero, 128, 339n16
Ciszek, Walter, 37
Clark, S. H., 314n155, 316n168
Claude, Jean, 532
Claudel, P., 53n11
Clayton, T., 422n191
Clement of Alexandria, 13, 130–32, 131n90, 132n91, 133n92, 258n30, 479
Clement of Rome, 86, 269
Clines, D. J. A., 241, 263, 263n44, 377, 379n13, 420n188, 440
Clouser, R. A., 415n166, 474n46, 476, 476n47
Cocceius, J., 88n16
Cochrane, C. N., 339, 339n17, 339n19, 340n20, 340nn22–24, 341n25, 341nn27–29, 341n31
Cockerill, G. L., 490n6, 494n630
Cody, A., 508n107
Cohen, J. J., 178n99
Cohen, M., 184n135, 185
Cohen, S. J. D., 161n7
Coleridge, S. T., 29, 393
Coles, R., 408
Colet, J., 153, 195n9, 196, 196n13
Collingwood, R. G., 117, 117n21, 212, 212nn97–98
Collins, J. J., 161n7, 168n51, 169n59
Cook, J., 165n32
Cooper, A., 98
Cooper, J. W., 445n50
Cornick, D., 526, 526n12
Cornutus, 127–28
Coventry, John, 73n109
Crawford, S. W., 162, 162n13, 162nn15–16
Crenshaw, J., 304n109
Croatto, S., 97n56
Croce, B., 395, 396, 416n170
Cross, F. C., 92
Crusius, C. A., 290
Cullmann, O., 63n63, 95, 344, 344n47
Cunningham, V., 408
Cyprian of Carthage, 134, 196, 262, 262n43
Cyril of Alexandria, 204n54, 248

Daane, J., 530, 530n34
Dalferth, I. U., 433, 433n8, 444, 444nn44–45, 445n47, 477n50
Dan, J., 178n99
Daniélou, J., 144, 144n160, 338n13, 338n15, 499, 499n64
Dannhauer, J. C., 286, 292
Dante, 388–89
Daube, D., 179n110, 180n118, 181
Davidson, R., 538n66, 541n72
Davie, G., 521n165
Davies, P. R., 248n245
Davies, W. D., 512, 512n123, 512n125
Davis, E., 483, 483n68, 525, 525n8, 532n43
Dawson, D. A., 128nn74–77, 130nn88–89, 416n169
Dearman, J. A., 204n53
de Certeau, M., 472n41
DeGregorio, S., 150nn181–82
de La Tour, G., 21
Delegue, Y., 154n196
de Man, P., 116n13
Demarest, B. A., 491n11, 507n104
Dempster, S. G., 264, 266n54
Derrida, J., 19n14, 27, 27n65, 31, 31n84, 118n22, 121, 122, 236, 306n117, 307n122, 313, 316, 325, 326, 356, 407, 408, 533, 534
Descartes, R., 207, 209, 310, 345–46, 345n48, 532
Dever, W. G., 365, 365n141
Dewald, C., 339n16
de Wette, W. M. L., 207, 208, 213–18, 220, 237, 292, 348
Dickson, G. G., 297n74
Dilthey, W., 203, 286, 308, 309, 350
Diodore of Tarsus, 127, 135–37
Docherty, S., 158, 158n1, 499n65
Dodd, C. H., 169n61, 498–99, 499n61, 510n117
Döderlein, J., 299
Dohmen, C., 256, 256n16, 256n18, 256n21
Donovan, M. A., 74n114
Dooyeweerd, H., 359n118
Drogo of Paris, 152
Droysen, J. G., 212, 286, 350, 354
Drusius, J., 202
Duke, P., 7n10
Dumbrell, W. J., 83, 97, 97n56, 99, 105, 169n57, 204, 440n32, 441n33
Dungan, P., 252, 252n5
Dunn, J. D. G., 229, 460, 460nn106–7, 500, 500n70
Dunnill, J., 494n29, 514, 514n136
Düringer, H., 320n188

Earnest, J. D., 58n40, 146n166
Ebeling, G., 120, 120n31, 283n9
Eco, U., 118n22, 122–23, 122n50, 123nn52–54, 531, 533–34, 534nn50–51, 534nn53–54
Edgar, A., 292n52
Edwards, M., 408
Edwards, O. C., Jr., 532n40
Eichhorn, J. G., 211, 212
Eichrodt, W., 250, 454, 454n81
Eisen, R., 187, 187nn152–55, 188n156, 189n168, 190n169–72, 191n176, 191n178
Eisenbaum, P. M., 519n158
Eliezer ben Jose ha-Galili, Rabbi, 182
Eliezer of Beaugency, 188, 189
Eliot, T. S., 396–97, 396nn85–86, 408, 409, 410n141
Ellingsworth, P., 490n6, 493n24, 494n29, 497n49
Ellis, E. E., 62–63, 62nn61–62, 63n63, 129, 129n83, 268n65, 275, 275nn101–2
Ellul, Jacques, 23, 23nn44–45, 23n47, 543n82
Elman, Y., 185, 185n137
Empson, W., 396
English, E. D., 392n69
Erasmus, D., 195–96, 199, 490n11
Ernest, J. D., 58n40, 298
Ernesti, J. A., 211
Evans, C. F., 155
Evans, C. S., 274n97, 300n95, 300n97, 301nn101–2, 304, 326, 371, 371n178, 374n97, 467, 467n19

Fahey, M. A., 134n106, 135n107, 262n43
Falque, E., 476n49
Farge, J. K., 153n192
Farrow, D., 74, 74n114
Feld, H., 494n29
Felde, J. von, 285
Feldmeier, R., 106–10, 106n114, 107nn115–21, 108nn122–26, 109nn127–30
Fichte, J. G., 213
Filson, F. V., 495n36
Fishbane, M. A., 123–24, 124n57, 183n126, 242, 418n175, 418n177
Fitzmyer, J., 155
Fiumara, G. C., 19–20, 19n14, 20nn15–16, 20nn18–24, 22, 24
Flacius Illyricus, M., 202–4, 285
Flint, P., 182n121
Fodor, J., 314n155, 315nn162–63, 316n167
Folks, E., 521n165

Ford, D., 322, 322n199, 433, 433n7, 434, 473, 473n42
Ford, J. M., 426, 428, 428n222
Foster, E., 339n16
Foucault, M., 313, 313n151
Fowl, S., 464, 464n5, 480n60, 481n63, 482, 482n67
Francis of Assisi, 133, 388
Frank, D., 186, 186n144, 186n146
Frankfort, H., 343, 343n42
Freedman, D., 166nn41–42, 330n219
Frei, H. W., 8, 67, 67n84, 237, 315n163, 410
Frendo, A. J., 336, 336n5
Freud, S., 27, 315
Freund, E., 114n4, 313n153
Freytag, G., 383–84
Friedlander, M., 191n173
Froehlich, K., 120–21, 120n32, 120nn35–36, 121n37
Frye, N., 408

Gabler, J., 86–88, 88nn13–15, 211, 352
Gadamer, H.-G., 20, 31, 31n86, 66, 114, 115, 117n21, 249, 249n248, 281, 281n3, 282, 282n4, 286, 310–12, 310nn140–41, 310n143, 314, 316–17, 317n170, 318, 322, 325, 326, 533
Galileo, 195, 445
Gamble, H. Y., 254–55, 255n10
Garbini, G., 364–65, 364nn135–38, 364nn139–40, 369, 370
Gardner, H., 401nn105–6
Garfinkel, S., 160n6
Gehring, H.-U., 115n6
Gelardini, G., 494n30
Gelles, B. J., 188n158
Gellner, E., 521n167
Gentry, P. J., 83n158
George, J. F. L., 218
Gerkin, C. V., 68–69, 69nn91–93
Gersonides, 191
Gerstenberger, E. S., 89n18
Gert, B., 321
Gesenius, W., 218
Gheorghita, R., 498n54, 498n56
Gibson, A., 362–63, 362n128, 363nn132–33, 370–71, 371nn174–75, 374, 374n191
Gibson, M., 152n185
Gilbert, P., 206n63
Gilkey, L., 90, 91, 92–94, 93nn32–35, 94n36, 94n40, 96–97, 361
Girard, R., 258, 258n29, 389, 408, 408n132

Author Index

Glassius, S., 202, 203
Glatzer, N. N., 179n109
Gleim, J. W. L., 299
Goethe, J. W., 220, 296, 299
Goheen, M., xn4, 41n132, 57n35, 59n46, 76n121, 77n124, 79–80, 82n154, 83n157, 83n159, 179n105, 207n67, 360, 360n122, 445n48, 465n9, 476n49, 477, 477nn51–52, 478, 480n62, 481n64
Goldingay, J., 89n18, 229, 229n170, 370n172, 506, 506n97, 506n101
Goldsworthy, G., 70, 70n96, 97
Goodman, L. E., 98, 98n67, 187n152
Goppelt, L., 129n83
Gorday, P., 58, 58n41
Gordon, C. H., 364, 364n134, 365, 365n142
Gordon, R., 467n30
Goshen-Gottstein, M., 98
Graf-Stuhlhofer, F., 261, 261nn40–41
Graham, G., 355, 355n93
Graham, M. P., 197n16
Gramberg, C. P. W., 218
Grant, G., 23n44
Grant, R. M., 198n19, 287n22
Grässer, E., 518n154
Grassi, E., 442
Green, J. B., 55, 55nn22–23, 55nn26–27, 56n34, 155, 180n116, 241, 338n11, 422n193, 423, 424–25, 424n205, 425nn210–12, 426, 426nn215–16, 427n220, 429n226, 430, 430n228
Greenberg, M., 98
Greene, T. M., 348n63
Green-McCreight, K., 236n203
Greenslade, S. L., 270n69, 271n79
Greenspoon, L., 165n32
Greenwood, D., 401nn108–9, 404, 404nn117–18, 404n122
Gregory I, Pope, 148–50, 148nn174–75, 149nn176–78
Gregory of Nyssa, 134–35
Gregory of Tours, 388
Greidanus, S., 70, 70n97, 74n117
Greimas, A. J., 403, 403n116, 404, 406
Griesbach, J. J., 213
Griffioen, S., 466n14
Griffiths, J. I., 520n164
Grillmeier, A., 74nn115–16
Grimal, N., 368, 368n162
Grondin, J., 197n17, 282n5, 284n12, 285n16, 286nn19–21, 292, 292n54, 306nn119–20, 307n122, 307n127, 308nn132–33, 350n72

Grossman, A., 184nn131–32, 186n145, 186nn147–48, 187n150
Grotius, H., 205
Grou, J. N., 21, 21n29
Gruber, M. I., 184n131, 188n159
Gruenler, R. G., 292, 292nn50–51
Grunhaus, N., 186n142
Guigo II, 40
Gunkel, H., 90, 124n57, 223, 400n103, 453
Gunn, D. M., 238, 238n209, 238n211
Gunneweg, A. H. J., 89n18
Gunton, C. E., 7, 87n10, 137n124, 438n25, 447, 447n55, 448, 449n60
Guthrie, D., 229
Guthrie, G. H., 488, 488nn2–3, 493n27, 496nn41–42, 497n49
Guthrie, S. R., 360n122
Gutiérrez, G., 447, 447n53, 543
Güttgemanns, E., 404

Habermas, J., 312, 313, 316, 317–23, 317n170, 318n171, 318n173, 318n175, 319n177, 319nn179–80, 320n181, 320nn183–88, 320n191, 324, 329, 442–43, 473
Hafemann, S., 219–20, 220n127
Hagen, K., 490n9, 490n11
Hagman, E., 43n141
Hahn, H. F., 223n140
Hahn, S. W., 172, 172n74, 209n76, 264–65, 264n45, 265nn46–48, 269n67, 371n177
Hailperin, H., 188nn160–61
Hamann, J. G., 74n114, 211n89, 281, 281nn1–2, 286, 293–97, 293n59, 294n63, 295n66, 297n74, 298, 299, 299n91, 300, 302, 305, 325, 325n206, 326, 465, 465n9, 468, 474, 479
Harbison, E. H., 196nn10–12
Harding, S. G., 415n166
Harlow, D. C., 161n7
Harnack, A. von, 274
Harris, H., 219n125, 220, 220n128
Harris, Max, 360n122
Harris, Murray J., 460, 460n105, 460n109, 461n110
Harris, Robert A., 189nn164–67
Harris, Roy, 121nn41–42, 122n45
Harrison, R. K., 228
Harrisville, R. A., 208n71, 287n22, 288n26, 296n72, 297n73, 297n76
Hart, T. A., 360n122
Harvey, V. A., 353n84
Hase, K., 208, 299

Hasel, G., 230
Hauerwas, S., 67, 67n85, 69nn94–95
Hauret, C., 54n18
Hawkes, T., 402, 402nn111–12, 403nn115–16
Hayes, J. H., 365n141
Hays, R. B., 64
Hazony, Y., 98, 98n66
Hebblethwaite, B., 7n14
Hecateaus, 339n16
Hegel, G. W. F., 207, 212, 213, 217, 219, 220–21, 295, 296, 302–3, 348–49, 350, 351
Heidegger, M., 20n17, 25, 46, 65, 286, 308, 309–10, 309nn134–35, 309n138–39, 535
Heim, K. M., 378n8
Held, J. S., 21n32
Hengstenberg, E. W., 228
Henry, C., 530, 530n36
Henry, M., 47n157, 343n39, 476n49
Heraclitus, 127, 128
Herder, J. G., 220, 286, 293, 295, 296, 297–300, 298nn80–81, 298n85, 305, 325, 352, 394, 394n77
Hermann, W., 353
Herodotus, 339, 339n16, 342, 365
Herrara, R. A., 342, 342n33
Herrington, A., 317n170
Heschel, A., 98
Hesse, M. B., 333–34n235
Hesse, Mary, 207n68
Hilary, 196
Hill, E., 144, 147, 147n170
Hill, R. C., 135n108, 136nn114–19, 137nn120–23
Hillel, 167, 181–82
Himmelfarb, G., 356, 356n99
Hippolytus, 36, 490
Hirsch, E. D., 313, 313n150, 530, 530n37, 533, 534
Hodge, C., 530n38, 532, 532n44
Hoffmeier, J., 365n144, 366, 366nn149–51, 368nn162–63, 369
Hofmann, J. C. K. von, 75n118
Holenstein, E., 400n102
Holmes, M. W., 269n68, 272n82, 273n87, 490n7
Holmstedt, R., 452n74
Holt, R., 541n74
Holub, R. C., 114n4, 118n22, 313n153
Holwerda, B., 74n117
Homer, 67n84, 284, 386–89
Honorius III, Pope, 133n93
Hort, F. J. A., 229
Horton, M. S., 94n40

House, P. R., 89n18
How, A., 317n107
Howard, T. A., 213n102
Hubert, M., 156
Hübner, H., 89n18
Hufnagel, W. F., 299
Hughes, P. E., 490n9
Hugh of St. Cher, 155
Hugh of St. Victor, 152, 204n54
Humboldt, W. von, 212, 350, 350n74, 351, 351nn75–76, 352, 354
Hume, D., 290n37, 294, 296, 353
Hurst, L. D., 89n18, 504, 504n86, 511, 511n121, 515nn142–43, 516n144–46
Hutton, J., 392nn67–68

Iggers, G. G., 351n79
Ignatius of Loyola, 206, 489, 522
Illyricus, 197n17
Ingarden, R., 66, 114
Ingraffia, B., 465n12
Irenaeus, 13, 58, 74, 86–87, 87n9, 137n124, 248, 271, 338, 338n15, 448, 480, 490
Irwin, W., 121n39
Isaac of Stella, 152
Isaacs, M. E., 493n20, 493nn25–26, 512
Iser, W., 66, 114, 118n22

Jacobi, F. H., 297, 297n78, 299
Jakobson, R., 402–3, 402nn113–14
Jang, J. Y., 491n14
Japhet, S., 189nn162–63, 269n67
Jasper, D., 408
Jauss, H. R., 3, 3n1, 12, 114, 115–17, 115nn5–12, 116nn13–16, 116n19, 117nn20–21, 118n22, 119nn24–26, 119n28, 121n44
Jeanrond, W. G., 141, 141n148, 211n90, 284, 284nn10–11, 285n13, 285nn15–16, 286n22, 317n169
Jedin, H., 205n57
Jefferson, A., 395, 395n80
Jeffrey, D. L., 56, 56n29, 391, 391n65, 392n69, 393, 393nn70–71, 393n74, 408–9, 409n140, 410n141
Jenkins, K., 323n202, 356, 356n98
Jenkins, P., 482
Jeremias, J., 159, 159n4, 179n108, 180, 180n114, 181, 428n221
Jerome, 45, 45n149, 135, 140, 141, 154, 196, 201, 204n54, 275–76, 376, 376n2, 388, 490
Jobes, K. H., 164n23, 164nn25–28, 164n30, 164n32, 165n33, 169n56, 170n65

Author Index

John of Jandun, 194–95
John of the Cross, 157
John Paul II, Pope, 481
Johnson, L. T., 423, 423n198, 425, 425n213, 426n214
Johnson, M., 333n234
Johnson, P., 194n3
Jones, L. G., 67n85
Joseph ben Isaac Bekhor Shor, 188, 189–90
Josephus, 161, 172, 175, 180n112, 269, 406
Josipovici, G., 512, 512n124, 518
Justin Martyr, 13, 130, 490

Kähler, M., 353
Kaiser, W., 97n56
Kalimi, I., 61n54, 99, 99n69, 183n127
Kalin, E., 266, 266n57
Kalman, J., 183n127, 187nn151–52, 191n177
Kannengiesser, C., 126, 126n66, 126n69, 127nn70–71, 135n110, 135n113, 138nn132–33, 139n134
Kant, I., 179, 207, 213–14, 213n103, 217–18, 286, 289–92, 294–96, 325, 346, 347–48, 347nn59–60, 468
Kara, A., 184
Karris, R. J., 154, 154n197, 155, 155nn201–3
Käsemann, E., 511, 511n122
Kass, L. R., 98, 98n63, 441, 452, 452n73, 456, 456nn89–90, 456nn92–93, 458, 467, 467n18, 543, 543n81
Keach, B., 202
Kealy, S., 422, 422n192
Keating, D. A., 156n205
Keble, J., 394
Keil, C. F., 211
Kellogg, R., 384n36
Kelsey, D., 439, 478, 478n55
Kennedy, G. A., 442n37
Kereszty, R. A., 36, 36nn103–5
Kermode, F., 237–38, 237n206, 288n26, 336, 336n2
Kessler, J., 89n18
Kidner, D., 229, 506, 506nn98–99
Kierim, R. P., 366–67
Kierkegaard, S., 19, 19nn9–12, 286, 296, 300–305, 300nn96–97, 301n98, 301n100, 302n103, 303nn104–5, 304n107, 305n110, 322n196, 325, 326, 349–50, 448, 468, 479
Kimball, C. A., 55n24
Kirwin, C., 139nn136–37
Kistemaker, S., 494n29
Kitchen, K. A., 365

Kiuchi, N., 330n220
Klein-Braslavy, S., 185n136
Kleuker, J. F., 299
Kline, M., 97
Klink, E. W., III, 98n57
Knierim, R. P., 366nn147–48, 366nn152–53, 367nn154–57, 437n22
Knight, D. A., 399
Koester, C. R., 491, 491n12, 492, 492n16, 493n20, 494, 494nn31–32, 495n37, 507n104, 508n108, 514n135
Kolb, R., 203nn50–51
König, A., 61n59, 458n99, 459, 459nn102–3, 461, 461nn111–12, 461n115, 462, 462nn116–19
Kraemer, H., 294, 294n60
Kraus, H.-J., 101n80, 369n169
Kraus, K., 27
Krentz, E., 208–9, 208n73, 211nn86–87, 211n91, 212, 212n96, 213n100, 219n124, 223n140, 224–27, 224n141, 224n143, 225n144, 225nn146–51, 226nn152–58, 227nn159–64
Kristeller, P. O., 194n4, 197n15
Kristeva, J., 116, 116n17, 121, 121n40
Kuczynski, M. P., 471n40
Kuenen, A., 352
Kugel, J. L., 98, 98n61, 170–72, 171n69, 172n72
Küng, H., 463, 463n2, 472n41, 542, 542n78
Kurianal, J., 506n97
Kuss, O., 495n36
Kuyper, A., 435, 448, 454, 454n83, 527n23, 532, 532n45

Lacan, J., 27
LaCocque, A., 52n6, 299n90, 447n54, 456–57, 457nn94–96
Lacoste, J.-Y., 18, 18n4, 33n92, 46–47, 46nn151–53, 47nn154–56, 47n158, 476n49
Ladd, G. E., 97
Lakoff, G., 333n234
Lampe, G. W. H., 153n192
Lancaster, I., 184n133
Lane, A. N. S., 200n38
Lane, W. L., 488, 488n4, 490n8, 491–93, 491n13, 492n15, 493n23, 493n27, 496, 496n40, 496n42, 497, 497n44, 497n50, 497n52, 498n54, 501n74, 503n78–79, 503n81, 504n84, 505nn88–89, 505n95, 507n104, 508nn105–6, 508n110, 510n118, 511n122, 513, 513nn128–29, 513nn131–32,

513n134, 514, 514n138, 517n148, 518, 518nn155–56
Lanfranc of Bec, 152
Langan, J., 390, 390n61
Lapide, C. à, 204n54, 206
Lash, N., 322n197
Lategan, B., 379, 379n14
Lateiner, D., 339n16
Law, T., 163n20
Lawee, E., 185nn138–39, 185n141
Leach, E., 404
Leclercq, J., 40nn127–28, 44, 44nn144–46, 152–53
Legarde, P. A., de, 169n56
Legaspi, M. C., 211n89
Legrand, L., 55n25
Leibniz, G. W., 195, 290n37, 346
Leiman, S. Z., 266n55
Leithart, P., 408–9, 408n134, 409n135
Lentricchia, F., 401n107, 407n128
Lerch, D., 120, 120nn33–34
Lessing, G. E., 220, 299, 346–47, 346nn52–53
Levene, N., 473n42
Levenson, J. D., 61n54, 98, 98n58, 243n233, 410–11, 411nn144–45, 411n147, 456n91
Lévi-Strauss, C., 122n46, 404
Levy, S., 125, 125n59
Lewis, C. S., 389n59, 391, 396, 408–9, 409nn136–37
Lichtheim, M., 343nn37–38
Liftin, D., 530n33
Lightfoot, J. B., 229, 461, 461n113
Lillback, P. A., 87n11
Lim, T. H., 55, 55n24
Lincoln, A., 7n10
Lindars, B., 494n29
Lindbeck, George, 8, 67, 237, 410
Linn, D., 39n120
Linn, M., 39n120
Linn, S. F., 39n120
Livy, 212
Lloyd, G., 355, 355n96
Lloyd-Jones, M., 35, 533, 533n49
Lockett, D. R., 98n57
Loewe, R., 285n13
Lohfink, N., 256, 256n19
Lombard, P., 44, 152, 153
Long, V. P., 336, 336n6, 354, 374
Longenecker, R. N., 129n80, 129n82, 164n32, 182nn124–25, 497, 498nn59–60, 499, 499n62

Longman, T., III, 336, 336n6, 354, 365, 374, 414n160
Loughlin, G., 72n105, 74n114
Lubac, H. de, 13n34, 40, 53–54, 53n15, 60, 60n49, 61, 61nn55–56, 61n58, 128n78, 129nn84–85, 142, 146n168, 150, 150n179
Lundin, R., 408
Luraghi, N., 339n16
Luther, M., 197–201, 198n24, 199nn25–26, 199nn28–29, 199n31, 200n37, 203, 233, 248, 276, 277, 441, 444, 490–91n11
Lyon, D., 291n46
Lyotard, J.-F., 313, 324

Machey, L., 391
MacIntyre, A., 63–64, 64nn65–66, 322, 326, 337, 337n8
Mackey, L. H., 391n64, 391n66
MacLeod, D. J., 493n27
Madison, G. B., 31n86
Magness, J., 168n50
Magrassi, M., 13, 13n37, 33, 33n95, 34n97, 36n106, 37, 37n110, 40, 40n121, 40nn123–26, 41, 42, 42nn133–35, 42nn137–39, 43, 43n142, 45n148, 487n1
Maimonides, 185, 189n168, 190, 190n169, 192, 288
Mandelbaum, M., 221n132, 399n99
Manguel, A., 46n150
Marcel, G., 22–23, 22nn42–43
Marcion, 86, 257, 438
Marcos, N. F., 164n32
Marenbon, J., 151n183
Marincola, J., 339n16
Marion, J.-L., 476n49
Marquard, O., 119
Marsden, G., 119n30, 466
Marshall, B. D., 6n8, 7nn11–13, 8, 8n16, 8n18, 9, 12nn33–34, 15n44
Marshall, I. H., 89n18, 179n108, 179n110, 180nn116–17, 423n202
Martens, E. A., 89n18
Martin, F., 245
Martin, G. D., 169n57
Martin, R., 229
Marx, K., 315, 348
Mason, E. F., 507n104
Mattes, M. C., 296n72, 297n73, 297n76
Maurer, W., 197n15
Mauthner, F., 27
Maximus the Confessor, 142–44, 143nn153–57
Maxwell Miller, J., 365n141

Mayeski, M. A., 146n165, 146n167, 148n173, 151, 151nn183–84
Mays, J. L., 377n6, 506, 506n102
McCann, C., 136, 377n6, 506
McCann, J. C., Jr., 11, 11n26
McCarthy, R. M., 466n14
McCarthy, T., 317n170
McClendon, J. W., Jr., 67, 67n86
McClure, J. S., 529, 529n28
McComisky, L. E., 204n53
McDonald, L., 252–53, 252n6, 259, 267, 267n60, 275, 277
McGrath, A. E., 432n2, 434, 434n14, 435, 435n17, 438n24, 448
McIntyre, A., 326n208
McIntyre, J., 62n60, 225n145
McKeever, M. C., 338n11
McKim, D. K., 202n48
McKnight, S., 179n110
McLay, R. T., 164–67, 164n29, 164n31, 165nn33–34, 166nn35–40
McLeod, F. G., 138nn127–30
McNamara, M., 177n95
McNicol, A. J., 508n107
Meek, J. A., 165n33
Meier, J. P. A., 260n37, 286
Melanchthon, P., 201, 203, 210
Melville, H., 21n31
Meyer, H., 219
Michaelis, J. H., 211, 298
Michalson, G. E., Jr., 217, 217n111, 217nn114–15, 217n117, 218n119, 346, 346n54, 347, 347nn55–58, 349n68, 353, 353nn86–88
Michel, O., 497
Middleton, J. R., 481, 481n65
Milbank, J., 325, 325n207, 464, 464nn3–4, 468n24, 472n41, 476
Milgrom, J., 330–34, 330nn220–21, 330n223, 331nn224–25, 331nn227–28
Millard, A. R., 369n170
Miller, P., 450, 450n65
Mitchell, B., 377n5
Mittleman, A., 98, 98n68, 187n152
Moberly, R. W. L., 24n48, 38n112, 89n18, 229, 245
Moessner, D. P., 423, 423n199, 424, 424n207
Molnar, P., 251, 251n2
Moltmann, J., 7, 53, 53n12, 448
Mommsen, T., 350
Montefiore, H., 504, 504n85, 515n141
Monti, D., 155n200
Mooney, M., 197n15

Moore, G. F., 182n120, 254, 254n7
Morgan, R., 31n85, 357, 411, 414, 414n162
Moritz, K. P., 214
Morris, L., 229
Moscati, S., 343n41
Most, G. W., 127n72
Motyer, J. A., 366n153
Mouw, R. J., 466n14
Moyise, S., 56, 56n31
Mudge, L. S., 315n157, 315nn160–61
Mueller-Vollmer, K., 197n17, 285, 285n17, 306n118, 310n142, 350n73
Muilenburg, J., 238
Mulchahey, M. M., 153n191
Muller, R., 198n23, 202, 202n49, 204–5, 204n52, 204nn54–55, 205n56
Müller-Sievers, H., 297, 297n79
Mumford, L., 484, 484n69
Munslow, A., 243n232, 244nn235–36
Murphy, R. E., 421n190

Nägele, S., 165n33
Nahmanides, 185, 186n142
Nairne, A., 499, 499n63
Neill, S., 11, 11n29, 219n126, 228, 228n166, 229n168, 246, 246n240, 248n244, 271n80, 335, 337
Nelson, E., 98, 98n64
Nestorius, 135
Neuhaus, R. J., 14, 14n41, 247–48
Neusner, J., 98, 161n10, 167, 167n45, 176–77, 176nn91–93, 178n97–98, 178nn100–104, 179nn106–7, 181n119
Newbigin, L., 5, 6n6, 6n8, 33, 33n96, 35n102, 42, 59–60, 59n47, 70, 70nn98–99, 71–73, 71nn100–101, 72n104, 72nn106–8, 73nn109–13, 80n145, 250, 387n46, 473, 473n44, 480, 536
Newman, C. C., 246n241
Newman, J. H., 438n24, 474
Newton, Isaac, 209
Nicholas of Lyra, 189, 204n54
Nicholson, E. W., 208n73, 218, 218n121, 308n132, 350, 350n72, 352
Nickelsburg, G. W. E., 160n5, 161n7, 168n50, 173nn78–79, 173n81, 174n84
Nida, E. A., 493n24
Niebuhr, B. G., 212, 350
Nietzsche, F., 6, 315, 356
Nissen, J., 428n221
Nobile, M., 89n18
Noll, M. A., 45n147, 337, 337n9, 466

Nolland, J., 55, 55n20, 56n28, 155
Nomoto, S., 508, 508n109
Norris, C., 242, 242n230, 286–87, 287n23, 288n26, 291n48, 313, 313n149, 317n169, 323n200, 324n205
Norris, R. A., Jr., 145n164
Nouwen, H., 539
Nussbaum, M., 355, 355n94

Oakes, K., 235n199
Obbink, D., 127n72
Ochs, P., 322, 473n42
Ocker, C., 153–54, 153nn190–92, 154n193, 154n196
O'Connor, M. P., 169n58
Oden, T., 14, 247–48
O'Donovan, O., 15n43, 32n89, 106, 249, 249n247, 324, 326n210, 441, 441n35, 458, 478, 478n54, 479, 509, 509n113, 523–24, 524n3, 544
O'Dowd, R. P., 157n210, 378n9
Oeming, M., 256n16
Ogletree, T. W., 357n103, 358n113, 359nn114–16
Olbrechts-Tyteca, L., 442
Old, H. O., 524n7, 525nn9–10, 533n46, 533n49
Olivier, J.-M., 135n112
O'Malley, J. W., 205n57, 205n60, 205n62, 206n65
O'Neill, O., 290, 290nn39–41, 291n42
Ong, W., 125, 283n7, 376, 376n1, 381–84, 381nn22–24, 382nn25–26, 382n28, 383nn30–32, 383n34, 384n35, 384nn37–38, 385, 399, 399n98, 408, 408n131, 421n190, 423–24, 424n206, 426, 428, 453, 453n76
Origen, 14, 58, 133–35, 133n97, 134nn98–103, 141, 196, 248
Orlinsky, H. M., 170n62
Orr, M., 116n18
Oshlag, R. S., 333n232
Östborn, G., 258, 258n31, 265nn49–51, 268, 268n63
O'Toole, C. J., 448n56

Palmer, R. E., 308, 308n130, 350, 350n70
Pannenberg, W., 246n241, 357, 357n101, 434–35, 435n15, 435n18, 439n27, 448
Papias, 272–73
Parker, T. H. L., 202n48
Parry, R. A., 183n127
Patrick, D., 105, 105n103
Pecknold, C. C., 322n199, 473n42

Pelikan, J., 464, 464n7
Perelman, C., 442
Perkins, W., 532
Perlitt, L., 220–21, 220nn129–31, 221nn132–35, 222nn136–37
Petersen, N. R., 433, 433n10
Peterson, E., 234n193, 377n6, 537n62, 538n66, 539n67, 541, 541n73
Petrarch, 195
Petrie, H. G., 333n232
Petronius, 387
Pettinato, 363
Peyrère, I. de la, 210
Pfister, M., 78–79, 78n137, 78n139, 79nn140–42
Phillips, A., 267n61
Philo, 130, 175, 182–83, 284n12, 499, 502n77, 507n104, 511, 512
Pico, 195
Pieper, J., 145nn161–63, 153nn188–89, 373n187, 374, 374nn189–90
Pitkin, B., 200n38, 200n40
Pitre, B., 179, 179nn110–11, 180n113, 180n116, 180n118
Plantinga, A., 8, 57, 192, 192n179, 235, 249, 291, 291n47, 308–9n133, 326, 326n209, 348, 361, 361n125, 445, 445n48, 466–67, 467n15, 467n17, 468
Plato, 122n48, 128, 132, 194, 338n12, 391, 442, 442n39
Plotinus, 147
Plutarch, 128
Polanyi, M., 72n107
Polk, T. H., 304n109, 305n111
Polliack, M., 186nn143–44
Polzin, R. M., 401, 401n109, 402n110, 404, 404n118
Pomponazzi, P., 194, 195
Pons, 304n108
Popovic, M., 165n32
Porquet, J.-L., 543n82
Prestige, G-L., 131, 131n90, 133nn94–96, 134n105
Preus, J. S., 211n88, 289n33
Preuss, H. D., 89n18
Prickett, S., 408
Propp, V., 403
Provan, I. W., 336, 336n6, 354, 365n143, 372n179, 372n184, 373n185, 374
Pseudo-Longinus, 394
Puckett, D. L., 198n21, 202n48
Pufendorf, S., 299

Quash, B., 359n117

Rabanus Maurus, 151
Rad, G. von, 245, 250, 362, 437, 447, 447n54, 450, 450n63, 451, 451n66, 471n38
Radcliffe, T., 328, 328nn215–16
Rae, M., 335, 335n1, 339n18, 340n21, 348, 348n65, 349n67, 375
Raeder, S., 197, 197n14
Rajak, T., 163n20
Ramus, P., 532
Randall, J. H., Jr., 194n4, 195nn5–6
Randolph, F., 7n108, 36n103, 37n108
Ranke, L. von, 212, 220, 350, 351–52, 351n77, 351n79
Rashbam, 184, 186n142, 188, 189, 190
Rashi, 184, 186n142, 188–89
Ratzinger, J., 320n188
Ray, J., 469
Reardon, B. M. G., 305–6, 305nn112–13, 306nn114–16
Redmond, M., 294n61
Reimarus, H. S., 299
Reist, T., 154nn198–99
Rembrandt, 21, 22, 23
Rendsburg, G. A., 364n134, 365, 365n142
Rendtorff, R., 89n18, 256, 256n15
Renz, T., 443n43
Reuss, E., 218
Reventlow, H. G., 53, 53n14, 54nn16–19, 87n9, 119n29, 207, 207n69, 209n78, 211n87, 286–87n22, 352, 352nn81–82
Richard of St. Victor, 152
Richards, I. A., 396–97, 398, 442
Richardson, A., 209–10, 210n81
Richardson, B., 423n200
Richardson, M. E. J., 368n159
Ricoeur, P., 27, 52, 52n6, 63–66, 64n68, 64nn70–71, 65nn72–7, 66nn78–82, 67, 79nn143–44, 141n147, 299n90, 312, 313, 314–17, 314nn154–57, 315nn158–59, 315n163, 316nn164–66, 317n170, 325, 326, 328n214, 329, 333n234, 341–42, 342n32, 344n46, 354, 354n89, 372, 372n183, 380, 380nn15–16, 381n20, 390, 410, 414, 414n161, 419, 443, 447n54, 449, 449n62, 452n72, 456n87, 457nn94–96, 462
Ridderbos, H., 6, 6n9, 74, 75n118, 97, 260–61, 261n39, 278, 278n110, 441
Rieff, P., 469–70, 469nn28–30, 470n31
Rimbaud, A., 27
Ritschl, A., 101

Rivetus, A., 202, 203
Roberts, J. T., 339n16
Robertson, O. P., 97
Robey, D., 395, 395n80, 396n83, 398n94
Robinson, D., 97n53
Robinson, F. C., 377n5
Robinson, H. W., 530, 530nn31–32
Robinson, W. C., 422, 422n195
Rogerius, C., 285
Rogerson, J. W., 89n18, 208, 208n74, 211n92, 212n93, 213, 213nn101–2, 213nn104–5, 214n106, 215, 215nn107–9, 217, 218n122, 219n123, 221–23, 222n138, 292n53, 321, 321nn189–90, 321nn192–93, 443n42
Rorty, R., 312, 313, 321, 324–25, 324n204
Rosenberg, D., 464, 464n6
Rosner, B. S., 97n54
Roth, N., 183n129, 185, 185n140
Rothen, B., 199n30
Routledge, R., 89n18
Rummel, E., 195nn8–9
Runge, S. E., 416n169
Rupert of Deutz, 204n54
Rush, O., 115nn5–6, 116n16, 118n22
Ryken, L., 408
Ryle, H. E., 265–66, 265nn52–53

Saadiah Gaon, 187–88
Saebø, M., 183n127, 195n7, 298n80
Sáenz-Badillos, A., 186n149
Saggs, H. W. F., 370
Said, E. W., 386nn40–42
Sailhamer, J. H., 89n18
Salters, R. B., 189n163
Sanders, J. A., 252n6, 255, 255n11, 259, 338, 426, 426n218
Saperstein, M., 191n175
Sasso, S. E., 183n126
Saussure, F. de, 115n11, 121–22, 121n41, 283, 402
Scheffler, I., 333n234
Schelling, F. W. J., 213, 214, 216, 296
Schenker, A., 165n32
Schlegel, F., 295
Schleiermacher, F., 93, 217n118, 218–19, 220, 283n7, 286, 305–8, 305n113, 306n117, 306n121, 307nn123–24, 308n128, 310–11, 328, 350, 352, 444, 537
Schmidt, K. L., 512, 512n125
Schnelle, U., 89n18
Scholder, K., 206–9, 206n66, 207n69, 208nn70–72, 209n75, 210nn82–83, 210n85

Scholes, R. E., 384n36
Schreiner, S., 200n36
Schreiner, T. R., 89n18, 97n56
Schürer, E., 374
Schwemer, A. M., 55n20
Scobie, C. H. H., 52n5, 87n8, 87n11, 88nn16–17, 89n19, 90n22, 92, 92n28, 103–6, 103nn89–95, 104nn96–101, 105nn102–8, 106nn110–13, 108, 250, 441
Scott, N. A., 27n67
Scroggs, R., 264n45
Scruton, R., 290nn37–38, 291, 291nn44–45
Seerveld, C., xn5, 137n124, 248, 248n246, 299n87, 299n90, 310n144, 311n145, 337n7, 390n60, 395n82, 408, 481
Segal, M., 173n81
Segalla, G., 89n18
Seitz, C. R., 8n20, 10n22, 13–14, 14n38, 14n40, 237, 245, 246, 246n238, 276, 276n106
Seldon, R., 396n87
Semler, J. S., 211, 298
Serforno, O., 191
Sertillanges, A. G., 22n40, 407n129, 463, 463n1, 465, 467n22, 484n70, 542n76
Sheeley, S., 423n201
Shinan, A., 123, 123nn55–56
Siegert, F., 494n32
Silva, M., 164n23, 164nn25–28, 164n30, 164n32, 165n33, 167n44, 169n56, 170n65
Silver, D. J., 175–76, 175n89
Silverman, H. J., 317n170
Simeon, C., 532
Simon, R., 185n138, 205, 206, 206n64
Simon, U., 183n127, 184n135
Simonetti, M., 135n109, 135n111
Skarsaune, O., 205, 205n59
Skillen, J. W., 466n14
Skinner, J., 538n66
Smalley, B., 151–52, 152nn186–87, 153n192, 154, 154nn194–95, 155n204
Smit, M. C., 342, 342n34
Smith, W. R., 352
Smolar, L., 177, 177n94
Söding, T., 256n16
Sokolowski, R., 60–61, 60nn50–51, 61nn52–53, 436n19
Sommer, B. D., 98, 98n65, 124n57
Soskice, J. M., 333n234
Sowers, S. G., 513n133
Spears, A., 41n129, 528n25, 529, 529n27, 529n29, 530–32, 530n30, 530nn35–37, 531nn38–39, 532n42, 533–35, 534n52, 534n55, 535nn56–57
Speiser, E. A., 364
Sperling, S. D., 99n70
Spicq, C., 497, 511
Spieckermann, H., 106–10, 106n114, 107nn115–21, 108nn122–26, 109nn127–30
Spinoza, B., de, 191, 195, 211, 286–89, 287n24, 288nn25–31, 289n32, 289n34, 292, 299, 325, 344nn49–51, 345–46
Spykman, G., 54, 251, 252n4, 437n22, 439–40, 440nn29–31, 444n46, 446n51, 449n61, 451n67, 458, 458n97, 477, 543n80
Staiger, E., 397n90
Stegemann, H., 168n50
Stegner, W. R., 495n32
Steiner, G., ixn1, 25–32, 26nn54–58, 26nn60–61, 27nn62–65, 28n68, 29nn75–78, 30nn79–81, 31nn82–83, 32nn87–89, 42, 327, 408–9, 408n130, 409n138
Steinmetz, D. C., 198n22, 200n38
Stek, J., 230, 440–41, 441n33, 454, 454nn79–80, 455, 455nn85–86
Stemberger, G., 187n150, 256n21
Stephens, W. P., 198n18, 200n35
Sternberg, M., 78n138, 99, 238–41, 239nn215–20, 240nn221–24, 241nn225–28, 242, 242n229, 334n237, 354, 354nn90–92, 379, 379n11, 390, 408, 411–13, 411n148, 412nn149–54, 413nn155–58, 415n167, 418n173, 419–20, 419n179, 420nn186–87
Stewart, J., 304n108
Stewart, R. A., 513n133
Steyn, G. J., 498nn53–54
Still, J., 121n38
Stiver, D. R., 67, 67n83
Stonehouse, N. B., 228
Storkey, A., 39nn118–19
Stott, J., 15, 15n45, 35, 481, 482, 536
Strauss, D. F., 221, 222, 349, 357
Strauss, L., 98, 98n60, 287n22
Stroup, G. W., 67–68, 67nn87–88, 68nn89–90
Struck, P. T., 127n72
Stuhlmacher, P., 89n18
Stump, E., 157, 157n211, 192, 192n179, 467, 467n16
Suleiman, S. R., 313n153, 421n189
Sundberg, A. C., 254
Sundberg, W., 208n71, 287n22, 288n26
Sweeney, M. A., 99, 99n70
Swetnam, J., 497n48
Symonds, J. A., 394
Szondi, P., 79n140

Author Index 621

Tacitus, 387
Taine, H., 395
Talbert, C., 422, 422n196, 423n204
Tallis, R., 121, 121n44
Talmage, F., 184n135
Tannehill, R., 423, 423n197
Tarnas, R., 293, 293n58
Tauler, J., 22, 22n37
Taylor, C., 64, 201, 293, 293nn55–56, 328, 328n214, 448, 470, 470n37, 475
Taylor, J. E., 170, 170n68
Taylor, M. C., 257n27
Teal, A., 135n109, 137nn125–26, 138n130
Terence, 376
Teresa of Avila, 248
Tertullian, 196, 258n30, 269–70, 270nn70–76, 271nn77–78, 338, 448, 490, 490n9
Terveen, J. L., 493n21
Theodore of Mopsuestia, 135, 137–38, 183
Theodoret, 135
Theodoric, 145
Thiele, R. A., 492n19
Thielicke, H., 308, 308n129, 448, 502, 502n76, 505, 505nn90–94, 505n96, 509, 509nn111–12, 509nn114–16, 524n7, 537, 537n59, 537n61, 541n71
Thielman, F., 89n18
Thiselton, A. C., 14, 14n39, 116n18, 121–22, 121nn42–43, 122n45, 122n47, 130n87, 216, 216n110, 235, 238, 238n214, 247n241, 251, 251n3, 282, 282n6, 283, 285n14, 286n22, 306n115, 307, 307n125, 308n129, 309nn136–37, 312, 312nn146–47, 313n149, 317n169, 381n20, 411, 411n147, 418n174, 418n177, 422n192, 438, 438n23, 438n26, 439n28, 448n59, 530n38, 534n51, 535
Thomas, D., 200n36
Thomas, H., 119n27, 126n67, 183n127
Thomas à Kempis, 135, 195, 201
Thomas Aquinas, 6, 6n7, 45, 58n42, 74n114, 94n39, 128, 128n79, 131, 153, 154n196, 155, 156–57, 156n208, 157n209, 178, 194, 197, 200, 201, 248, 337, 444, 448, 468, 472n41, 492, 542
Thompson, J. A., 514–15, 513n133, 539n68
Thompson, M. D., 199n27
Thompson, T. L., 364, 365, 370
Thucydides, 339–40
Thulstrup, N., 349, 349n69
Thurneysen, R, 230
Thyen, H., 495n32
Tillich, P., 448

Tjørhom, O., 451–52, 451n68, 452nn69–70
Torrance, T. F., 198n20, 251, 251n1, 257n23, 257n28, 259, 259n32, 259n36, 448
Torrell, J.-P., 156nn206–7
Toulmin, S., 209, 209n79, 220, 442
Tov, E., 162, 162n14, 164n24, 164n32, 169, 169n57
Tracy, D., 67, 198n19, 287n22
Trigg, J. W., 275n103, 276nn104–5
Troeltsch, E., 226, 352–53, 353n85
Troubetskoy, N. S., 402
Turner, J., 45, 45n147, 127n72, 337, 337n9
Turrentinus, 211
Tyconius, 140

Ulrich, E., 182n121, 254n8
Urbach, E. E., 98

Valdes, M. J., 380n17
Valla, 195
Van de Beek, A., 85, 85n1
Van de Mieroop, M., 368, 368n159, 368nn164–66, 369n167
Vanderburg, W. H., 23n44, 23nn46–47
Vander Goot, H., 305n112
VanderKam, J. C., 167n46, 168, 168nn49–50, 168nn52–53, 170n66, 171n71
Van der Toorn, K., 368n165
van der Watt, J. G., 61n59
Van Dyke, H., 19n7
Vanhoozer, K. J., 8n21, 10–11, 10n25, 12n34, 13n36, 33n91, 78, 78nn129–35, 245, 246–47, 247n242, 283, 314n155, 315n162, 410n143, 411, 432–33, 433n5, 434, 439n28
Vanhoye, A., 495n38, 496, 496n39
Vanier, J., 13, 13n35, 47, 47n160, 422
Van Leeuwen, R. C., 241, 378n8
van Ruiten, J., 173n81
Van Seters, J., 364, 365, 366n145, 370
Van Til, C., 230, 230n171, 431
Van Til, H. J., 441n33
van't Spijker, W., 193, 193n1
Van Winden, J. C. M., 452n74
Vatke, J. K. W., 218, 220–21, 222, 223
Vaughan, R., 542n75, 542n77
Vaux, R. de, 179n111, 370
Veltri, G., 165n32
Vermès, G., 159, 159n3, 161, 161n12
Virgil, 377
Vischer, L., 120, 120nn33–34
Voegelin, E., 342–44, 342n35, 343n36
Voltaire, 210

Vos, G., 74, 250
Vriezen, T. C., 38nn113–14, 250

Walfish, B. D., 183n127
Walker, A., 82–83, 82n155
Wallace, M., 64, 64n67
Walsh, B. J., 481n65
Walsh, K., 152n186
Walters, J., 498, 498n57
Waltke, B. K., 89n18, 168–69, 168n54 169n58
Walzer, M., 98, 98n62
Ward, B. K., 470n37
Ward, George, 25n52
Ward, Graham, 236, 236n201
Ward Holder, R., 198n20
Warnke, G., 312n148, 318n174, 323n200
Warren, A., 397n89, 414, 414n159, 416n170
Watson, D. F., 494n28
Watson, F., 10n22, 59n48, 95–96, 95n47, 96nn48–49, 96n52, 122n51, 235, 245, 246, 246n239, 274n99, 283, 379n13, 410n143, 411
Weaver, R., 442
Weber, O., 454n82, 458n98
Webster, J. B., 12n34, 17, 17n1, 235, 245, 257, 257nn25–26, 257n28, 260
Weemes, J., 202
Weigel, G., 481
Weinandy, T. G., 156n205
Weinfeld, M., 124n57
Weiss, H.-F., 494n31
Weiss, M., 394n79, 397n88, 397n90, 398n93, 399–401, 399nn96–97, 400nn101–4
Weitzman, S., 169n55, 276–77, 277n108
Wellek, R., 394n78, 395–96, 395n81, 396n84, 397n89, 399n99, 414, 414n159, 416n170
Wellhausen, J., 207, 208, 218, 220–23, 229, 237, 337, 348, 348n62, 352
Wellum, S. J., 83n158
Wendel, F., 201, 201n44
Wengert, T. J., 197n16, 201nn42–43
Wenham, G. J., 188n157, 228n165, 229, 230, 230n173, 241, 249n246, 362n128, 363n131, 365, 367n154, 370n171, 370n173, 371n176, 423n205, 452n74, 453, 453n77, 503n80, 507, 507n103
Wesley, J., 248
West, A., 377n6
Westbrook, R., 369n169
Westbury, J. R., 416n169

Westcott, B. F., 229, 254, 497n46, 497n51, 515n141
Westermann, C., 76n122, 124n58, 125n61
Westfall, C. L., 496n41
Westphal, M., 291n48
Wetzstein, J. G., 211
Whately, R., 532
Whitaker, W., 202, 203
White, H., 323n202
Whitelam, K., 336, 336nn2–3
Whybray, R. N., 170, 170n62
Wicks, J., 205n58, 205n61
Widdowson, P., 396n87
Wiesel, E., 184n131
Wiker, B., 209n76
Wilckens, U., 225, 225n146
Wilken, R., 86, 86nn4–6, 87n7, 87n10, 126, 479, 479nn56–59, 480
William of Thierry, 152
Williams, B. A. O., 355, 355n95
Williams, Ronald. J., 368, 368n163
Williams, Rowan, 433, 433n6
Wills, L., 494n32
Wilson, G., 377n6
Wilson, P. S., 528n24, 528n26
Wilson, R. D., 228
Wimsatt, W. K., 397, 397n88, 398, 398nn91–92
Windelband, W., 209n77
Wiseman, D. J., 369n170
Witherington, B., 229
Wittgenstein, L., 27, 122n49, 147n172, 535
Wold, D. J., 333n230
Wolters, A., 24n50, 477n51
Wolterstorff, N., 8, 77n126, 179, 179n105, 192, 192n179, 283, 292, 292n49, 326, 328n217, 361n124, 380–81, 380n20, 381n21, 418n176, 418n178, 445, 445n47, 466, 469, 469n27, 537n64
Wood, A. W., 289, 289n35, 290, 291n43
Wood, C. M., 12, 12n32
Wood, D., 152n186
Worton, M., 121n38
Wright, C., 106
Wright, D., 367–69, 368nn160–61
Wright, G. E., 75, 90, 91, 91n25, 91n27, 97n55, 343n40, 361–62, 362n129, 365n141, 372
Wright, N. T., 11, 11nn28–29, 55, 55n21, 56, 56n30, 56nn32–33, 76–82, 76n123, 77nn125–26, 78nn127–28, 81nn146–50, 82nn151–53, 118, 118n23, 125–26, 161, 161nn8–9, 161n11, 162n17, 167n47, 168n48, 171, 171n70, 172, 172n73, 172n75, 173,

173n77, 173n80, 174n83, 175, 179n108,
180, 228, 228n166, 229, 229n168, 238,
238nn212–13, 245, 246, 246n240, 247,
250, 271n80, 274n97, 326–27, 327n211,
329, 360, 371–75, 372nn180–82, 373n187,
374n188, 378, 401, 404–7, 404nn120–21,
406nn123–27, 411, 413n158, 415n167, 425,
429, 433, 433n9, 433nn11–13, 436, 441, 480,
481, 499–500, 499n67, 500nn68–69, 512,
512n126, 513n127, 519, 519n159
Wyschogrod, E., 31n84
Wyschrograd, M., 98

Yocum, J. P., 156n205
Young, E. J., 228

Young, F. M., 57, 57n37, 58nn38–39, 135n109,
137nn125–26, 138n130
Yu, C., 89n18

Zabarella, G., 194
Zachman, R. C., 200n41, 201n45
Zaharopoulos, D. Z., 138n131, 140
Zahn, T., 254
Zahrnt, H., 224n142
Zakovitch, Y., 123, 123nn55–56
Zarhnt, H., 446, 446n52
Zenger, E., 256, 256n20
Zizioulas, J., 7
Zwingli, H., 198n18, 199n32, 200n35, 525–26

www.ingramcontent.com/pod-product-compliance
Lightning Source LLC
Chambersburg PA
CBHW020259010526
44108CB00037B/155